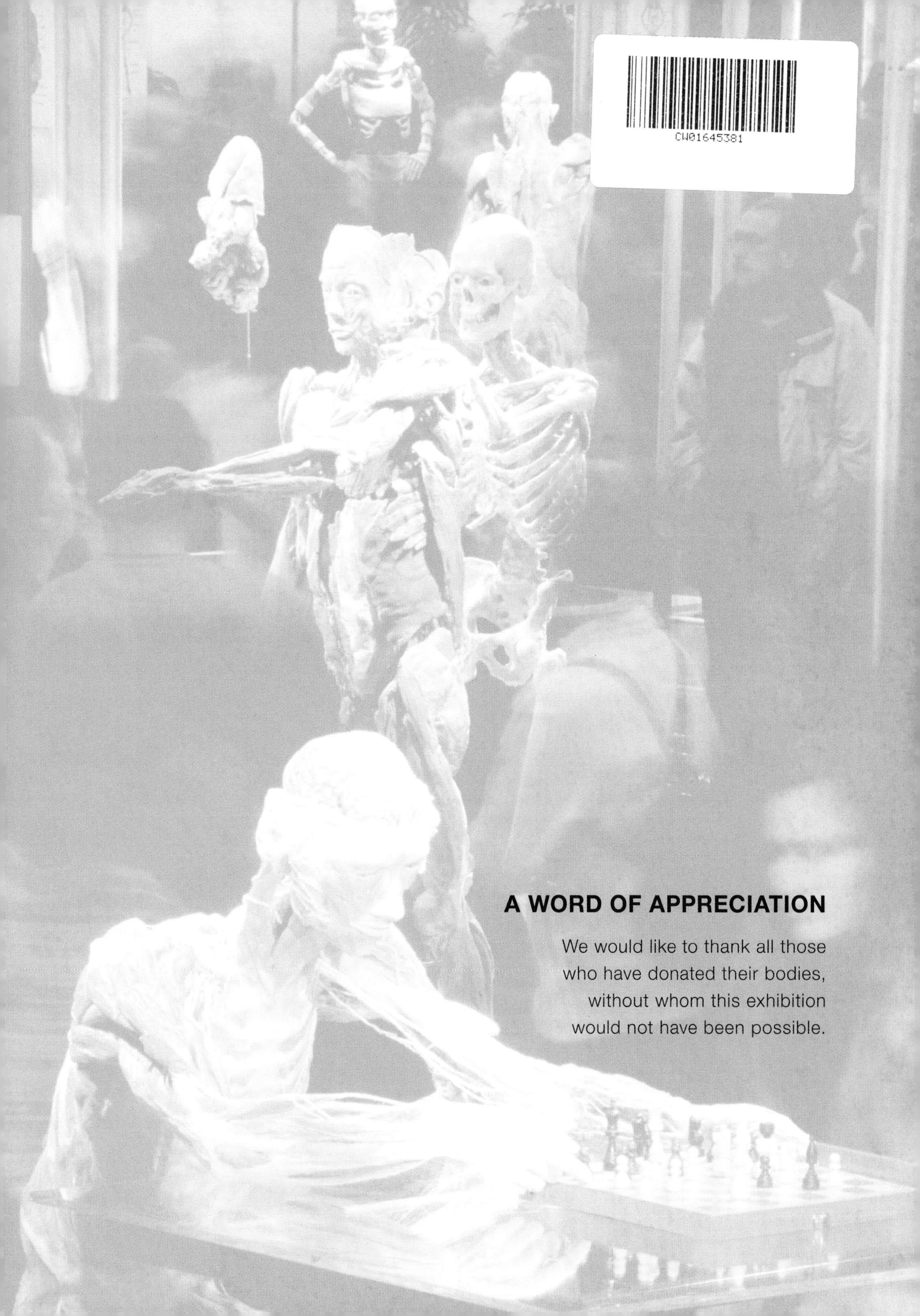



## A WORD OF APPRECIATION

We would like to thank all those who have donated their bodies, without whom this exhibition would not have been possible.

Gunther von Hagens'

# BODYWORLDS

## CATALOGUE ON THE EXHIBITION


Franz Josef Wetz
**Foreword**

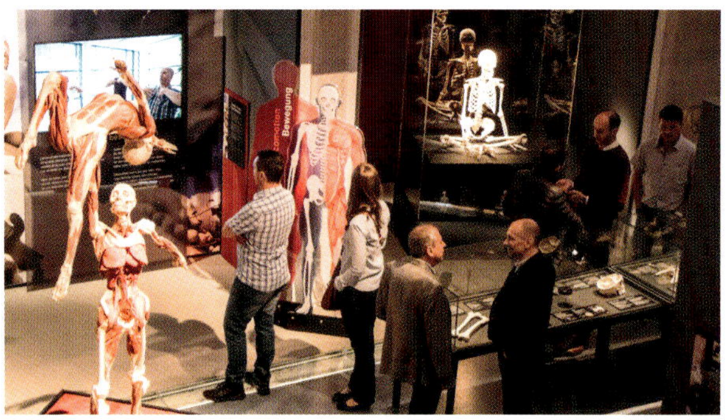

5

Gunther von Hagens
**Anatomy and Plastination**

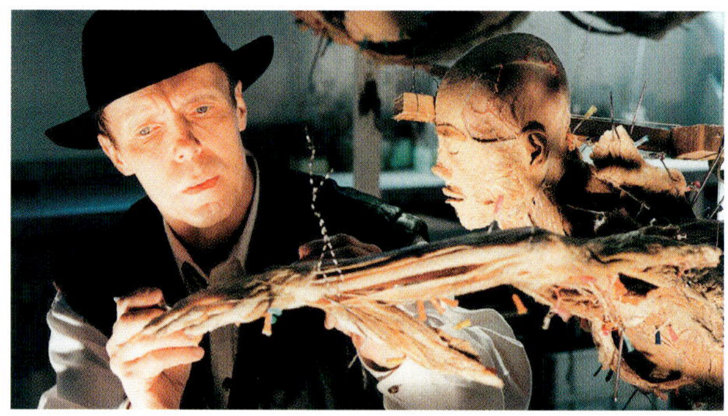

9

1. History of Anatomy ........ 9

2. Plastinated Specimens and Plastination ........ 22

Definitions ........ 43


**BODY WORLDS** is also known as
**KÖRPERWELTEN** and **LE MONDE DU CORPS** in some countries.

Gunther von Hagens' **KÖRPERWELTEN**   Gunther von Hagens' **LE MONDE DU CORPS**

Angelina Whalley
**The Human Body – Anatomy and Function**

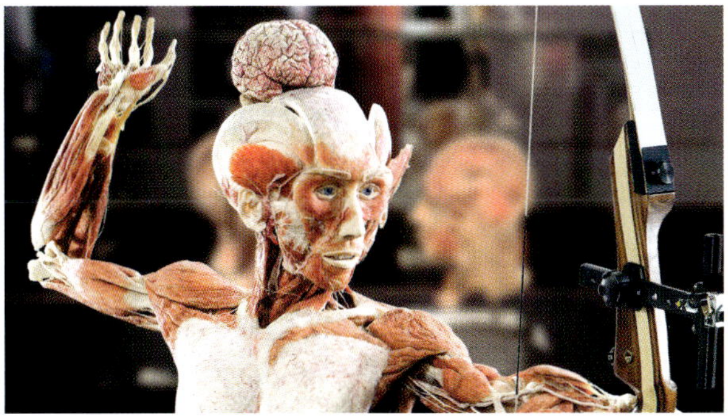

45

1. The Locomotive System ........................................ 47

2. The Nervous System ........................................ 65

3. The Respiratory System ........................................ 79

4. The Cardiovascular System ........................................ 93

5. The Digestive System ........................................ 111

6. The Urinary Tract ........................................ 131

7. The Reproductive Organs ........................................ 139

8. Prenatal Development ........................................ 149

9. Whole-Body Plastinates ........................................ 163

Franz Josef Wetz
**The Public Corpse**

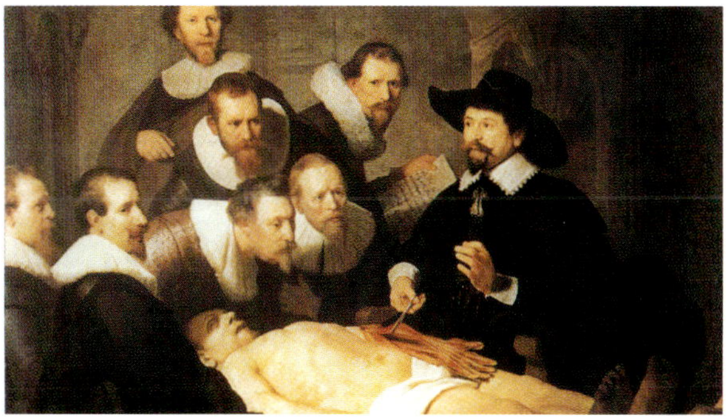

212

The Dignity of Man ........................................ 212

Modern Anatomical Theatre ........................................ 230
– The First Public Autopsy in 200 Years

Franz Josef Wetz

# Foreword

The universal appeal of BODY WORLDS is remarkable and beyond compare. At this writing, more than 47 million people across Europe, the Americas Africa, Asia and Australasia have seen the exhibitions.

The authenticity of the specimens on display is certainly the foremost reason for the considerable public interest. But sheer curiosity and mixed emotions such as *angstlust*, the German term for the thrill associated with fear, are also persuasive and compelling rationales to attend.

Anatomy is an attempt at illuminating the dark of life with the light of death. The exhibition covers the twilight between life and death that has always been fascinating for humans. Its producers utilise this inherent fascination of anatomy itself.

While there are many impressive individual organs on display, the whole-body plastinates – entire bodies set in life-like poses – mesmerize the visitor. These figures are awe-inspiring visual objects and technically brilliant instructional specimens. More than mere repositories of anatomical information, they are also representational symbolic expressions. In addition, they are sensational attractions.

BODY WORLDS is a cultural event promising a stimulating experience. And yet, some visitors experience a feeling of unease, even timidity, before entering the exhibition hall for the first time. They are unsure of what to expect, but curious enough to actually enter. Once inside, their anxiety tends to be quickly alleviated by the aesthetic and pleasing presentation of the plastinates.

The visitor's behaviour inside the exhibition hall is notably quiet, solemn, and disciplined, rather unusual in today's societies. Considering, however, that the exhibition offers every visitor an unusual perspective of his or her own life, this behaviour is less surprising. In this exhibition, by looking at a foreign body one discovers one's own body in a whole new way. It is comparable to looking at oneself – without a mirror.

Viewed this way, the reason for solemnity and quiet is not a state of shock, caused by seeing something gruesome, like some of them may have expected. Rather, their thoughtfulness results from being enthralled by self-discovery.

The exhibition intends to be a place of anatomical education and information. The visitor's state of awe additionally makes it a sacred site with a special aura.

The exhibition presents insights into the body's interior, providing an understanding of its structure, and of the functions of its organs. The depth of the education provided depends both on the previous knowledge and the degree of interest on the part of visitors. Admittedly, many of them simply seek to be allowed to see the real, authentic interior of the body, a legitimate interest as well.

The fact that the bodies shown are real, increases the value of this experience, making it more intense and the exhibition extremely trustworthy. This exhibition brings one particularly close to oneself.

At the same time, however, it also urges us to remember our own mortality, as it illustrates life, which eventually will lead to death, using the dead. The purpose of creating this awareness of one's own transience is not to induce us to turn away from our mortal life, but rather to prompt us to attend to it more carefully, taking care of our health. In this way, the exhibition also promotes a new form of body culture without succumbing to a cult of the body.

BODY WORLDS needs to be viewed against the backdrop of the growing body consciousness of our time. Today, "working on the body" more and more often replaces "working with the body". The less we need our bodies just to survive, the more we can worry about them as the vessel and embodiment of life. As a result, we become more health conscious.

Health is an unstable state that may rapidly decline; it cannot be expected to last. Health remains rather improbable, and, in old age, it is a lucky coincidence. In modern societies, health is considered a valuable good. However, it now no longer is seen simply as a godly or natural gift, but also as the result of one's lifestyle - even as an important task in life. In order to achieve this good, major efforts are undertaken because one not only wants to be healthy, but also to feel healthy.

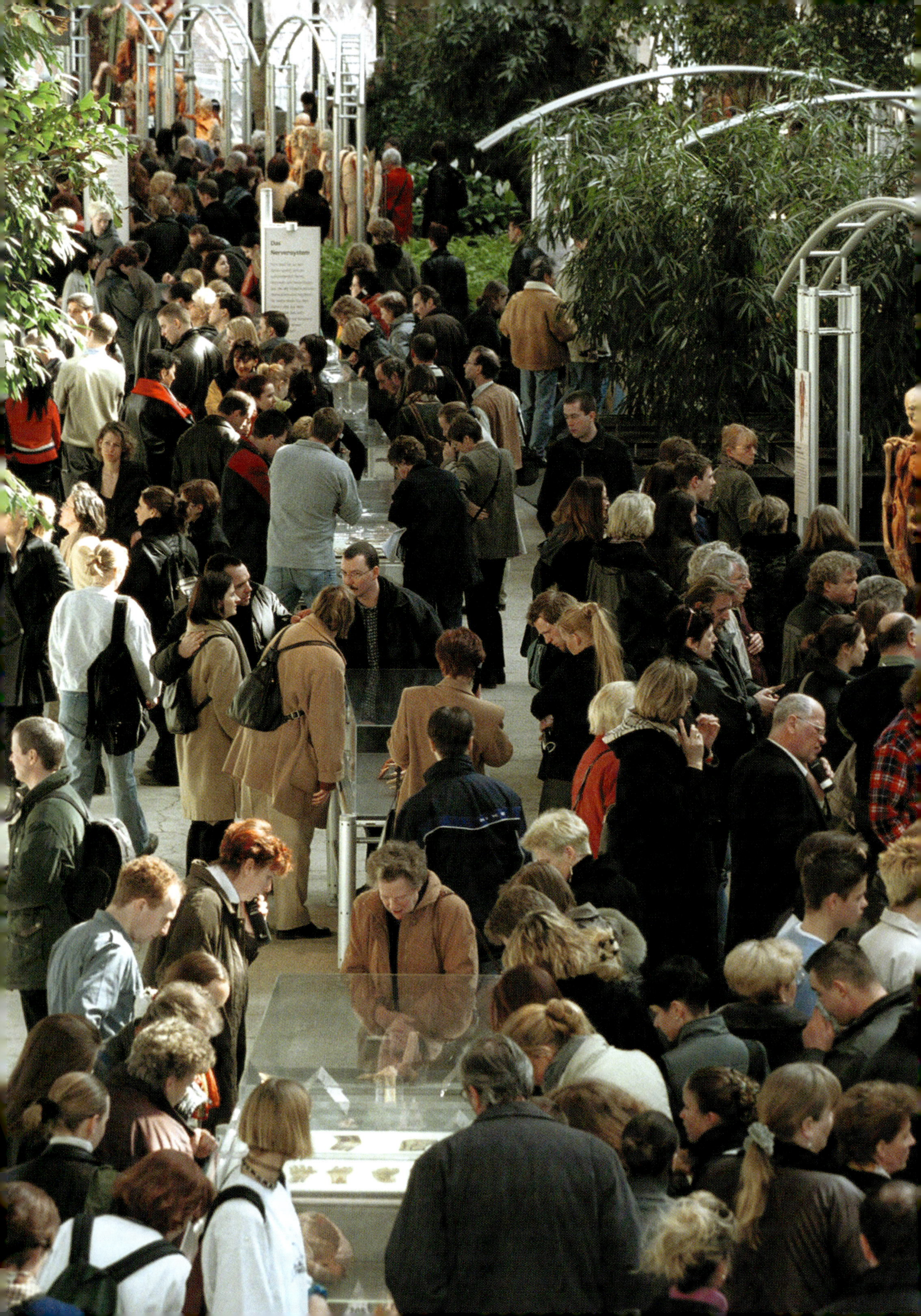

The exhibition confronts us with health and sickness, life and death, strength and weakness, and the uniqueness and vulnerability of our bodies. It not only educates visitors about their bodies' interior structures, but also inspires them to choose a healthier, more conscious lifestyle. In doing so, BODY WORLDS makes both the misery and the magnitude of human existence visible. The exhibition shows the vulnerability of life, inspiring at the same time awe and respect in detailing the fine structures and complexity of the body.

While providing all this, the exhibition does not prescribe a specific view of humankind. Thus, visitors from very diverse cultural backgrounds and religious denominations, with widely differing philosophical viewpoints, can appreciate the exhibition. This is possible because the exhibition remains neutral regarding our world view. Only this neutral stance allows it to be interpreted in various religious or philosophical ways, depending on the personal views and beliefs of the individual visitor.

In this sense, the exhibition is not merely about anatomical education. It also aims to contribute to a more conscious lifestyle for its visitors, to strengthen their attention towards their own well-being, to show them the abilities and limits of the human body, and to inspire them to contemplate the question of the meaning and importance of humankind. In order to do so, BODY WORLDS delivers both factual information and highly unusual sensual impressions that will touch the visitor at the emotional level and leave her or him thoughtful.

**Prof. Dr. Franz Josef Wetz**
Professor of Philosophy at the University of Education
in Schwäbisch Gmünd, Germany

Gunther von Hagens

# Anatomy and Plastination

## 1. The History of Anatomy

### Anatomy and Hunting; Ritual Anatomy

Anatomy refers to the science of investigating the body's internal structures. There have always been specialists on the body's interior; hunters were among these specialists in man's early history. Animals killed during the hunt had to be gutted, and the meat had to be removed from the bones; a certain understanding of anatomy was an advantage in this regard. 'Kitchen anatomy' therefore concerned the anatomy of animals. Initial interest in human anatomy presumably arose among cannibals, whose motives were primarily ritual in nature. They believed that by consuming their enemies they could absorb their strength. In the earliest advanced civilizations, procedures were developed for immortalising the bodies of the dead – at least when the deceased had been persons of importance. Preserving entire corpses in this way was known in many cultures. The most famous instance is that of the mummies of ancient Egyptian pharaohs and other dignitaries, whose gutted bodies had been treated with fragrant resins and sodium bicarbonate, and then dried; this was to allow the deceased to live on after death. At its high point in South America, mummification even led to the establishment of entire cities of the dead. Ritual anatomy did not achieve any great anatomical insights, however, because the focus of preservation efforts was the mortal shell of the person, the skin in particular. The organs themselves, the failure of which was responsible for the individual's death, fell prey to decay.

The major impetus for acquiring detailed anatomical knowledge has always come from medicine. At first, this knowledge lay in the hands of shamans and priests; shortly before the beginning of the Common Era (AD), the profession of physician came into being, a vocation for which training was largely of a philosophical nature.

### First Anatomical Studies in Greece and Egypt

At around 500 BC, the Greeks founded medical schools such as those in Crotona (lower Italy) and Cyrene (Africa), where they explored the anatomy of animals, examining even such tiny structures as the organ of equilibrium located in the temples. Aristotle (384–327 BC) was the first known anatomist, even though he is better known today for his philosophical writings. A student of Plato and a teacher to Alexander the Great, Aristotle drew a distinction between nerves and tendons, and described how major arteries branched out into smaller blood vessels.

Shortly after 400 BC, the Greek philosopher Plato came to the conclusion that there must be a fundamental difference between body and soul. He saw the body as only a temporary housing for the soul. This school of thought, known as the dualism of body and soul, provided the necessary foundation for preserving human specimens. The conviction that the soul exists independently of the body made it permissible to open up the body once the soul had departed after death. It was in this spirit that Herophilos and Erasistratos undertook the first dissections of human bodies in Alexandria, where, following the death of Alexander the Great, King Ptolemy I had established a medical school in 320 BC. Dissections were performed on the bodies of executed prisoners – probably in public.

Although first expressed by Plato, the philosophical premise of the dualism of body and soul later found its way into the Bible, where Paul says the following about the new body to come after the resurrection: "But someone will ask, 'How are the dead raised? With what kind of body will they come?' ... But God will give them a body as he sees fit..." (Cor. I, 15:35–38)

### Anatomy in Europe in the Common Era

When the Romans conquered Egypt in 30 BC, the medical school of Alexandria declined in importance. The teachings of Galen of Pergamum (131–201 AD), a doctor whose conclusions were based on the study of animals, would now dominate the field. Having studied in Alexandria, Galen settled in Rome and produced some 150 medical writings. It is assumed that he never dissected human bodies, but instead studied monkeys and other animals – his anatomical works were flawed accordingly. Galen was a difficult, high-handed individual, whose arrogance was expressed in his books as follows: "Anyone looking for fame simply has to familiarise himself with all that I have achieved." Galen did, in fact, enjoy an excellent reputation as a doctor – even Emperor Marcus Aurelius refused to go without his services.

Over the course of time, Galen published 200 books and influenced anatomical thought and medicine for the next 1,300 years. During this time, dissections of the human body remained an exception to the rule. Only a very few historical sources confirm that doctors dissected human bodies, but these dissections served mainly to preserve the identity of the medical profession at that time. A professor would read from Galen's books while his assistants dissected a cadaver, lending the words of the ancient master more significance than was attributed to any anatomical findings revealed by opening the body. Anatomical drawings were correspondingly faulty.

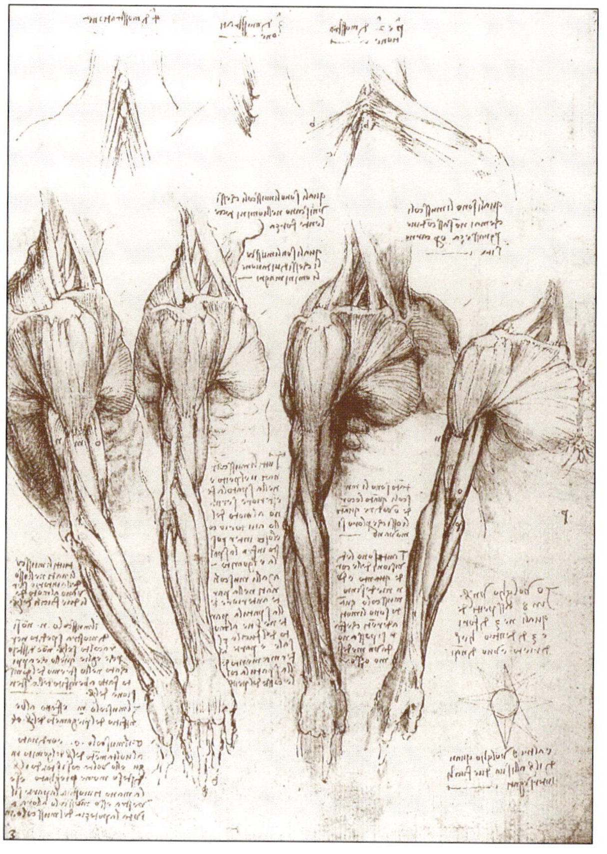

*Fig. 2: Anatomical studies of Leonardo da Vinci, 1510.*

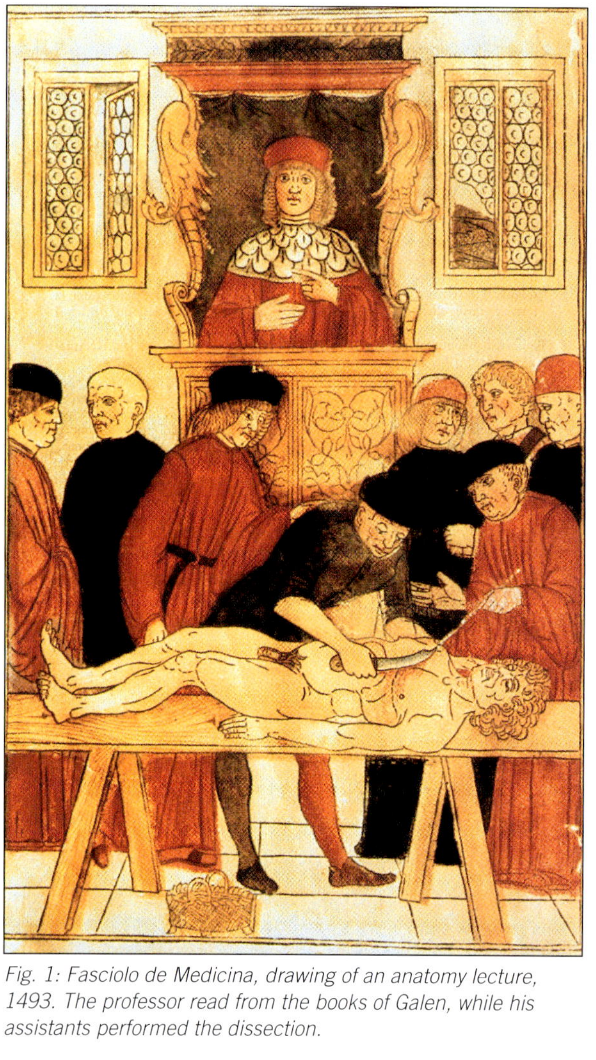

*Fig. 1: Fasciolo de Medicina, drawing of an anatomy lecture, 1493. The professor read from the books of Galen, while his assistants performed the dissection.*

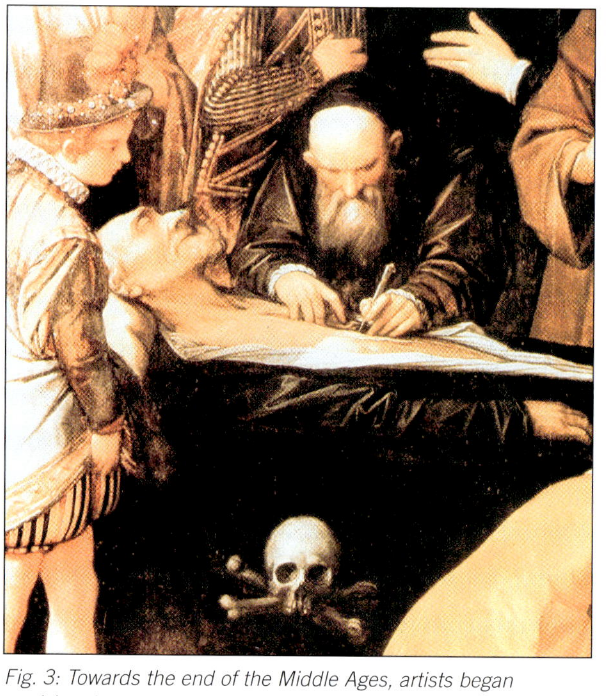

*Fig. 3: Towards the end of the Middle Ages, artists began studying the structure of the human body. This illustration presumably shows Michelangelo dissecting a corpse.*

A change in attitude towards the teaching of anatomy first appeared at the end of the Middle Ages, when artists in particular began to investigate the structure of the human body. Today the most well-known artist and scientist of that time is Leonardo da Vinci (1452–1519), who privately performed anatomical dissections of human corpses. These formed the basis for his famous, highly detailed anatomical sketches. For the first time, he provided realistic, correctly proportioned illustrations of the body's interior, even though the details of his drawings were often incorrect. da Vinci's work made a significant contribution to society's acceptance of studying human bodies.

Leonardo da Vinci passionately studied the human body. Under cover of night, he climbed cemetery walls, stole bodies, and dragged them into his studio. In his notebook, dated around 1510, he wrote:

> *"I have dissected more than ten human corpses, digging deep into each limb, pulling back the minutest bits of flesh. If this subject excites you, you may feel a natural repulsion, or even if you're not put off, you may still dread spending the night among cut-up, flayed, ghastly-looking cadavers. If all that still doesn't deter you, you may lack the artistic talent indispensable for this science."*

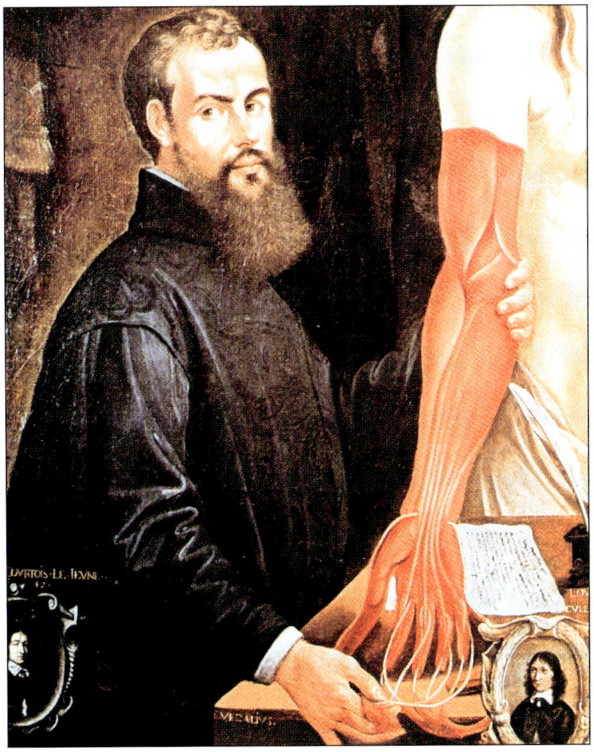

*Fig. 4: Andreas Vesal (1514–1564), founder of the science of anatomy.*

A short time later, the famous anatomist Andreas Vesalius (1514–1564) had the courage to criticise publicly the practice of limiting anatomical dissections to animals. In his monumental work, *De Humani Corporis Fabrica*, Vesalius describes the anatomy of the human body according to what he had observed at recently introduced public dissections at the "Anatomical Theatres." He is considered the founder of the science of anatomy. The drawings by his illustrator Kalkar were more exact than anything that had been previously produced. The sketches also introduced a new aesthetic quality, showing dissected bodies in nearly lifelike poses, standing in nature and surrounded by everyday items. According to available evidence, Andreas Vesalius was also the first person to assemble real bones into an upright structure. He named this a skeleton after 'ho skeletos', which means 'dried up' in Greek. This was revolutionary, as no one had ever before dared to do anything similar with cadavers; he more or less pulled the dead out of their graves and put them back into society. A skeleton assembled by Vesalius can still be found at the Institute of Anatomy of the University of Basel.

Anatomy as it was shown in the drawings of that time was initially a very individual type of anatomy. The specimen and all of its unique anatomical features were copied in as great detail as possible. Certain artistic means were employed to demonstrate the authenticity and individuality of the illustration; shadows caused by the light coming in through a window, for example, made it clear what time of day that particular specimen was dissected. A fly on the drawing symbolised the momentary nature of the illustrator's art, as in a photograph.

That all changed with Bernhard Albinus (1697–1747), whose illustrator Wandelaer not only enriched contemporary understanding of anatomy with his drawings of animals; he also compiled the many variations that he found into a standard, thereby clearing the way for the statistically average anatomy. Organs were no longer sketched individually or as they were found in the body; instead, they were drawn together with their associated functional structures, thus emphasising systems of organs. A kidney, for example, was not just drawn along with the adrenal gland in the surrounding fatty tissues; the ureters and bladder were included as well. The brain was no longer shown solely from the perspective of the open skull; it was now sketched along with the spine and the peripheral nerves. This provided the foundation for developing schematic diagrams of the anatomy – an abstraction that arose from a more functional understanding of the body.

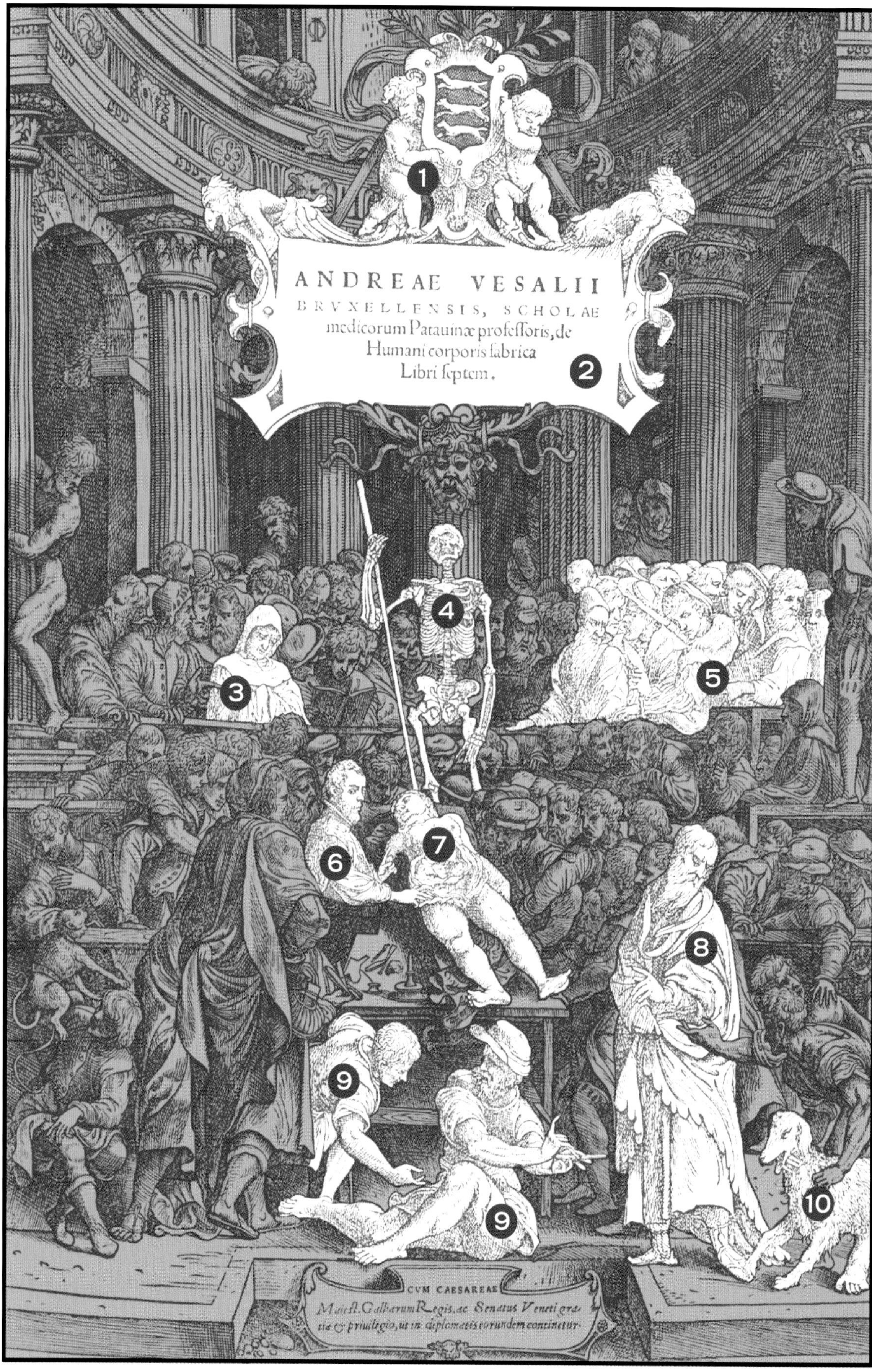
ANDREAE VESALII
BRVXELLENSIS, SCHOLAE
medicorum Patauinæ professoris, de
Humani corporis fabrica
Libri septem.
CVM CAESAREAE
Maiest. Gallarum Regis, ac Senatus Veneti gra-
tia & priuilegio, ut in diplomatis eorundem continetur.
1
2
3
4
5
6
7
8
9
9
10

## Anatomical Theatres

Artistic passion inspired the anatomists of the Renaissance, and interest in anatomy grew among the masses. More and more, physicians, as well as the general public, wanted to see the human body with their own eyes. "Autopsy" hails from the Greek phrase, "To see with one's own eyes." Anatomical theatres were built in many cities. Rich and poor alike would flock to the public dissection presentations.

The picture on the left is the front piece illustration for Andreas Vesal's seven-volume opus *On the Fabric of the Human Body*. It shows Vesalius performing a dissection in a crowded theatre. Like many Renaissance paintings, this illustration is filled with symbolisms and allegories. Here are a few that have been deciphered:

(1) Cherubs hold up Vesalius's coat of arms, showing three weasels. The name Vesalius is a Latin version of the Flemish surname von Wesel.

(2) The writing on the plaque states, "Andreas Vesalius of Brussels, Professor in the School of Physicians of Padua; his seven books On the Fabric of the Human Body".

(3) The hooded figure, perhaps a monk, represents the Church watching over Vesalius's work.

(4) The large skeleton symbolises that humans are mortal and that death is in the room. The skeleton looks toward heaven, striking a pose used by Renaissance artists when depicting saints or Christ.

(5) Many in the crowd are thought to have been members of the wealthy nobility. Some of these noblemen may have financially or politically supported Vesalius's work.

(6) Andreas Vesalius carries out the dissection himself. In previous times, a barber-surgeon would have performed the dissection, while a professor lectured from a nearby lectern.

(7) The cadaver is female. During the Renaissance, nature was often seen as having a female persona. Vesalius exploring the female cadaver implies that he is exploring nature and is part of the great line of natural scientists.

(8) The robed man may represent the classical anatomist Galen (129–200 AD). Galen's books on human anatomy dominated medicine up until the Renaissance. Galen's information was based on the dissection of pigs, large monkeys and other animals, since the dissection of humans was forbidden by Roman law. Vesalius was one of the first to publish tracts on human anatomy based on his dissections of human bodies.

(9) The two men represent barber-surgeons. With Vesalius doing the dissection himself, the gentlemen are left to just sharpen the scalpel-knives. Normally barber-surgeons did the dissections.

(10) The dog (and the monkey on the left side) symbolise Galen's study of human anatomy through the dissection of animals. Vesalius admired Galen, but through the examination of human cadavers, he soon realised that Galen had made a number of mistakes. These mistakes are symbolised by the dog's rear foot, which is clearly human.

The father of cross-sectional anatomy was Russian anatomist Nikolas Pirogov (1810–1881). In his *Anatomia topographica, sectionibus per corpus humanum*, he published two hundred and thirteen cross-sectional illustrations of the human body, including one of a pregnant woman. The cadavers were frozen during the Russian winter in St. Petersburg. The stone printing plates used for his work exist to this day.

The introduction of the microscope allowed 17th century anatomists to study the microstructure of the body; as a result, many anatomists lost interest in macroscopic anatomy, which was increasingly considered to have no more research potential. In Western countries, this trend intensified in the 1950s with the use of the electron microscope and with constantly evolving research in cell and molecular biology. As a result of their research in cell biology, western anatomists have lost nearly all interest in anatomical studies on cadavers.

### Anatomy and Art

In the 16th century, the human body was the focus of an entire era in the history of art. At precisely that moment in history when the sculptures and paintings of the Renaissance had elevated the beauty of the human body to an aesthetic ideal, and natural beauty stood at the heart of our understanding of art, artists also discovered the beauty of the body's interior. In their longing for perfection, painters and sculptors wanted to see the actual muscles upon which they modelled their works of art. First, they observed anatomists, but it was not long before they took the scalpel into their own hands. In Italy and the Netherlands, guilds of doctors, apothecaries and artists even banded together.

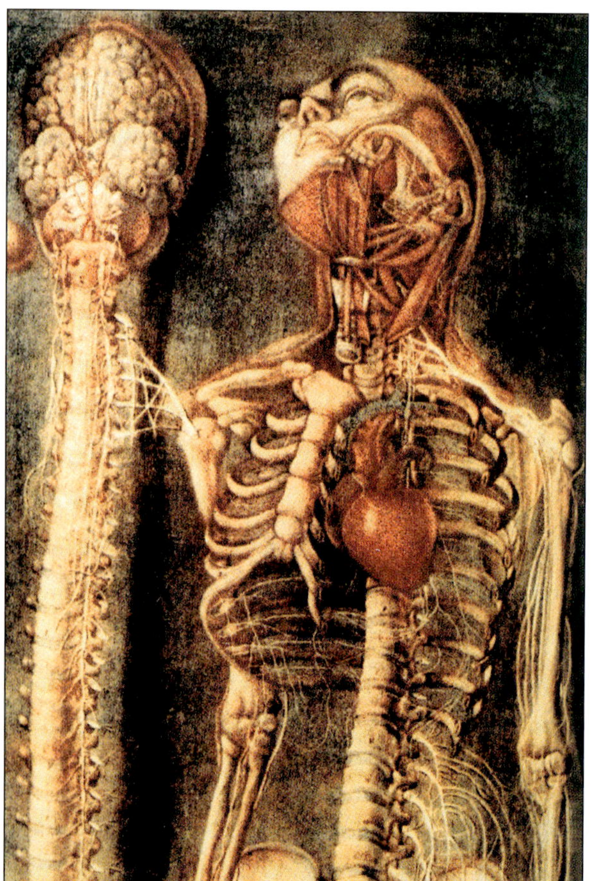

*Fig. 6: Bernhard Siegfried Albinus. As anatomy became better understood, organs were sketched more and more frequently in systems representing specific functions.*

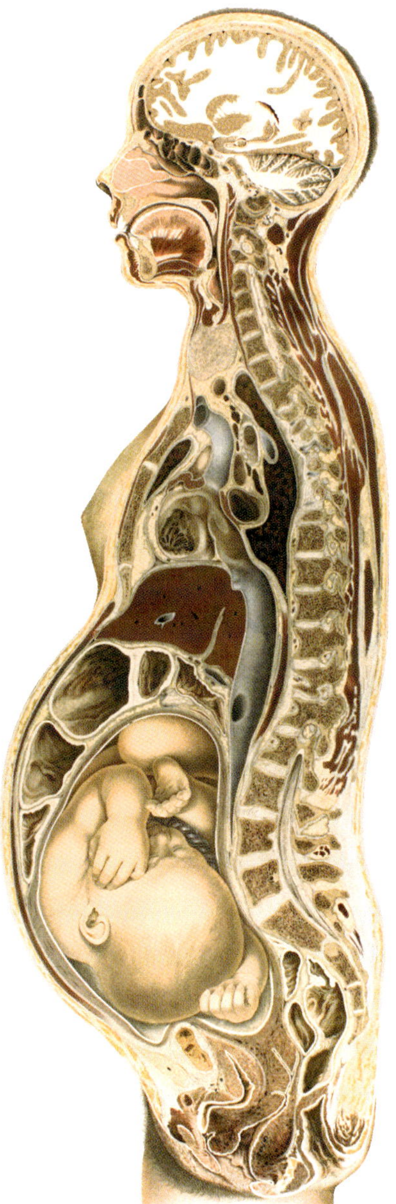

*Fig. 7: Cross-sectional drawing of the body of a pregnant woman by Russian anatomist Nikolas Pirogov, 1855.*

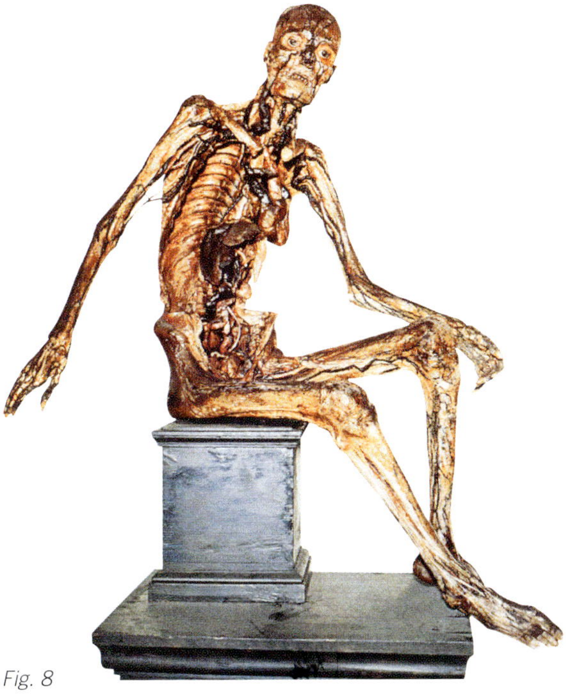

*Fig. 8*

Only when the skeletal systems and musculatures of entire bodies had been studied in detail could the famous paintings and sculptures of the day come into being. During this era, when artistic talent and anatomical knowledge were combined, the most artistic works in the history of anatomy were created. Surviving anatomical illustrations, which are now considered part of man's cultural heritage, were clearly not drawn from memory – real specimens served as models. Due to the lack of appropriate preservation techniques, however, cadavers decomposed shortly after they had been dissected.

Only a very few of them could be preserved, and these can still be seen today at the Italian Museum of Anatomy. Bodies were first dried and their surfaces were treated with oils; in some cases, specimens were injected with metal alloys as a means of highlighting arteries.

The dissected bodies were displayed in aesthetically pleasing, life-like poses that are expressive in a way that brings out the individual character of their anatomy. Some of the bodies are even shown in a manner that makes them seem to exude charm and humour. What is so fascinating about surviving pictures is that, in addition to providing a detailed depiction of the specimen, they also surround the specimen with ancient landscapes. The resulting surreal atmosphere created by these illustrations is astonishing; take, for instance, a drawing in which a rhinoceros makes its way into the scene, its proverbial thick skin forming a contrast to the dissected, skinless human being. BODY WORLDS is presented here as natural art. The beauty of the medieval specimens manifests itself in their perfection, in the harmonious contours of the specimens, in the pleasing, perfect balance of their components and the clarity of anatomical detail. By performing precise studies of anatomical relationships and sharing the results of these studies, anatomy artists established anatomy as a science. They sought the source of truth in the original and made seeing for themselves, i.e., the 'autopsy,' the foundation of their scientific endeavours. As the science of anatomy developed further, the significance of the artist as such was increasingly relegated to the background. Anatomy was gradually reduced to medical courses on dissection and dissection in the service of pathology; as a result, it gradually became the sole privilege of doctors. Finally, the invention of photography made artists largely dispensable.

Today an artist's place in the science of anatomy is mostly limited to occasional modifications to existing anatomical illustrations and to sketching anatomical findings yielded by surgery. If artists wished to study a real cadaver, they would now have to go begging to anatomists; being granted this privilege, however, is generally an exception rather than the rule. It, therefore, comes as no surprise that the aesthetic quality of anatomical drawings made of the human body during the Renaissance has remained unrivalled to this day.

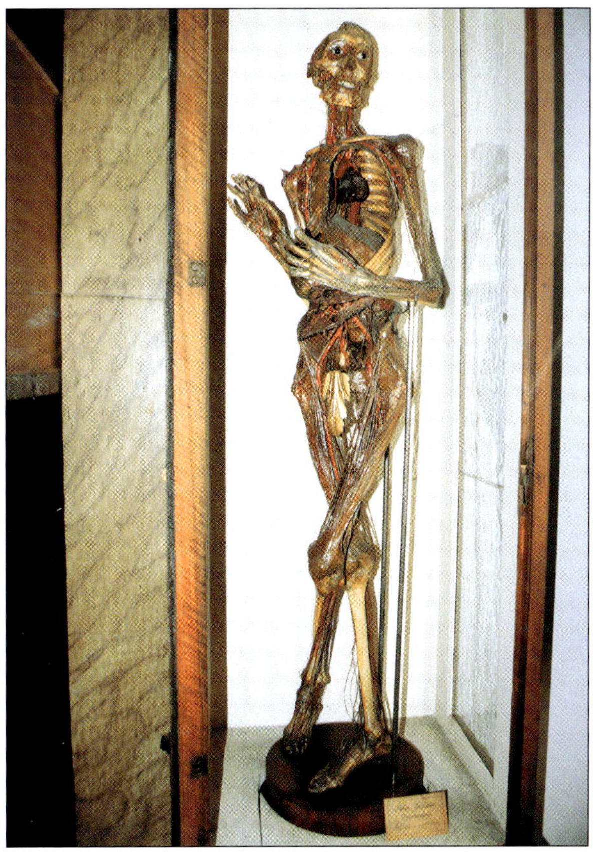

*Fig. 8 and 9: These roughly 200-year-old whole-body anatomical specimens, which can still be seen in Florence and Modena, have been preserved with varnish.*

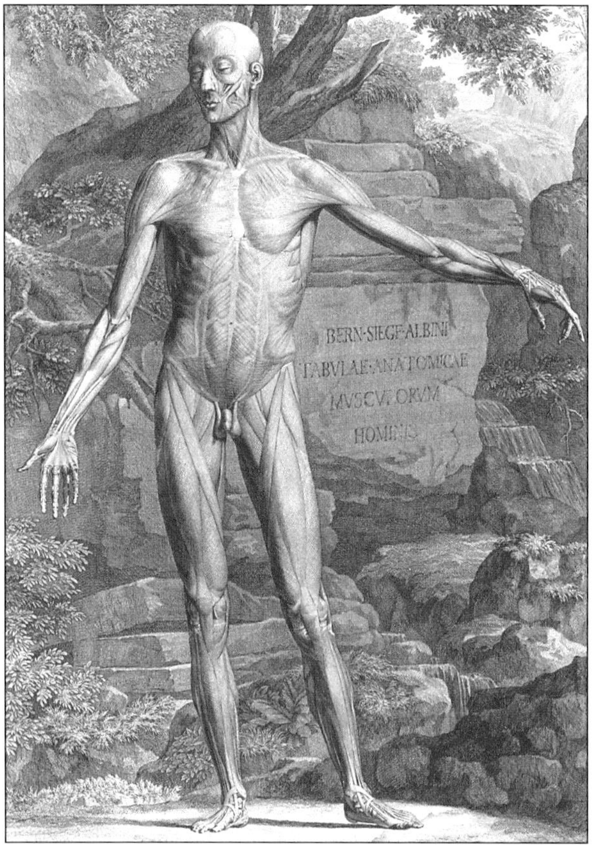


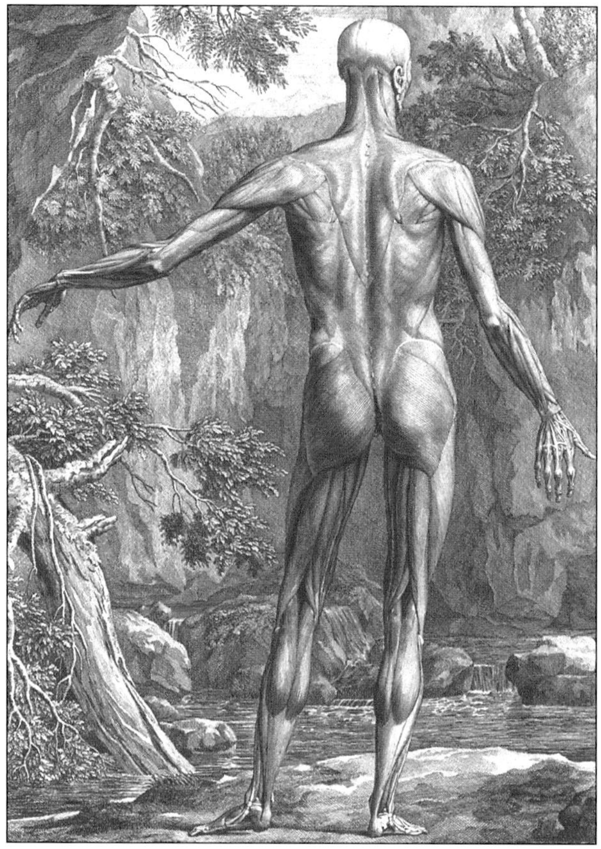

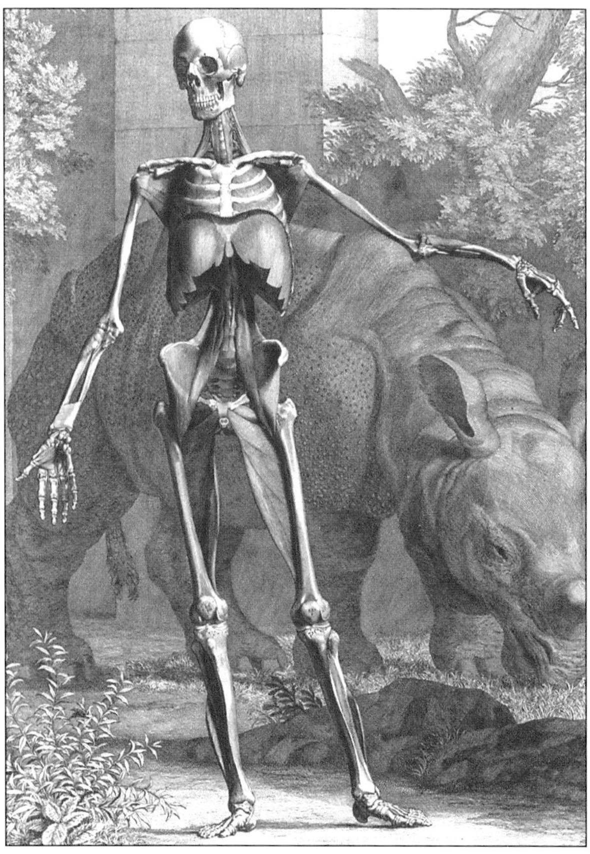

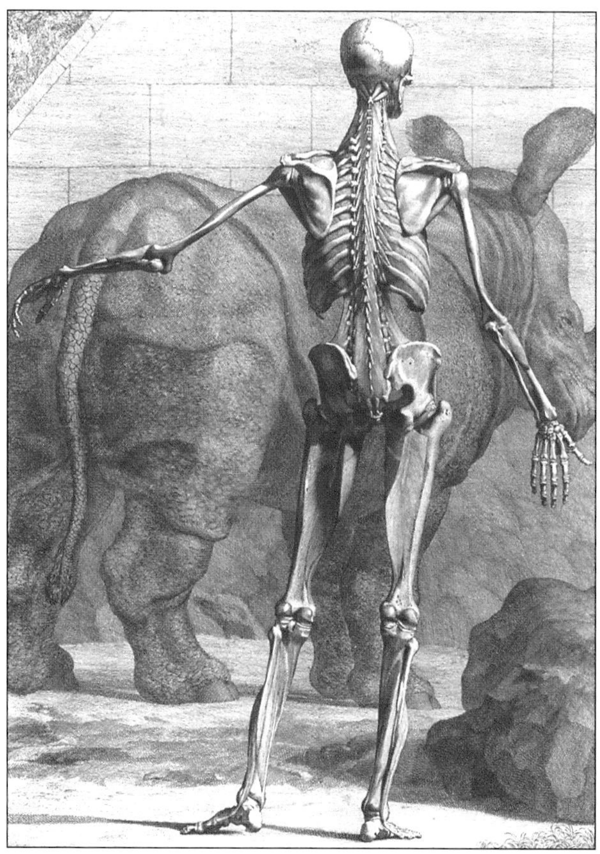

*Fig. 10-13: Depictions of Bernhard Siegfried Albinus (1697–1747), anatomist at the University of Leiden in Holland, 1747.*

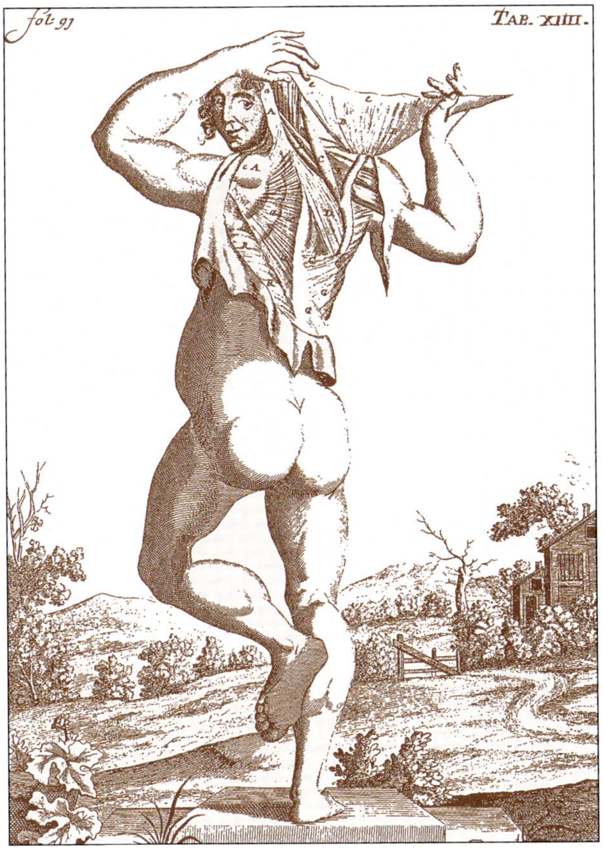

*Fig. 14: Dissected bodies were shown in life-like poses, their gestures accentuating the individuality of their anatomy.*

**Anatomy and the Papacy**

Today's medical profession has laid sole responsibility for the over 1000-year stagnation of anatomical studies at the feet of the church. De sepulturis, the papal bull issued by Pope Bonifacius VIII in 1300, is gladly interpreted as evidence of the animosity towards anatomical science on the part of the church. The purpose of this decree was quite different, however: crusaders had begun the practice of dismembering the corpses of their fallen comrades, boiling their bones and sending them back home. The reason for this was that they could thus be buried on consecrated ground in their native lands; the time-consuming custom weakened the troops' fighting ability, however, and this was the reason that the papal bull was intended to put a stop to it. Over-zealous clerics interpreted it as a general ban on dissection.

A notable example of how well-disposed the church was towards anatomy is that the body of Pope Alexander V was dissected in the year 1410. Popes Sixtus IV and Clement VII expressly permitted the dissection of human cadavers in Padua and Bologna. The Museum of Anatomy in Bologna owes its existence to support from Pope Benedict XIV, who had always been very open-minded regarding modern science. Even when he was still the archbishop of Bologna, Benedict had indicated the importance of anatomy and stressed the necessity of dissecting cadavers. The Holy See expressly permitted corpses to be opened during epidemics of bubonic plague.

Without the Christian belief of the dualism of body and soul mentioned earlier, anatomical dissection would never have originated and become established in Italy, a country ruled by the papacy. Similarly, without this belief, the Catholic tradition of preserving ritual relics would never have developed. Even today, relics can be found in many Catholic churches, and many old cemeteries have what are known as ossuaries – charnel houses with stacks of bones and skulls reaching to the ceiling.

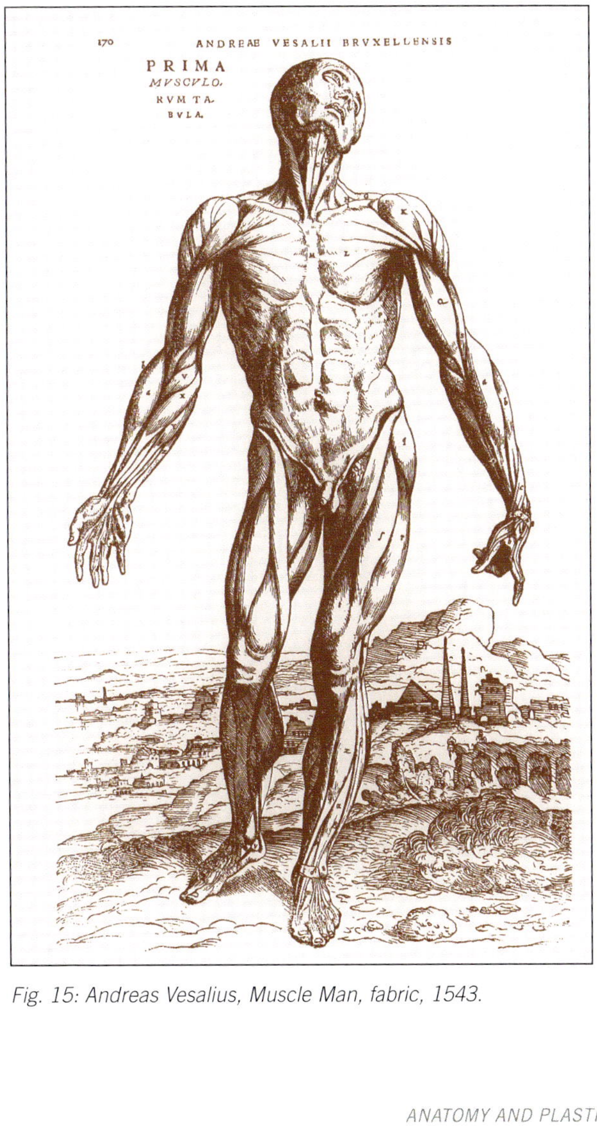


*Fig. 15: Andreas Vesalius, Muscle Man, fabric, 1543.*

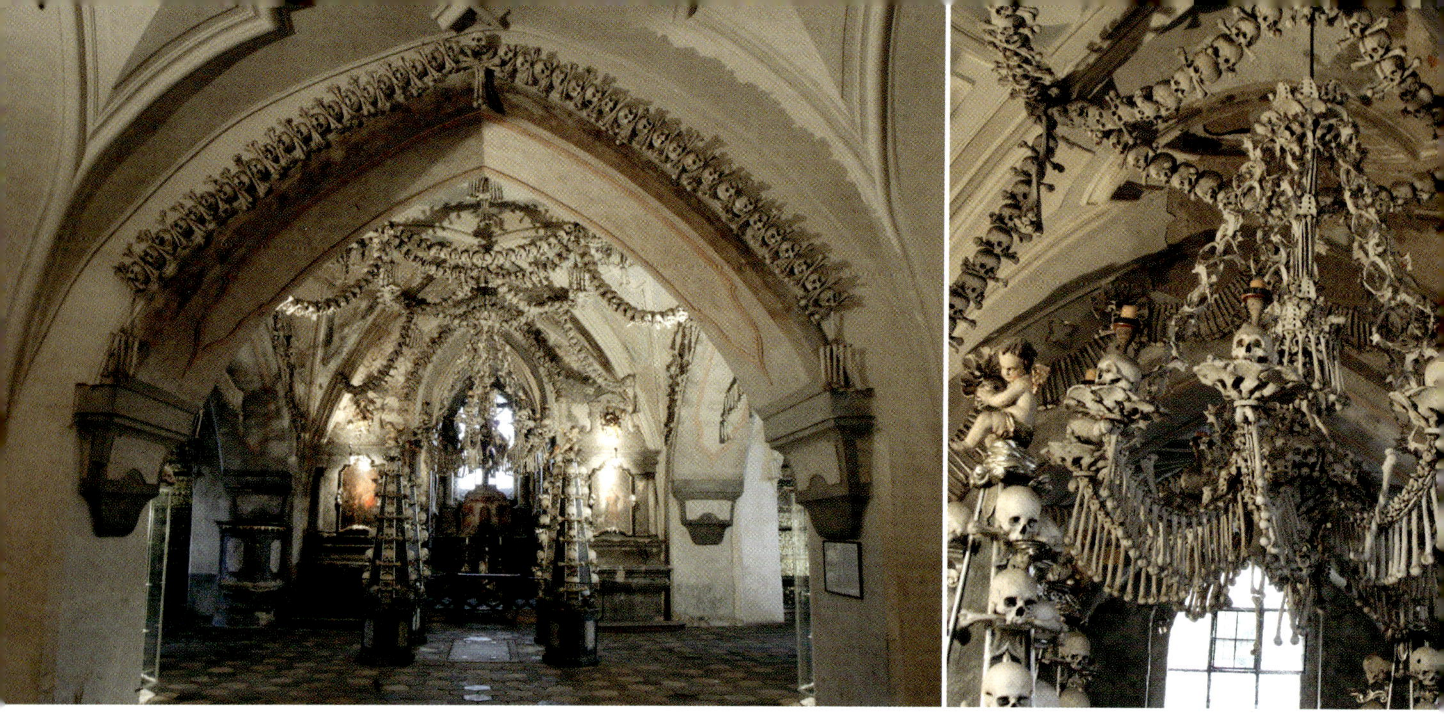

*Fig. 16: In 1860, a wood carver named Frantisek Rint artistically adorned the charnel house of the All Saints Church in Kunta Hora, Czech Republic, with the bones of 40,000 people.*

**The History of Procuring Cadavers**

Anatomists of the Renaissance dissected the corpses of executed prisoners, disputing the right of criminals to their own bodies. This was the case in England, where Henry VIII (1491–1547) commanded that the bodies of criminals hanging from the gallows be handed over to anatomists. Dabbling in anatomy became so popular, in fact, that dissections began to be carried out in public theatres of anatomy so that anyone having an interest could satisfy his or her curiosity. It was not long before bodies became so scarce that people began robbing cemeteries. Parish councils received frequent complaints; in one such complaint, it was reported that thieves had stolen seven adult cadavers and three children's bodies during the nights from Thursday, January 12, to Friday, January 13, 1786. In this case, it was claimed that young anatomists had, in attempts to hide the remains from the neighbours, burned the bones and used the fat from the dead as heating fuel in the winter. Robbing graves became an established profession; its representatives were known as 'resurrection men.' Because of the public interest in educating medical students, a blind eye was turned to this practice, until 1828 when two Scots named Burke and Hare began strangling people in order to deliver the bodies directly to anatomists. The public was so horrified that the English parliament immediately passed the Anatomy Act in 1832, a law that would secure the supply of bodies to anatomists, thereby depriving grave robbers of their economic base. Since that time, England has had an official anatomy examiner bearing the title 'Her Majesty's Inspector of Anatomy.' In Germany, there was also an effort made by the state to offset shortages of cadavers for anatomical purposes. In Prussia, for instance, circulars from 1889 saw to it that unclaimed cadavers were delivered to anatomical institutes. Bodies found, for which no survivors could be identified, formed the basis for the supply of corpses at anatomical institutes up until the 1960s. Bodies were transferred to institutes of anatomy by such public institutions as the Social Welfare Office.

In the 1960s, German anatomical institutes switched over to the practice of seeking bequeathments, in which individuals stated that, upon their deaths, their bodies should be donated to the nearest anatomical institute. Since then, the supply of cadavers has so greatly outpaced demand that most institutes of this type no longer need to accept unclaimed corpses.

How cadavers are procured for anatomical purposes varies greatly from one country to the next, and depends on the cultural and religious context. In the United States, for instance, where this is a state issue just as it is in Germany, institutes of anatomy either operate their own body donation programs or they obtain bodies from independent, state-run organisations (State Anatomy Boards), which are responsible for supplying cadavers to interested institutes. Such organisations also run special donation programs for obtaining bodies. In addition to this, federal law holds that unclaimed cadavers are to be sent to State Anatomy Boards, where, for example in Maryland, they are chemically preserved and turned over to any interested institutions for a small fee (to cover costs).

## History of Preserving Cadavers

Man's desire to be immortalised is as old as the human race. Cave paintings, Egyptian pyramids, art collections, endowments and monuments all testify to this. It, therefore, comes as no surprise that there has always been a desire in all civilizations to protect one's own body and those of relatives from decomposition, or at least to slow the process down and to prevent the body from becoming a transitory object immediately following death. In the past, however, permanent preservation was reserved for only a few wealthy individuals. Yet it was not simple death rituals that led to the development of methods for preserving cadavers; fear of apparent death also played a role. Up until the 18th century, the processes of death and dying were not well known, and people were very unclear and unsure as to when the actual moment of death occurred. It was believed that the body lived on in some diminished state, especially for however long the flesh was still on it. Comments such as "Corpses are ravenous and devour their own garments!" or "Corpses can hear!" were not uncommon in documents of the time. If the ground over a grave sank or if the gases that result from decay caused it to rise (mass graves were common at the time, and a significant amount of gas was produced as a result), the tombstone would rise and sink, thereby sending out what appeared to be encoded messages from the dead. It was not until people understood the circulatory system and the functions of the brain that the moment of death could be defined as a unique event in time. Finally, the development of appropriate preservation methods was extremely important for the advance of medicine, as the study of human anatomy had previously been greatly impeded by the process of decay.

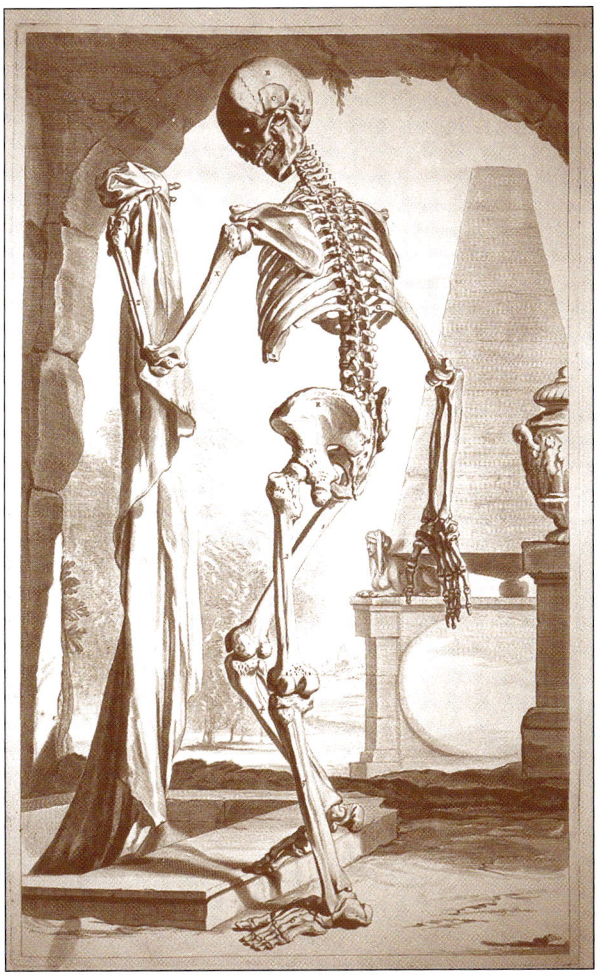

*Fig. 17: Because of ignorance regarding the process of decomposition, it was a long-held belief that the body lived on in some diminished state.*

Artificial preservation methods undertaken by man are not the only means of preserving corpses. Natural preservation can also take place, and requires that the cadaver dry out in a relatively bacteria-free environment over a long period of time, as happens to a body when kept in an airtight sarcophagus or in a crypt ventilated with dry air. The same is true for bodies buried in moors where they are preserved by the humic acid found there. Many natural mummies, including Ötzi (the oldest and most well-known European mummy) prove that the degree to which they have been preserved is no worse than in the case of the mummies of the Pharaohs, for which such great pains had been taken.

## Cultic Preservation of Bodies

The idea has persisted throughout nearly every epoch, culture and religion that death does not mean the end of our individual existence. When death is seen as a transition of the soul to a spiritual world, as is the case with Jews, Christians, Buddhists and other religious societies, then the body is considered to be of secondary importance; rituals accompanying death are kept relatively simple.

It was different with early cultures that were often convinced of a somatic life after death. Here the deceased were buried with a rich array of burial objects, commensurate with their social status. Moreover, the question arose on how to preserve the bodies of the dead from decomposition. Notably, the Egyptians developed embalming and mummification methods over several thousand years, the results of which can even today be admired in museums throughout the world.

Why it was the Egyptians who developed such methods can presumably be explained by the following. Because of the annual flooding of the Nile Valley, the people were forced

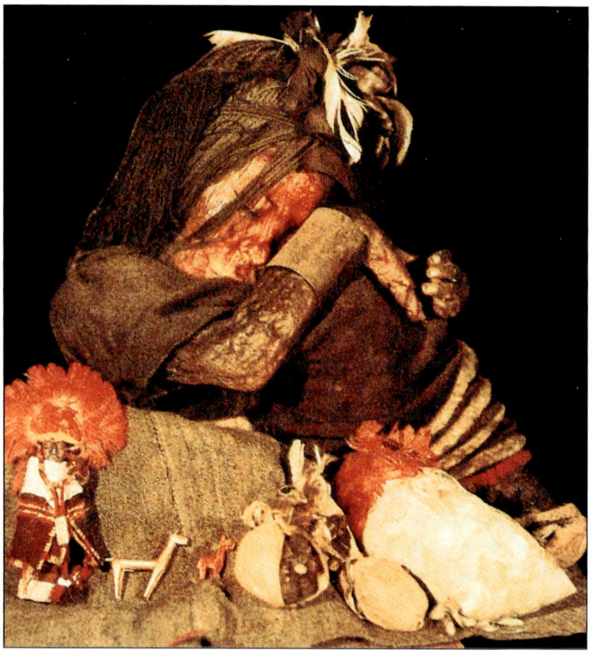

*Fig. 18: "The little Inca prince", approximately 500-year-old ice mummy. National Museum in Santiago de Chile.*

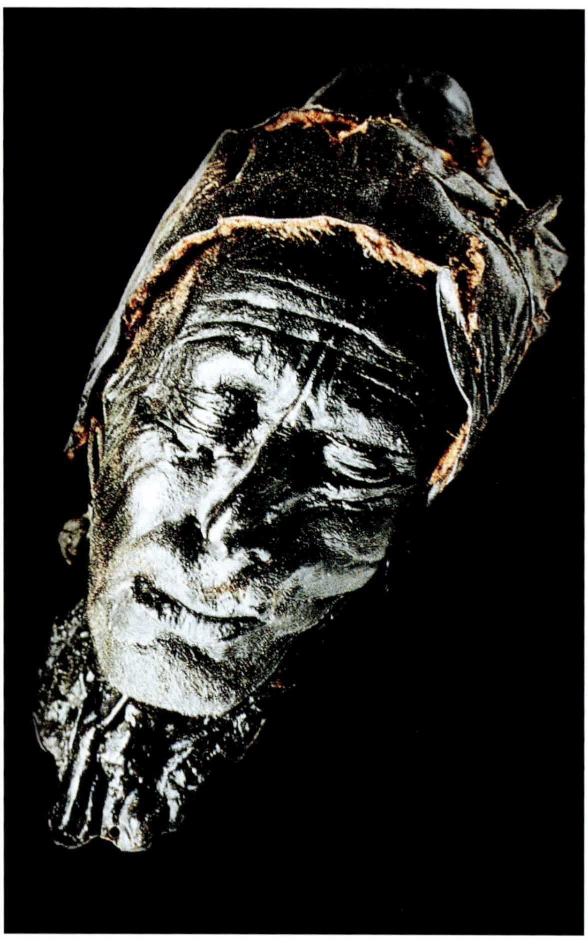

*Fig. 19: Tollund man, one of the best-preserved bog bodies from the pre-Christian era.*

to bury their dead beyond the reach of the floodwaters, in other words, in the dry, hot sand or rocks of the surrounding desert regions. Here the conditions were ideal for natural mummification: warm, dry sand that could dehydrate the body while at the same time stabilising it in its outward form. The steady draughts prevailing in these desert regions additionally favoured the drying-out process. Finally, finding natural mummies by the Egyptians themselves must have contributed to making the idea of a somatic afterlife a central part of their religious world view.

The art of embalming in Egypt reached its zenith in the period from 1700–1100 BC. It confined itself, however, to the 'mortal shell' of the corpses. The organs, whose failure was the cause of death, such as the lungs, liver, kidneys and brain, could not be sufficiently preserved. Their fate was as follows: First, the brain was removed through the nose with the aid of a hook. After opening the abdominal cavity through a slit along the left side of the body, the viscera were taken out except for the heart; they were then washed in palm oil and preserved in an alcohol solution in canopic jars. They nevertheless quickly fell prey to decomposition because the essences (natron, resins) only had a superficial effect. The body cavity was also washed and filled with powdered myrrh, resins and perfumes. The slit was then sewn back together. Next, the body was placed in a solution of potassium nitrate or saltpetre for 70 days.

Finally, it was again washed, rubbed with oils or resin and wrapped repeatedly in complicated layers of linen bandages. It was thus possible to preserve permanently only the skin and the bones, which could hardly rot under such dry conditions, anyway.

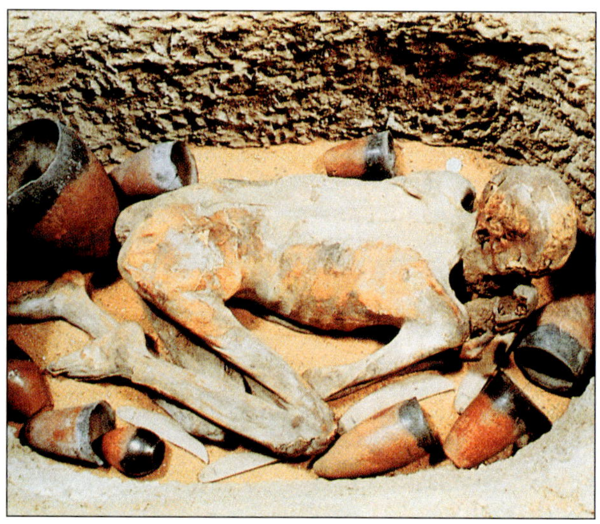

*Fig. 20: "Ginger" – the oldest, fully preserved dry mummy in the world. About 3200 years ago, she was buried in the hot desert sands of Egypt. British Museum, London.*

Methods of preservation similar to those of the ancient Egyptians are also utilised by the natives on the Canary Islands, in Africa (Guinea, Congo, Sudan and the Ivory Coast), in Asia (inter alia, India, Sri Lanka and Tibet), in Oceania (inter alia, Melanesia and Polynesia), America (in many Indian tribes of North and South America) and in Europe. In fact, they are partially still in use even today, for example by headhunters in the Amazon region, in Assam, Burma, Malaysia and New Guinea, to produce shrunken heads as trophies.

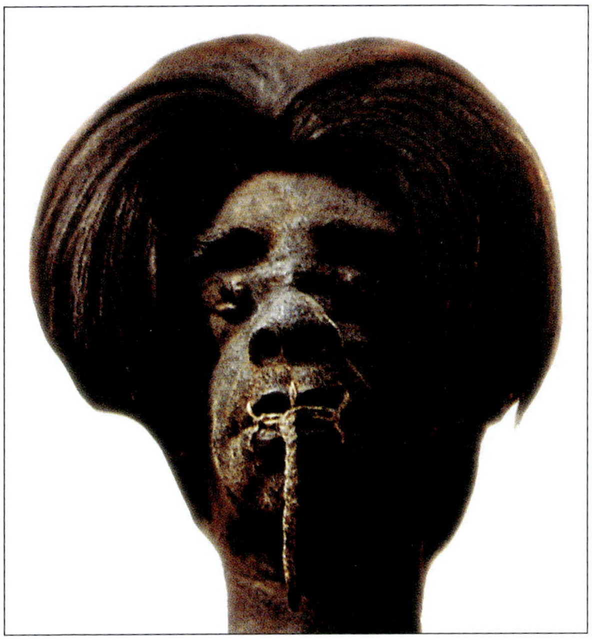

*Fig. 22: Shrunken head of a Jivaro. Trophies of human heads were supposed to convey the power and strength of an enemy to the victor.*

The complex processes of mummifying corpses developed from methods used to preserve food, for example, drying (dried fruits and meats), curing with smoke, salts, acids and protective solutions (pickling fluids, honey, sugar or alcohol). Two famous examples of using methods for preserving food to protect corpses were: 1) the body of Alexander the Great, which was kept in honey for the return to Macedonia after his untimely death; and 2) the body of Horatio Nelson, which spent the return journey from the victorious battle of Trafalgar, which had ended fatally for the admiral, in brandy.

**Modern Embalming**

Until the 17$^{th}$ century, corpses were preserved with the embalming methods developed by the Egyptians. The embalming methods commonly used today differ from the old ones both in the substances employed for preservation as well as the technology. Here we can primarily mention the introduction of new chemicals for preservation, especially formaldehyde, and the development of embalming through arterial injection. The latter was first made possible when William Harvey published his revolutionary ideas on the circulatory system. During his research, Harvey had injected dyestuffs

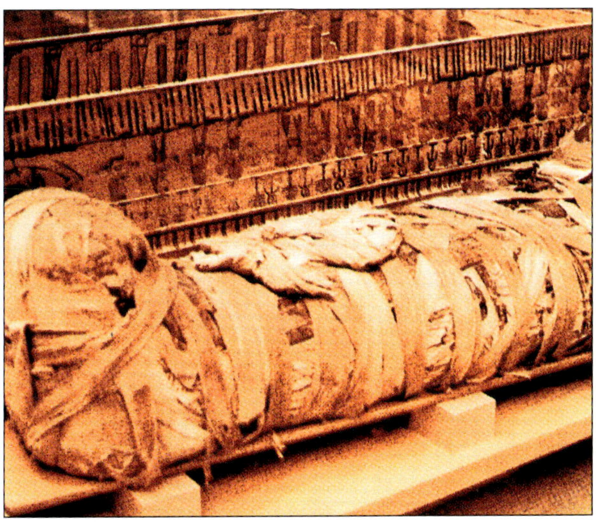

*Fig. 21: Egyptian mummy. Vatican Museum, Rome.*

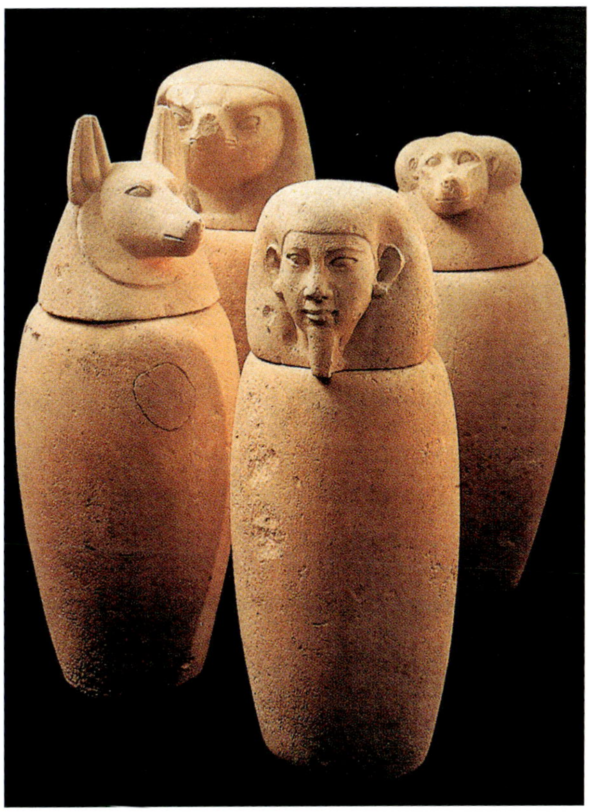

*Fig. 23: Canopic jars. They were used to hold the viscera of Egyptian mummies.*

into the blood vessels of cadavers. This new principle of arterial injection was first used successfully by Frederick Ruysche (1665–1717), who taught anatomy in Amsterdam. Unfortunately, Ruysche neglected to record exact information about the chemicals that he used. Detailed descriptions on arterial embalming were first written by the famous Scottish anatomist, William Hunter (1718–1783). He employed a solution consisting of turpentine and resinous oils, mixed with dyes, which he chose to inject in the femoral artery. In 1868, chemist August Wilhelm von Hofmann discovered formaldehyde that was later integrated into preservation techniques. Some years before, Laskowski (1886) had already introduced his Genevan embalming fluid, glycerin (discovered by Scheele in 1779), to protect specimens from dehydration and phenol (introduced as a disinfectant by Lister in 1867) to preserve them.

The importance that these discoveries had for practical preservation is shown by a survey that was published by Grönroos in 1898. Of the 44 anatomical institutes in Europe surveyed by the study, all of them utilised arterial injection for embalming. Embalming fluids that had gained Europe-wide acceptance were those that used solutions with formaldehyde (embalming and hardening), phenol (to inhibit the formation of fungi) and glycerin (moisture-retentive as it is a humectant). By the beginning of the 20$^{th}$ century, all of the substances had already been introduced, which have remained relatively unchanged until today and have been most frequently used to preserve cadavers. These include formaldehyde, phenol, glycerin, ethanol and water. A typical example is the preservation fluid used in the Institute of Anatomy at the University of Heidelberg: formaldehyde 3%, Lysoformin (contains formaldehyde, glutaraldehyde and a wetting solution) 1%, phenol 6%, glycerin 15%, alcohol 30% and water 45%.

## 2. Plastinated Specimens and Plastination

### What are Plastinated Specimens?

Approximately 70% of our bodies consist of fluids. They are indispensable both for living and for decomposing. With plastination, fluids in our tissue are replaced by reactive plastics, such as silicone rubber, epoxy resin or polyester resin, in a special vacuum process. Body cells and the natural surface relief remain identical with their condition prior to preservation down to the microscopic level. The specimens are dry and odourless and are thus 'graspable' in the most literal sense of the word. Thanks to these properties, plastinated specimens are of extremely high value both in educating medical students and in enlightening interested laypersons.

With the invention of plastination, it has become possible for the first time to preserve natural anatomical specimens in a durable, realistic and aesthetic manner for instructional and research purposes as well as for general education. Natural specimens are especially valuable for medical studies and also for laypersons as the complicated structure of the locomotor system and organs as well as their relative positions and relationships to one another cannot be fully comprehended in their three-dimensional complexity when only books are used. Regardless of the quality of the pictures, they cannot replace the original. Artificial anatomical models can also make only limited contributions to understanding anatomy as they are schematised at best, are not capable of showing fine details and cannot convey the individuality of the human body. One model is the same as the next one. Anatomical variations, however, are significant from one individual to another. For this reason, a thorough, practical anatomical education for medical students using dead, human bodies has been laid down by law in most of today's advanced societies.

Beyond their didactic qualities, plastinated specimens also radiate a certain fascination, based primarily on their authenticity. Plastination stops decomposition and dehydration so completely that the insides of bodies cease to be objects of revulsion. Observers are not bothered by any kind of offensive odours.

Plastination creates beautiful specimens as a sensuous experience that are frozen at a point between death and decay. Thanks to this realistic quality, plastination represents the most attractive form of exhibiting durable human specimens. This becomes particularly evident in the transparent body slices that provide a window into structures that are indispensable to life even in areas which would normally be viewed with a magnifying glass. To achieve the unlimited durability of a specimen, an inordinately large amount of time-consuming dissection work is now justified, which was heretofore not justifiable. One thousand and more hours of dedicated work are necessary to create one whole-body specimen dissected to show minute details. Plastinated specimens far exceed the expressive power of untreated specimens, for example, when – thanks to dyed plastics – grey brain matter is more obviously distinguishable from the white matter than would be possible with an unplastinated brain.

## New Types of Specimens through Plastination

Plastination permits us to produce completely new types of specimens because it makes otherwise soft body parts such as muscles or the skin rigid, for example, in 3-millimeter thick body slices. Plastination also makes it possible to produce 'exploded-view' specimens, 'open-door' specimens and 'open-drawer' specimens. With 'exploded-view' specimens, body parts are shifted in all directions.

These specimens are particularly instructive when the body parts are 'exploded' in only one direction, for example, in the longitudinal. Instructional 'open-door' specimens also succeed in that hinges are attached in such a way that an open view into the innermost realms of the body is provided. Finally, parts of the body can be shifted forward like open drawers, thereby giving a clear insight into the body.

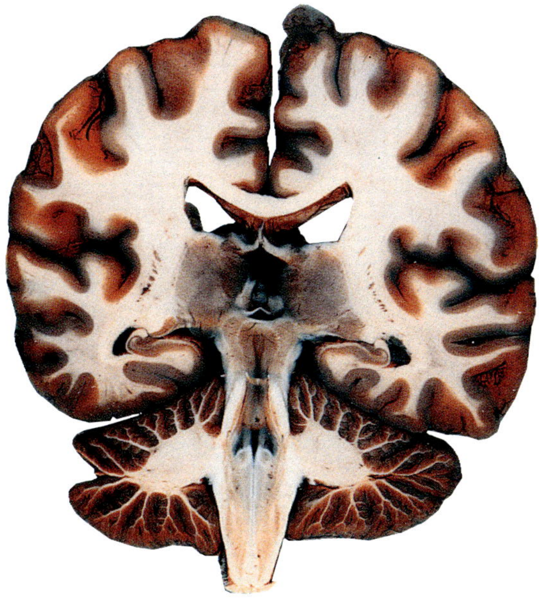

*Fig. 25: In plastinated brain slices, the grey matter of the cerebral cortex and the nuclei are clearly distinguishable from the white matter.*

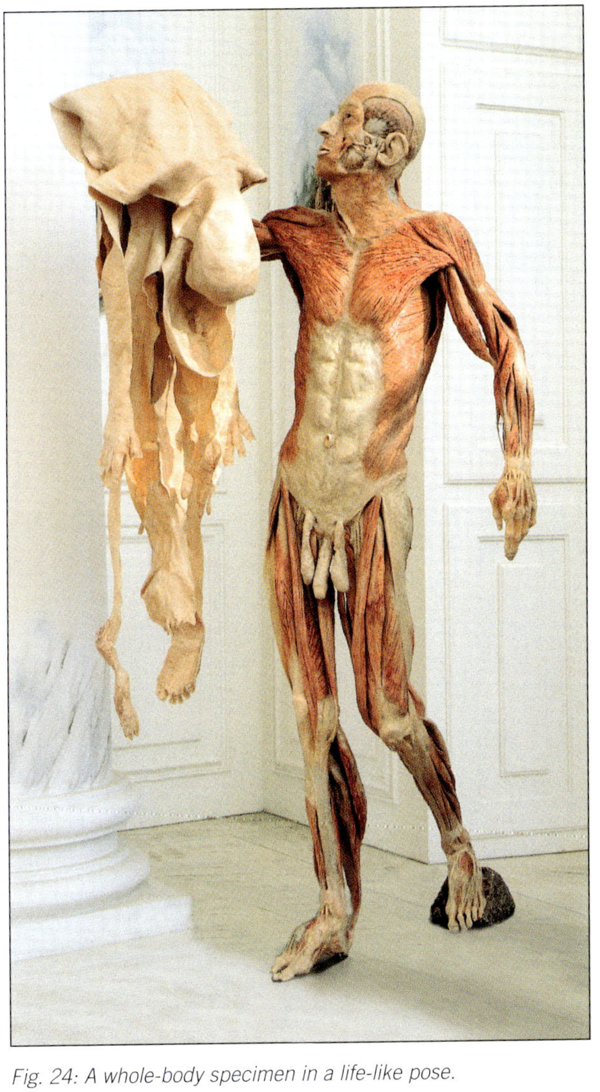

*Fig. 24: A whole-body specimen in a life-like pose.*

These interstitial specimens that permit the observer to shift back the individual parts of the body to their original position in the mind's eye and reduce the body to its original shape and size contrast with traditional 'removal dissections' practiced at universities. Here, each succeeding layer is removed from the bodies. The major disadvantage of this procedure is that by the end of the course, students have often forgotten which parts were removed at the beginning.

### The Technology of Plastination

In principle, plastination is relatively simple. As shown in the Figure 31, plastinated specimens are created through two essential exchange phases: In the first phase, bodily fluids are replaced by acetone through diffusion. In the second phase, the acetone still in the body is replaced by reactive plastics. It is then removed from the plastic bath to be cured into a fully plastinated specimen.

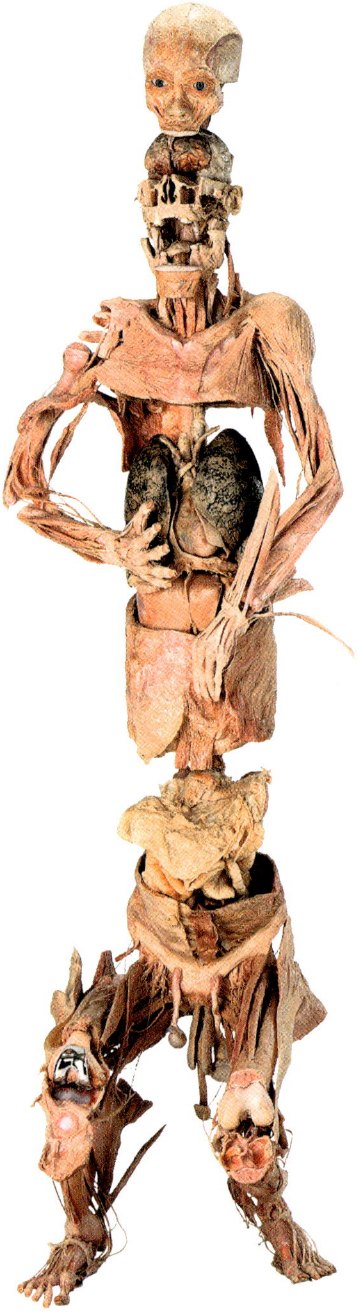

*Fig. 26: The Longitudinally Expanded Body.*

The decisive trick, with which liquid plastic can be infused into the last cells, is forced vacuum impregnation. Just as babies use a partial vacuum to suck the milk out of their mothers' breasts, acetone is sucked from the specimen in the vacuum. In this way, the vacuum created in the specimen keeps a steady supply of plastic flowing into the tissue. Gradually the specimen fills up with plastic. Seen physically, the process takes advantage of the difference in pressure between the volatile acetone and a plastic solution with a high boiling point. Thin body slices take only a few days for this; conversely, with whole-body specimens, this can take weeks. Only when the vacuum falls below one-hundredth of normal atmospheric levels (<5mmHg) and only individual acetone bubbles squeeze out of the specimen is it removed from the plastic bath and cured.

The advantages of this "forced impregnation with plastic in a vacuum," which is the main step in plastination, are primarily the following:

1. Impregnation can be done with a number of liquid, polymerisable plastics.
2. By regulating the vacuum, the speed of impregnation can be adapted to the type of specimen, its thickness and the viscosity of the plastics used.
3. Impregnation can be used to minimise shrinkage at low temperatures, e.g., at –25°C.

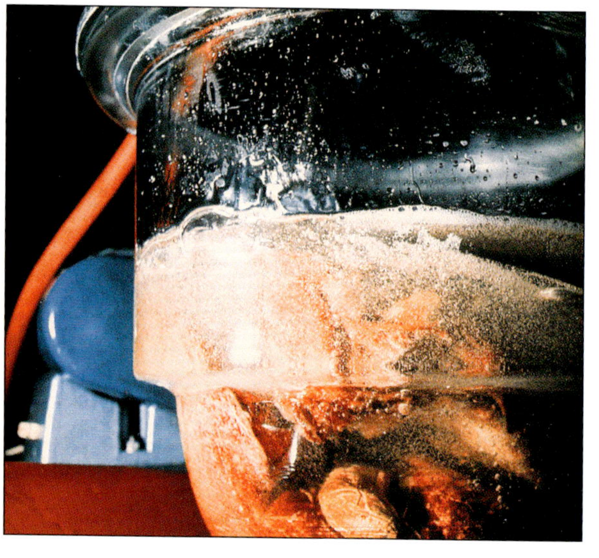

*Fig. 27: Forced impregnation. Acetone is squeezed out of the specimen and is constantly sucked away.*

# PRESERVATION BY PLASTINATION

**1. Embalming and Anatomical Dissection**

The first step of the process involves halting decay by pumping formalin into the body through the arteries. Formalin kills all bacteria and chemically stops the decay of tissue. Using dissection tools, the skin, fatty and connective tissues are removed in order to prepare the individual anatomical structures.

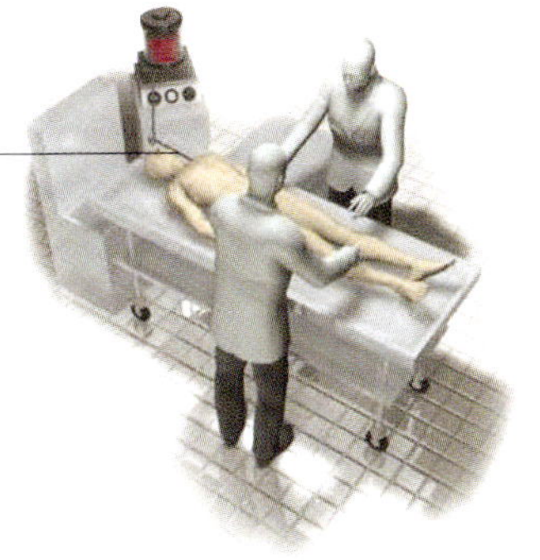


**The process of plastination**

is based on two exchange processes:

**2. Removal of Body Fat and Water**

In the first step, the body water and soluble fats are dissolved from the body by placing it into a solvent bath (e.g., an acetone bath).

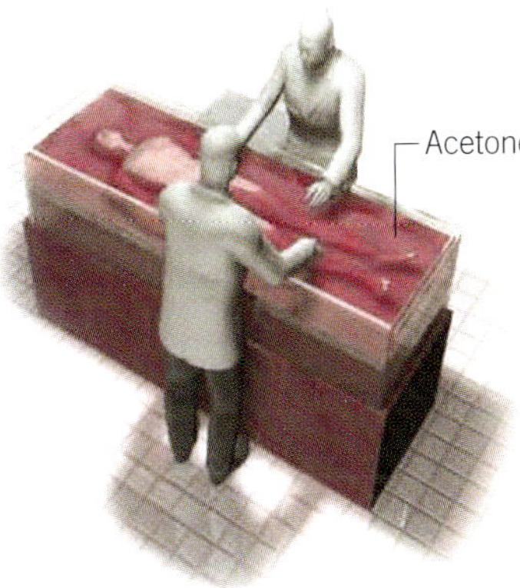


**3. Forced Impregnation**

This second exchange process is the central step in plastination. During forced impregnation a reactive polymer, e.g., silicone rubber, replaces the acetone. To achieve this, the specimen is immersed in a polymer solution and placed in vacuum chamber. The vacuum removes the acetone from the specimen and helps the polymer to penetrate every last cell.

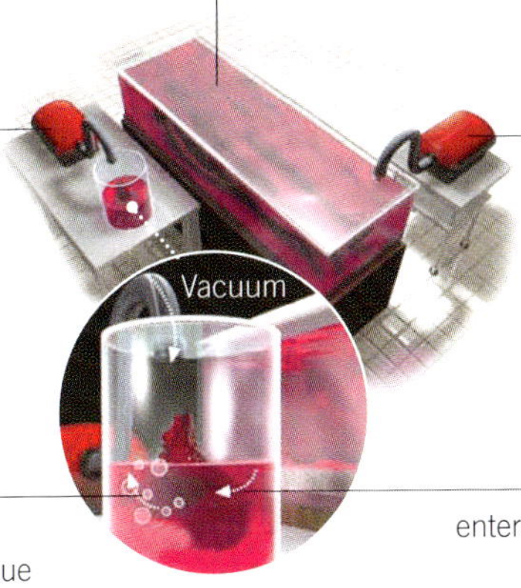


**4. Positioning**

After vacuum impregnation, the body is positioned as desired. Every single anatomical structure is properly aligned and fixed with the help of wires, needles, clamps, and foam blocks.

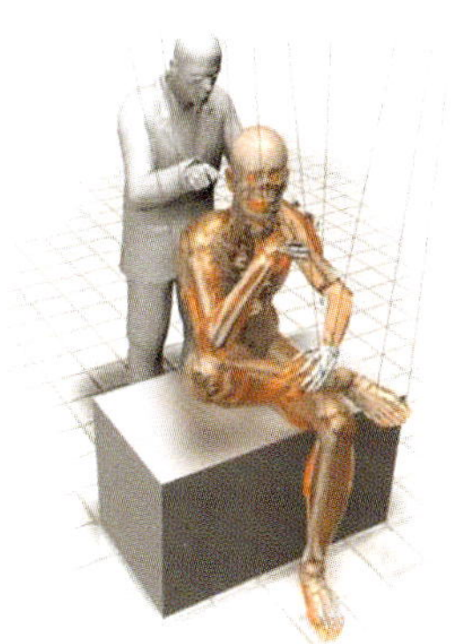

*Illustrations courtesy of the DENVER POST*

**5. Curing (Hardening)**

In the final step, the specimen is hardened. Depending on the polymer used, this is done with gas, light, or heat.

Dissection and plastination of an entire body requires about 1,500 working hours and normally takes about one year to complete.

# PLASTINATION PROCESS

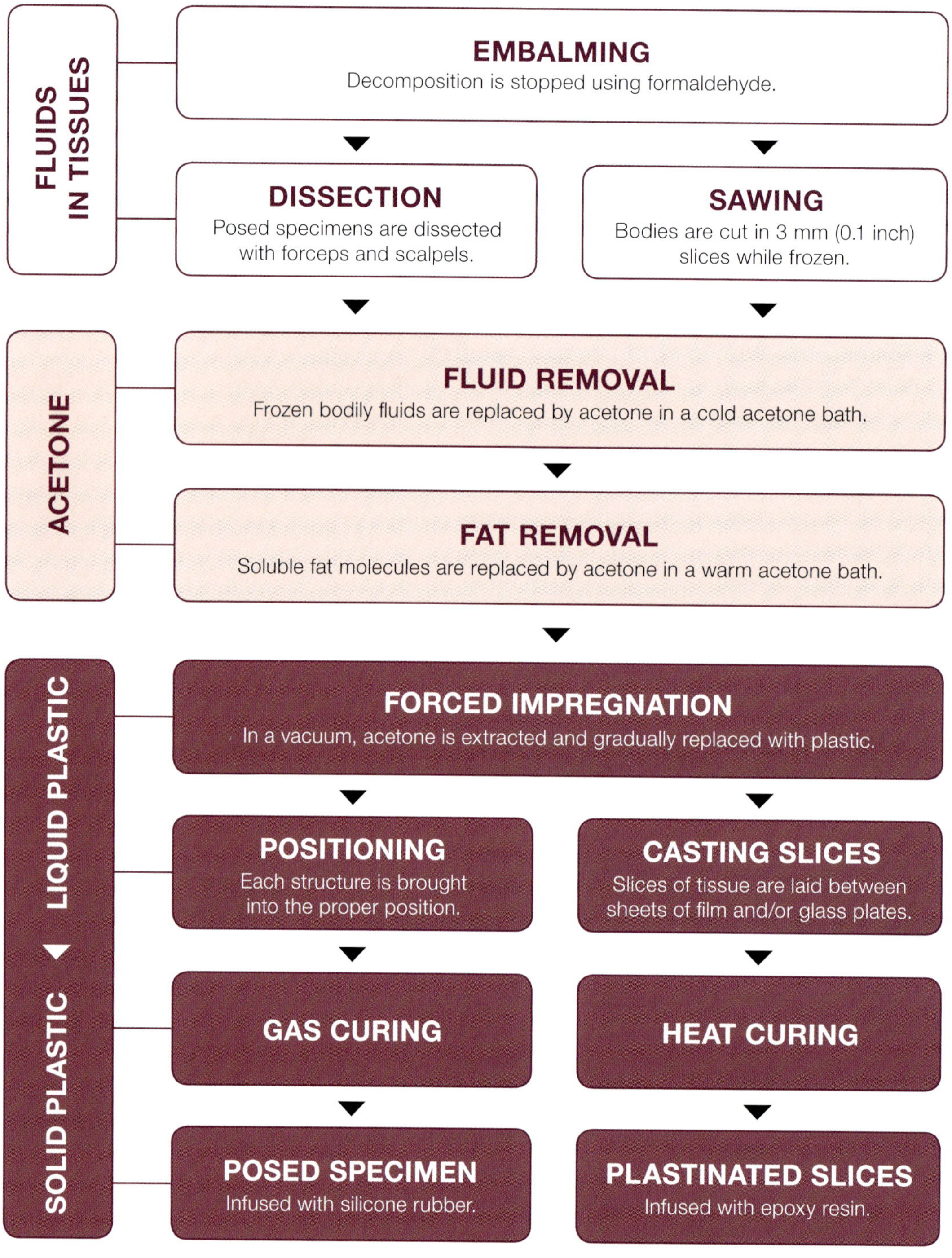

In this way, the plastination process permits numerous possibilities for variation. It also means that the process can be very complex in individual details on the one hand; however, its strengths come just from these complexities on the other hand. If optimum results are desired, the choice of plastics and the type of plastination technology can be adapted to the respective specimen. Here are some examples:

Most specimens, especially bones and intestines, must first be defatted in acetone at room temperature. Conversely, brains would shrink substantially in size if subjected to such a treatment. The same applies for specimens still covered with skin, such as embryos and fish, which therefore require additional infusion with plastic. Freezing specimens may also cause their volume to expand, and when this occurs too slowly, ice crystals can form. Emulsifying plastics cause swelling so that newcomers to the process often wonder why a brain plastinated with these materials no longer fits into its skull. Transparent series of slices should be approximately 6 millimetres (1/4inch) thick through the abdomen while slices of the head should be approximately 3 millimetres (1/8inch) thick. All of this depends still on a number of different factors, such as age, distribution of fat, venous congestion and others.

*Fig. 28: Specimens plastinated with silicone are cured with a special gas.*

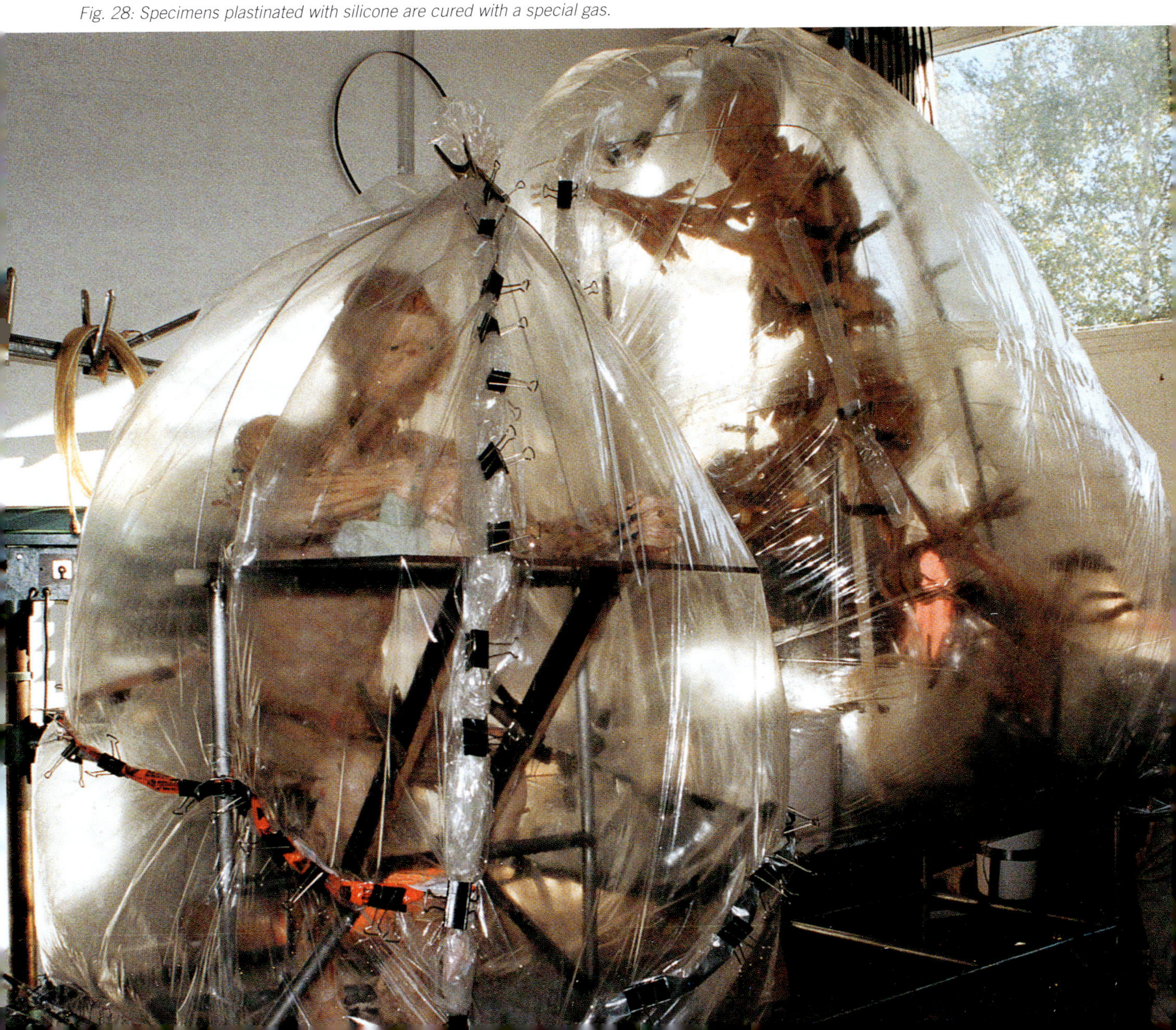

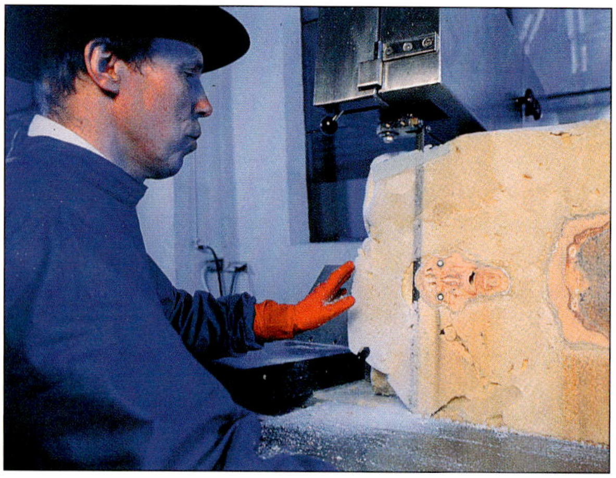

*Fig. 29: A body that has been frozen at –70°C and infused with polyurethane is sawn into approximately 1/8-inch-thick slices.*

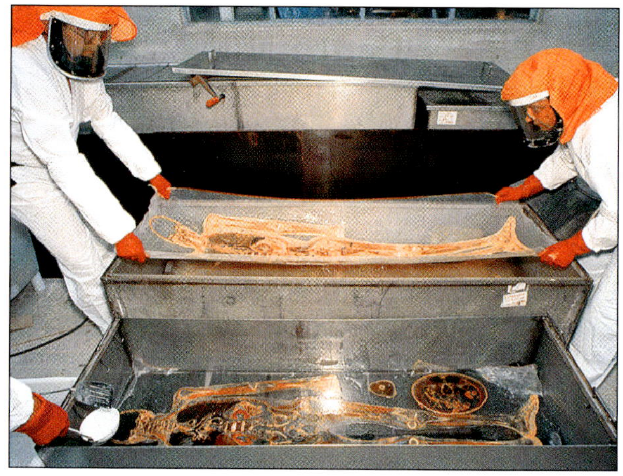

*Fig. 30: Body slices dehydrated with acetone are then placed in a polymer solution.*

The demand for research is still enormous despite all of the progress until now. A particular focus is on retaining the colour of tissue, optimum presentation of blood vessels as well as improving the plastination of slices and treating specimens that are difficult to preserve, such as jellyfish. An International Society for Plastination, a professional journal and biennial conferences are the main forums for discussing advances in plastination.

**Plastics used in Plastination**

Developments in plastination have always been closely associated with development of suitable plastics, as the mechanical and optical properties of the plastics employed largely determine the character of the specimens. The plastics normally used are silicone rubber, epoxy resins and polyester resins.

After curing, silicone rubber is elastic and thus lends elasticity to the specimens. It only refracts light very weakly, which accounts for the natural look of specimens infused with silicone. For this reason, silicone rubber is used to plastinate whole organs (in contrast to slices); here plastination of whole-body specimens is a more recent development. A very thin-bodied silicone provides the best results with whole-organ packages. Gas-curing is used to harden the specimens after all of the anatomical structures have been properly positioned. Plastination with silicone rubber is the simplest of all the techniques used in this process and thus has the most users worldwide.

The highly refractive properties of epoxy resins allow the slices of saturated tissue to appear transparent when the surface is smooth. Because polymerised epoxy resin is also extremely hard, epoxy resin blends were chosen as the polymer of choice for plastinating cross-sectional specimens. The resins are heat-cured.

The use of epoxy resins for plastination is highly suitable for solving clinical problems, because plastinating bodies that have been cut into a series of slices makes it possible to perform precise, three-dimensional analyses of the specimens. In the past, this has allowed scientists to investigate such complex issues as the blood supply in the kneecaps and wrist bones, and the paths taken by the tiny muscles and nerves around the prostate gland that are critical for sexual potency.

A highly refractive polyester resin cured by ultraviolet light is only used for slices of the brain. Polymerisable emulsions that turn white during the curing process are used for thick, natural-looking specimens.

Scientists just getting started with plastination work with one to two types of polymer systems; experienced scientists will use up to ten. Polymers utilised for plastination must have low viscosity, should withstand yellowing and should be compatible with the tissues being plastinated; also, the time available for processing these polymers should be as long as possible, or, even better, unlimited. For this reason, only special polymer blends developed specifically for plastination are used.

## The Idea behind Plastination

I developed the plastination techniques at the University of Heidelberg's Institute of Anatomy in 1977, patented it between 1977 and 1982, and have been continually improving the process ever since. When, as an anatomy assistant, I saw my first specimen embedded in a polymer block, I wondered why the polymer had been poured around the outside of the specimen as having the polymer within the specimen would stabilise it from the inside out. I could not get this question out of my mind. A few weeks later, I was to prepare a series of slices of human kidneys for a research project. The usual process of embedding the kidneys in paraffin and then cutting them into thin slices seemed like too much wasted effort to me, as I only needed every fiftieth slice. Then one day, I was in the butcher shop in the university town where I was studying, and as I watched the sales woman slice ham, it dawned on me that I ought to be using a meat slicer for cutting kidneys. And so a 'rotary blade cutter,' as I called it in the project-appropriation request, became my first plastination investment. I embedded the kidney slices in liquid Plexiglas and used a vacuum to extract the air bubbles that had formed when stirring in the curing agent. As I watched these bubbles, it hit me: It should be possible to infuse a kidney slice with plastic by saturating it with acetone and placing it under a vacuum; the vacuum would then extract the acetone in the form of bubbles, just as it had extracted air before. When I actually tried this, plenty of acetone bubbles emerged, but after an hour the kidney was pitch black and had shrunk. At this point most people would have dismissed the experiment as a failure, and the only reason I went ahead and repeated it a week later using silicone rubber was because my basic knowledge of physical chemistry told me that the blackening effect was due to the index of refraction of the Plexiglas, and that the shrinkage could be attributed to having permeated the specimen too quickly. The next time, I carried out this process more slowly, using three successive silicone baths as a means of preventing a single bath (along with its contents) from curing too quickly. After curing the specimen in a laboratory kiln, I had the first presentable sample of plastination. That was on January 10, 1977, the day that I decided to make plastination the focus of my life. The roots of this decision go back to January of 1968, following my arrest for unsuccessfully attempting to defect from East Germany. While I was being detained in a Bratislava jail, a Czech official gave me the opportunity to escape. I stood before an open window, but could not make up my mind to flee. I was convinced that the East German secret police would not incarcerate me – that conviction cost me two years in an East German prison for "deserting the Republic." That is the reason that in 1977 I made a clear decision in favour of uncertainty, because uncertainty always represents an opportunity.

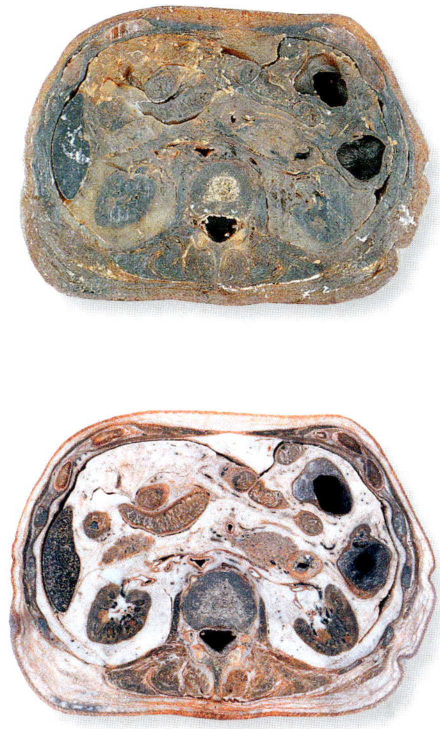

a)

b)

*Fig. 32: Slices of bodies impregnated with a polymerisable emulsion, a) before curing and b) after curing. Emulsification during the curing process lightens the colour of the specimen.*

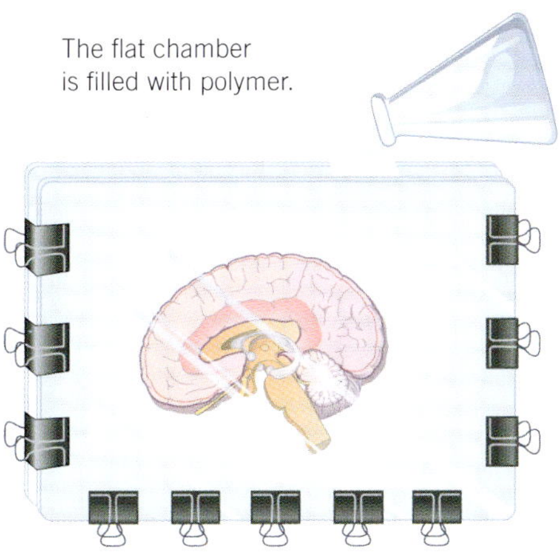


*Fig. 31: Cross-sectional plastination. Tissue slices that have been saturated with polymer are placed in a flat container where additional polymer is poured over them.*

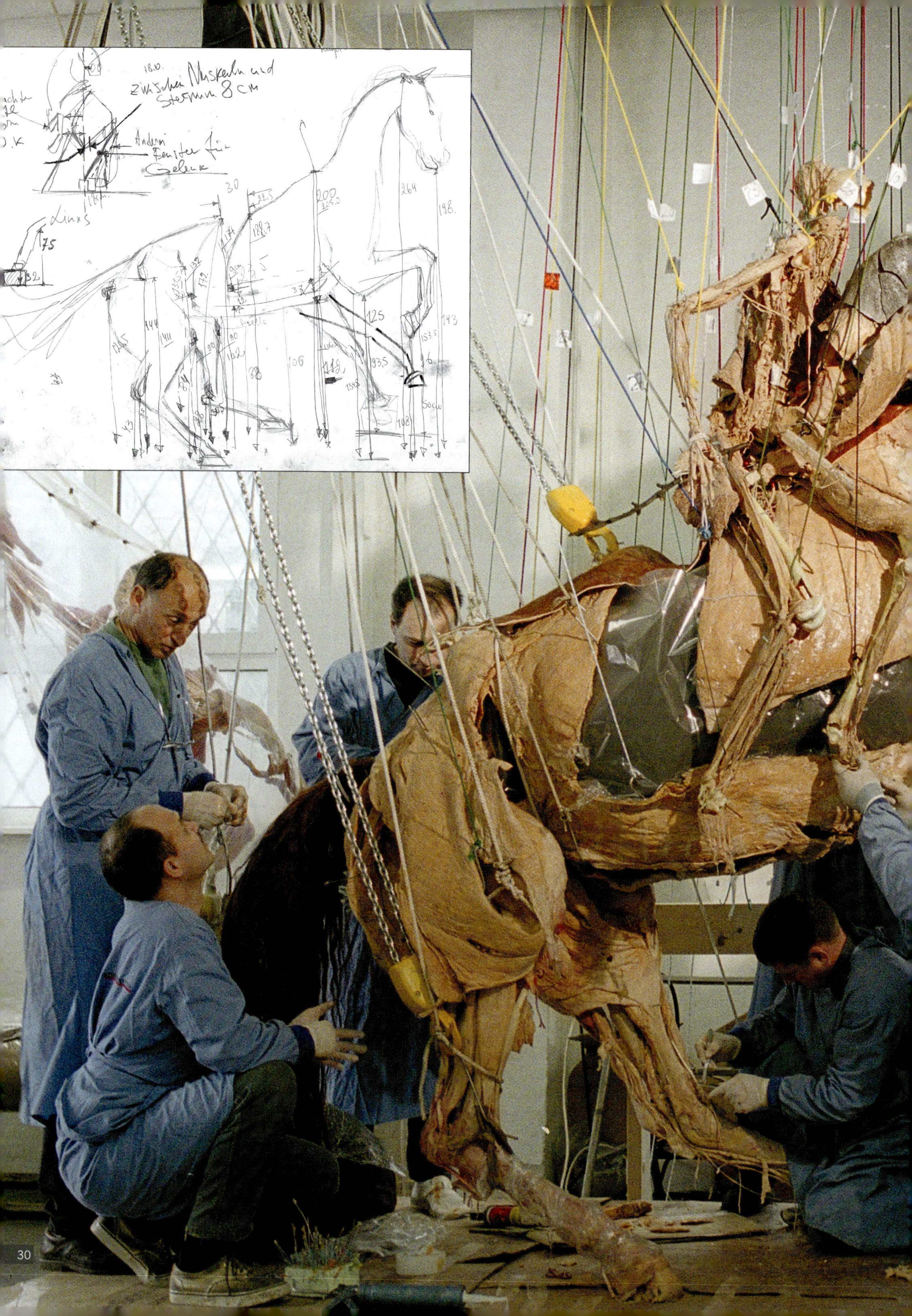
zwischen Muskeln und
Sternum 8 cm
Andere
Fenster für
Gelenk
Links

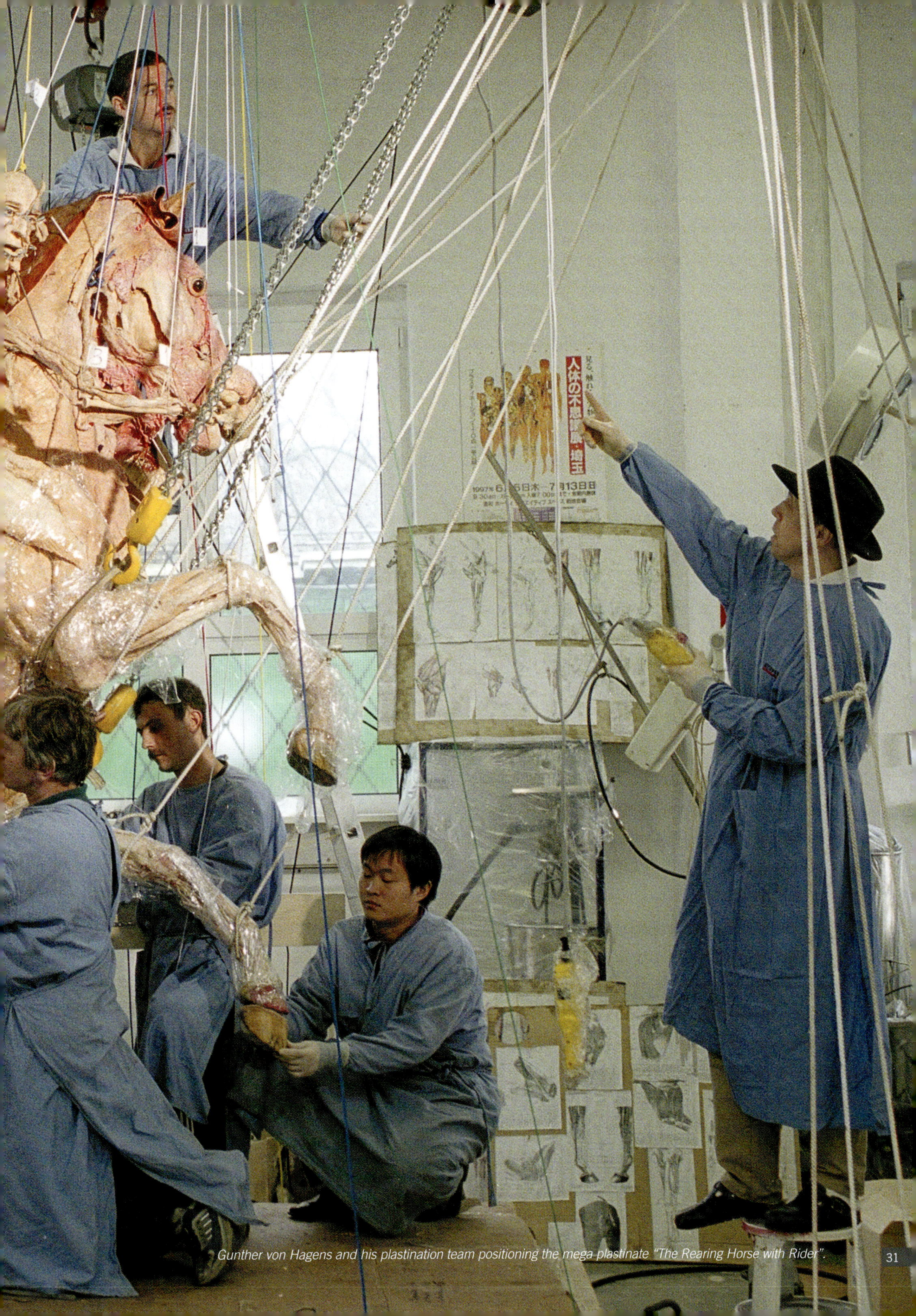

Gunther von Hagens and his plastination team positioning the mega plastinate "The Rearing Horse with Rider".

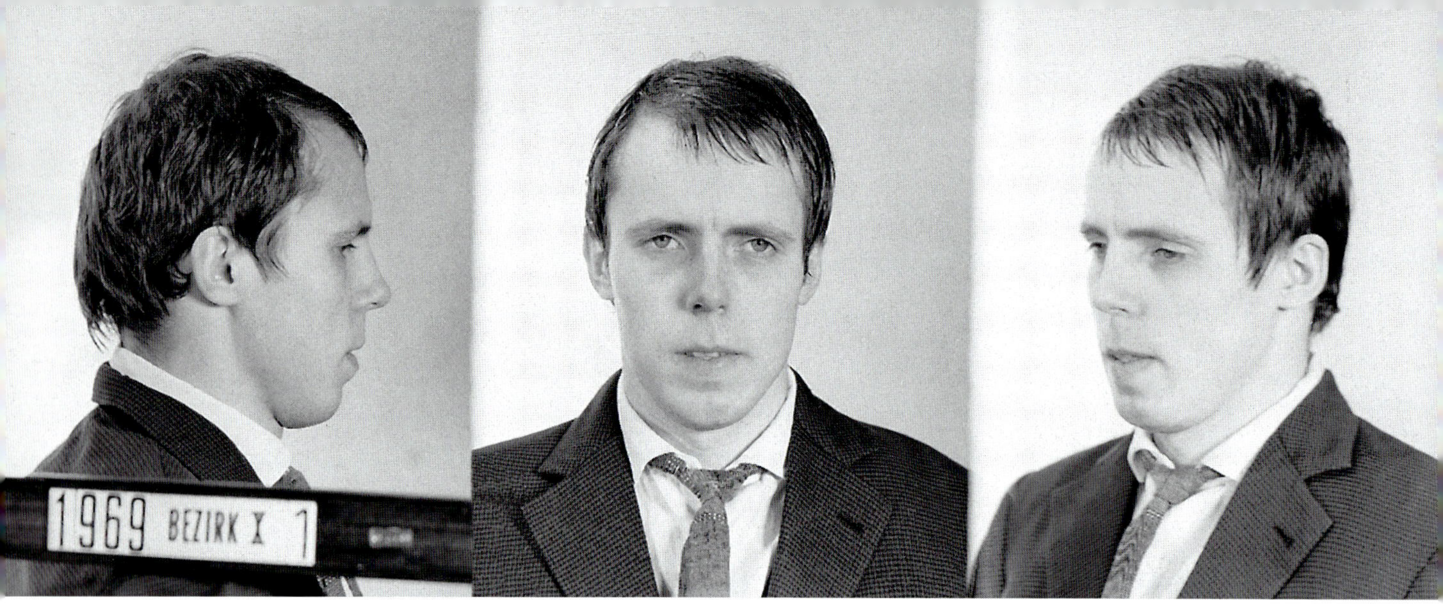


*Fig. 33: Prison photo of Gunther von Hagens, taken in 1969 by the East German Ministry for State Security.*

The first round of plastinated specimens looked anything but promising. Their surfaces were smeared with polymer, transparent tissue slices were full of air bubbles, and it often happened that specimens met their end in polymer baths that had cured prematurely. Only a series of further developments over the following 20 years have made it possible for me to transform plastination from a largely impractical idea to an internationally recognised preservation technique. Significant innovations and developments included the following:

1. The ability to delay curing of the impregnation bath while simultaneously speeding up the curing process once a specimen has been completely infused with polymer. Specimens saturated with silicone rubber in a vacuum, for instance, are not cured until placed in a gas atmosphere. This even makes it possible for large specimens such as entire bodies to be saturated over the course of several months without running the risk that the impregnation bath will cure too early. After the specimens are taken out of the bath, they are further dissected and positioned – only then are they subjected to curing.

2. The development of plastinating slices, in which tissue sections are infused with polymer in flat glass containers or between plastic sheets.

3. The use of highly refractive polyester resin copolymers for plastinating slices of the brain. These copolymers create an excellent colour distinction between the cerebral cortex, medulla oblongata and the nuclei.

4. Development of a new class of polymers that do not emulsify until the curing process has begun, thereby yielding firm, yet natural-looking specimens.

5. The development of perfusion plastination. The first steps in this process are to drain and rinse all of the blood from an organ, position it and allow first acetone and then silicone to flow through it. The specimen is then cured by means of a gas perfusion technique that sends the curing agent through the organ's vascular system. Entire systems of organs can be plastinated in this way, yet because their vascular system is hollow (only the cells themselves are permeated with polymer), they remain light-weight and flexible.

The term 'plastination' is a word of my own invention. In my initial patents of 1977/78, I referred to the procedure as "Polymer Impregnation of Perishable, Biological Specimens," but I did not think that it was very catchy; it was also completely inappropriate for popularising the technology, particularly abroad. Because the term 'plasticise' was already used in the field of polymer chemistry to mean something else, I came up with the following little jingle during a visit to a Viennese pub in 1979: "Plastination teaches the

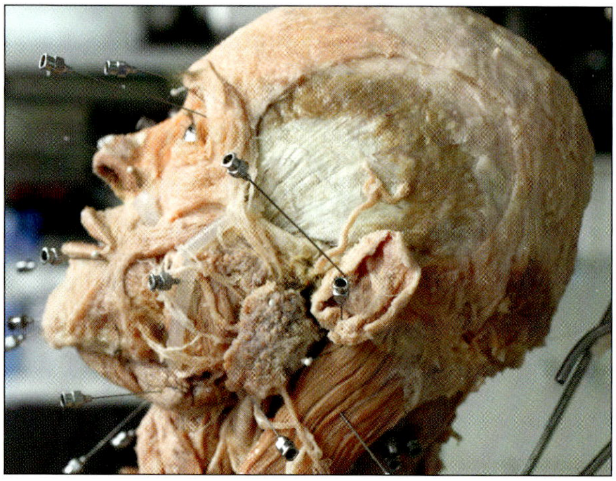

*Fig. 34: Positioning anatomical structures before gas curing.*

nation, because BIODUR® (a trade name for polymers used in plastination) retains the structure." In the 19th edition of the Brockhaus Encyclopaedia (1992), on the other hand, the term plastination is shown to be derived from the Greek (from plassein = to mold, form).

### The Inventive Process

Society praises its living conformists and honours its deceased rebels. As a result, people are caught up in a conflict between individuality and group consensus. If an individual conforms to the group, he will be popular. If he goes his own way, he will lose the group's approval and quickly come to be considered an oddball. The lure of this status is enhanced by ever increasing specialisation, which offers a previously unknown degree of choice and potential for personal development, thereby permitting individuality to a degree never seen before. The more individualism a society allows, the more inventors it will produce. Inventions have always been created by individuals – particularly when these have been individualists. Groups do not invent; their existence is dependent upon conformist thinking. Inventions under socialism tended, therefore, to be rare.

An invention must be new for it to be patentable; it must represent an advance in technology and must be acknowledged as surprisingly good even by experts in the field. In the language of patent law, "surprisingly good" is expressed by the words "inventive merit." As such, it is distinct from simple modifications to existing inventions. The door to invention has never been open to as many people as it is today. A computer, for example, is the only investment software developers need to begin inventing. The essential invention behind plastination, i.e., introducing polymers into every cell in a tissue sample, was not expensive.

During my forty years of working on plastination, I have produced a whole series of individual inventions. Again and again, people have asked me how I come up with these ideas and what steps I take.

The inventive process that I utilise corresponds to the usual four stages of invention: recognising the problem, analysing it, working out solutions and applying those solutions.

(1) Recognising the problem: I question everything as a matter of principle. Anything that is good can be improved because better is superior to good. Recognising that infusing a specimen with polymers must be superior to embedding it in a polymer block (as had been done up to that point) was the central problem that led me to develop the Plastination process. The problem was to put that idea into practice.

(2) Analysing the problem: Not only do I try to recognise the problem at hand; I also try to imagine what sorts of additional questions might arise from the problem. This includes studying handbooks, textbooks, patent literature and company brochures, and regularly visiting trade fairs.

(3) Solving the problem: As a matter of principle, I am never completely satisfied with a solution. Instead, I always have several irons in the fire, letting three to five potential solutions compete simultaneously with each other for a relatively long period of time. It is also important that I not settle on any one solution too soon. When following up on an approach to a solution, my gut feeling tells me that the solution in question will be the one that will work, even if I know that it is nonsense from a purely objective standpoint. I always have to go back and rethink the problem and factor in my own mistakes. When discussing suggested solutions with experts, I am often inclined to believe that the more emotionally a given potential solution is rejected, the more revolutionary and essentially feasible it must be.

(4) Applying the solution: This is where studying company brochures and visiting trade fairs again becomes important. Constantly updating my technical expertise in the field and constantly thinking through ways of applying solutions is indispensable. As a result, I think about plastination nearly all the time: before I get up in the morning, when I am looking at my schedule for the day, when I am in the shower, driving my car, or doing my shopping. That is how a pudding mould becomes a cranium, a meat slicer becomes a cutter for making anatomical slices of the brain, a pancake turner becomes a turner for brain slices, an aquarium pump becomes a vaporizer for the gas-curing process, and clamps to hold price tags in store windows are "recycled" to hold the plates of the shallow containers used to infuse slices with polymer. Adapting and recycling established technologies in this way is the stuff that enriches the inventive spirit.

I often try out impossible, utterly ridiculous options; decisive insights frequently arise from trying out nonsense. Hence, I sometimes allow mistakes to happen or even make them consciously. Odd experiments, mistakes and coincidences are a productive part of the inventive process. A key development in plastination, for instance, was the use of a gas-curing technique for silicone rubber. This invention came about while attempting to extend as much as possible the time available for preparing a specimen. I hoped to achieve this by placing infused specimens in a curing bath; the curing agents that I was using, however, partially dissolved the polymer, causing it to leach back out again.

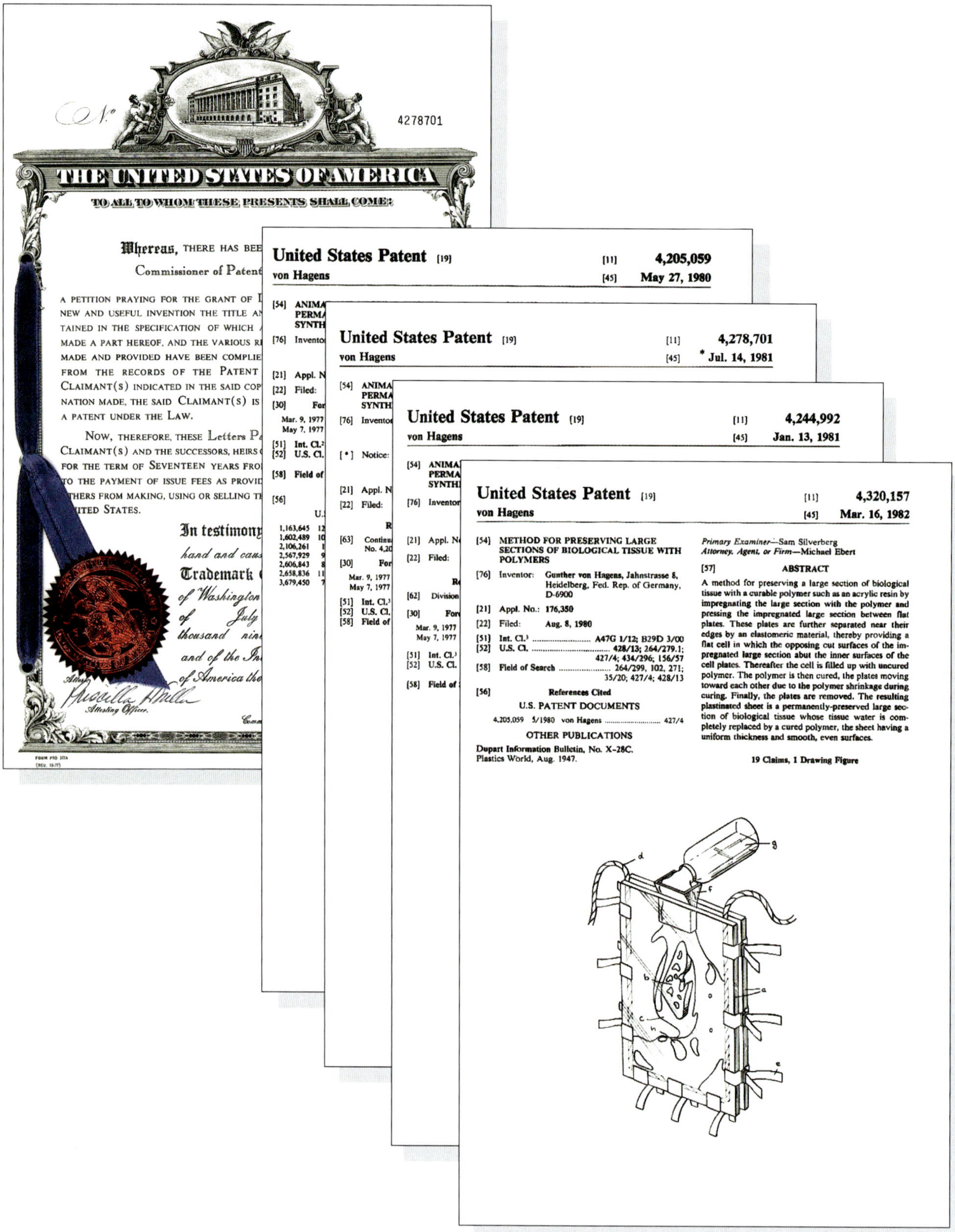

United States Patent [19] [11] 4,205,059
von Hagens [45] May 27, 1980

United States Patent [19] [11] 4,278,701
von Hagens [45] * Jul. 14, 1981

United States Patent [19] [11] 4,244,992
von Hagens [45] Jan. 13, 1981

United States Patent [19] [11] 4,320,157
von Hagens [45] Mar. 16, 1982

[54] METHOD FOR PRESERVING LARGE SECTIONS OF BIOLOGICAL TISSUE WITH POLYMERS

[76] Inventor: Gunther von Hagens, Jahnstrasse 8, Heidelberg, Fed. Rep. of Germany, D-6900

[21] Appl. No.: 176,350

[22] Filed: Aug. 8, 1980

[51] Int. Cl.³ .......... A47G 1/12; B29D 3/00

[52] U.S. Cl. .......... 428/13; 264/279.1; 427/4; 434/296; 156/57

[58] Field of Search .......... 264/299, 102, 271; 35/20; 427/4; 428/13

[56] References Cited

U.S. PATENT DOCUMENTS

4,205,059 5/1980 von Hagens .......... 427/4

OTHER PUBLICATIONS

Dupart Information Bulletin, No. X-28C.
Plastics World, Aug. 1947.

*Primary Examiner*—Sam Silverberg
*Attorney, Agent, or Firm*—Michael Ebert

[57] ABSTRACT

A method for preserving a large section of biological tissue with a curable polymer such as an acrylic resin by impregnating the large section with the polymer and pressing the impregnated large section between flat plates. These plates are further separated near their edges by an elastomeric material, thereby providing a flat cell in which the opposing cut surfaces of the impregnated large section abut the inner surfaces of the cell plates. Thereafter the cell is filled up with uncured polymer. The polymer is then cured, the plates moving toward each other due to the polymer shrinkage during curing. Finally, the plates are removed. The resulting plastinated sheet is a permanently-preserved large section of biological tissue whose tissue water is completely replaced by a cured polymer, the sheet having a uniform thickness and smooth, even surfaces.

19 Claims, 1 Drawing Figure



**Patent Rights**

The plastination process is protected by a series of patents, particularly in the United States. Plastinating specimens for non-commercial purposes such as medical instruction or museum exhibits, however, is not subject to any such limitations.

As the polymer leached out of a specimen, it created countless polymer bumps on its surface, nearly covering it completely. I knew this before performing an experiment, in which I left a brain in the curing bath overnight. Because the container that I was using no longer held sufficient curing bath, I had propped it up at an angle so that the brain would be completely submerged. The next morning, I found that the container had fallen over, and only the base of the brain was still in the bath. This section had hardened, and, as expected, was covered with little plastic knobs that would require a great deal of effort to remove. The real excitement, however, came when, much to my surprise, I discovered that the major portion of the brain, which had been sticking out of the curing bath, had also hardened, but in fact had done so perfectly, without any annoying bumps. This could only have been the result of the evaporated curing bath, i.e., the gaseous vapours of the curing agent. I quickly repeated the experiment, having procured even more volatile hardening agents. Thus, the gas-curing process was born, a technique that has significantly influenced further development of plastination with silicone polymers, and which is now used in 38 countries.

The constant effort to find new ideas, to see what has never been seen before, does, however, affect my personality. My penchant for hats, for instance, is not reflective of an artistic demeanour; it has more to do with my self-image as an inventor. My hat symbolises my internalised individualism, which is born of the conviction that an unusual outward appearance fosters non-conformist thinking. A look that flies in the face of social conventions has a nurturing effect on my creativity.

**Donating Bodies for Plastination**

Exhibiting real human specimens is made possible most of all by countless donors. During their lifetimes, these people willed that, upon their deaths, their bodies should be plastinated and thus made available for educating doctors and providing instruction for anyone else with an interest in medicine. They have expressly waived their right to burial. The Institute for Plastination also accepts donations of bodies that have been provided by survivors, provided that neither the deceased nor any relatives have voiced any objections. Finally, the Institute also accepts specimens from old anatomical collections when such collections are liquidated. This particular exhibition includes, for example, a plastinated hydrocephalic baby, a phenomenon that, thanks to advances in medicine, no longer occurs in today's highly developed societies. In some cases, these specimens are over 100 years old, and the Institute either purchases them outright or procures them in return for its plastinated specimens.

**Motivations of Donors**

Reasons for donation are as varied as life itself. The desire to donate one's body as a way of aiding a good cause is a common theme. Emotional rejection of decomposition and cremation, a desire to save burial expenses, or simple enthusiasm for plastination are often given as reasons. Comments such as the following indicate the wide variety of opinions (partially abridged):

"I would like to make the human body – 'the natural work of art' – more accessible to anyone who's interested."

"Through my many years of work with the Institute for Plastination I have had the opportunity to become very familiar with plastination, and it fascinates me more and more all the time."

"Since I've been helped over and over again by blood transfusions, it's important to me to help future generations by allowing research to be performed on my body."

"After my death I would prefer being like this to being consumed and metabolised by worms and tiny organisms."

"If I were displayed as a whole-body specimen, my body might make visitors stop and think."

"I've abused, neglected and ignored my body. But it still works, renews itself and tests its limits. Gratitude for that is a major reason for me to donate."

"Maintaining a grave site is just one last way of pulling the wool over other people's eyes."

"Ever since I heard about the plastination process, the prospect of my own death hasn't bothered me at all."

"Using plastination as a way of furthering the development of art and culture is what fascinates me most."

"I've always felt a need to donate my body to science, and the idea of being plastinated fills me with a sense of inner tranquillity and happiness."

"When this world comes to an end and Christ returns, He will raise me to new life with a new body, as is written in the Bible."

"I'm a Bible-believing Christian and I know that man has a soul, and when he dies, the breath of life within him will return to God, and when Christ returns I will be raised to new life in a new body, as is written in the Word of God."

"As a former Heidelberg student, I feel very attached to the city of my alma mater. I see your program as a way for me to return to Heidelberg."

"You've 'cut through' a taboo, as it were, and for that I'm particularly grateful to you. And there's one thing I'm now sure of: when I've breathed my last, my body will perform an important function for mankind. Mind and spirit will gaze upon it with envy... I even dreamed that I had been cut into fine slices and was admiring myself. It was a lovely dream."

"Plastination has added a new dimension of memory to anatomical thought. It will be my pleasure to contribute to its progress!"

"Because the medical arts have saved me from death several times, I feel a need to show at least a small token of my appreciation to medicine by donating my body."

**Transforming a Cadaver into a Plastinated Specimen**

Terms are usually defined according to such criteria as form, quality, function or an administrative act. Because a purely descriptive definition of a cadaver slated for burial is not clearly distinct from that of a mummy, relic, specimen, skeleton or plastinated specimen, we must draw upon additional qualities such as intent, administration and qualitative change. Intent can be seen in bodies that have been donated for plastination to promote education and research; the administrative act consists of accepting bodies for plastination, transferring documents and assuring anonymity; the qualitative change is the first step in plastination, i.e., preserving the body for plastination (with formalin or by freezing). Transforming a body into a plastinated specimen (either an entire body or a part of the body) is accomplished by curing a polymer inside the specimen. Ensuring anonymity is important for distancing the body from its plastinated counterpart, as it is the only sure way of ending the sense of reverence surrounding that body, i.e., the sense of personal and emotional attachment to the deceased. Anonymity also makes sense, because it fits in with anatomical traditions, thereby distinguishing plastinated specimens from relics and mummies of persons known by name. Conversely, the only time that plastination should be non-anonymous is in exceptional cases where there is ample justification. It goes without saying that every human specimen continues to possess human qualities. That also means that a plastinated specimen must be used for educational purposes, as dictated by the testamentary disposition of the donor.

**Plastination, Art and Knowledge**

Dissection and plastination are done by hand. In 1860, anatomist Joseph Hyrtl said, "Dismemberment is the heart and soul of anatomy. It is a craft, however, that requires skill if it is to be successful. The art of dismemberment must be learned. Beyond that, it also requires an innate talent for technical work. Anyone not possessing this talent will not make much progress towards solving the mysteries of the grave."

The most difficult aspect of this is plastinating entire bodies. Whole-body plastination is an intellectual achievement requiring the ability to see the finished specimen in the mind's eye just as a sculptor envisions the completed statue while he is carving it. If the specimen has soft, flexible tissues such as muscles when it leaves the silicone rubber bath, it will need to be positioned, a process guided by both aesthetic and educational considerations. The Chess Player's nervous system, for instance, is highlighted specifically. The plastinated pregnant woman is protecting both her genitals as well as the foetus in her uterus. Specimens that have been plastinated without such gestures often appear doll-like by comparison.

Experience at exhibitions has shown that the aesthetic aspects of posed specimens make such an impression that visitors consider a number of these to be works of art. There is no dispelling that conclusion either, because "art is in the eye of the beholder." No anatomical works of art have been created; they become works of art through the judgment of the visitors to exhibitions.

From my perspective, however, plastinated specimens are not works of art, because they have been created for the sole purpose of sharing insights into human anatomy. Art, unlike the products of skilled trades and the sciences, is not created for a purpose. Unless the term 'artist' is used in the inflated sense in which Beuys uses the word, a plastinator is at most a skilled labourer in the field of art, but not an artist as such. It would be completely misguided to refer to posed specimens as works of art, because (modern) art is a term subject to interpretation; as a result, everyone projects his or her own personal understanding of art and morality onto the motivation underlying my efforts.

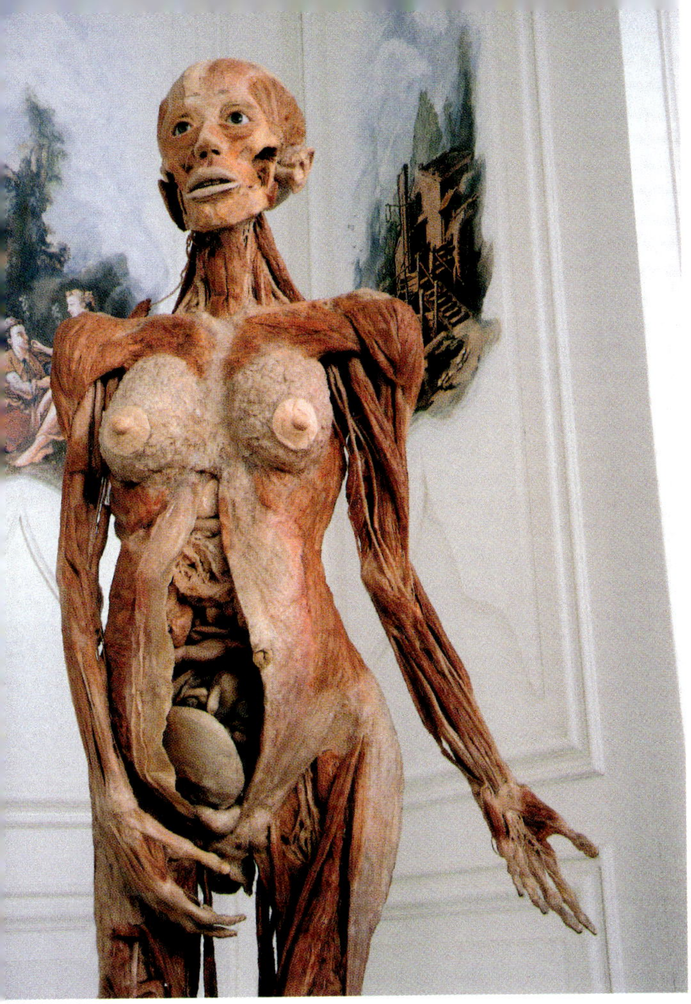

*Fig. 36: A plastinated body in a realistic pose.*

In order to avoid misunderstandings and to depersonalise discourse, I have introduced the term BODY WORLDS, by which I mean the "aesthetic and instructive presentation of the body's interior." 'Presentation' in this case can be understood in two ways: both in the sense of an artistic rendering and in the sense of the work performed by a skilled labourer in the field of art. The instructive component of this presentation likewise has two meanings: on the one hand, it refers to making us aware of our physical nature, of nature within us; on the other hand, it can be understood as a concrete act of sharing anatomical information. Only in this sense do I consider myself to be an artist – an anatomy artist.

BODY WORLDS falls within the tradition of the Renaissance when art was a product of ability; plastination has brought anatomy art a step further by making it possible to take soft tissues such as muscles or fat and fix them permanently in any given pose. This gives rise to completely new types of specimens, including slices of bodies only 3 millimetres (1/8 inch) thick, which are as transparent and colourful as stained glass. The ability to position soft tissues permanently also makes it possible to fragment the body in ways that are both aesthetic and instructive. Displacing these fragments and opening doors cut in the body provide new perspectives for viewing the body. The novel forms that arise from such techniques, such as a body that was expanded lengthwise, are necessary results of displacing fragments; they do not, however, reflect a dominant, recurring theme of the dissection process.

Even though plastinated specimens are not intended to meet any artistic demands, and even though I do not create the specimens in pursuit of any artistic goals, they may well satisfy certain artistic criteria. Like works of art, attractively posed specimens have a certain aesthetic effect and emotional content, which is attested to by, among other things, the fact that half of the visitors to the BODY WORLDS exhibition in Mannheim went precisely because of the aesthetic appeal that the specimens held for them (this according to a scientific survey taken by Dr. Lantermann of the University of Kassel's Institute of Psychology). These are qualities not generally possessed by objects that are of purely scientific interest.

Posed specimens provide an optical bridge to self-awareness. Immanuel Kant said that man's powers of awareness are twofold. By that he was referring to emotional and rational awareness; whereas the former is conveyed more by aesthetics and feelings, the latter is imparted by intellect and instruction. Emotions and intellect are both involved when making visual sense of plastination exhibits, particularly when these are whole-body specimens. Feelings, i.e., emotional awareness, have a direct effect without our really being conscious of it. This type of insight leaves many visitors feeling fascinated and moved. The aesthetic pose, which is occasionally criticized, is what helps dispel revulsion; because it is so powerful, it also promotes emotional awareness.

In an exhibition for laypersons, who are not attending an anatomy lecture but who have instead come to the museum just to "have a look," it is especially important that objects be directly understandable without lengthy explanations. The whole-body specimens achieve this most successfully. The intellectual awareness of the visitor is aroused by components of whole-body specimens, such as organs, muscles and bones. Achieving awareness in this way is a greater and more satisfying accomplishment than is the case when studying individual organs or body parts. Seeing a skeleton likewise leads to a greater understanding of the body than does seeing an individual bone.

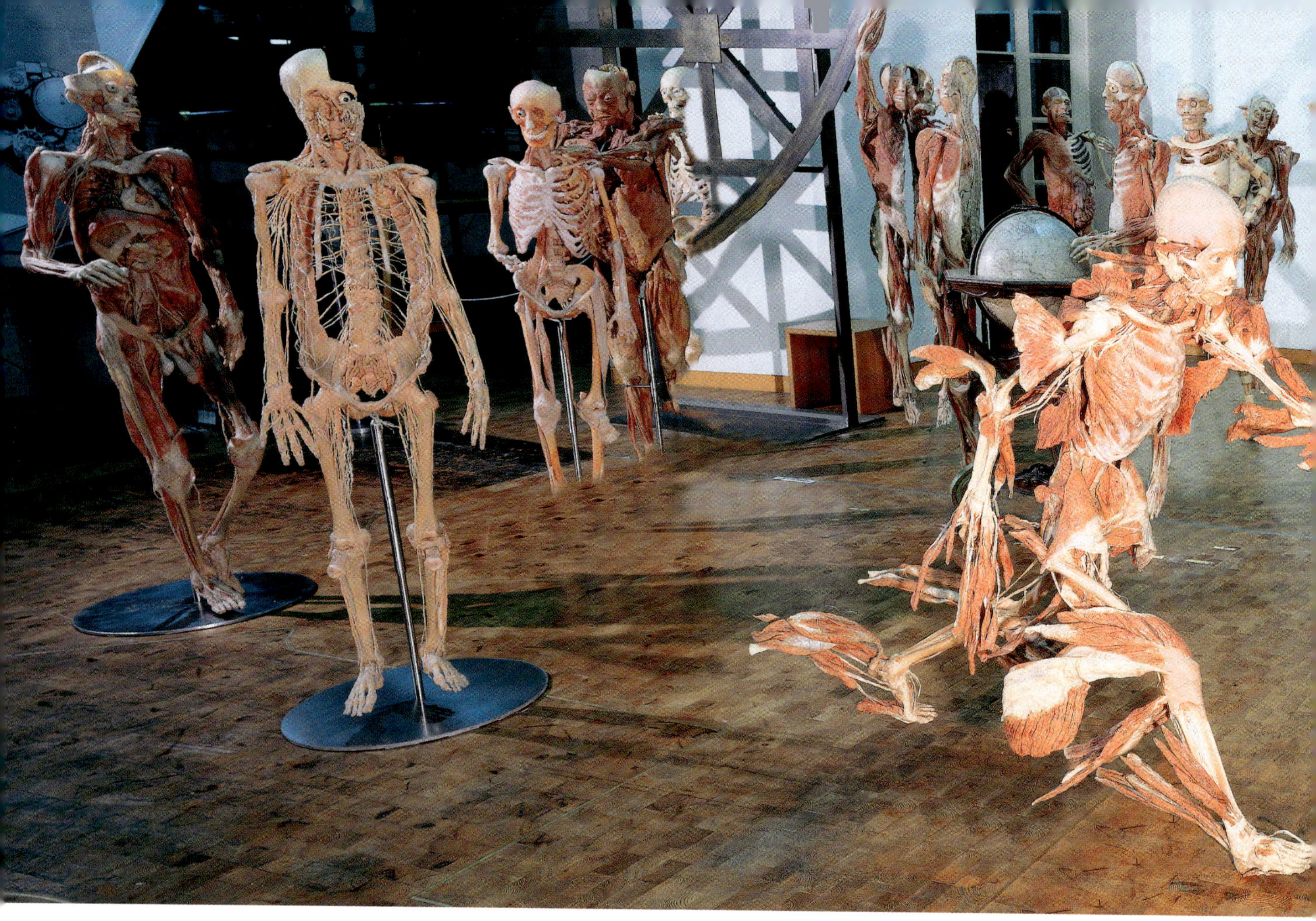

*Fig. 37: Whole-body plastinates. Displaying these specimens in realistic, life-like poses carries on the tradition begun by the founding fathers of anatomy.*

The realism of the specimens contributes greatly to the fascination and power of the exhibition. Particularly in today's media-oriented world, a world in which we increasingly obtain our information indirectly, people have retained a keen sense for the fact that a copy has always been intellectually 'regurgitated,' and as such is always an interpretation. In this respect the BODY WORLDS exhibition satisfies a tremendous human need for unadulterated authenticity.

**Living Anatomy**

The anatomy of a corpse is not very interesting in and of itself. It is significant only because through it we can study the anatomy of living human beings to a certain degree. Whereas the human skeleton has been standing upright ever since Vesal's work during the Renaissance, the wet, dripping corpses of anatomical institutes have had to remain on the dissecting table. Lying there, with either their front or back hidden from the researcher's view, is how an intact body has traditionally been presented.

As a student I always found it difficult to follow the advice of our anatomy professor and associate the pleasant bodies on display at the swimming pool with the utilitarian study of surface anatomy. The difference between the stiff corpse lying on the dissecting table and the interplay of muscles in swimming, running and sitting people was just too great.

"Living anatomy" was always a popular subject with students, although rather neglected by classical anatomy. In this course, students would feel each other and then project and paint muscles and organs on each other's skin. Neither a hobby anatomist nor a beginning anatomy student is interested in the anatomy of the dead because a real patient is living, moving and posing. Hence, it is only natural that plastinated whole-body specimens should be positioned upright and realistically – and thus imparting the information that they are intended to convey – in the living environment from which they came.

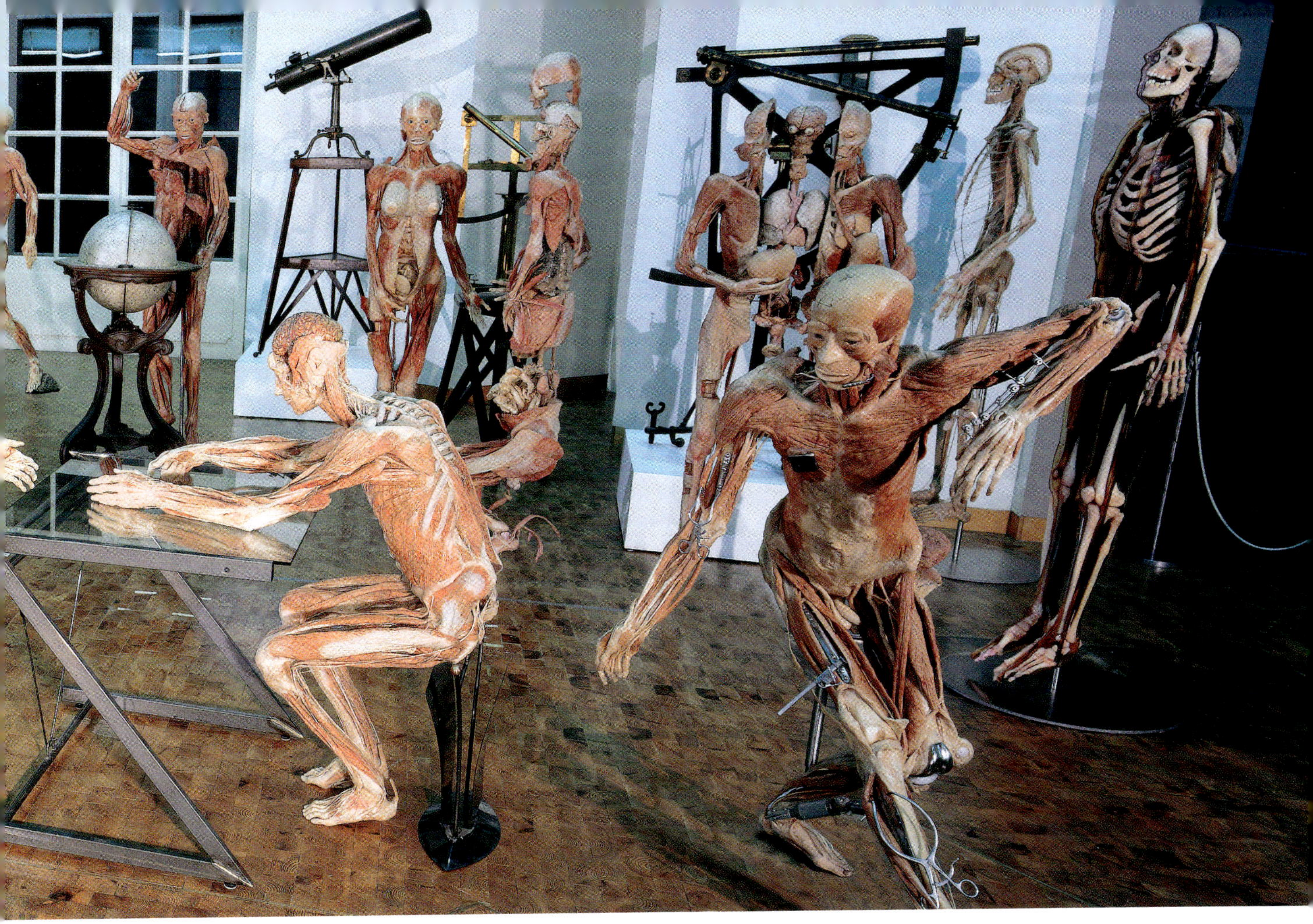

Plastination allows us to solidify soft tissue and as a result has made it possible to stand entire bodies in upright positions. Doing so carries on the tradition begun by the founding fathers of anatomy. As the Tokyo exhibition was nearing – the first major public plastination exhibition – our colleagues at the National Science Museum in Tokyo clearly recognised the unique qualities of the posed whole-body specimens, and discussed this with us for weeks. The issue under debate was the horizontal display of whole-body specimens, but the decision that came out of the discussions favoured living anatomy and the new dimension that it adds to the way we view the body as a whole. In the foyer of the Heidelberg Institute of Anatomy is a sign that reads, "Hic gaudet mors succurrere vitae," which means, "Here Death is happy to rush to the aid of the living." And it should do it standing upright. This realistic pose creates anatomical individuality. A whole-body specimen is attractive when its pose is compatible with dissected anatomy and its function within a living being.

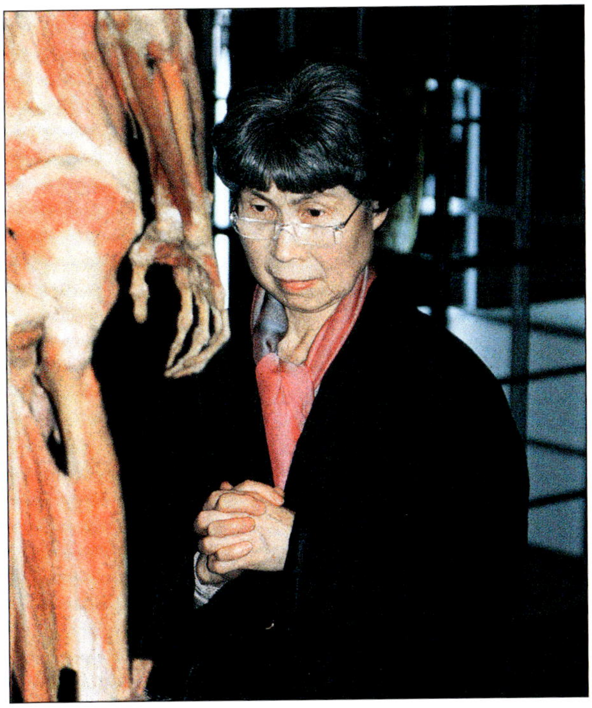

*Fig. 38: A woman attending the exhibition in Japan.*

## The Face Within

Whole-body plastinates join the ranks of skeletons and mummies as a new means of determining our post-mortem existence for ourselves. In addition to an external face associated with our personalities, we all possess a face within. This internal face is a great deal more variable and unique than our external faces. Even slices of a head, torso or arm no more than 3 millimetres (1/8 inch) thick are individual representatives of their donors, and can be distinguished by their shape, size, colour and tissue composition. The aesthetics of the human body, celebrated during the Renaissance, visibly lives on in the body's interior – even at a microscopic level. Donors demonstrate their natural anatomical individuality, regardless of whether the body has been plastinated in its entirety or whether it is displayed as a series of slices. The manner and quality of both the dissection and the plastination work will determine which outward appearance the face within will acquire.

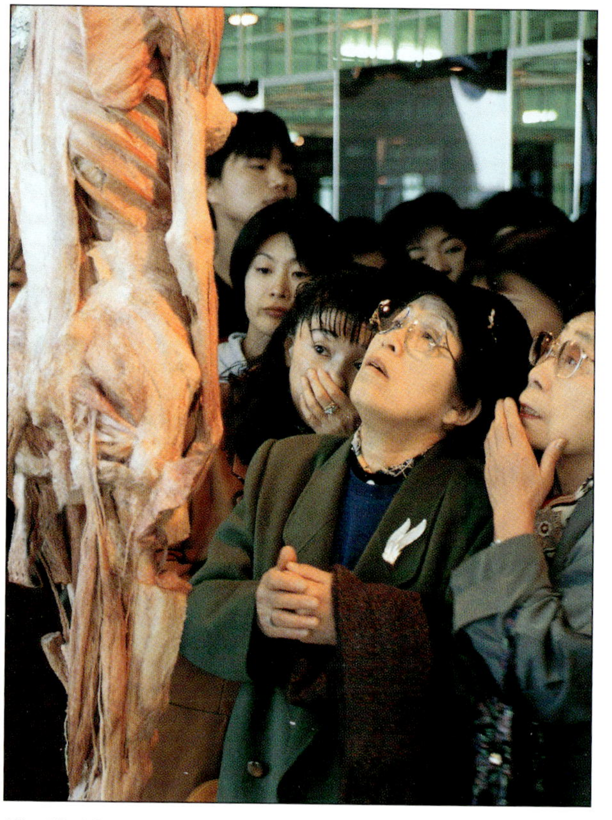

*Fig. 39: Mixed reactions at the exhibition in Japan.*

A posthumous change in identity is really nothing new. In Japan, the deceased have been given new names since time immemorial. Plastination, however, also represents a shift in value from a useless corpse to a plastinated specimen, which is useful, aesthetically instructive and produced by nature.

Austrian philosopher Ludwig Wittgenstein once said, "The human body is the best picture of the human soul." For a physician, that statement is only too understandable. The external face, the human countenance, has always been considered the mirror to the soul.

The soul, on the other hand, also has an effect on the body. Happiness and worry have visible effects on the face within – just look at anorexia or stomach ulcers. Does that mean that an entire plastinated body is also an embodiment, a reflection of the soul? Thinking along these lines does not, however, bring us any further in our search for the individual soul. The closest that I have come to the location of the soul is when I am plastinating a brain. The function of brain cells and the memories stored within them collapse when the person dies. That makes it likely that death also erases our ability to remember. Yet without memory there is no awareness of the self, and without awareness of the self, there is no individual soul. The decisive question is therefore whether there is not some individual capacity for memory associated with the brain. If so, does that fly away as part of the soul, leaving the brain behind as an empty container?

Plastination is the most modern, lasting and vivid means of preserving specimens of the human body for educational purposes. The process is therefore especially well suited for honouring the desire of donors to make a posthumous contribution to the education of future generations. Like marble statues, they outlast the lifetimes of their creators. Life is short, but plastination will endure (and will educate) for a long time.

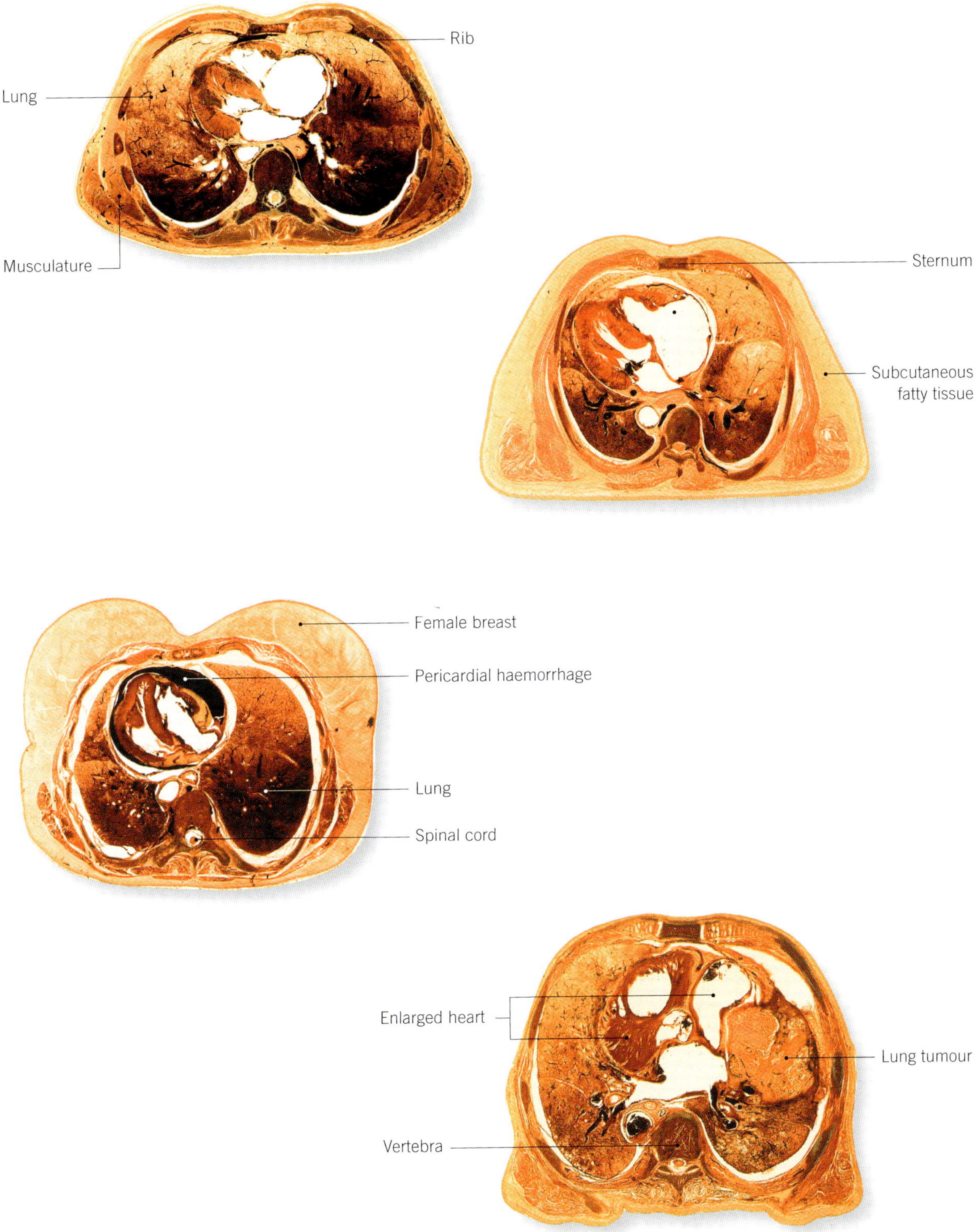


*Fig. 40: The inner individuality: These chest slices were all taken from different donors. Even though they were all cut at the same height, they look completely different depending on, among other things, individual body size, distribution of fat and blood, organ size, age and disease.*

**A Word of Appreciation**

I would like to thank those people who have donated their bodies to plastination, who in turn have made the existence of the Institute for Plastination and the development of public exhibitions of plastinates possible. I would also like to express my gratitude to my co-workers in the plastination Institutes in Heidelberg and Guben, Germany for their dedication and commitment. I would like to thank my distinguished teacher, Prof. Wilhelm Kriz, for supporting me with unswerving foresightedness during my university years and for allowing me the room to develop that is so vital for success.

Finally, I would like to thank all of my critics for their qualified and also their unqualified criticism, which has gone a long way in helping me continually to assess and to reassess my work.

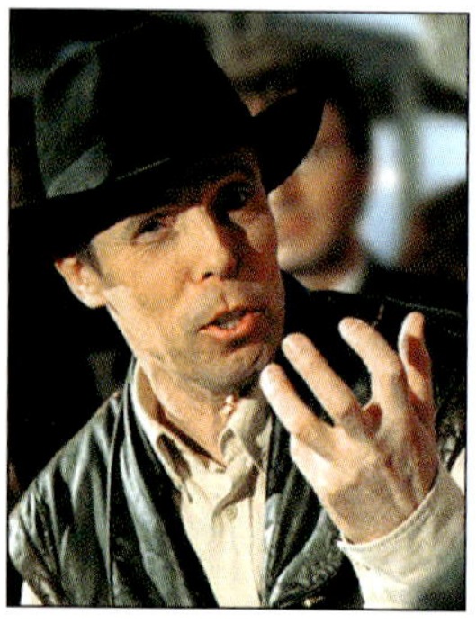

Dr. Gunther von Hagens began his medical studies at the University of Jena in 1965. He was arrested while attempting to flee East Germany after distributing leaflets in protest against the invasion of Czechoslovakia by Warsaw Pact troops. In 1970, West German authorities secured his freedom. He completed his medical studies at the University of Lubeck in 1973 and a year later he received his license to practice medicine. He then moved to the University of Heidelberg, where he completed his doctorate in the Department of Anaesthesia and Emergency Medicine. In 1975, he began to work at the Institutes of Anatomy and Pathology, which ignited his passion for invention and to teach anatomy in a new way.

It was in 1977 at the University of Heidelberg that he invented plastination, a vacuum technique to permanently preserve anatomical specimens with reactive plastics specially developed for this purpose. He subsequently founded BIODUR® Products to market the respective polymers and equipment to other institutions around the world. In order to bring plastination to a wider audience, he founded the Institute for Plastination in 1993. Soon after, together with his colleague and wife Dr. Angelina Whalley, he created the first anatomical exhibition of real human bodies, titled BODY WORLDS, which has now seen by more than 47 million people worldwide. They later launched ANIMAL INSIDE OUT, the first exhibition dedicated to plastinated animals, in 2010.

His popular success in Plastination has been accompanied by academic accolades. In 1996, he became a visiting professor at the School of Medicine in Dalian. That same year he became Director of the Plastination Centre at the State Medical Academy in Bishkek, Kyrgyzstan, where he was awarded the title of Honorary Professor. Since 2004, he has been a visiting professor at New York University College of Dentistry.

In 2006, he established Gubener Plastinate GmbH, a plastination laboratory in Guben, Germany. It is considered the world's leading plastination research, development and preparation facility. The campus also houses the PLASTINARIUM, which promotes public anatomy by granting access for all visitors to observe the preparation of permanently preserved, anatomical human and animal specimens.

The international Association of Science-Technology Centers (ASTC) honoured him in 2013 with a lifetime achievement award for outstanding contribution to the public understanding of science.

## Definitions

In discussions on the ethical justification of utilising human specimens, varying ways of understanding certain terms have frequently been the cause of misunderstandings. This list of definitions should aid in preventing such misunderstandings in the future.

**Anatomy art**
Aesthetically instructive presentation of bodily interiors.

**Anatomical cadaver**
Preserved corpse that is anatomically dissected and is buried upon completion of dissection.

**Corpse**
A deceased human body, which will decompose and for which a funeral will be prepared. In contrast to an anatomical specimen, it is the object of personal grief or human sympathy.

**Dignity**
Personal right to humane treatment guaranteed in the German constitution. It is subject to moral standards, which may vary in accordance with social progress and development.

**Dissection**
Removing anatomical structures and/or making them visible.

**Ethics**
Principles and norms that are generally valid in leading one's life, derived from an individual's responsibility towards others.

**Funeral**
Burial or cremation of a corpse.

**Gestalt plastinate**
Aesthetic, instructive whole-body specimen positioned in a life-like pose.

**Inner individuality**
Anatomical individuality of bodily interiors, which have been made visible through plastination.

**Morals**
System of ethical norms and standards of behaviour based on tradition, social conventions and religion that sets the rules for interpersonal conduct for a given time frame.

**Mummy**
Preserved human body, whose human form is essentially complete in the assembly of its parts and whose death goes back several generations; it is no longer an object of human grief.

**Plastinate**
Specimen of a human or animal, whose cells have been infused and hardened with reactive plastics.

**Plastination**
Method for the preservation of putrefiable biological specimens. The structural elements of the specimens are fixated, dehydrated (preferably with acetone), and under vacuum conditions are saturated with reactive polymers such as silicone rubber. Subsequently, the specimens are hardened (cured).

**Plastination craftsmanship**
Skilled craftsmanship in producing high-quality, aesthetic and instructive plastinated specimens.

**Privilege of viewing bodies**
Privilege of physicians, medical students and other representatives of the medical professions to view the insides of bodies. This privilege evolved with the development of medical science. The freedom to make use of this privilege by interested laypersons gained through the Enlightenment at the beginning of the modern era was lost when the anatomical theatres of the Renaissance were transformed into dissection halls for students and autopsy halls for pathologists.

**Relics**
Human remains, preferably individual bones, but also personal objects of deceased religious authorities, e.g., saints.

**Reverence**
A feeling of profound awe and tactful respect shown towards the dead.

**Robbing the dead**
Stealing the personal effects of deceased persons.

**Specimen**
Demonstration exhibit for research and instructional purposes, existing either as a decomposable, fresh specimen or as a preserved, permanent specimen.

**Whole-body plastinate**
Deceased human body, whose human form is essentially complete in the assembly of its parts and whose identity remains anonymous; it is no longer an object of human grief and has been plastinated.

**Whole-body specimen**
Deceased human body, whose human form is essentially complete in the assembly of its parts and has been preserved; it is no longer an object of human grief and its identity remains anonymous. It will be converted into one or more permanent anatomical specimens.

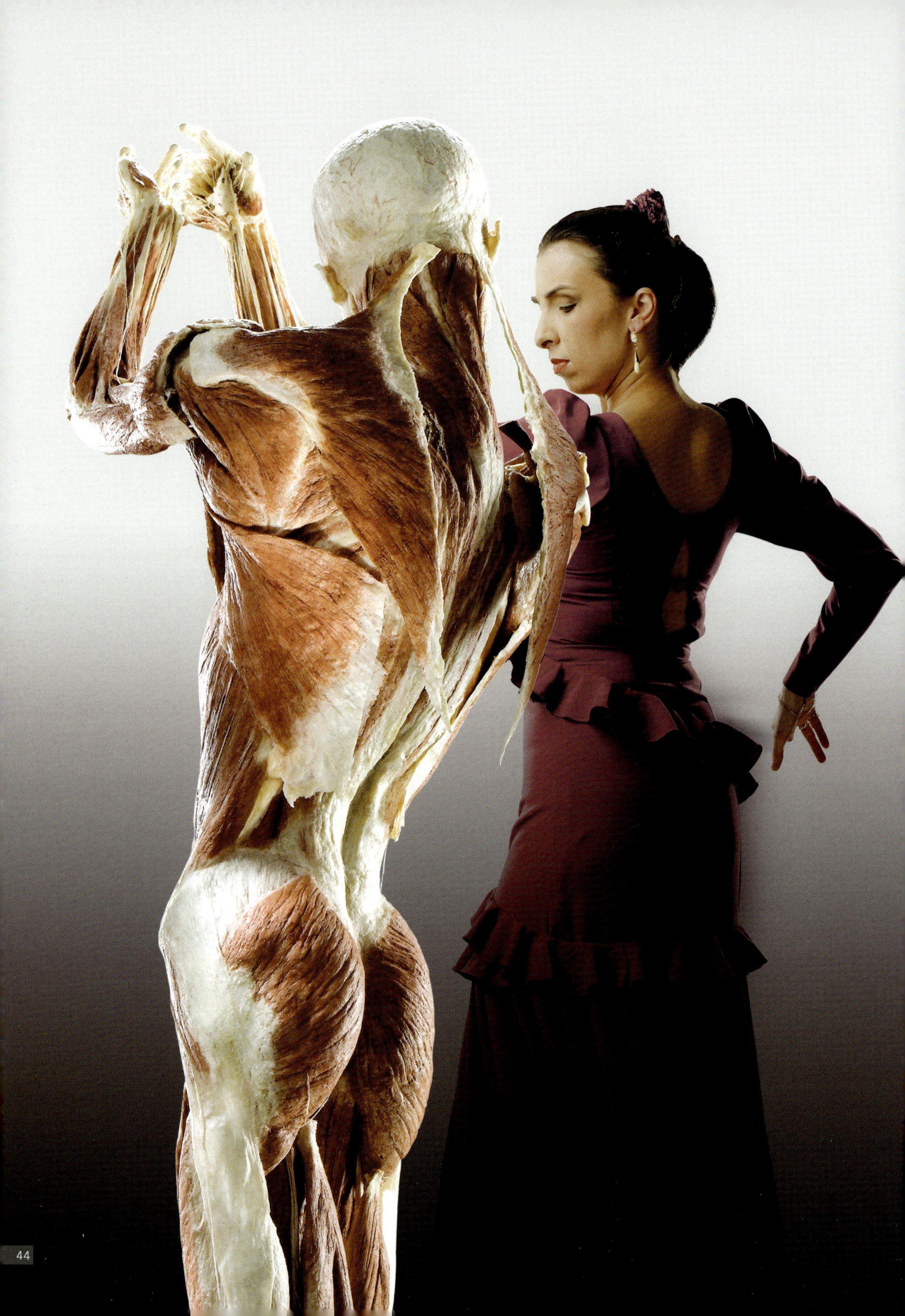

Angelina Whalley

# The Human Body – Anatomy and Function

Just like all of the plants and animals that exist today, man is the offspring of primordial, single-cell organisms – the result of more than 3.5 billion years of continuing evolution. And just like all higher organisms, every human individual develops from one single cell, a fertilized egg. When grown to maturity, we consist of approximately 60 billion cells of immense variety. Nevertheless, they form a unity of a manageable number of various organic systems that cooperate in an orderly fashion in order to perform all of our complex bodily functions.

Using plastinated specimens that have been permanently and durably preserved, the structures of the human body and their functions will be explained according to the outline below.

The pictures in the following chapters show a selection of plastinates in all BODY WORLDS exhibitions. Moreover, some additional specimens are shown, which are not displayed in the exhibitions.

- The Locomotive System
- The Nervous System
- The Respiratory System
- The Cardiovascular System
- The Digestive System
- The Urinary Tract
- The Reproductive Organs
- Foetal Development
- Whole-Body Plastinates

Dr. Angelina Whalley started her medical career at Freie Universität in Berlin and completed her doctorate with an experimental dissertation on kidney physiology at the University of Heidelberg in 1986. The same year, she obtained her license to practice medicine. For several years, Dr. Whalley did scientific research at the Institute of Anatomy as well as at the Institute of Pathology for the University of Heidelberg.

Dr. Whalley has been the creative and conceptual designer of all BODY WORLDS exhibitions since their debut in 1995. As exhibition curator, she introduced the concept of comparative anatomy in the exhibitions, and is responsible for presenting BODY WORLDS in a meaningful way that optimizes the aesthetic and educational value of plastination. Her memorable, thematic story-telling as well as her accessible teaching approach has inspired more than 47 million people around the globe to discover the wonders of the human body and adopt healthier lifestyles along the way.

In ANIMAL INSIDE OUT, the first exhibition of plastinated animals, she created a symbiosis of anatomy and didactics, in a captivating presentation, aiming at increasing awareness for the wonders of nature and the endangered biodiversity on our planet.

Since 1997, Dr. Whalley has also been the Director of the Institute for Plastination in Heidelberg, Germany and Director of BIODUR® Products, a company that markets plastination formulas and auxiliaries to more than 400 medical schools and universities worldwide. In 2003, she founded Arts & Sciences Exhibitions and Publishing GmbH, a company planning and touring scientific exhibitions worldwide as well as publishing related materials. She is the author of several best-selling books and catalogues that chronicle the exhibitions and is producer of a related documentary.

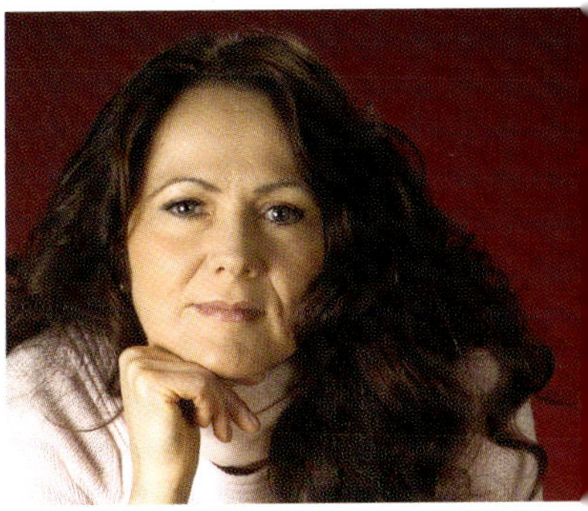

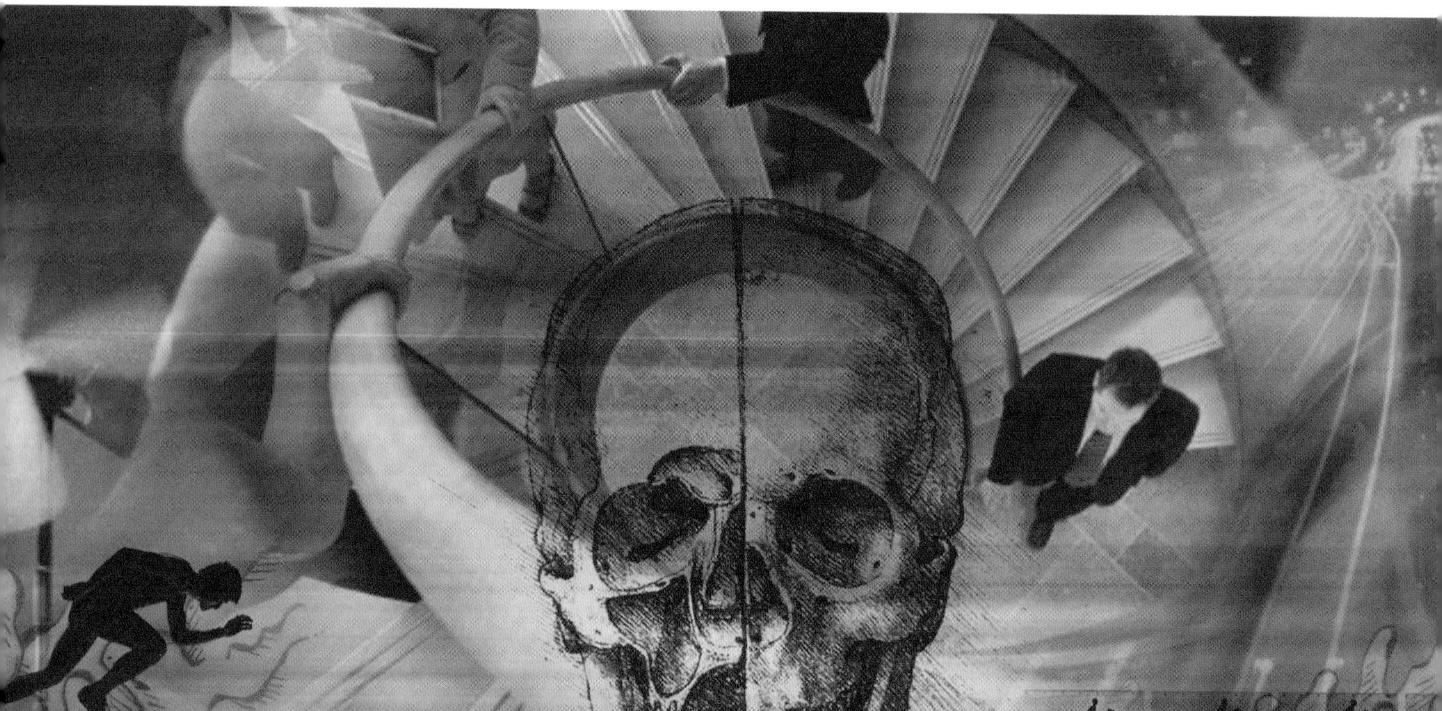

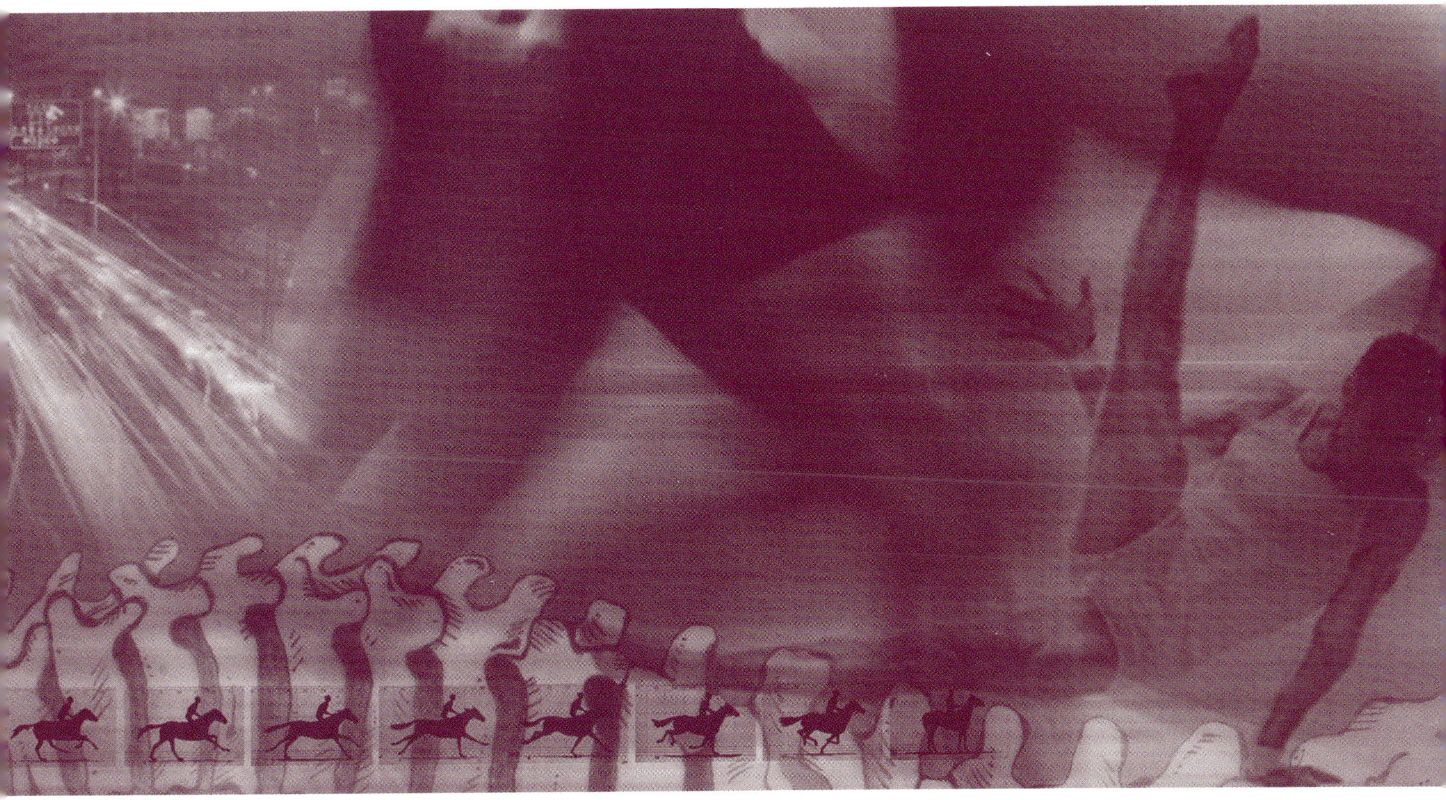

# 1. THE **LOCOMOTIVE** SYSTEM

The human body is composed
of various organ systems working together
in an orderly fashion to form a unified whole
and to perform the functions of life.
The body's movements, including both
stationary and forward motion,
constitute a significant portion of these functions.
Movements are made possible
by what is known as the locomotive system
which consists of the bones,
muscles, and joints.

# The Skeleton – The Internal Framework

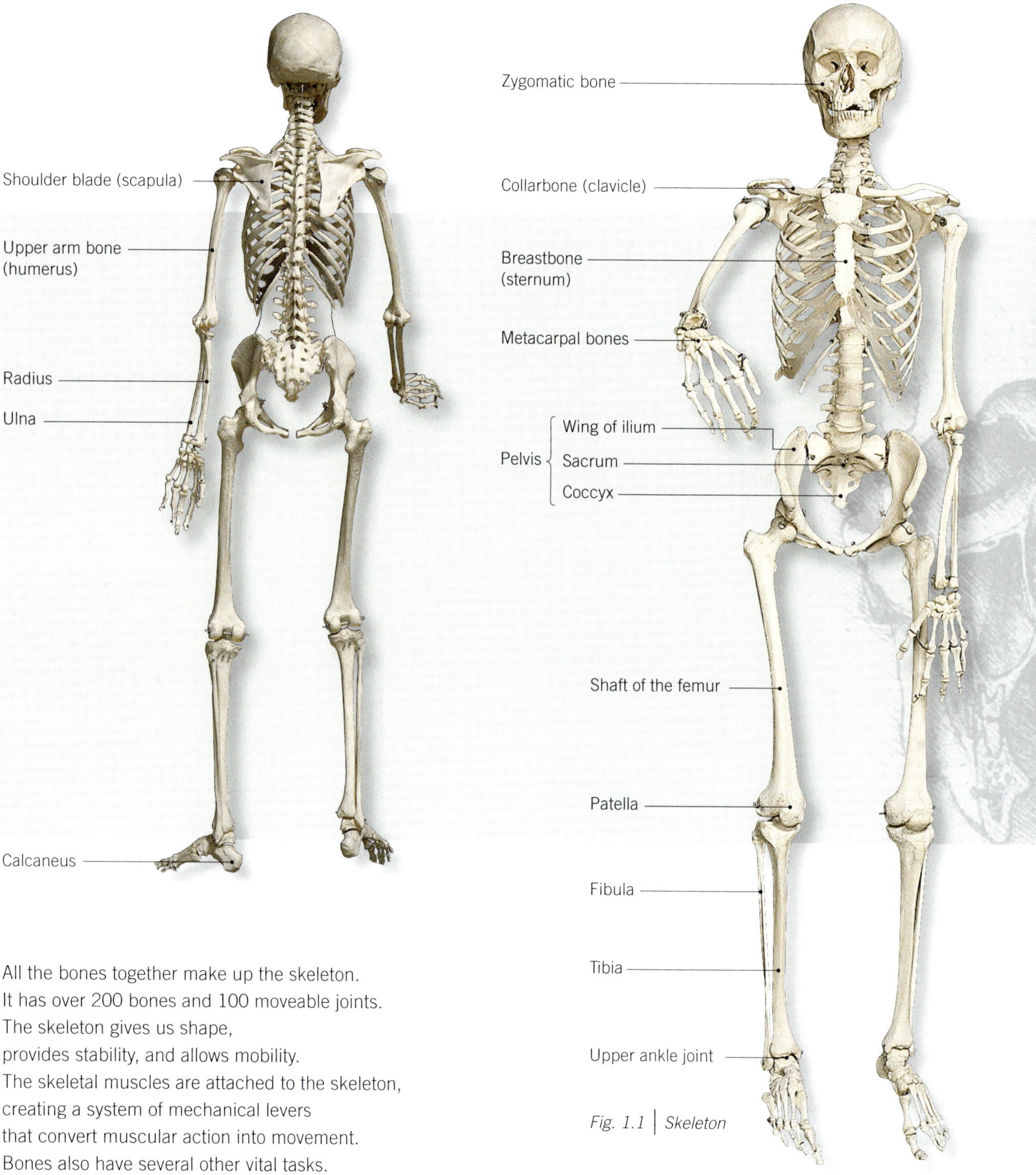


*Fig. 1.1* | *Skeleton*

All the bones together make up the skeleton.
It has over 200 bones and 100 moveable joints.
The skeleton gives us shape,
provides stability, and allows mobility.
The skeletal muscles are attached to the skeleton,
creating a system of mechanical levers
that convert muscular action into movement.
Bones also have several other vital tasks.
They protect delicate internal organs
and store mineral salts needed for metabolism.
The bone marrow inside the bones
produces the blood cells.
The main blood cell production sites
are in flat bones, such as the breastbone,
ribs, shoulder blades, and pelvis.

**Joints**

The point at which two bones meet
is called a joint or articulation.
Most joints are mobile, allowing the bones to move.
Some joints only move a little, such as the vertebrae.
A few joints are fixed – for example the skull bone plates
held by fibrous connective tissue.

The shape of joints corresponds to the respective type and scope of movement required.
Their names are derived from their similarity to technical, articulated connections, such as:

- hinge joints, as in the fingers, knees, elbows, and toes. They allow only bending and straightening movements.
- Ball-and-socket joints, such as the shoulder and hip joints, allow backward, forward, sideways, and rotating movements.
- Pivot joints, such as the neck joints, allow limited rotating movements.

Most joints are stabilised by tough bands of connective tissue, the ligaments. External ligaments attach to the bone on either side of the joint, forming a fibrous capsule that completely encases the joint. The capsules contain synovial fluid. This helps lubricate the joints and cushions the impact of movement. Most joints are synovial joints.

The articular surfaces of the bones are covered with cartilage to reduce the friction of movement.

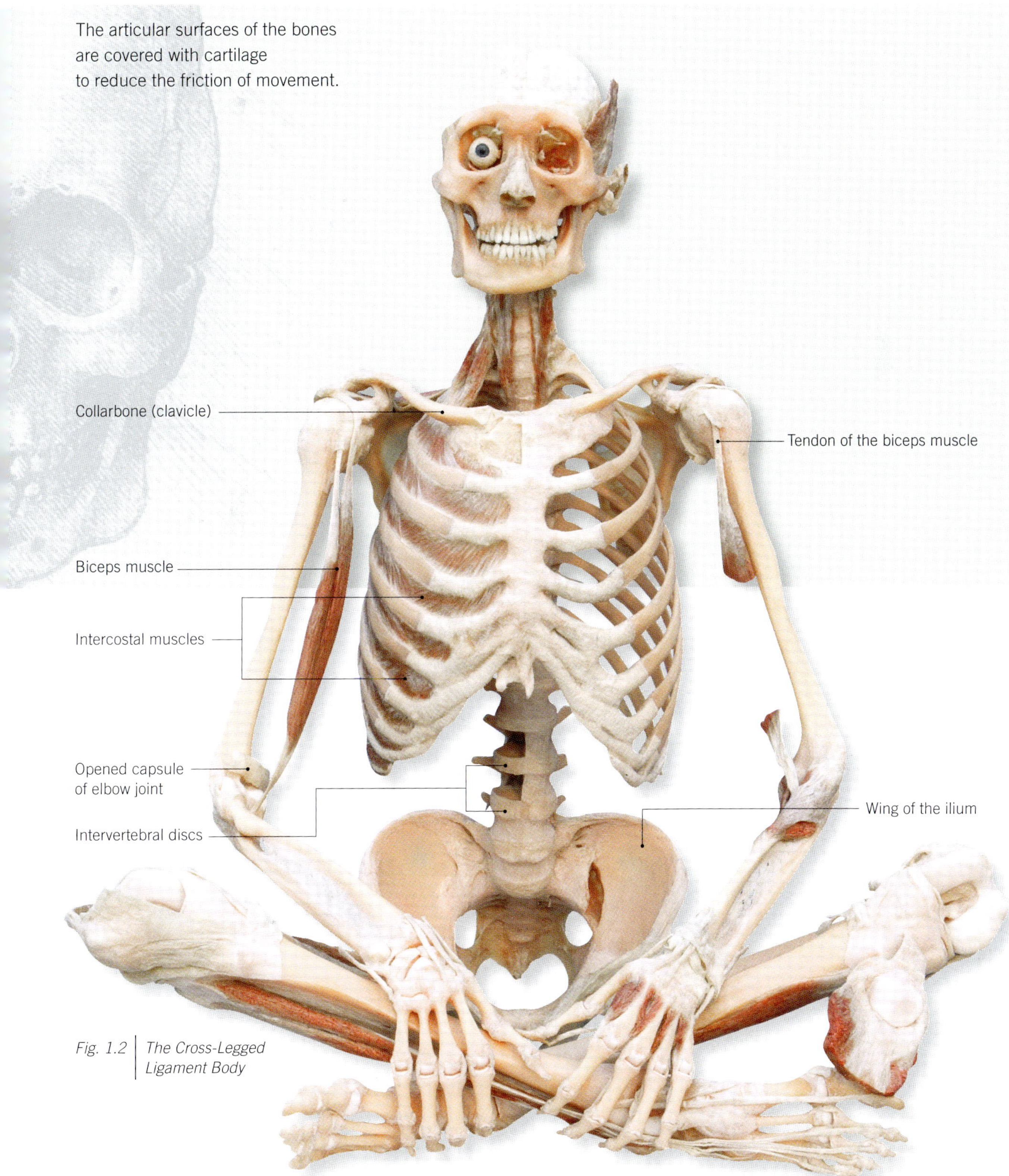


*Fig. 1.2 | The Cross-Legged Ligament Body*

# Joints

**Shoulder Joint**
The shoulder joint is a ball-and-socket joint.
It connects the upper arm bone (humerus)
to the shoulder blade (scapula)
and has the greatest movement of any joint.

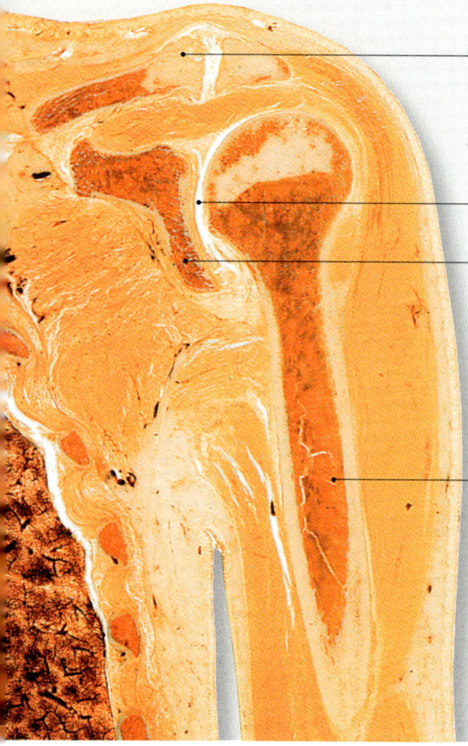


*Fig. 1.3 | Femoral slice of a shoulder joint*

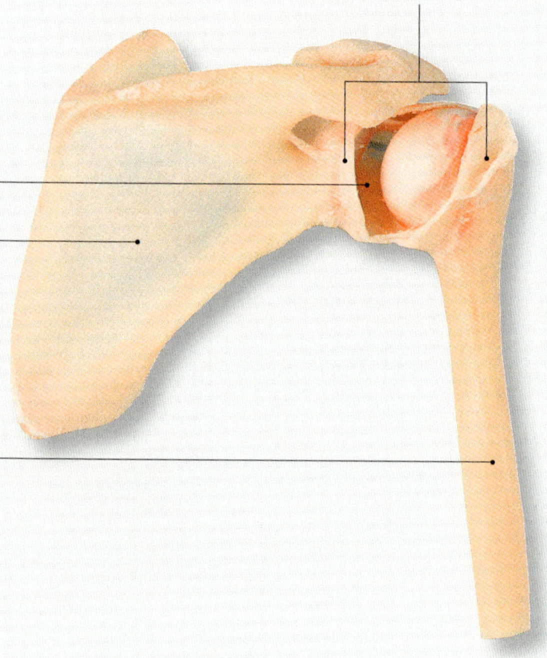


*Fig. 1.4 | The shoulder joint (seen here from behind)*

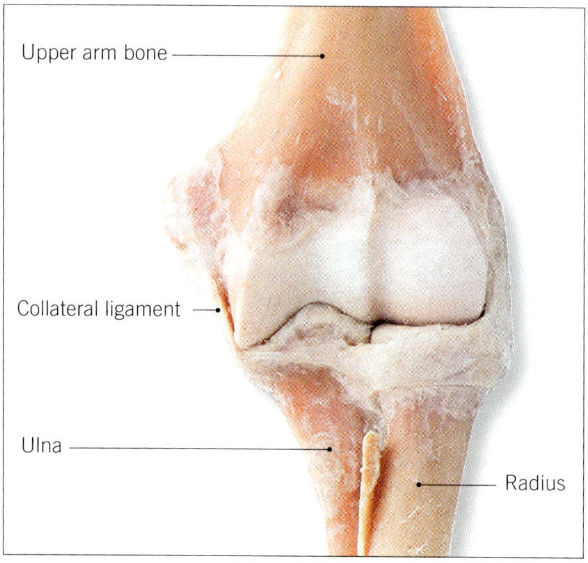


**Elbow Joint**
The elbow comprises three bones:
the humerus, the radius, and the ulna.
This allows three kinds of forearm movements:
flexing, extending, and turning.

If we knock the humerus –
the 'funny bone' at the elbow –
it produces an unpleasant tingling sensation,
shooting all the way down the arm.
This feeling is caused by the ulnar nerve
which is close to the skin surface there.

*Fig. 1.5 | Elbow joint, viewed from the front*

**Hands and Feet**

Hands and feet are similar in their skeletal design.
The human hand has 27 bones,
controlled by 37 skeletal muscles.
They allow for a wide variety of movement
with exceptionally fine motor functions
and a powerful gripping action.
In particular, it is the ability to bring the tips
of the thumb and the fingers together
that gives human hands their unique dexterity.

Feet and toes are crucial for walking upright.
They bear and distribute body weight
when we walk or run.
They also help the body keep its balance.
Each foot has 26 bones and over 100 ligaments.
Some of the 33 foot muscles
actually originate in the lower leg.

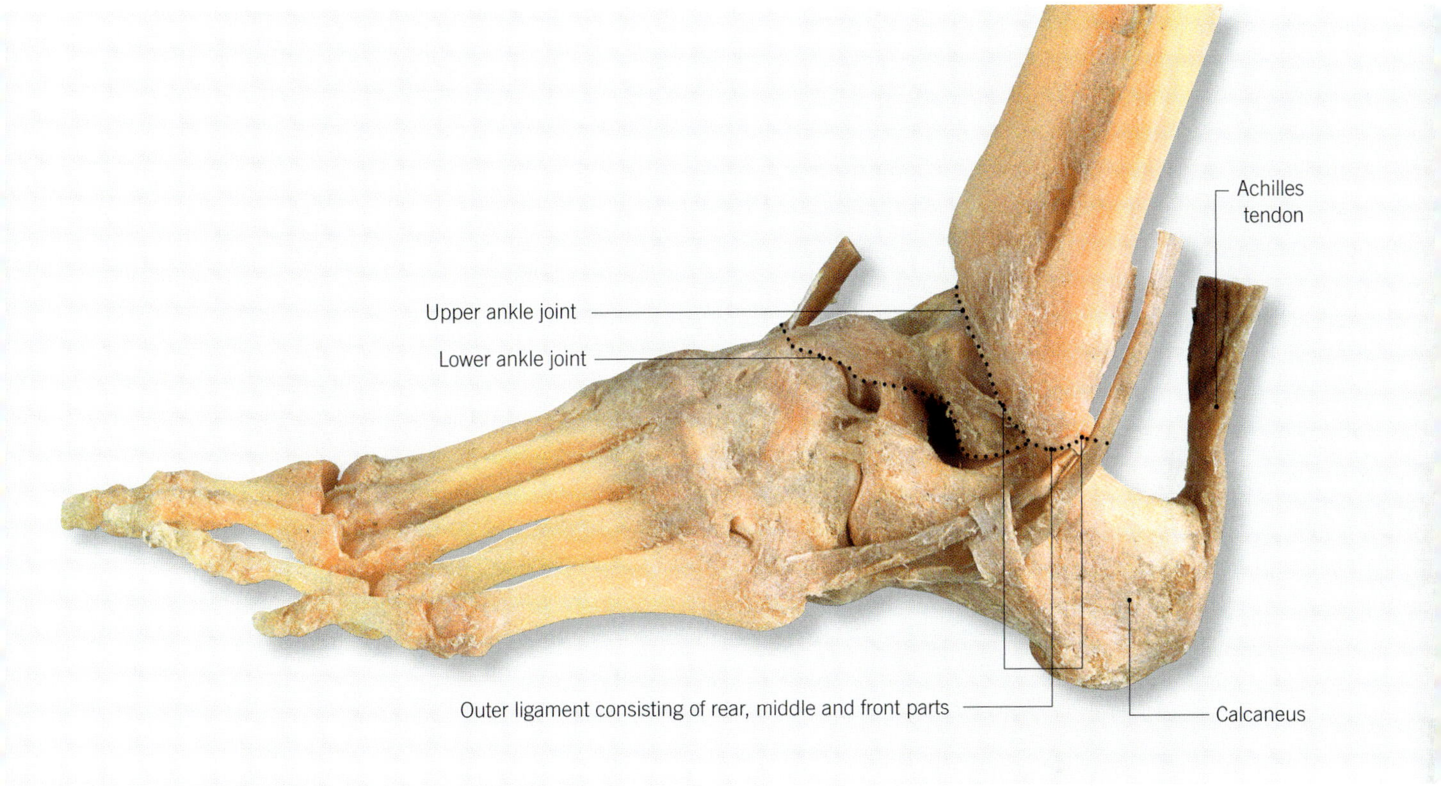


*Fig. 1.6 | Dissection of foot showing ligamentous structures*

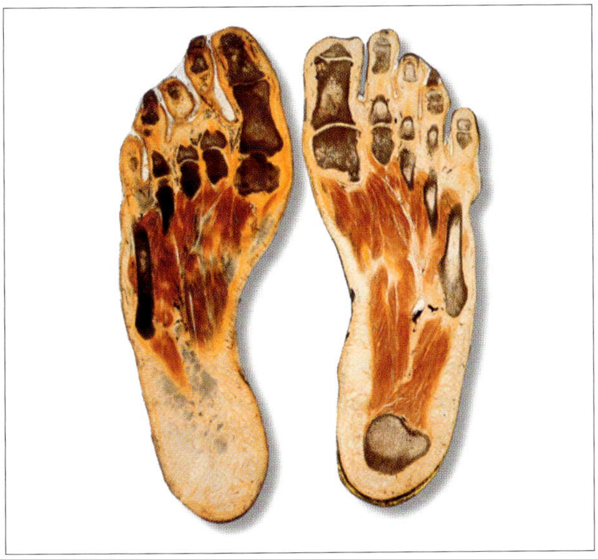

*Fig. 1.7 | Horizontal slices of the feet*

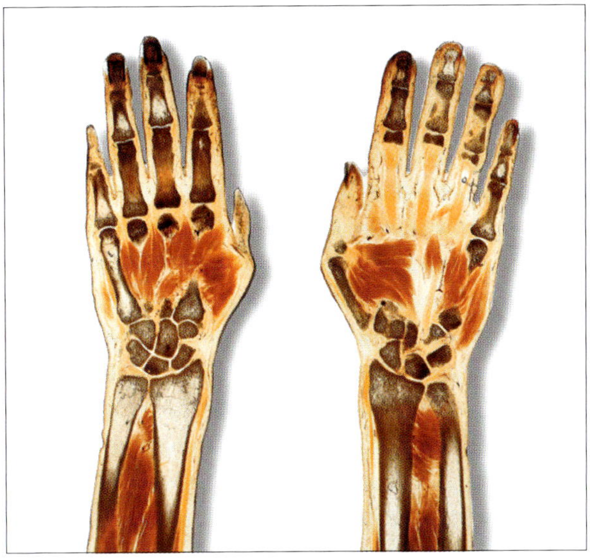

*Fig. 1.8 | Frontal slices of the hands*

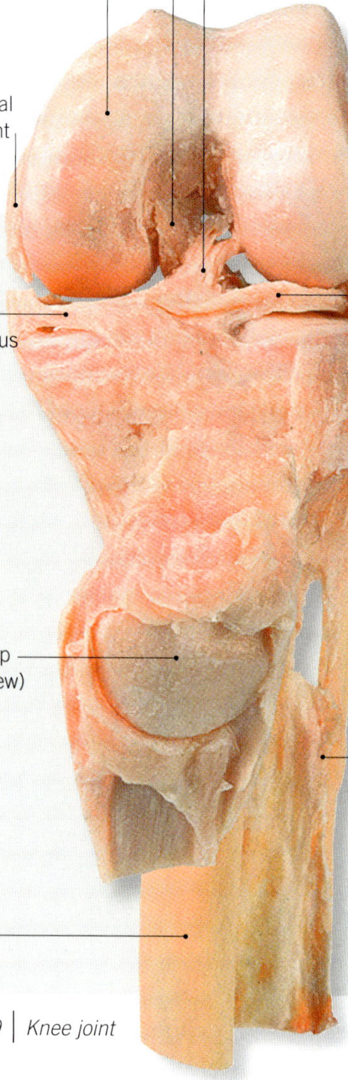


*Fig. 1.9 | Knee joint*

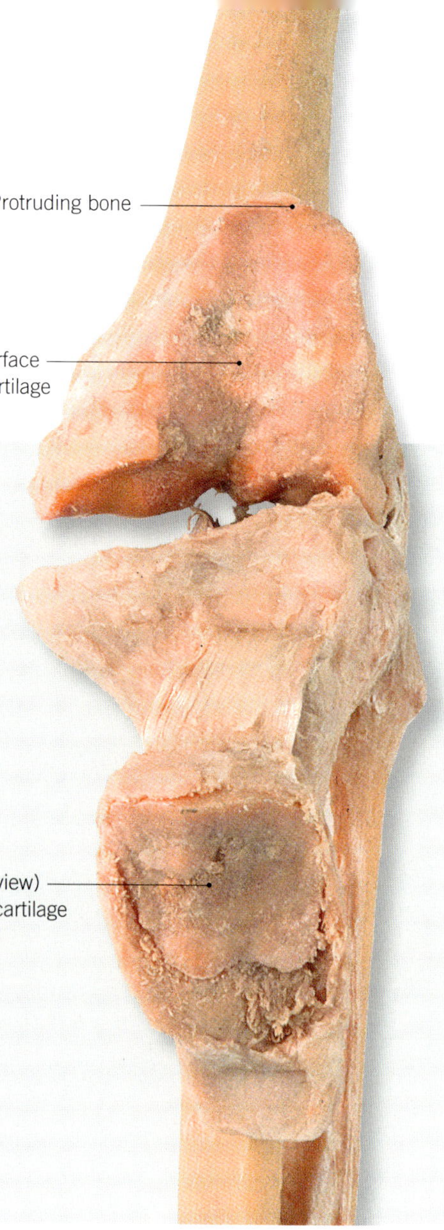


*Fig. 1.10 | Knee joint with severe arthritis*

**Knee Joint**

The knee has to be extremely stable.
It bears the greatest load of any joint.
It joins the thigh bone and tibia –
the weight-bearing bone in the lower leg.
One part of the knee joint is the kneecap.
This is held in a sheath of tendons.
To be stable, the knee needs 13 muscles
plus collateral and cross ligaments.
The knee joint bones are not a perfect fit.
To fill the gap, they have two
crescent-shaped cartilage wedges (menisci).

**Arthritis**

Since the knee has to support our body weight,
it suffers severe wear and tear over a lifetime.
The damage may cause chronic pain,
and the knee may even become inflammatory.
In a diseased or worn joint,
the cartilage loses its elasticity.
It becomes brittle and splinters,
and may even be destroyed completely.
Such cartilage damage is called arthritis.
In very advanced arthritis,
also the bones may begin to wear down,
leading to protruding bone growths.
It mostly affects patients over 50 years of age
and is more common in people who are overweight.
Weight loss tends to reduce the symptoms
associated with knee or hip arthritis.
There is also a genetic predisposition
of this condition.

## Hip Joint

The hip joins the torso and legs via the pelvic bones. The pelvis is a flexible ring formed by three major bones: the two hipbones and the rear sacrum bone. Thanks to this ring structure, the legs can handle the torso's weight.

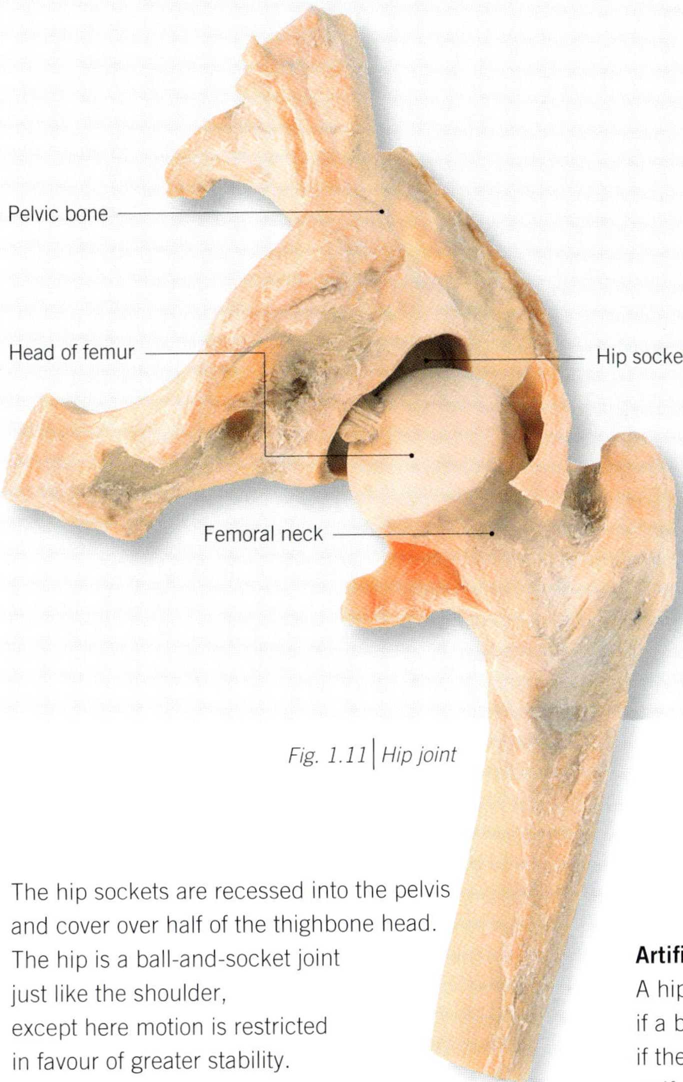


*Fig. 1.11 | Hip joint*

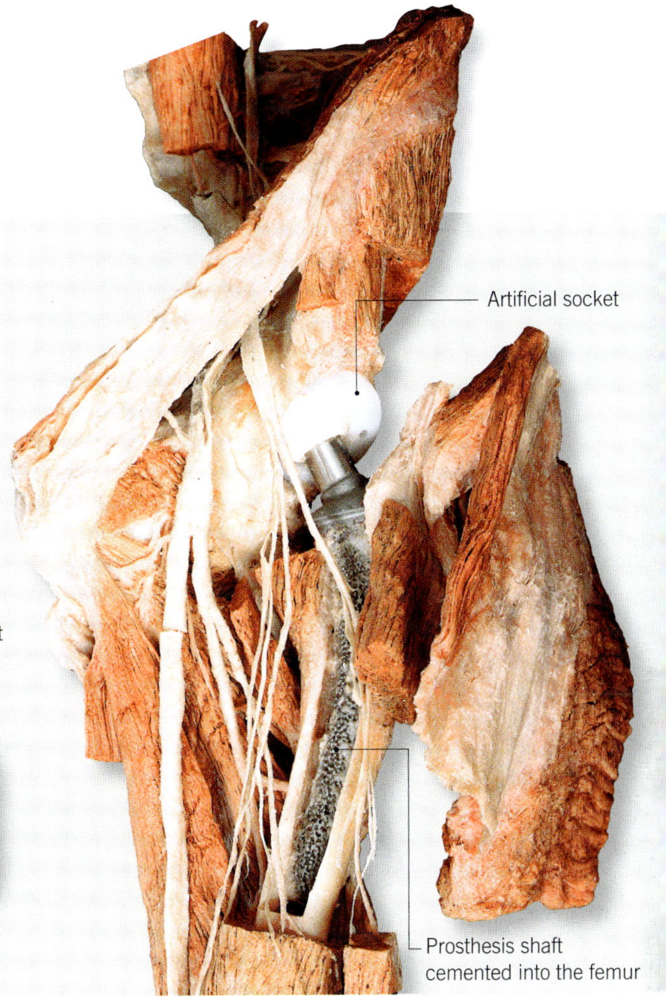


*Fig. 1.12 | Artificial hip joint*

The hip sockets are recessed into the pelvis and cover over half of the thighbone head. The hip is a ball-and-socket joint just like the shoulder, except here motion is restricted in favour of greater stability.

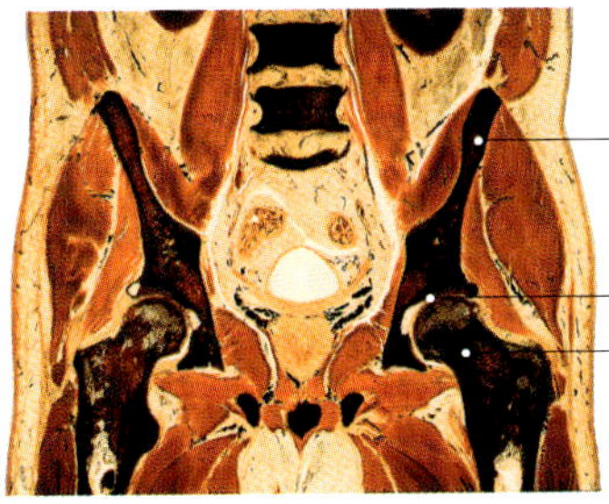


*Fig. 1.13 | Frontal slice of the pelvis*

## Artificial Hip Joint

A hip replacement may be necessary if a bone becomes severely worn (arthritis), if the neck of the femur becomes fractured or if any other change takes place in the hip that significantly limits its function. Artificial hips mimic both the spherical shape of the head of the femur as well as the angle at which the neck of the femur is inclined in a natural joint.

Its long stainless steel shaft is cemented into the bone marrow canal of the femur. The joint socket is made of Teflon.

# The Skull

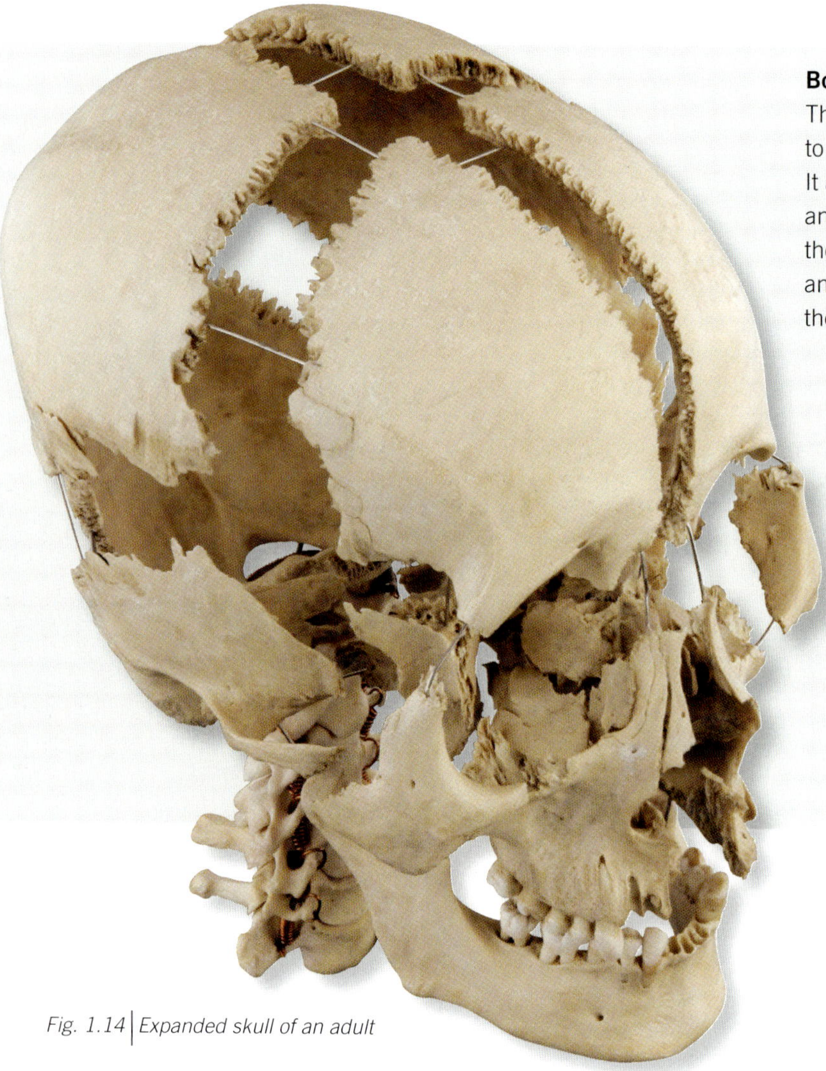

Fig. 1.14 | *Expanded skull of an adult*

**Bones of the Skull**
The skull's most important role is to enclose and protect the brain. It also gives shape to the head and face and houses the main sensory organs: the eyes, nose, tongue, and, at the base of the cranium, the inner ears.

The bone plates of a newborn baby's skull are linked by cartilage bridges. This allows the bone plates to overlap slightly like shingles when passing through the narrow birth canal. During childhood, the separated bones yield to facilitate growth of the skull and brain. By adulthood, all the bones are fused together.

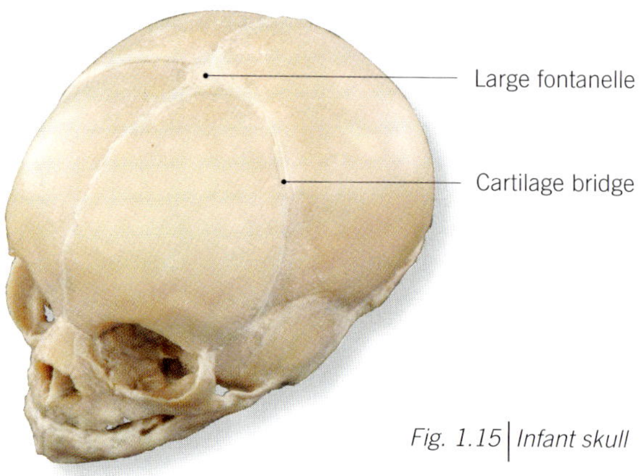


Fig. 1.15 | *Infant skull*

# Hearing

**Ossicles**
The ossicles of the middle ear
are the smallest bones in the body.
They are named after their shapes:
the hammer (malleus), the anvil (incus)
and the stirrup (stapes).

The ossicles form a bony chain behind the eardrum
at the end of the external auditory canal
and transmit sound to the inner ear.
The ossicles and the ear drum form the middle ear.

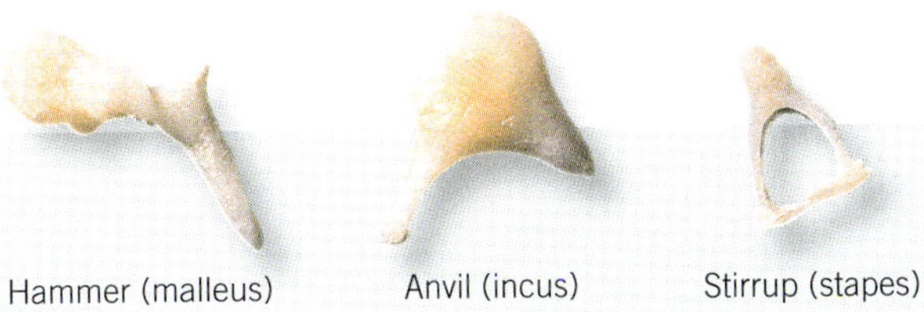


*Fig. 1.16 | Auditory ossicles*

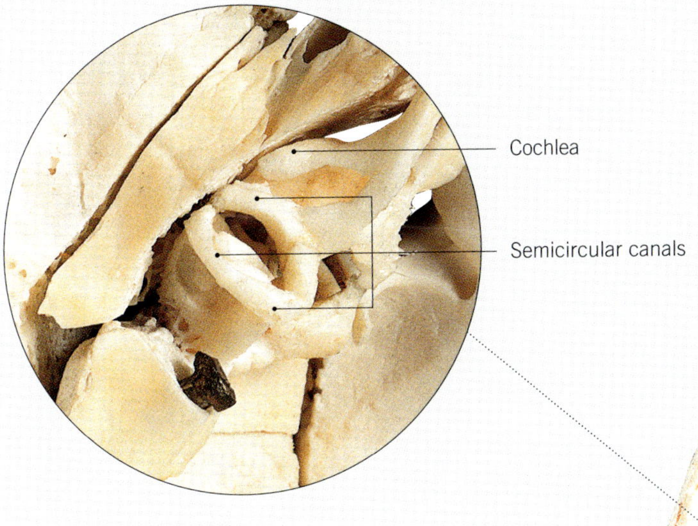


*Fig. 1.17 | Inner ear at skull base*

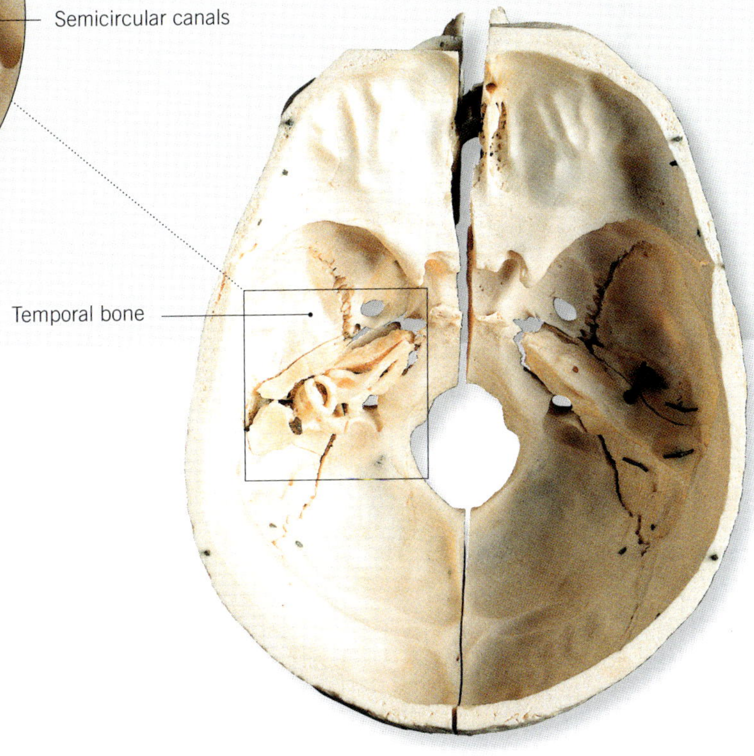


*Fig. 1.18 | Skull base with inner ear dissected*

**Inner Ear**
The cochlea is our organ of hearing.
The semicircular canals next to the cochlea
are our organ of balance.
Both systems make up the inner ear.
They are embedded in the temporal bones
at the base of the skull.

The cochlea is full of liquid.
When sound waves travel down the auditory canal
the liquid vibrates, stimulating special sensory cells.
These cells convert the vibrations
into electrochemical messages.

The data are then carried along the auditory nerve
to the brain where the signals are interpreted.

The semicircular canals have a similar system
to convert head and body movements
into signals interpreted by the brain.

# Bone Structure and Growth

Although the skeleton of an adult weighs only about 7–9 kilograms (15–20 pounds), it is stronger than reinforced concrete. By comparison, steel rods of the same size would probably weigh 4 to 5 times as much. This is due to the structure of the bones.

Our bones are usually made of two parts: a hard, compact outer layer and spongy cancellous bone inside. The structure of cancellous bone is designed to cope with forces of pressure and contraction. So bones can remain lightweight, yet have considerable stability.

The soft, spongy tissue produces the cellular components of blood: white cells, red cells, and platelets. It is also the most radiation sensitive tissue of the body.

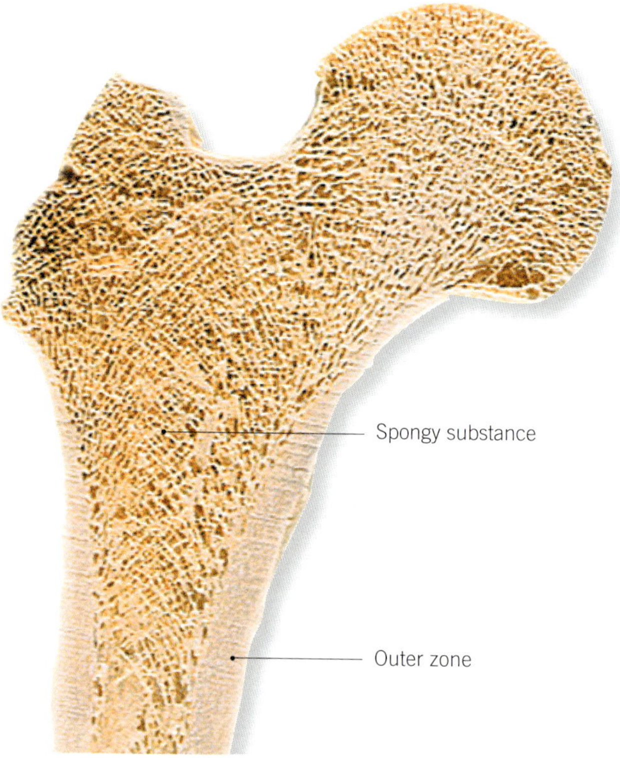


*Fig. 1.19 | Adult thighbone (femur), longitudinally cut*

**Bone Growth**
In embryonic development, the skeleton is initially cartilage. Gradually as the body grows, the cartilage is replaced by bone. In a newborn baby, there are still cartilage zones at the ends of the long, tube-like bones to provide starting points for bone growth. The process of ossification continues until the age of about 18 years.

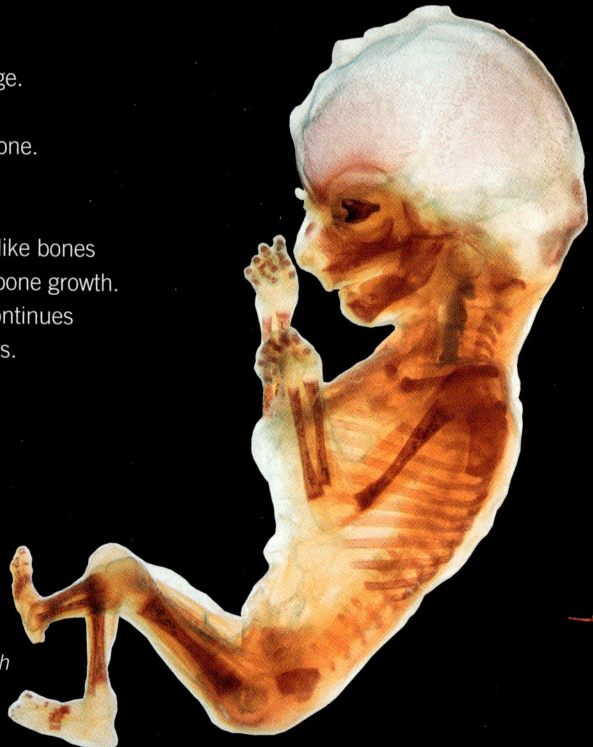

*Fig. 1.20 | Foetus in the 3rd month*

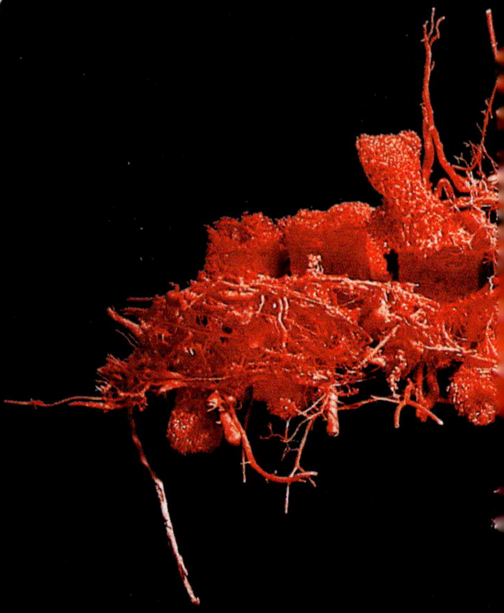

Bone is made up of living cells,
as well as protein, mineral salts, and water.
The bone cells are constantly regenerating.
Specialised bone cells create new bone,
while other cells remove older ones.

**Osteoporosis**

As people age, bone tissue renewal slows down.
By the age of 70, most people's skeletons
have become about a third thinner and lighter
than they were at the age of 40.
This loss of bone density is called osteoporosis.
It makes bones more fragile and likely to break.
Such osteoporotic fractures typically occur
in the hip, spine, and wrist.

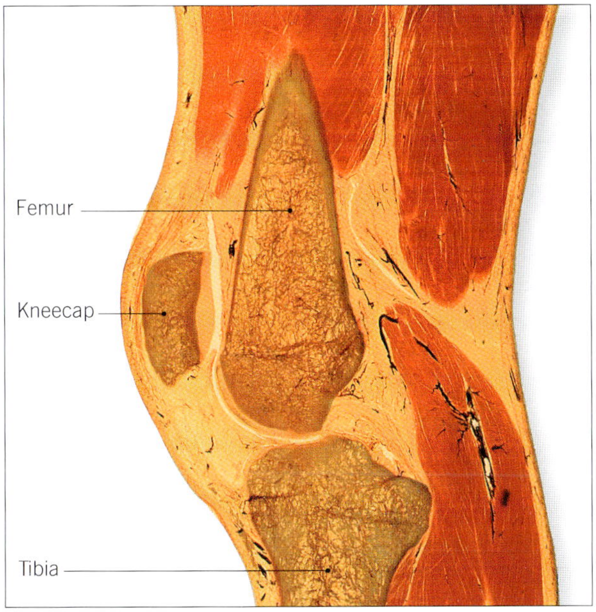


*Fig. 1.21 | Longitudinal slice of knee joint with normal bone structure*

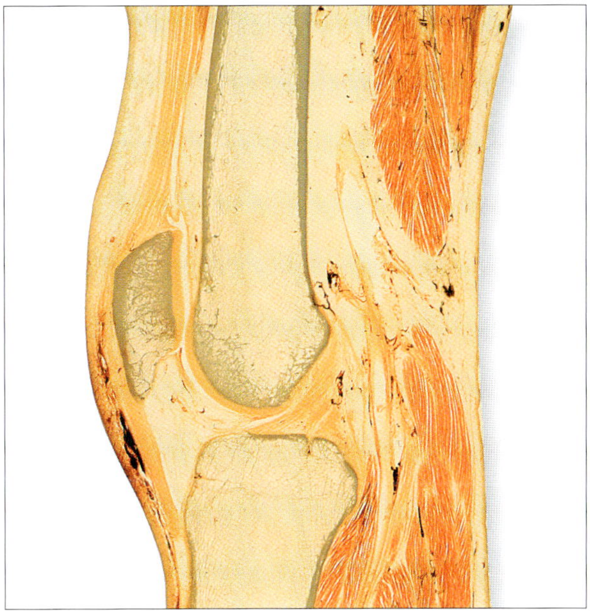

*Fig. 1.22 | Longitudinal slice of knee joint with osteoporosis*

**Blood Supply of the Bone**

Bone has a rich vascular supply,
receiving 10–20% of the cardiac output.

The blood supply varies
with different types of bones,
but blood vessels are especially rich
in areas that contain red bone marrow.

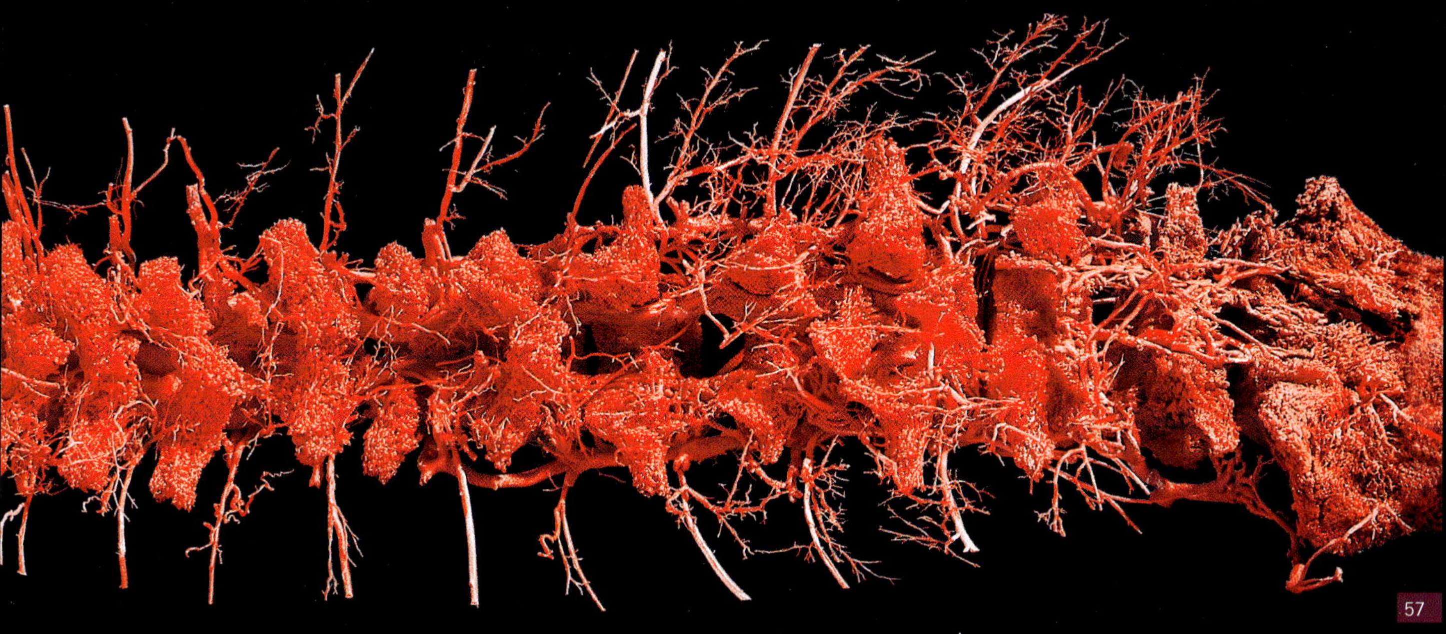

*Fig. 1.23 | Blood vessel configuration of the spine*

# Bone Disorders

Bones may be deformed for several reasons:
genetic or metabolic disorders,
improperly healed bones, inflammation,
or poor load distribution.

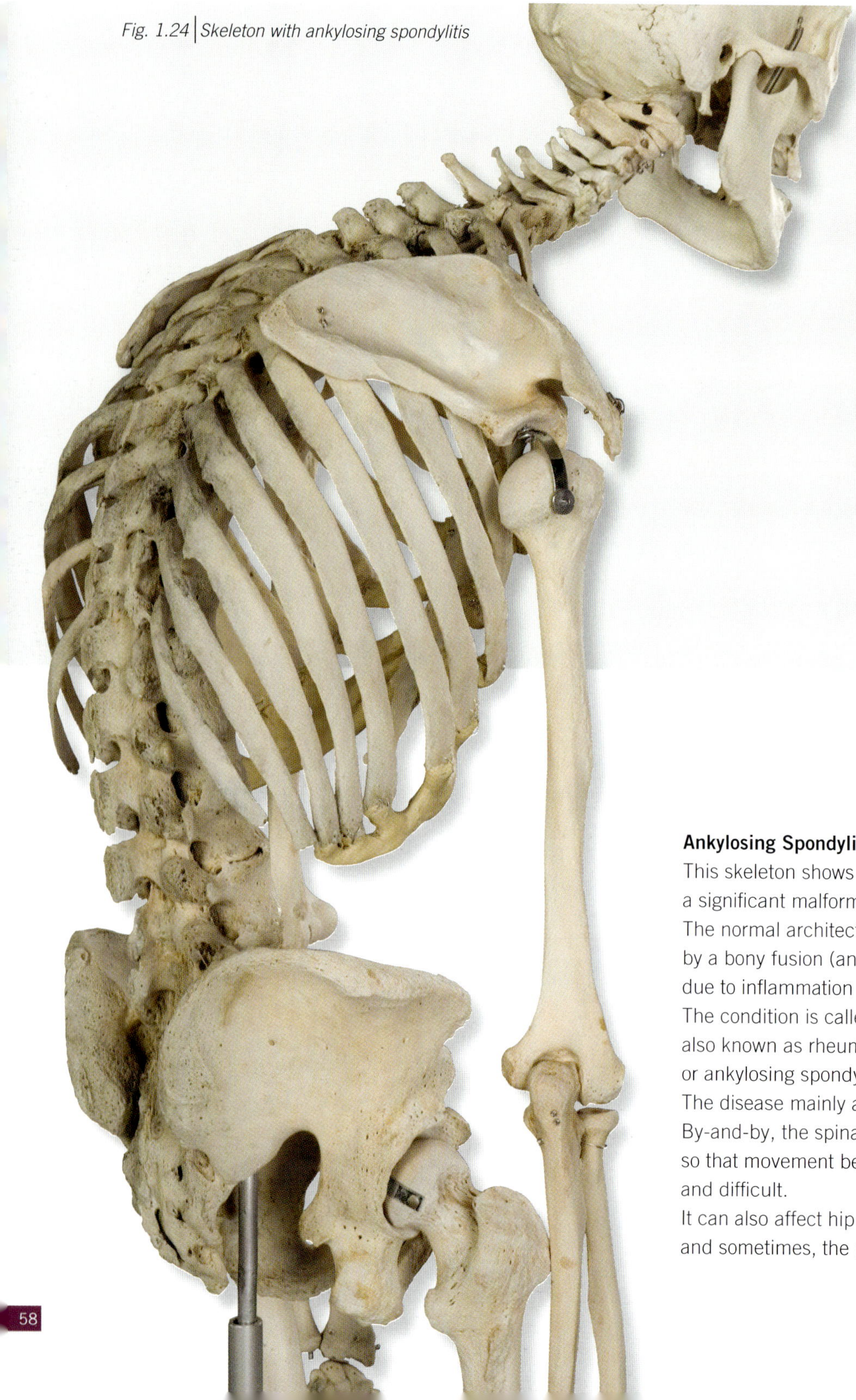

*Fig. 1.24 | Skeleton with ankylosing spondylitis*

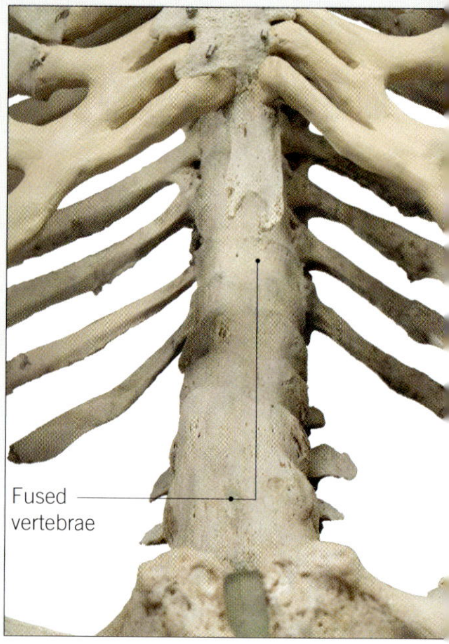


*Fig. 1.25 | Close-up of a spine affected by ankylosing spondylitis*

**Ankylosing Spondylitis** (Bechterew's Disease)
This skeleton shows
a significant malformation of the spine.
The normal architecture of the spine is replaced
by a bony fusion (ankylosis) of the vertebrae
due to inflammation of the vertebral joints.
The condition is called Bechterew's Disease,
also known as rheumatoid spondylitis,
or ankylosing spondylitis.
The disease mainly affects young males.
By-and-by, the spinal joints and ligaments stiffen
so that movement becomes increasingly painful
and difficult.
It can also affect hip and shoulder joints,
and sometimes, the peripheral joints.

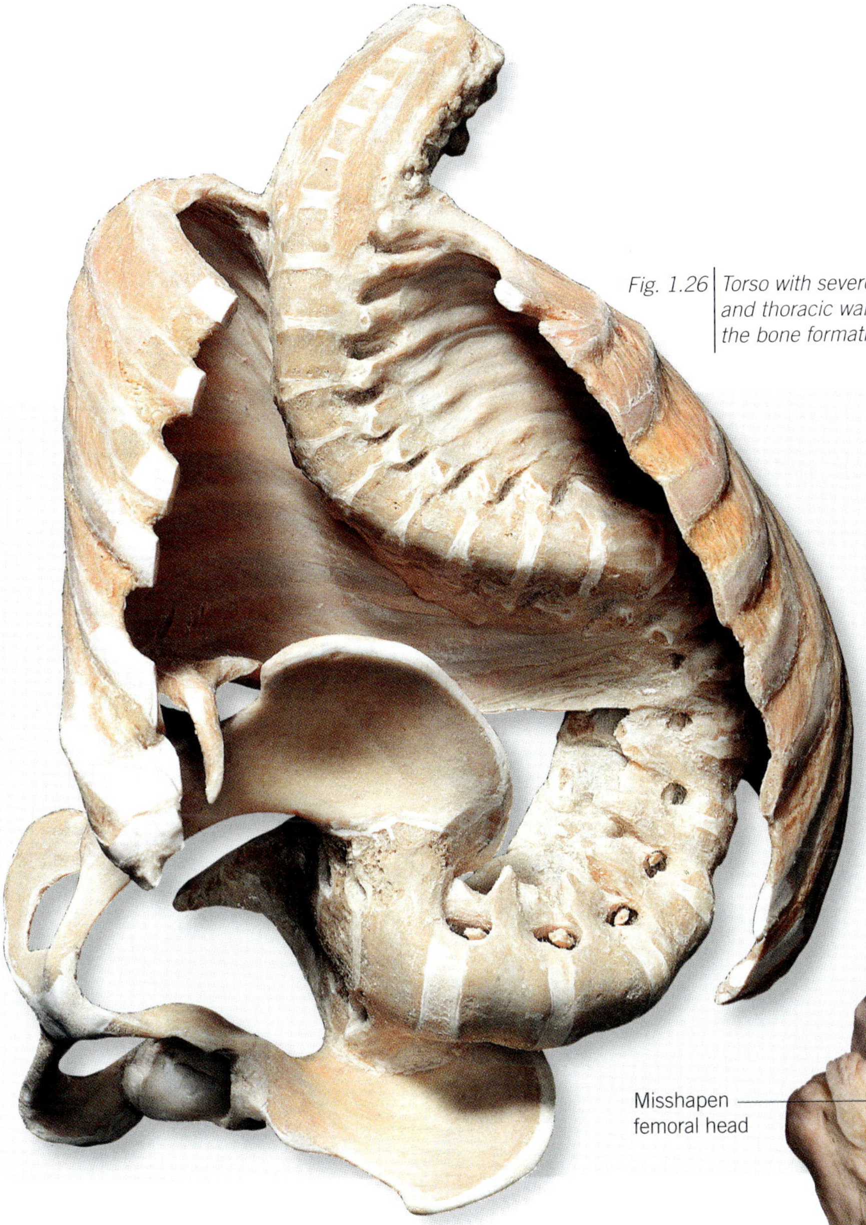

Fig. 1.26 | *Torso with severe deformation of the spinal column and thoracic wall caused by a hereditary disorder of the bone formation and development*

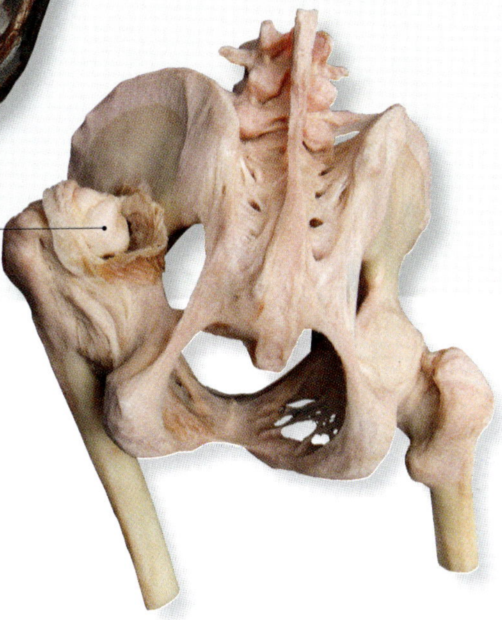


Fig. 1.27 | *Congenital hip dysplasia (left side)*

**Deformation of the Spinal Column**

The distortion of the spinal column above is due to a genetic bone disorder. The internal organs' size and shape had to adapt to the unusually twisted torso. A deformed torso particularly affects lung function.

**Congenital Hip Dysplasia**

This left hip joint in Fig. 1.27 shows a severe abnormal formation known as congenital hip dysplasia. The femoral head is not deeply and tightly held by the socket of the hip bone (acetabulum). Instead of being tightly fit, it is loose and dislocated.

Also the femoral head and acetabulum are not smooth and round but are misshapen, causing abnormal wear and tear and friction within the joint as it moves. A congenital hip dysplasia is already present at birth. Genetic factors may play a role in this disorder.

# Bone Repair

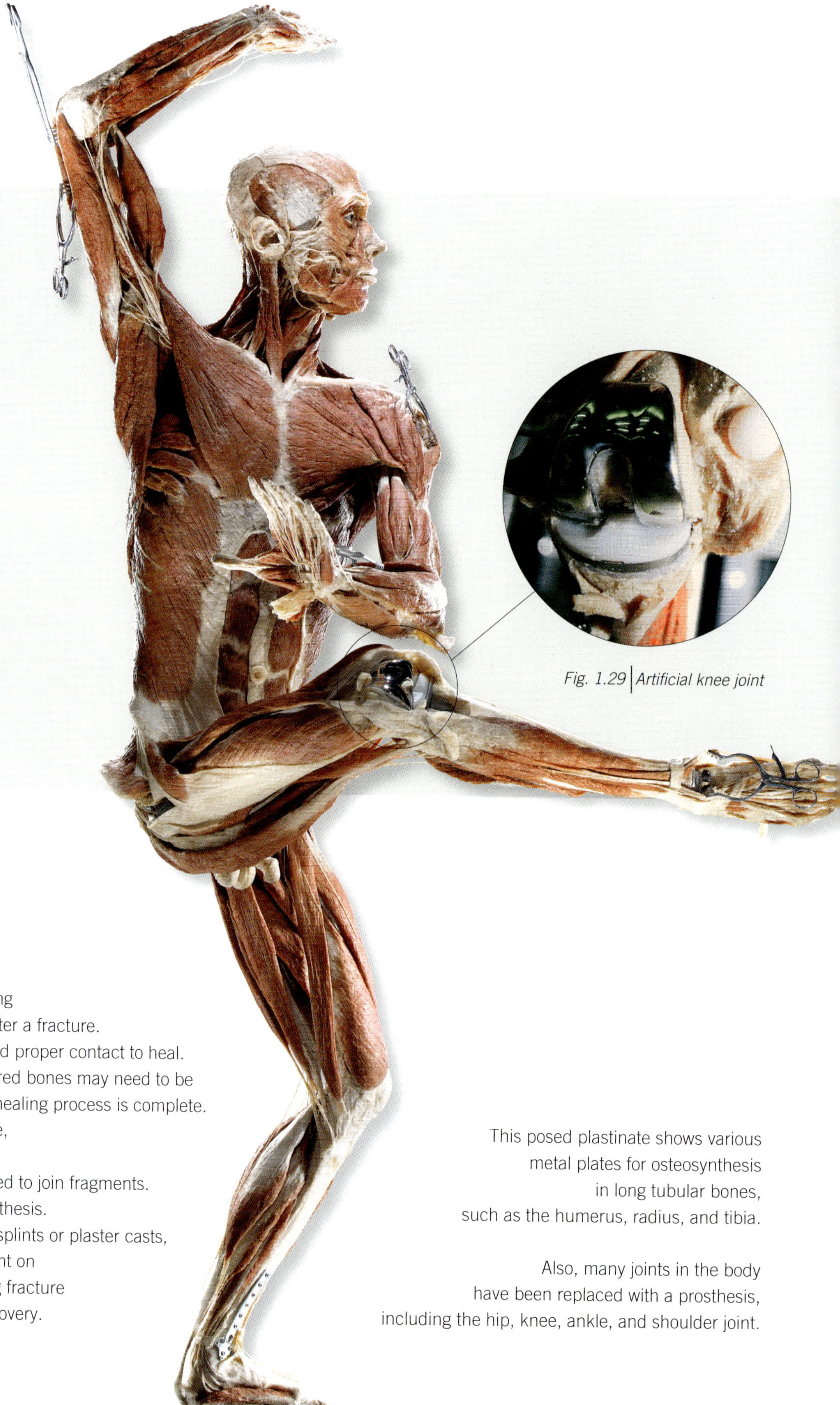

Fig. 1.29 | *Artificial knee joint*

Fig. 1.28 | *Tai Chi Man*

Bone has an astonishing ability to mend itself after a fracture. But the fragments need proper contact to heal. For this reason, fractured bones may need to be immobilised until the healing process is complete. If the fracture is severe, stainless steel screws, plates, or wires are used to join fragments. This is called osteosynthesis. Even without external splints or plaster casts, a patient can put weight on an internally stabilising fracture at an early point in recovery.

This posed plastinate shows various metal plates for osteosynthesis in long tubular bones, such as the humerus, radius, and tibia.

Also, many joints in the body have been replaced with a prosthesis, including the hip, knee, ankle, and shoulder joint.

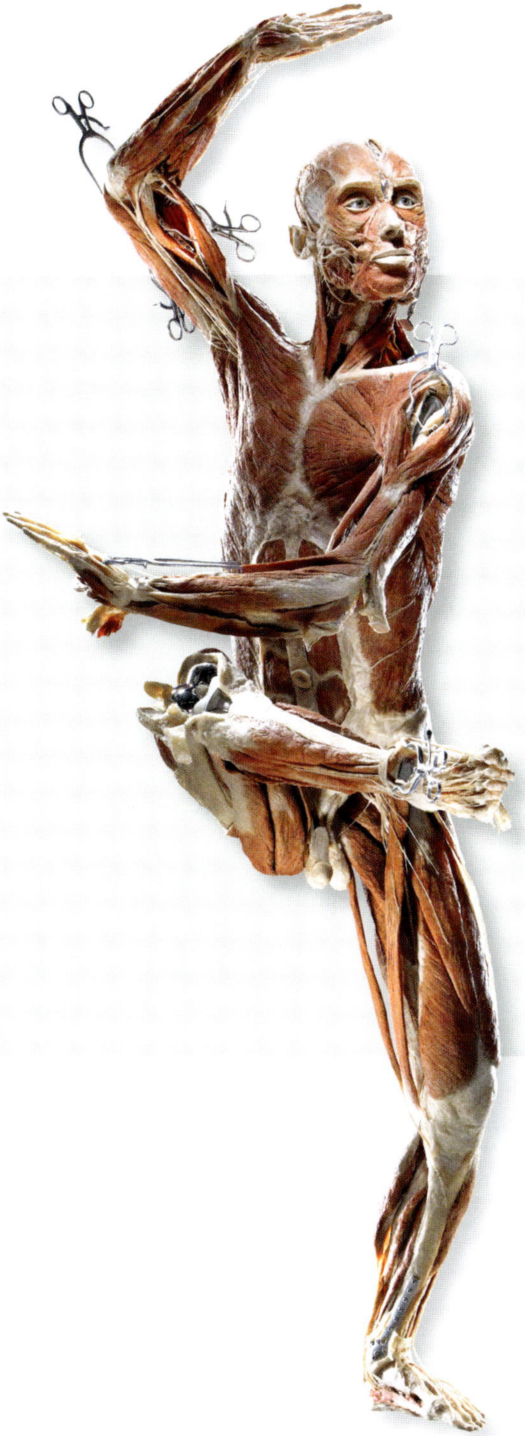

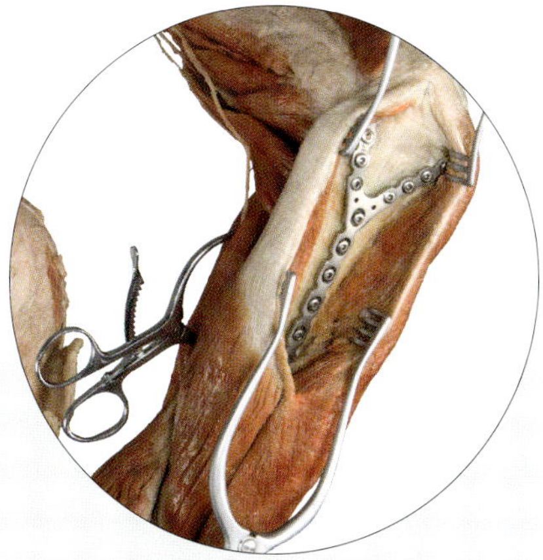

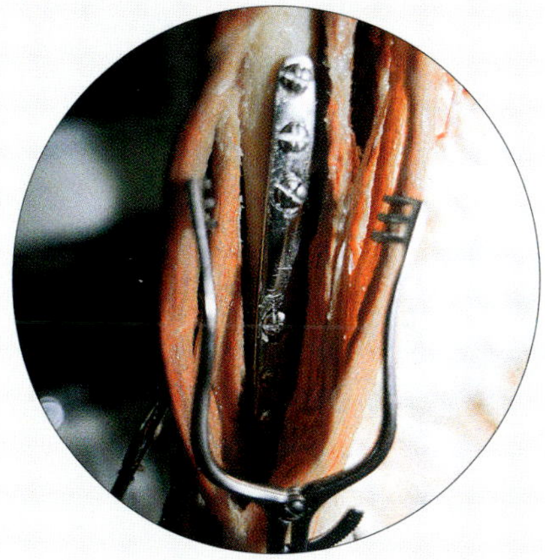

Fig. 1.30 | Osteosynthesis with metal plates

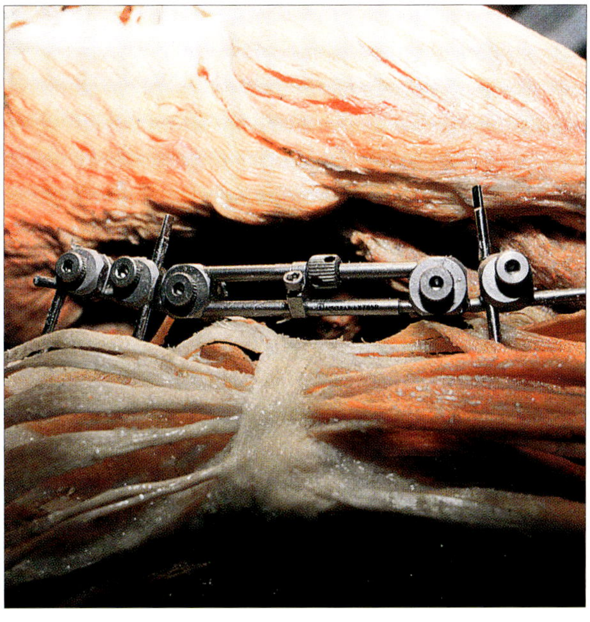

Fig. 1.31 | External wrist fixation

In complicated bone fractures,
external fixation might become necessary.
This is accomplished by placing pins or screws
into the bone on both sides of the fracture.
The pins are then secured together
outside the skin with clamps and rods.
The clamps and rods are known as the "external frame".

# Muscle System

A muscle is a biological flexor.
It functions in that its fibres contract
to become shorter.
There are three types of muscles.
They each perform different roles and
have different structures:

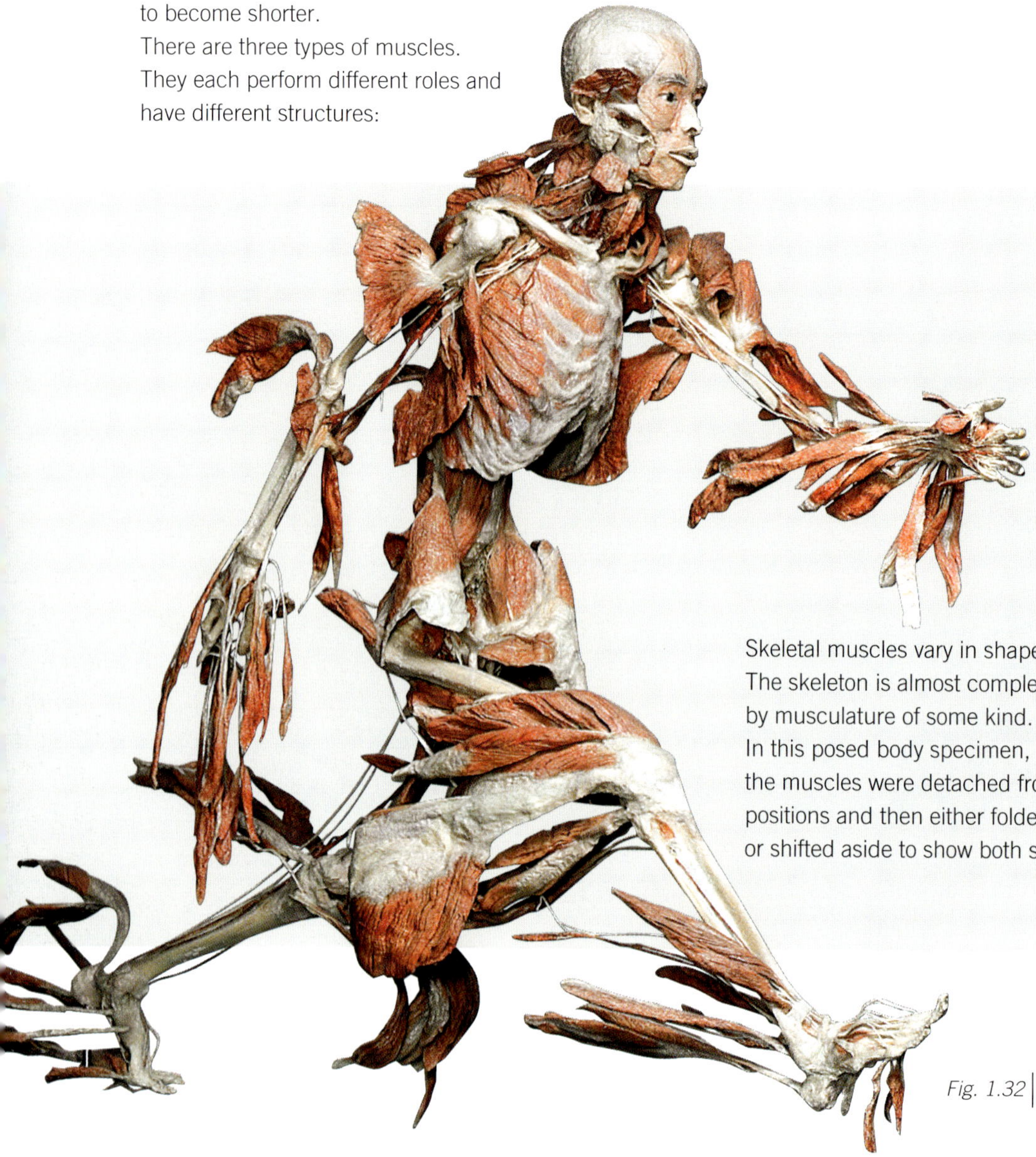

Skeletal muscles vary in shape and strength.
The skeleton is almost completely covered
by musculature of some kind.
In this posed body specimen,
the muscles were detached from their original
positions and then either folded back
or shifted aside to show both systems simultaneously.

*Fig. 1.32 | The Runner*

a) Skeletal muscles perform voluntary movements.
They can contract quickly, but only for a short time.

b) Smooth muscles perform unconscious actions,
such as propelling food along the digestive tract.
They contract slowly but can continue in a state
of contraction for long periods.

c) Cardiac muscles are involuntarily controlled.
They contract rhythmically and continuously
in order to pump blood around the whole body.

A typical muscle stretches from one bone to another,
crossing a joint.
They are attached to bones with tendons
which are made of connective fibres.

Muscles are usually arranged
in pairs with opposing functions.
The biceps, for instance, flexes the elbow,
while the triceps does just the opposite
and serves to extend the elbow.
When the biceps contracts,
the triceps inhibits any excessive movement.
This makes our movements fluid and controlled.

Muscle movement requires signals
from the brain and nerves.
When we want to move something,
the brain sends electrical signals
down nerve pathways to the muscles.
When the signals arrive,
the filaments in the muscle fibres
respond by contracting.
This moves the bones relative to one another.

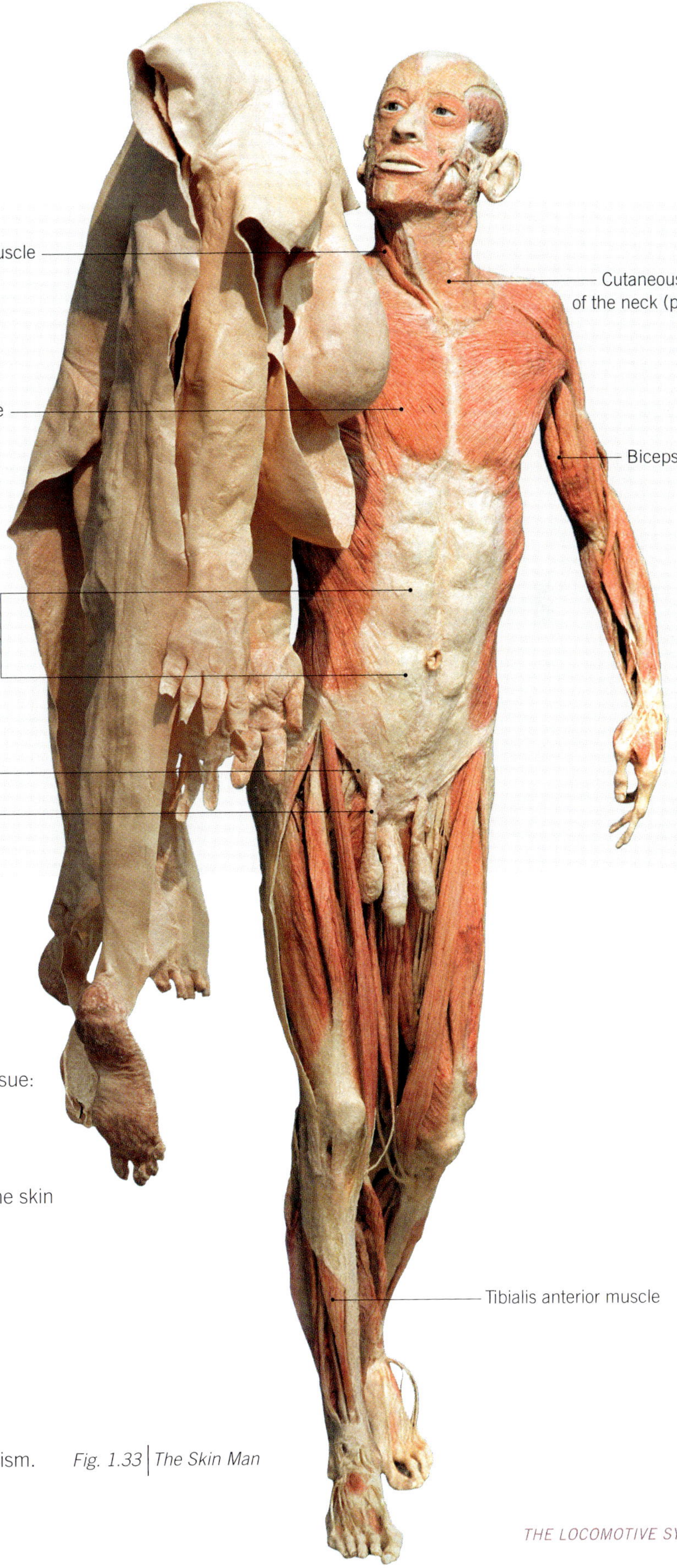


The posed plastinate on the right
shows all the muscles just below the skin.
Muscles play a big role in the way we look
and make up the largest proportion of our tissue:
roughly 23% of body weight in women
and 40% in men.

This plastinate also points up the nature of the skin
as an independent organ.
The skin is our largest and heaviest organ
without which we could not exist.
The skin lends individuality to our exterior.
It imparts beauty and age.
Its most important functions are
to shield the body from the outside world,
pass on pressure and tactile sensations,
and regulate temperature and water metabolism.

*Fig. 1.33 | The Skin Man*

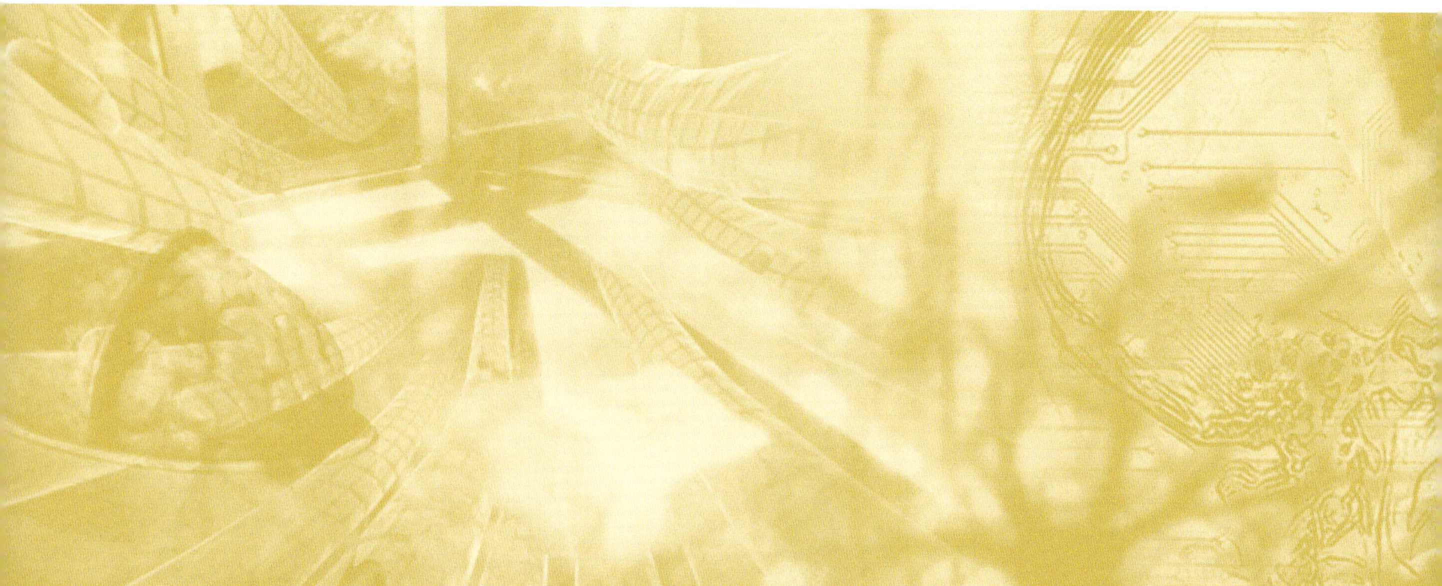

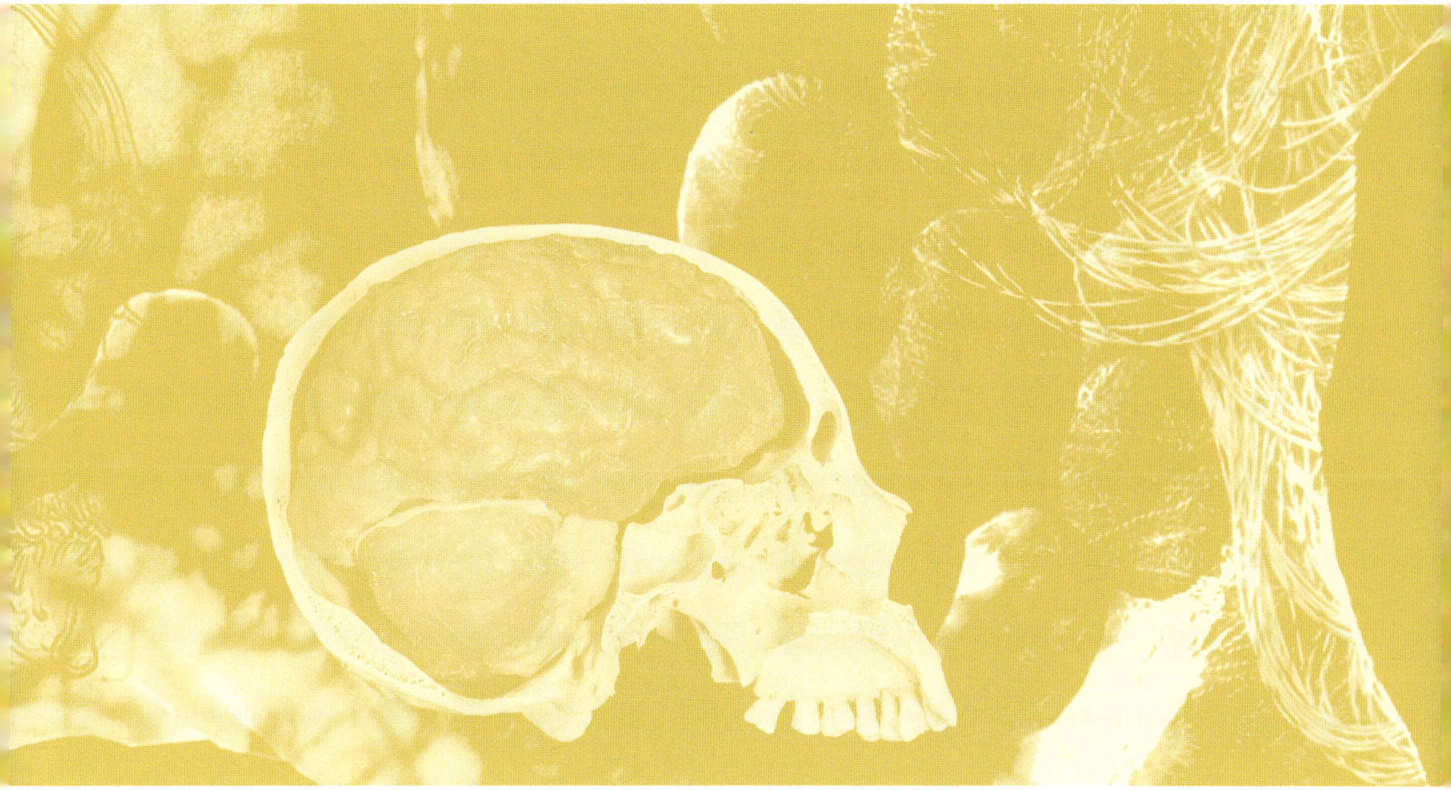

# 2. THE **NERVOUS** SYSTEM

Without a central communication system
with connections that encompass
an entire country from one end to the other,
a modern nation would soon become ungovernable.
It is the same with the human body and its nervous system.
The nervous system regulates
hundreds of activities simultaneously.
It monitors and controls almost all bodily processes,
ranging from automatic functions
of which we are largely unconscious,
such as breathing and digestion,
to complex activities that involve thought and learning.
It is also the source of our consciousness, intelligence,
and creativity, and allows us
to communicate and experience emotions.

# Central and Peripheral Nervous System

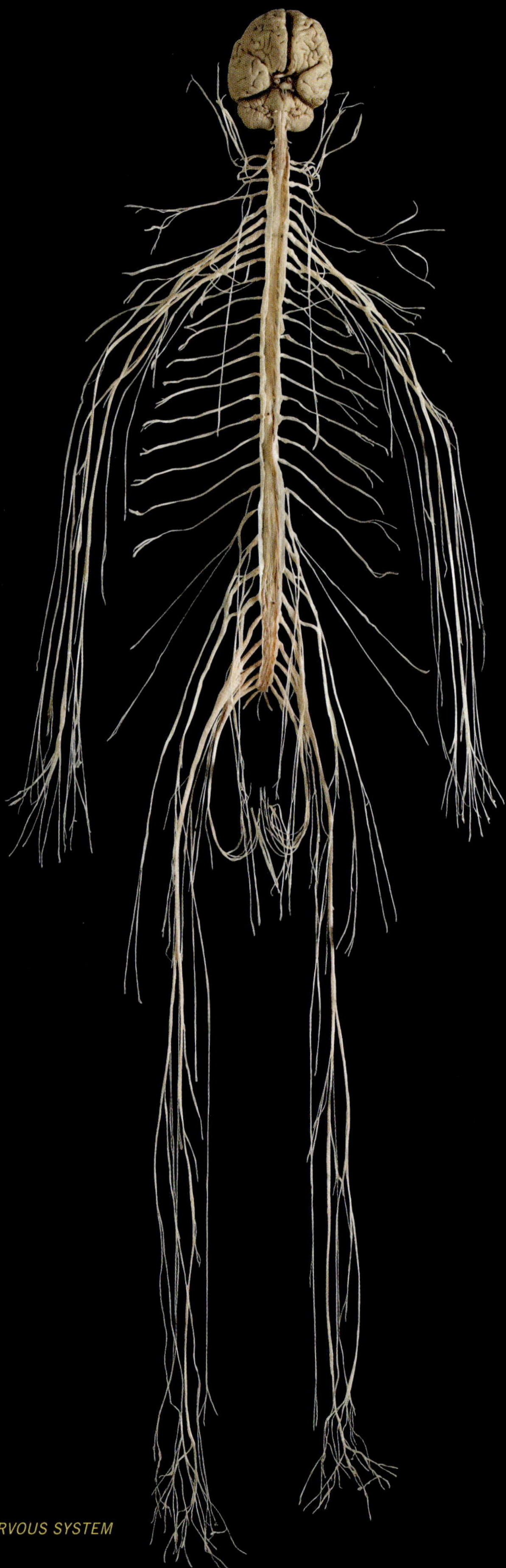

The nervous system can be divided into two parts:
a) The central nervous systems,
composed of the brain and the spinal cord.
It regulates bodily activities by
processing and coordinating nerve signals.

b) The peripheral nervous system
is made up of all the nerves that emanate
from the central nervous system and
branch out throughout the body.
They transmit the signals
between the central nervous system
and the rest of the body.

The basic units are nerve cells.
When parts of the body communicate,
they use weak electrical signals
emitted by the nerve cells.
These signals can travel at up to 400 km/h (250 mph).

The peripheral nerves originate directly
from either the brain or spinal cord
and become increasingly fine as they branch out
into the peripheral regions of the body.
Here, only the main peripheral nerve branches are shown.

*Fig. 2.1 | Isolated central and peripheral nervous system*

# The Brain

The brain is the body's command centre.
It processes sensory information,
coordinates most movement and thinking,
and allows us to feel, remember, and communicate.

The skull bones protect the brain,
like a shell around a walnut.
As humans evolved, the cerebrum,
formed by the two cerebral hemispheres,
gradually grew and expanded.
This is where voluntary action is coordinated.
To grow within the restricted skull space,
the surface became convoluted and furrowed.
The furrows hide roughly two thirds
of the brain's surface.
Spread out flat, the cerebral cortex
would be approximately 1.5 sq. metres (16 sq. feet).

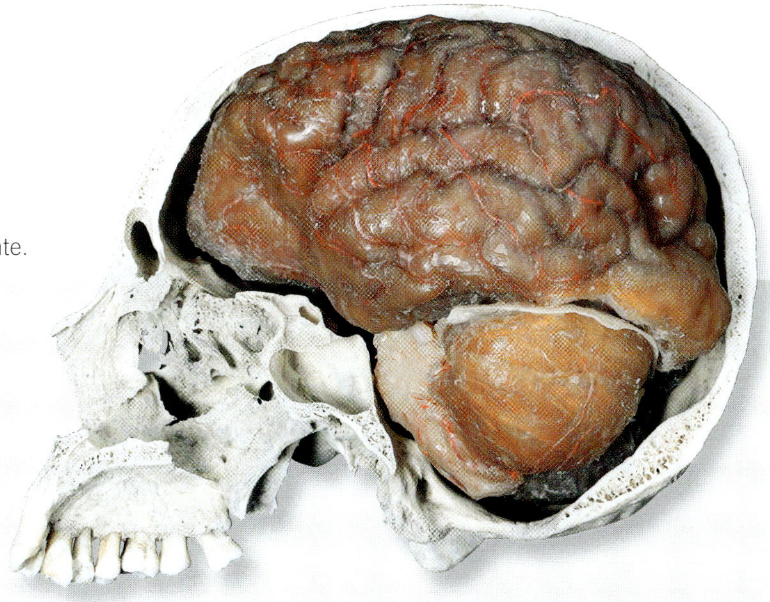

*Fig. 2.2 | Brain in half skull*

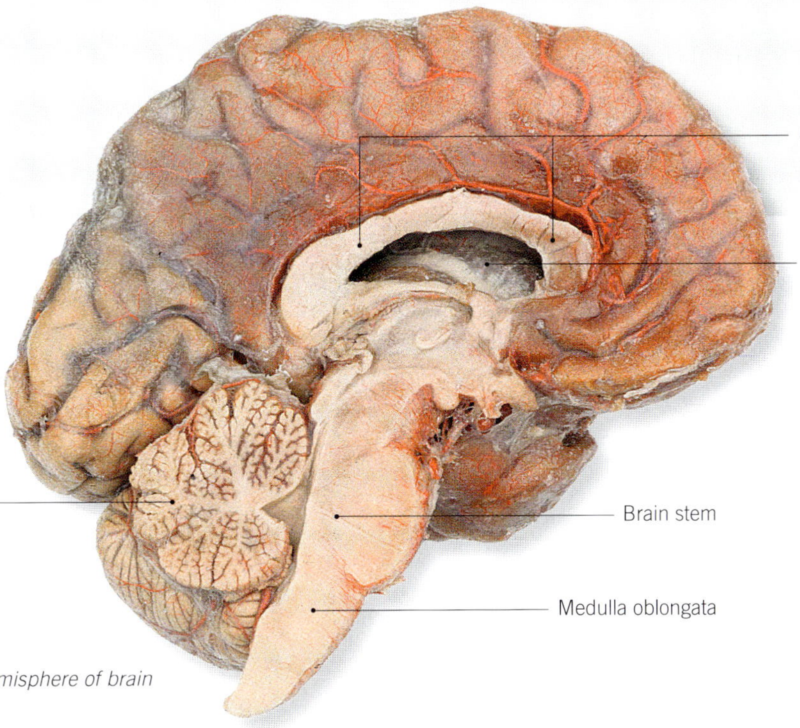


*Fig. 2.3 | Left hemisphere of brain*

The cerebrum is the largest part of the brain.
A groove runs down its convex shape,
dividing it into two cerebral hemispheres.
At its bottom, the corpus callosum is visible.
It joins both cerebral hemispheres.

Much of the inter-hemispheric communication
in the brain is conducted across the corpus callosum.
Beneath that are the brain stem and cerebellum.
The brain is connected to the spinal cord
by the medulla oblongata.

# Inside the Brain

Both the brain and the spinal cord contain areas of grey and white matter; as can best be seen in a cross section.

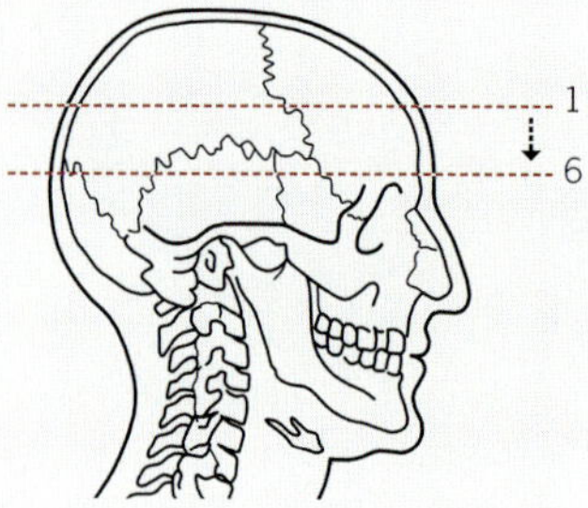


The outermost layer of the cerebrum (cortex) and a group of nuclei deep in the hemispheres (basal ganglia) are composed of densely packed nerve cells (neurons).
They are referred to as grey matter.
Due to the polymers used for plastination, the grey matter appears brownish.
In grey matter, nerve impulses are processed.

The cerebral cortex plays a key role in memory, attention, perceptual awareness, thought, language, and consciousness.

The basal ganglia pre-process millions of nerve signals going into or out of the cortex.
They also send signals on to the relevant brain "centres" for further analysis.
Among other functions, they help coordinate movement.

White matter consists of nerve fibres.
They interconnect the different regions of the central nervous system and transmit the nerve impulses.

*Fig. 2.4* | *Series of horizontal brain slices*

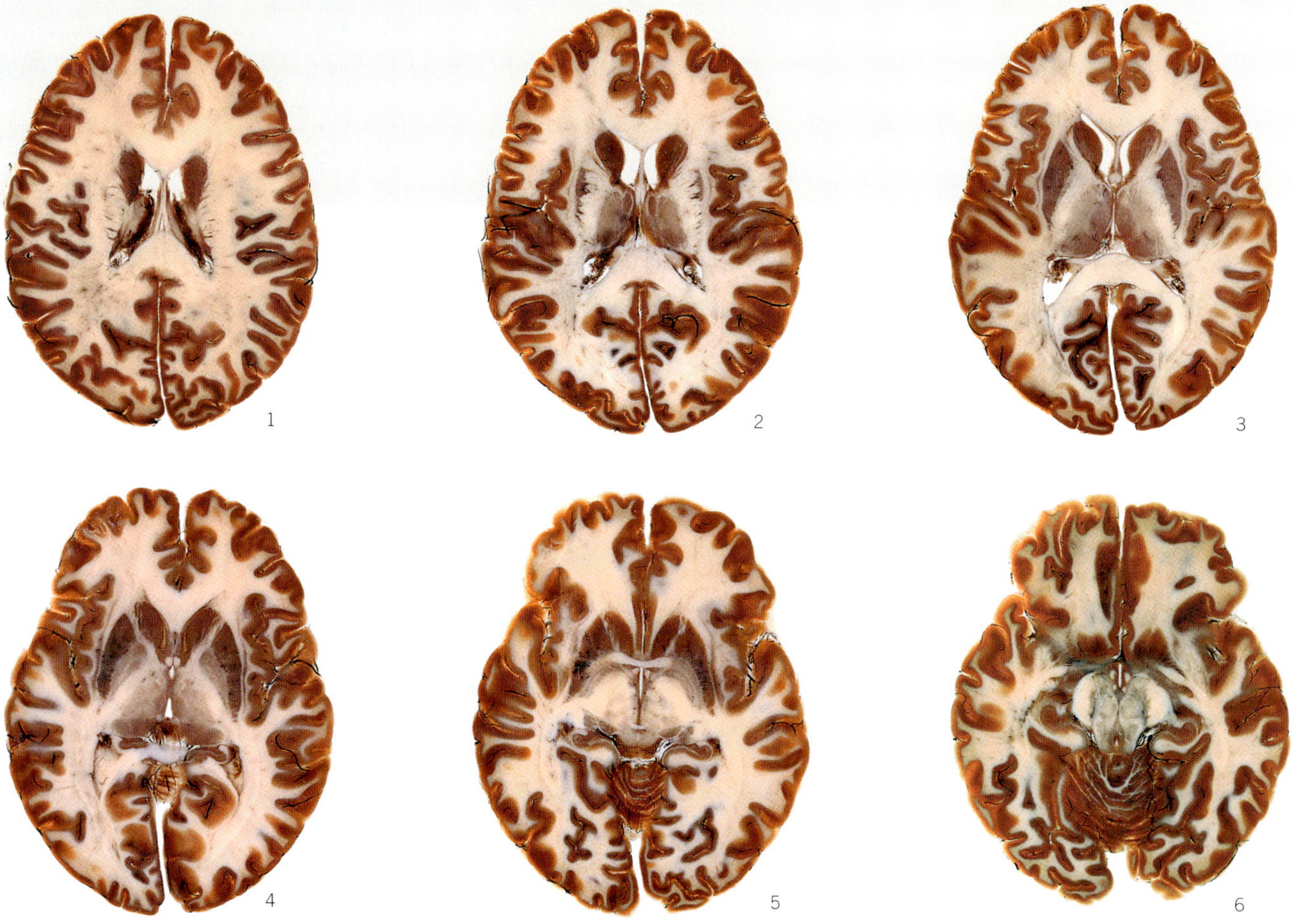

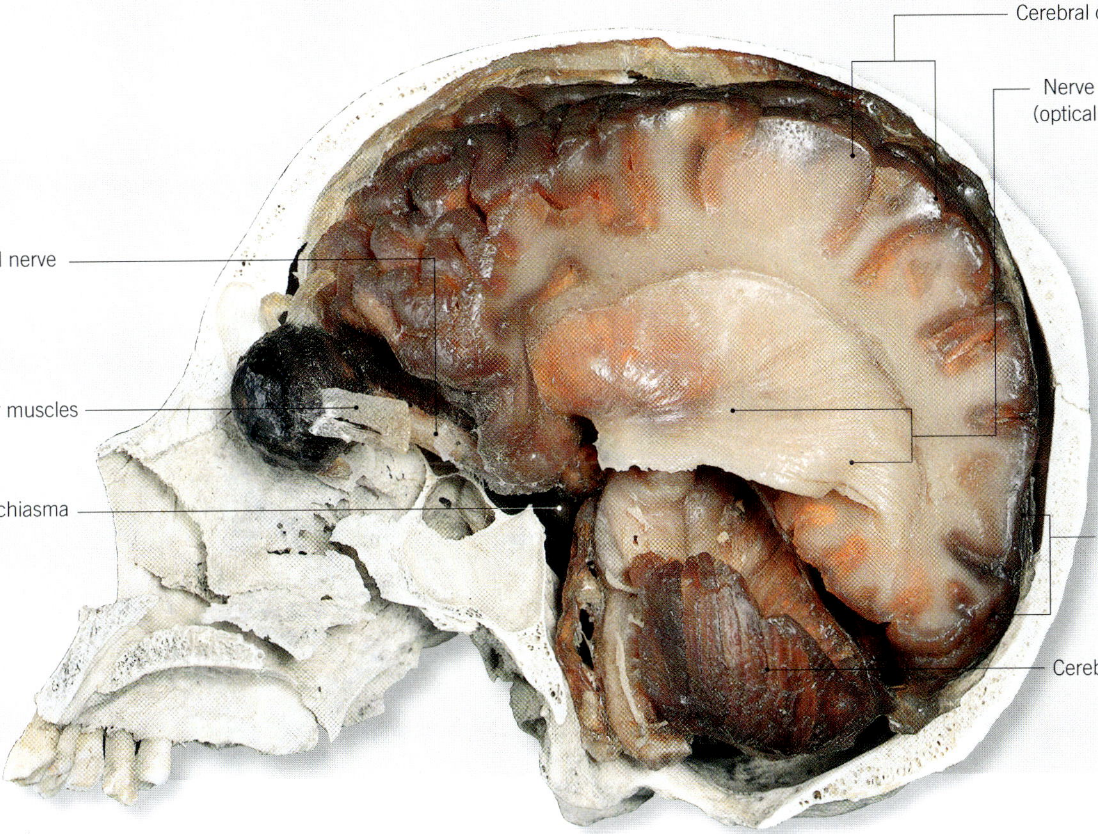


*Fig. 2.5* | *Brain in half skull with dissection of the nerve fibres*

In the brain specimen shown above, the optic nerve fibres are exposed that run from the eyes to the visual cortex at the back of the brain.
Visual information is received via the retina of each eye. This information passes down the two optic nerves, which meet at a junction called the optic chiasma.
Here, half of the nerve fibres from each eye cross to the other side of the brain.
The fibres continue along the optic tract all the way up to the visual cortex.
Here, the brain integrates the signals into a composite colour image.

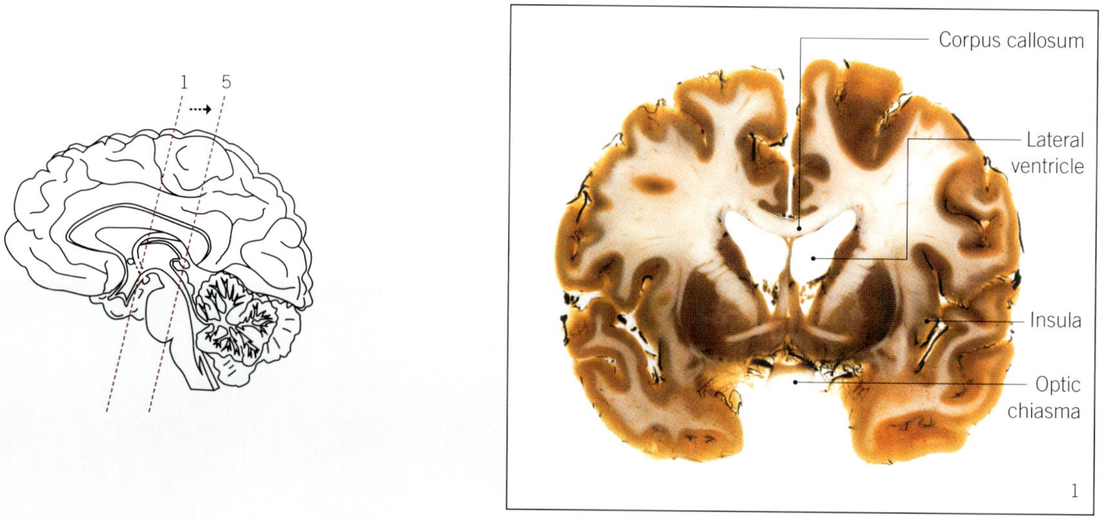


Fig. 2.6 | Series of frontal brain slices

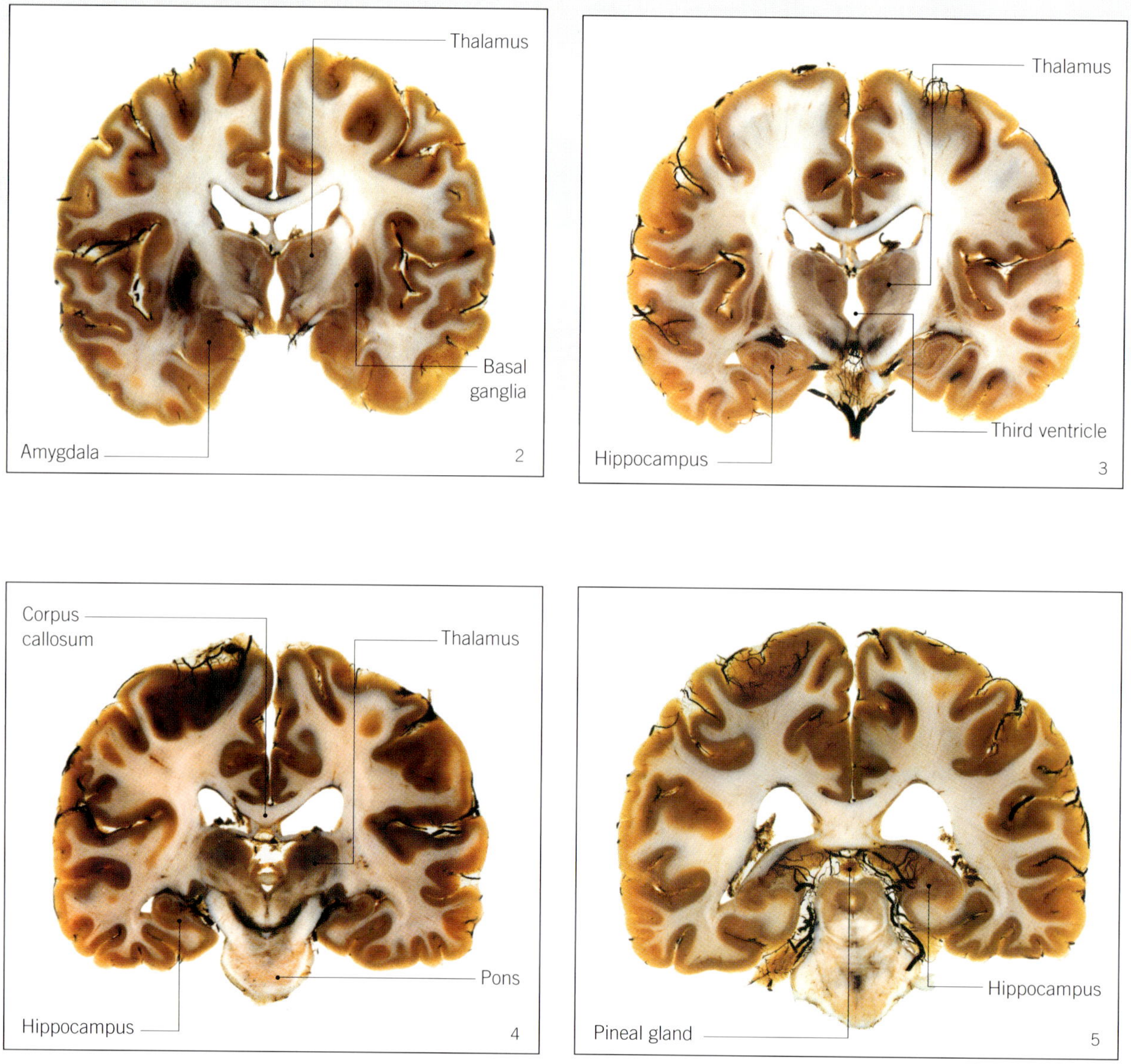

## Brain Ventricles

The brain has four interlinked cavities called ventricles.
Fluid circulates within these ventricles.
Among other functions,
the fluid serves as an internal shock absorber.

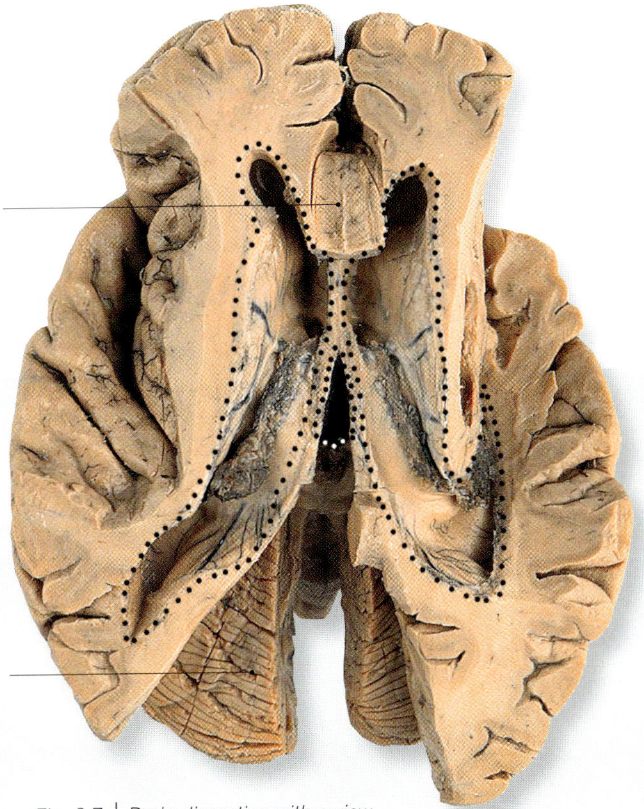


*Fig. 2.7* | *Brain dissection with a view of the ventricle system (marked area)*

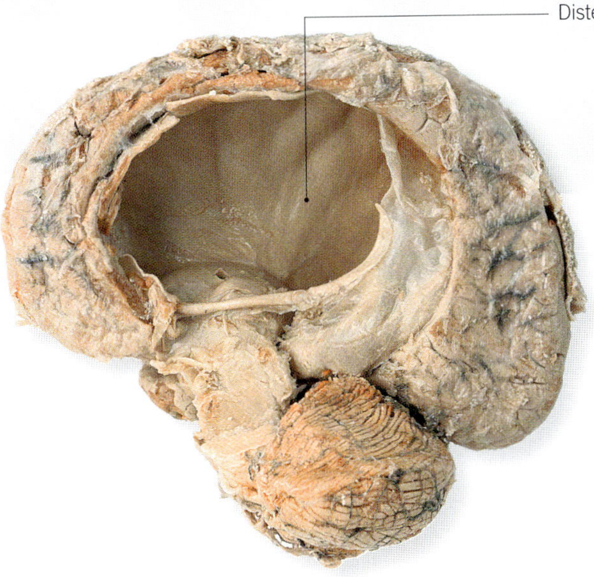


*Fig. 2.8* | *Right brain hemisphere with hydrocephalus*

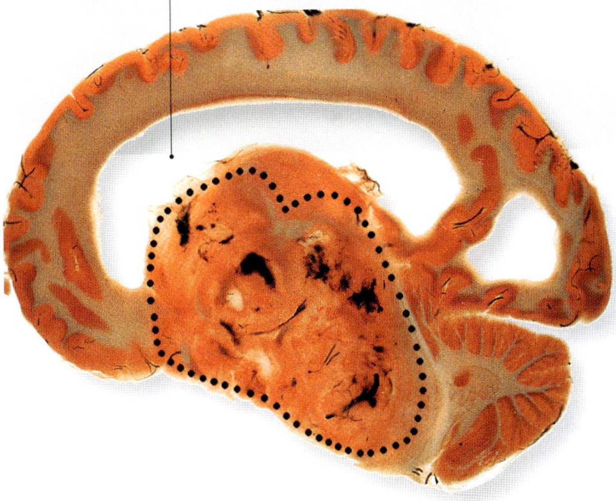

*Fig. 2.9* | *Brain slice with brain stem tumour (marked area) and hydrocephalus*

## Hydrocephalus

When the flow within the ventricles is blocked,
the amount of fluid will increase.
This causes the ventricles to expand,
thereby compressing and damaging brain tissue.
This condition is also known as “water on the brain”.
It can be caused by tumour growth,
inflammation, or congenital malformation.

The malignant tumour growth shown in Fig. 2.9
has taken over a large portion of the brain stem,
putting pressure on and blocking the ventricles.

# The Diseased Brain

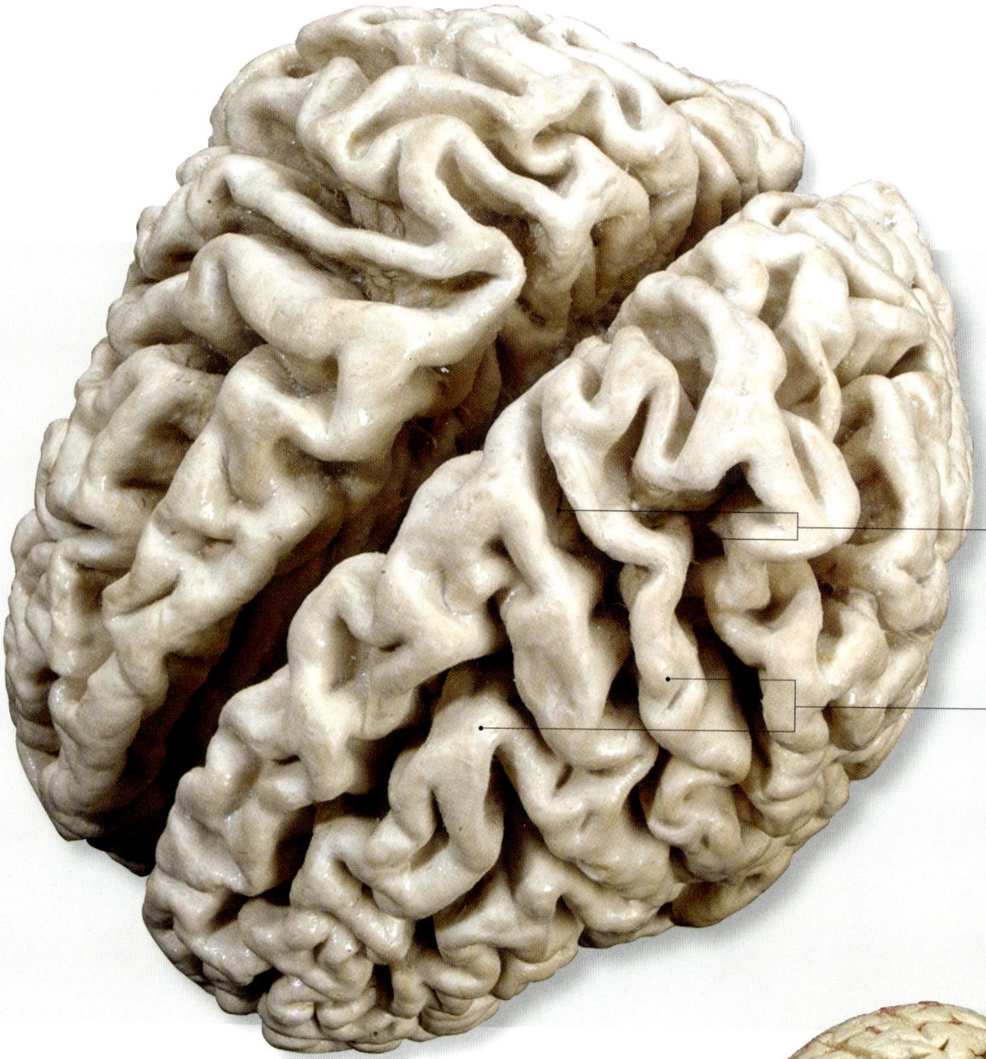


*Fig. 2.10* | *Brain with Alzheimer's disease*

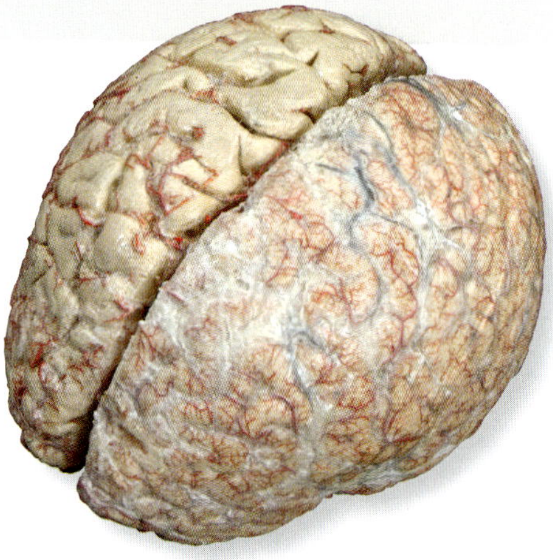

*Fig. 2.11* | *Normal brain. In the left hemisphere, the meninges (pia mater) are left intact.*

**Alzheimer's – The Long Goodbye**
The word "dementia" is used to describe
a collection of symptoms that include a decline in memory,
reasoning, and communication skills and a gradual loss of
the ability to carry out daily activities including personal care.

These symptoms are caused by
structural and chemical changes in the brain.

Alzheimer's disease is the most common form of dementia.
During the course of the disease,
plaques and tangles develop in the structure
of the brain, causing brain cells to die.
The physical effects of the disease can be seen here
as the significant widening of the grooves in the cortex.

Dementia can affect people younger than 65
but is most common in older people.
One in six people older than 80 live with a form of dementia.

**Blood Supply to the Brain**

The brain is only 2% of our total body weight but needs 20% of our blood supply. If the blood flow to the brain is interrupted for only 10 seconds, we lose consciousness. If it is interrupted for longer than 10 seconds, we can suffer severe brain tissue damage.

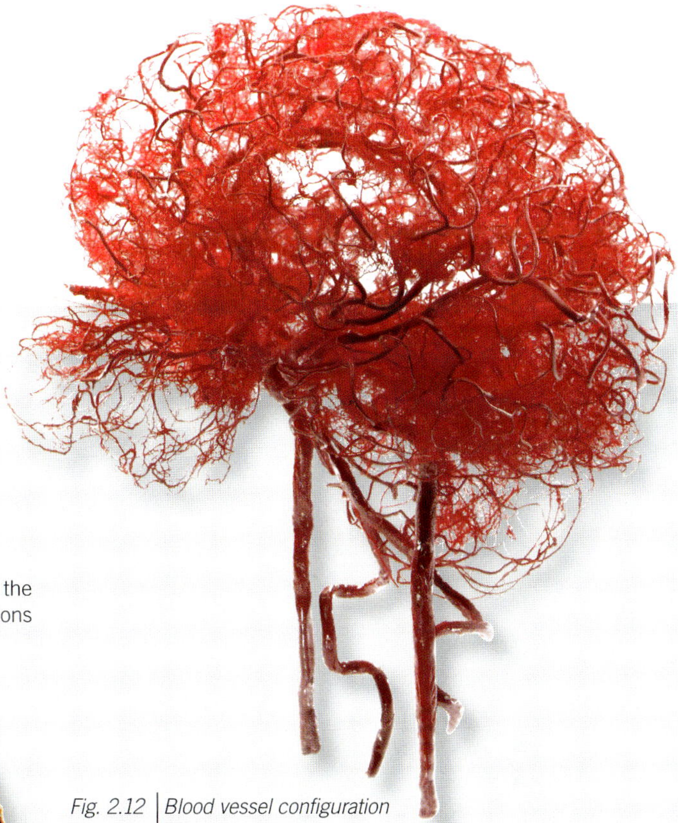

Fig. 2.12 | *Blood vessel configuration of the brain*

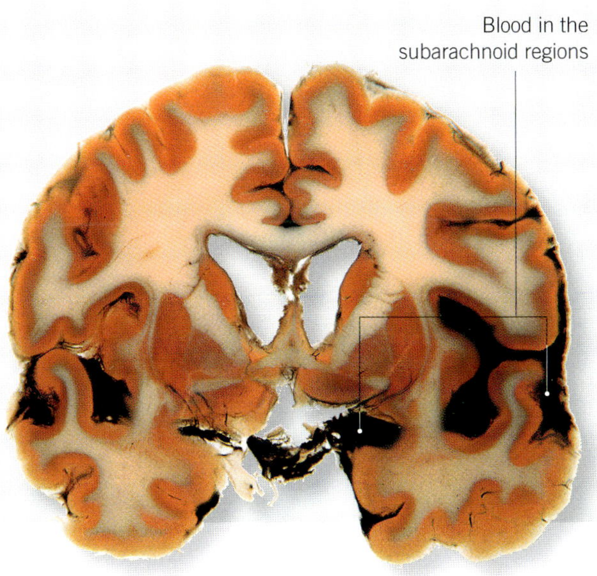


Fig. 2.13 | *Brain slice with a haemorrhage in the brain stem*

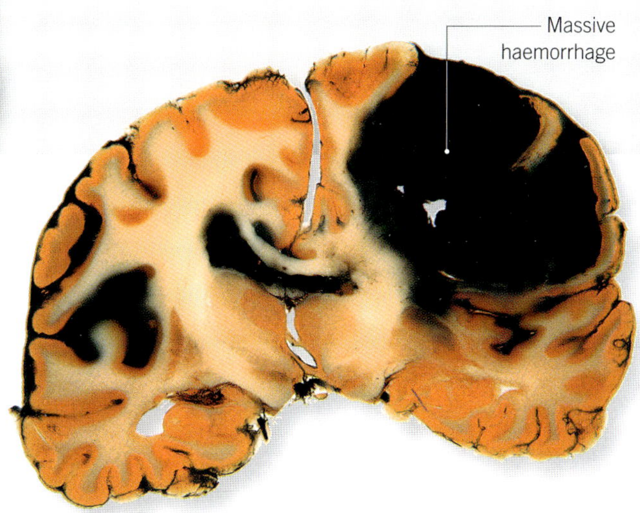


Fig. 2.14 | *Brain with a massive haemorrhage following a stroke*

**Stroke**

In a stroke, an artery to the brain is blocked or blood leaks from a ruptured blood vessel. Both can seriously damage brain tissue. The symptoms of a stroke develop rapidly and depend on the size and location of the affected area. They can include severe disabilities, such as numbness, paralysis, slurred speech, and sudden death.

Damages on the brain blood vessels are often due to high blood pressure. But long before it creates a health emergency, hypertension often takes a subtle toll on mental faculties. It can reduce attention, learning, memory, and decision-making skills.

# The Autonomic Nervous System

This plastinate shows all the major nerves.
The spinal cord down our backbone
is like a main cable joining body and brain.

Many nerves around the spine
belong to the autonomic nervous system (ANS).
The ANS automatically regulates bodily functions,
including circulation, respiration, and digestion.

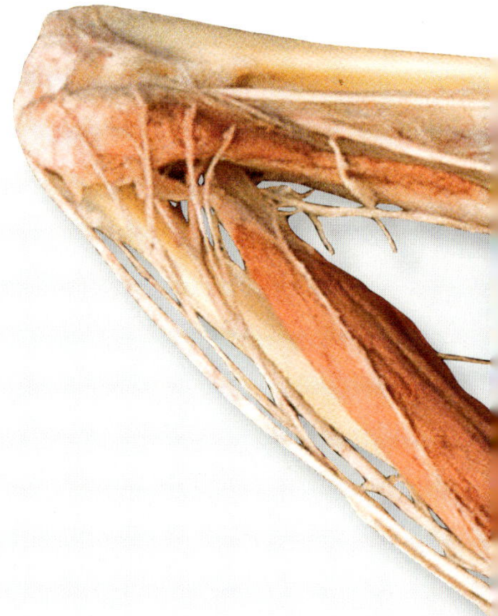

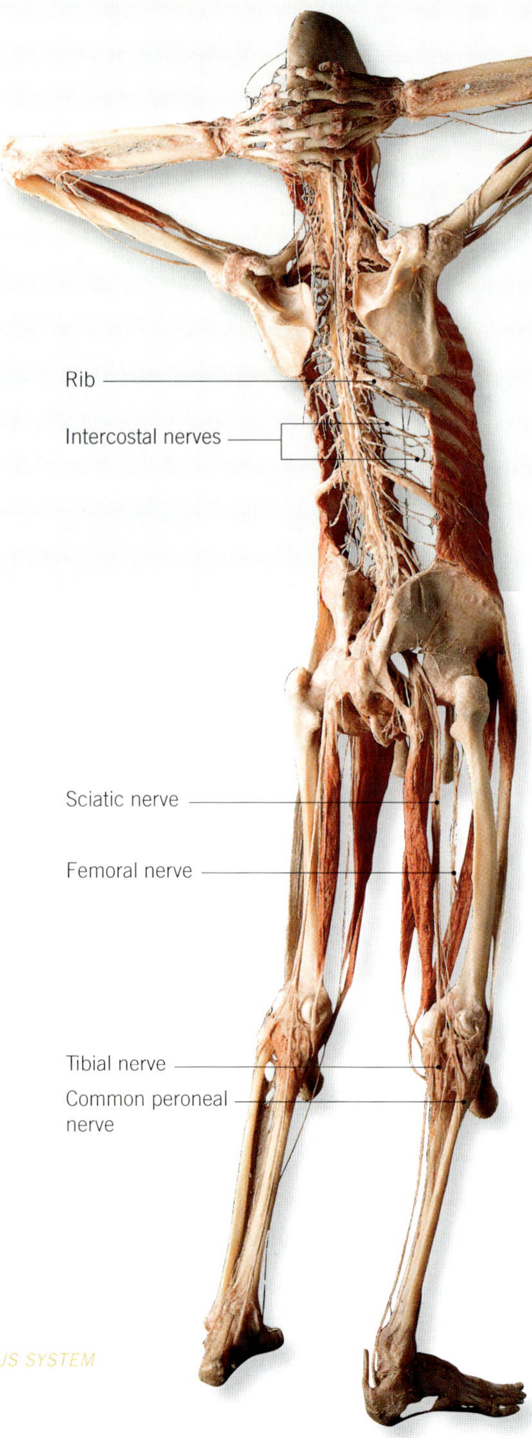


There are two types of autonomic nerves:
sympathetic and parasympathetic.
They have opposing effects
and are not under conscious control.

The sympathetic nervous system stimulates the body
for action and prepares it at times of stress.
For example, it increases the rate and strength
of the heartbeat, dilates the bronchial tubes,
and releases glucose from the liver.

The parasympathetic nervous system, also called vagus,
influences the organs to maintain energy
or to relax and restore energy.
The vagus nerve is for instance stimulated
by the sight, smell, and taste of food.
It increases stomach acid secretion
and triggers peristalsis, pushing the food
through the digestive tract.
In the cardiovascular system, the vagus nerve
decreases the rate and strength of the heartbeat.

*Fig. 2.15 | Man at Leisure*

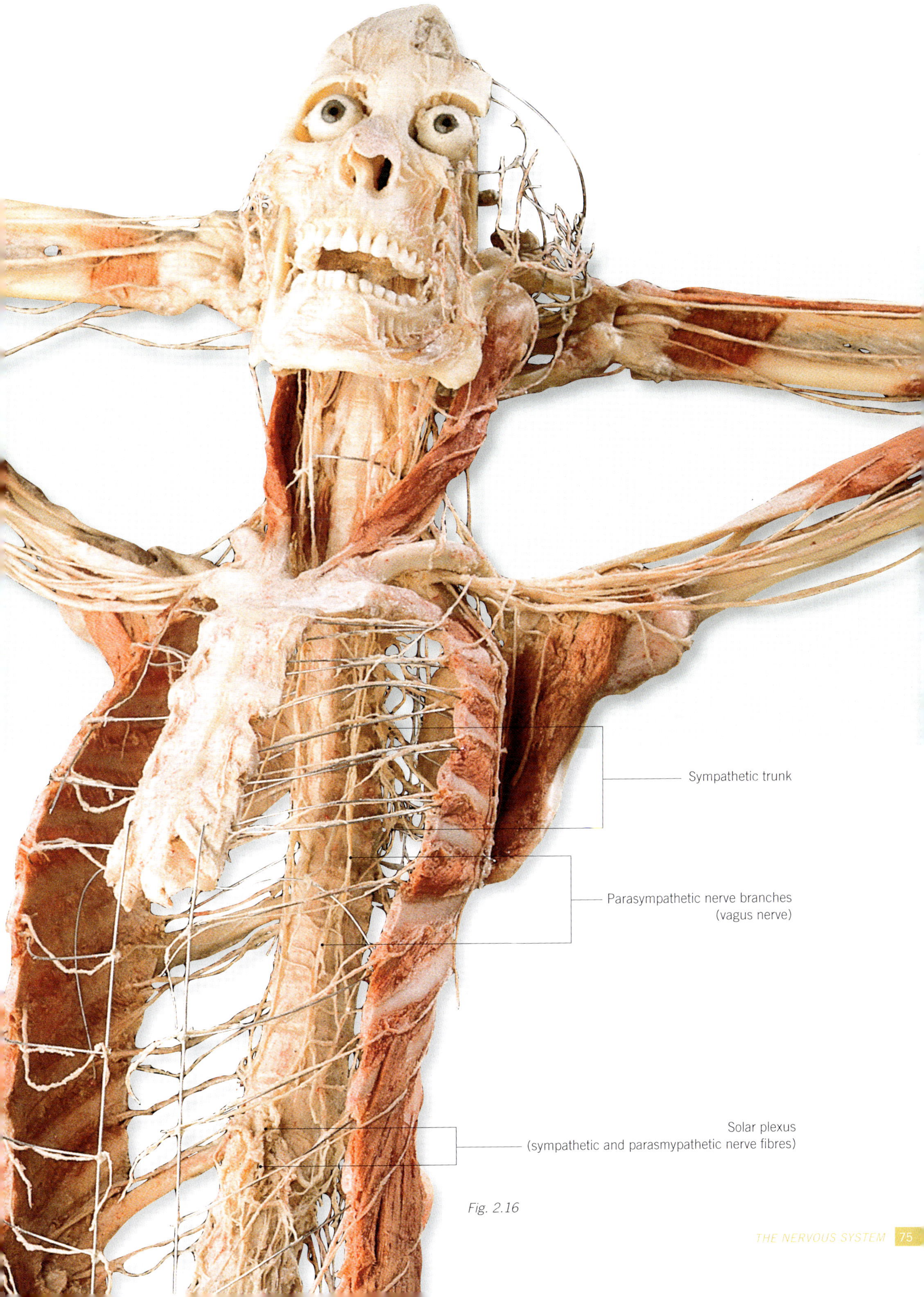
Sympathetic trunk
Parasympathetic nerve branches
(vagus nerve)
Solar plexus
(sympathetic and parasmypathetic nerve fibres)

*Fig. 2.16*

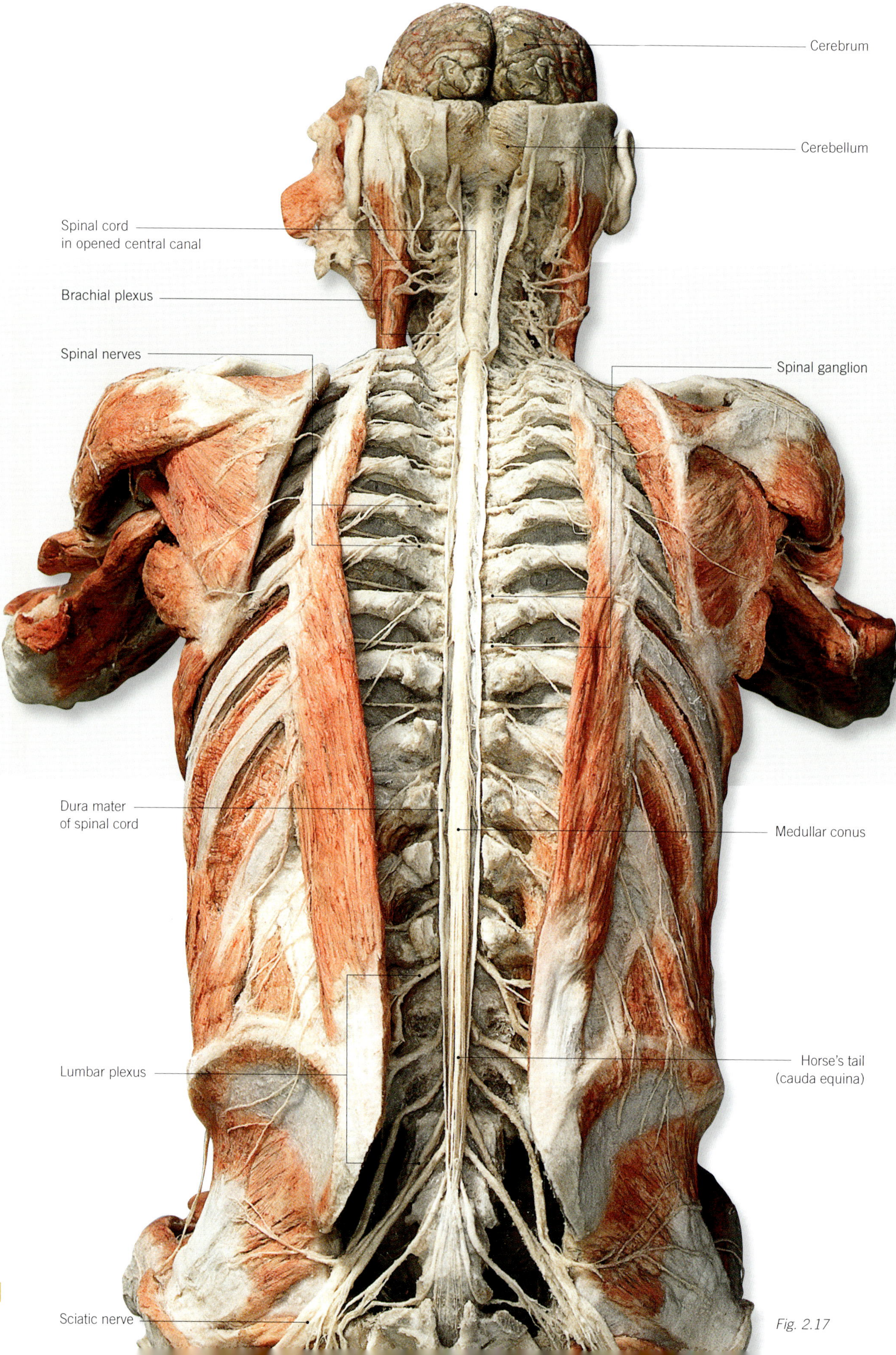
Cerebrum
Cerebellum
Spinal cord
in opened central canal
Brachial plexus
Spinal nerves
Spinal ganglion
Dura mater
of spinal cord
Medullar conus
Lumbar plexus
Horse's tail
(cauda equina)
Sciatic nerve

*Fig. 2.17*

## The Chess Player

This posed plastinate has been given the posture of a person deep in thought to illustrate how nerve fibres run throughout the entire human organism.
The pose emphasises the special character of this plastinate – its anatomical identity.

The brain is visible in the opened skull.
From there, the spinal cord extends down through the spinal column that is open towards the back.
From between the vertebrae, 31 pairs of spinal nerves connect the spinal cord to the rest of the body.

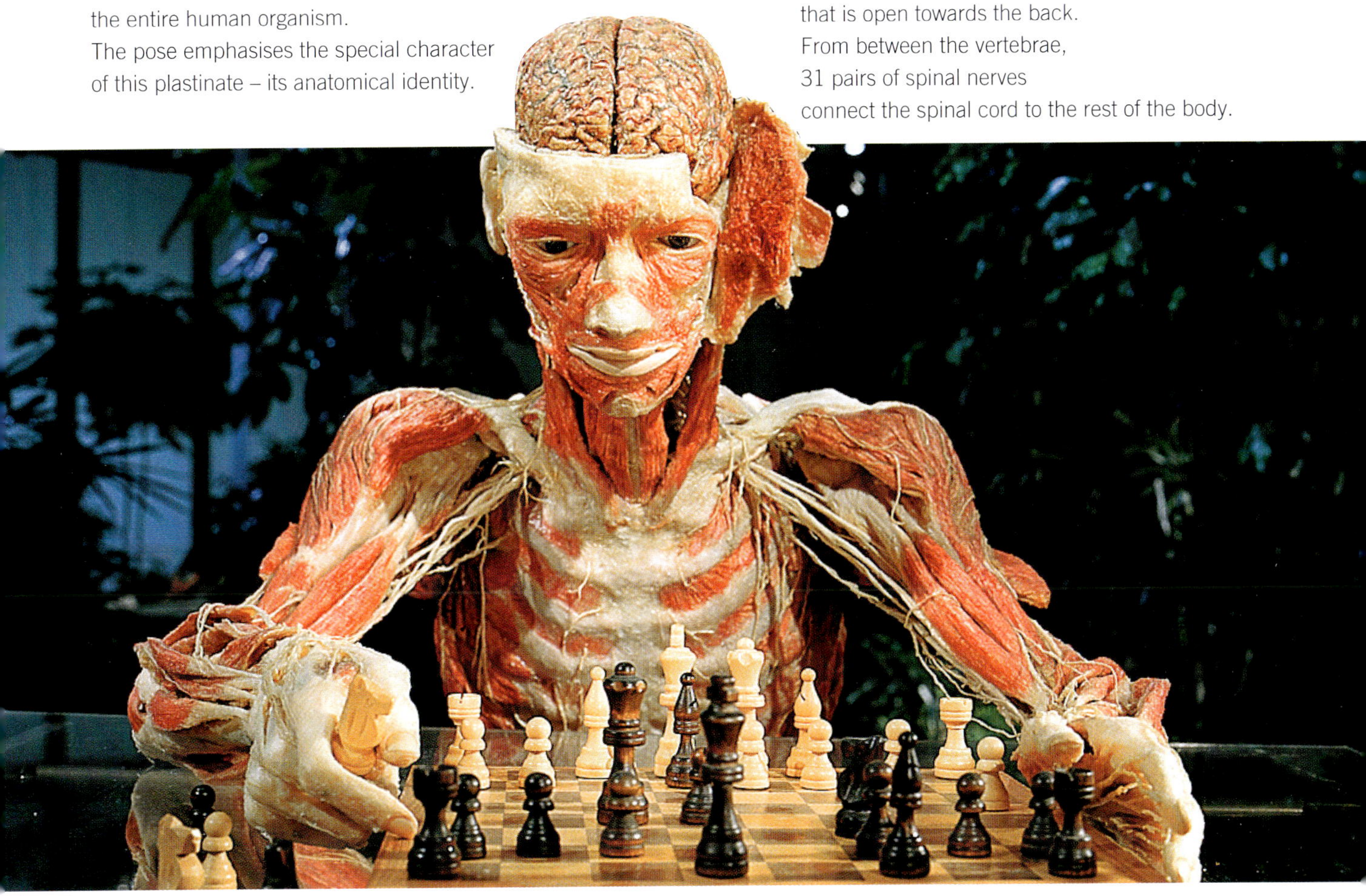

*Fig. 2.18 | The Chess Player*

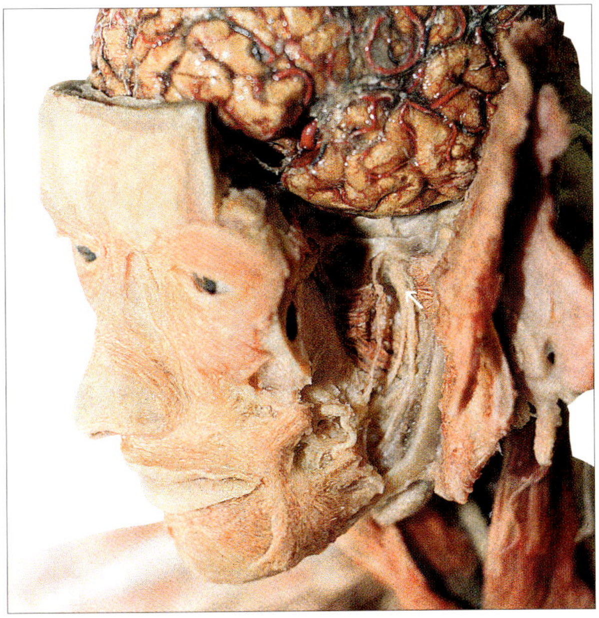

The bundle of nerves at the base of the spine is the cauda equina – the "horse's tail".
The two sciatic nerves run from the lower spine behind the hip joint down the leg.
They are the largest and longest nerves in the body.

*Fig. 2.19 | Dissection of the facial nerves (Trigeminal nerve; arrow)*

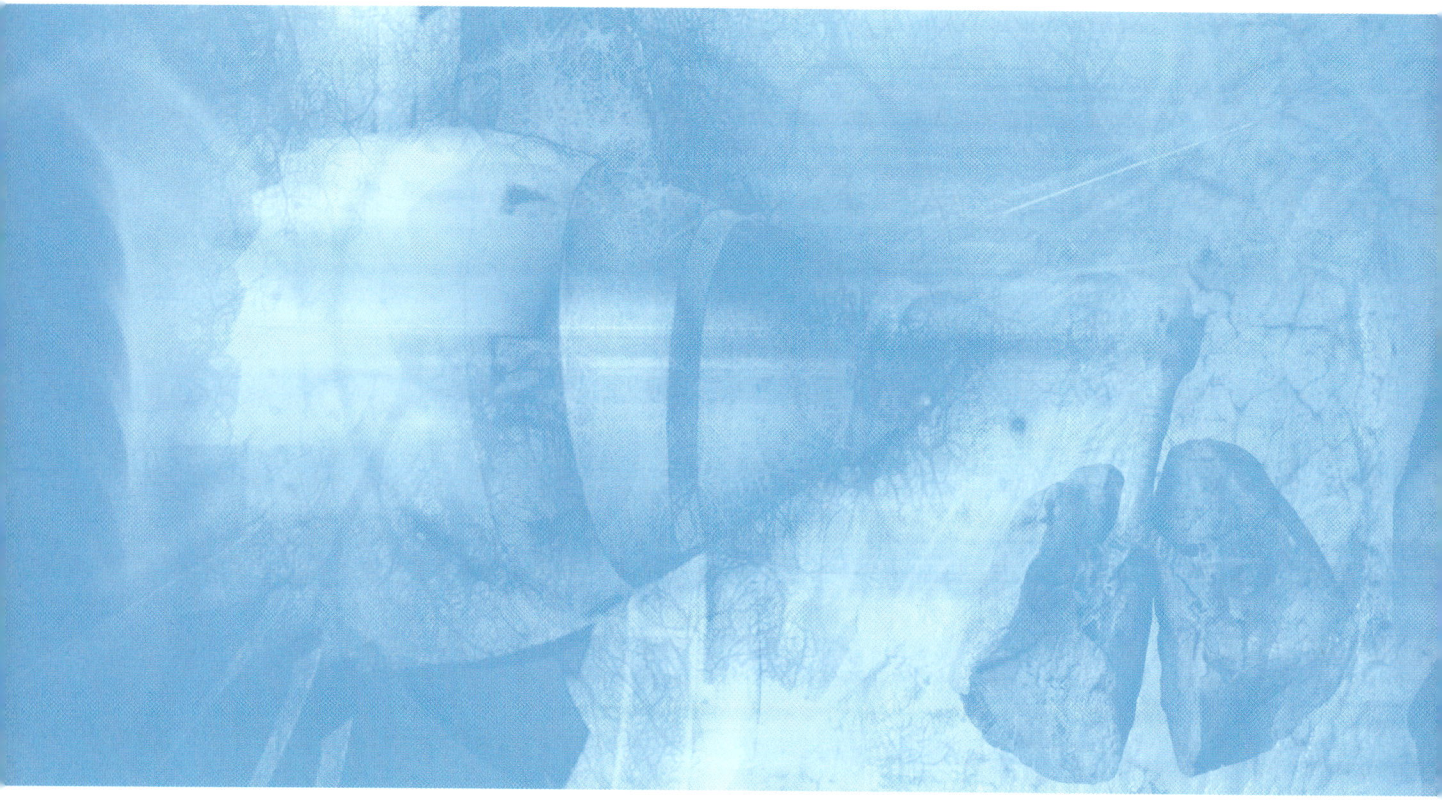

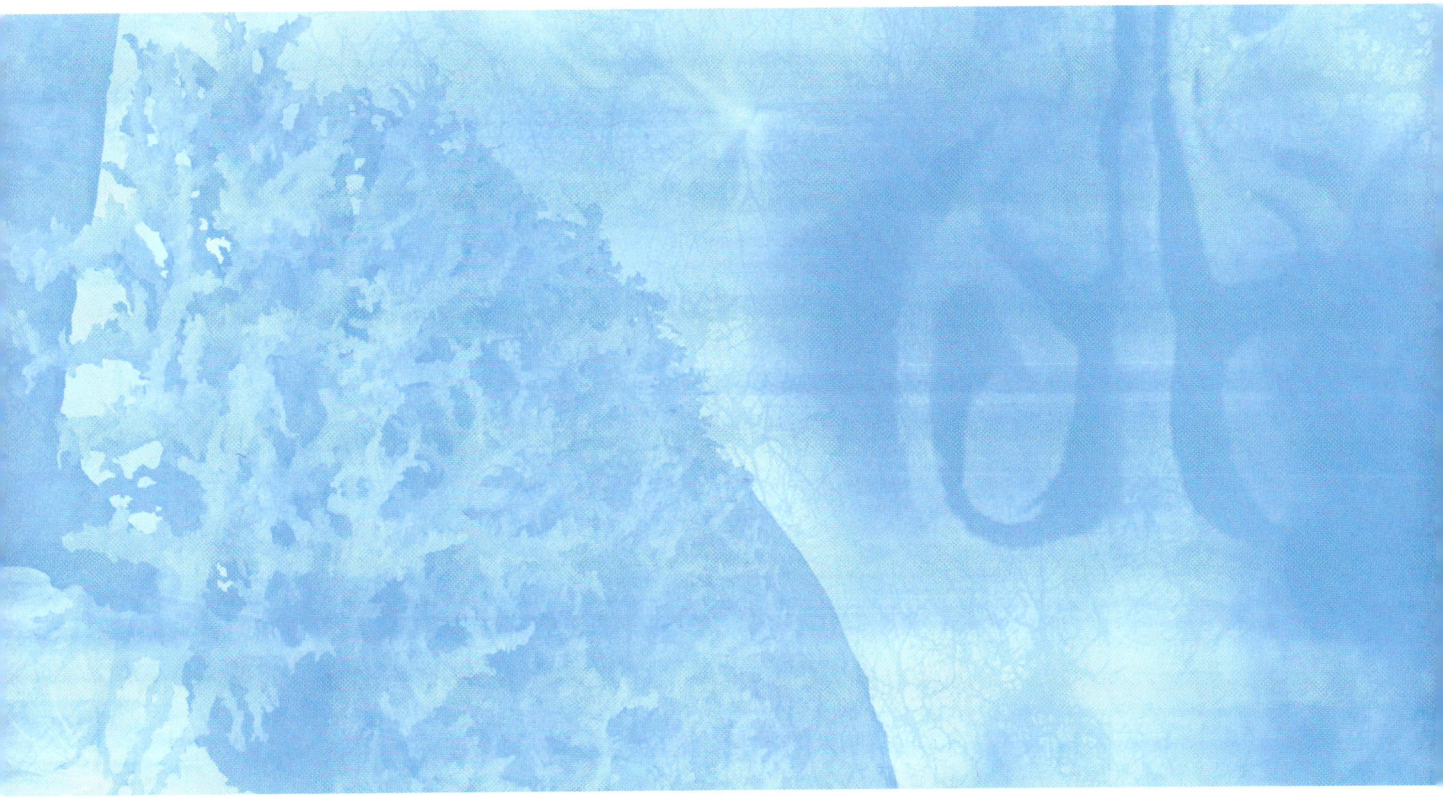

# 3. THE **RESPIRATORY** SYSTEM

Human life requires a continuous supply of oxygen,
which we extract from the air.
Without this element, most of the body's cells
would not be able to survive more than a few minutes.
Oxygen is indispensable for cell metabolism,
a process that transforms nutrients into energy
to keep the body functioning.

# Getting Air into the Lungs

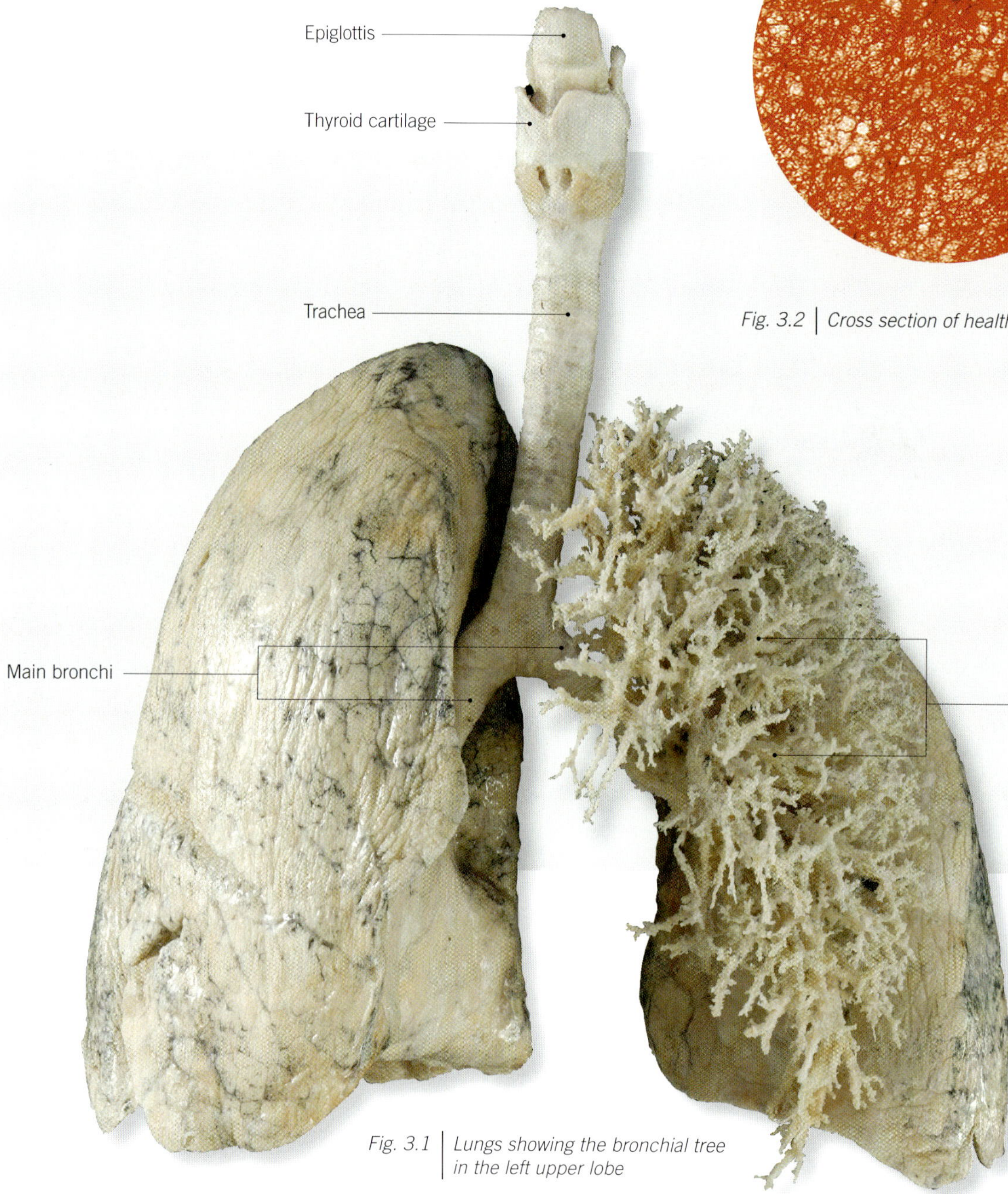


*Fig. 3.1* | *Lungs showing the bronchial tree in the left upper lobe*

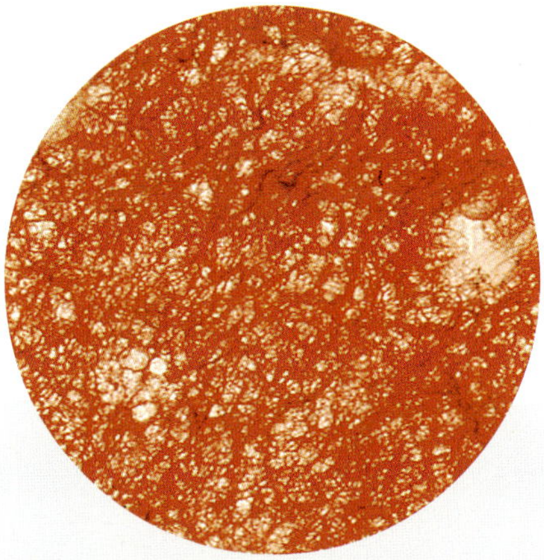

*Fig. 3.2* | *Cross section of healthy lung tissue*

The lungs absorb oxygen from the air
and pass it on to the blood.
Every minute, about 5–6 litres (11–13 pints)
of air pass into the lungs.
To reach the lungs,
the air first passes the nose and mouth,
and then the larynx and trachea.
The trachea divides into two major bronchi,
one leading to each lung.

Rather like the branches of a tree,
the bronchi subdivide into ever smaller parts,
as shown in the upper lobe of the left lung here.

The trachea and bronchi
contain supporting cartilage
so they stay rigid and open at all times,
no matter how much the air pressure fluctuates.

The bronchial passages in the lungs
lead into clusters of tiny air sacs (alveoli)
that give the lungs a sponge-like appearance.
This can best be seen
in an enlarged cross section of lung tissue.
Each alveolus is surrounded
by a network of capillaries,
where oxygen and carbon dioxide are exchanged.
Each lung contains 300 to 450 million alveoli.
Spread out flat, they would cover
between 80 and 120 sq. metres
(860 and 1,300 sq. feet).

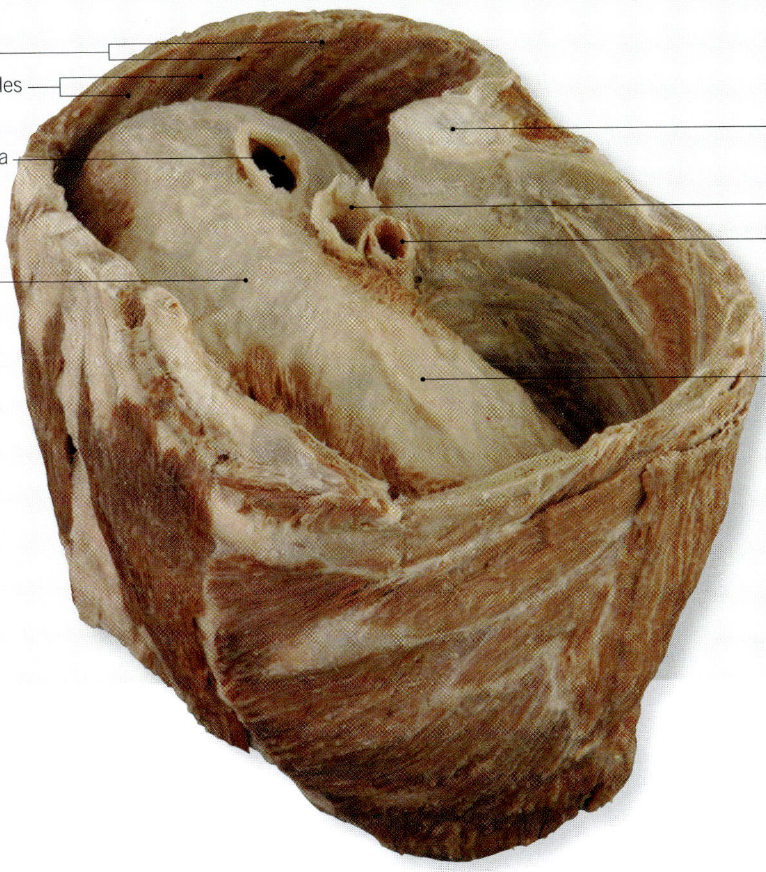


*Fig. 3.3 | Diaphragm*

When we breathe in,
muscles work to expand the chest.
The primary respiratory muscle is the diaphragm.
This is a thin dome-shaped muscular partition
that separates the chest from the abdomen.
When its muscle fibres contract,
the diaphragm drops
and the thoracic cavity enlarges.
The intercostal muscles between the ribs
additionally enlarge the thoracic cavity
by pulling the chest up and out.
As the lungs expand, the air flows in.

To exhale, the diaphragm and intercostal muscles
simply relax and return to their resting position.

Although we can influence our breathing,
it is usually controlled subconsciously
by the respiratory centre in the brain.
If the spinal cord is severely injured,
breaking the nervous system link
between the brain and the muscles,
the person dies unless artificially ventilated.

# Taking a Breath

As air flows from the nose into the trachea, it first passes over the nasal conchae. Their fine hairs filter dust and bacteria, while the mucous membrane heats and moistens the inhaled air. Our smell receptors are located at the top of the nasal cavity.

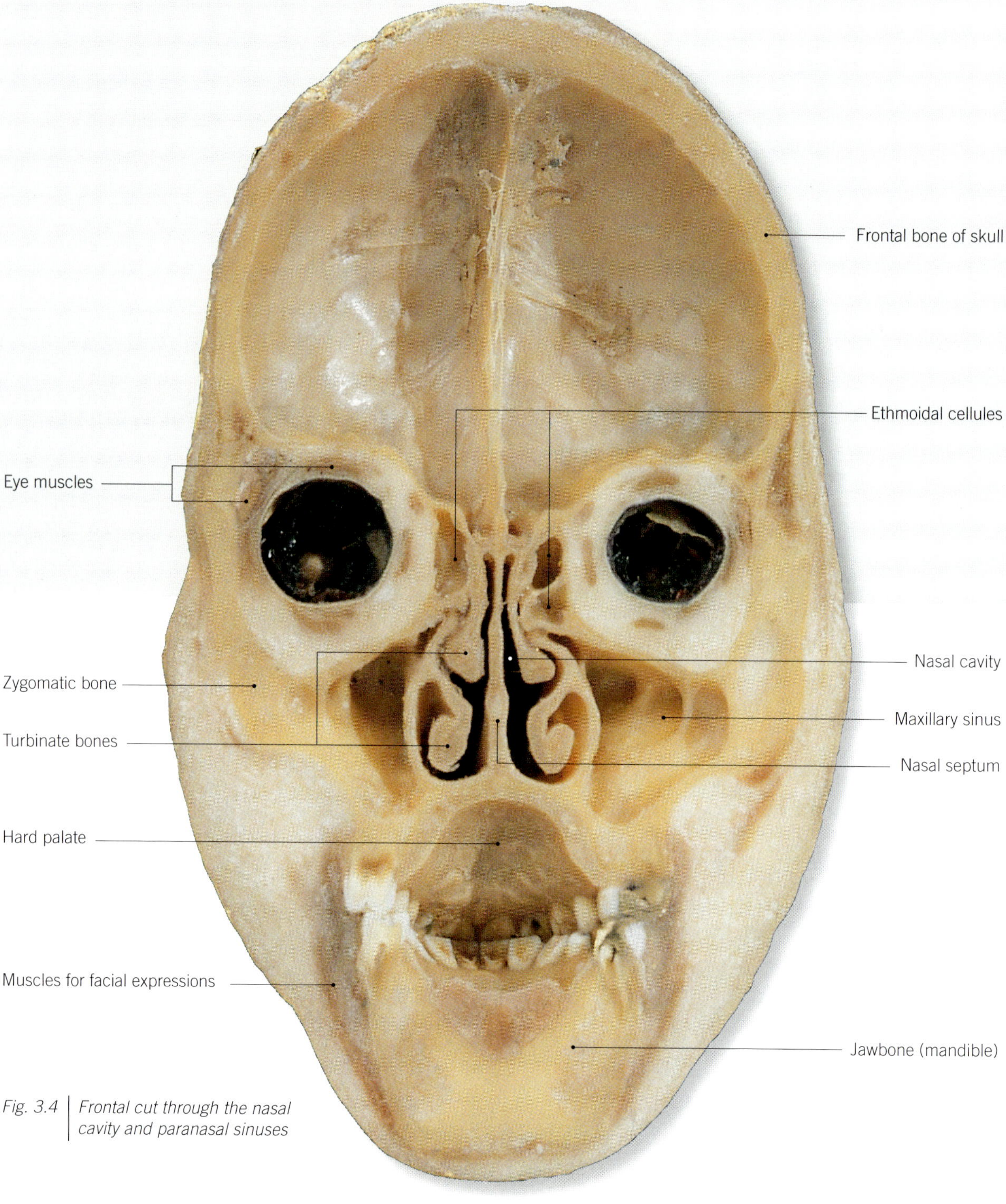


*Fig. 3.4* | *Frontal cut through the nasal cavity and paranasal sinuses*

# Producing Sounds

Breathing exchanges oxygen and carbon dioxide and also allows us to produce sounds. The key organ for sound is the larynx, located between the oral cavity and the trachea.

The upper part of the larynx is the epiglottis. When we swallow, this cartilage flap covers the trachea entrance, directing food and liquid into the oesophagus. The vocal cords are in the middle of the larynx, adjusted by a series of delicate muscles, allowing us to modulate our voice.

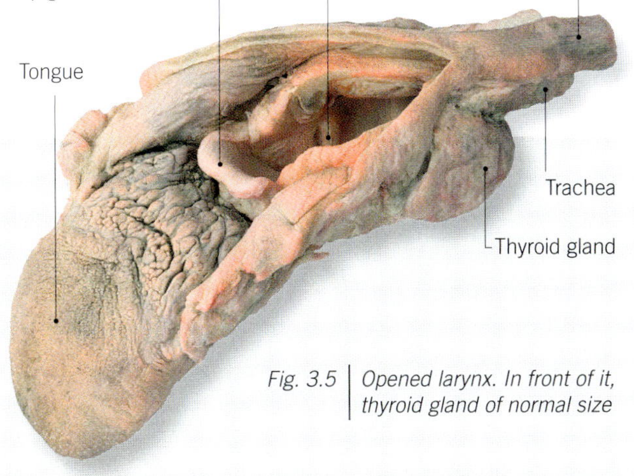


*Fig. 3.5* | *Opened larynx. In front of it, thyroid gland of normal size*

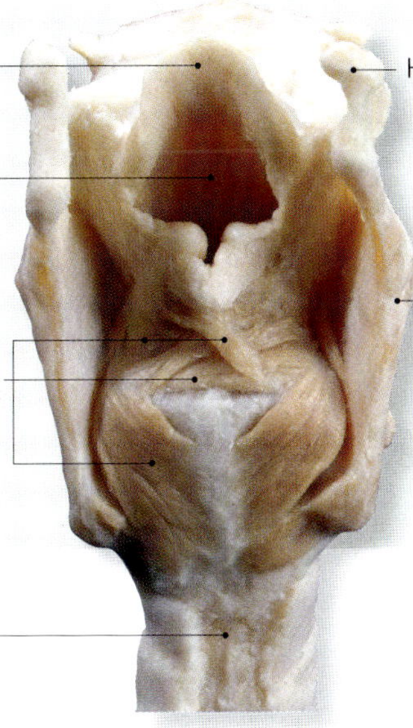


*Fig. 3.6* | *Larynx, rear view*

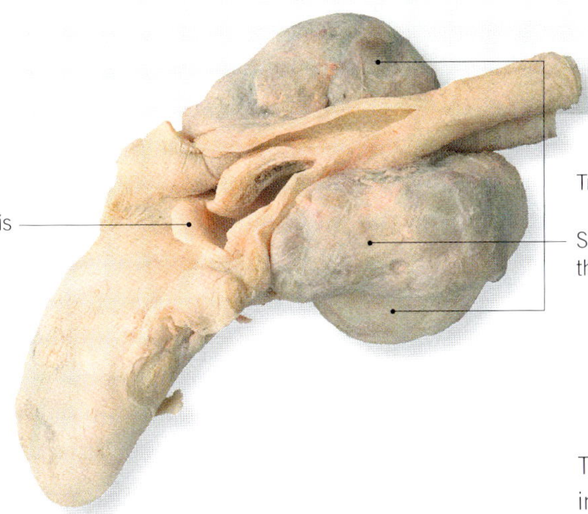


*Fig. 3.7* | *Enlarged thyroid gland (goiter)*

There is a gland located directly in front of the trachea below the larynx, the thyroid. The thyroid produces hormones that regulate metabolic functions and the body's level of activity. It can significantly enlarge and cause the neck to swell, a condition known as goiter. If the swelling is very severe, it can constrict the trachea and impair breathing. Goiters can have different causes, including iodine deficiency.

# The Diseased Lung

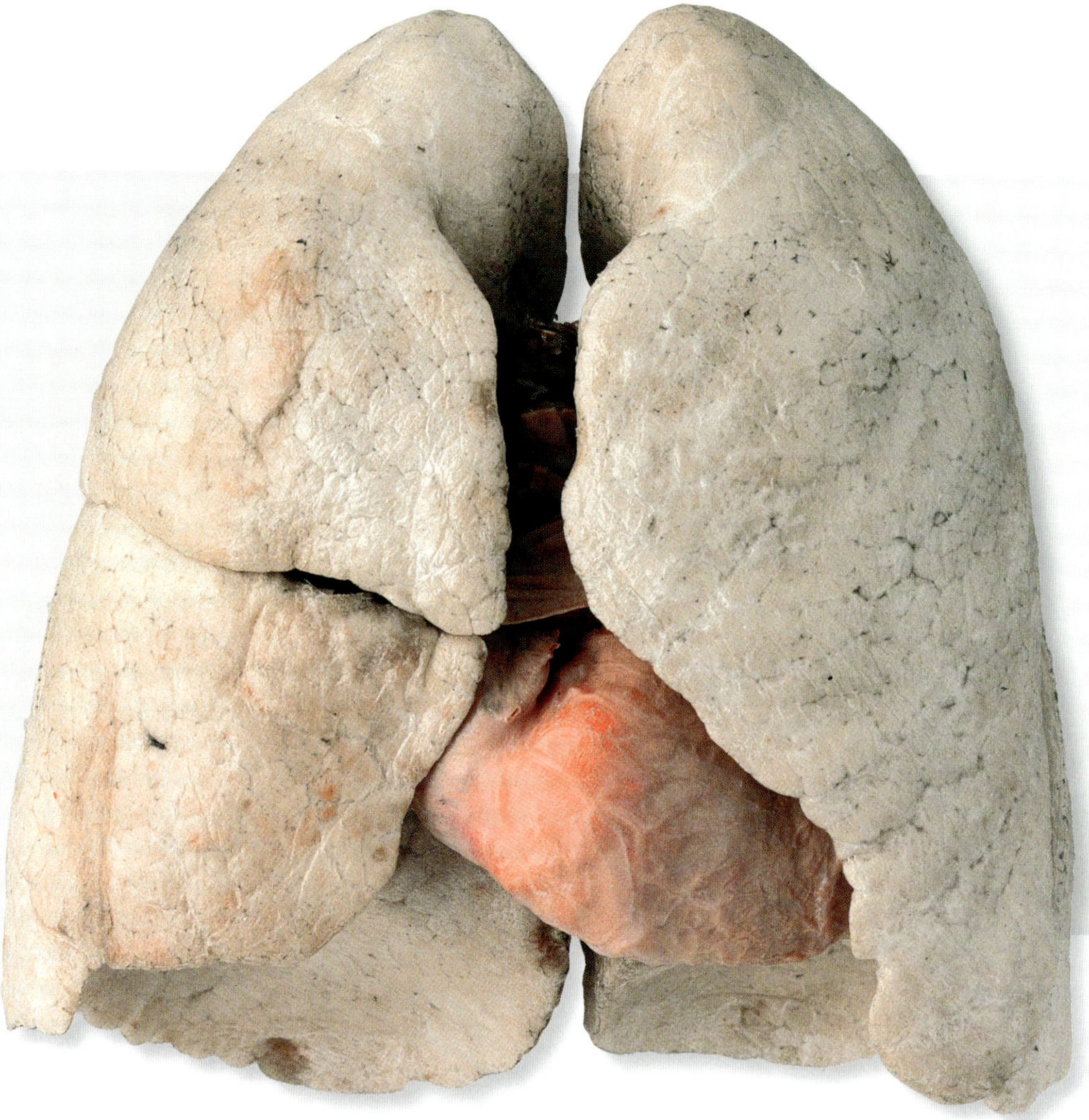

*Fig. 3.8* | *Non-smoker's lungs.*
*The heart is in between the two lungs*

The heart is surrounded by the lungs.
Since the heart is located left of centre,
the left lung is slightly smaller than the right.
The lungs have horizontal and diagonal fissures
dividing them into individual lobes:
three on the right and two on the left.

When we breathe in,
we also inhale fine particles of dust,
that form deposits in the lung tissue.
These deposits usually disappear in time.
As we grow older, though,
the lung often exhibits small surface marks
similar to those on this lung.

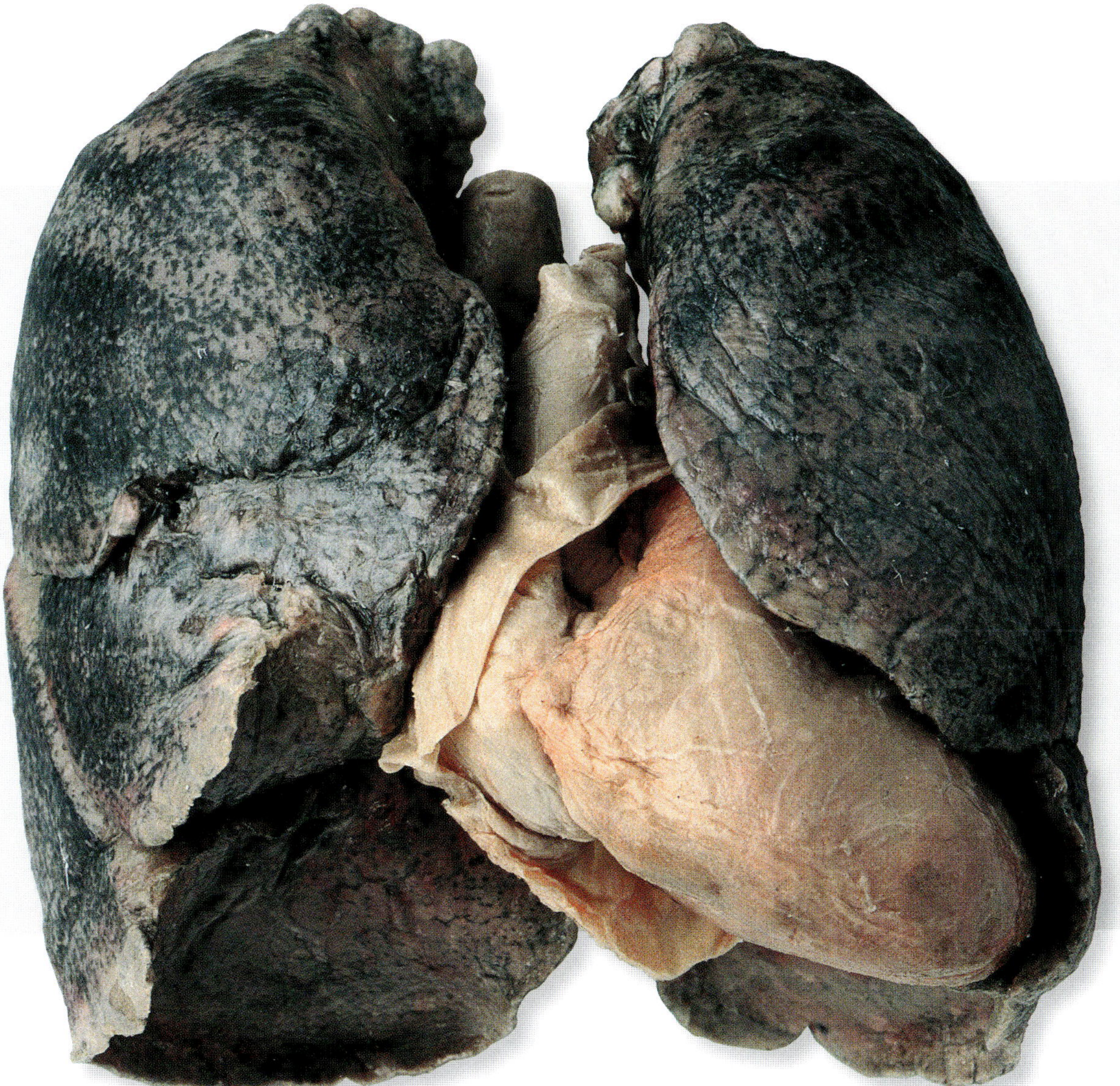

*Fig. 3.9 | Smoker's lungs*

Tar and soot particles from cigarette smoke
form deposits in the pulmonary tissue.
The deposits turn the lung black.
Just 20 cigarettes a day
produce an annual 150 millilitres (5 fl. ounces) of tar.
That is about the volume of a full coffee cup.

When smoking a cigarette, it only takes about 8 seconds
for the nicotine to reach the brain.
Breathing speeds up, the arteries narrow,
blood pressure and heart rate rapidly increase,
and the central nervous system is stimulated.

Nicotine raises the levels
of a neurotransmitter called dopamine
in brain areas linked to pleasure and reward.
This effect of nicotine may explain
why many people find it so hard to stop smoking.

After quitting smoking, the tar will gradually decompose
and the lungs will recover –
even after many years of smoking.
Also smoking related health risks can greatly be reduced.

### Lung Cancer

Smoking negatively affects the body in different ways and can shorten a person's life by an average of five years. One of the dangers of long-term smoking is the development of lung cancer.

Lung cancer is 20 times more common in smokers than non-smokers and is the most common cause of death in men. It is the most lethal malignant tumour worldwide, causing up to 3 million deaths annually.

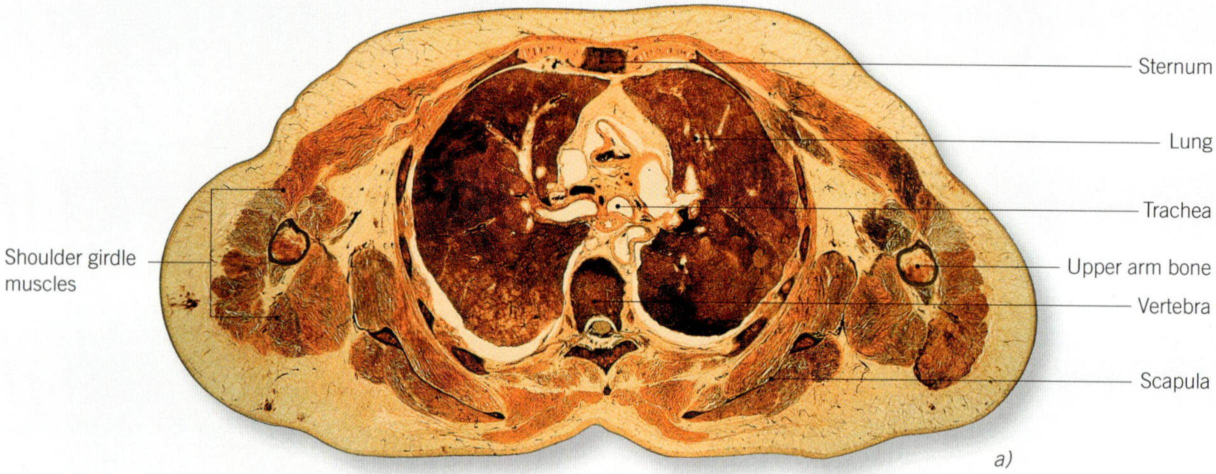


*Fig. 3.10 Cross sections of the thoracic cavity with a) a non-smoker's lungs and b) a smoker's lungs*

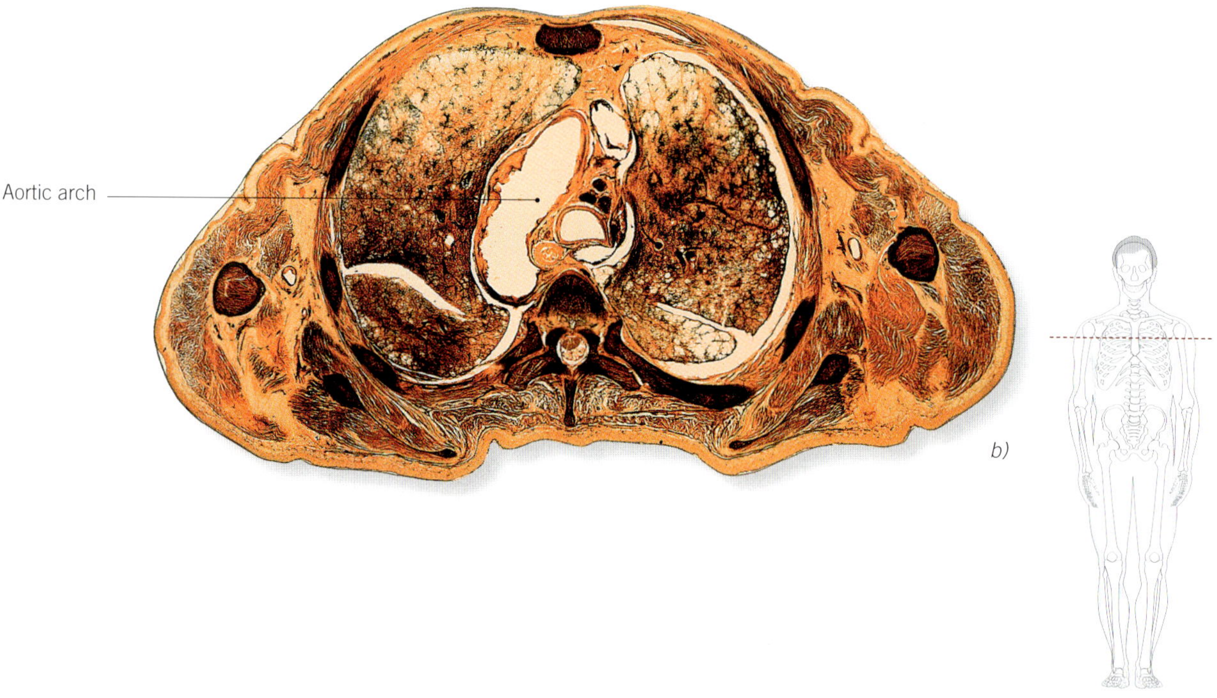

Most lung cancers originate from the bronchial walls. Thus, they are also called bronchial carcinoma. The bronchi get in direct contact with our immediate environment and inhaled carcinogens such as tobacco smoke. This can directly affect the bronchial walls and contribute to local tumour growth.

In the lungs shown in Fig. 3.12 a solid tumour originating from the bronchial wall is considerably narrowing the air passage to the right lung.

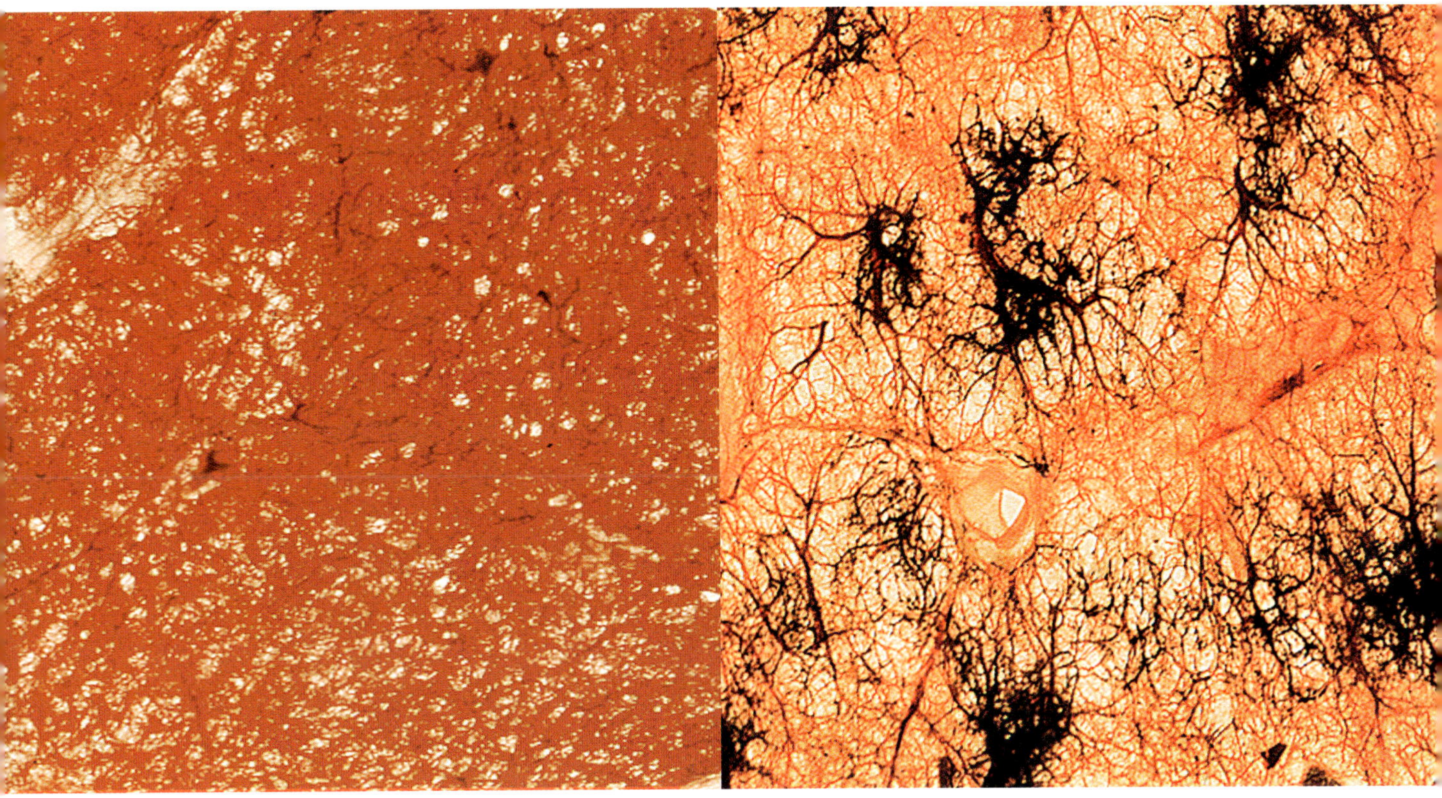

*Fig. 3.11 | Enlargements of sections of lung tissue taken from a non-smoker (left) and a smoker (right)*

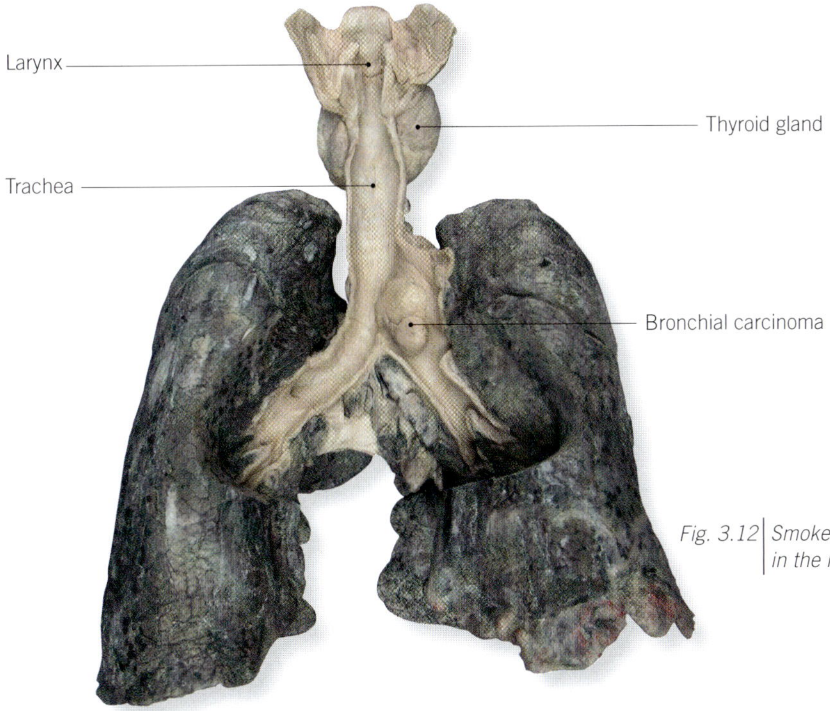


*Fig. 3.12 | Smoker's lung with bronchial carcinoma in the right main bronchi*

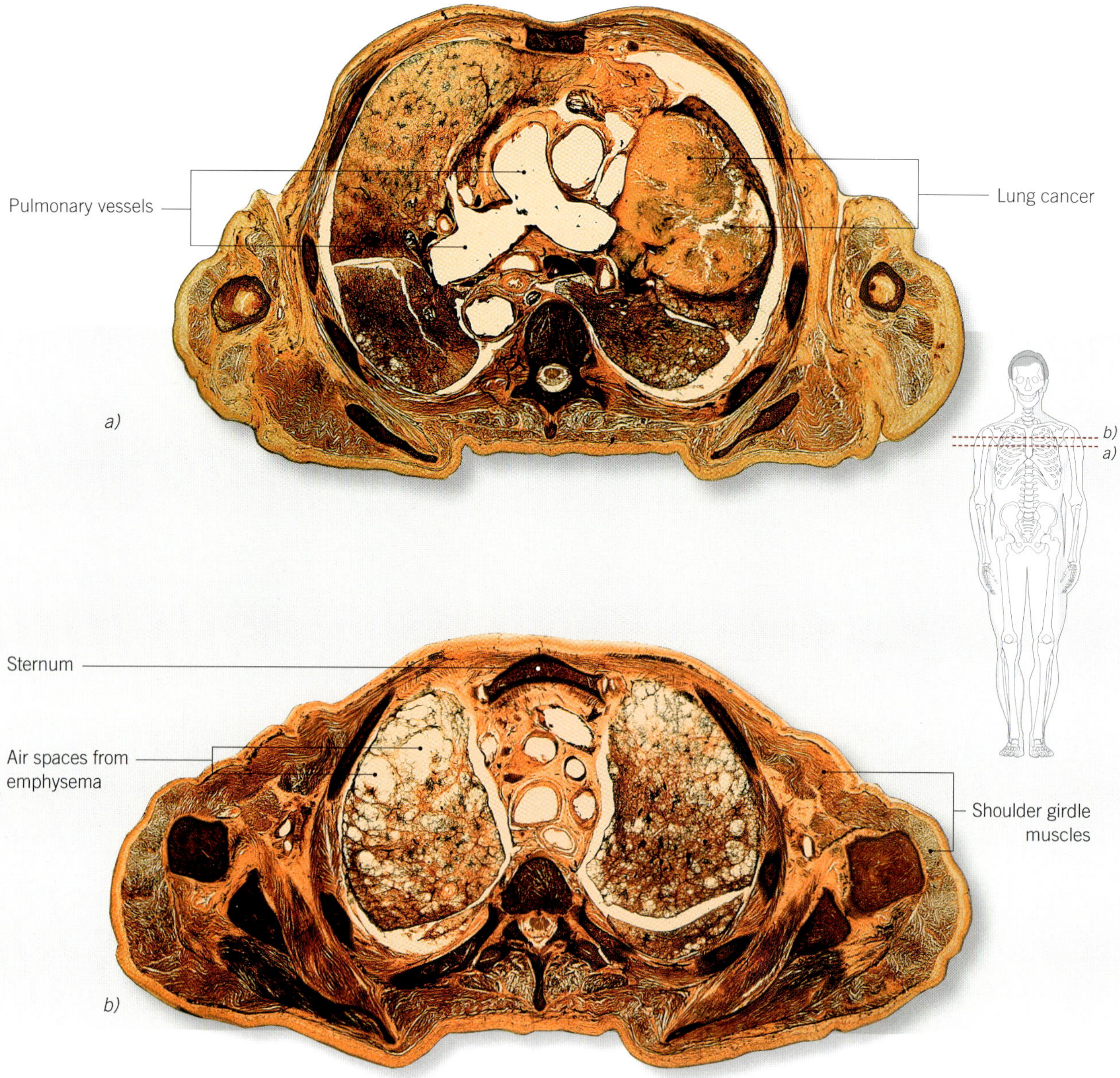


*Fig. 3.13* | *Cross sections of the thoracic cavity with a) a smoker's lungs with lung cancer and b) a smoker's lungs and emphysema*

**Lung Emphysema**

Another danger of long-term smoking
is the development of emphysema.
Emphysema is a relatively common disease.
It doesn't develop suddenly
but comes on very gradually.
Air sacs in the lungs are irreversibly destroyed,
leaving behind cavities in the lung tissue.
These cavities reduce the lung surface available
for the exchange of oxygen and carbon dioxide,
causing shortness of breath.
Many older people naturally experience
increasing lung emphysema.
In many cases today, however,
emphysema is the result of years of smoking.
Lung emphysema also puts a strain
on the right side of the heart:
The more lung tissue is destroyed
the smaller the capillary bed of the lungs gets.
This eventually raises the vascular resistance
and pulmonary artery pressure,
'overloading' the right ventricle.
If left untreated, the person may suffer
right-sided heart failure.

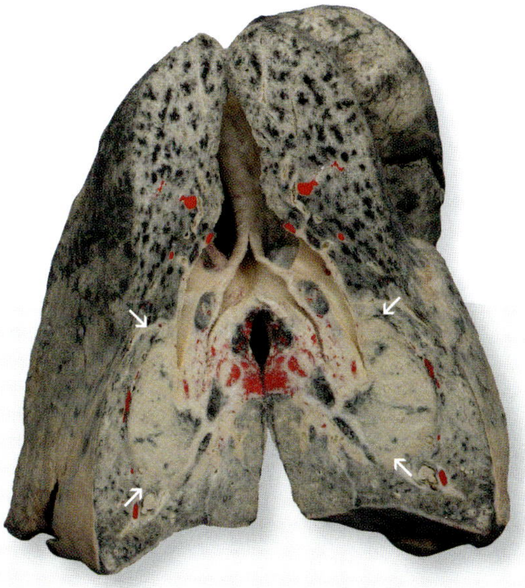

*Fig. 3.14* | *Smoker's lungs with lung cancer.*
*The solid, whitish looking tumour has invaded almost the complete lower lobe.*

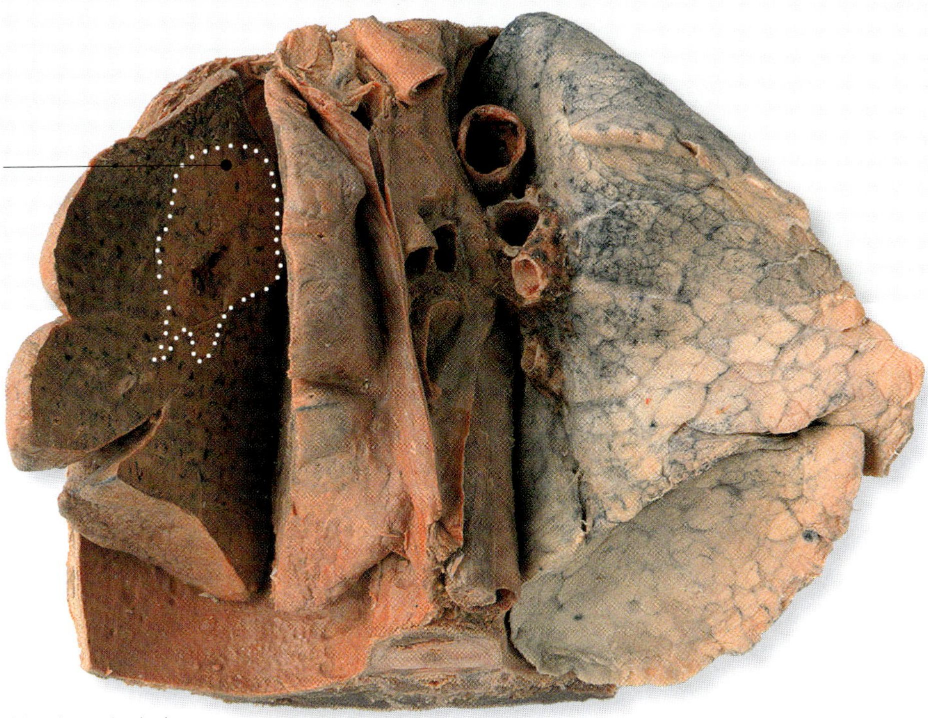


*Fig. 3.15* | *Lungs with tubercular lesion*

**Tuberculosis**

In principle, tuberculosis bacilli could attack any organ. Primarily, though, they infect the lungs. Tuberculosis is characterised by an inflammatory lesion with a cavern.

This is thickened tissue collapsed at centre. Tuberculosis may also affect other organs, such as the brain. When it takes the form of meningitis, it is a life-threatening condition.

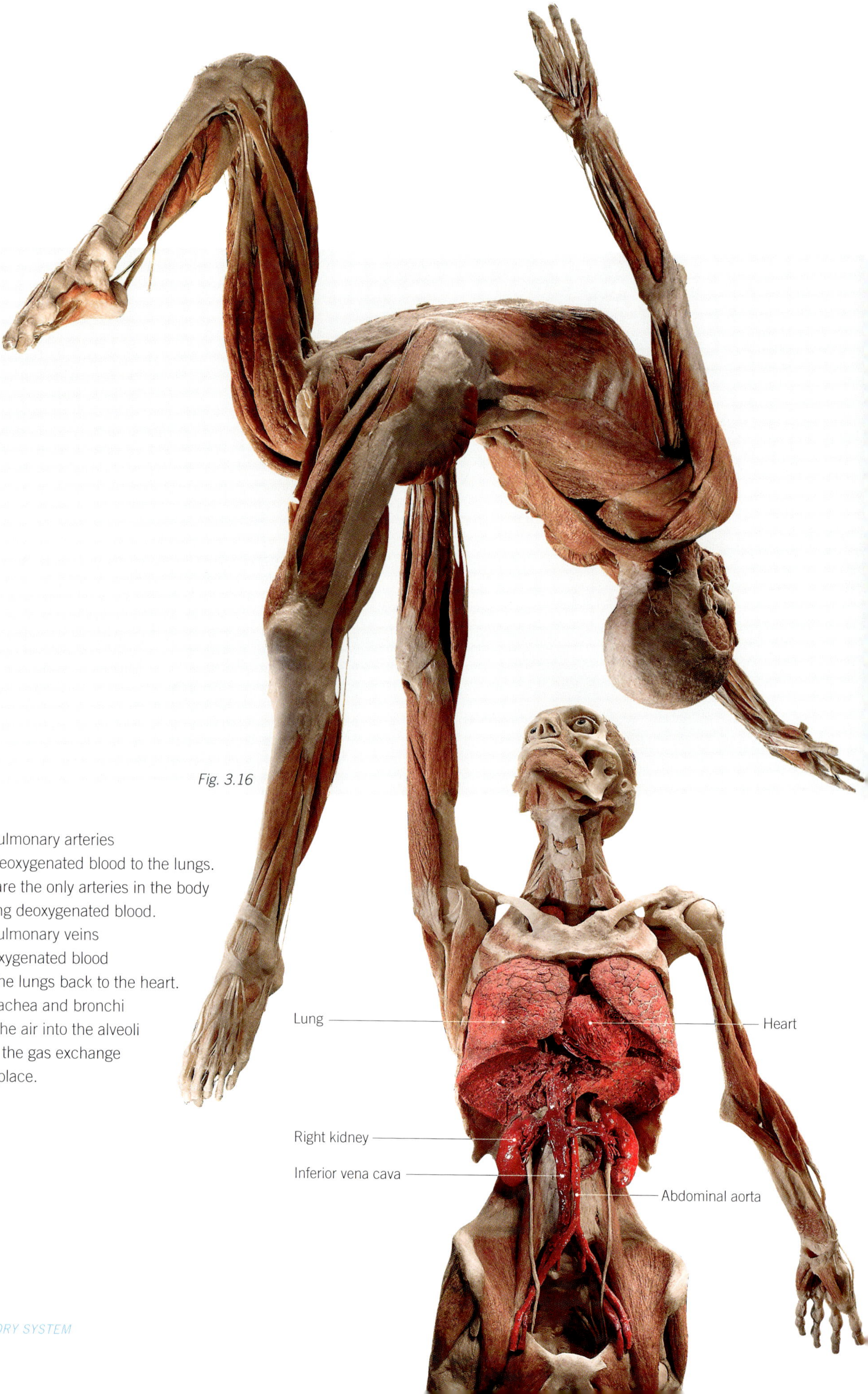


*Fig. 3.16*

The pulmonary arteries take deoxygenated blood to the lungs. They are the only arteries in the body carrying deoxygenated blood. The pulmonary veins take oxygenated blood from the lungs back to the heart. The trachea and bronchi carry the air into the alveoli where the gas exchange takes place.

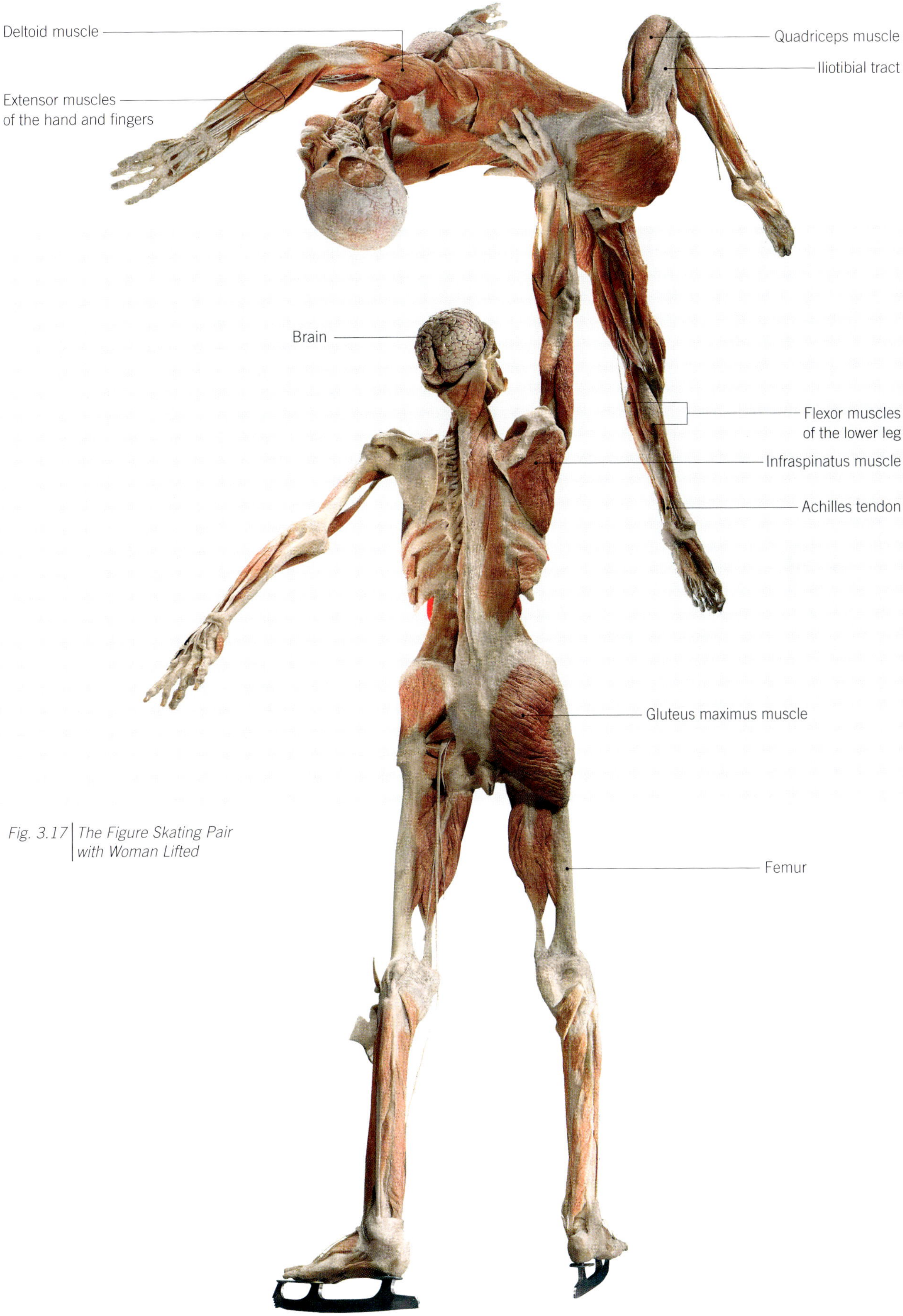


*Fig. 3.17* | *The Figure Skating Pair with Woman Lifted*

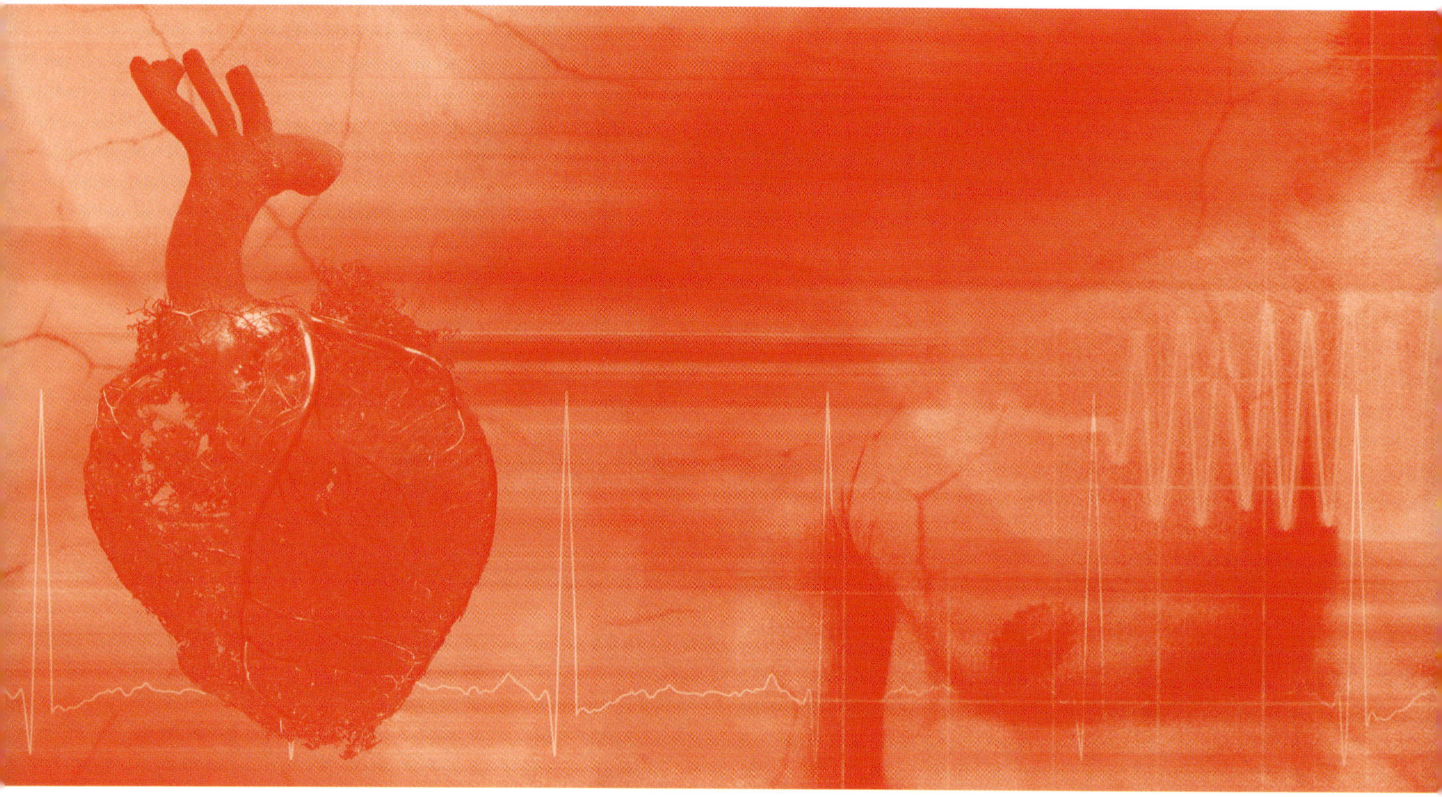

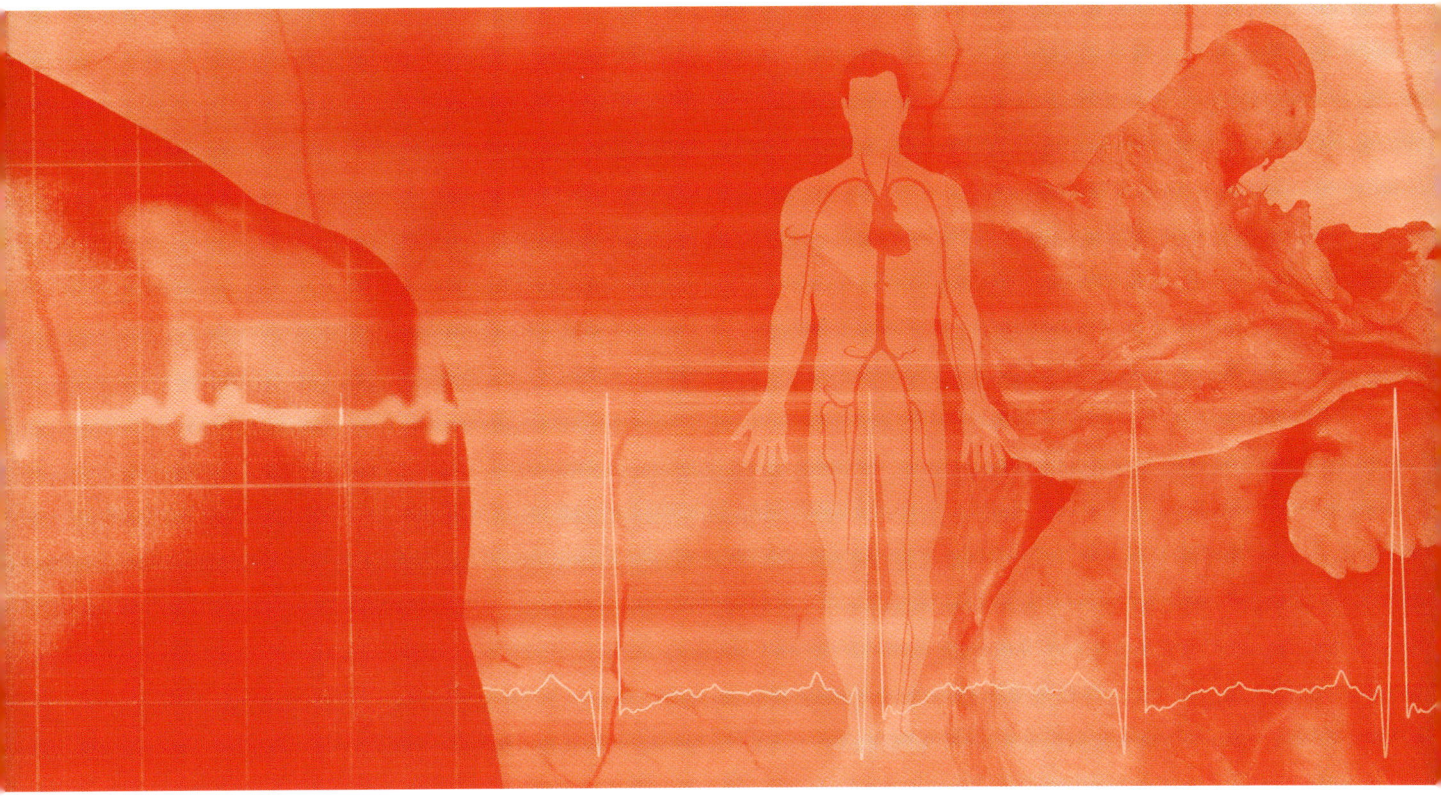

# 4. THE **CARDIOVASCULAR** SYSTEM

The cardiovascular system is an
organism's major transport system.
Not only does it distribute nutrients,
oxygen and hormones to individual regions of the body;
it also collects metabolic by-products
which are then eliminated.
The heart is the engine of this system,
and the dense network of blood vessels
form the transport routes.

# Circulation

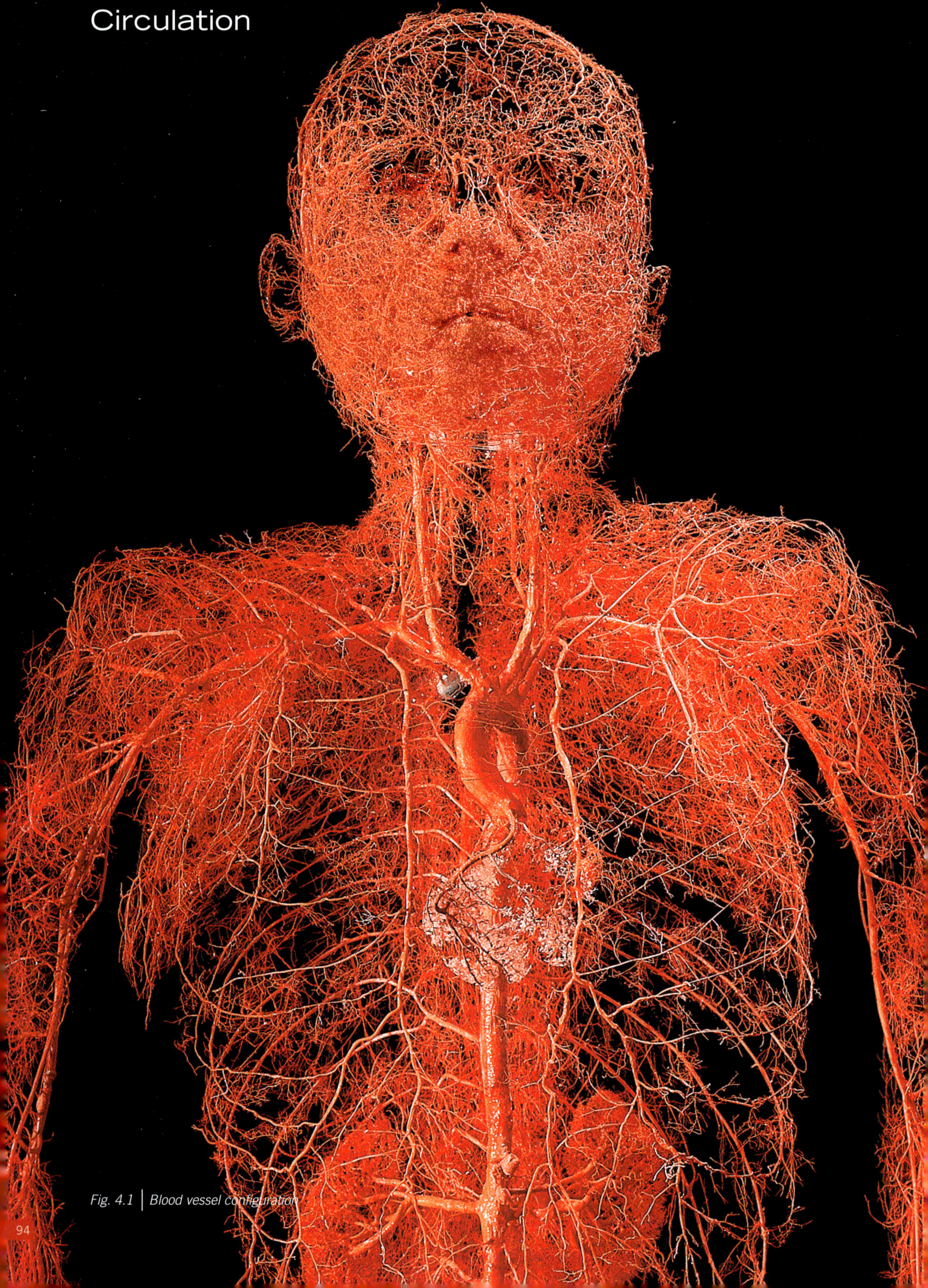

Fig. 4.1 | Blood vessel configuration

Generally speaking, the vessels represent major highways that distribute blood to the body. They taper down more and more as they pass into the organs and tissue to form an intricate network of minute, hair-like vessels called capillaries. It is here that the interchange of nutrients, oxygen, and other substances takes place between the blood and tissue cells.

The dense network of arteries, veins, and capillaries that carry blood to and from the heart is more than 96,500 kilometres (60,000 miles) long. Laid end to end, the cardiovascular network of an average adult would wrap around the earth more than twice.

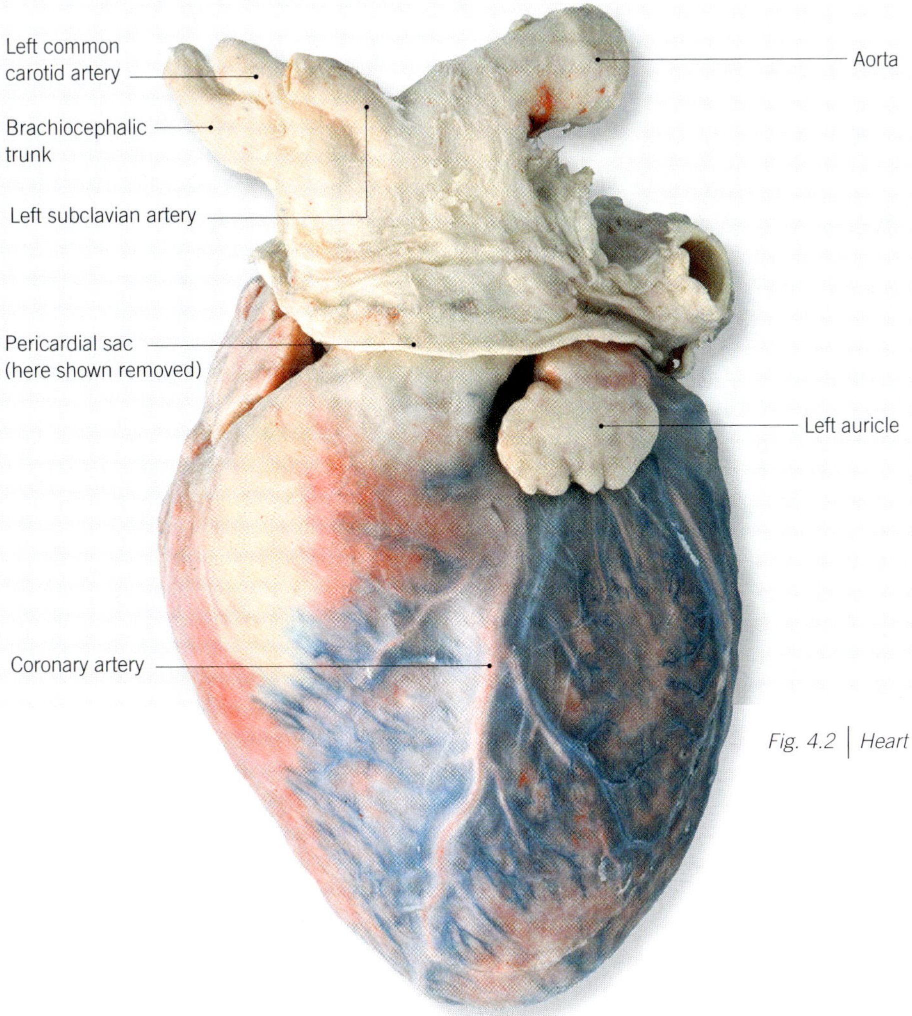


*Fig. 4.2* | *Heart*

The heart is the engine of the cardiovascular system. The hollow, muscular organ constantly pumps blood around the body. Its muscle fibres run spirally so that it can contract the chambers on all sides. The size of the heart is roughly that of our fist and weighs approximately 300 grams (11 ounces).

At rest, the heart has about 70 beats per minute and pumps about 75 millilitres (3 ounces) of blood through the body with each beat. This adds up to about 1 million barrels of blood during an average lifetime of around 75 years. That is enough to fill more than 3 super tankers.

# The Body's Pump

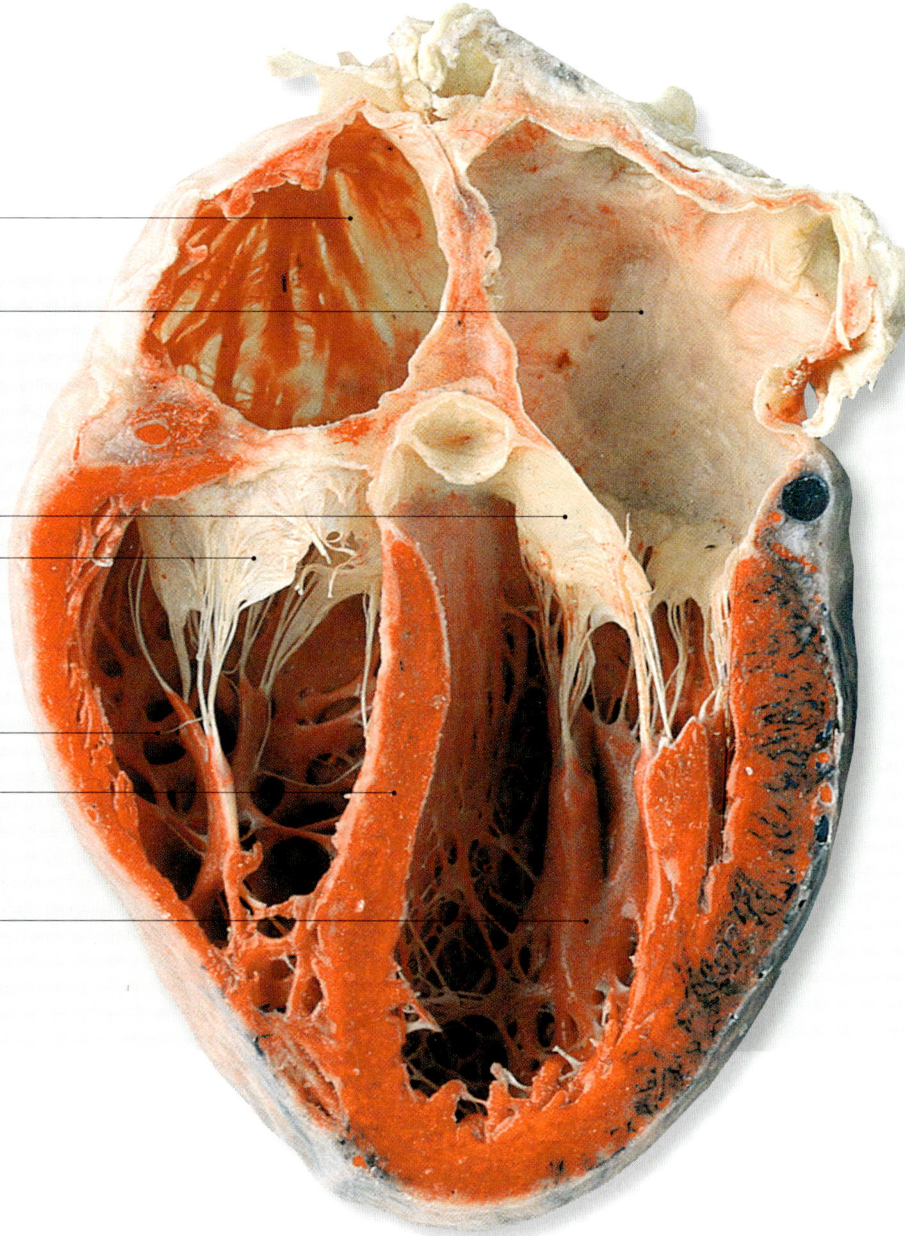


Each side of the heart
has an atrium for incoming blood
and a ventricle to pump blood out.
The left ventricle of the heart distributes
the oxygen-rich blood from the lungs
to all the body's cells.
Here, oxygen and nutrients are exchanged for waste
through the web-like beds of capillaries.
The oxygen-poor blood drains through veins
back to the right heart
and from here to the lungs for replenishment.

To get enough oxygen to all of the body's organs,
all of our blood must pass through the lungs
and around the body at least once a minute.

The gas exchange is incredibly fast.
The blood in the capillaries of the lungs
comes into contact with air
for only about 0.75 seconds
but is fully oxygenated after about
a third of this time.

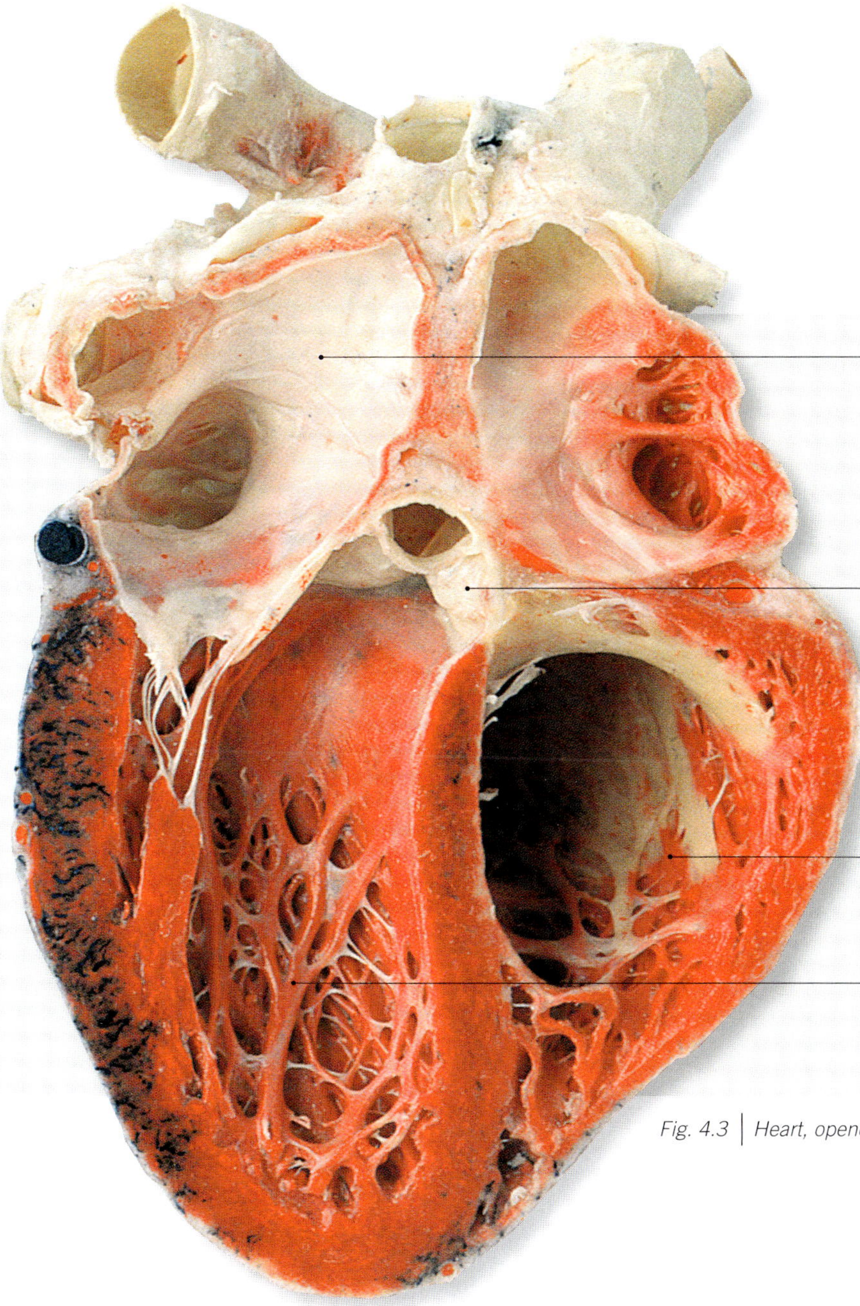


*Fig. 4.3 | Heart, opened longitudinally*

The heartbeat is regulated
by special muscle fibres in the heart walls.
These fibres are not visible to the naked eye.

The rhythm of our heart accompanies us
throughout our lives, without a moment's rest.
The sound – lub-dub, lub-dub, lub-dub – is created
by the four heart valves as they direct blood flow
through the heart's four chambers.

The closing of the two valves
between the atria and the ventricles –
mitral and tricuspid – creates the first part
of the heartbeat, the lub.
The second part of the heart beating – dub –
is the closing of the aortic and pulmonary valves
that separate the ventricles from the arteries.

If the valves do not close properly and leak,
the sound will be muffled.

# Controlling Blood Flow

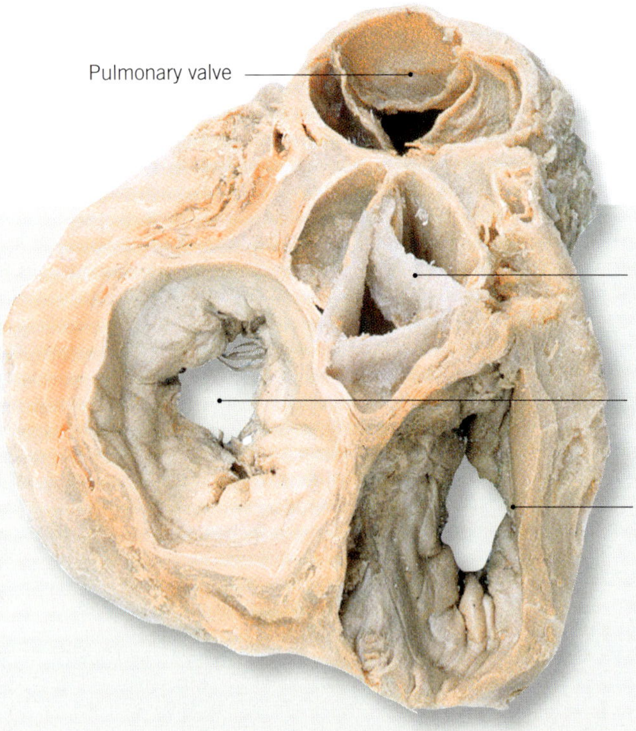


*Fig. 4.4* | *View of the cardiac valves from above*

**Heart Valves**
Blood flow between the atria and ventricles is controlled by one-way valves.
These are flaps of fibrous tissue, called cusps.
As the ventricles begin to contract, the pressure inside the ventricles rises and slams the cusps tightly shut.
There are also valves at the openings to the aorta and pulmonary arteries to prevent backflow.
The heart in Fig. 4.4 is dissected to show all four valves viewed from above.

**Aortic Valve Infection** (Endocarditis)
The endocardium is the heart's inner lining.
Endocarditis is an inflammation of the lining and the heart valves.
After the infection has healed, permanent scars and growths may remain on the valve, as shown in Fig. 4.5.
These scars impair the heart's function:
If a valve fails to work properly, the heart needs greater pressure to pump the same volume of blood.
If an endocarditis is bacterial, it can lead to serious complications, including heart or kidney failure.

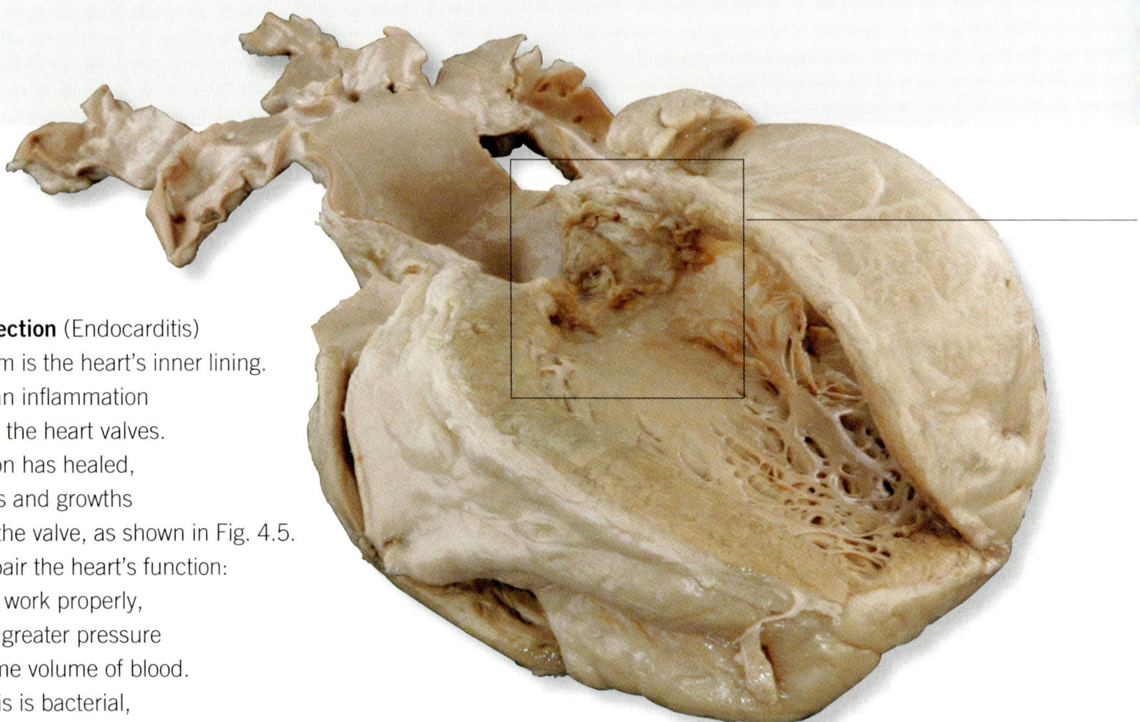

*Fig. 4.5* | *Opened heart with endocarditis of aortic valve*

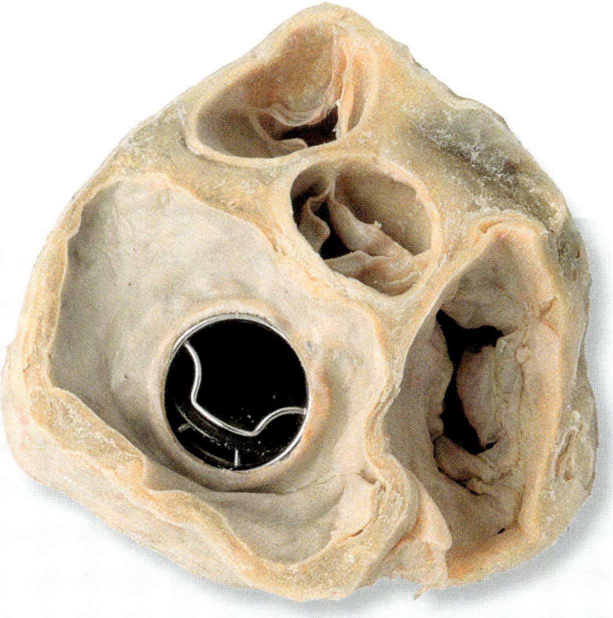

Fig. 4.6 | Cardiac valves from above with mitral valve prosthesis

Fig. 4.7 | Heart with mitral and aortic valve prosthesis

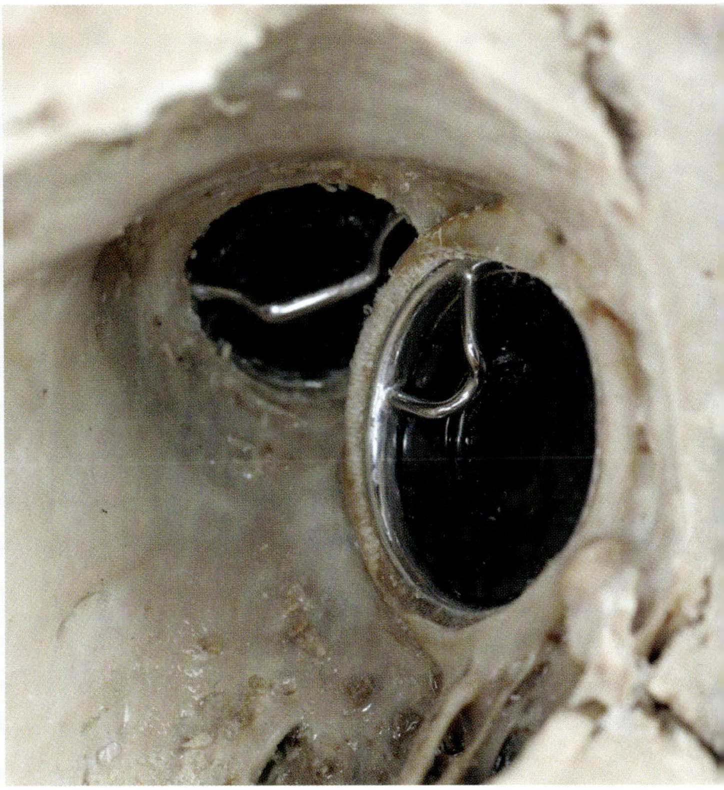

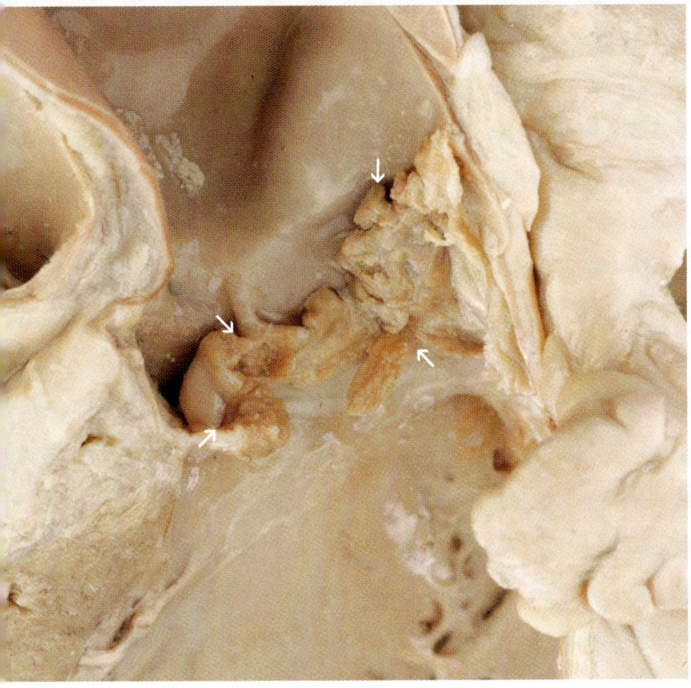

**Artificial Valves**

Bacterial or rheumatic infections (endocarditis) can deform the heart valves so much that they can no longer open sufficiently or close properly.

In severe cases, the affected valves have to be replaced with artificial ones.

Above, both the aortic semilunar valve (the valve between the left ventricle and the aorta) and the mitral valve (the valve separating the left atrium and the left ventricle) are replaced with prostheses.

Fig. 4.8 | Close-up of aortic valve with endocarditis

# Blood Supply of the Heart

The cardiac muscle has its own blood vessels to supply it with oxygen and nutrients. They are called coronary arteries. Two main arteries branch from the aorta and subdivide into smaller blood vessels that penetrate the heart muscle.

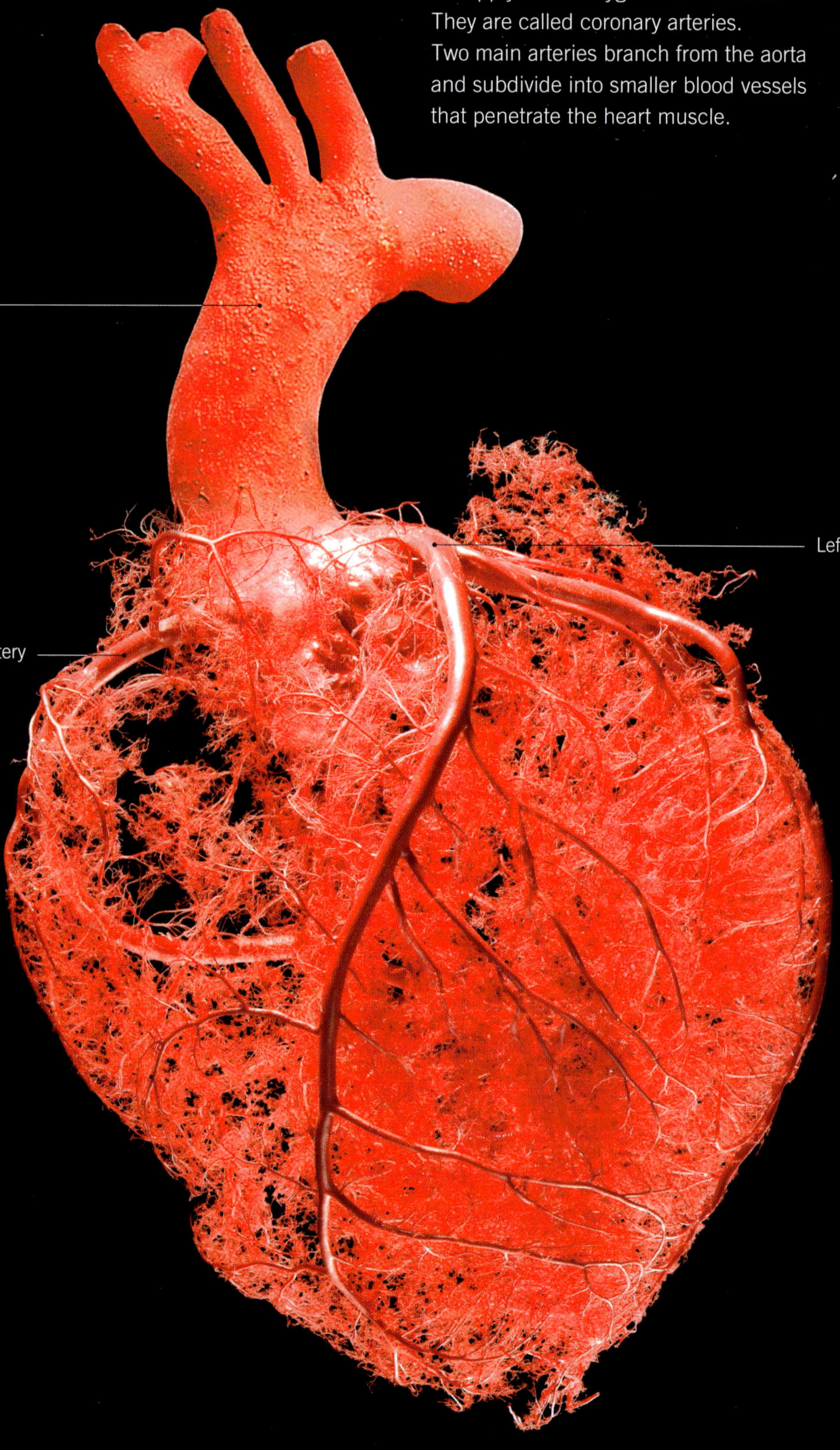


*Fig. 4.9 | Configuration of the coronary arteries*

# Coronary Artery Disease

In a diseased artery,
a fatty substance called plaque
forms on the arterial walls.
The plaque may gradually become
a bulge that obstructs blood flow.

When a coronary artery is affected,
it causes angina with symptoms, such as
chest pains and shortness of breath.

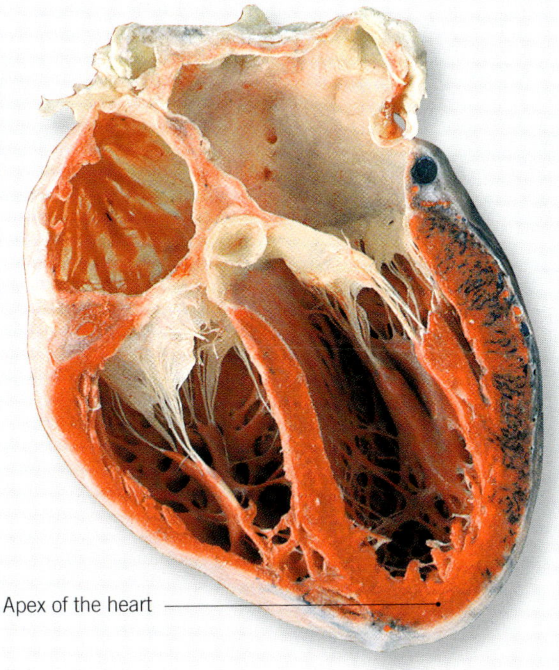


*Fig. 4.10 | Normal heart, opened longitudinally*

**Heart Infarct**

When the blood flow in a coronary artery is interrupted,
the muscle cells it supplies die.
This condition is known as heart attack.
If only a small section of the heart is affected,
it can continue to pump blood through the body,
and the person will survive the heart attack.
But the heart functions will be weakened.
Gradually, a white scar of connective tissue
will replace the dead cells.
The heart wall is then
significantly thinner in the affected area.

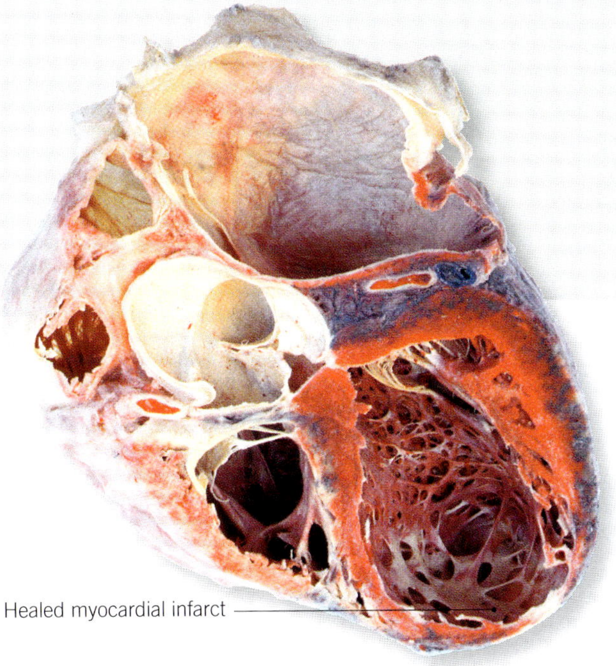


*Fig. 4.11 | Old, healed infarct in the apex of the heart*

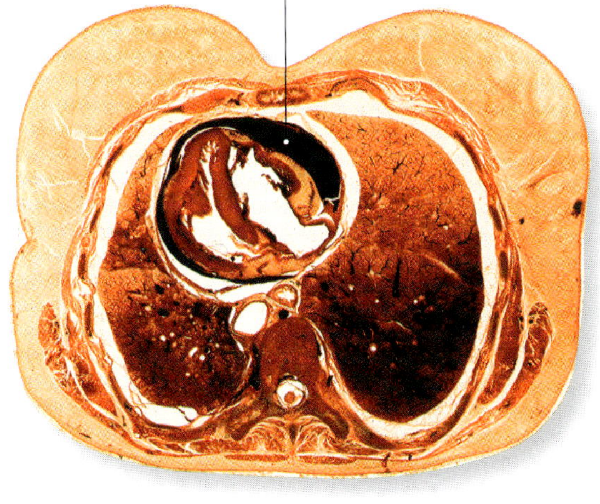


*Fig. 4.12 | Cross-section of the thoracic cavity with pericardial tamponade*

A heart attack can also be so severe
that the cardiac wall tears.
Blood then flows into the pericardium,
compressing the heart from outside.
This condition is called 'pericardial tamponade'
and is usually fatal within minutes.

## Heart Hypertrophy

All muscles increase with exercise
and so do our heart muscles.
An athlete's heart can even weigh
over 500 grams (18 ounces).

However, the heart also enlarges under strain,
for example, high blood pressure,
defects in the heart wall,
or faulty heart valves.
The massive hypertrophy shown here,
the heart weighs 800 grams (1.7 pounds),
was due to a heart muscle disease.

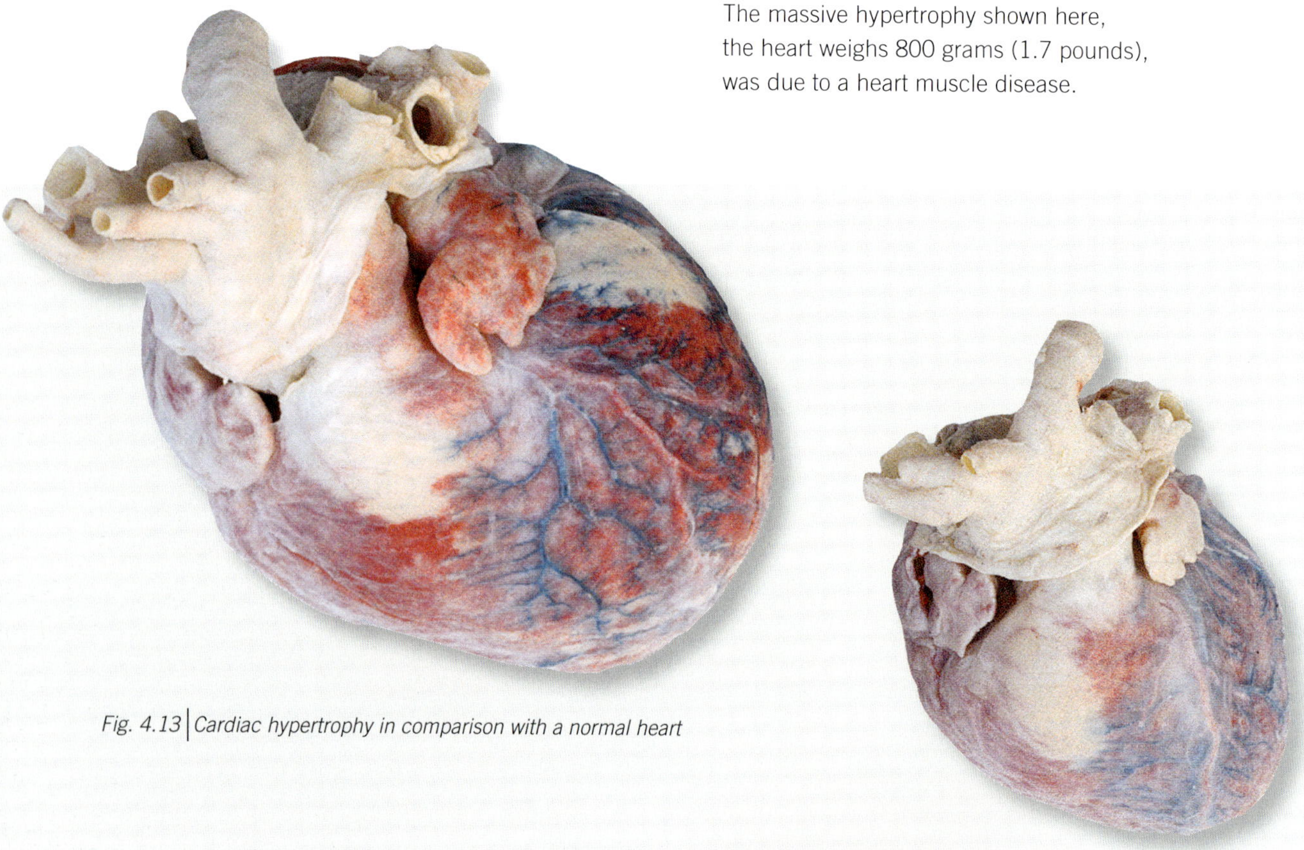

*Fig. 4.13 | Cardiac hypertrophy in comparison with a normal heart*

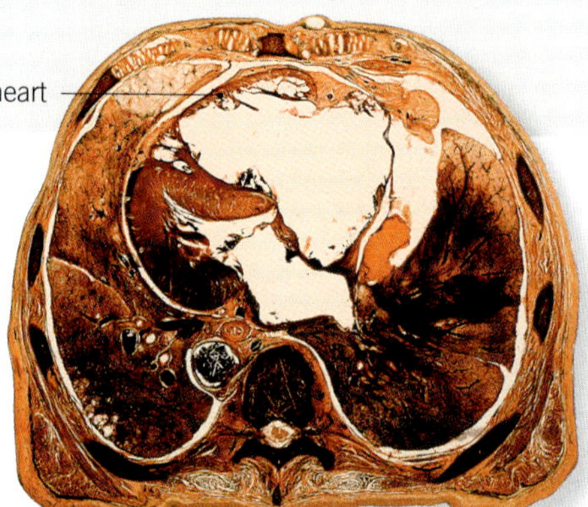


*Fig. 4.14 | Cross-section with enlarged heart*

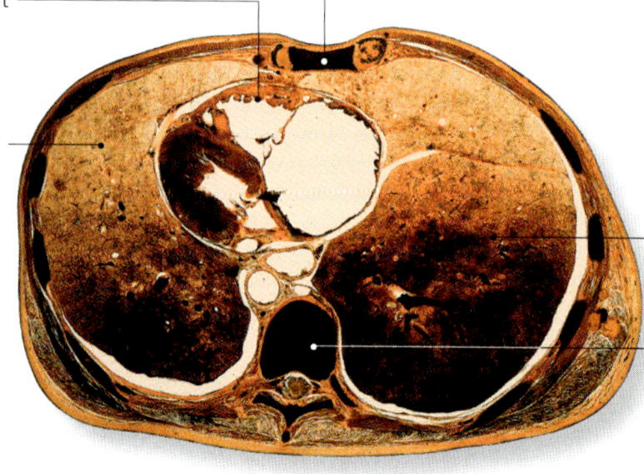


*Fig. 4.15 | Cross-section with heart of normal size*

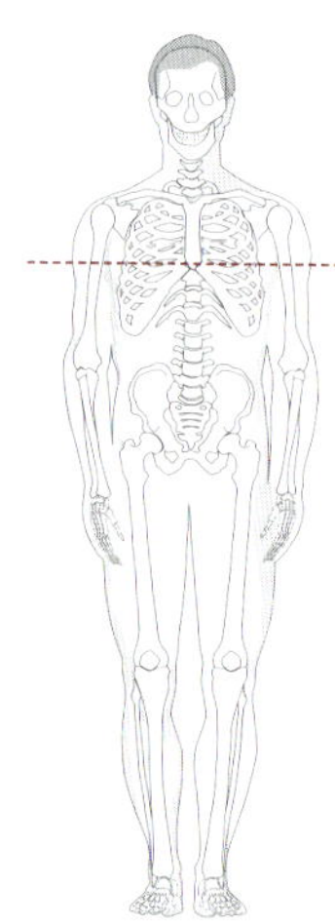

# Blood Vessel Configurations

Blood vessel configurations are perfect samples of the inner profiles of blood vessels. Here, only the main arterial branches are shown. If the capillaries were also injected, the arterial network would look so dense that one could not look through.

The vessels are first injected with a dyed plastic. By the time the plastic has cured, it has taken the shape of the vessels. The surrounding soft tissue can then be removed mechanically and chemically with the aid of ferments.

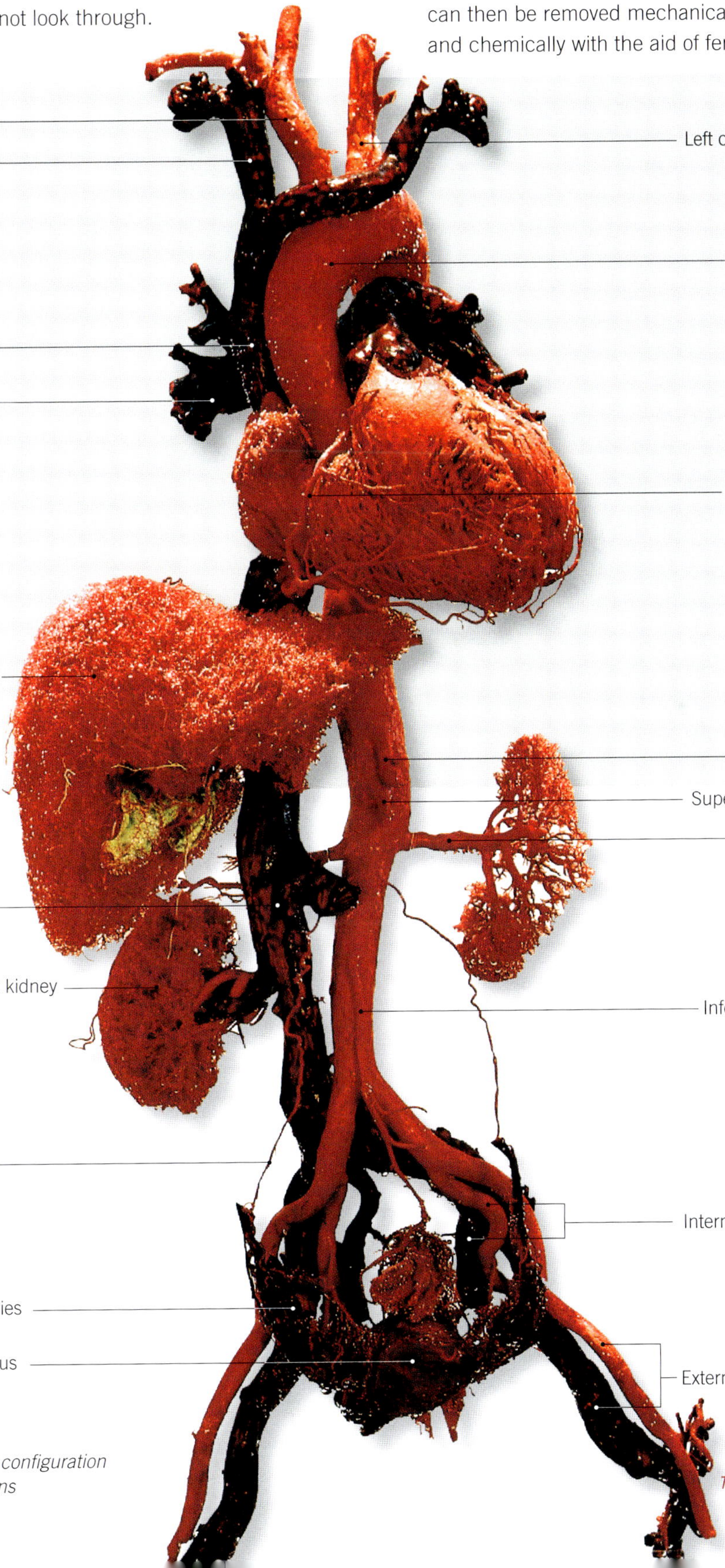


*Fig. 4.16 Blood vessel configuration of inner organs*

# Arteries

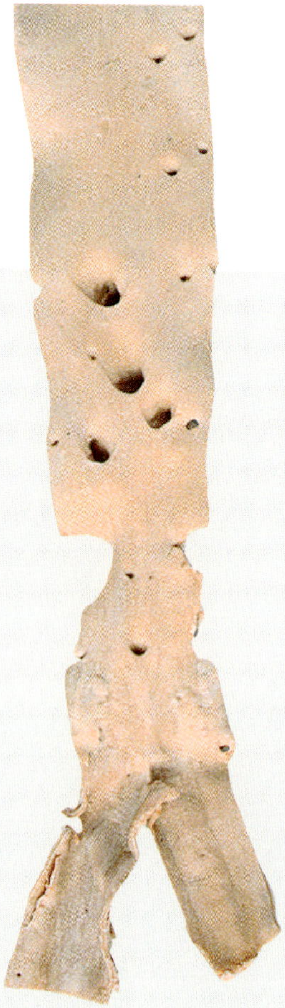

*Fig. 4.17* | *Inner lining of a healthy aorta*

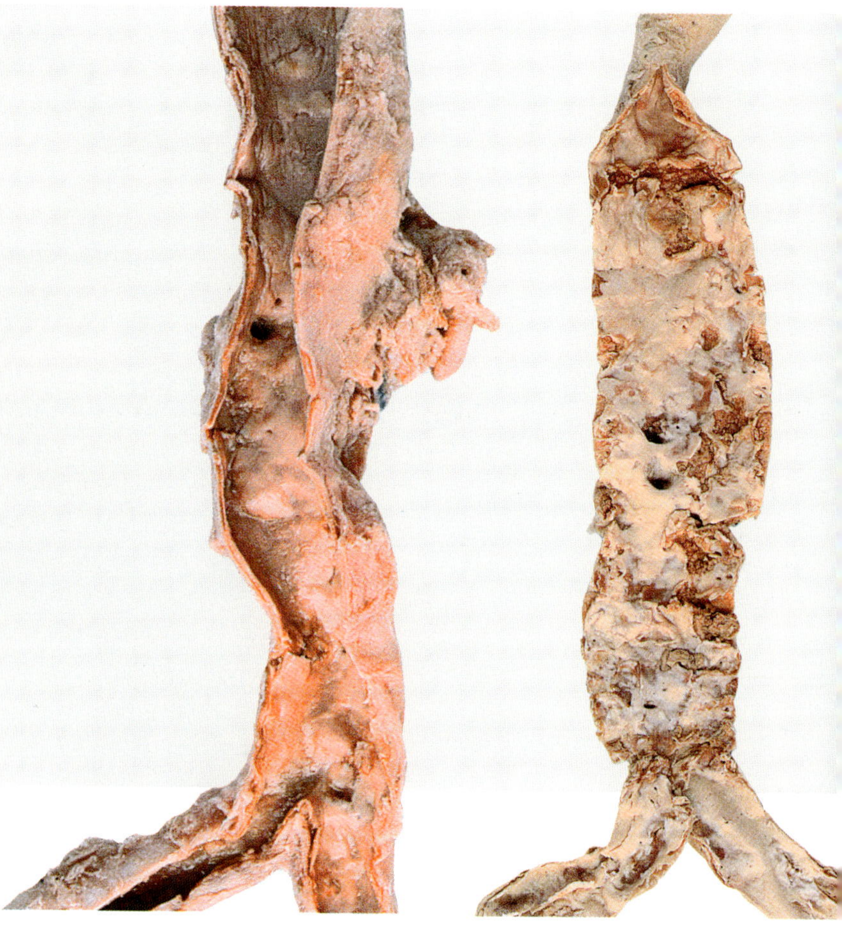

*Fig. 4.18* | *Inner lining of aortas with varying degrees of hardening of the arteries (arteriosclerosis)*

Arteries have a thin layer of muscles
in their walls, helping the heart pump the blood.
When the heart beats, the artery expands
as it fills with blood.
When the heart relaxes, the artery contracts,
exerting a force that is strong enough
to push the blood along.
This rhythm between the heart and the artery
constitutes our pulse.

The aorta is the largest artery in the body.
It is almost as thick as a garden hose.
Capillaries, on the other hand,
are so thin that it takes ten of them
to equal the thickness of a human hair.

The interior wall of a young, healthy artery
is completely smooth as is the aorta shown above.
To guarantee the blood supply to our organs,
our bodies monitor and regulate
the blood pressure in the arteries.
If arterial pressure is too low,
not enough blood reaches the body tissue.
If pressure is too high,
it could damage blood vessels and organs.
Responses are controlled by the
autonomous nervous system within seconds.

**Arteriosclerosis**
The aortas on the left show arteriosclerosis – the process of arteries gradually hardening. This is due to fats, proteins, and minerals deposited on the blood vessel walls. As the disease progresses, the internal walls of the blood vessels start to deteriorate and form ulcers. Blood clots collect on the ulcers, narrowing the arteries even more, until they become completely clogged.

**Aorta with Aneurysm**
Normally blood vessel walls are elastic. If wall segments become hard, they develop weak points that dilate under high blood pressure. As in the opened aorta on the right, the dilated areas interfere with circulation and cause blood to clot. Since these "pouches" (aneurysms) usually have thin and weak walls, high blood pressure can rupture them. The result is severe, often fatal, haemorrhaging. Large quantities of coagulated blood can clearly be seen here in the aneurysms of the arterial wall.

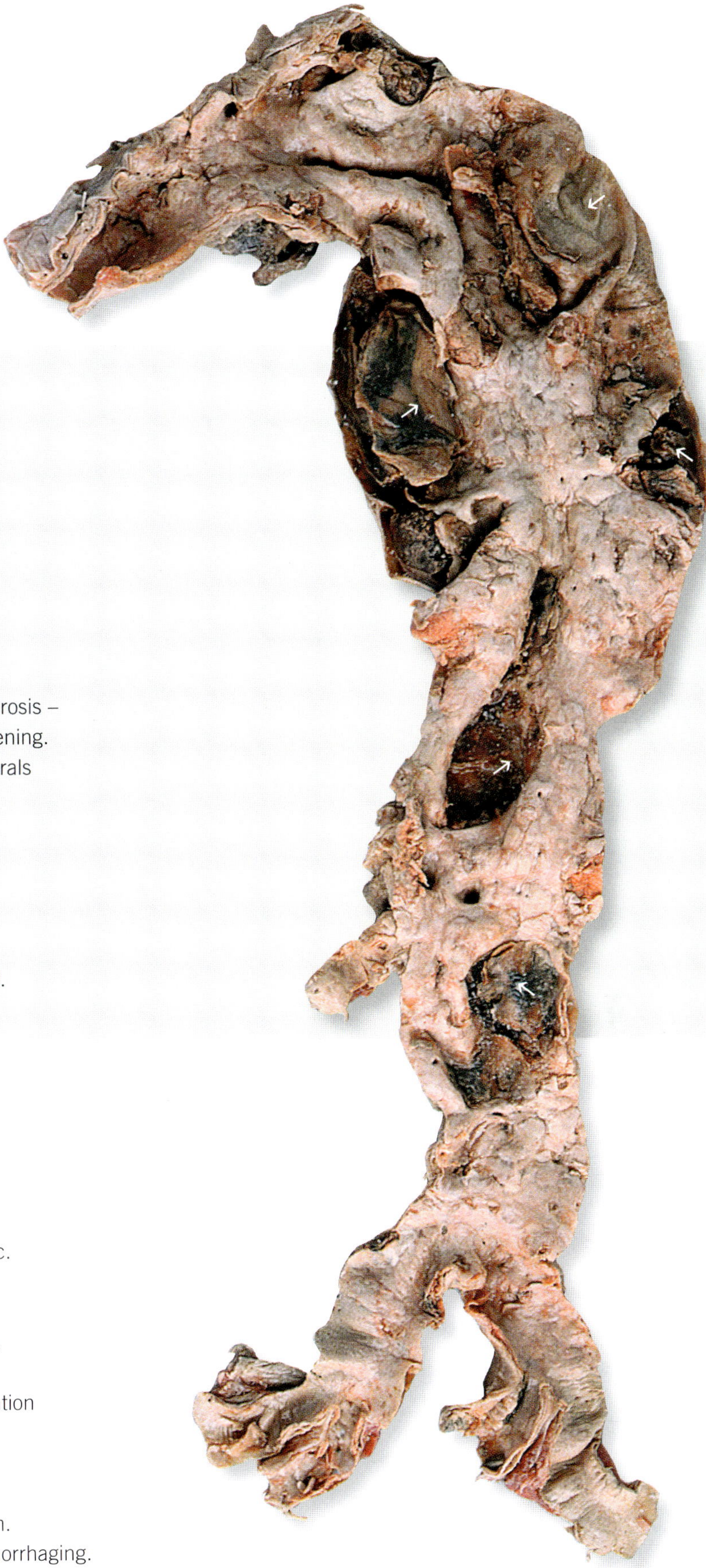

*Fig. 4.19 | Aneurysms in the aorta, filled with blood clots.*

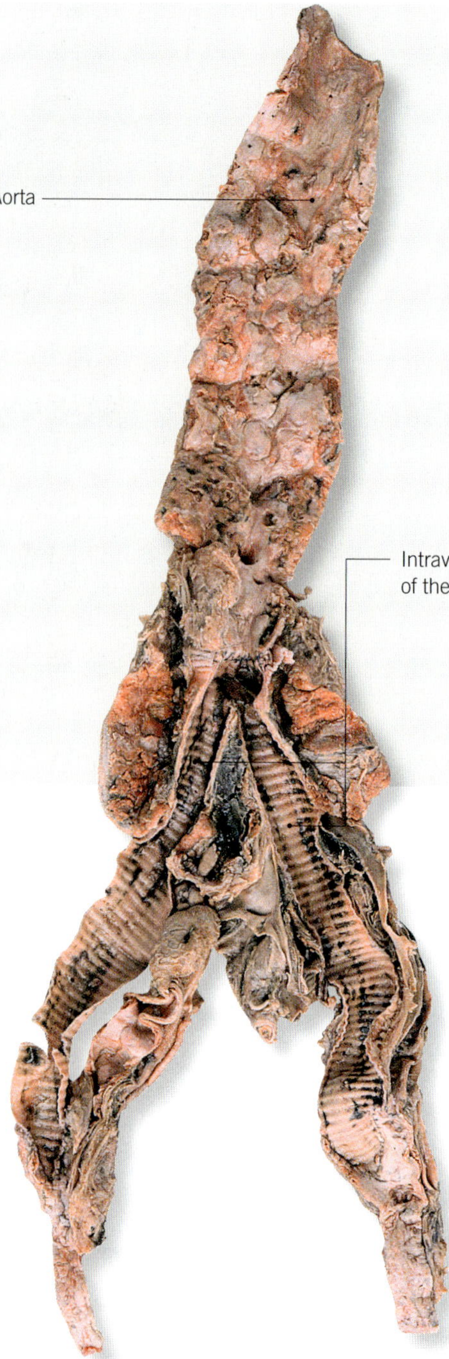


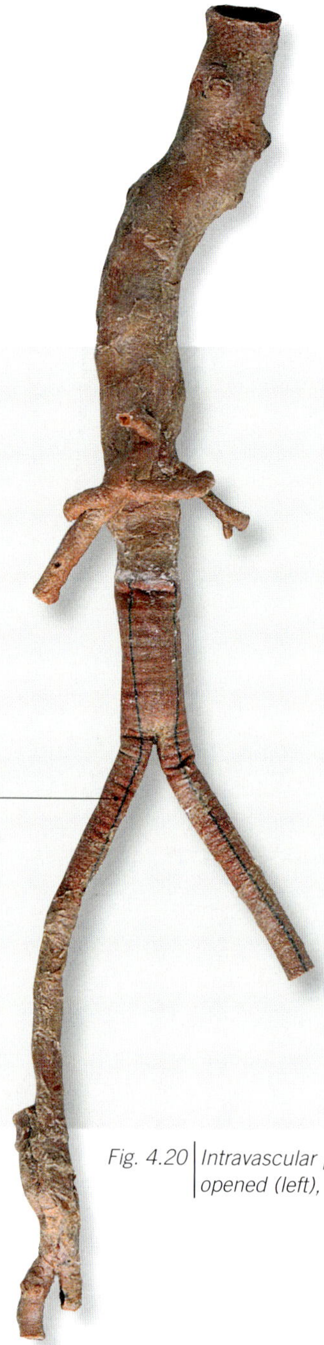

*Fig. 4.20* | *Intravascular prosthesis, opened (left), closed (right)*

**Vascular Prosthesis**
When blood vessels become narrow, the flow of blood to the regions of the body normally supplied by the affected arteries is significantly reduced, and the functions of these areas are consequently impaired.

The use of an intravascular prosthesis has long been practiced to replace constricted sections of larger arteries or arteries affected by an aneurysm.

# Blood

Blood consists of a pale liquid called plasma in which billions of red and white blood cells and platelets float.
Red blood cells are by far the most numerous. They transport oxygen and carry away carbon dioxide.

A red blood cell can circumnavigate the entire body in less than 20 seconds.
The colourless white cells are part of the body's built-in defence mechanisms.
Platelets are involved in blood clotting.

Together, these three kinds of blood cells make 45% of the blood tissue (55% is plasma).

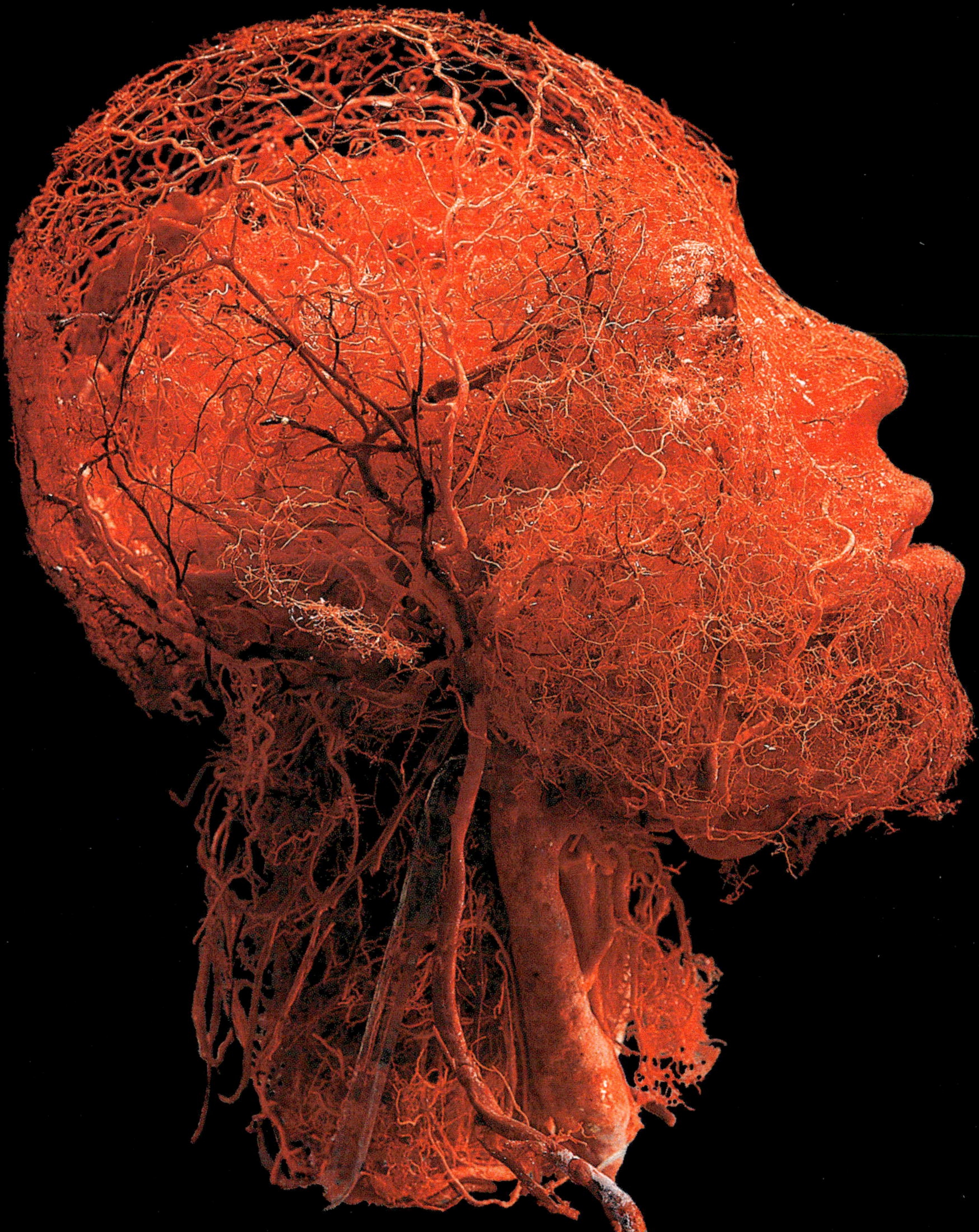

*Fig. 4.21 | Blood vessel configuration of the head*

This plastinate combines the vascular system of the arteries throughout the entire body with its bones and ligaments.

Body position significantly influences our cardiovascular system. For example, if a person changes from a lying position to a standing one, gravity causes about half a litre (1 pint) of blood to pool in the veins of the legs and lower body.

The body quickly responds to a decrease in blood pressure: The heart beats faster and more forcefully to increase its output of blood, and the small arteries (arterioles) constrict to increase resistance to blood flow.

Regular exercise, such as dancing or walking, reduces many of the established risk factors for cardiovascular disease. It improves the strength of the heart, can help reduce blood pressure, can reduce 'bad' cholesterol levels in the blood, and helps weight reduction. As fitness goes up, the incidence of heart disease goes down.

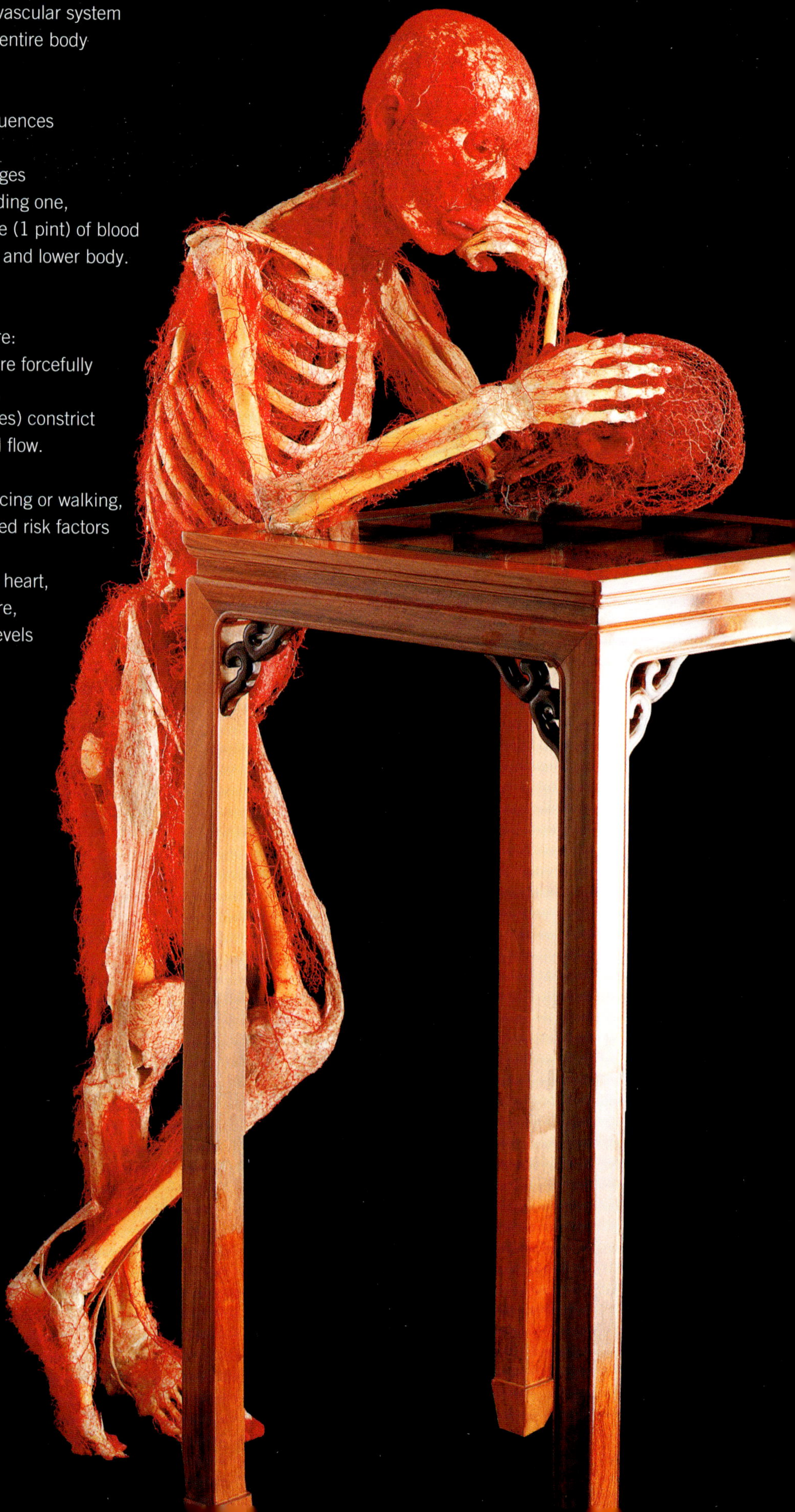

*Fig. 4.22* | *The Thinker*

**Spleen**

Old blood cells are broken down by the spleen.
Consisting of lymphatic tissue,
the spleen also plays a key role in the body's immune system.
The spleen is roughly 12 centimetres (5 inches) long
and weighs about 85–130 grams (3–5 ounces).
It is located on the left of the upper abdomen,
right next to the stomach and pancreas.

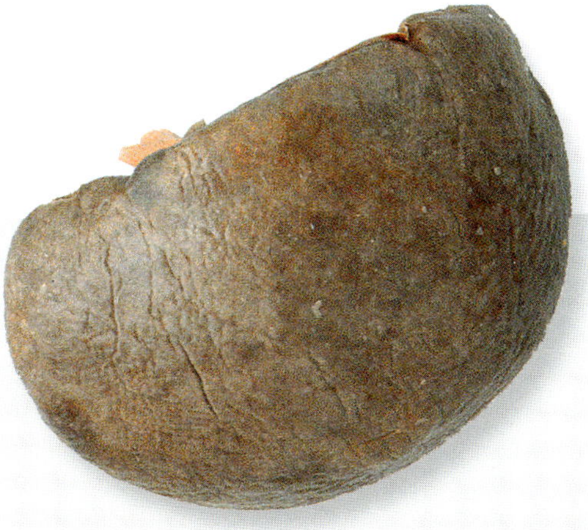

*Fig. 4.23* | *Normal spleen*

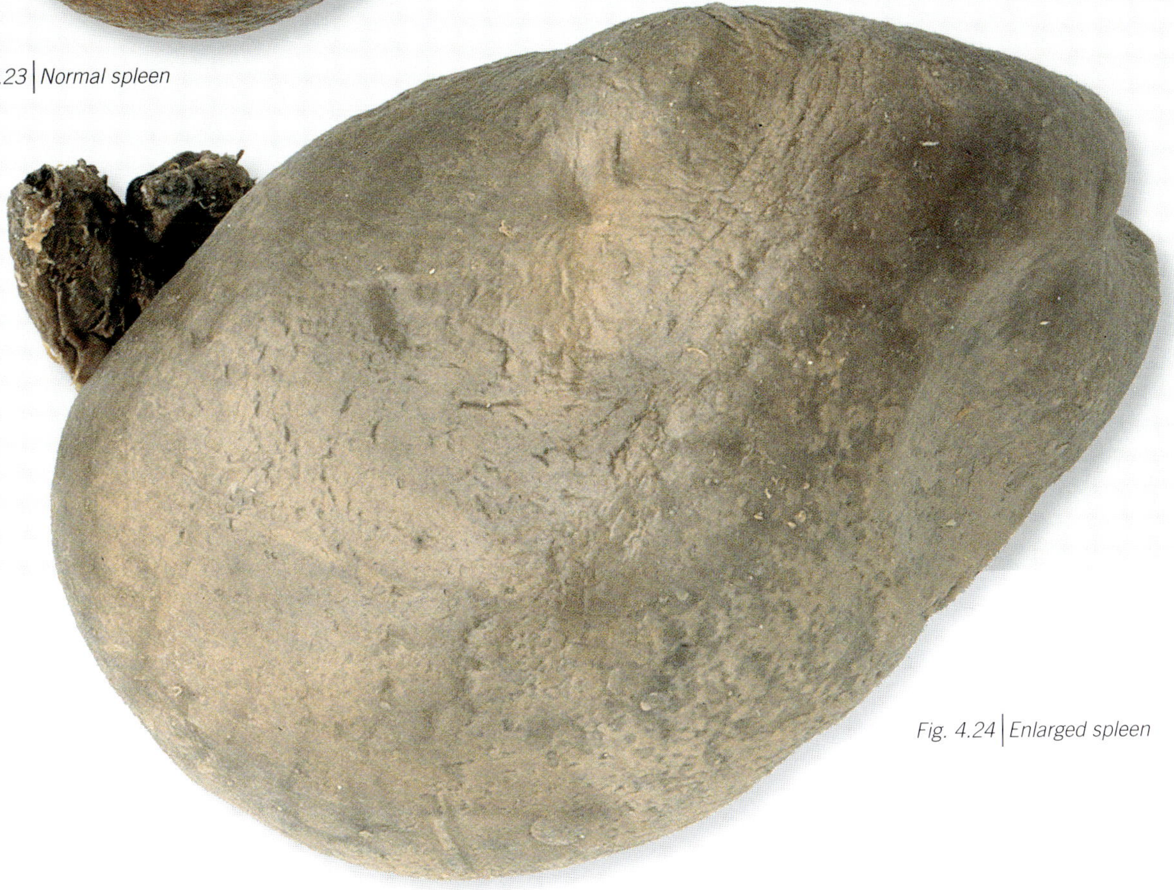

*Fig. 4.24* | *Enlarged spleen*

**Enlarged Spleen due to Leukaemia**

Leukaemia is a malignant disease
of the bone marrow and blood.
It leads to the production of large numbers
of non-functioning white blood cells
which must be broken down in the spleen.
To cope with this enormous strain,
the spleen enlarges.
In very extreme cases,
an affected spleen can weigh up to 9 kilograms
(20 pounds).

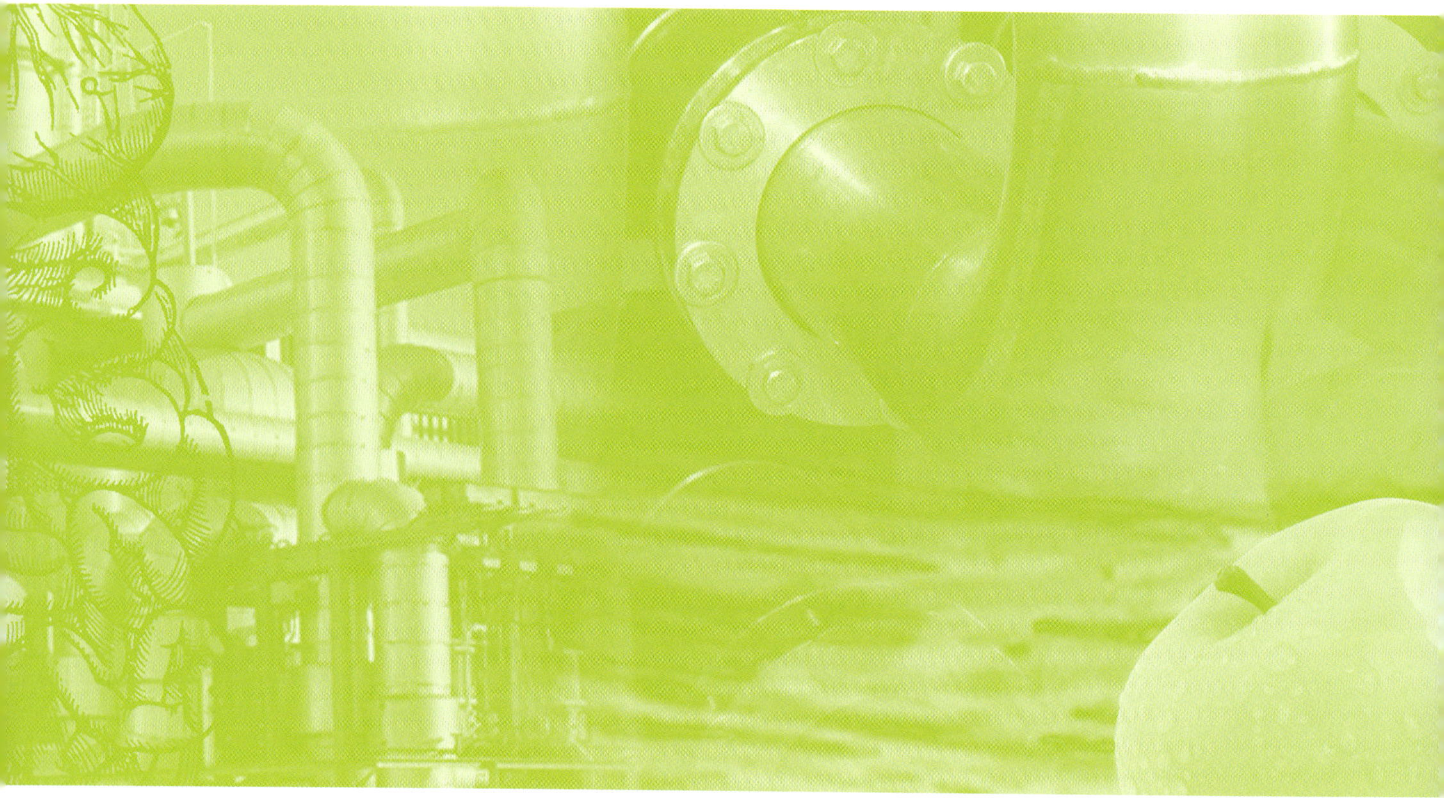

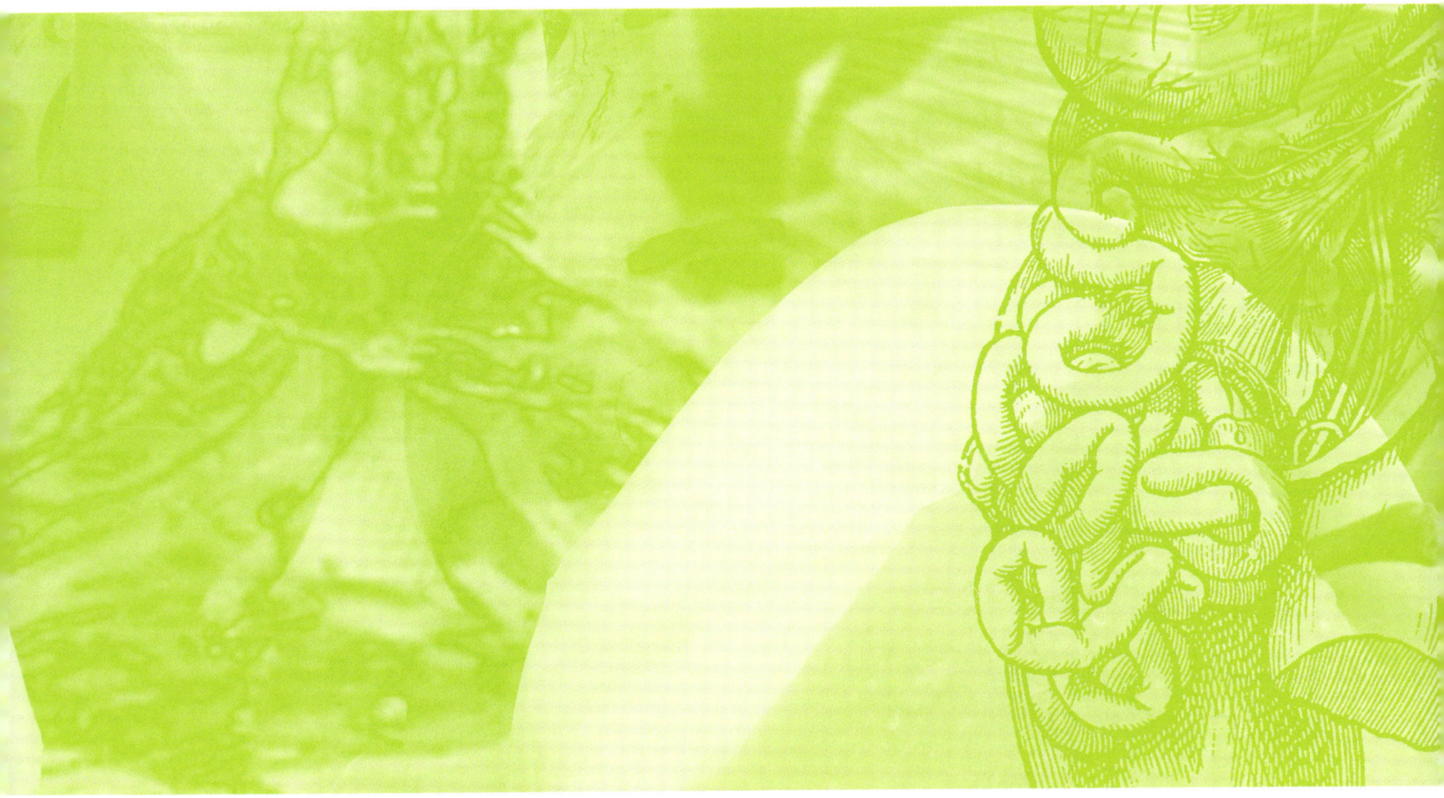

# 5. THE **DIGESTIVE** SYSTEM

All of the organs of the human body require an uninterrupted supply of energy if they are to perform their functions properly. Once they have been processed chemically, the nutrients present in food and absorbed through the digestive tract provide the organism with the energy that it requires. The organs of the digestive tract break down food both mechanically and chemically in a way that allows the nutrients to pass into the blood, where they can be transported to each individual cell.

# Fuelling the Body

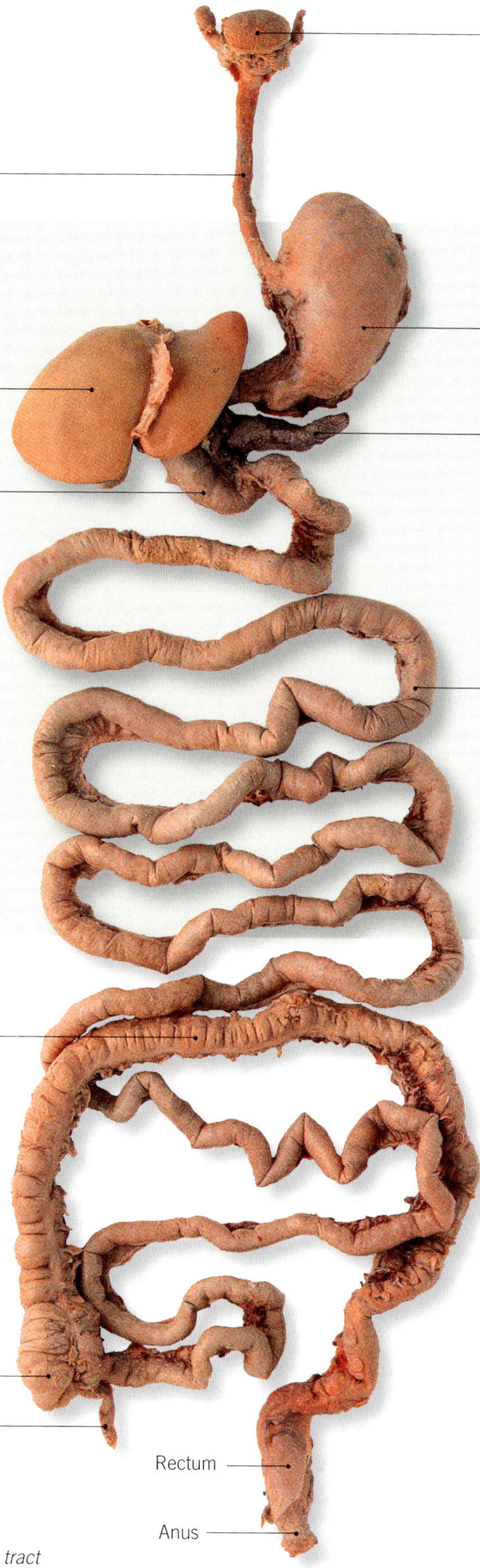


*Fig. 5.1* | *Digestive tract*

**The Organs of the Digestive System**

The digestive tract is like a long tube – roughly 9 metres (30 feet) in length. Food is first coarsely broken down in the mouth, then passes through the oesophagus and into the stomach. Gradually, it is fed into the duodenum where digestive enzymes from the liver and pancreas are added. The small intestine is a main site of digestion, where nutrient molecules are absorbed into the bloodstream. Indigestible food particles pass into the large intestine where water is extracted. They are then excreted through the rectum. The entire digestive process takes up to 20 hours.

The organs are tightly packed
in the abdominal cavity.
They are enclosed in the peritoneum,
the sheet of body tissue that lines the abdomen.
The peritoneum also produces a mucous fluid,
a lubricant to enable the organs to move.

The stomach and intestinal tract muscles
move the food by peristalsis,
a rhythmic, wave-like muscle movement.
Peristalsis is involuntary.
It can be stimulated by food
or even the smell of food,
or, if necessary, by medication.

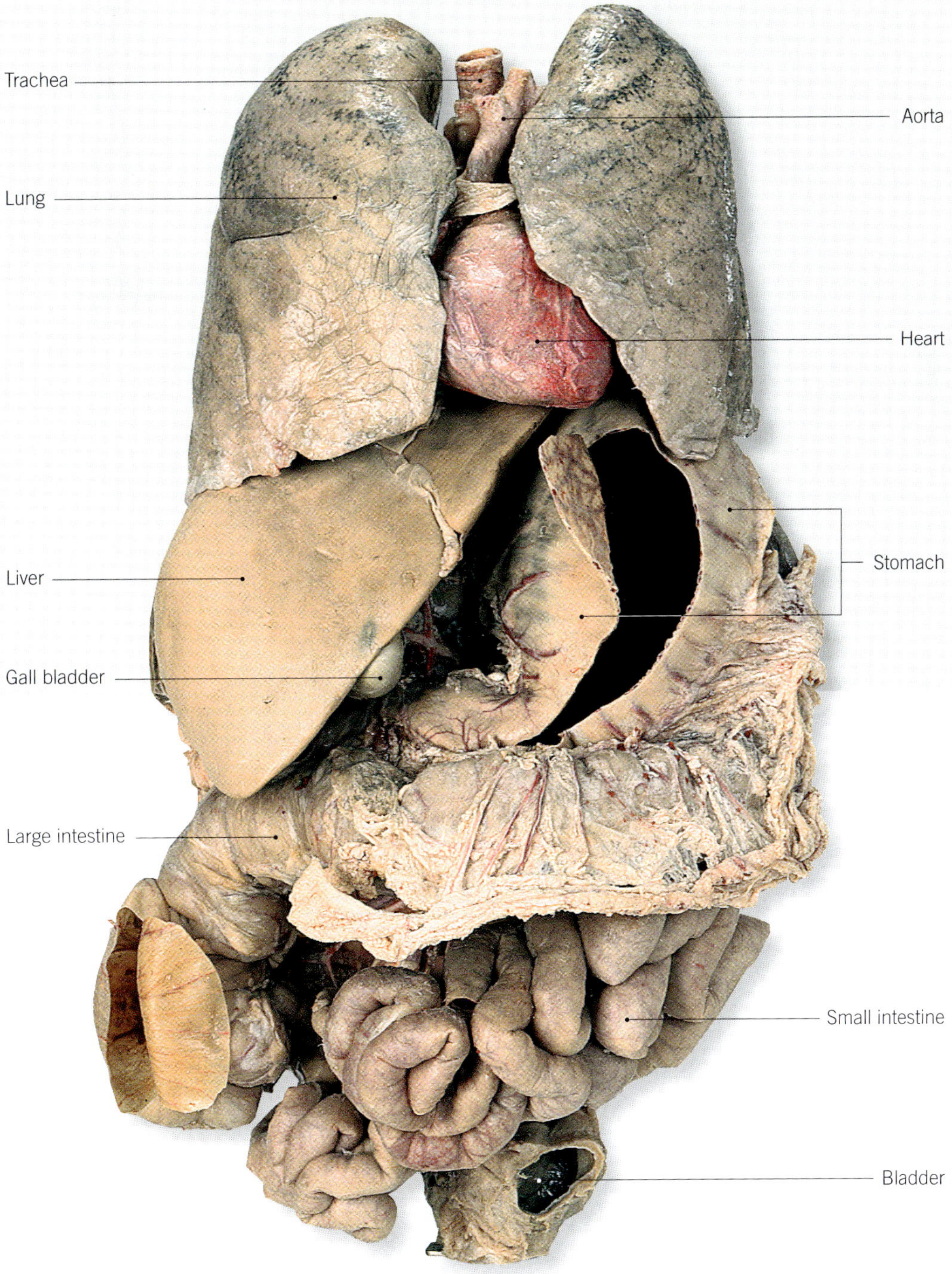


*Fig. 5.2* | *Thoracic and abdominal organs in their natural relationships and positions*

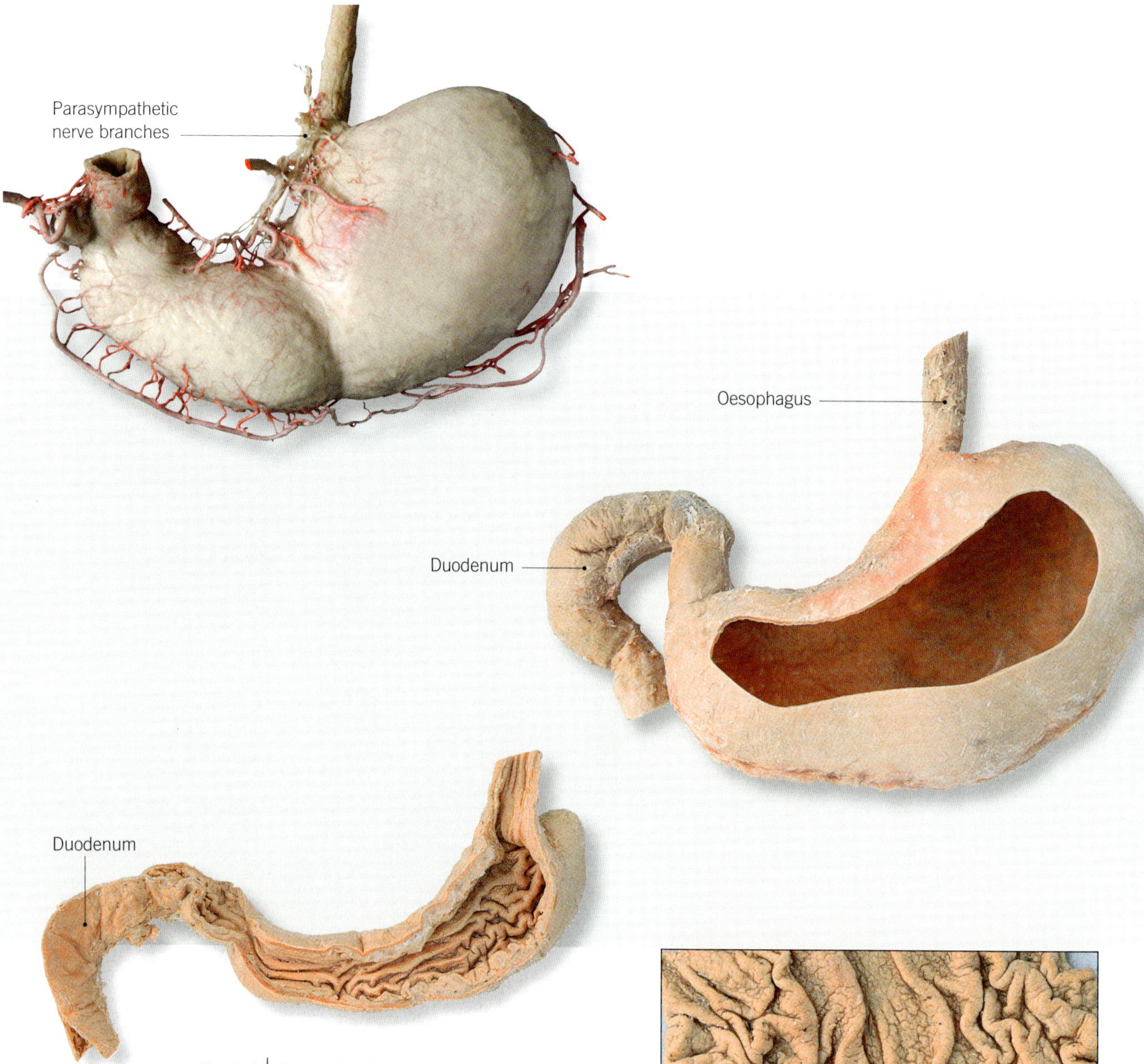


*Fig. 5.3* | *Stomachs of varying size and shape*

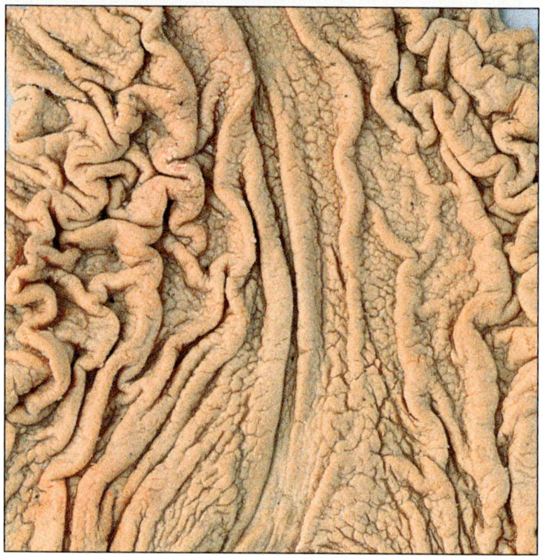

*Fig. 5.4* | *Mucous membrane of stomach lining*

**Stomach**

The stomach is a hollow, muscular organ, capable of holding 2–3 litres (4–6 pints). It stores food and initiates chemical and mechanical digestion, slowly releasing its contents into the intestines. The stomach's size, shape, and position depend on the amount of food in it, the position of the body, and the person's age and eating habits. The stomach's inner wall is lined with a furrowed mucous membrane. It has roughly 5 million glands, secreting around 2 litres (2 quarts) of gastric juices each day.

The juices mainly contain hydrochloric acid and enzymes that break food down into proteins. The glands also secrete a type of mucus to stop the stomach from digesting itself.

Fig. 5.5 | Inflammation of the mucous membrane with dot-like signs of bleeding

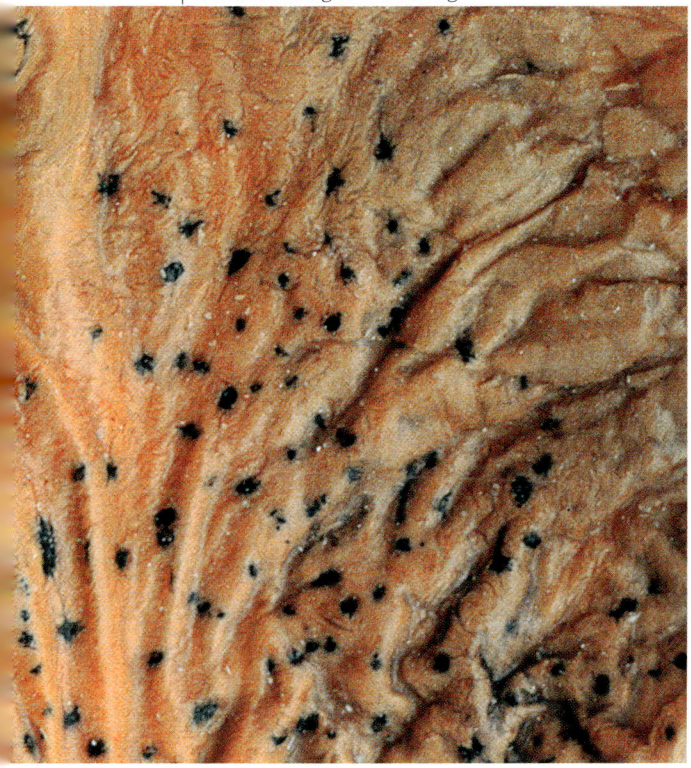

Fig. 5.6 | Stomach ulcer

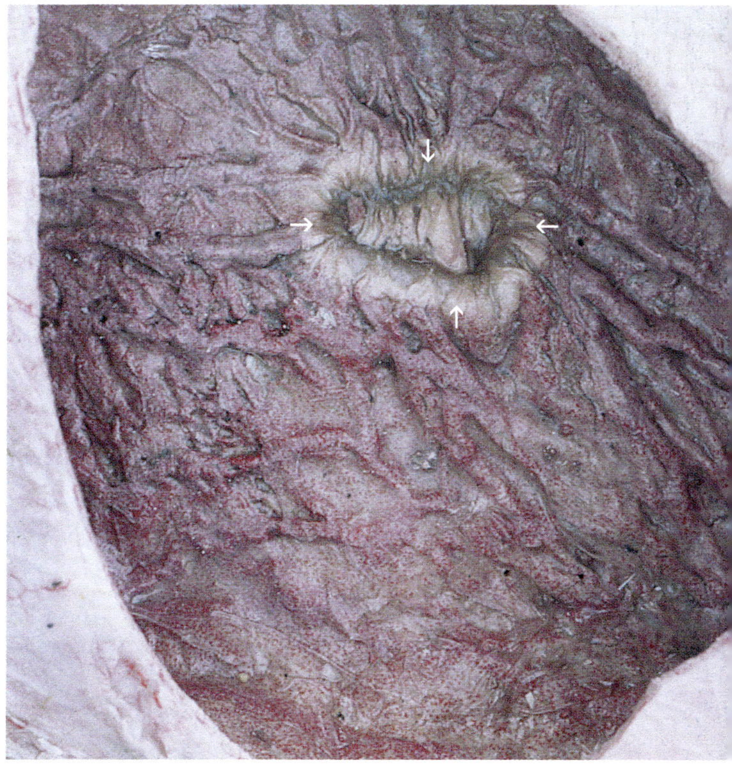

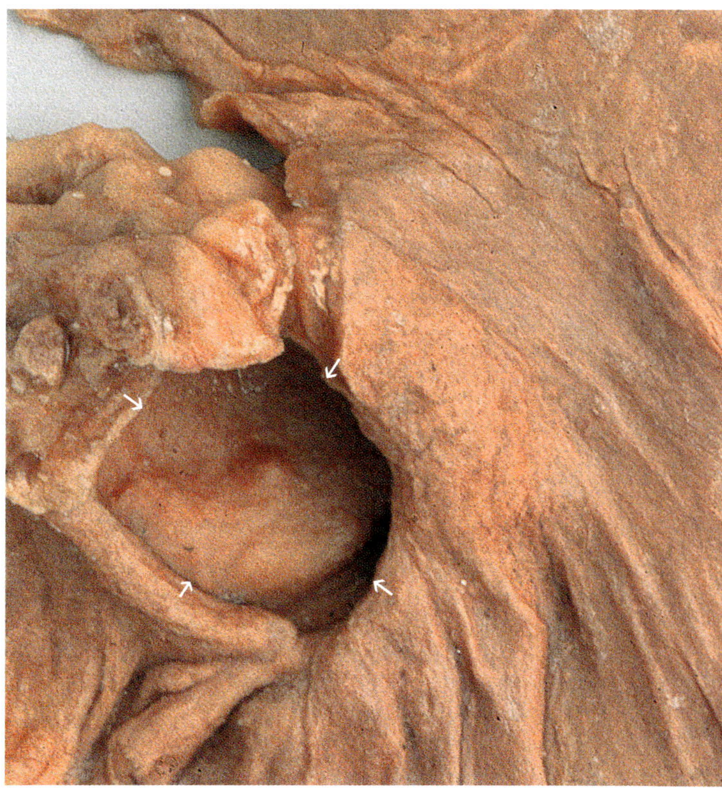

**Stomach and Duodenal Ulcers**

The opened stomachs in Fig. 5.6 and 5.7 have circular lesions at their inner lining, a stomach and duodenal ulcer, respectively. Overproduction of hydrochloric acid can damage the lining of the stomach and especially that of the duodenum. Ulcers readily form if this condition exists concurrently with a bacterial infection, particularly that of Helicobacter pylori. Ulcers can cause symptoms of indigestion, including severe pain.
They can usually be treated with medicines but, if left untreated, can lead to serious complications, including bleeding or perforation of the stomach.

Fig. 5.7 | Duodenal ulcer

Fig. 5.8 | Relief of membranous lining of small intestine

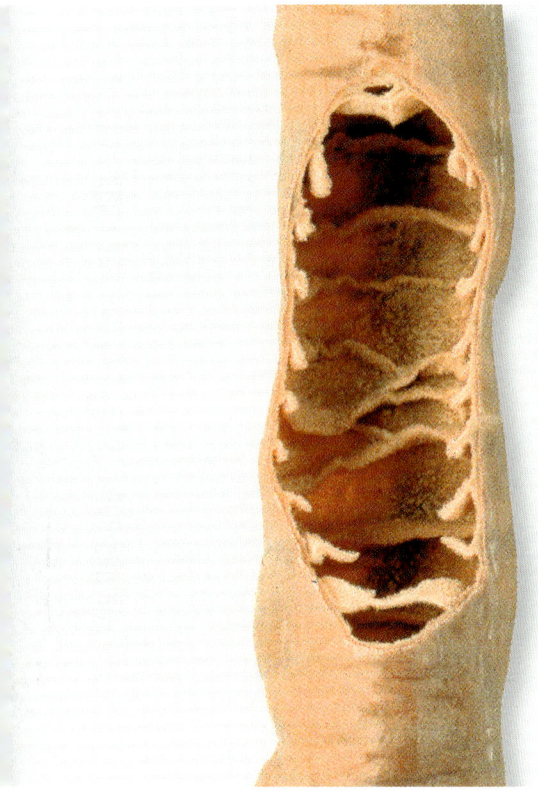

Fig. 5.9 | Small intestine in opened abdominal cavity

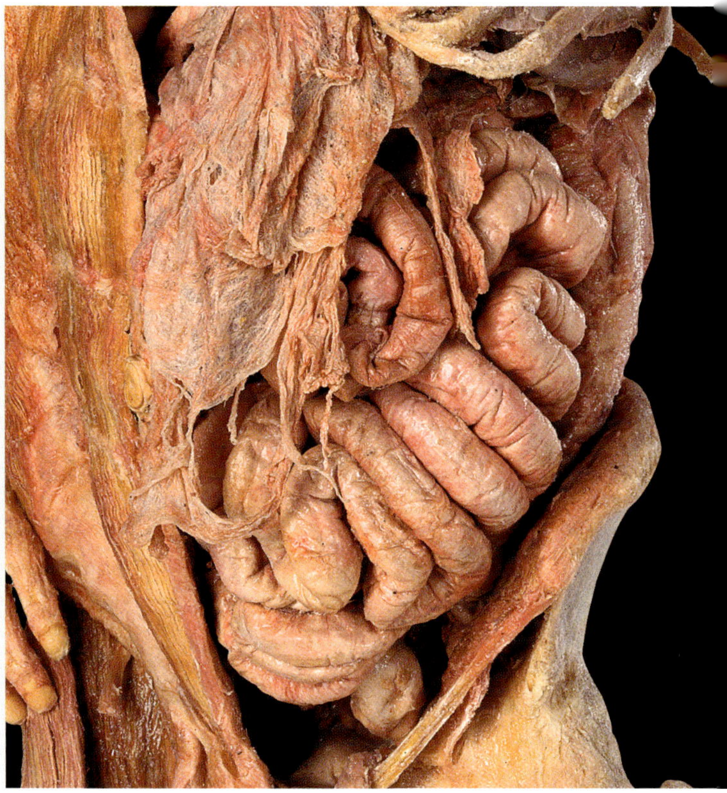

**Small Intestine**

Most digestion occurs in the small intestine. Nutrients are chemically broken down and released into the bloodstream. To increase the area for absorbing nutrients, the small intestine has ring-shaped folds and a dense network of finger-shaped villi, each 1 millimetre (0.04 inches) in length. The villi cells also form tiny projections, like the bristles of a microscopic brush. Each projection is only 1 1/2 thousandth of a millimetre (60 micro inches) long. If laid out, 3 metres (10 feet) of small intestine would expand to 30–40 sq. metres (320–430 sq. feet).

The small intestine absorbs almost all nutrients into the blood stream. To accomplish this, the small intestine's lining is equipped with an extraordinarily fine network of blood vessels. After a meal, blood supply to the intestines increases considerably. The absorbed nutrients flow to the liver via the portal vein for further processing.

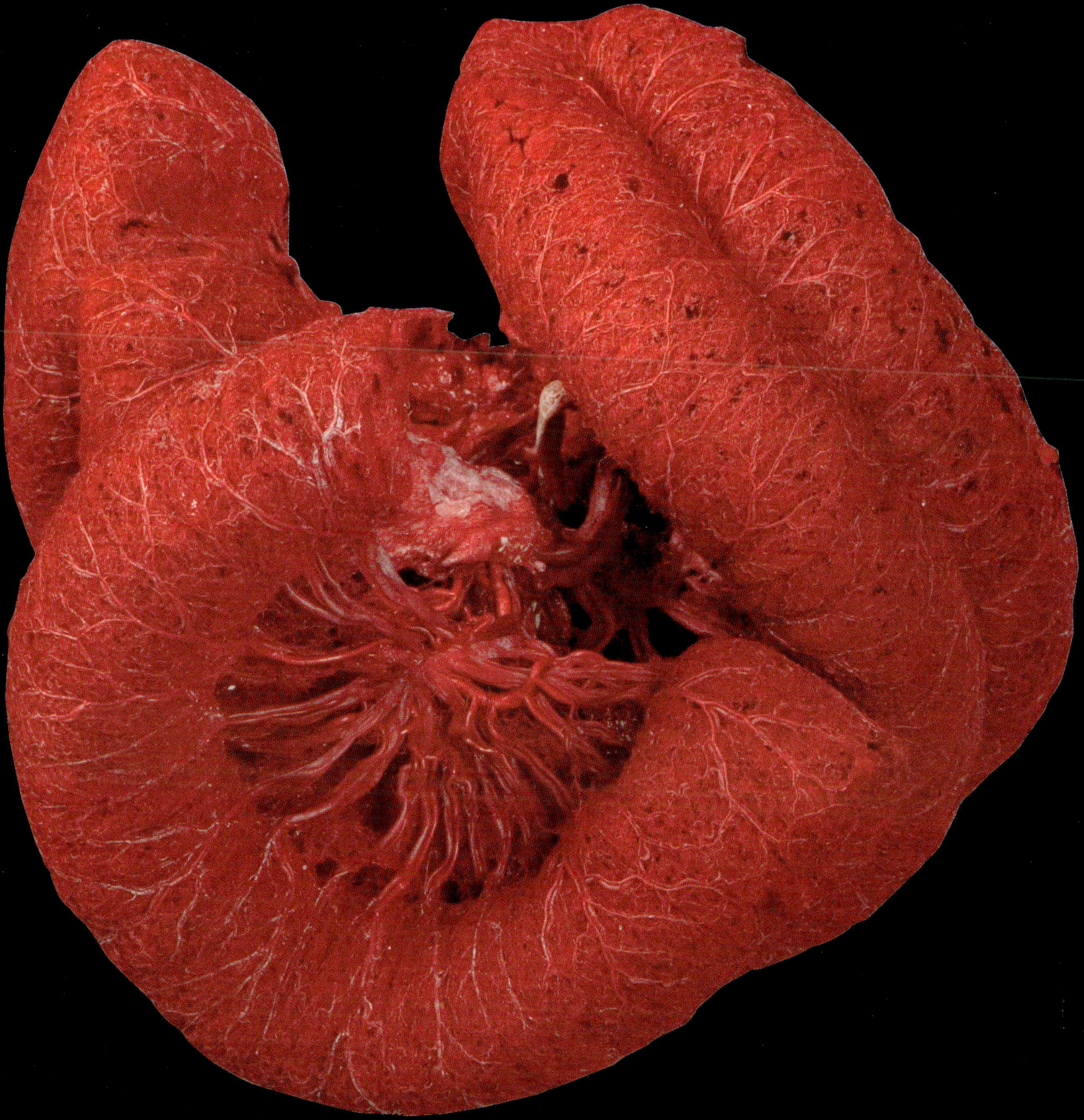

*Fig. 5.10* | *Blood vessel configuration of intestines*

Fig. 5.11 | Caecum with appendix

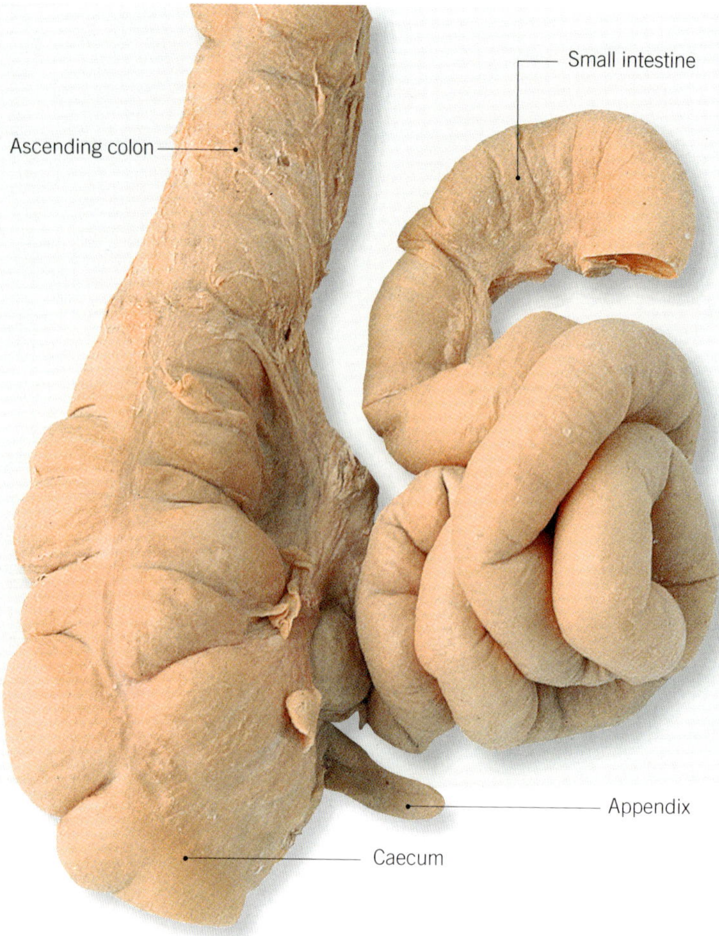


Fig. 5.12 | Section of large intestine

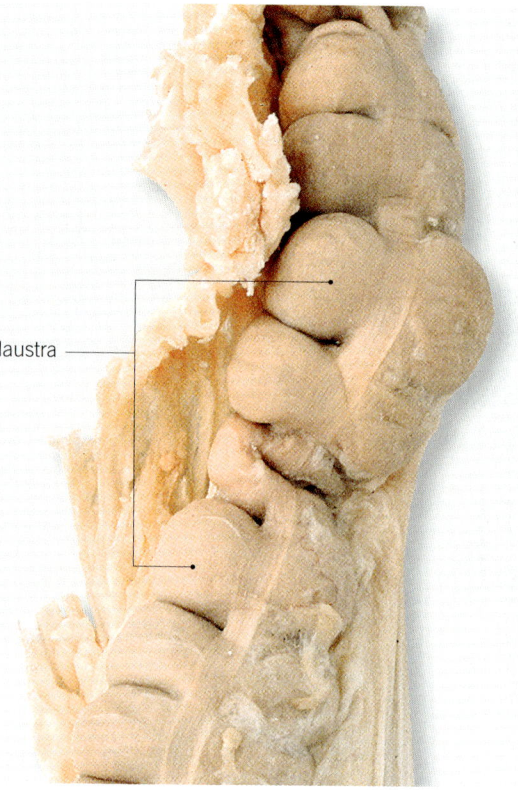


**Large Intestine** (Colon)

Indigestible material from the small intestine is released to the large intestine. There, water is absorbed to thicken the waste products. It also absorbs vitamins that are produced by billions of bacteria in the colon. The large intestine appears segmented due to its various "pouches" (haustra).

The caecum, the first part of the large intestine, is on the right-hand side of the lower abdomen. Attached to the caecum is the appendix. It varies from 1.5–20 centimetres (0.6–8 inches) in length and 0.5–2 centimetres (0.2–0.8 inches) in thickness. It does not fulfil any essential function and may be an evolutionary leftover. Its position in the abdominal cavity also varies. Removal of the appendix due to appendicitis is one of the most common surgical procedures.

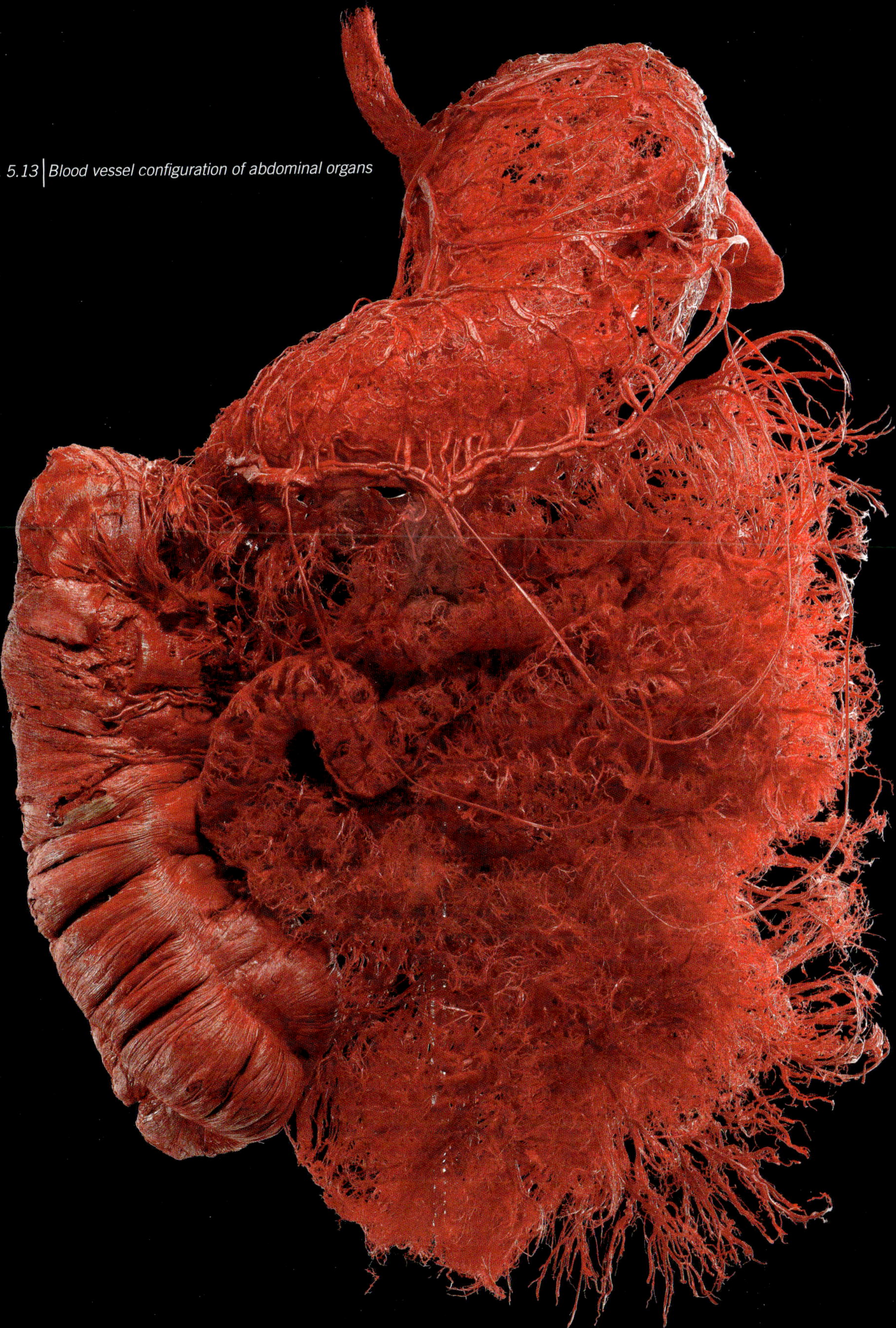

*Fig. 5.13* | *Blood vessel configuration of abdominal organs*

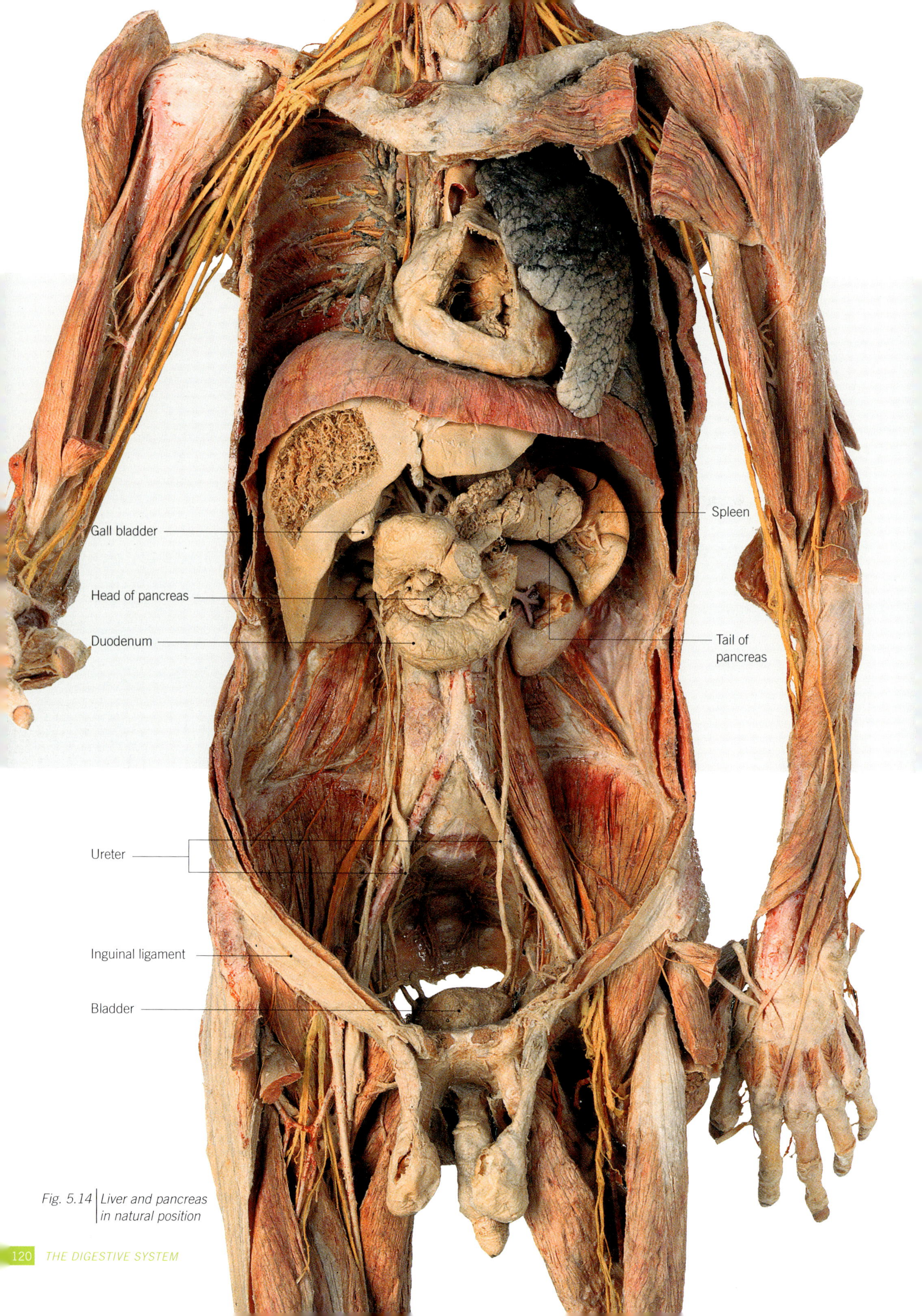


*Fig. 5.14* | *Liver and pancreas in natural position*

# Digestive Juices

### Pancreas

The pancreas produces a powerful juice that breaks down fat, proteins, and carbohydrates. The juice is released into the duodenum in response to the arrival of food in the digestive tract.

The pancreas also secretes two hormones, insulin and glucagon, directly into the bloodstream. These regulate the sugar levels in the blood. If the pancreas does not produce enough insulin, sugar levels in the body rise uncontrollably. This condition is known as diabetes mellitus. It causes damage to the heart and blood vessels.

The pancreas is located across the back of the abdomen, behind the stomach. The right side, called the head, is the widest part of the organ and lies in the curve of the duodenum – the first section of the small intestine. The tapered left side extends slightly upward, called the body of the pancreas, and ends near the spleen, called the tail.

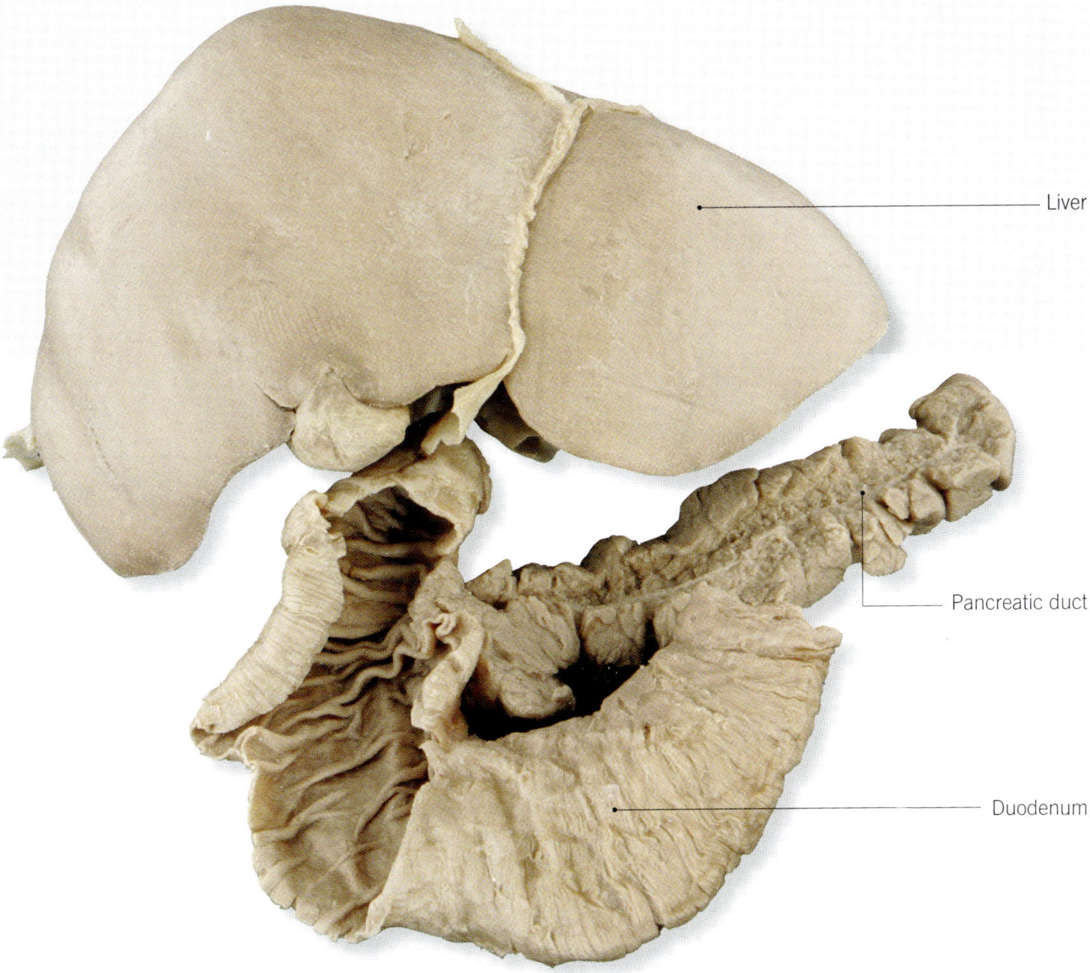


*Fig. 5.15 | Liver, pancreas, and duodenum in their natural relationships*

**The Liver**

The liver is the largest organ in the body.
On average, it weighs approx. 1.5 kilograms (3.3 pounds).
Its key function is to metabolise
carbohydrates, fats (lipids), and proteins.
It also absorbs toxic substances from the blood,
transforming them into harmless waste products.

Every minute, about 1.5 litres (1.6 quarts) of blood
flow through the liver.
Most of it comes from the digestive tract.
The digested nutrients are delivered to the liver
for further processing or storage.

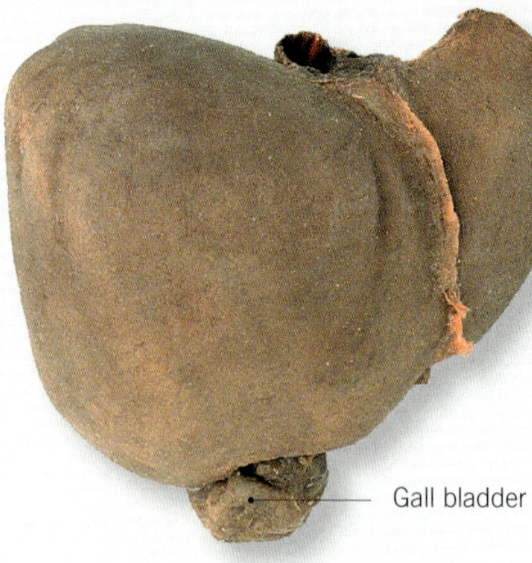


*Fig. 5.16 | Liver of an older person*

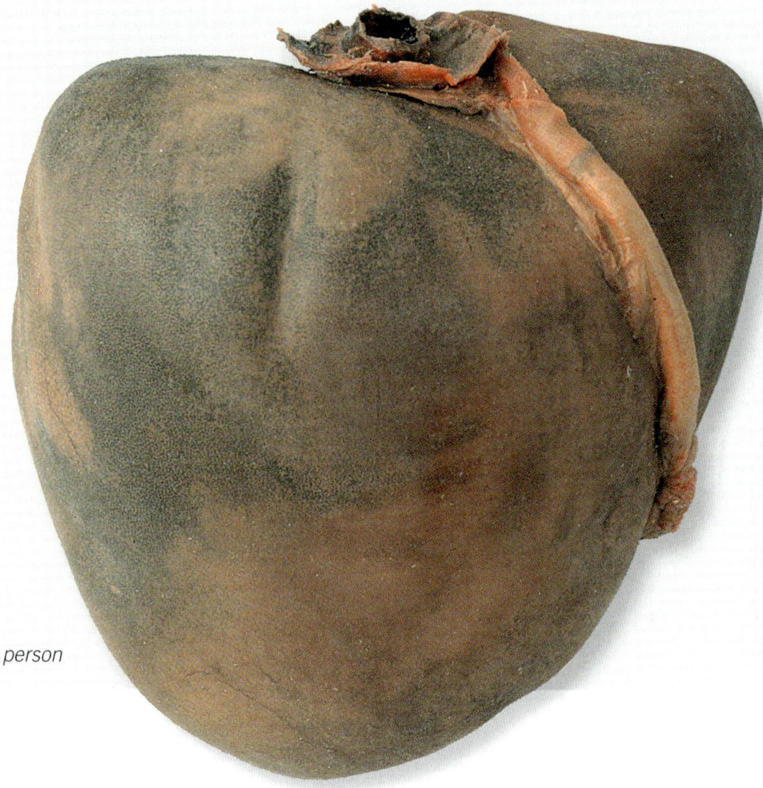

*Fig. 5.17 | Liver of a younger person*

*Fig. 5.18 | Cross-section through the upper abdomen*

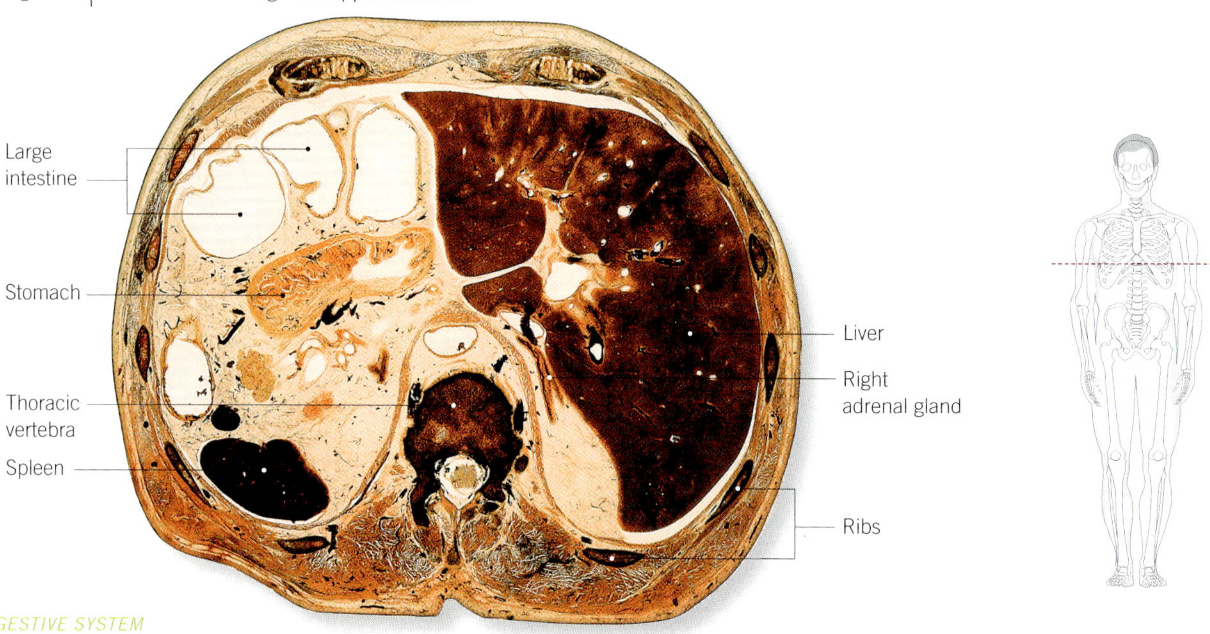

In a body slice taken from the upper abdomen (Fig. 5.18)
one can see that the liver takes up nearly all
of the upper right abdomen.
The dark-reddish colour of the liver and spleen
is due to the rich blood flow through them.
The spleen is much smaller,
and is located in the upper left abdomen.

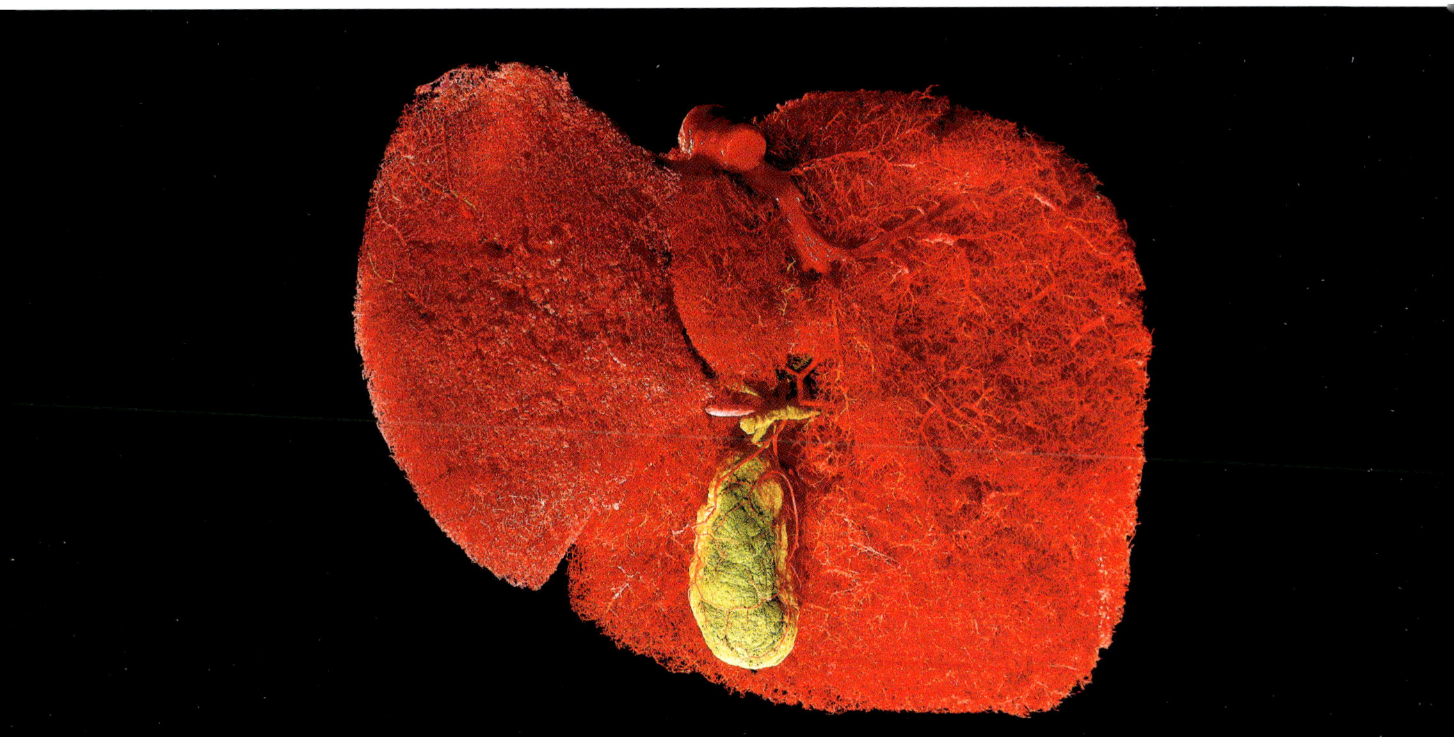

*Fig. 5.19 | Blood vessel configuration of the liver (rear view)*

Liver cells also produce bile –
0.7–1.2 litres (3–5 cups) each day.
The bile is stored in the gall bladder.
If no digestion is taking place,
the bile is stored temporarily,
in thickened form, in the gall bladder (above in yellow).

If it has an unbalanced chemical composition,
bile can harden into gallstones.
Gallstones can be as small as a grain of sand,
or as large as a golf ball.
They cause inflammation and discomfort,
with symptoms similar to indigestion,
especially after a fatty meal.
If a stone becomes lodged in the bile duct,
it will cause severe pain.

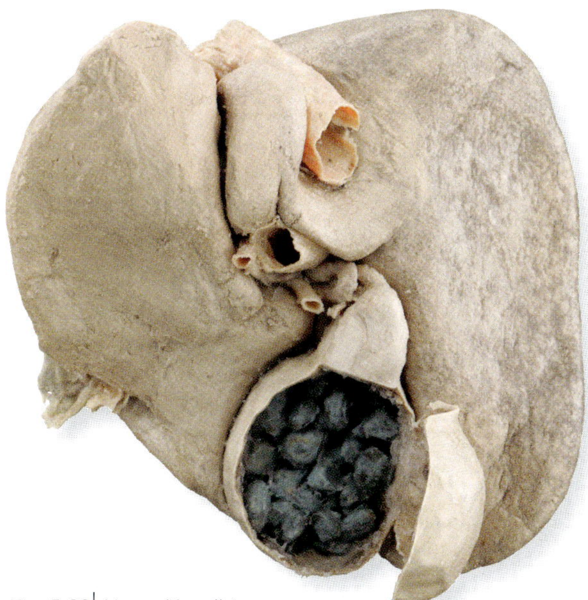

*Fig. 5.20 | Liver with gallstones*

# The Diseased Liver

**Fatty Liver**

The liver also breaks down and detoxifies alcohol. Excessive drinking causes fat to accumulate in liver cells. As a result, the liver enlarges and turns yellowish. But refraining from alcohol abuse, it can recover.

Fatty liver may also be associated with diabetes mellitus, high blood triglycerides, and other metabolic abnormalities. Just consuming a high-fat diet does not result in fatty liver.

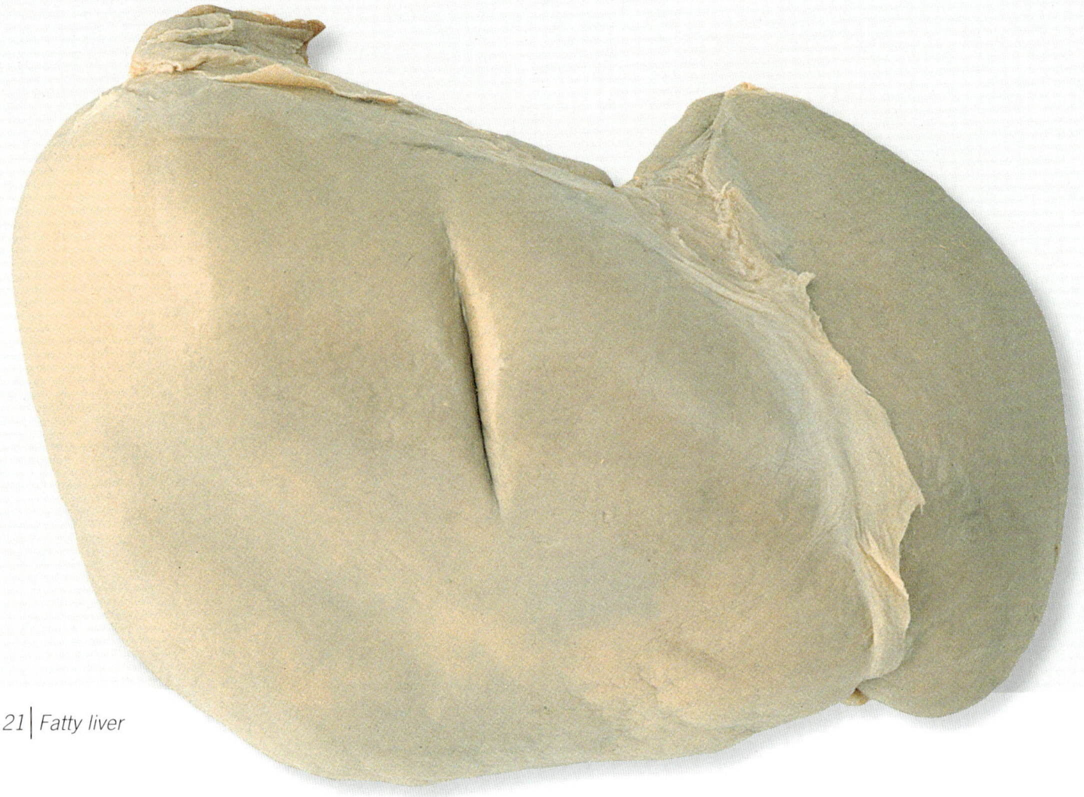

*Fig. 5.21* | *Fatty liver*

**Liver Metastases**

Due to its rich blood supply, the liver is frequently affected by tumour metastases. When a tumour invades the circulatory system, individual cells may break off the main tumour and enter the bloodstream. They may then stick in the capillary network of other organs as if trapped in a filter and grow into new tumours. They mostly appear as light-coloured lumps.

*Fig. 5.22* | *Liver slices with metastases (←)*

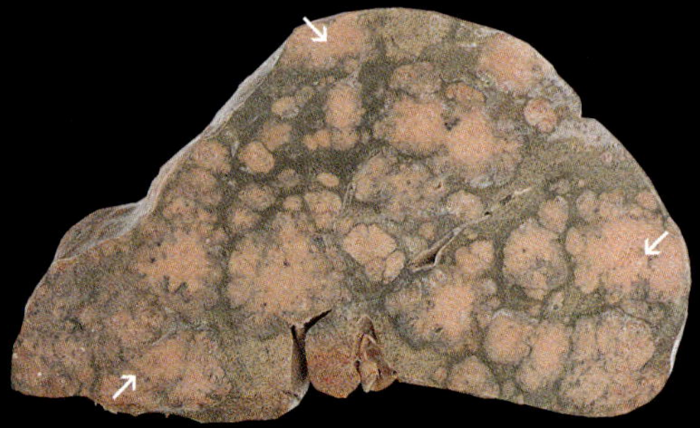

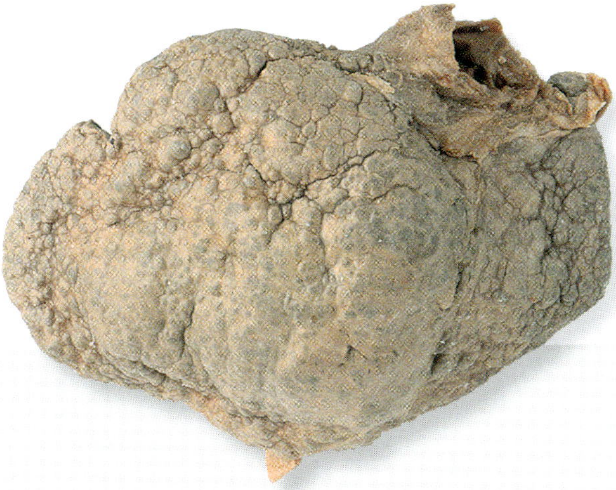

*Fig. 5.23* | *Whole liver and liver slice with cirrhosis*

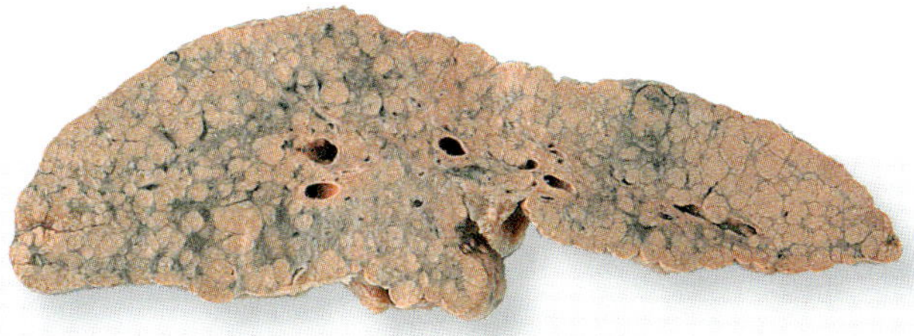

**Shrunken Liver** (Cirrhosis)
Frequent, heavy consumption of alcohol can cause permanent liver damage. Here, connective tissue scars spread like a net through the entire organ and have replaced the dead liver cells. Functioning cells in the shrunken liver form small islands or nodules, visible both on the surface and on a slice of the liver. As the disease becomes more advanced, liver functions become increasingly restricted.

*Fig. 5.24* | *Liver with metastases*

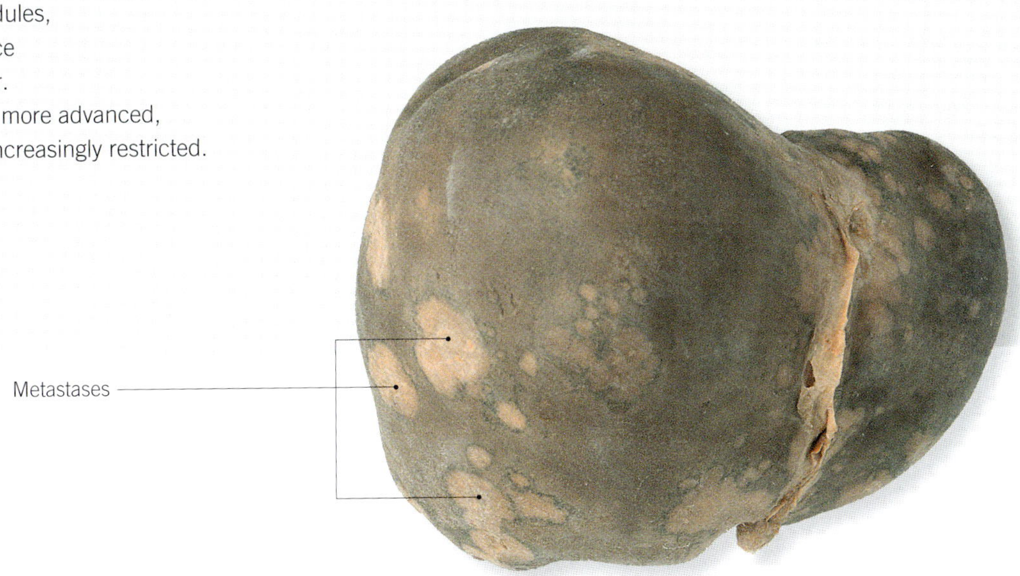


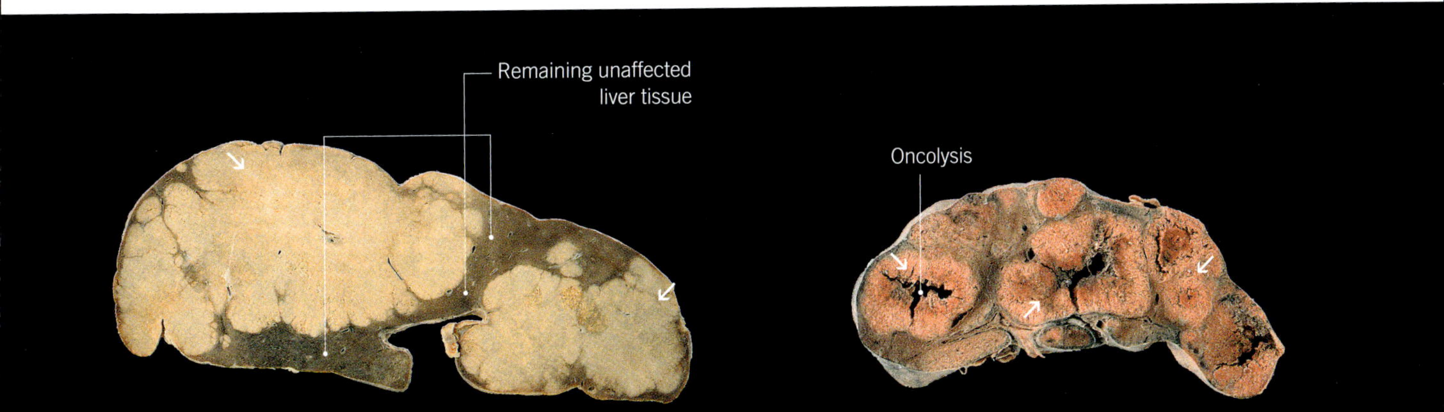

# Obesity Revealed

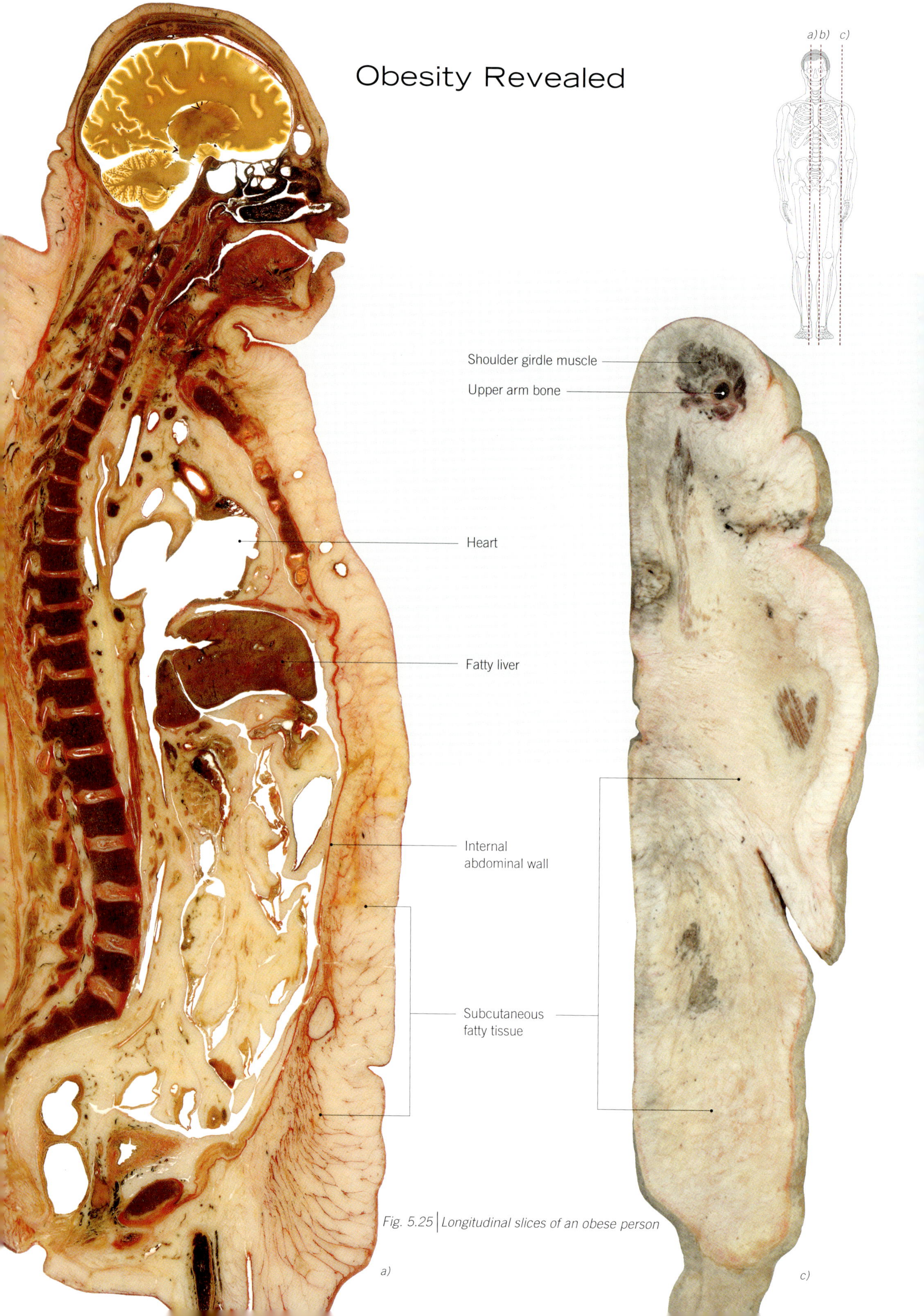


*Fig. 5.25 | Longitudinal slices of an obese person*

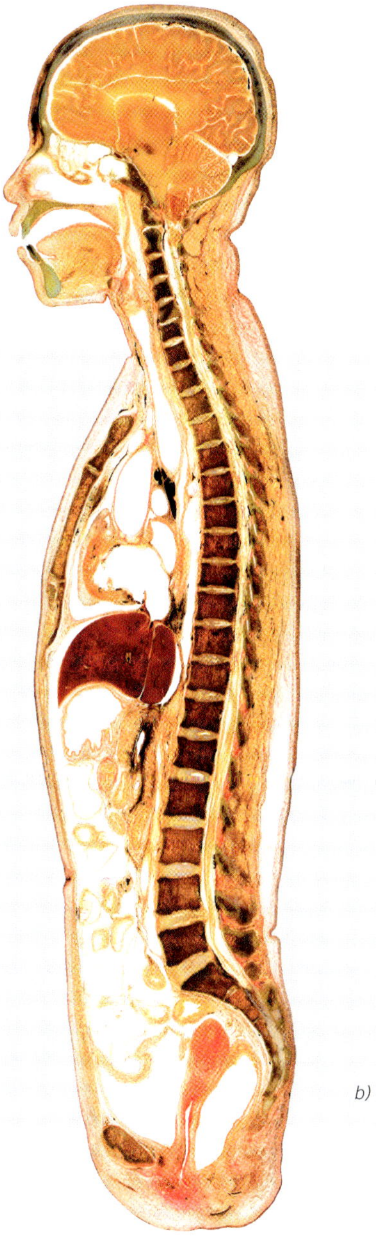

Fig. 5.26 | *Longitudinal slice of a normal person*

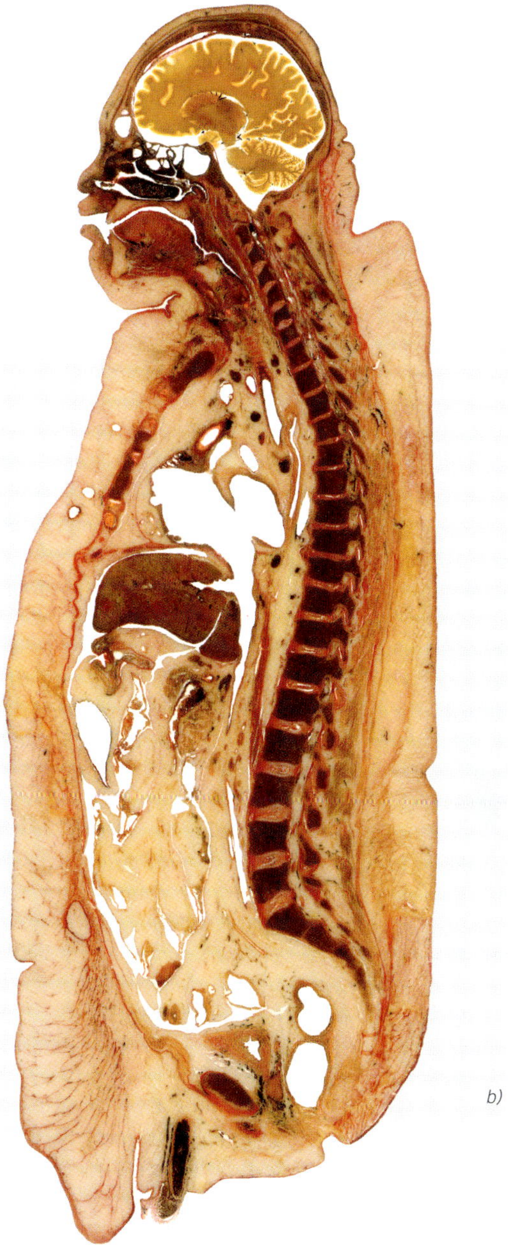

Fig. 5.27 | *Longitudinal slice of an obese person*

The longitudinal body slices in Fig. 5.25 and 5.27 show a severe degree of obesity.
Obesity means having too much body fat.
Here, the subcutaneous fatty tissue is notably thickened.
But also the fat inside the abdominal cavity is considerably increased.
This person's weight was about 136 kilograms (300 pounds).

Obesity occurs over time when we eat more calories than we need.
The balance between calories-in and calories-out differs for each person.
Factors that might tip the balance include the genetic makeup, overeating, eating high-fat foods and not being physically active.

Being obese increases the risk for chronic diseases such as diabetes, high blood pressure, arthritis, stroke, and some forms of cancer.
It especially puts a strain on the heart.
This obese man's heart is enlarged.
He died from a heart malfunction when he was only about 50 years old.

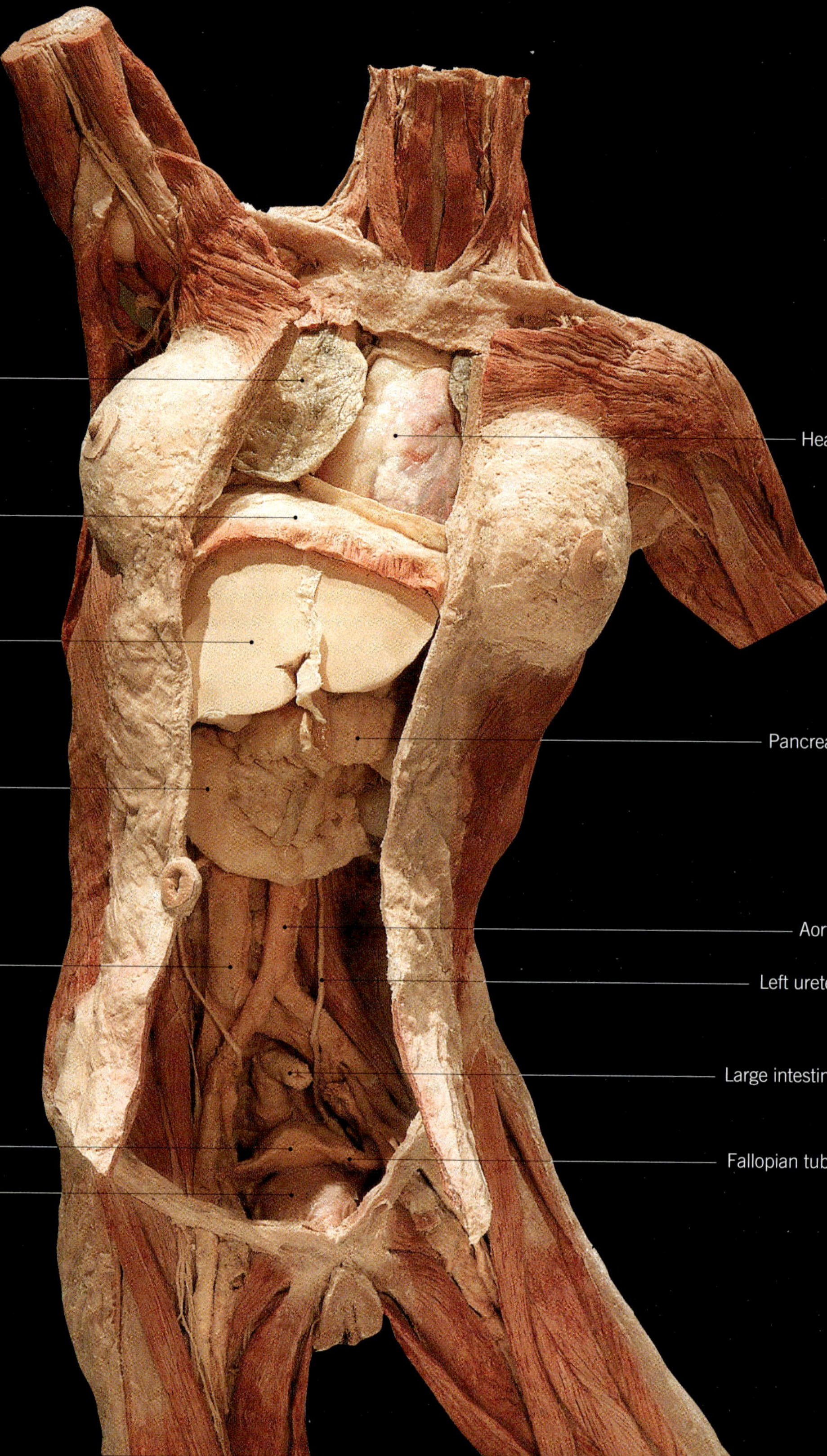


**Female Torso**

This opened torso shows the internal organs of the chest and abdominal cavities in their proper positions. The stomach as well as the large and small intestines have been almost completely removed to permit a view of the organs located between the abdominal cavity and the wall of the back, known as the retroperitoneum. These include the ureters, the aorta and the lower vena cava, as well as the pancreas and the duodenum. In the small pelvic cavity, the bladder can be seen, and behind it, the uterus, which is inclined forward with the Fallopian tubes emerging from the sides. The large intestine extends downward behind the uterus.

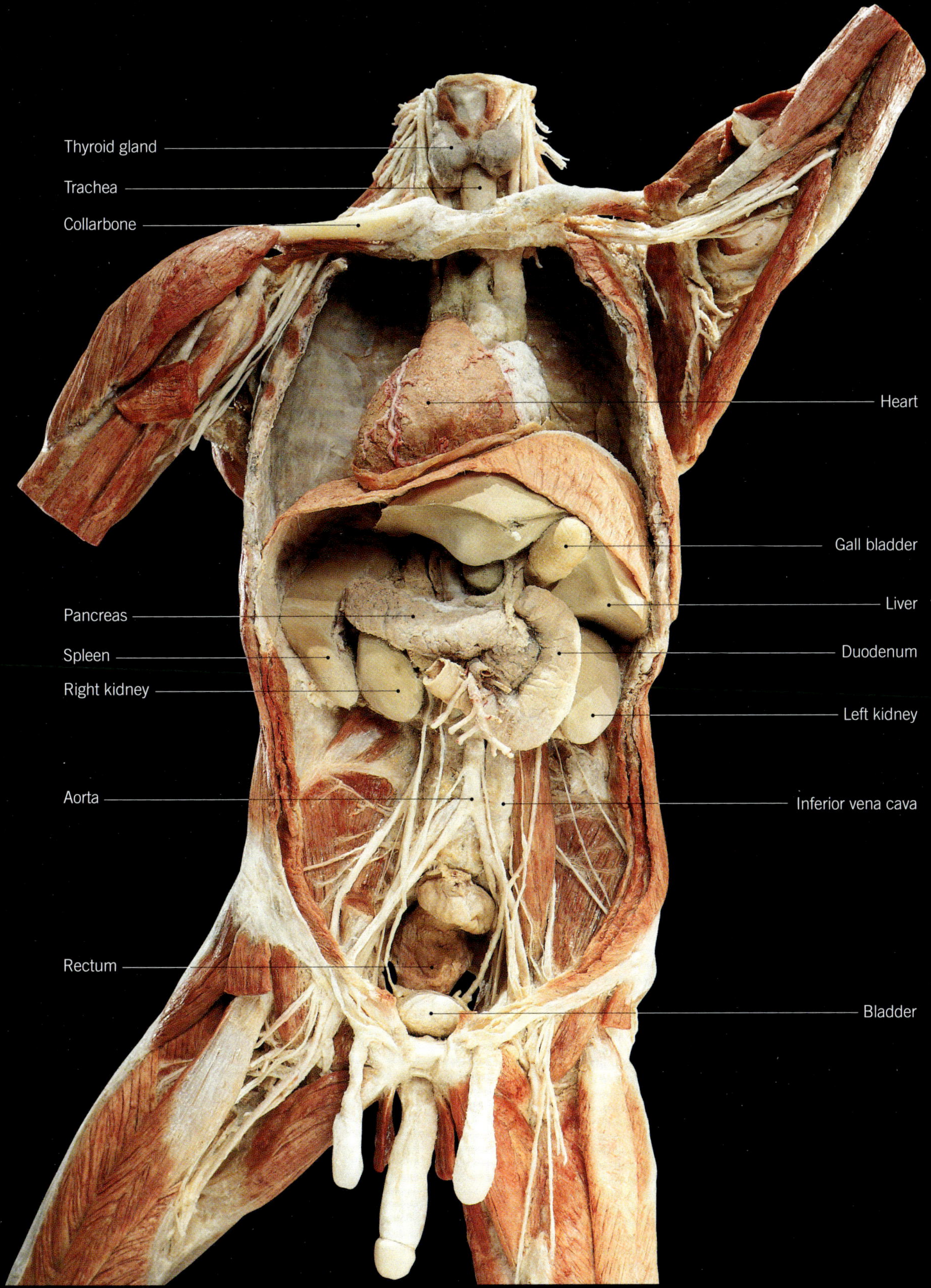


**Male Torso with Situs Inversus**

This torso displays a rare anatomical variation, known as situs inversus. Here the organs of the chest and abdominal cavities are transposed through the sagittal plane, showing a reversed mirror-image: the apex of the heart points to the right instead of the left; the liver is on the left side of the body while the spleen is on the right; and the pancreas extends from left to right across the spinal column instead of vice versa. This anatomical variation does not cause any disorders. The incidence of this phenomenon is about 1 in 25,000. The bladder can be seen in front of the rectum in the small pelvic cavity.

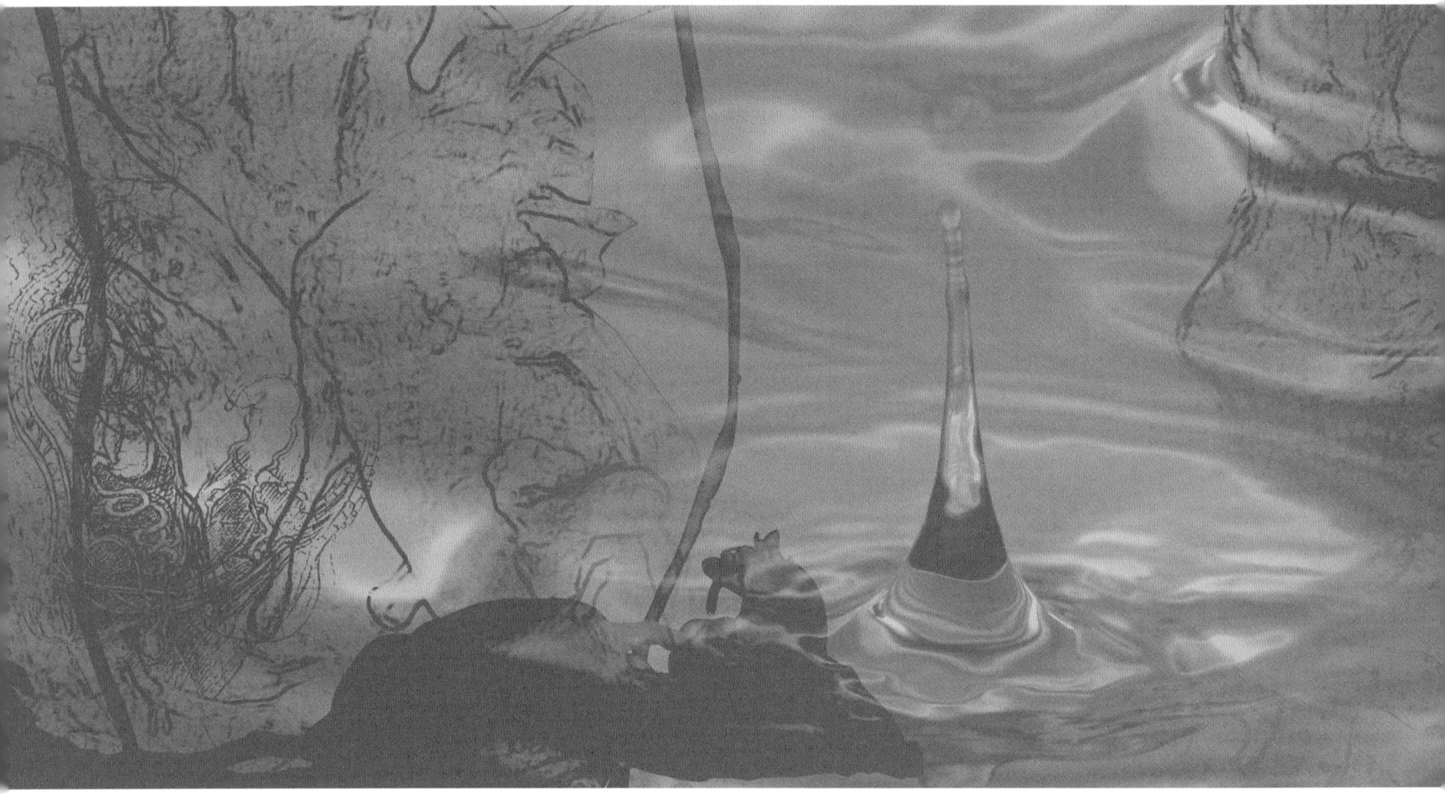

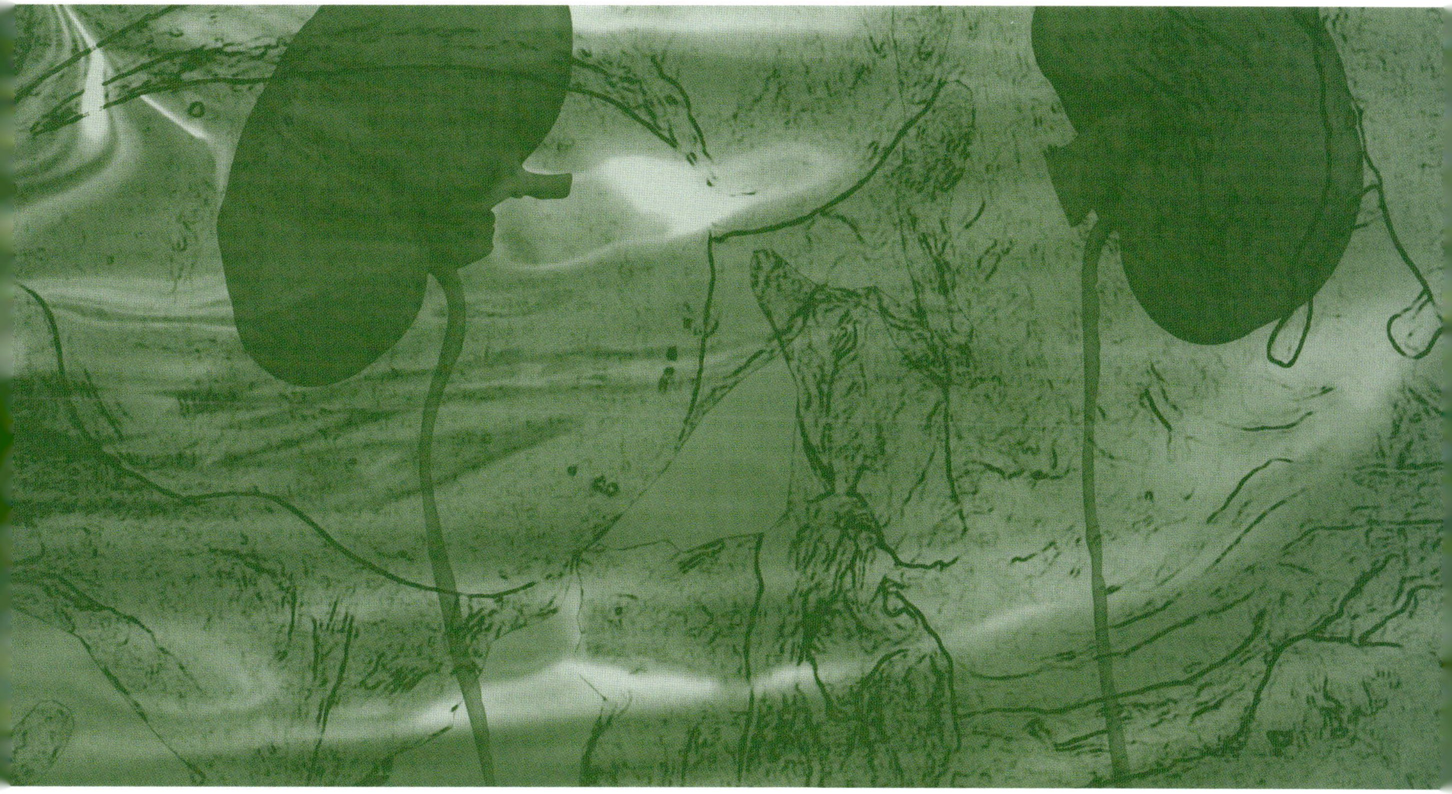

# 6. THE **URINARY** TRACT

Like any organism,
the complex human body also produces waste.
Part of these waste products are discharged through urine.
In addition, the kidneys constantly filter
dissolved waste products and water out of the blood.

# Filtering Waste

**Urinary Tract**

The kidneys filter water-soluble waste products from the blood and expel them in the urine. The urine first collects in the renal pelvis which is a part of the ureter in the kidney. Then the urine flows down the ureters into the bladder, where it is stored. Finally, it leaves the body via the urethra.

The male urethra runs from the bladder, through the prostate gland, to the tip of the penis.

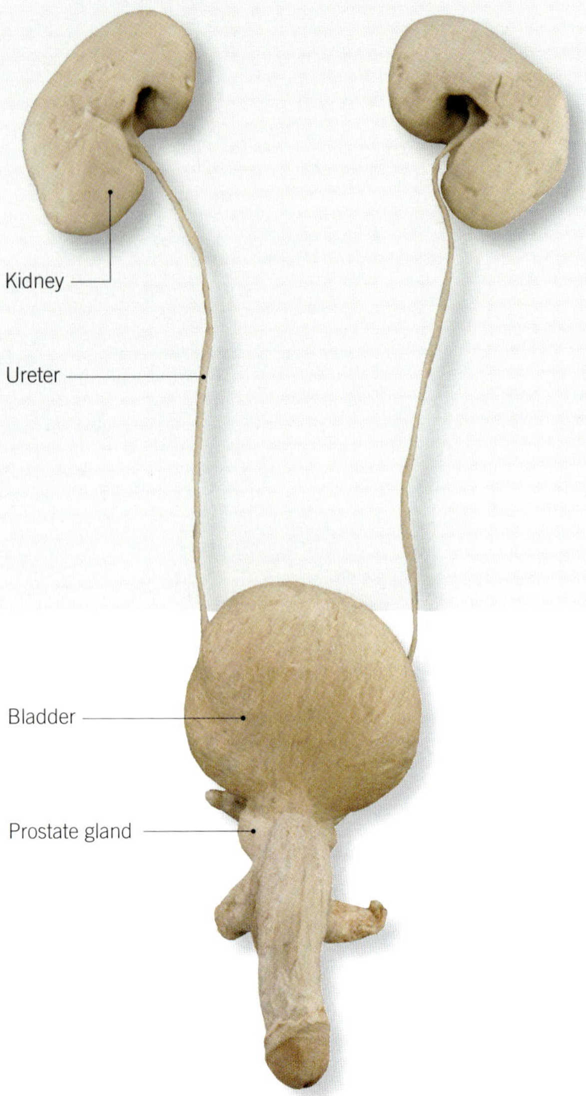


*Fig. 6.1* | *Male urinary tract*

The female urinary tract is in the lesser pelvis near the reproductive organs. The uterus and its adjoining structures are directly behind the bladder. When the bladder fills with urine, the uterus becomes increasingly upright so that it is visible in ultrasound imaging.

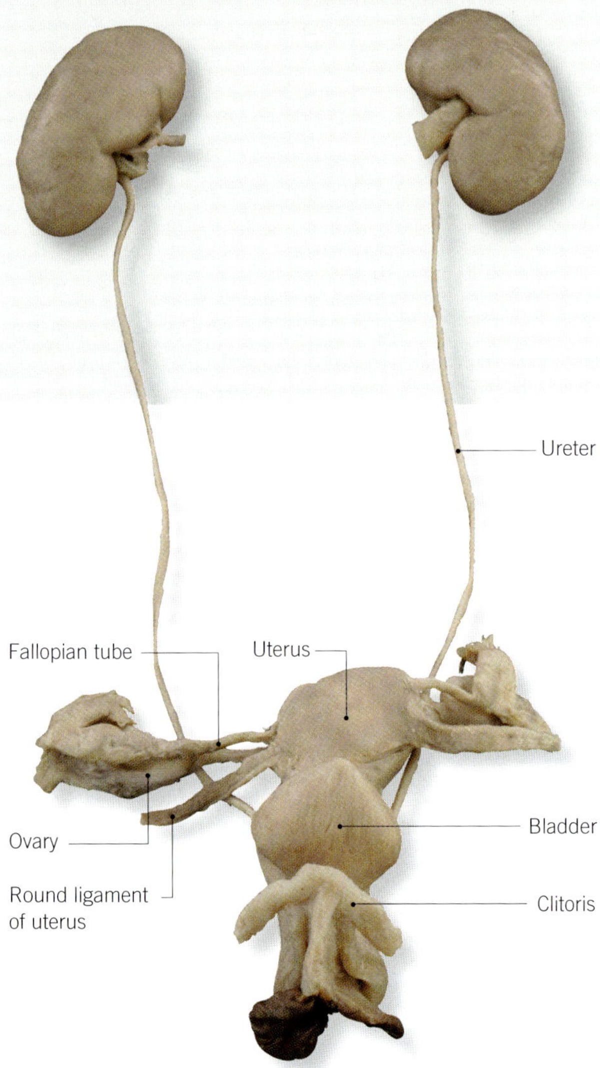


*Fig. 6.2* | *Female urinary tract*

*Fig. 6.3 | Kidney*

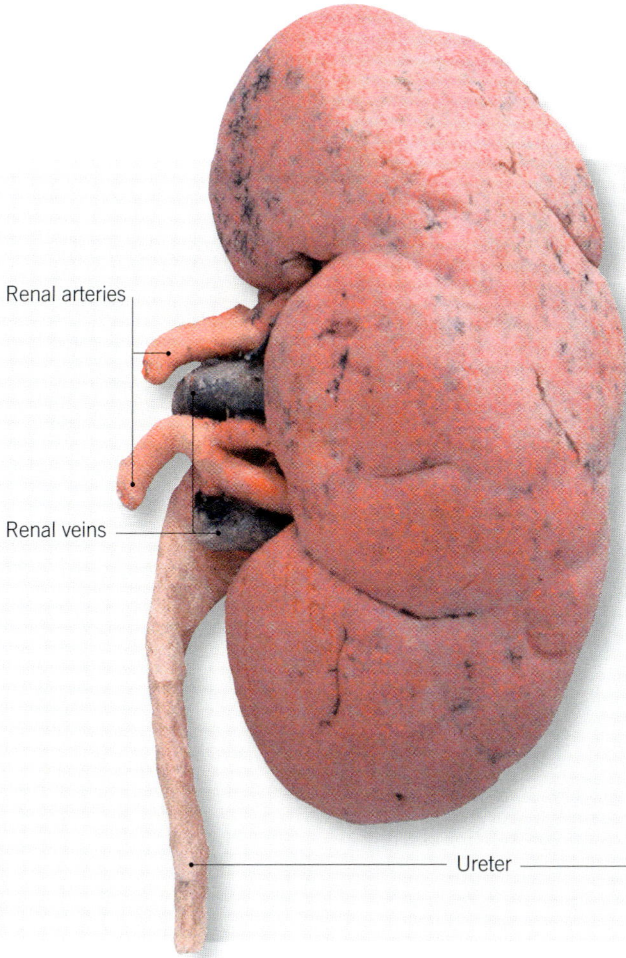


*Fig. 6.4 | Longitudinal section through the kidney*

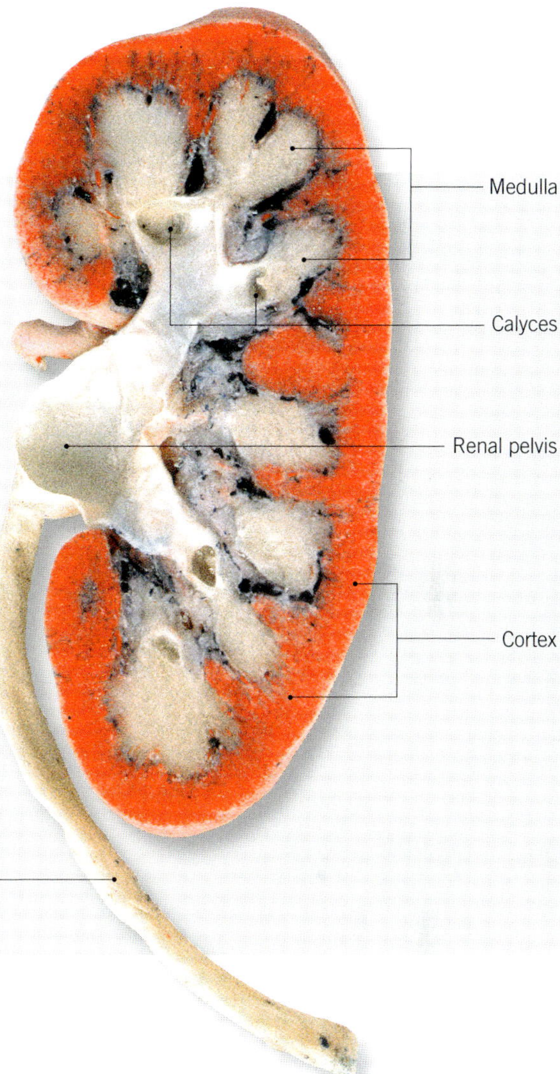


**Kidneys**

The kidneys are two bean-shaped organs,
each weighing 115-200 grams (4–7 ounces).
They are located on either side of the spine.
They are set in the renal bed, the perinephrium,
held in a thick layer of fatty tissue,
and protected by the ribcage.

A section through the kidney exposes the cortex,
where the blood is filtered,
and the inner medulla,
the white, cone-shaped blocks of tissue,
where the urine is concentrated.
The medulla's fine collection structures
open into cup-like calyces.
From there, the urine empties into the renal pelvis.

The body's entire volume of blood
flows through the kidneys
around 15 times each hour.
The blood is filtered by the renal corpuscles
and their fine clusters
of blood vessels (glomeruli).

Kidneys play a major role
in the regulation of blood pressure
by keeping the body fluids balanced.
Extra fluid in the body
increases the amount of fluid
in the blood vessels
and raises the blood pressure.

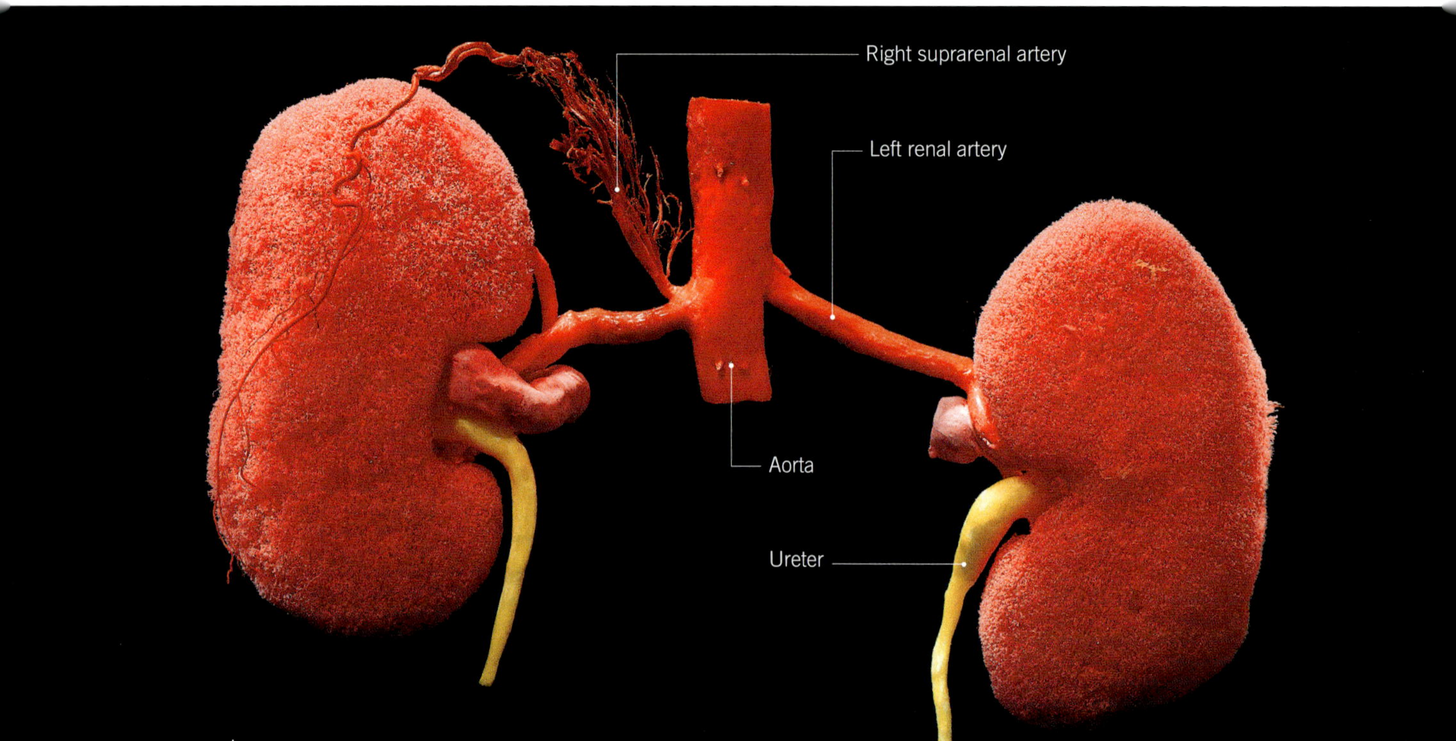


*Fig. 6.5* | *Blood vessel configuration of the kidneys.*

**Adrenal Glands**
Kidneys have a triangular-shaped gland on top.
These are the adrenal glands.
They are supplied with blood via the suprarenal artery.
The adrenal glands are part of the endocrine system.
They influence energy use and stress response
through the synthesis of hormones,
including cortisol and adrenaline.
In stressful situations,
the released adrenaline speeds our heartbeat,
thereby increasing circulation,
and recirculates stored glucose,
which provides a sudden burst
of energy and strength.

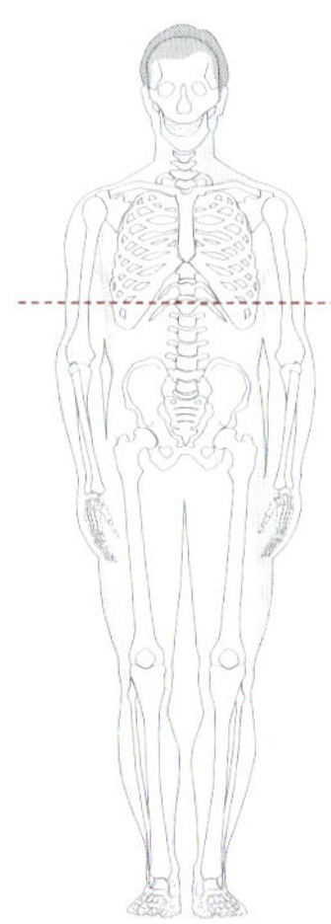

Fig. 6.6 | Cross-section of kidney, detail

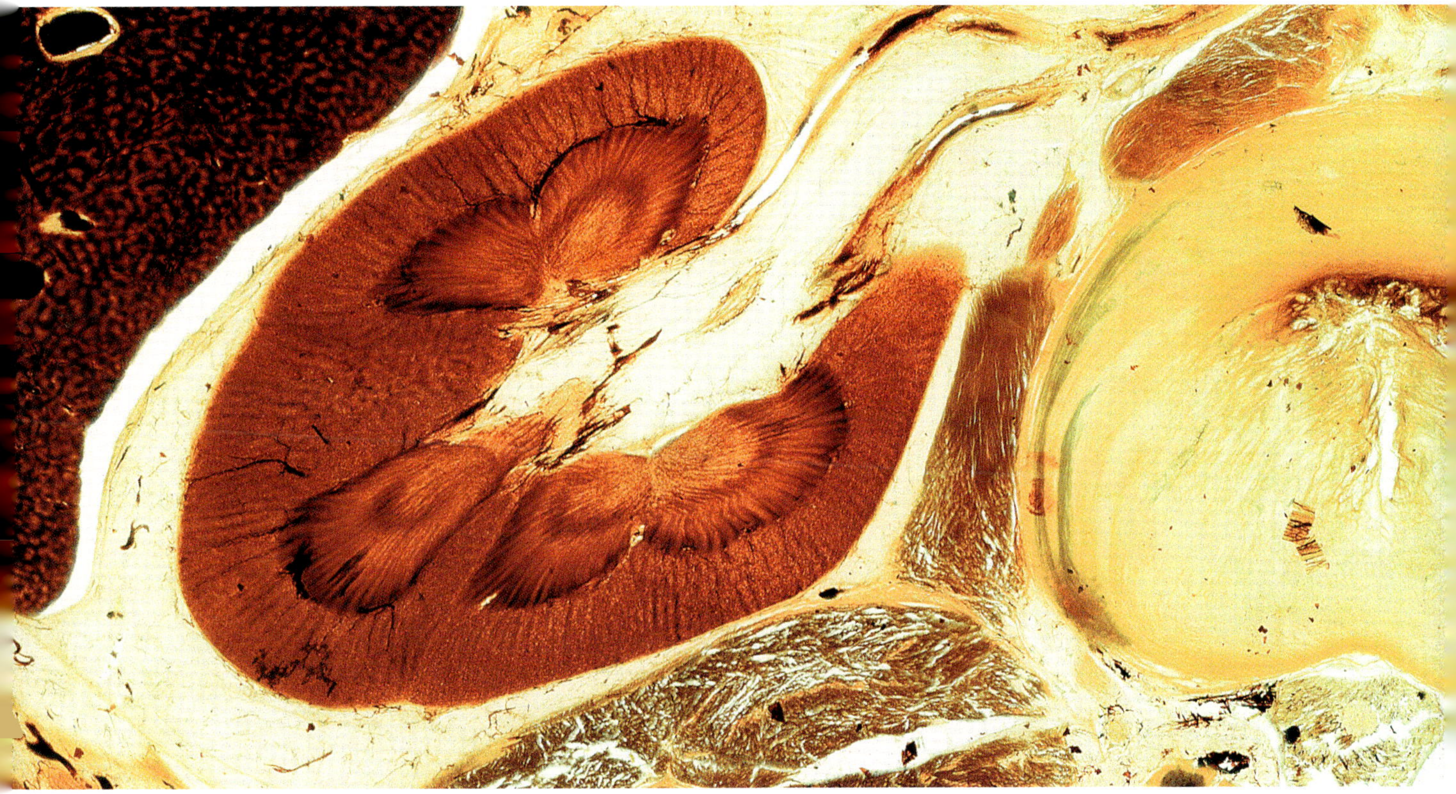

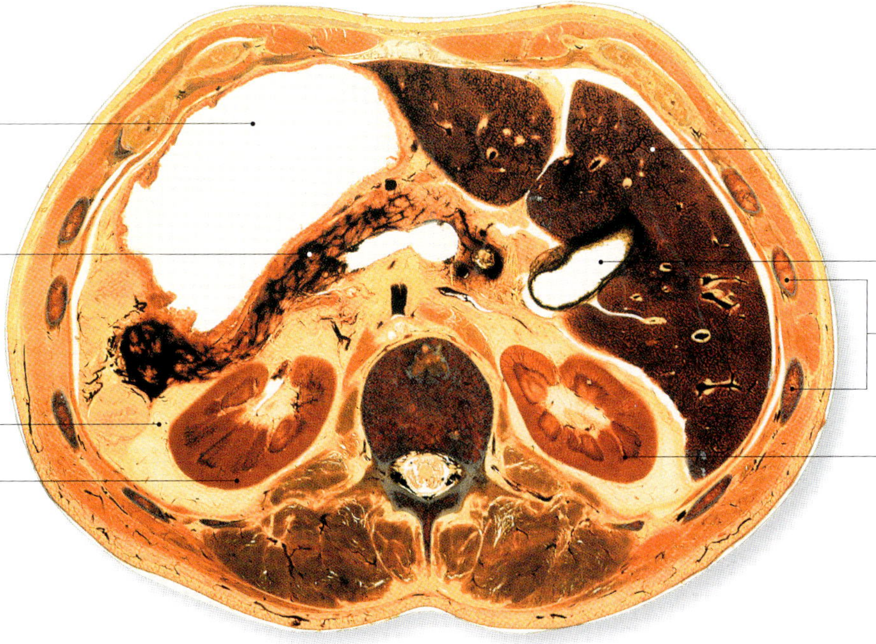


Fig. 6.7 | Cross-section through the upper abdomen

# The Diseased Kidney

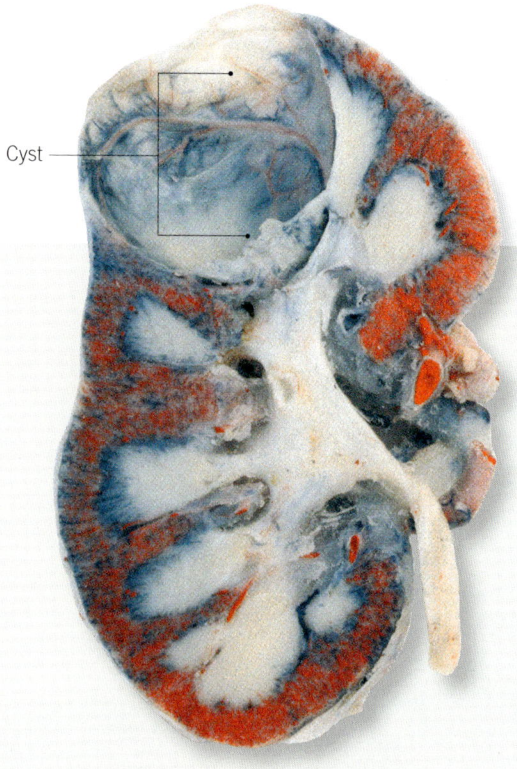


Fig. 6.8 | *Kidney with single cyst*

**Kidney Cysts**
Around one in ten people have kidney cysts, fluid-filled, sac-like cavities.
Generally they do not cause any problems and are often only detected by chance, e.g., during ultrasound of the abdomen.

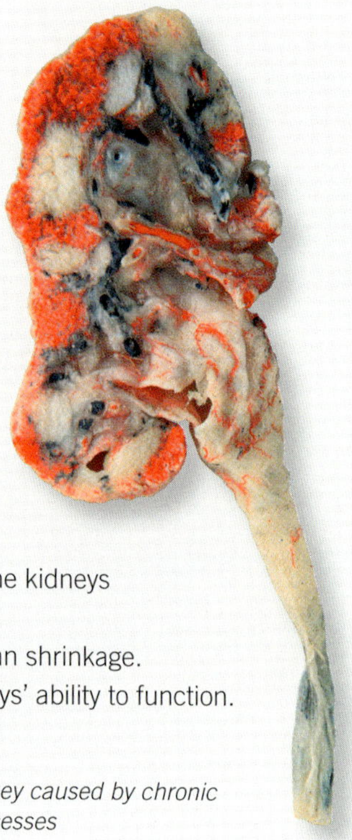

**Shrunken Kidney**
Chronic infections in the kidneys destroy kidney tissue, causing scars and organ shrinkage.
This restricts the kidneys' ability to function.

*Fig. 6.9* | *Shrunken kidney caused by chronic infectious processes*

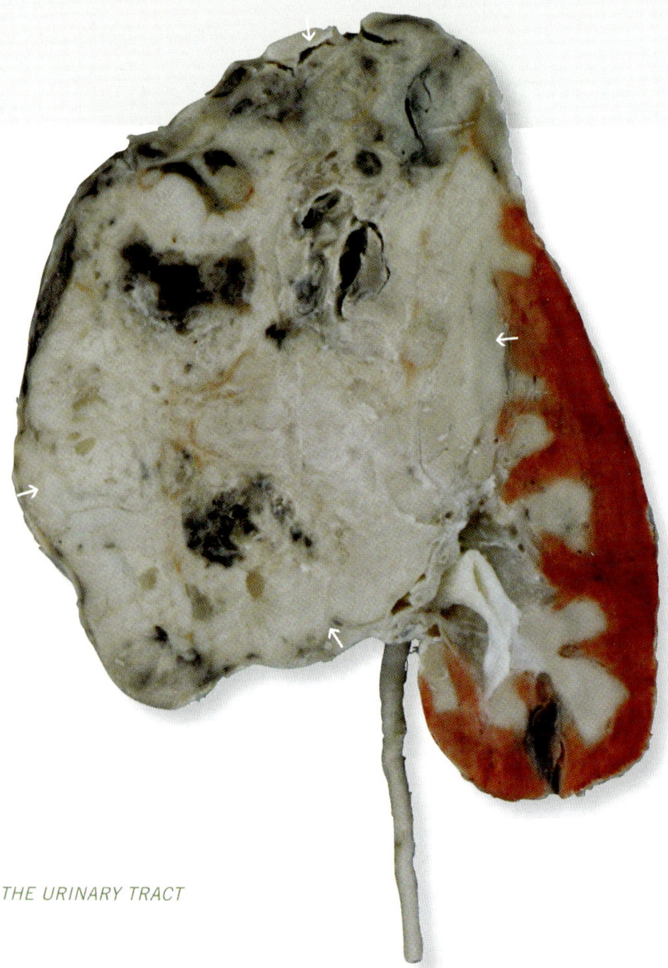

**Kidney Cancer** (Hypernephroma)
In adults, the most common type of kidney cancer is renal cell carcinoma, which begins in the cells that line the small tubes within our kidneys.
If the tumour invades the renal pelvis, blood will be visible in the urine.

*Fig. 6.10* | *Kidney with tumour*

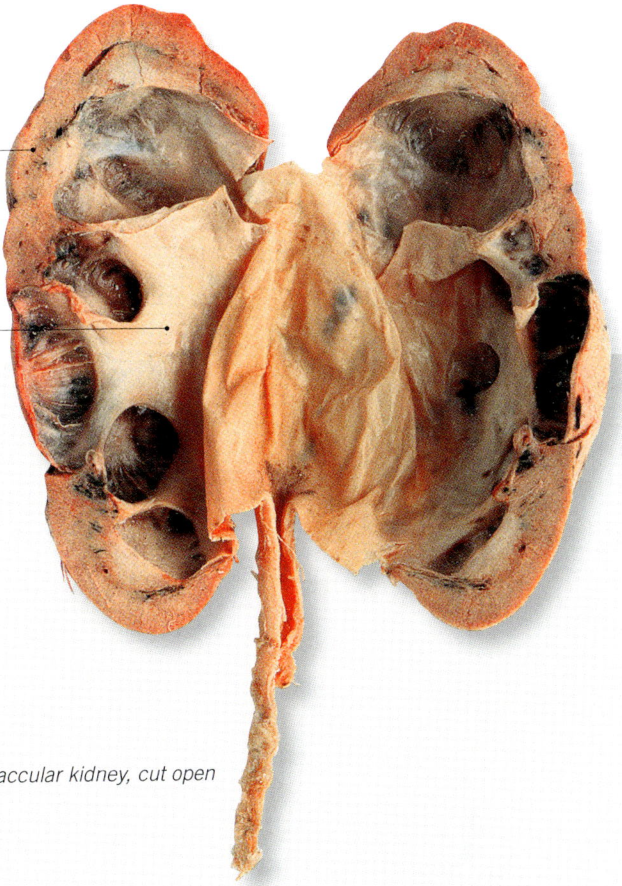


**Saccular Kidney** (Hydronephrosis)
The internal diameter of ureters is less than 3 millimetres (0.1 inch). Therefore they can easily be blocked, for example by a kidney stone or by external compression, such as a tumour. As urine is constantly being produced, such blockage causes it to back up in the renal pelvis, which in turn makes it distend and stretch the kidney tissue.

*Fig. 6.11 | Saccular kidney, cut open*

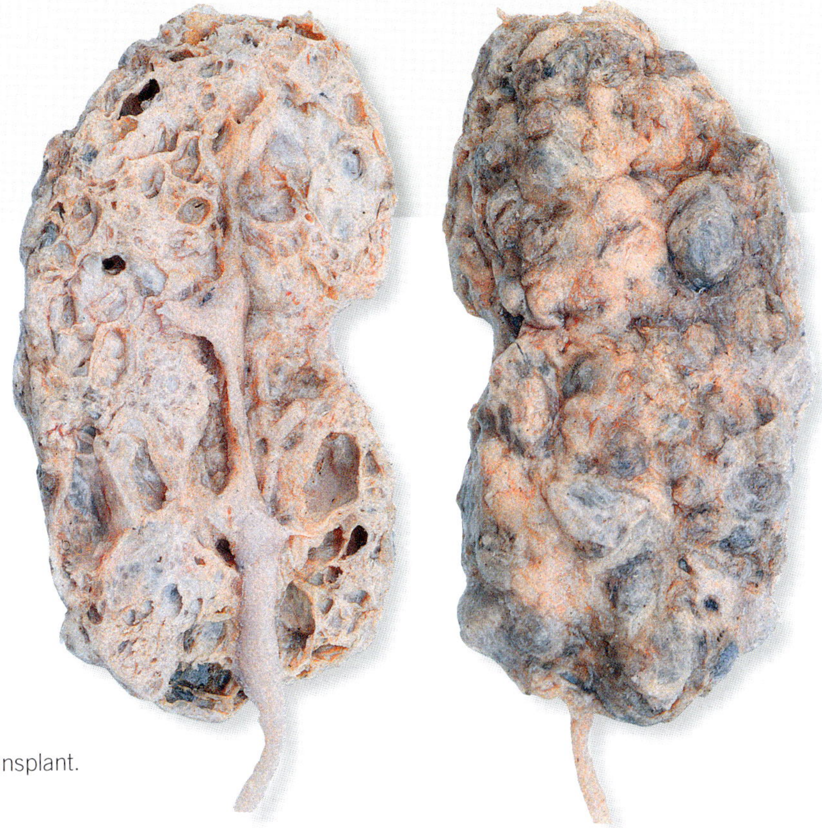

**Polycystic Kidney** (Cut open)
In this congenital kidney deformation, the entire organ is infiltrated with cysts, small, fluid-filled cavities. This disorder causes severe dysfunction and requires haemodialysis or a kidney transplant.

*Fig. 6.12 | Polycystic kidney, a) longitudinal section* *b) surface*

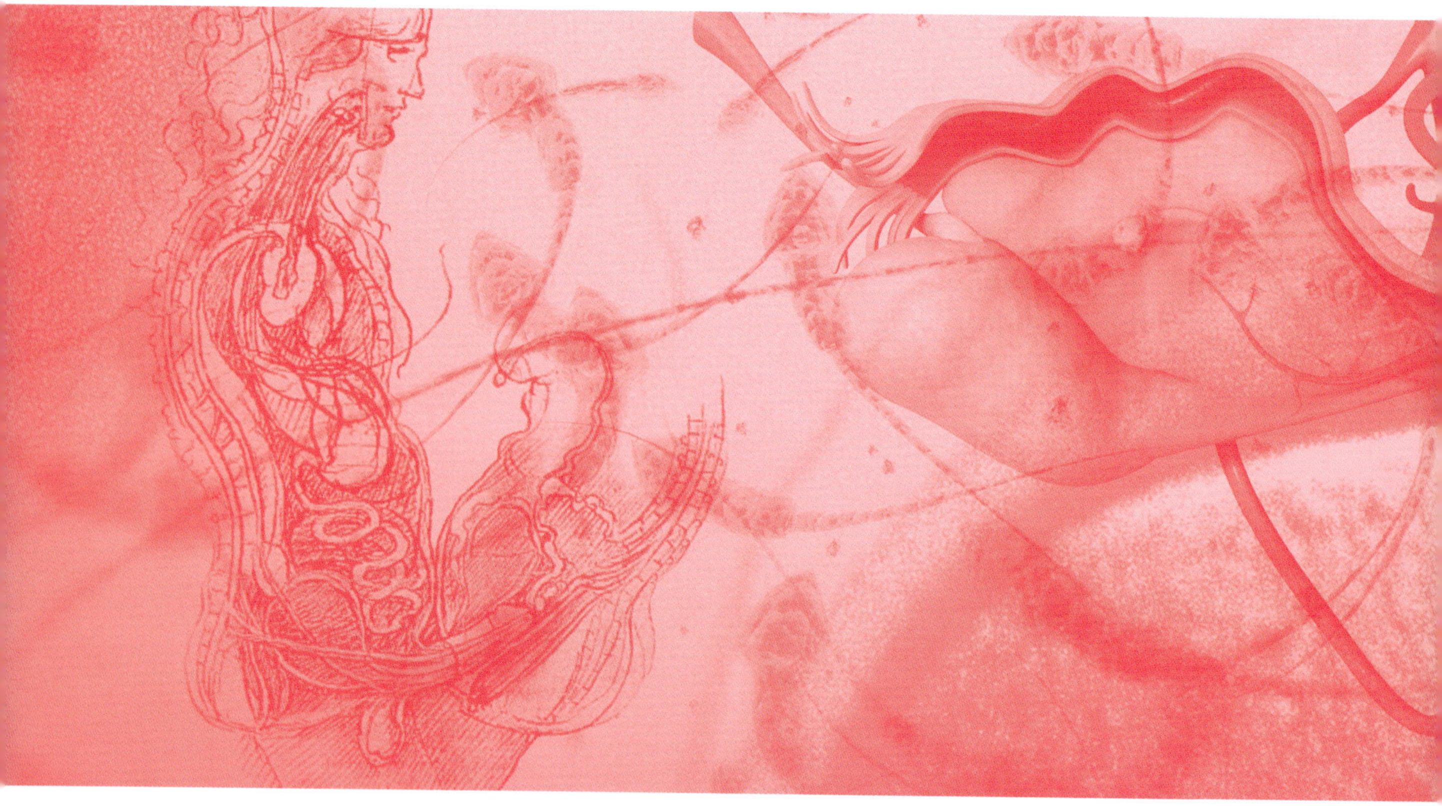

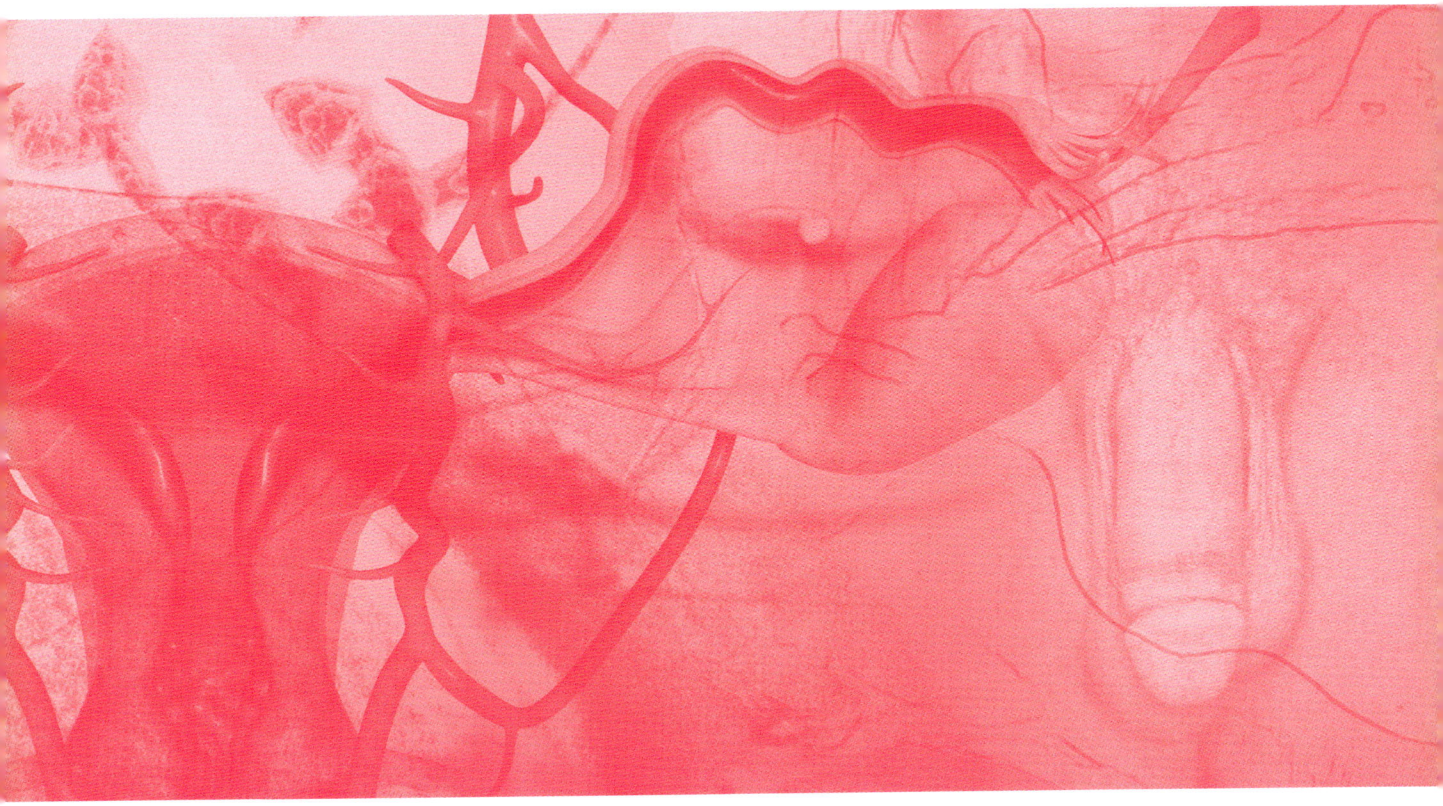

# 7. THE **REPRODUCTIVE** ORGANS

The external male and female genitals
mark the end of the urinary system.
The invisible internal genitals
are the true reproductive organs,
where eggs and sperm are produced.
Reproduction is an essential aspect of life.
New life is created when a male sperm
fertilises a female egg.

# Male Reproduction

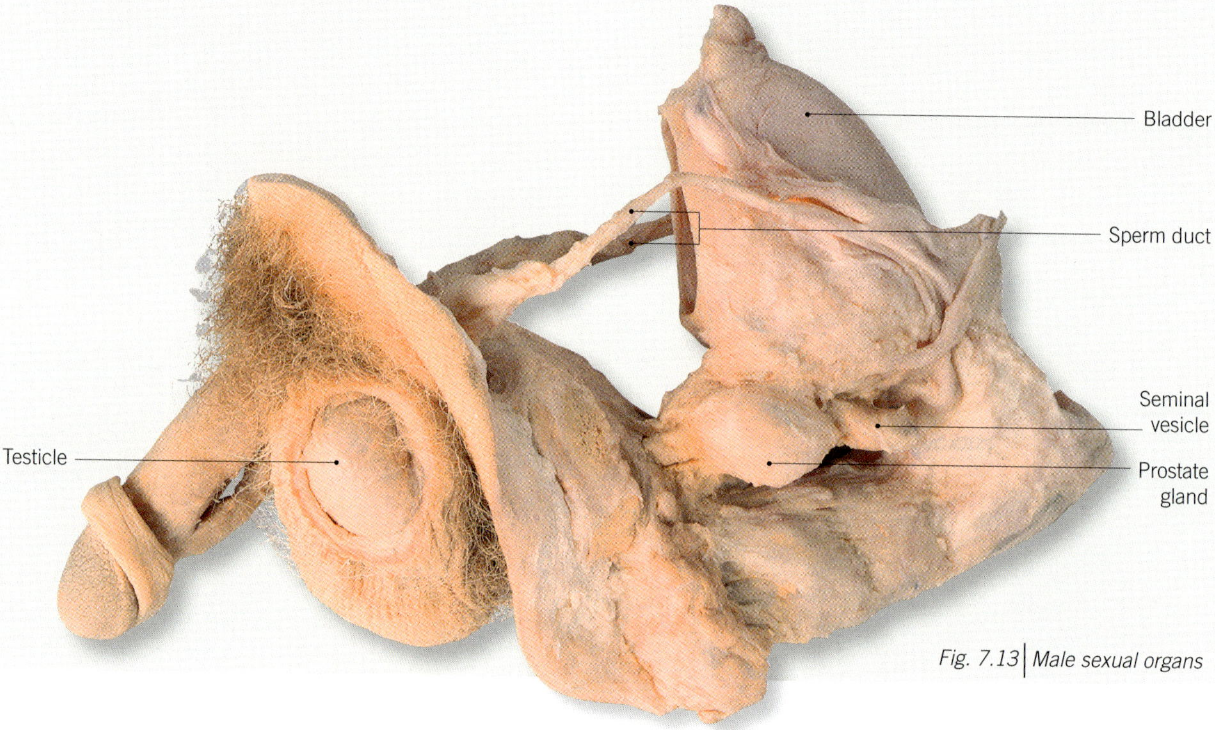


*Fig. 7.13 | Male sexual organs*

**Male Reproductive Organs**

The penis and the scrotum
are the visible male reproductive organs.
The scrotum contains two egg-shaped testes
and the epididymides, tubes to transport sperm.
Male reproductive organs also include
the seminal vesicles in the body,
the prostate gland, and the sperm duct,
as well as other connecting tubes.
The cascade of hormones in sexual arousal
is controlled by the hypothalamus,
located in the centre of the brain.

**Testes**
The testes are roughly the size of walnuts.
In their thousands of finely coiled tubes,
the seminiferous tubules,
about 300 million sperm mature every day.
Sperm are stored in the epididymides –
tubes that envelope the testes like a hood.

During orgasm, rhythmic contractions
pump the sperm through the vas deferens.
Where the vas deferens joins the urethra,
the fluids from the prostate gland
and the seminal vesicles mix with the sperm.
Rhythmic contractions of the urethral muscles
ejaculate the sperm.

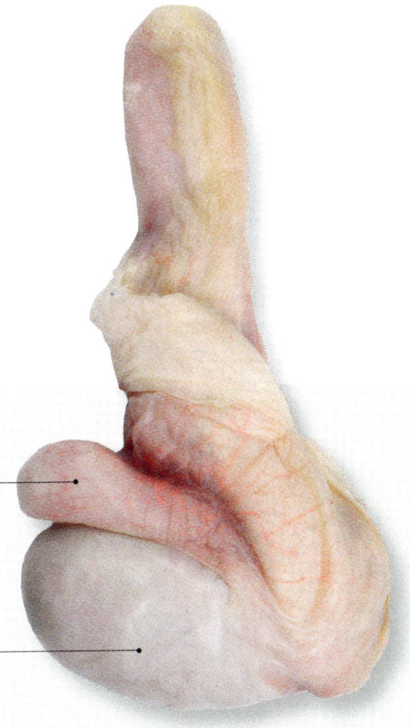


*Fig. 7.14 | Testicle with epididymis*

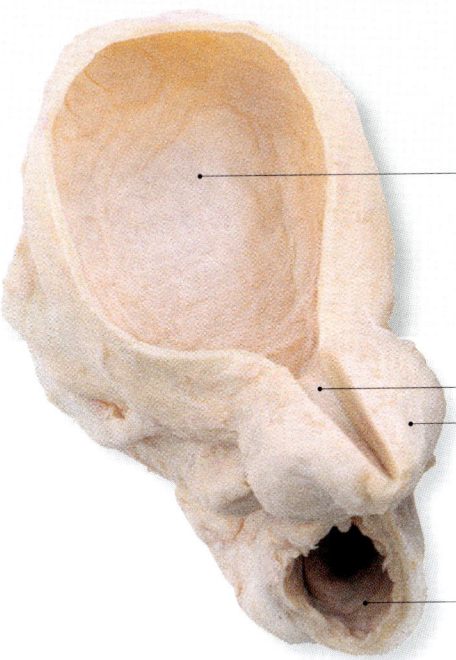


*Fig. 7.15 | Bladder with prostate gland*

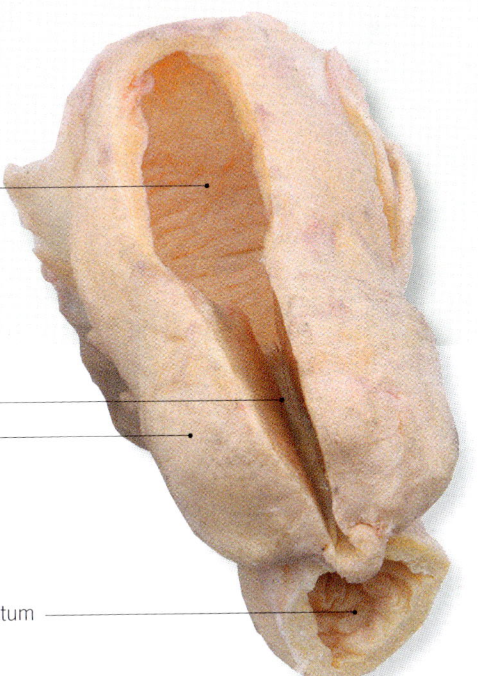

*Fig. 7.16 | Bladder with severely distended prostate gland*

**Prostate Gland**
The prostate is directly below the bladder
and surrounds the urethra.
At ejaculation, the prostate's secretions
are mixed with semen
to facilitate the movement of the sperm.

**Prostate Gland Enlargement**
With advancing age,
the prostate gland tends to distend,
narrowing the urethra
and partially blocking the urine flow.
This condition is also known as benign prostatic
hyperplasia.

# Female Reproduction

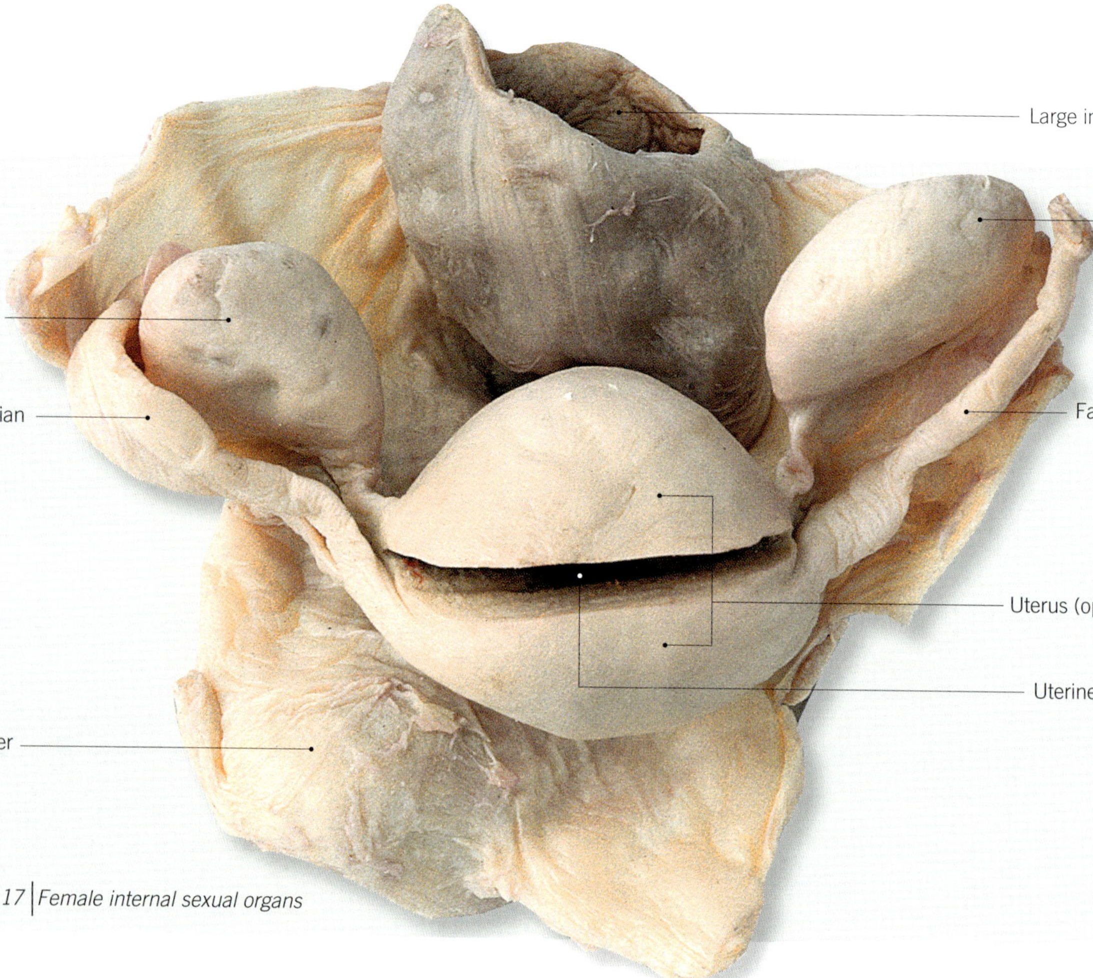


*Fig. 7.17 | Female internal sexual organs*

**Female Reproductive Organs**

The female reproductive organs
are largely within the body:
the two ovaries and Fallopian tubes,
the uterus, and the vagina.
The released eggs from the ovaries
pass down the Fallopian tubes into the uterus
where the fertilised egg can develop.

The external female genitals
are collectively referred to as the vulva.
The labia minora are the inner lips of the vulva.
They consist of thin stretches of tissue
within the labia majora that fold and protect
the vagina, urethra, and clitoris.
The opening to the urethra
is just below the clitoris.
It is not related to sex or reproduction
but is instead the passage for urine.

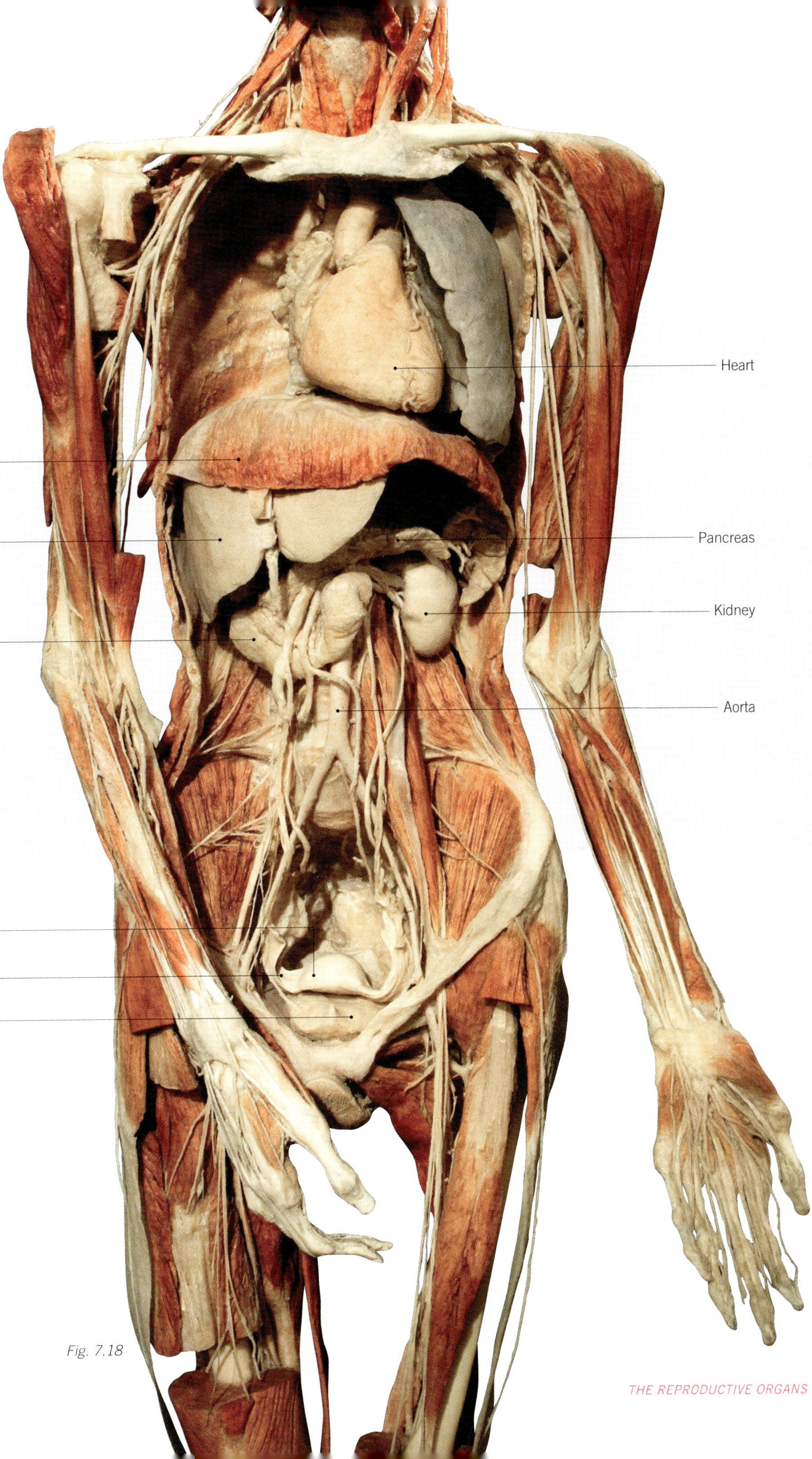
Heart
Diaphragm
Liver
Pancreas
Kidney
Duodenum
Aorta
Uterus
Fallopian tube
Bladder

*Fig. 7.18*

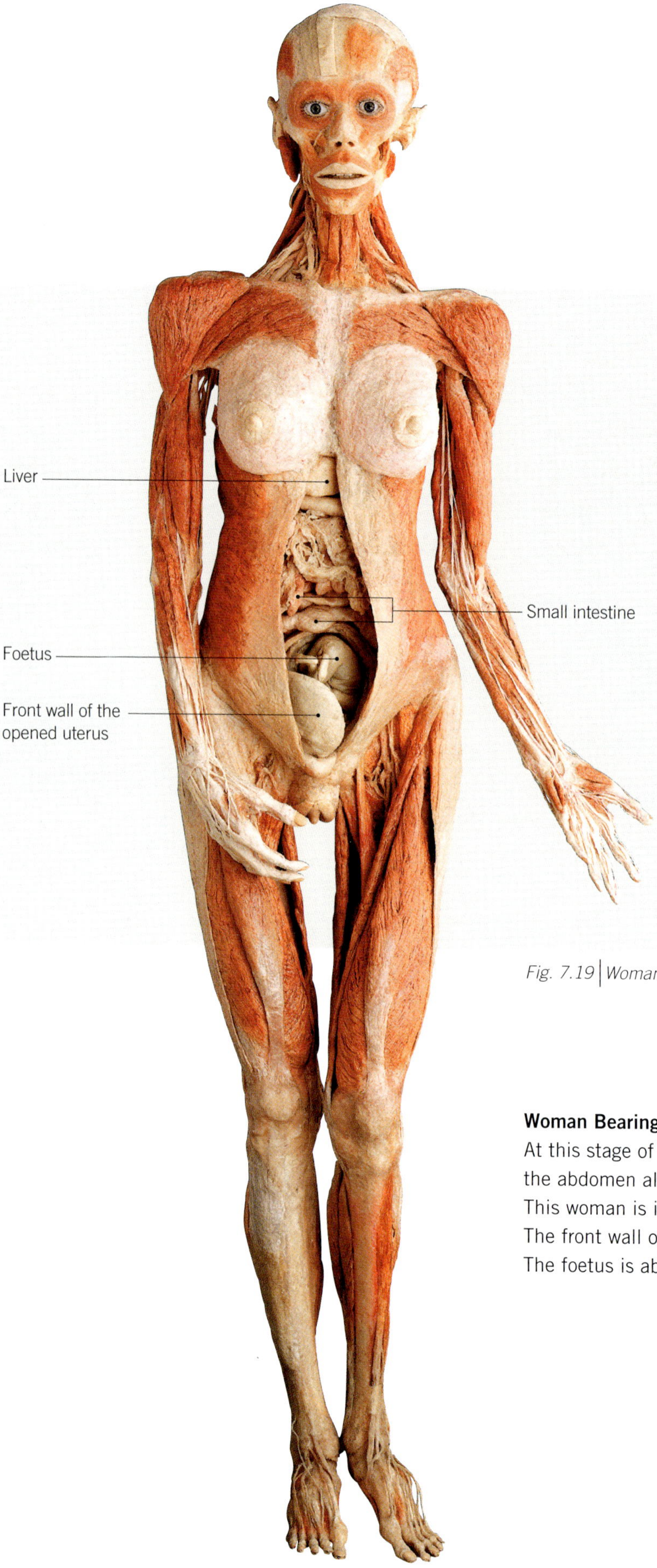


*Fig. 7.19 | Woman Bearing Life*

**Woman Bearing Life**
At this stage of pregnancy,
the abdomen already starts to bulge.
This woman is in the fifth month.
The front wall of the uterus has been opened.
The foetus is about 17 centimetres long (7 inches).

**Myomas**
Myomas are uterine fibroid tumours.
Since the wall of the uterus is muscle,
myomas are also made of muscle tissue.
Here, the uterine walls are covered
with numerous myomas.
Myomas are benign.

However, they can cause discomfort,
menstrual disorders,
or complications during pregnancy.

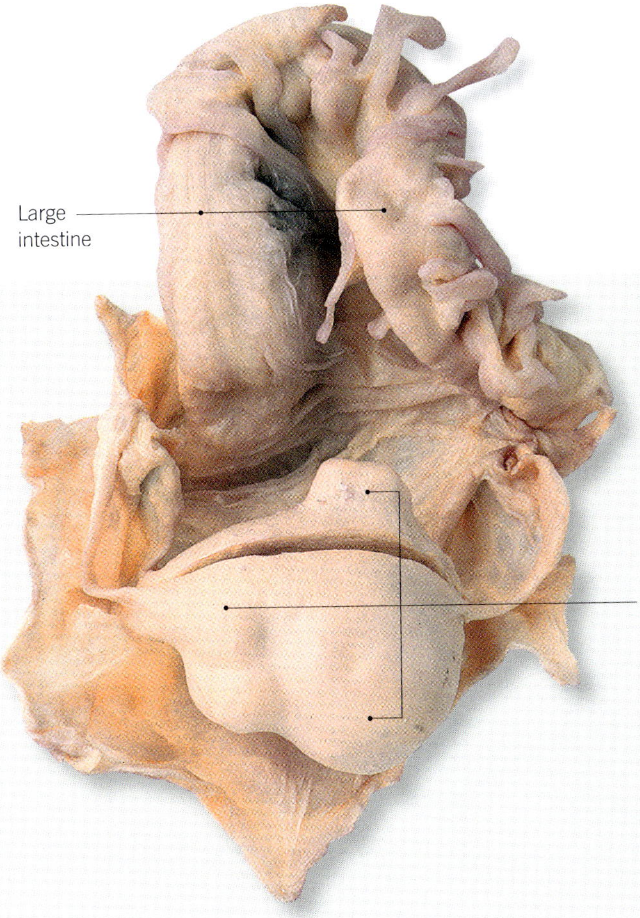


*Fig. 7.20* | *Myomas (benign tumours made of muscle fibres) on the uterus*

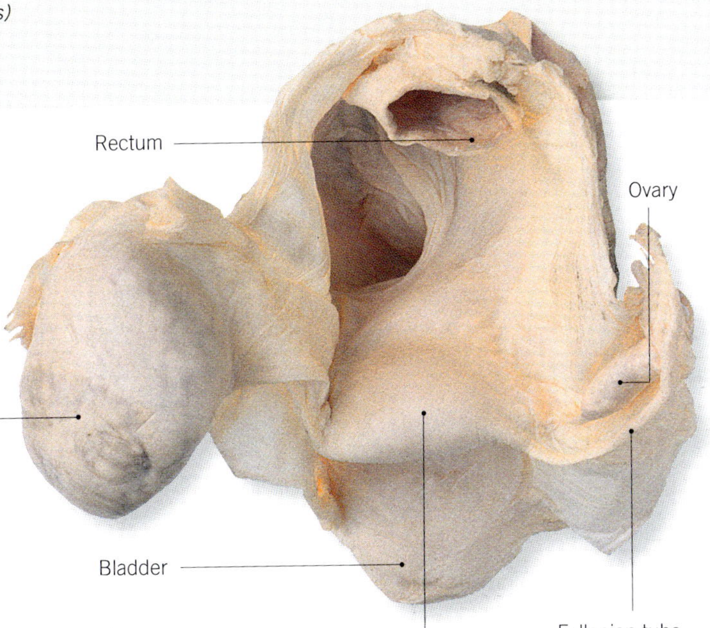


*Fig. 7.21* | *Ovarian tumour*

**Ovarian Tumour**
Here, the right ovary has ovarian tumour.
The tumour growth has enlarged the ovary
and given it an irregularly shaped surface.
Many ovarian tumours are benign.
However, malignant ovarian tumours
are very fast growing
and can pass from early to advanced stages
within just twelve months.

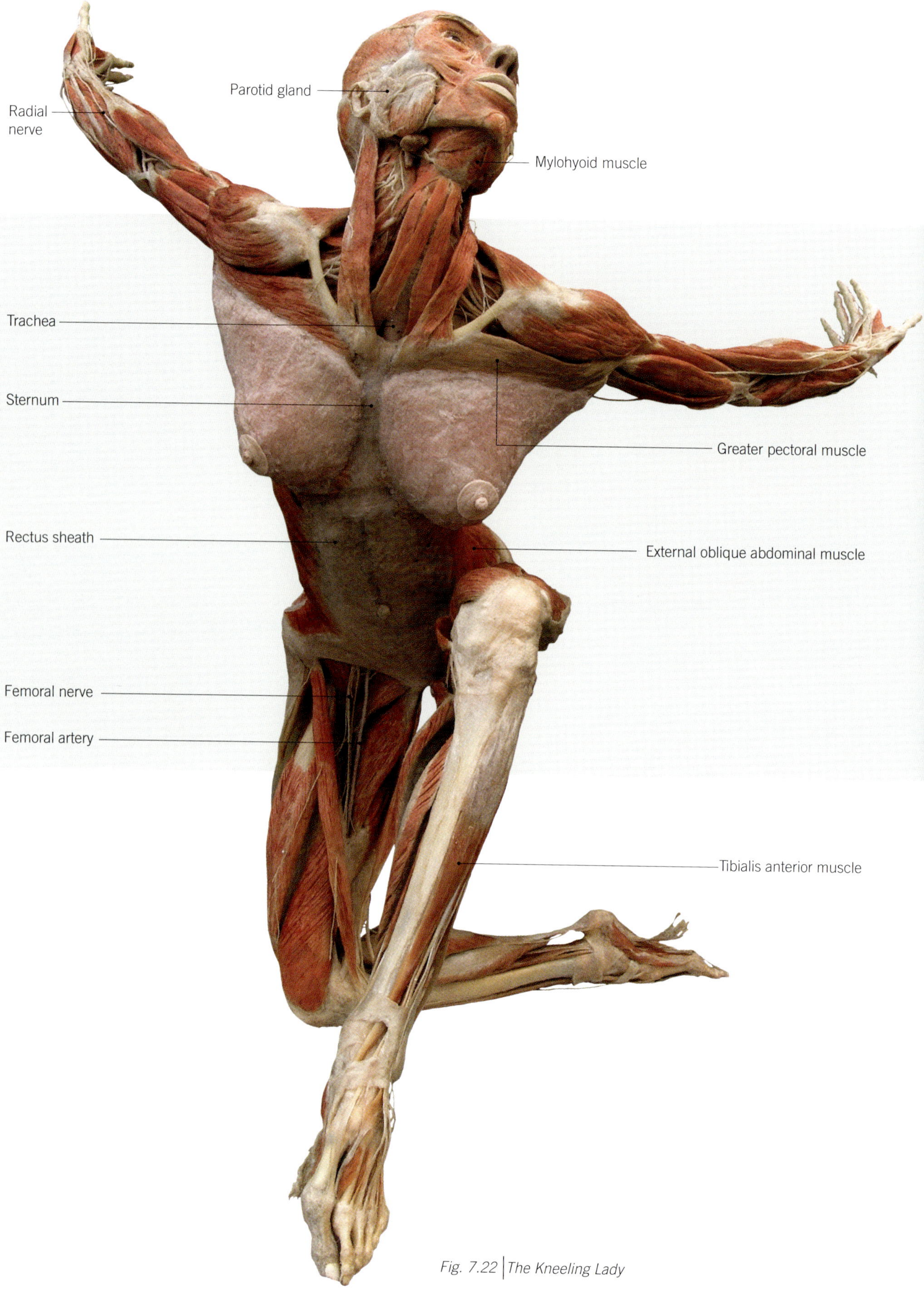


*Fig. 7.22* | *The Kneeling Lady*

*Fig. 7.23 | Longitudinal slice through a female breast*

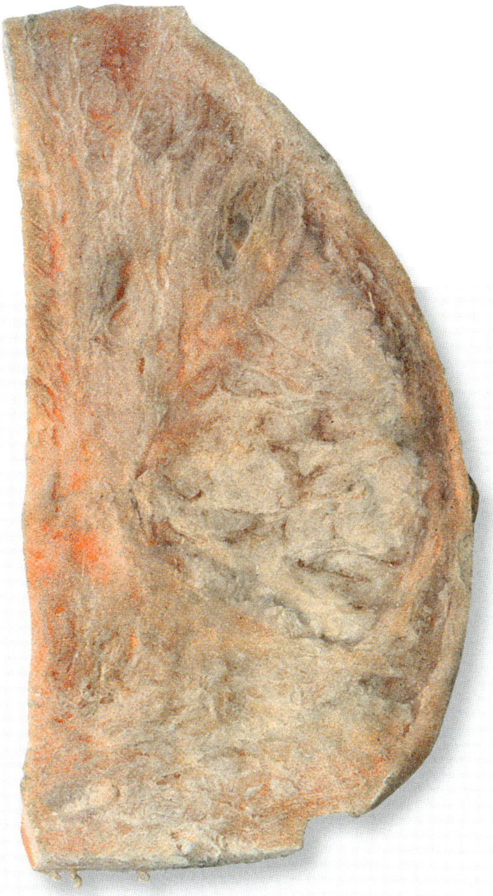

**Mammary Glands**
The mammary glands produce milk to feed the young and are part of a woman's external sexual organs.

They consist largely of fatty tissue, permeated by milk glands and a glandular duct network so fine, it is hardly visible to the naked eye. Small milk ducts empty into ever-larger collection ducts that finally find an outlet at the nipple. During pregnancy, the body releases hormones which increase the number of milk glands and glandular ducts significantly.

*Fig. 7.24 | Longitudinal slice through a female breast with breast cancer (marked area)*

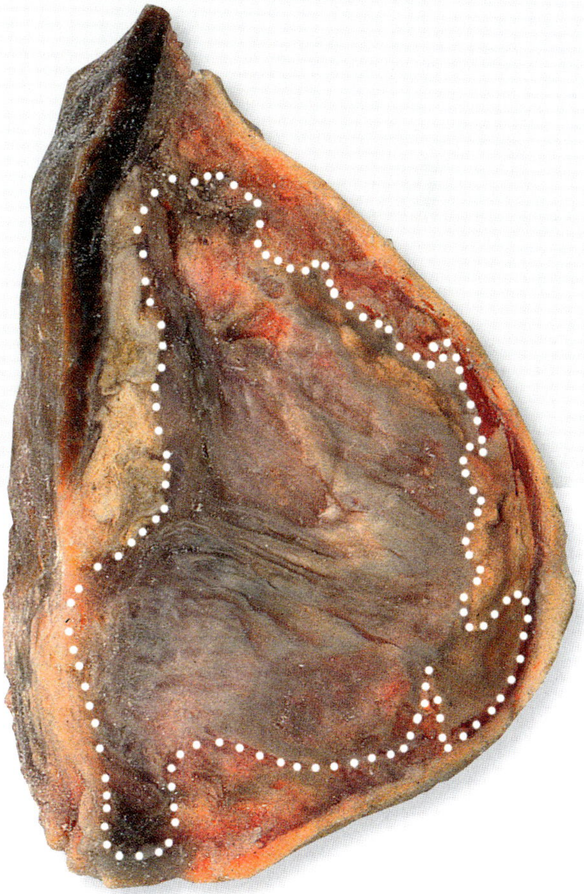

**Breast Cancer** (Mammary Carcinoma)
Breast cancer is the most common cancer in women. This longitudinal slice shows a female breast almost completely infiltrated by the hard tissue of breast cancer.

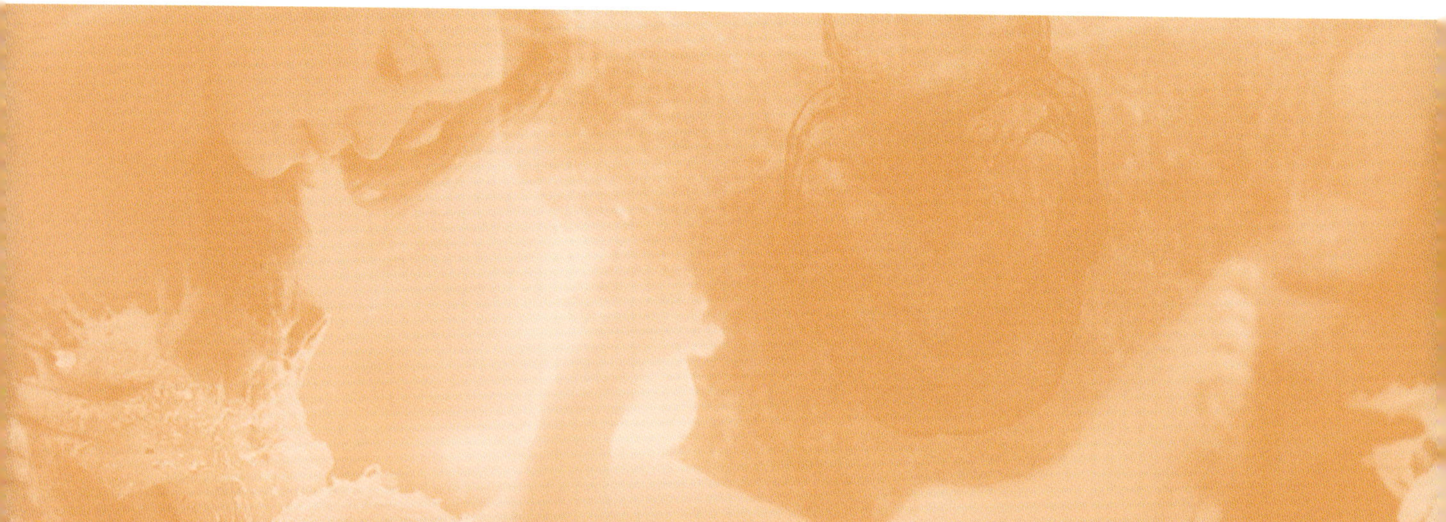

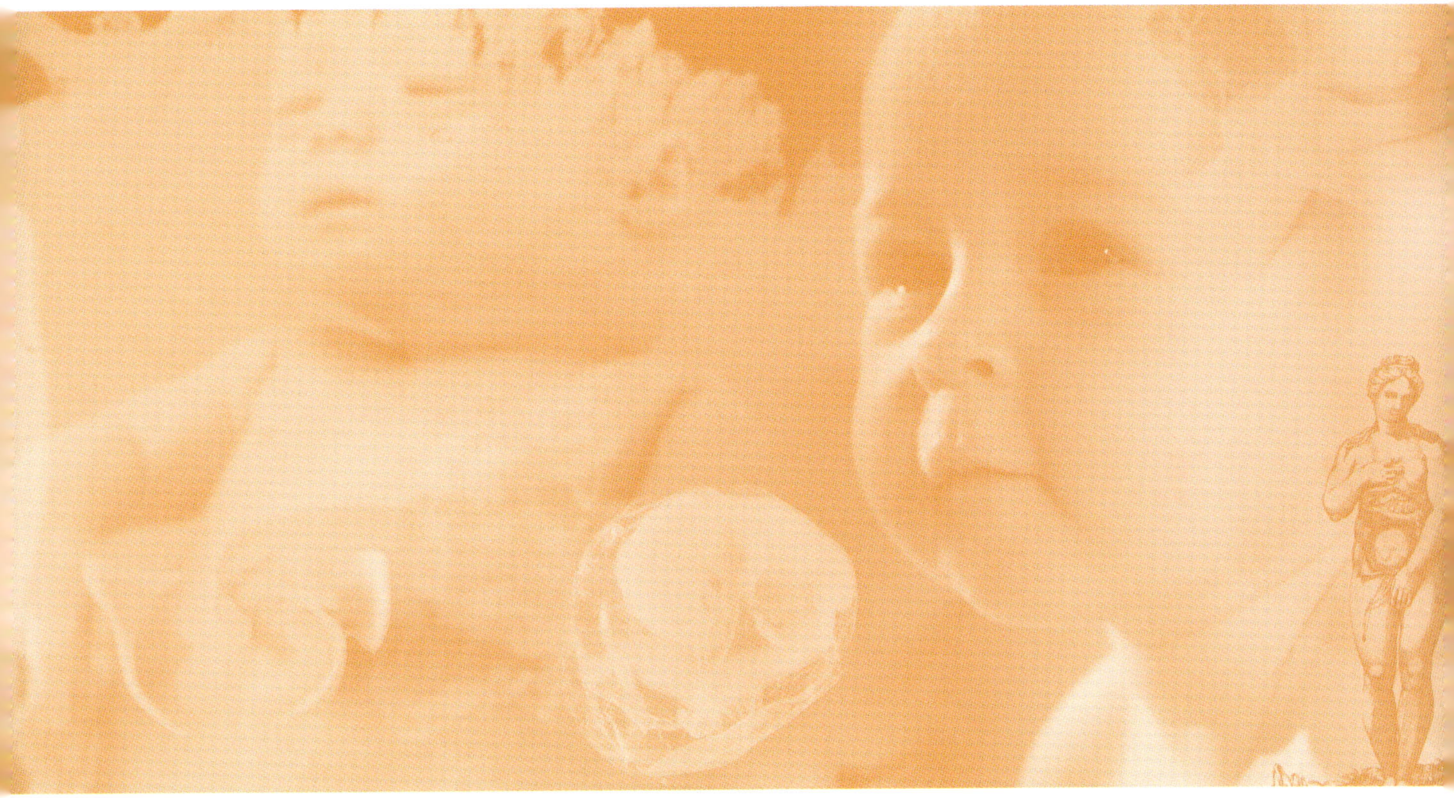

# 8. PRENATAL DEVELOPMENT

The first period of human life
takes place invisibly in the mother's body.
A single cell, or zygote, is formed
when the father's sperm fertilises the mother's egg.
It carries its own unique set of chromosomes
that determine the characteristics and traits
of the conceived human being.
The zygote is hardworking and tireless.
About 30 hours after conception,
it begins to divide
and starts travelling down the Fallopian tube.
On its way it continues to divide into multiple cells.
On the sixth day after conception,
it attaches to the wall of the uterus.
After approximately 266 days,
a new human being enters the stage of life.

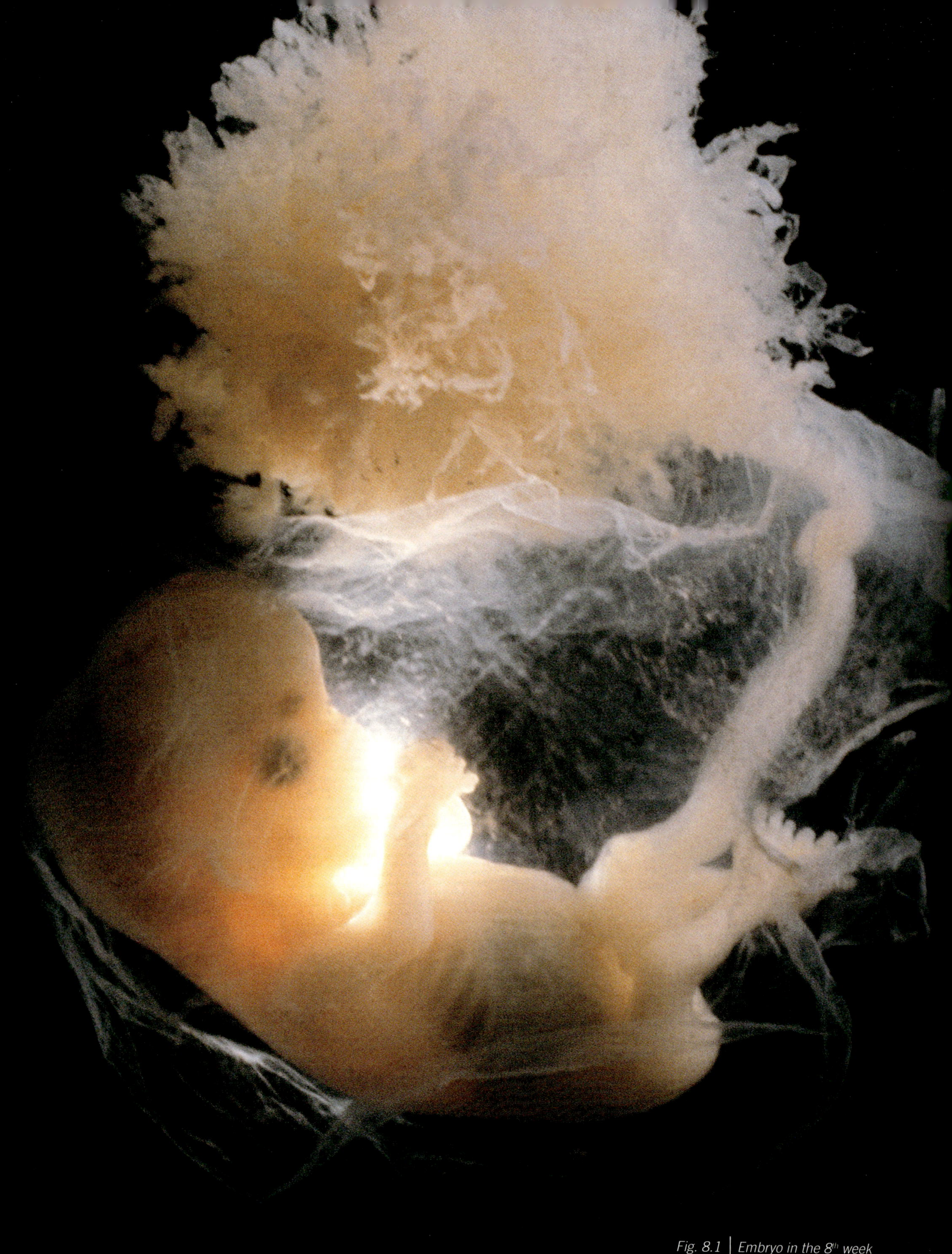

Fig. 8.1 | Embryo in the 8th week

# A Human Takes Shape

*Fig. 8.2* | *Developmental stages from the fourth to the eighth week of pregnancy. During the first eight weeks of pregnancy, the developing organism is called an embryo. During this time, all organs are formed.*

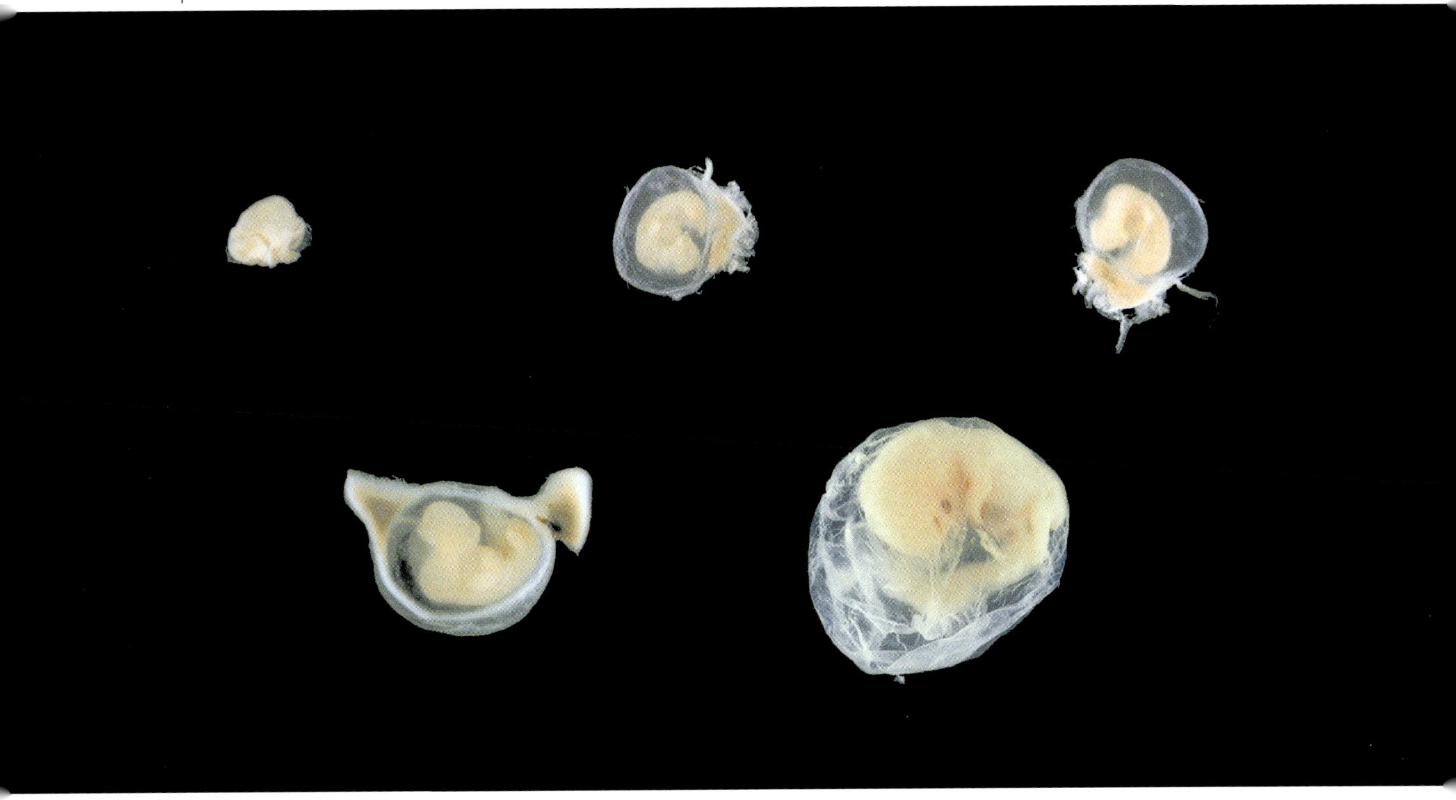

**Embryonic Development**
When the fertilised egg
travels down the Fallopian tubes,
it divides several times before
embedding itself in the lining of the uterus.
There the cells continue to divide.
Soon the cells start to specialise,
creating different tissues and organs.
After only four weeks,
an embryo already has a heart and eyes.
It also has four buds,
the start of its arms and legs.
After eight weeks,
organ differentiation is largely completed.

**Foetal Development**

The developing child is called a foetus
after the ninth week of pregnancy.
This is a phase of growth and organ maturation.
By the fourth month,
the liver and pancreas are developed,
together with the intestines and kidneys.
Hair and nails begin to grow.

In the fifth month,
the nervous system starts to mature,
and the mother can feel the foetus move.
After the seventh month,
the foetus could survive a premature birth.
In the last two months,
the foetus mainly gains in size and weight.

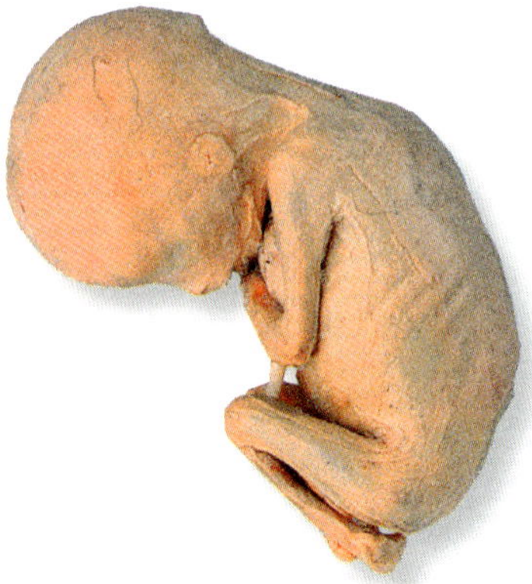

*13th Week of Pregnancy*

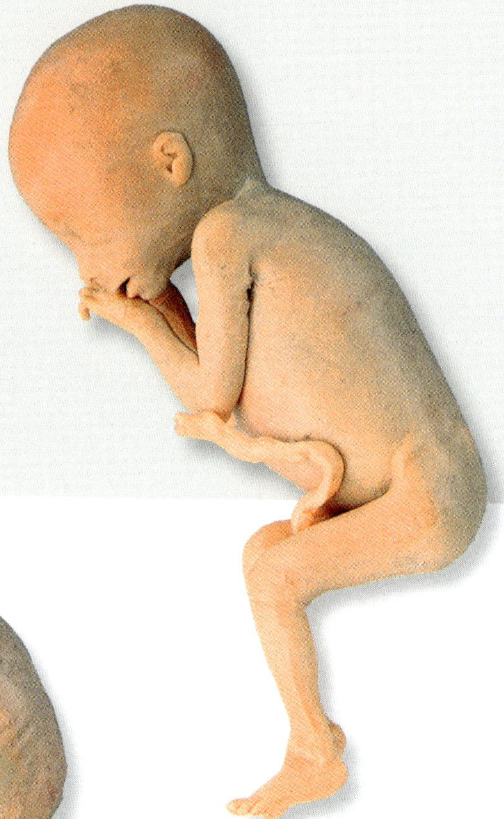

*17th Week of Pregnancy*

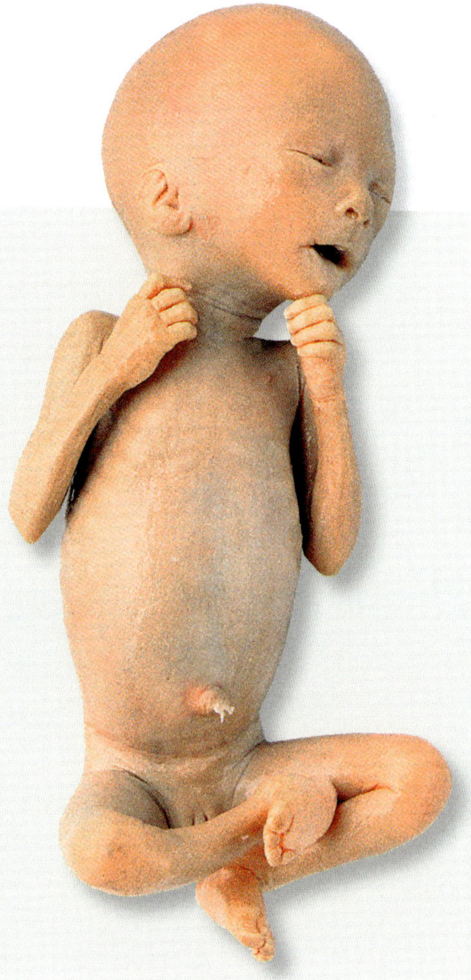

*19th Week of Pregnancy*

*Fig. 8.3*

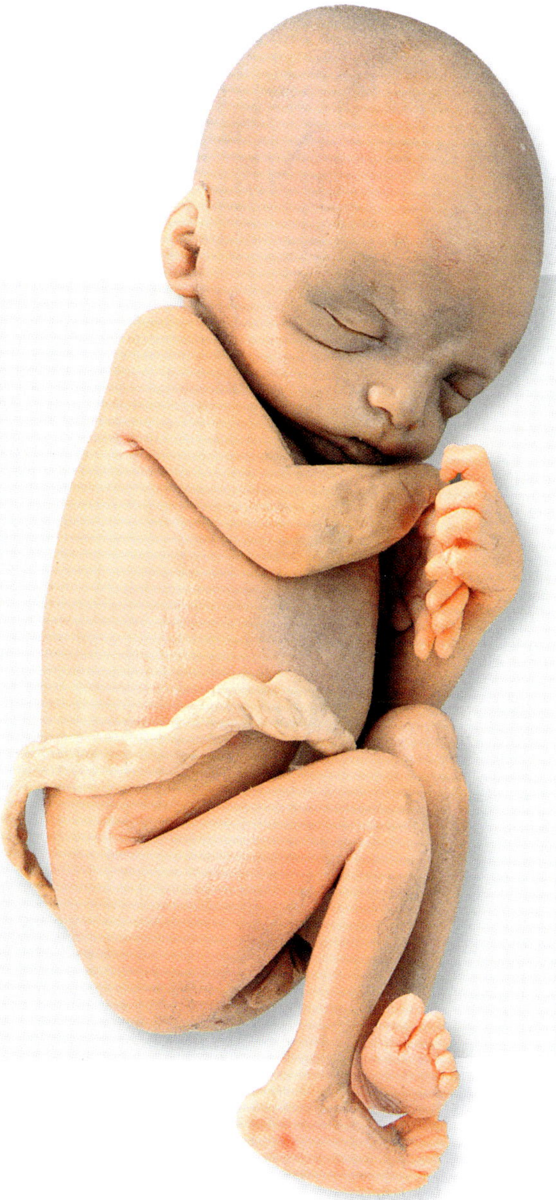

23rd Week of Pregnancy

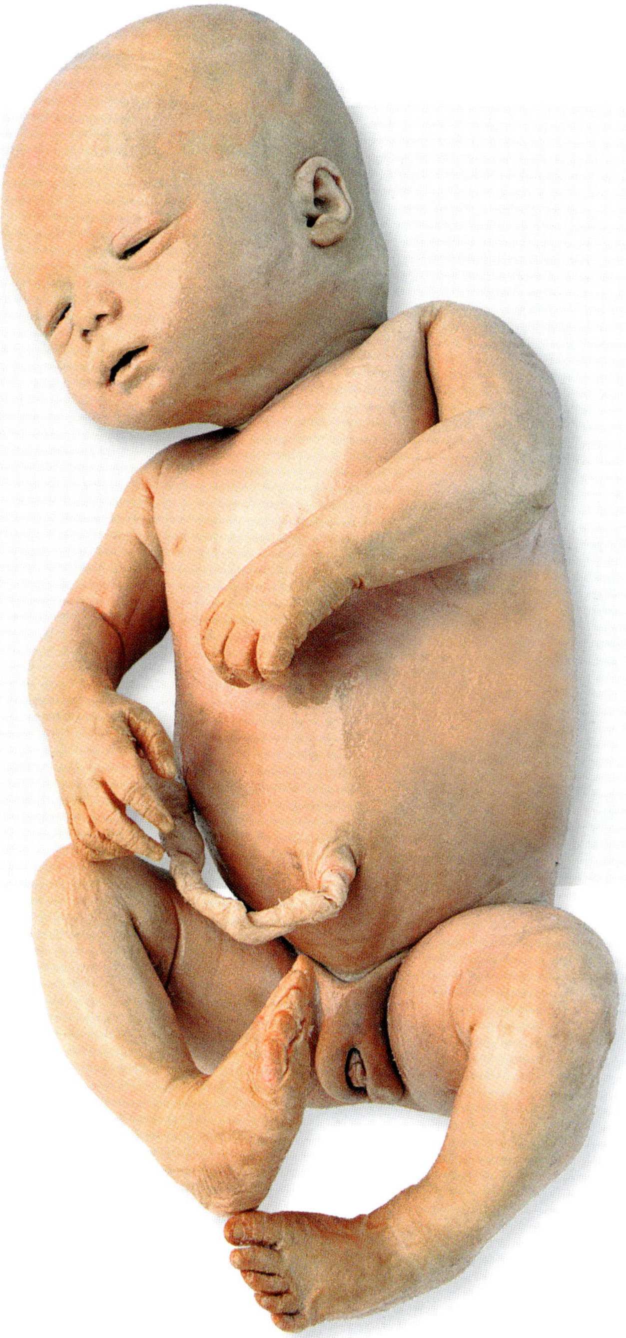

32nd Week of Pregnancy

**The First Weeks**

Roughly 30 hours after fertilisation,
a tiny human egg begins to divide
into two identical daughter cells.
These cells keep dividing
and form a cluster of cells, the blastocyst,
which migrates down the Fallopian tube.

It settles in the uterus as an embryo
on the sixth day after fertilisation.
Pregnancy will last about 260 days from that point.

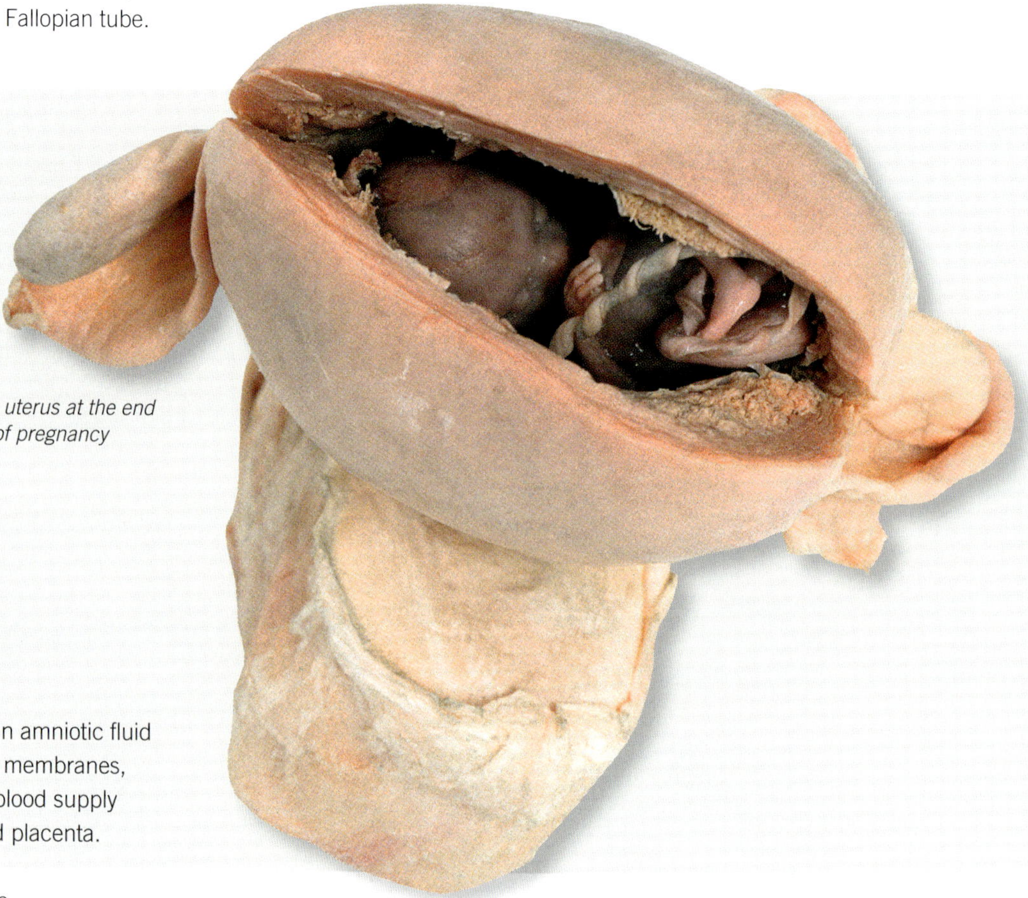

*Fig. 8.4* | *Foetus inside the uterus at the end of the 3rd month of pregnancy*

The embryo, suspended in amniotic fluid
and surrounded by foetal membranes,
is linked to the maternal blood supply
via the umbilical cord and placenta.

During the first four weeks,
the embryo is roughly 4 millimetres (0.15 inches) long.
It will grow to 3 centimetres (1.2 inches)
and weigh 4 grams (0.1 ounce)
by the end of the eight week.
All of the organs will be in place by the end
of this period, after which the developing child
is referred to as a foetus.
The length and weight of the foetus
then begins to increase significantly,
as it proceeds through further stages of development.

**Week 13 to 14**

Coordinated movements will begin,
although the mother is not yet able to feel them.
The relatively large head will straighten up,
the lower extremities are already well developed,
and the toenails will begin to grow.

**Week 15 to 16**

The foetus is now 15 centimetres (6 inches) long
and can weigh up to 200 grams (7 ounces).
Its gender can be detected via ultrasound,
and its skeleton will show up clearly on x-rays.
Its body becomes more proportioned.
Foetal blood begins to develop in the liver.
Ovaries have already developed in female foetuses.

**Week 17 to 18**

Foetal growth has slowed;
the weight of the foetus has increased to 300 grams
(10.5 ounces).
The skin is still thin,
because the (white) subcutaneous fatty tissues
have not yet developed.
However, brown fatty tissues have begun to form,
allowing the small organism to produce its own heat.
The uterus has developed in female foetuses.
Mothers can feel the foetus move from this point on.

**Week 19 to 20**
Toward the end of this phase, the foetus will be 28 centimetres (11 inches) long and weigh up to 450 grams (1 pound). The body and head of the foetus are now covered with fine hair which contains little pigment.

**Week 21 to 24**
The foetus begins to gain weight more rapidly again, and its proportions resemble more of a baby. The fingernails will start to grow, and the skin is still red and wrinkled. The lungs are capable of breathing, if insufficiently, because there is not yet any coordination between them and the nervous system. This lack of coordination could cause more or less severe damage to the brain, if the baby is born at this stage.

**Week 25 to 28**
The lungs are now fully capable of breathing, which means that the foetus is capable of living outside the womb.

During week 26, the eyes can open, and subcutaneous fatty tissue has given the body a more rounded shape. Until this point, the spleen has been producing blood; during week 28, bone marrow takes over this function. The foetus weighs more than 1,300 grams (2.8 pounds).

**Week 29 to 32**
The foetus' body will grow to over 42 centimetres (16.5 inches), and its weight increases to 1.5 to 2.1 kilograms (3.3 to 4.2 pounds). The fingernails grow to the tips of the fingers, and the skin will now be pink and smooth. The eyes respond to light by means of the pupillary reflex, and the hands respond to stimulus with a "grasping" reflex. Infants born during week 33 will usually survive.

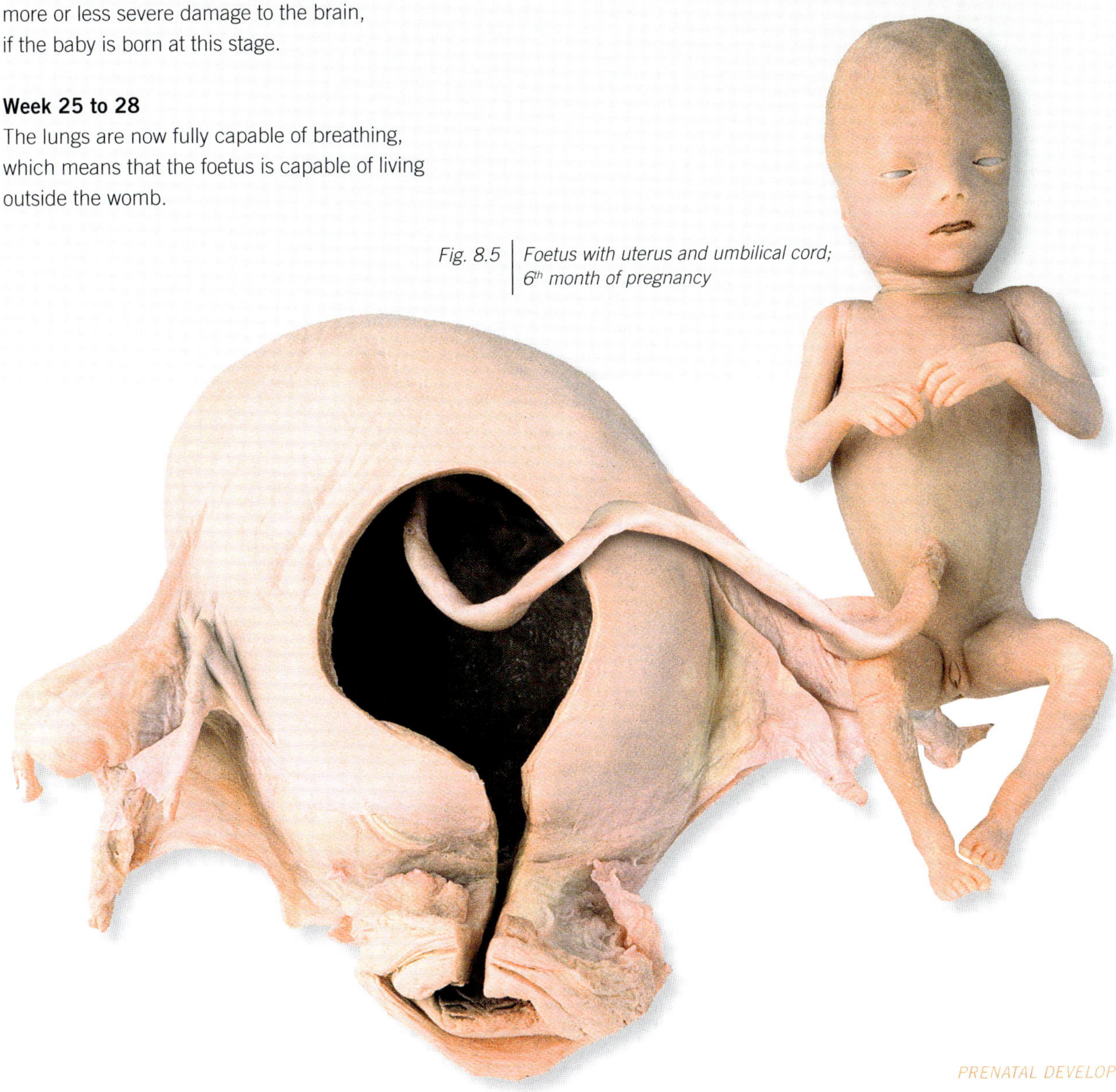

*Fig. 8.5* | *Foetus with uterus and umbilical cord; 6th month of pregnancy*

# Nourishing the Foetus

**Placenta**
The placenta exists only during pregnancy.
During the first ten weeks of pregnancy,
it develops at the point
where the fertilised egg embeds itself
in the lining of the uterus.

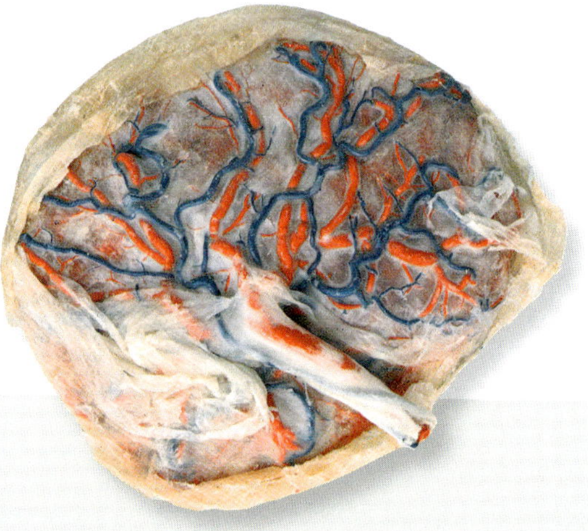

*Fig. 8.6* | *Placenta. On the surface of the foetal side, the arteries and veins of the umbilical cord vessels branch out*

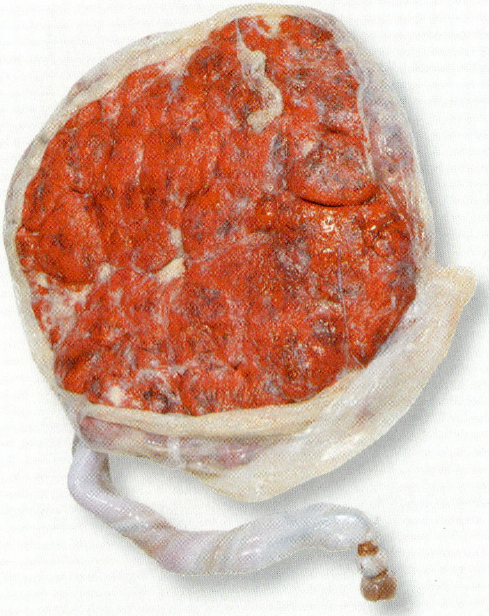

*Fig. 8.7* | *Placenta. The uterine side shows the dense vascular bed, in which the exchange of nourishment and oxygen takes place.*

The placenta is connected to the foetus
via the umbilical cord
and provides it with nourishment.
The blood vessels of the umbilical cord
branch out on the surface of the foetal side.
The foetus' heart pumps blood
through the umbilical cord artery
to the vascular bed of the placenta.
This is bathed in the mother's blood
from the lining of the uterus.
Here, substances, such as oxygen and nutrients,
as well as waste and $CO_2$, are exchanged.
This exchange can then occur
without mixing the mother's and child's blood.
Oxygen- and nutrient-enriched blood
flows back to the foetus via the umbilical vein.

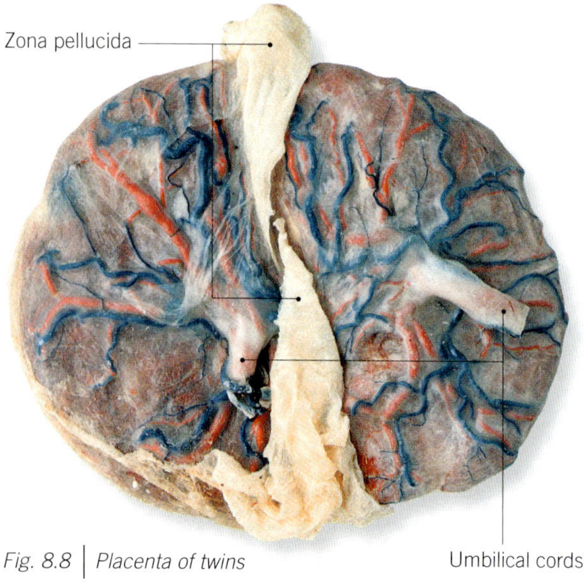


*Fig. 8.8* | *Placenta of twins*

**Placenta of Twins**
Twins are conceived
when a fertilised egg divides into two embryos
or two fertilised eggs develop simultaneously.
In the first case,
the twins share the same genetic code
and are identical or monozygotic twins.
They are always of the same sex.
In the second case,
the twins are fraternal or dizygotic twins.
They are genetically as similar or different
as any other non-identical siblings.
Identical twins can either share one placenta
or have separate ones.
Non-identical twins always have separate placentas.

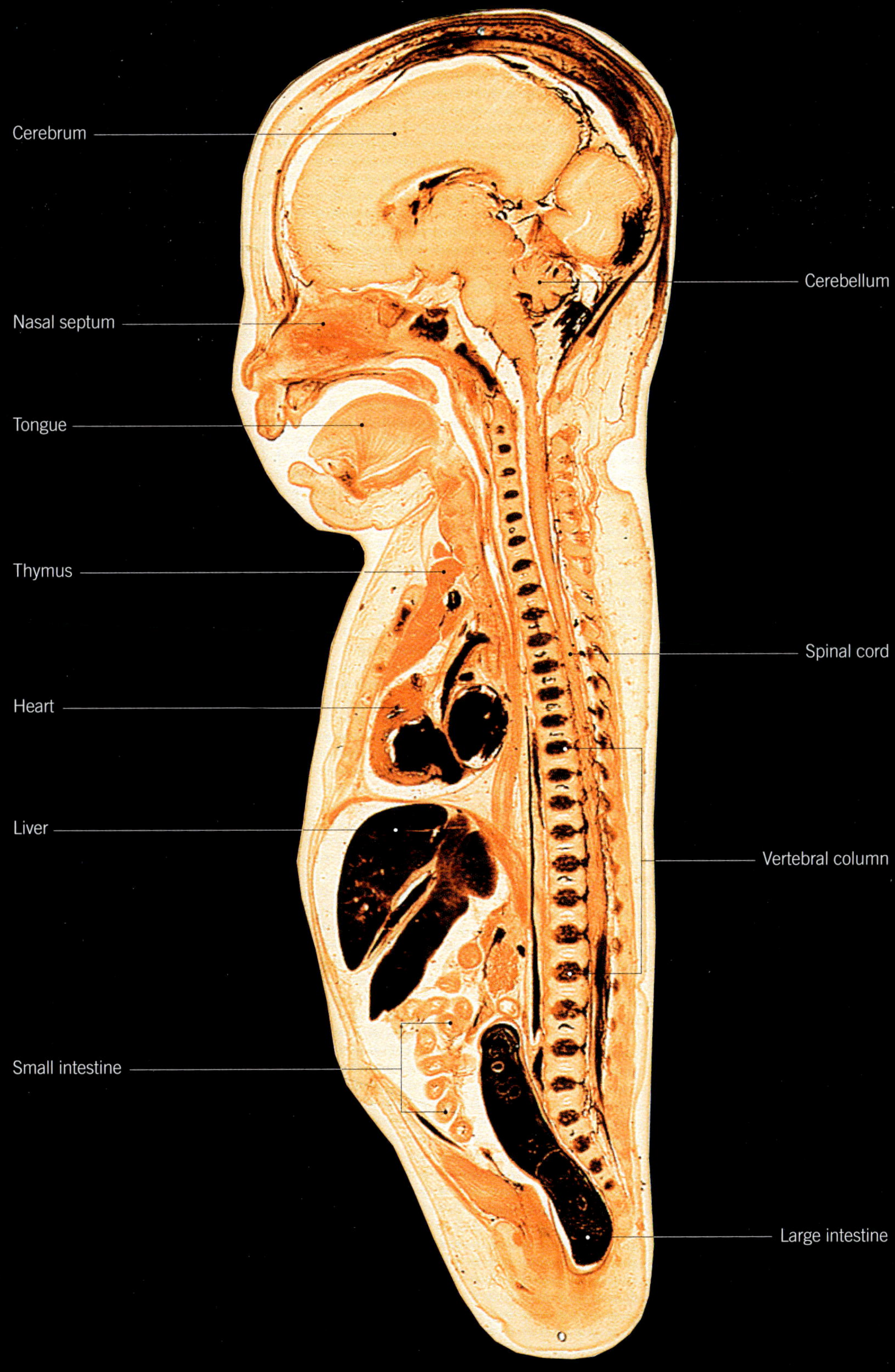


## Longitudinal Slice of a Foetus in the 7th Month

The position of the various organs
already corresponds to those in an adult body.

*Fig. 8.9*

# Congenital Deformities

Congenital deformities can either be the result
of pathological factors
or abnormal development of the foetus
caused by damage form external sources,
such as alcohol or drug abuse of the mother
or from infectious diseases.

From the third to the eighth week of pregnancy,
embryos are especially susceptible to such influences.
During this time the rate of cell division is particularly high
and organ differentiation is in progress.
Abnormal development of individual cells
can lead to malformation of the entire organism.

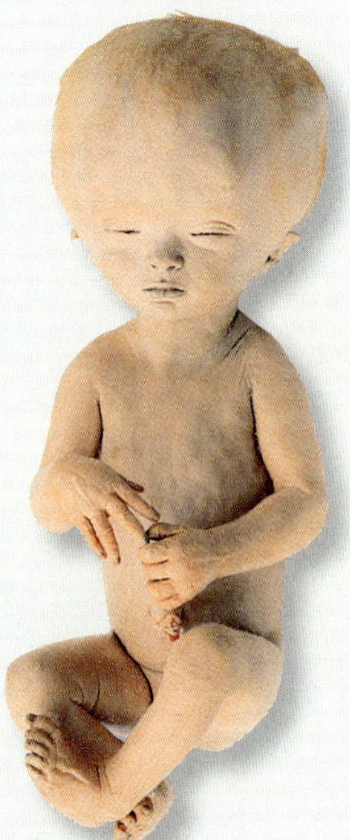

*Fig. 8.10 | New-born child with hydrocephalus*

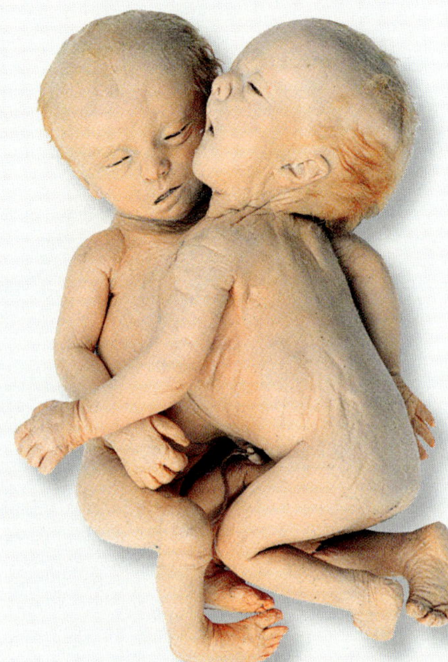

*Fig. 8.11 | Conjoined twins*

**Hydrocephalus**
Congenital hydrocephalus is caused
by an imbalance between the brain's production
of cerebrospinal fluid
and the body's ability to distribute or absorb it properly.
In foetuses and small children
it causes the entire skull to expand.
The reason for this is that the cranial sutures
have not yet become ossified
because of anticipated cranial growth;
they thus give way to the increased internal pressure.
This condition is also known as "water on the brain".
The excess fluid can increase pressure in the baby's brain,
possibly resulting in brain damage
and loss of mental and physical abilities.

**Conjoined Twins**
Conjoined twins originate from a single fertilised egg.
Malformations of this type occur
when individual cells or tissues fail to divide completely
during the first two months of pregnancy.
The foetuses then share either the skin alone
or internal organs.
Chances of survival and operability depend on
the extent to which shared organs are critical for survival.

The best known conjoined twins were
Eng and Chang Bunker, born in Siam in 1811,
hence the name Siamese twins.

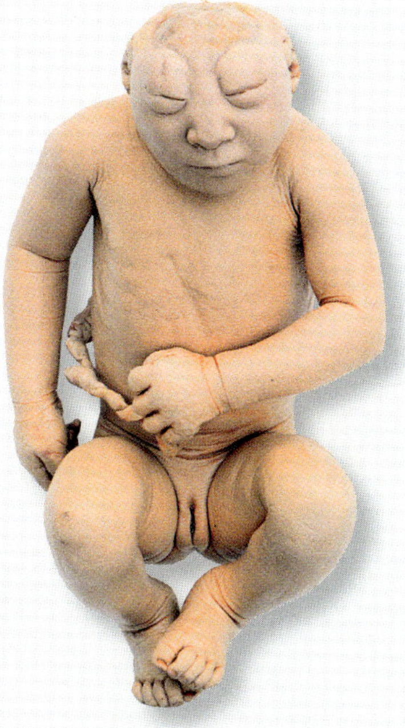

*Fig. 8.12* | *Foetus with anencephaly*

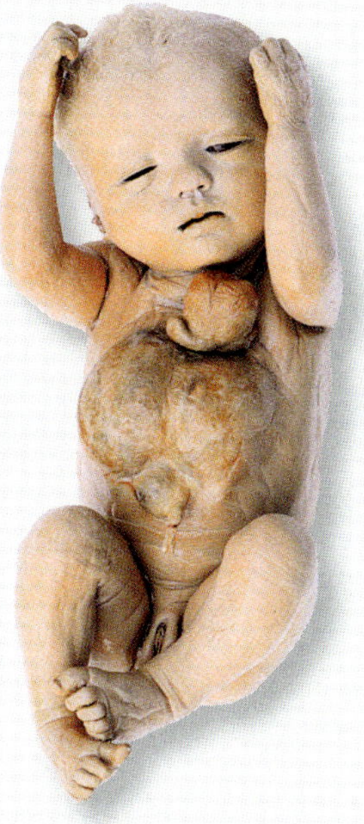

*Fig. 8.13* | *Foetus with chest and abdominal defects*

**Anencephaly**

Anencephaly is a congenital birth defect in which the top of the skull is missing and degenerated tissue is all that is left where the brain should be.
It occurs in about one out of 1,000 pregnancies.
If ultrasound images indicate such a serious defect, it can be confirmed early via amniocentesis.
Life expectancy for a baby with anencephaly after birth is just a few hours, sometimes a few days at most.

**Chest and Abdominal Wall Defect**

Abdominal wall defects occur when a child's abdomen does not develop fully while in the womb.
This causes the intestine to develop outside the abdomen.
In this case, also the heart protrudes from the body.

Chest and abdominal wall defects are very rare.
It is not exactly known what causes them.

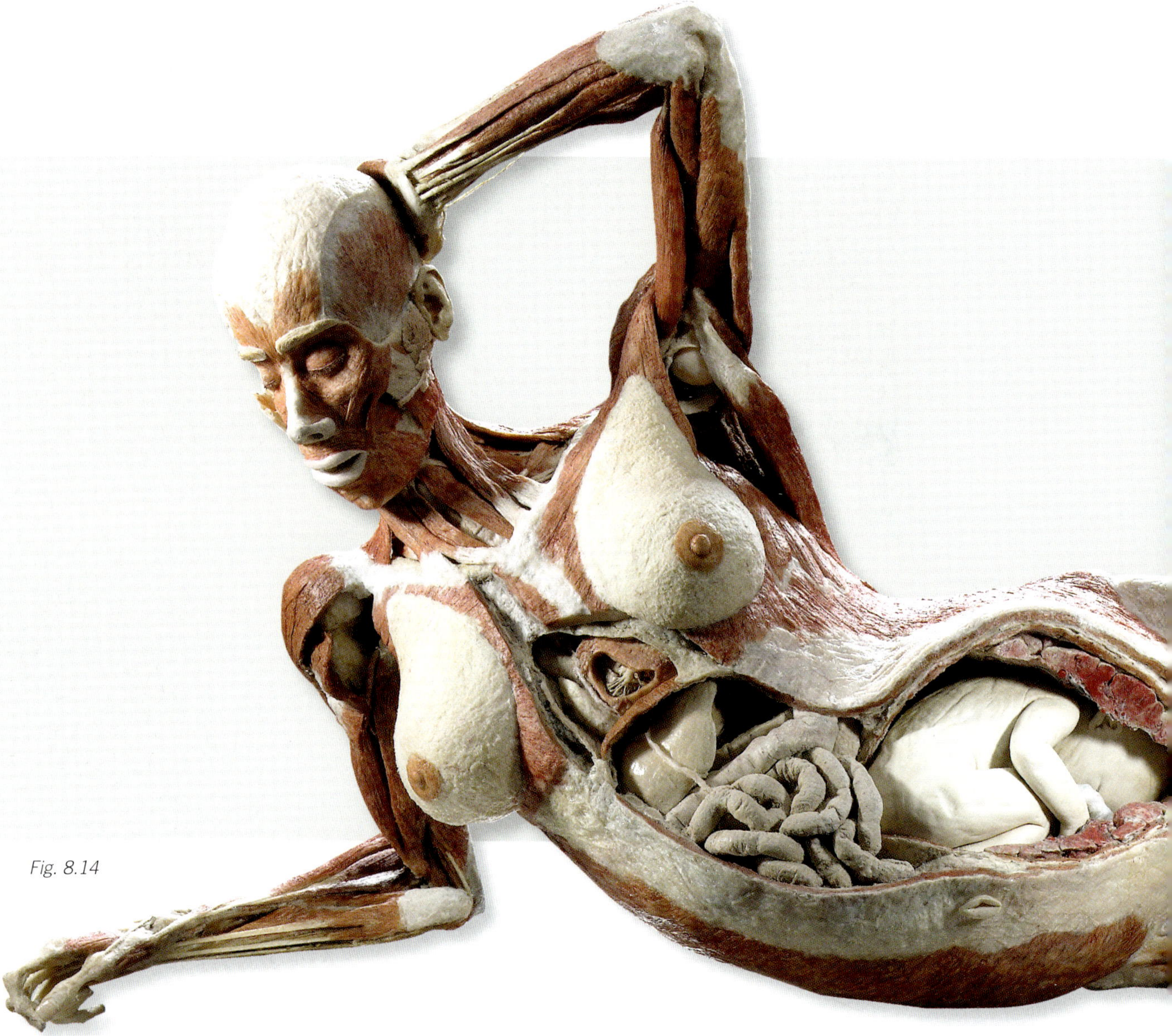

Fig. 8.14

## Reclining Pregnant Woman

The foetus and the placenta
can be seen in the opened uterus
which has been cut through at its front wall.
The child already measures 28 centimetres (11 inches)
and is pressing the abdominal organs
of the mother upwards.

The mother's liver can be seen
under the right arch of her rib cage
while the opened stomach is under the left one.
Below these are horizontal parts of the large intestine
and loops of the small intestines.

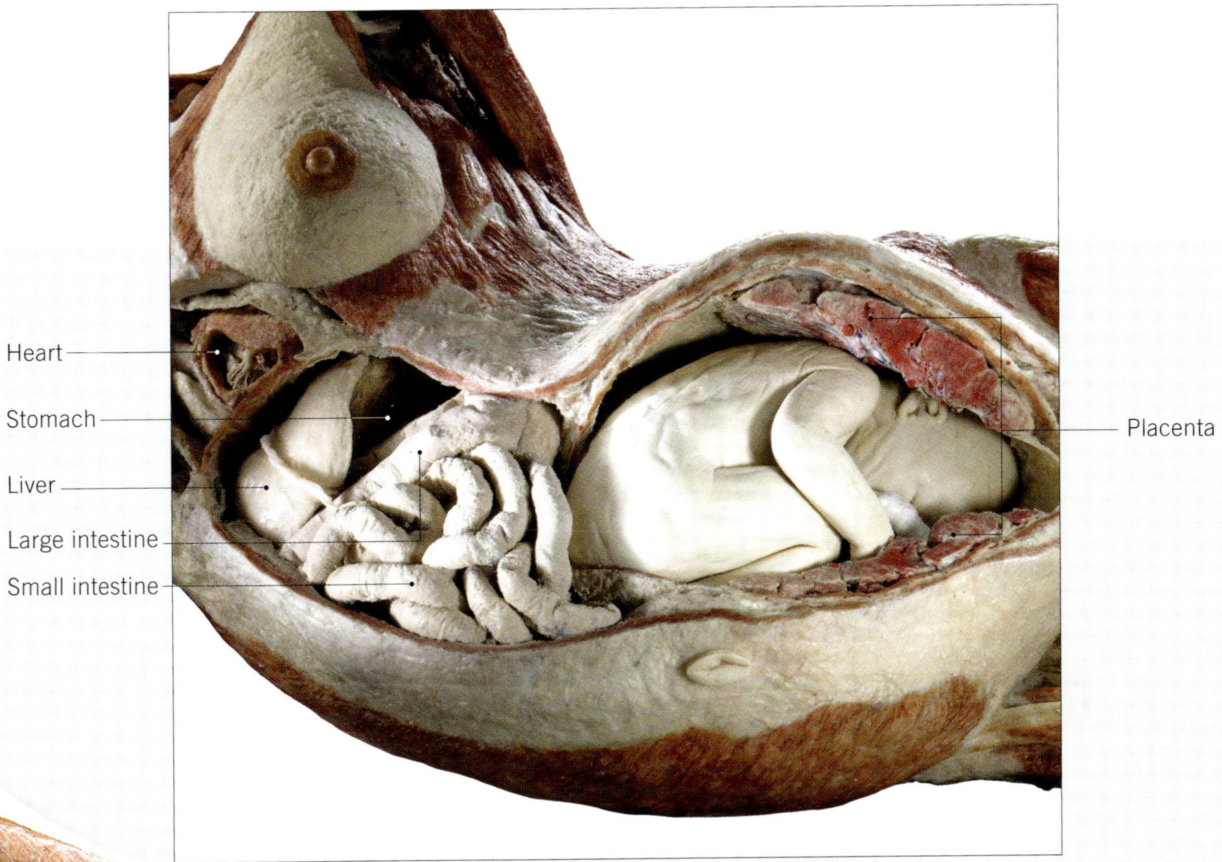

Heart
Stomach
Liver
Large intestine
Small intestine
Placenta


*Fig. 8.15*

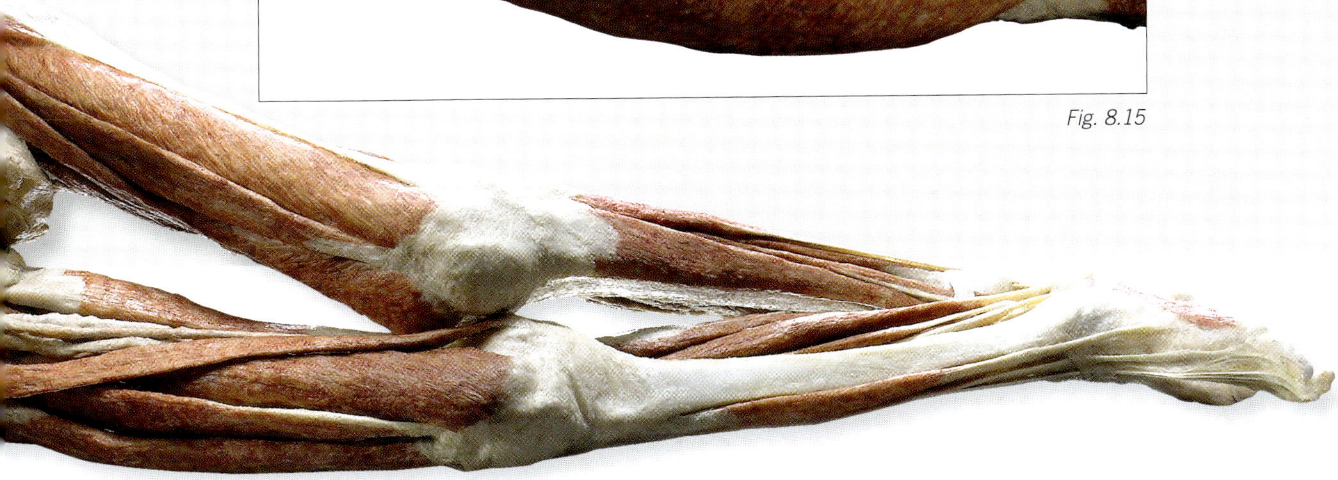

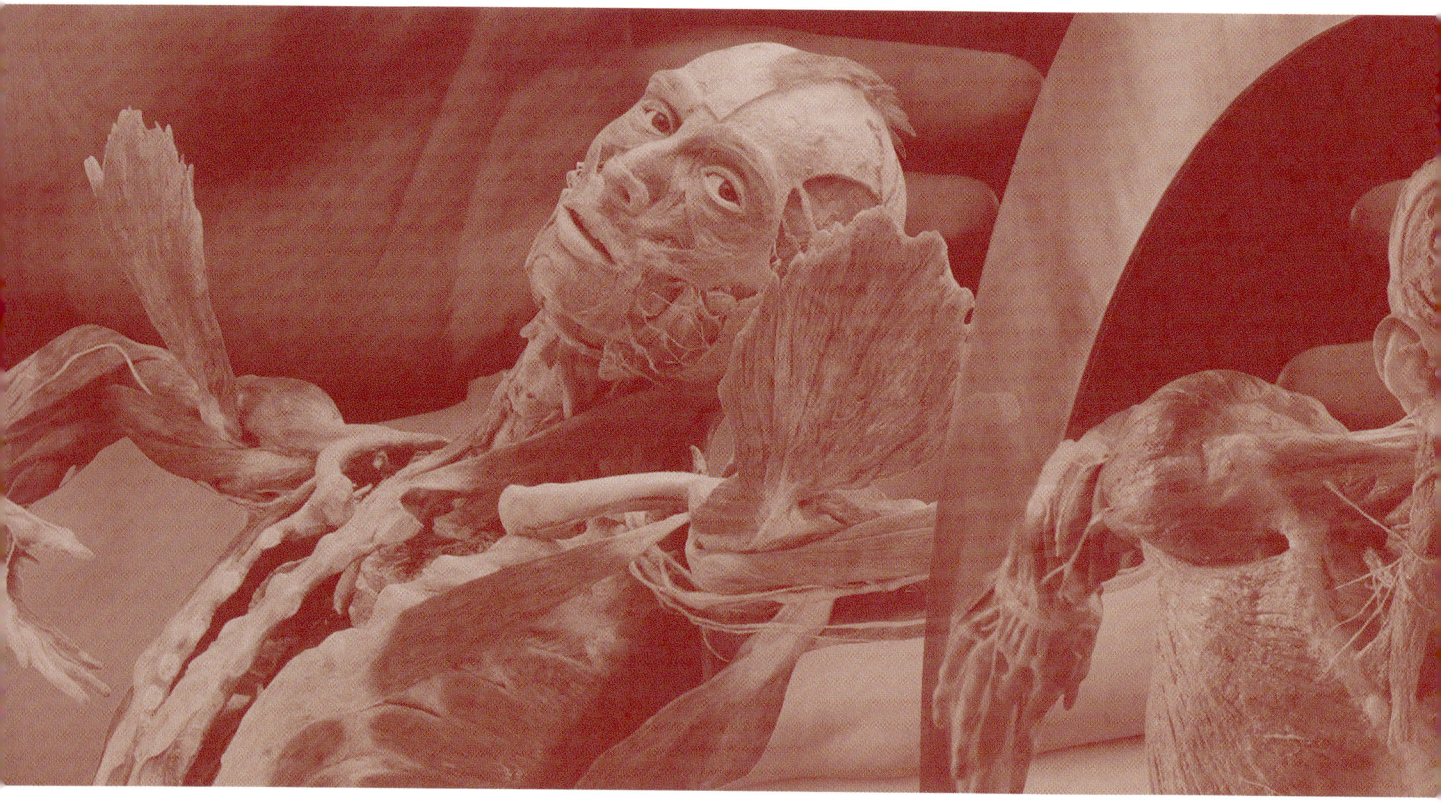

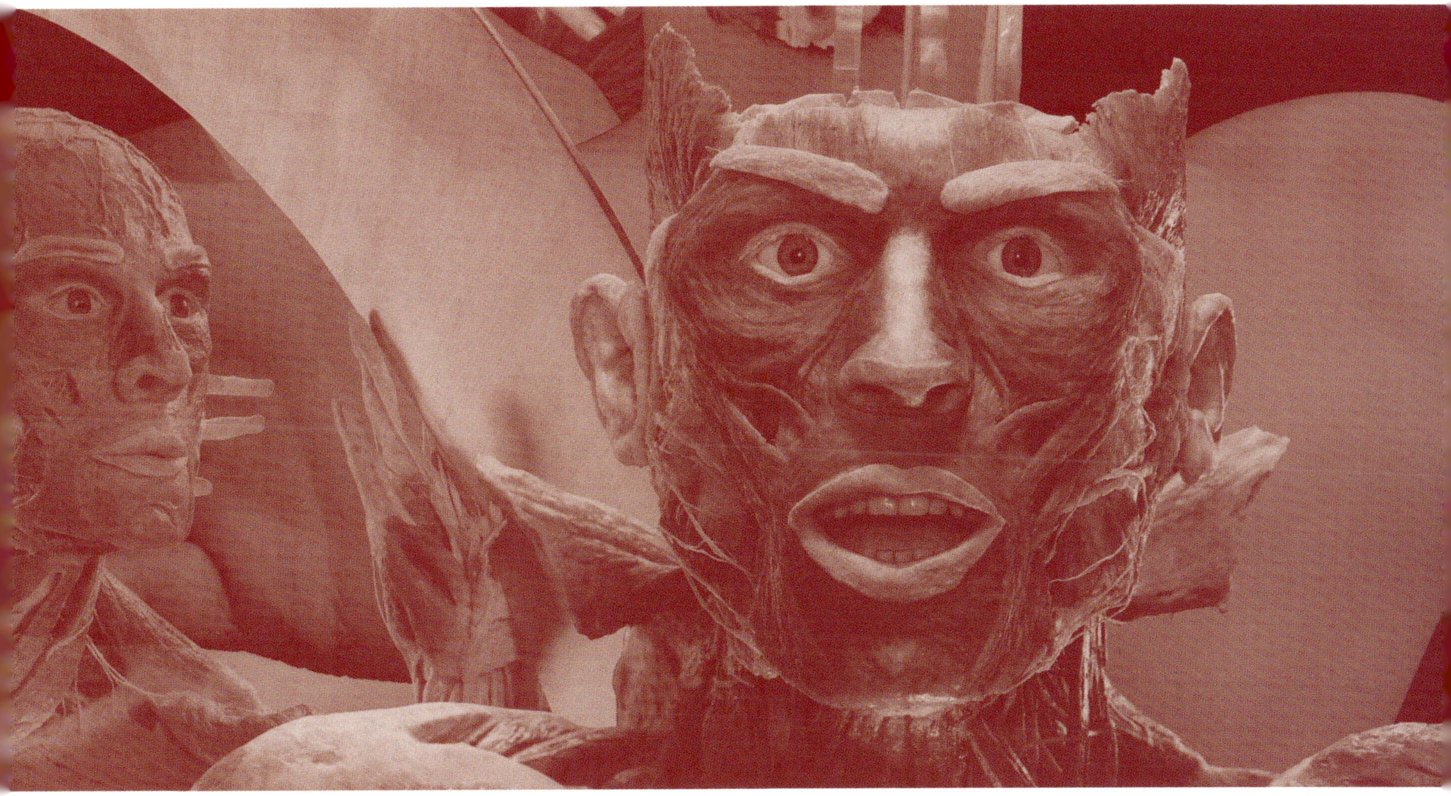

# 9. **WHOLE-BODY** PLASTINATES

Andreas Vesalius (1514–1564),
personal physician to Emperor Charles V
and King Philip II of Spain,
was the first to assemble a complete skeleton.
Since then such internal bony structures
of the human organism have served
as instructional and visual models.
At that time, it was not possible
to obtain a corpse complete with flesh,
much less to be able to erect it.
The soft tissue would have quickly putrefied
or it would have dried out as in mummies, at best.

As a consequence,
we have only inherited depictions
discovered by the founding fathers of anatomy
during their dissections,
which were occasionally executed in pictures
according to their perceptions.

Creating durable whole-body plastinates
and positioning them in lifelike poses
was first made possible by plastination
in the early 1990s.
The old Latin proverb of anatomy,
"Hic gaudet mors succurrere vitae"
(Here Death enjoys standing by Life),
can thus be realised in its truest sense.

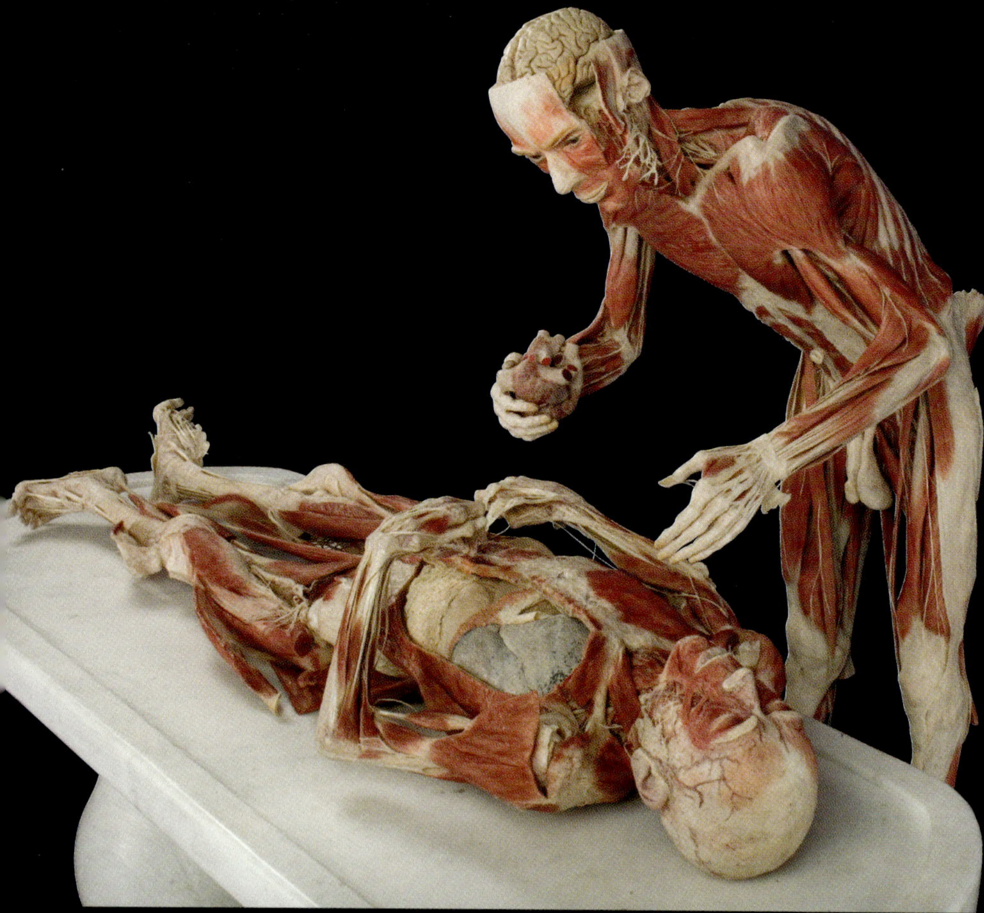

Fig. 9.1

## Surgery in Still Life

BODY WORLDS is firmly set in the grand tradition
of aesthetic, scientific anatomy
that began during the Renaissance.
Largely portrayed realistically,
anatomical specimens were posed in natural positions
and positioned in front of a landscape,
or painted carrying out an everyday activity.

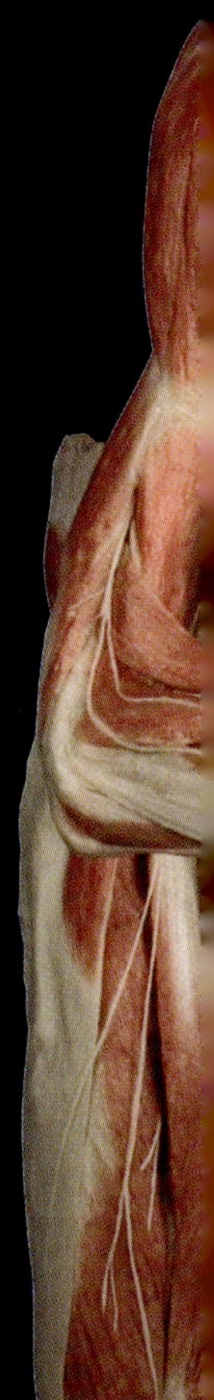

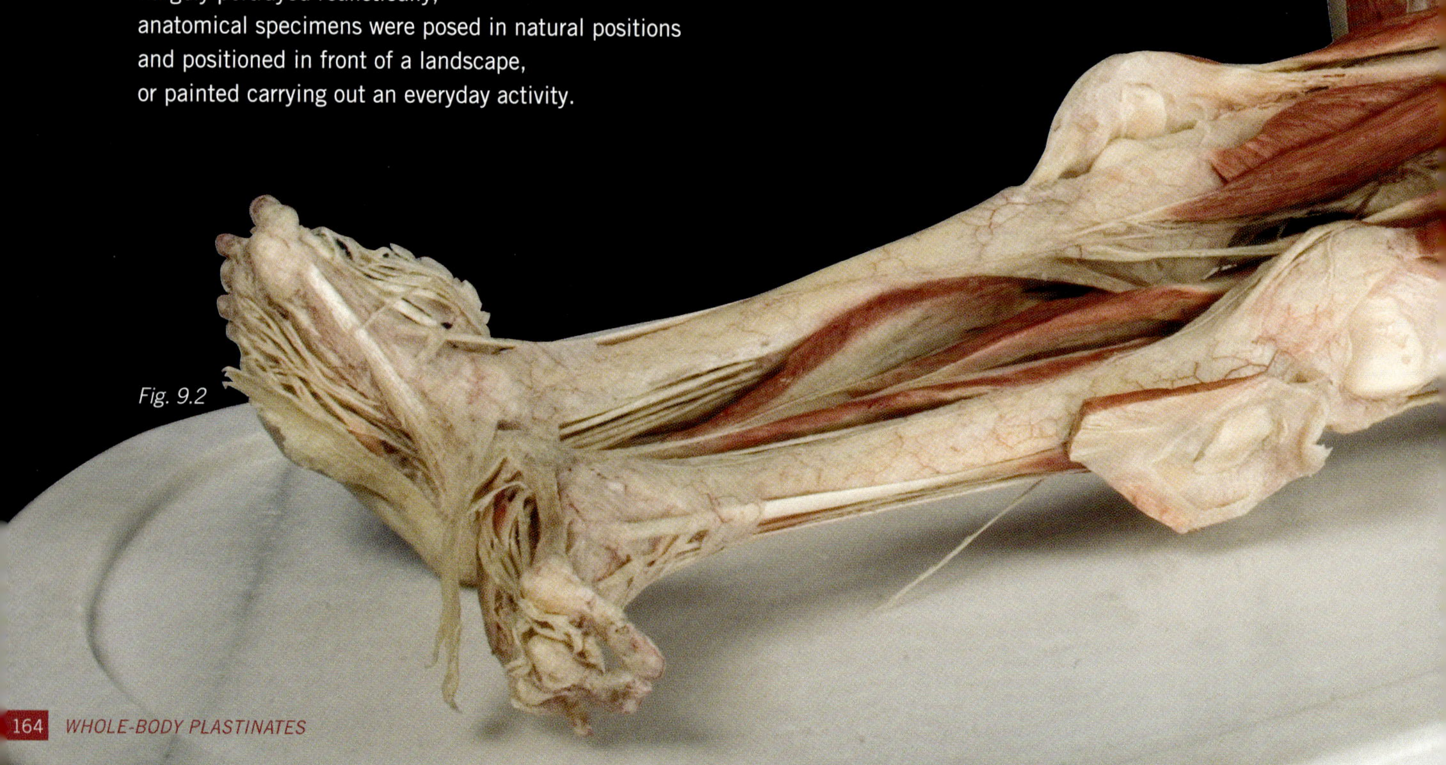

Fig. 9.2

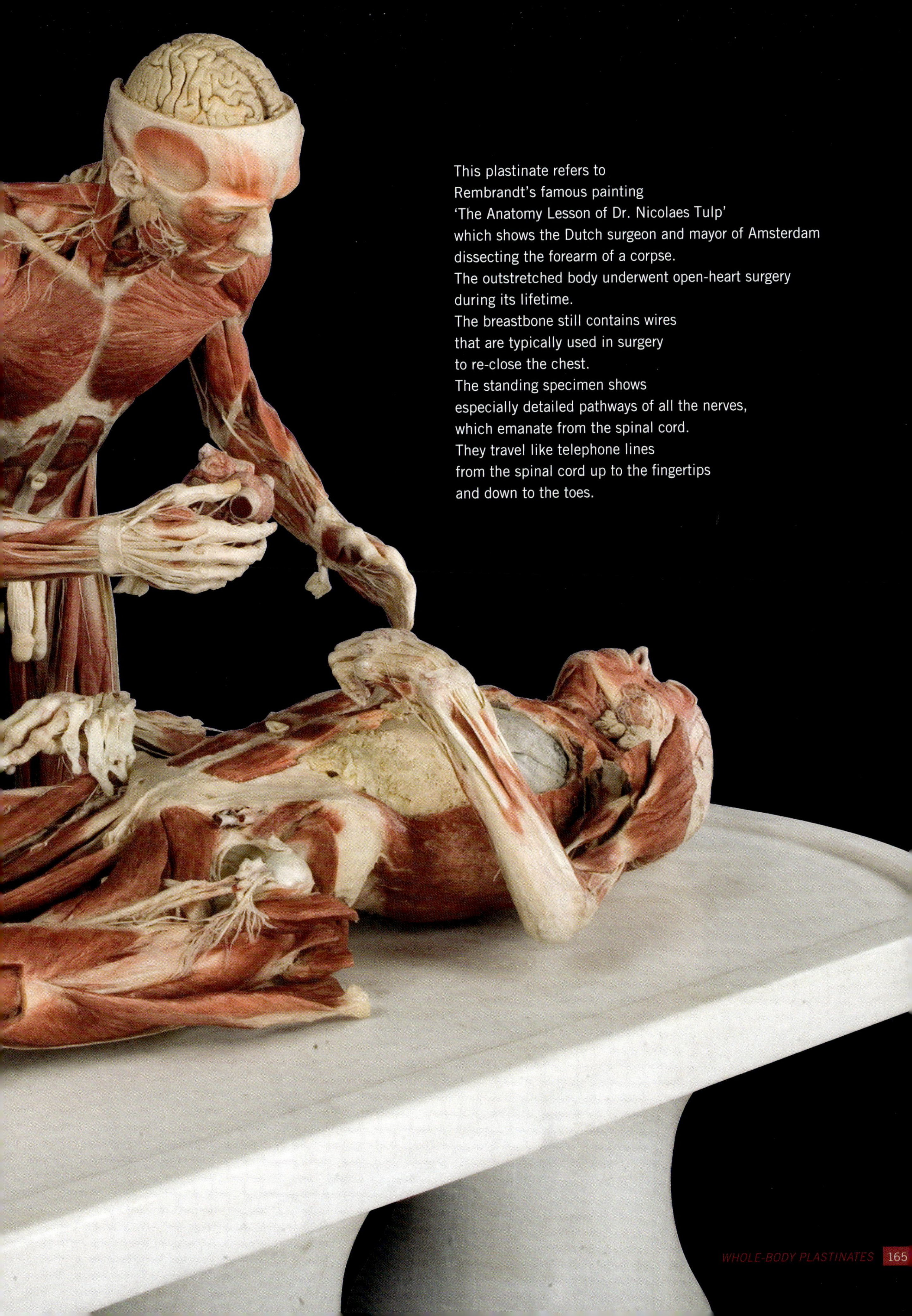

This plastinate refers to
Rembrandt's famous painting
'The Anatomy Lesson of Dr. Nicolaes Tulp'
which shows the Dutch surgeon and mayor of Amsterdam
dissecting the forearm of a corpse.
The outstretched body underwent open-heart surgery
during its lifetime.
The breastbone still contains wires
that are typically used in surgery
to re-close the chest.
The standing specimen shows
especially detailed pathways of all the nerves,
which emanate from the spinal cord.
They travel like telephone lines
from the spinal cord up to the fingertips
and down to the toes.

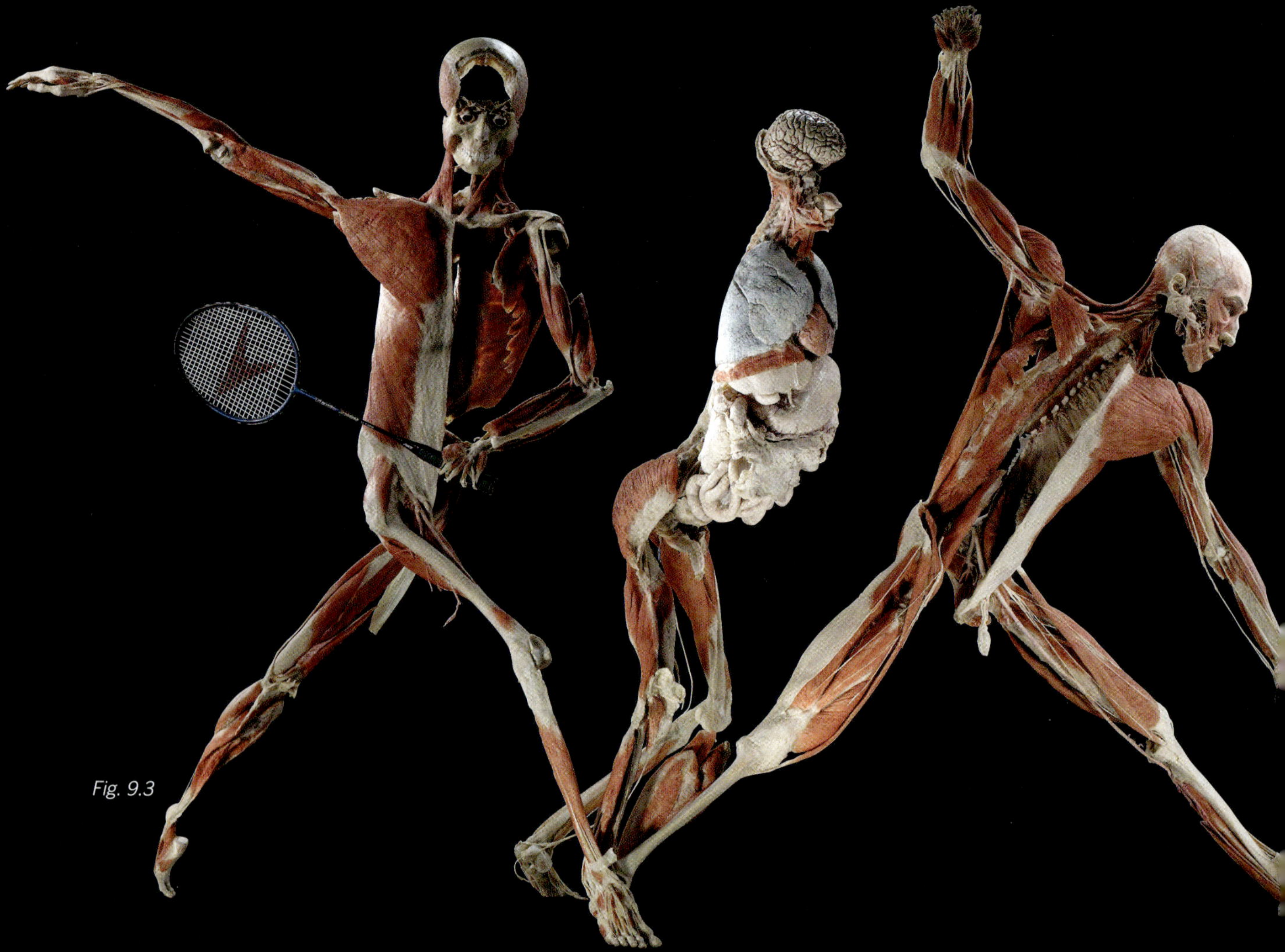

Fig. 9.3

## The Badminton Player

Plastination allows for completely new kinds of anatomical dissections, such as dissection by expansion. Here, like in an exploded view, anatomical structures are opened up and shifted apart. This creates artificial spaces, allowing all organs in the body to be viewed, even if they overlap or cover one another. Extended bodies are made possible only with plastination, since it gives the tissue the necessary stability.

In this posed plastinate, the body shell as well as the limbs were split frontally along functional structures and then pulled apart. For example, in the left upper arm, the extensor muscles that stretch out the arm were left with the front part, whereas the flexor muscles bending the arm were left with the rear part. In the middle is the spine together with all internal organs.

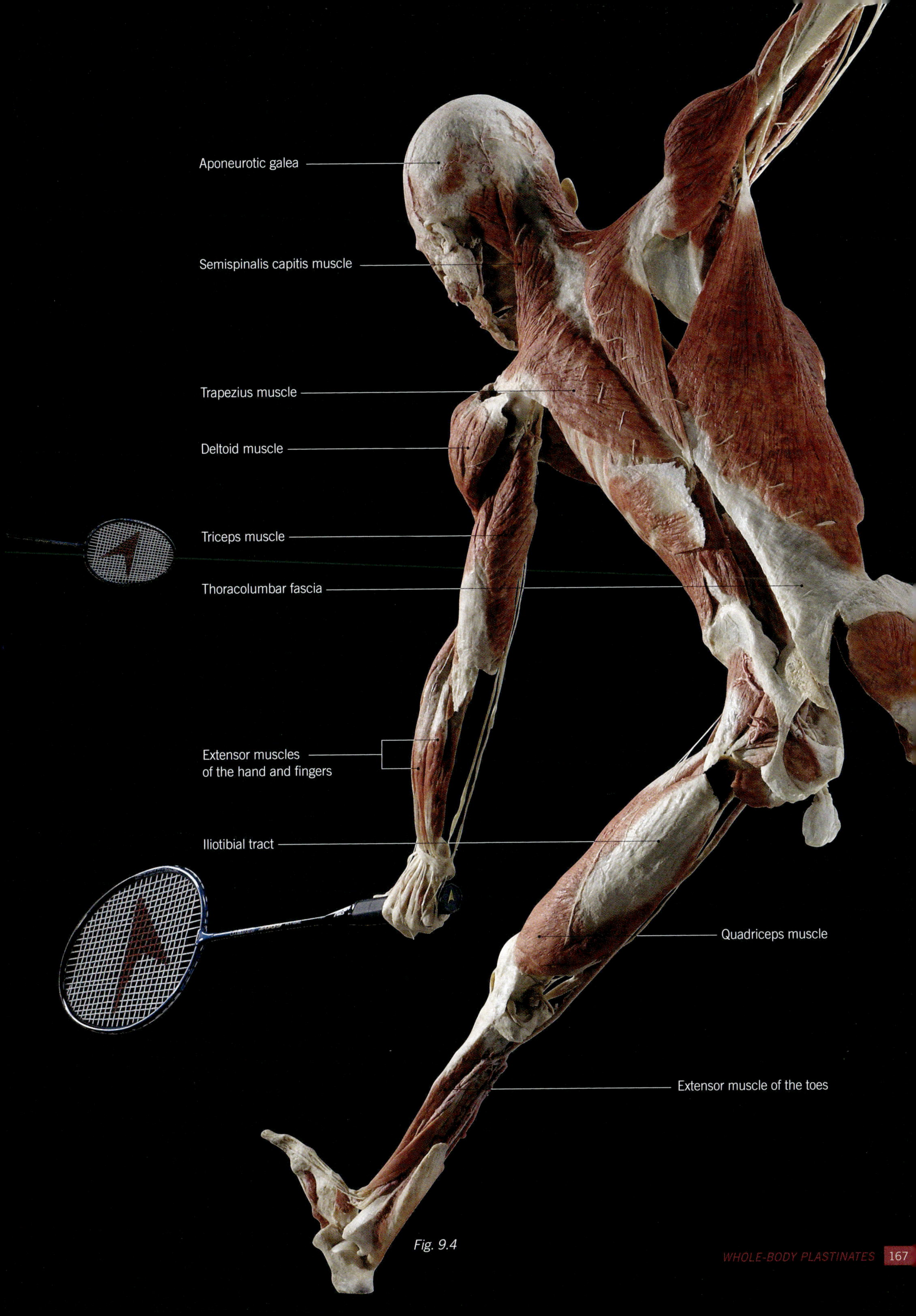
Aponeurotic galea
Semispinalis capitis muscle
Trapezius muscle
Deltoid muscle
Triceps muscle
Thoracolumbar fascia
Extensor muscles
of the hand and fingers
Iliotibial tract
Quadriceps muscle
Extensor muscle of the toes

*Fig. 9.4*

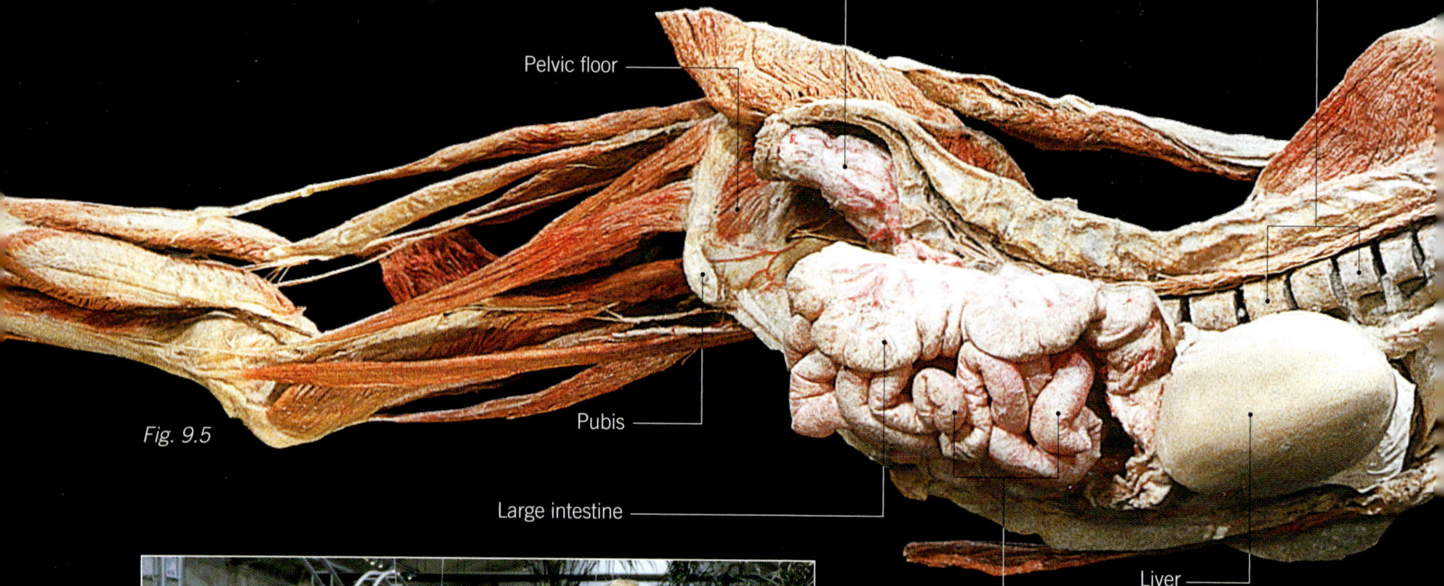


*Fig. 9.5*

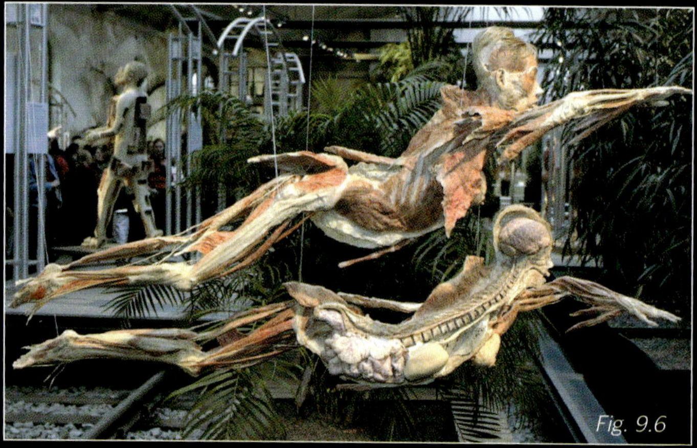

*Fig. 9.6*

## The Swimmer

The body shell has been laterally separated into two halves. However, the inner organs have been left in their original positions either in the left or right body half. On the corresponding side and opposite each organ, cavities indicate the position, form, and size of the organs that have been removed.

The vertebrae can thus be seen in the left half, with the oesophagus in front, and the liver and the intestines in the abdominal cavity. The inter-vertebral discs can be seen in the right half, as well as the uterus with the ovaries and Fallopian tubes in the pelvic cavity.

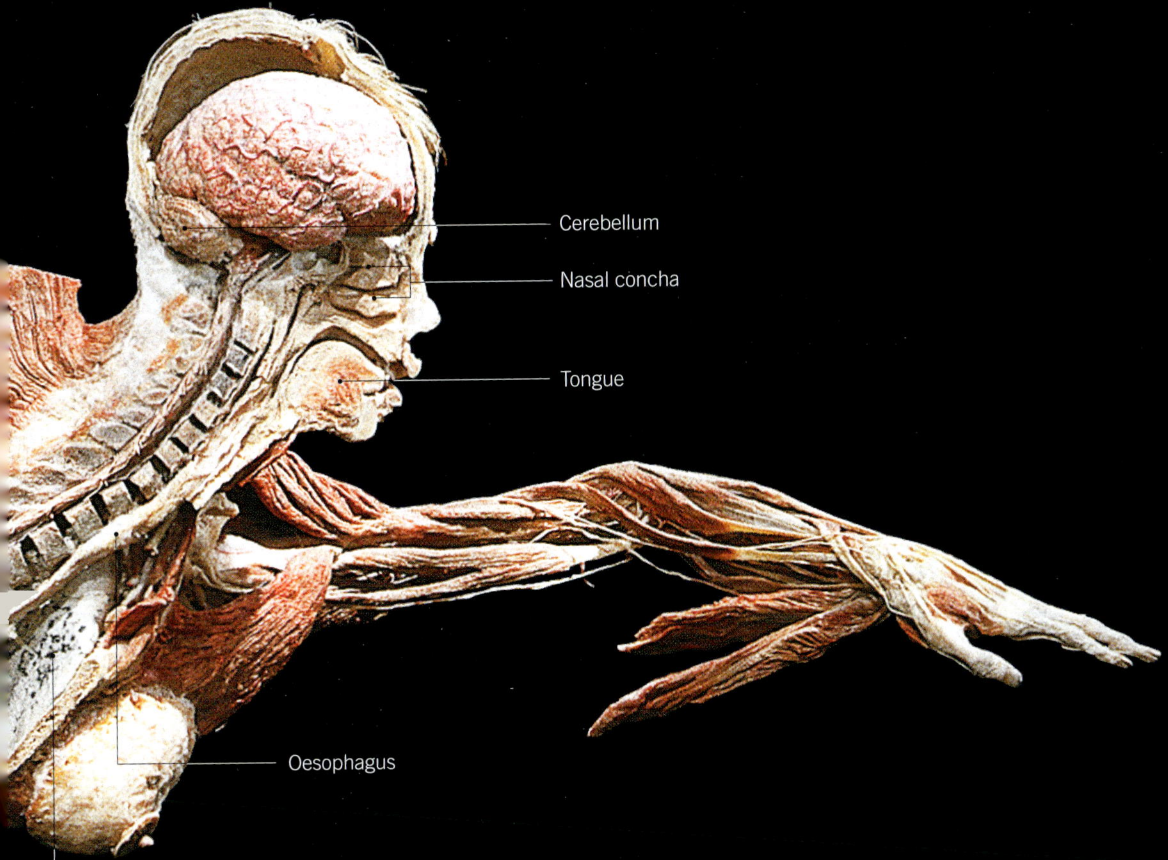
Cerebellum
Nasal concha
Tongue
Oesophagus
Left lung

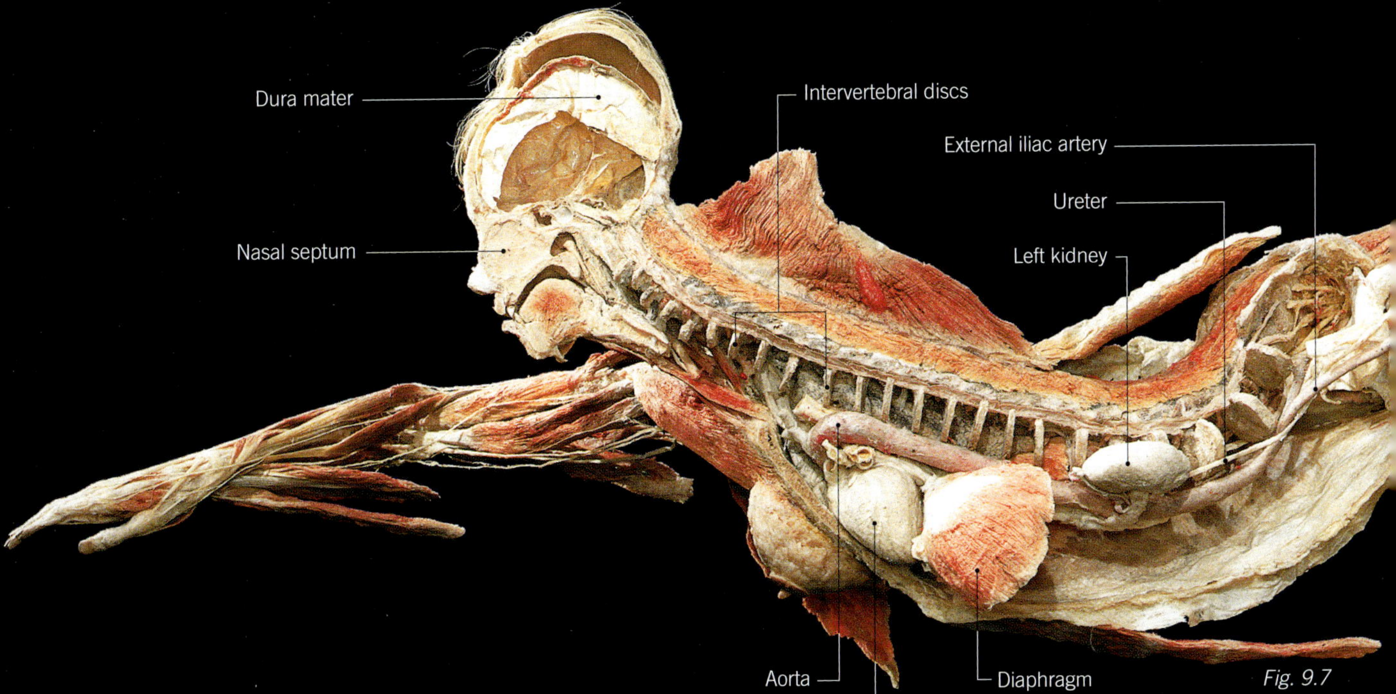
Dura mater
Intervertebral discs
External iliac artery
Ureter
Left kidney
Nasal septum
Aorta
Heart
Diaphragm

*Fig. 9.7*

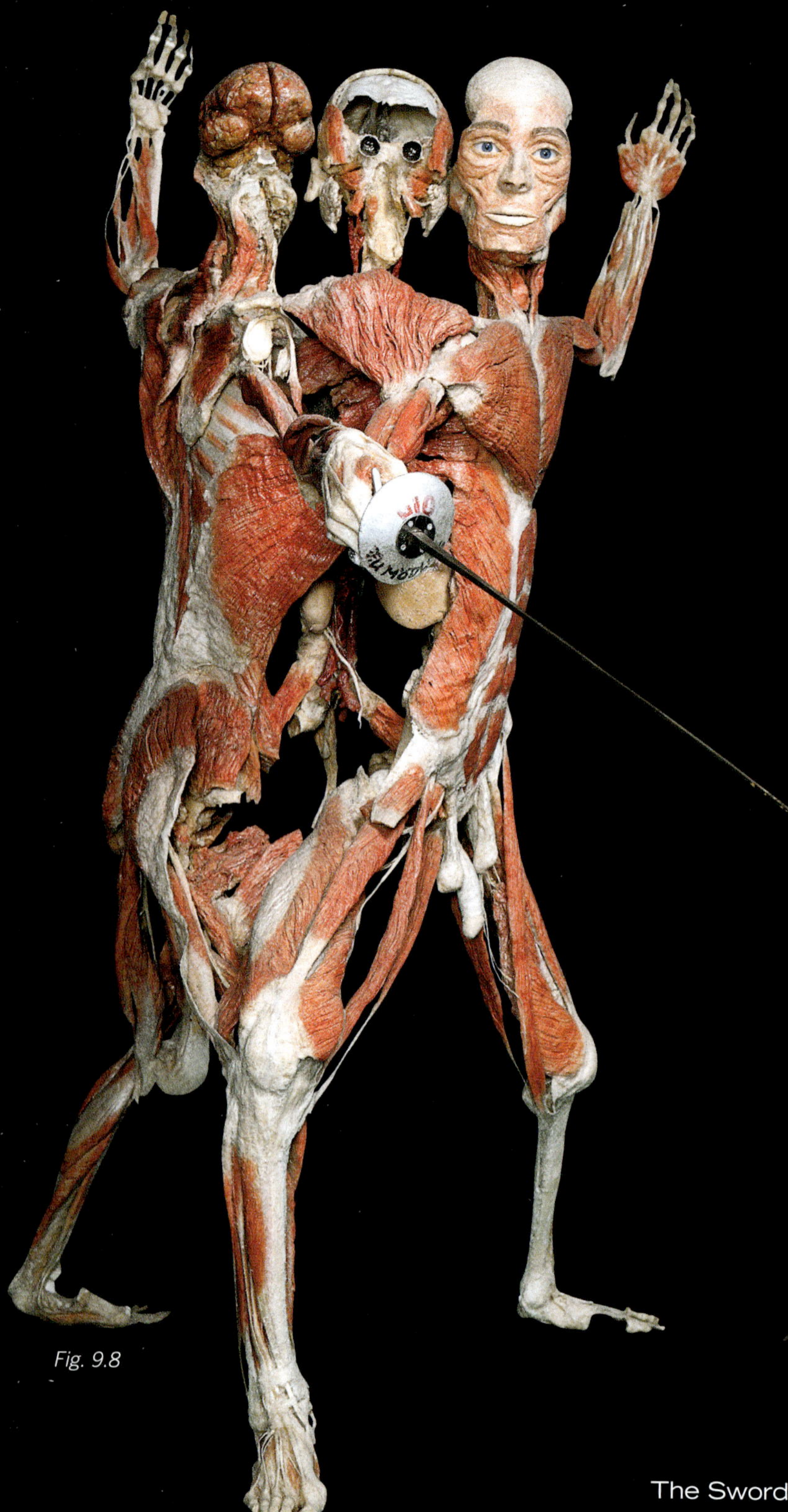

Fig. 9.8

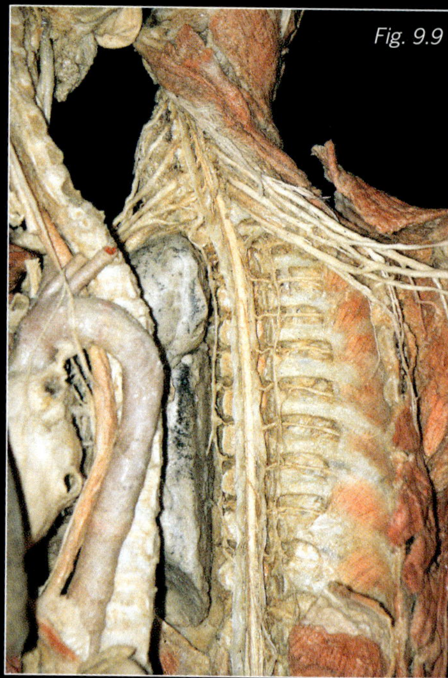

Fig. 9.9

## The Swordsman

The left side of this posed specimen
was first opened sagittally;
then the two halves of the body were forced apart
to permit a view of the internal organs.
The inclination of the head imparts a sense
of the complex functional anatomy of the cervical spine
with its emerging nerve endings.

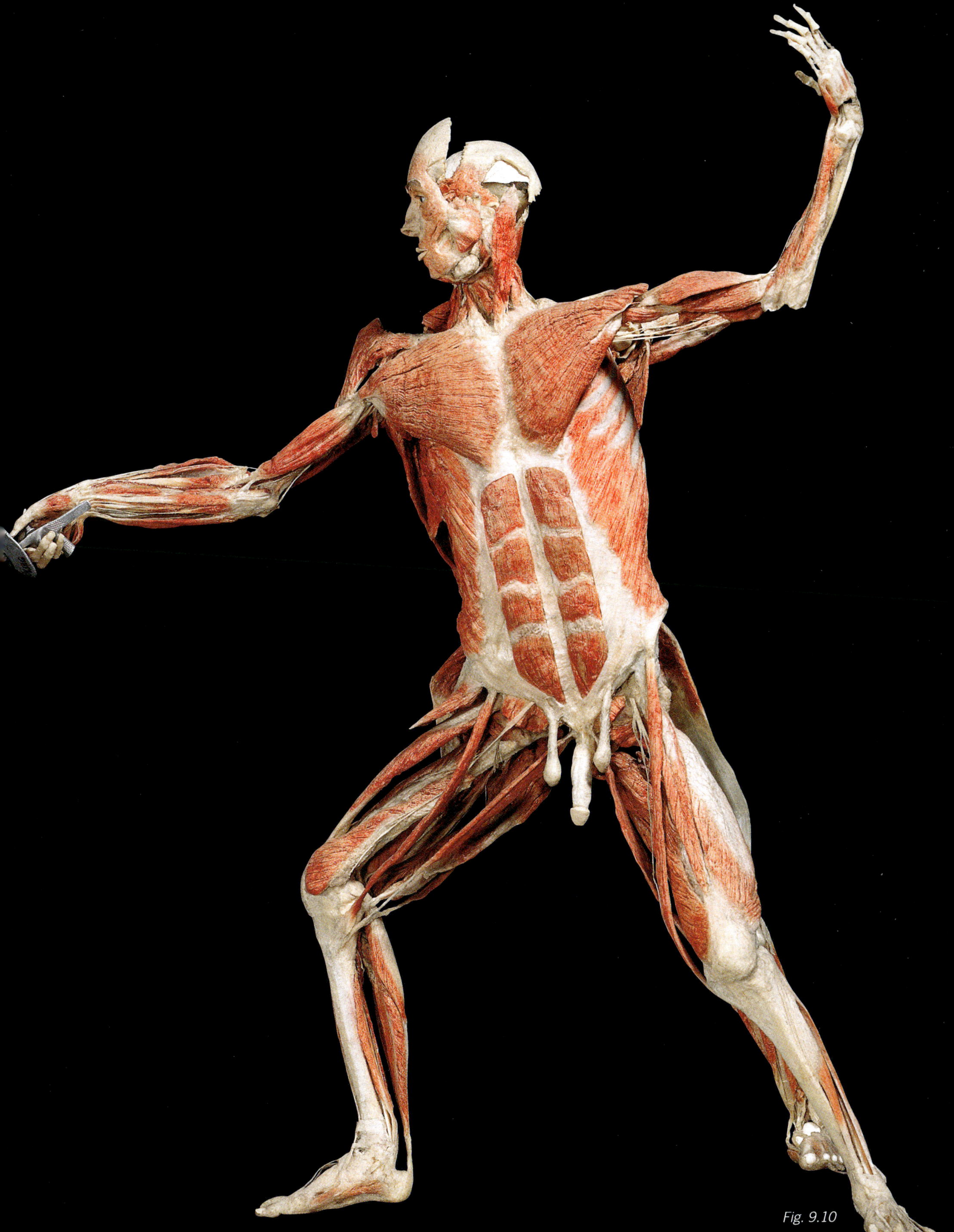

Fig. 9.10

## The Basketball Player

The Basketball Player plastinate demonstrates the skin modelling muscles of our body in a very dynamic posture. The skull has been opened to reveal the brain. The intestines have been removed in order to show the large back muscles at the rear of the abdominal cavity. The urinary bladder rests at the bottom of the small pelvis.

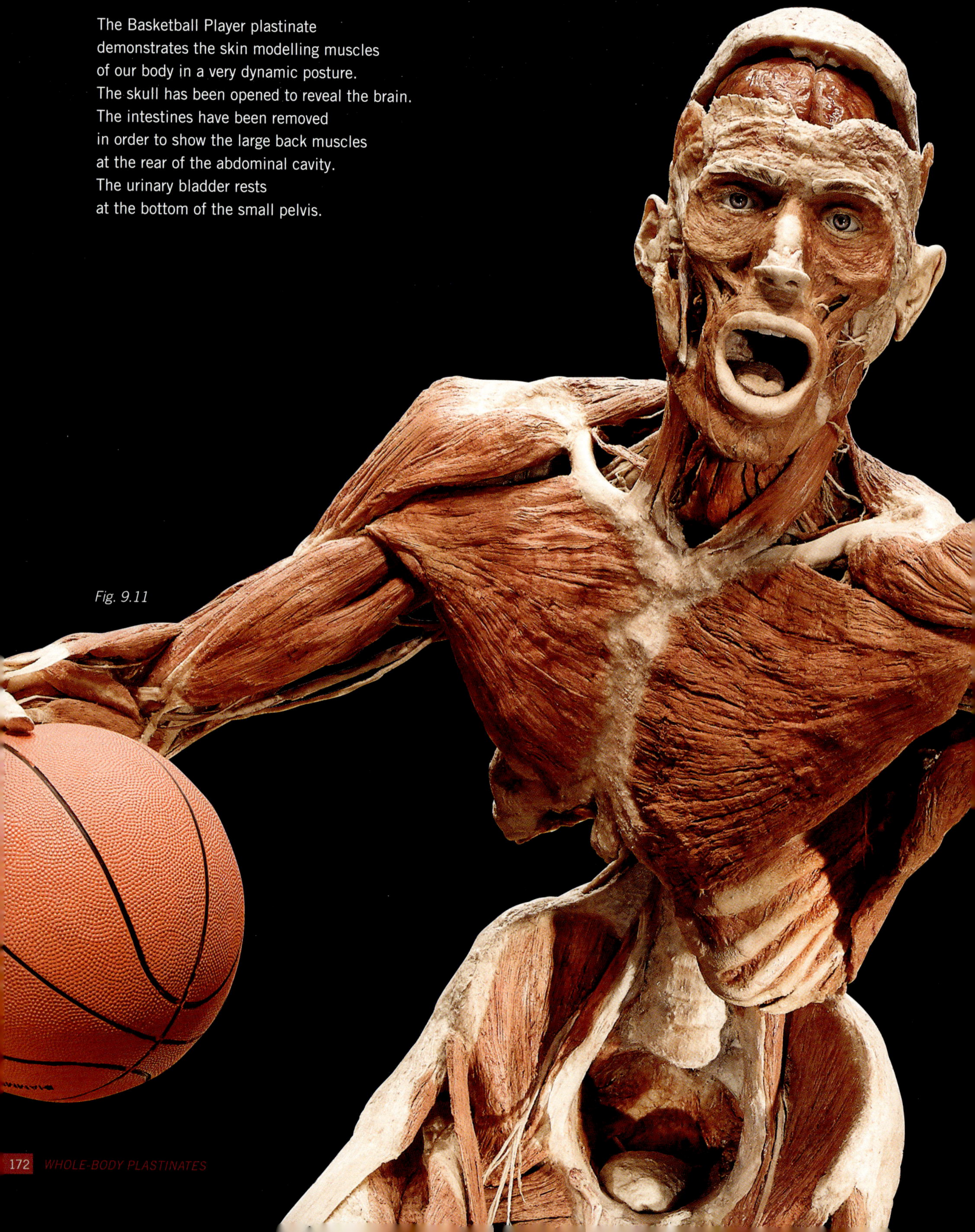

*Fig. 9.11*

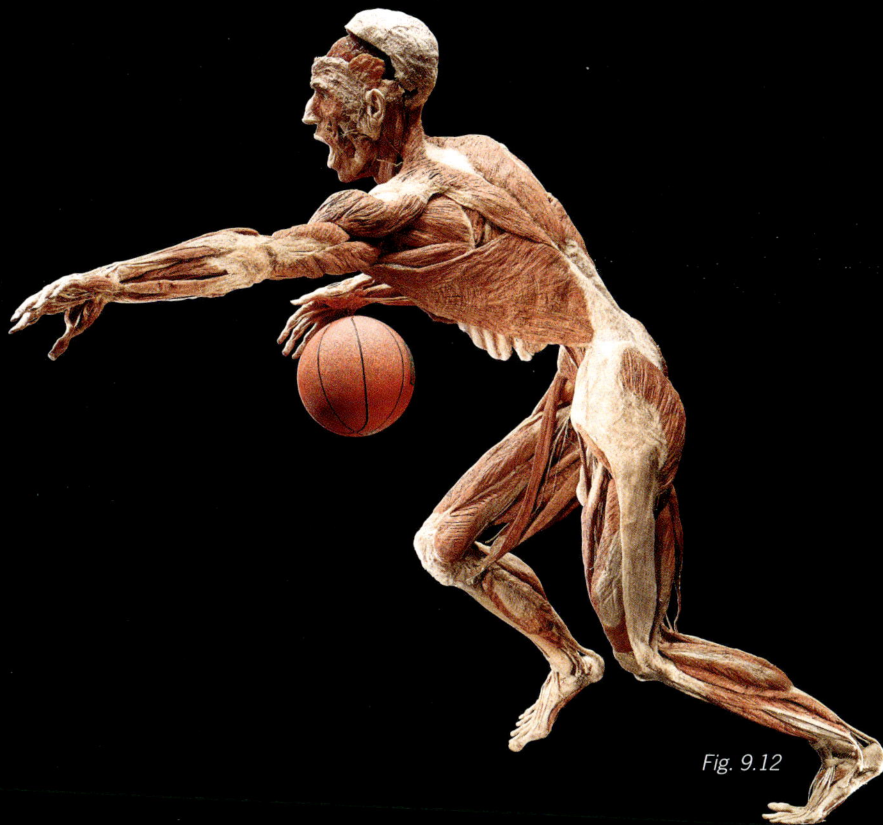

Fig. 9.12

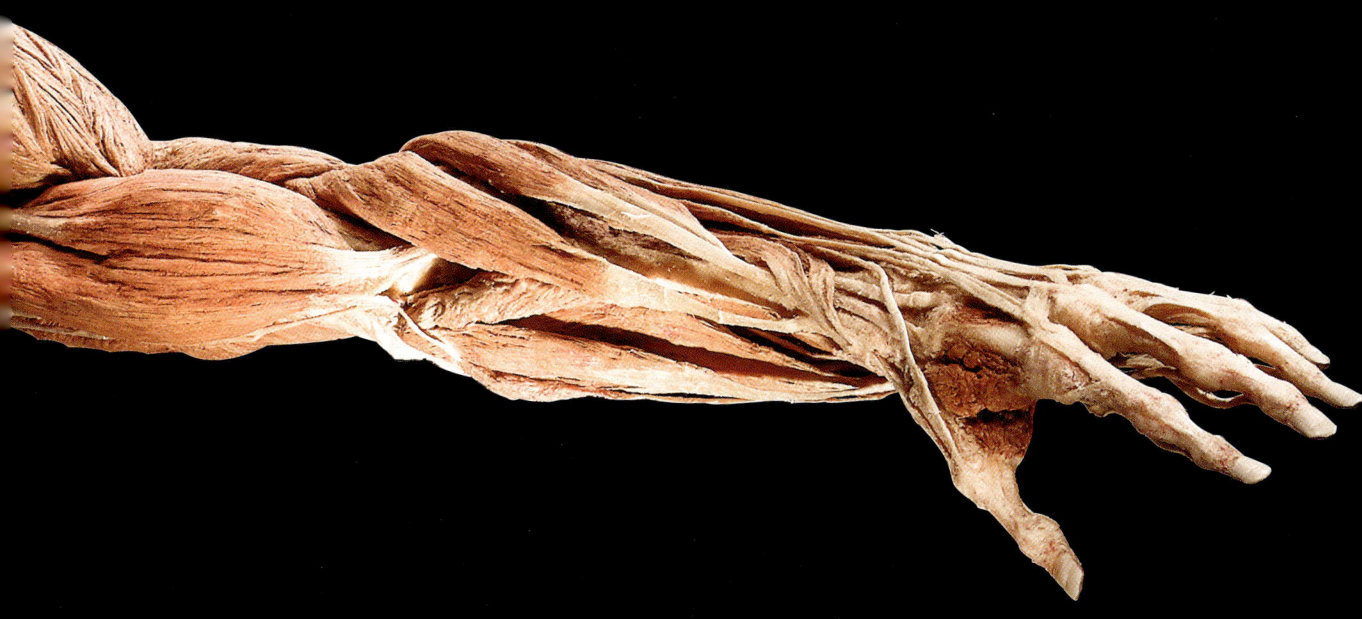

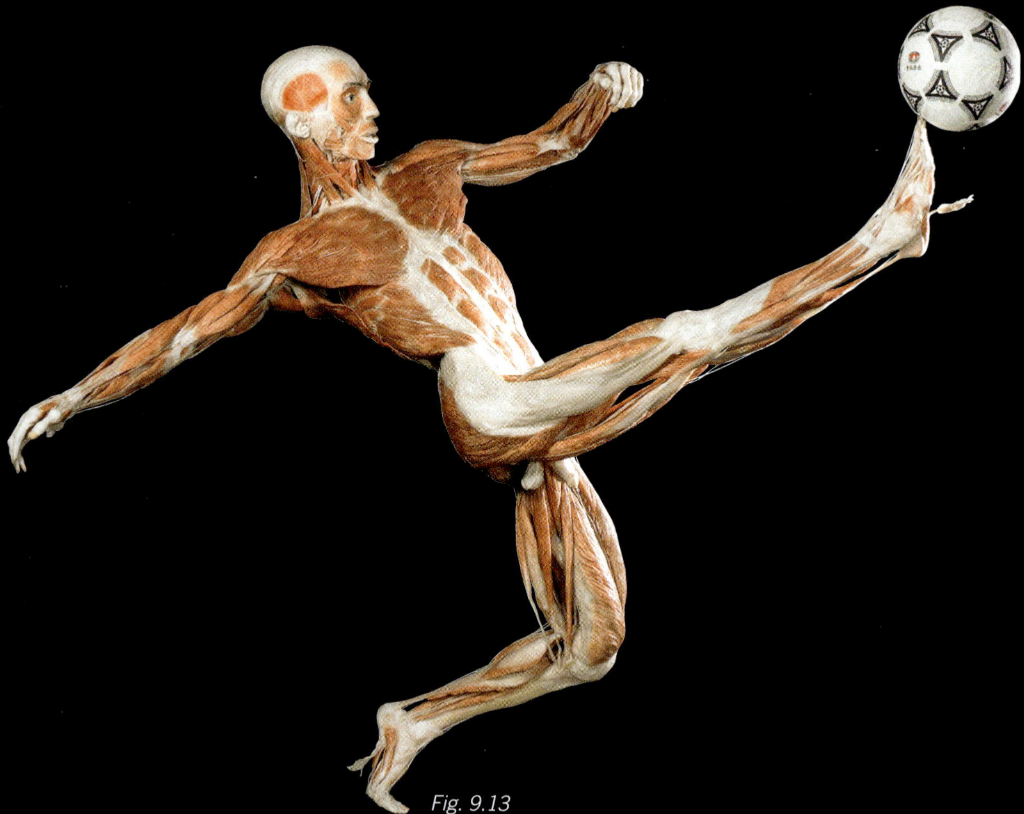

Fig. 9.13

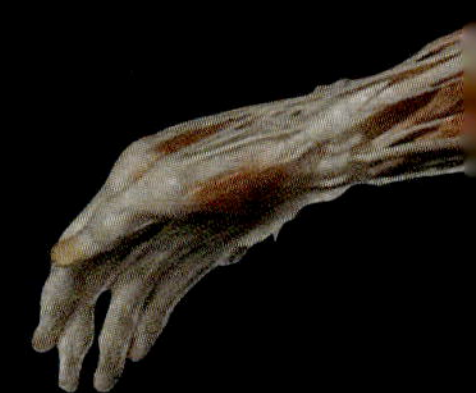

## The Soccer Player

Skeletal muscles make up
almost half the weight of our body.
We use these muscles when we sit, stand, or move.
The skeletal muscles vary in shape and strength.
The muscles that surround the spine
are the most powerful ones.
They give us posture.
This plastinate shows the interplay
between surface and intermediate muscles
when they work together in movement.

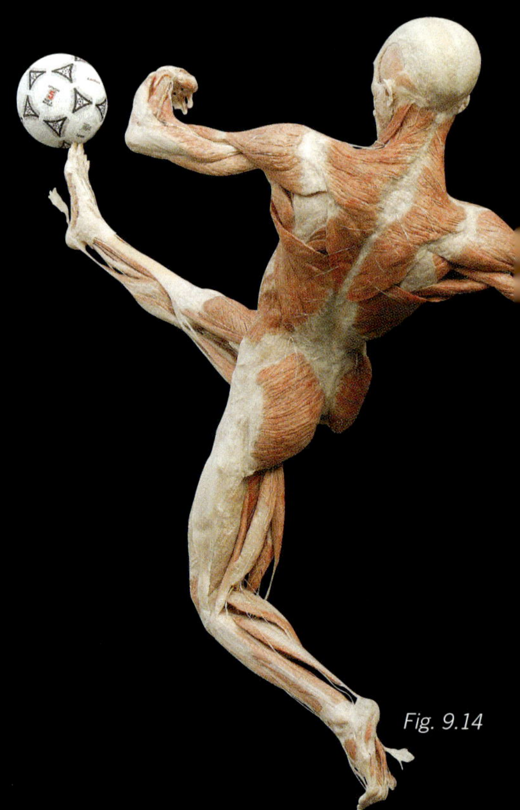

Fig. 9.14

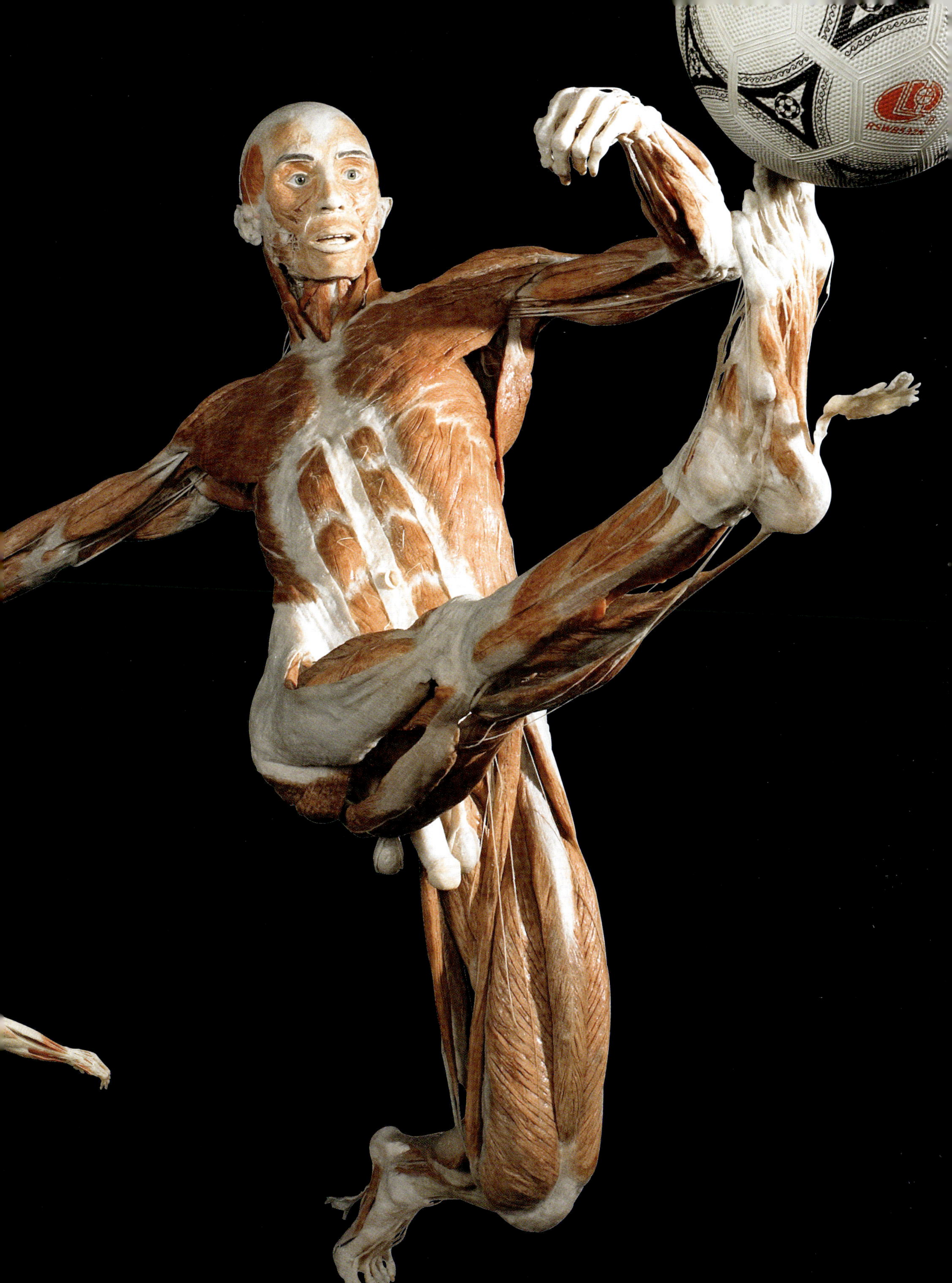

Fig. 9.15

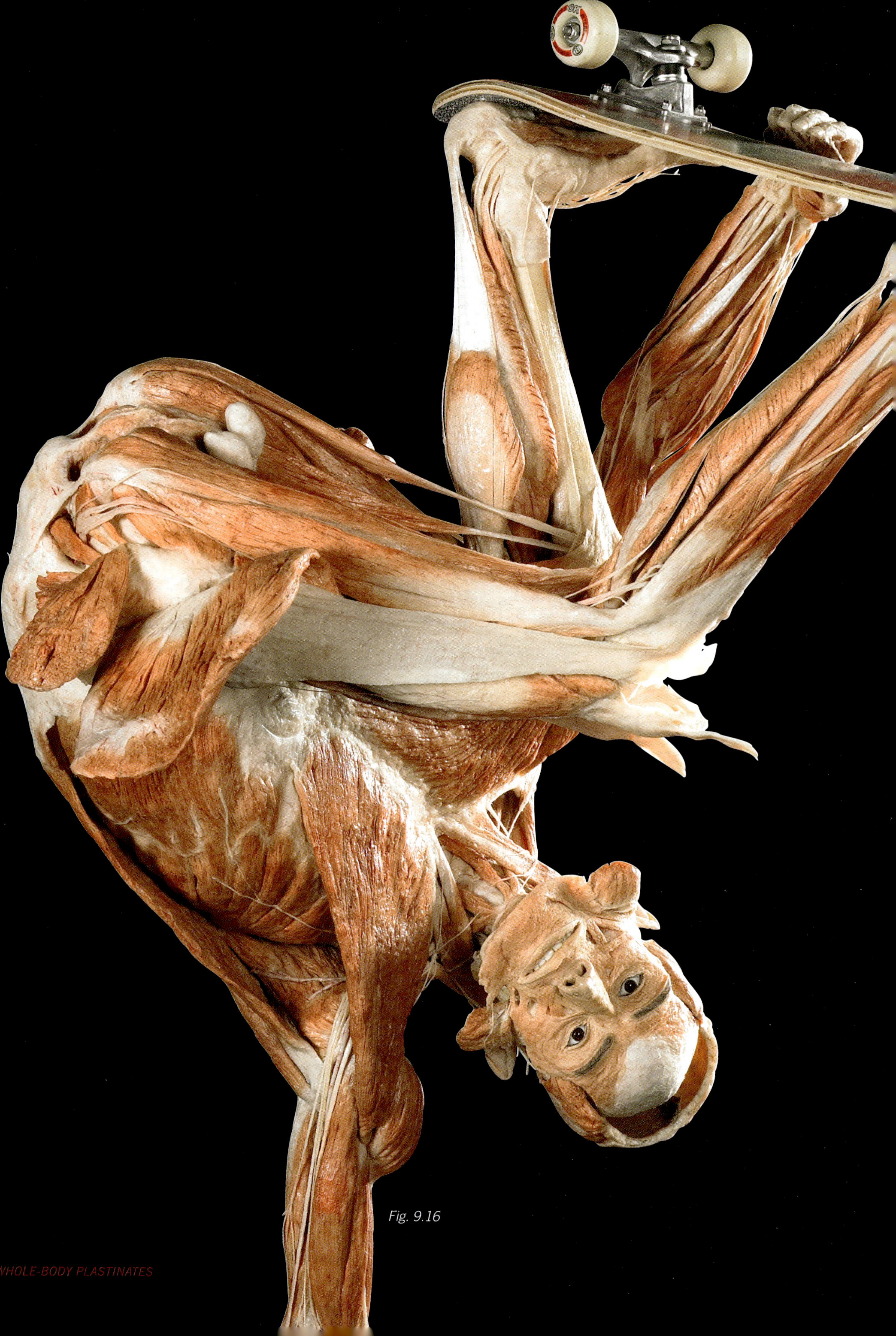

Fig. 9.16

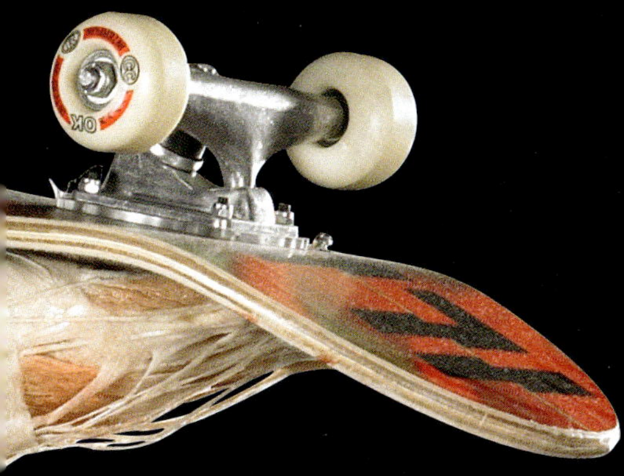

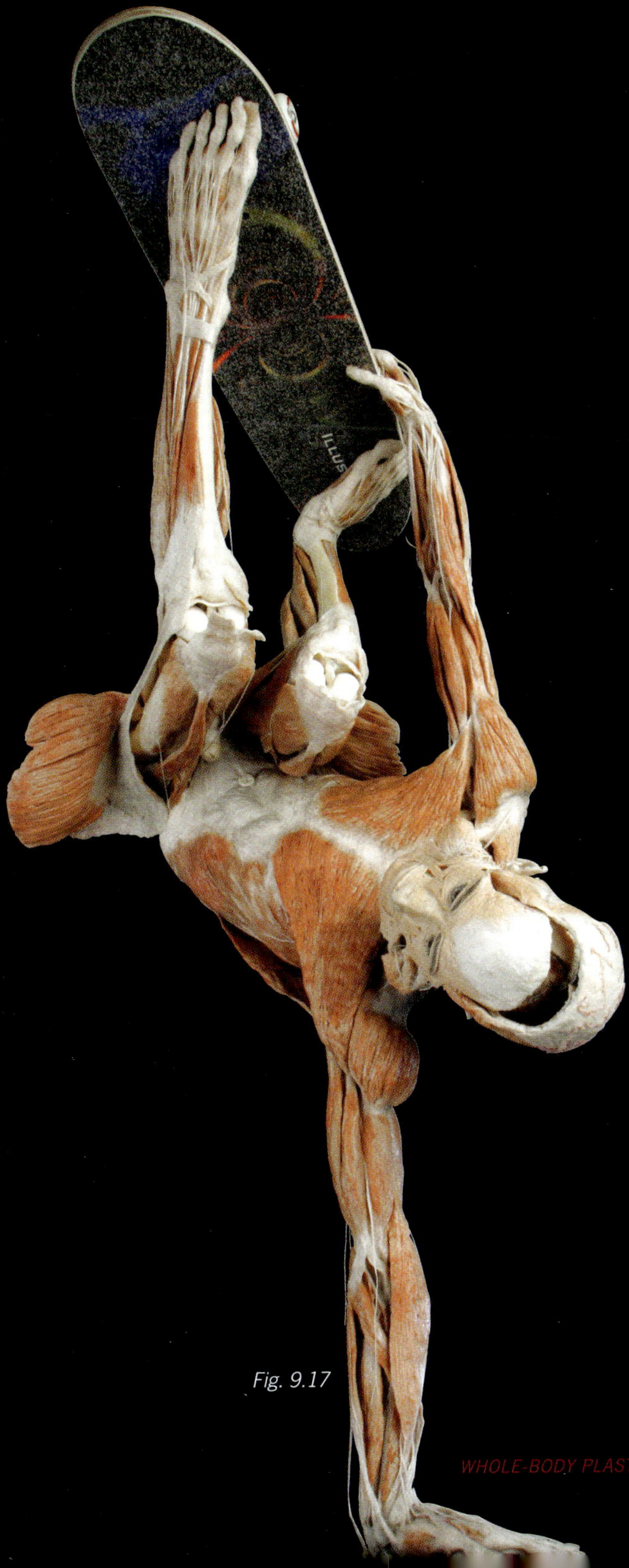

## The Skateboarder

This skateboarder's upside-down trick offers
an insight into the anatomy of the buttocks.
The buttocks comprise three gluteal muscles.
The largest – the gluteus maximus
is one of the body's strongest muscles.
Here, the muscles are flapped back
to reveal the thick band of the sciatic nerve
running underneath past the sitting bone of the pelvis.
Skateboarding is demanding on the knee joints.
Here, the kneecaps have been lifted.
The knee joint is a hinge joint
and, like most joints in the body,
contains a lubricating fluid called synovial fluid.
Since the knee supports much of the body weight,
obesity may make knee osteoarthritis more likely.

*Fig. 9.17*

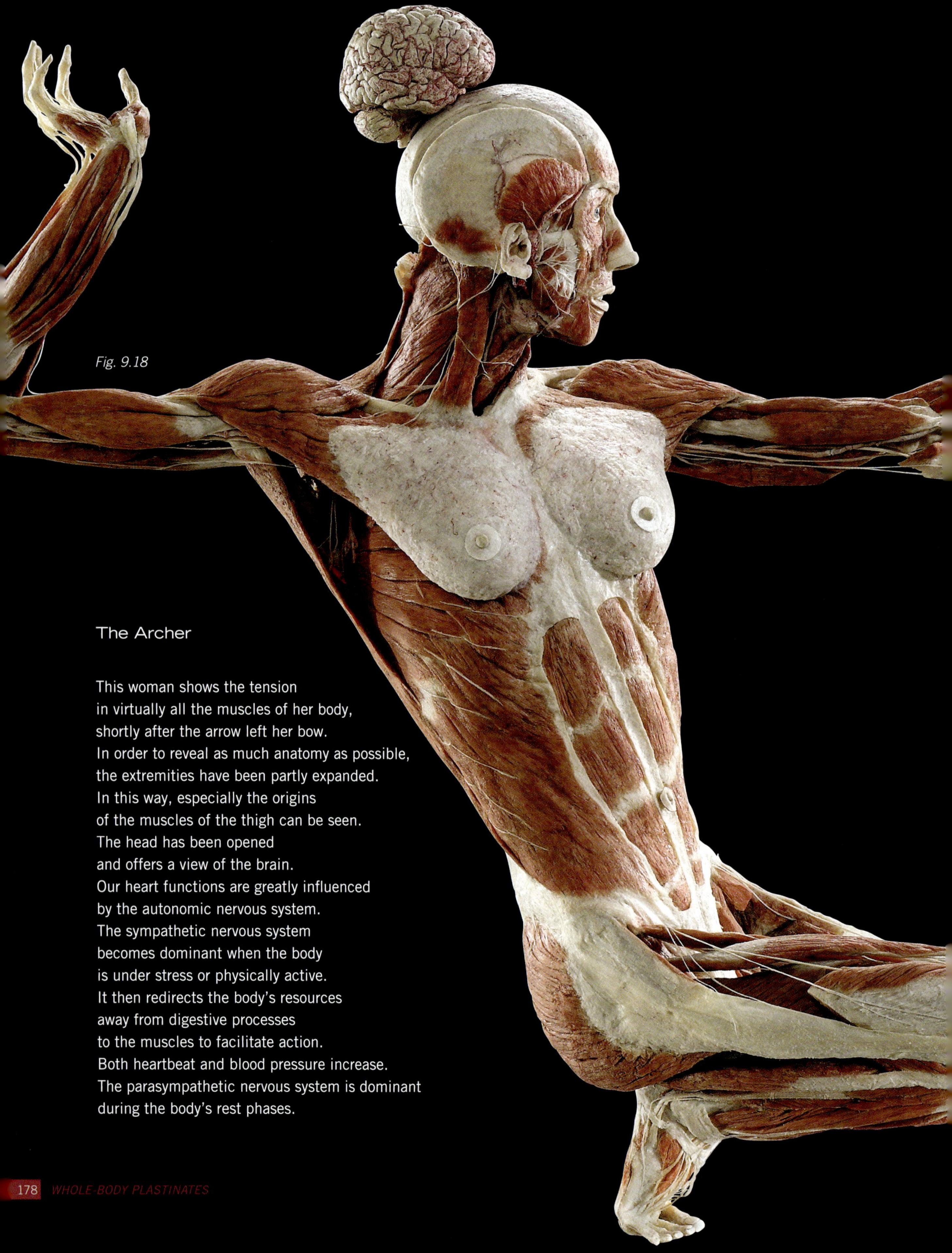

Fig. 9.18

## The Archer

This woman shows the tension in virtually all the muscles of her body, shortly after the arrow left her bow. In order to reveal as much anatomy as possible, the extremities have been partly expanded. In this way, especially the origins of the muscles of the thigh can be seen. The head has been opened and offers a view of the brain. Our heart functions are greatly influenced by the autonomic nervous system. The sympathetic nervous system becomes dominant when the body is under stress or physically active. It then redirects the body's resources away from digestive processes to the muscles to facilitate action. Both heartbeat and blood pressure increase. The parasympathetic nervous system is dominant during the body's rest phases.

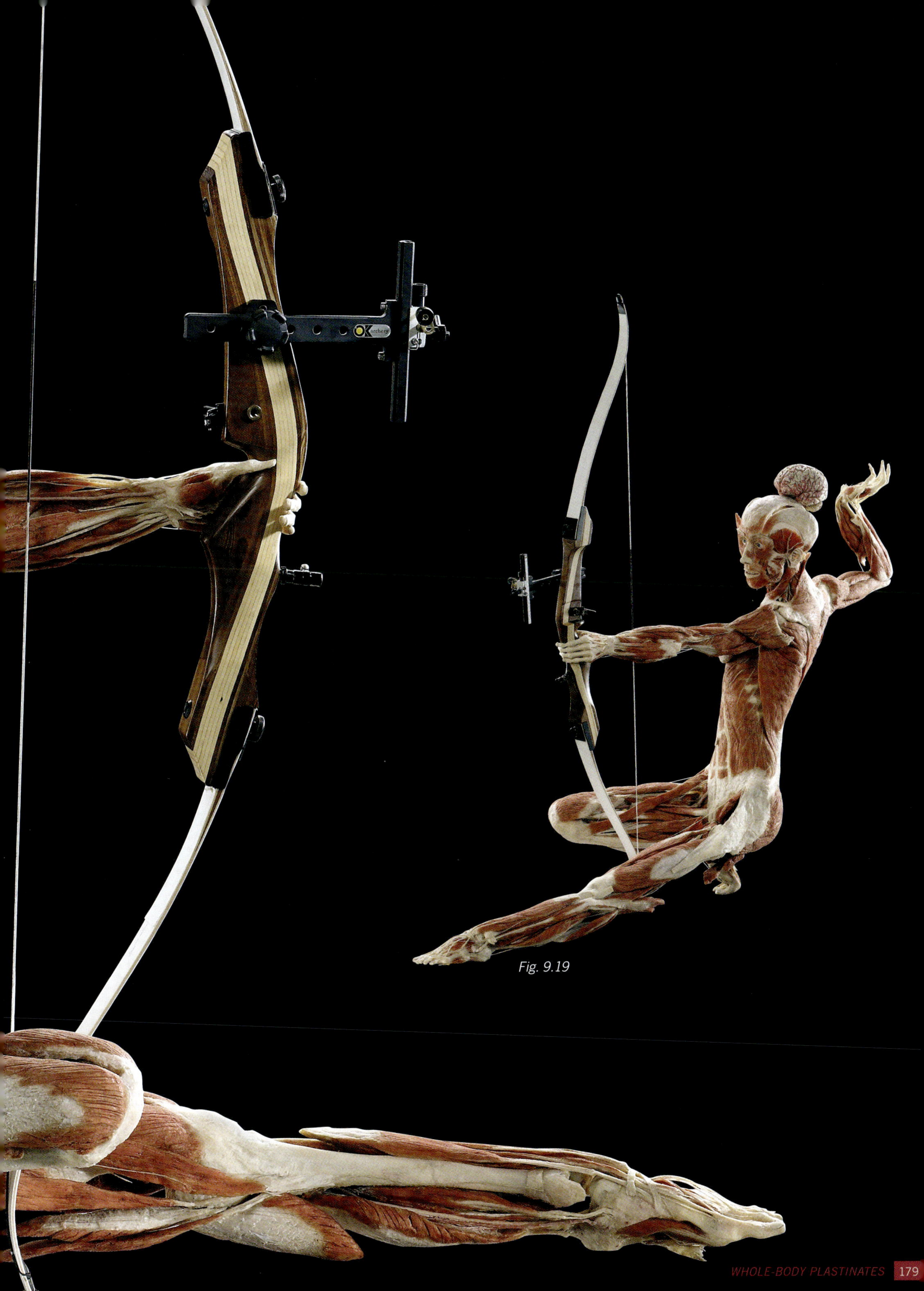

Fig. 9.19

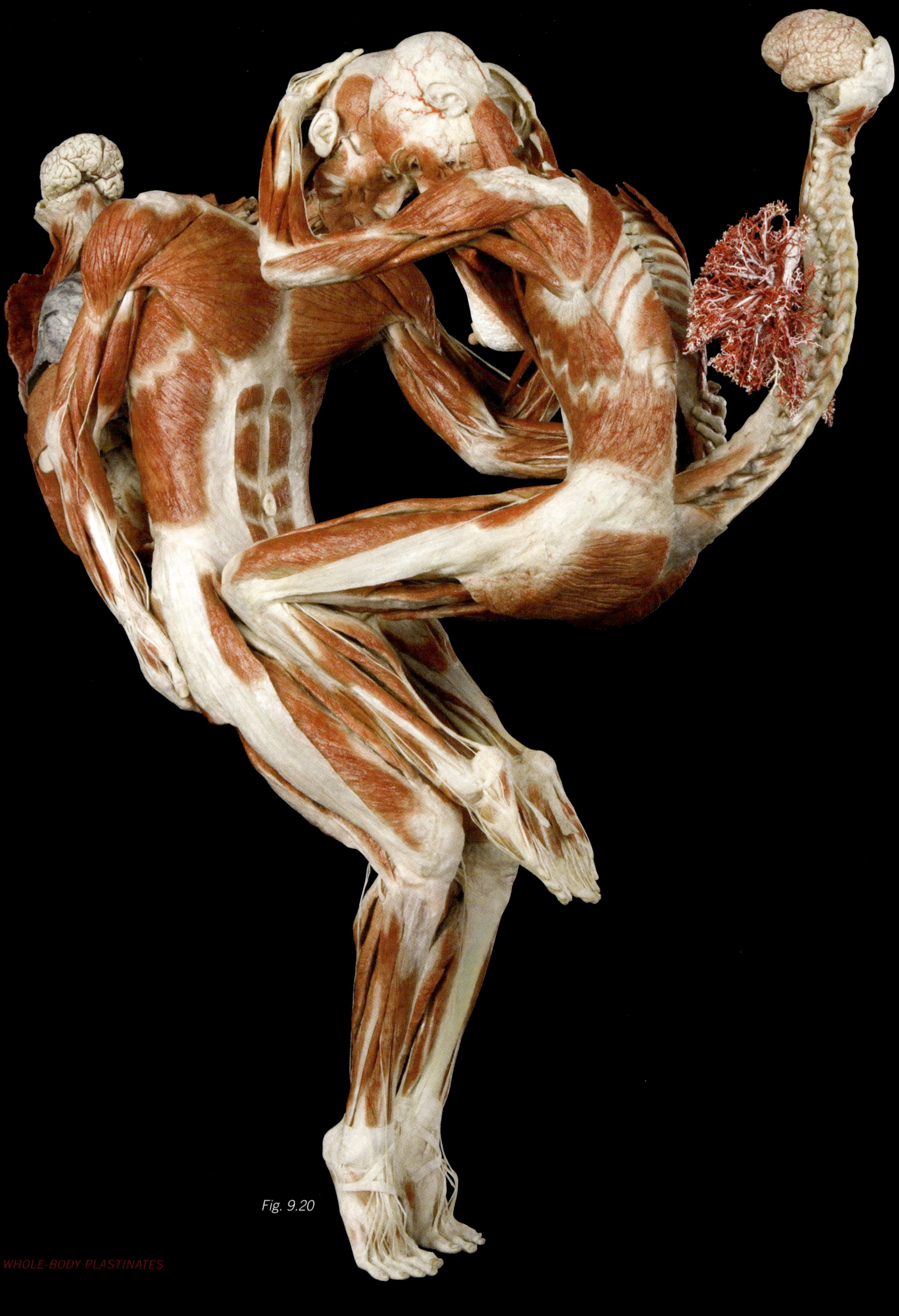

Fig. 9.20

## The Juxtaposed Couple

The juxtaposed plastinates embody
the relationship between the heart and the brain,
both physiological and physical.
The relationship between the two organs,
though still not fully explored,
is best explained by injuries and disease.

The skull, and thoracic and abdominal cavities
are opened from behind.
The brain rests on top of the occipital bone,
which in turn sits at the top
of the vertebral column.
The woman's lung is represented
by a cast of the bronchi (white)
and the large lung vessels (red).
In the male body, the lungs can be seen
with the heart resting on the diaphragm,
our primary respiratory muscle.

The brain with its cool logic,
and the heart with its volatility,
act alone as well as in concert – juxtaposed –
to make up our essential selves.
But the heart alone is viewed as the vessel
of love and malice, compassion and cruelty,
good and evil.

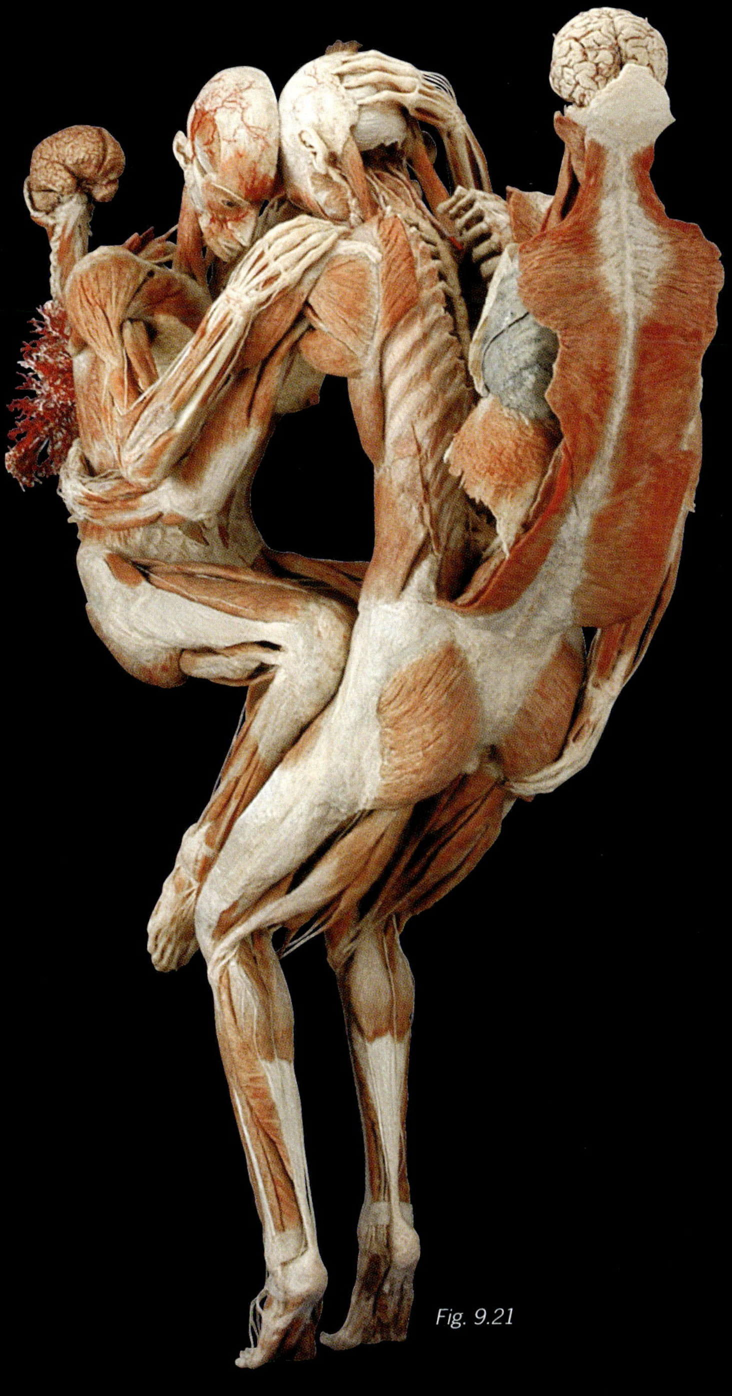

*Fig. 9.21*

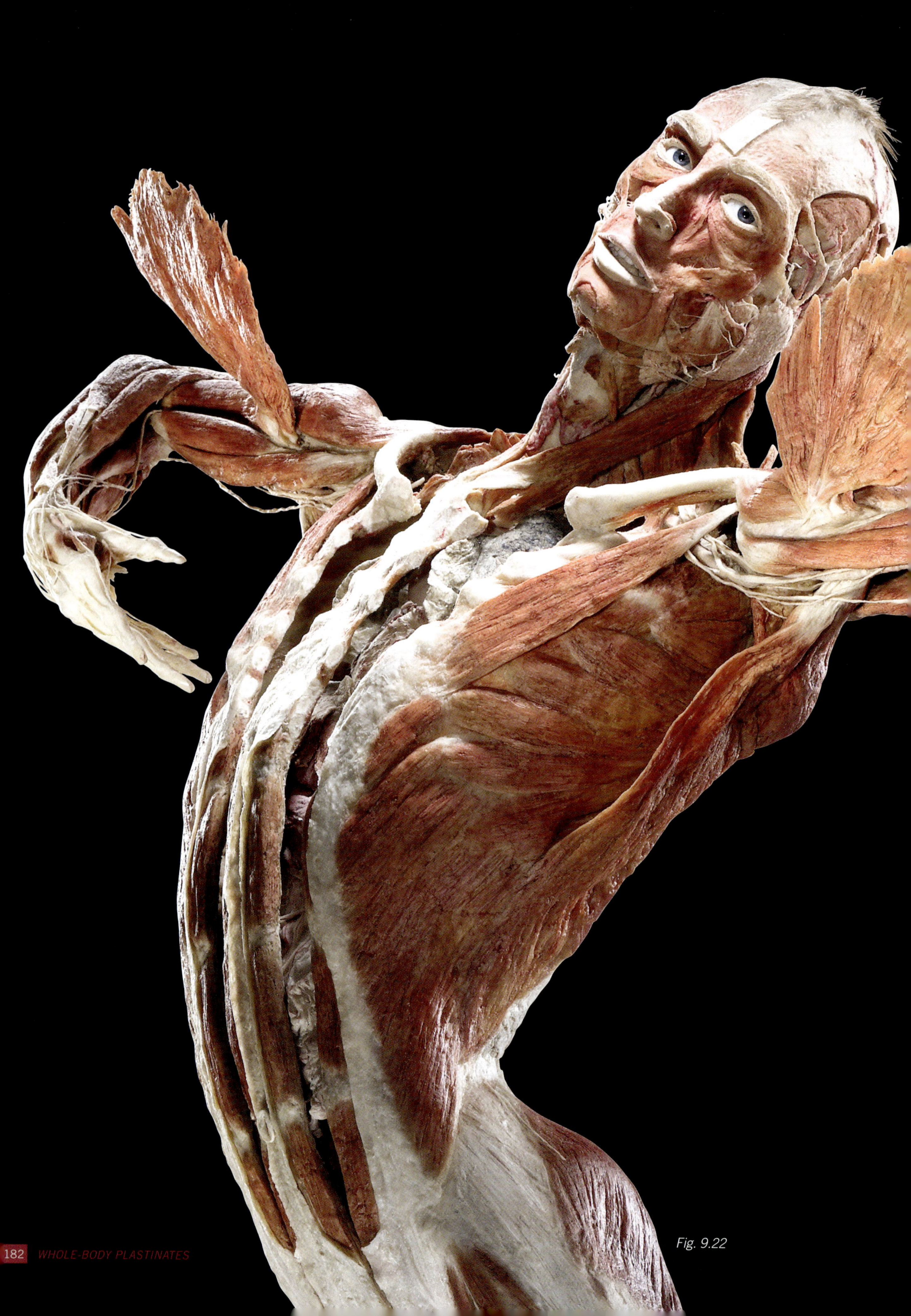

Fig. 9.22

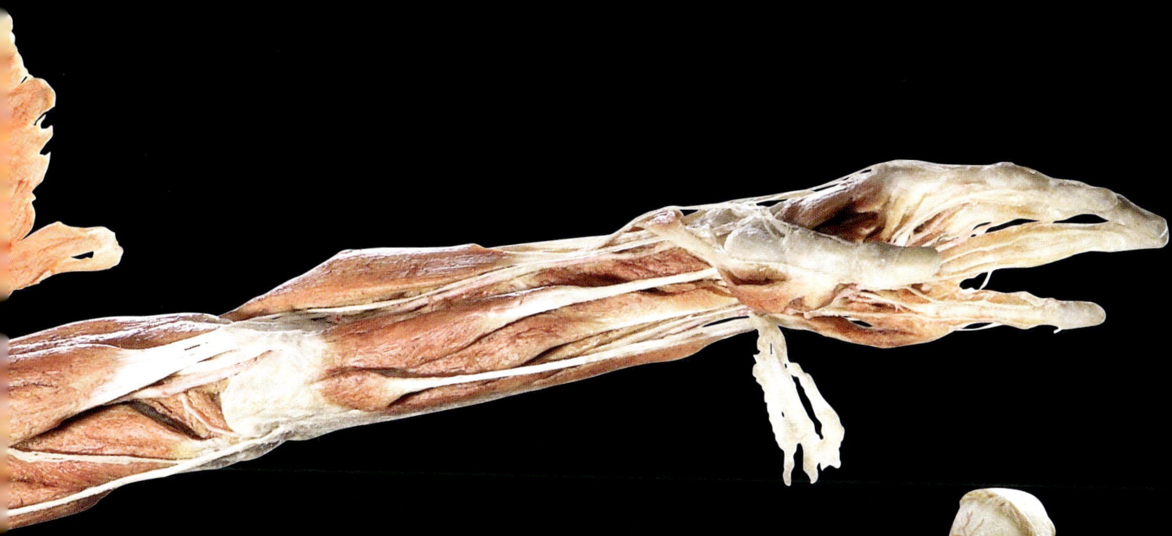

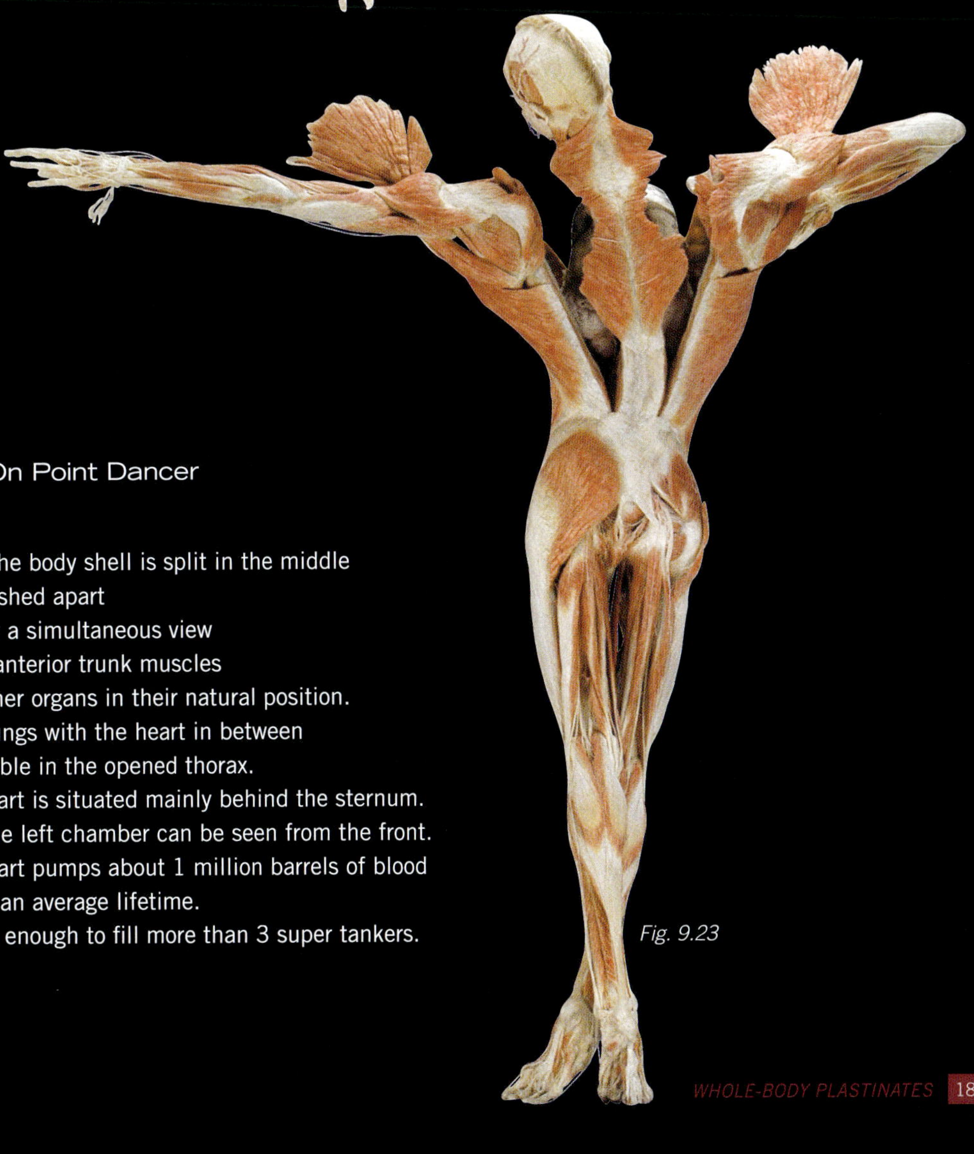

## The On Point Dancer

Here, the body shell is split in the middle
and pushed apart
to offer a simultaneous view
of the anterior trunk muscles
and inner organs in their natural position.
Both lungs with the heart in between
are visible in the opened thorax.
The heart is situated mainly behind the sternum.
Only the left chamber can be seen from the front.
The heart pumps about 1 million barrels of blood
during an average lifetime.
That is enough to fill more than 3 super tankers.

*Fig. 9.23*

## Limber Gymnast with Organs

While balancing on three wooden balls
with outstretched legs, this plastinate
presents his internal organs
with lungs, heart, liver, and intestinal tract.
Those organs were taken out from behind.
The spine is flipped up,
offering a view into the thoracic
and abdominal cavities.

The ability to maintain balance
depends on information that the brain receives
from the eyes,
the muscles and joints,
and the vestibular organs in the inner ears.
All three of these sources send information
in form of nerve impulses
from sensory receptors to our brain.
Our body's posture is largely maintained
by reflexive, involuntary control.

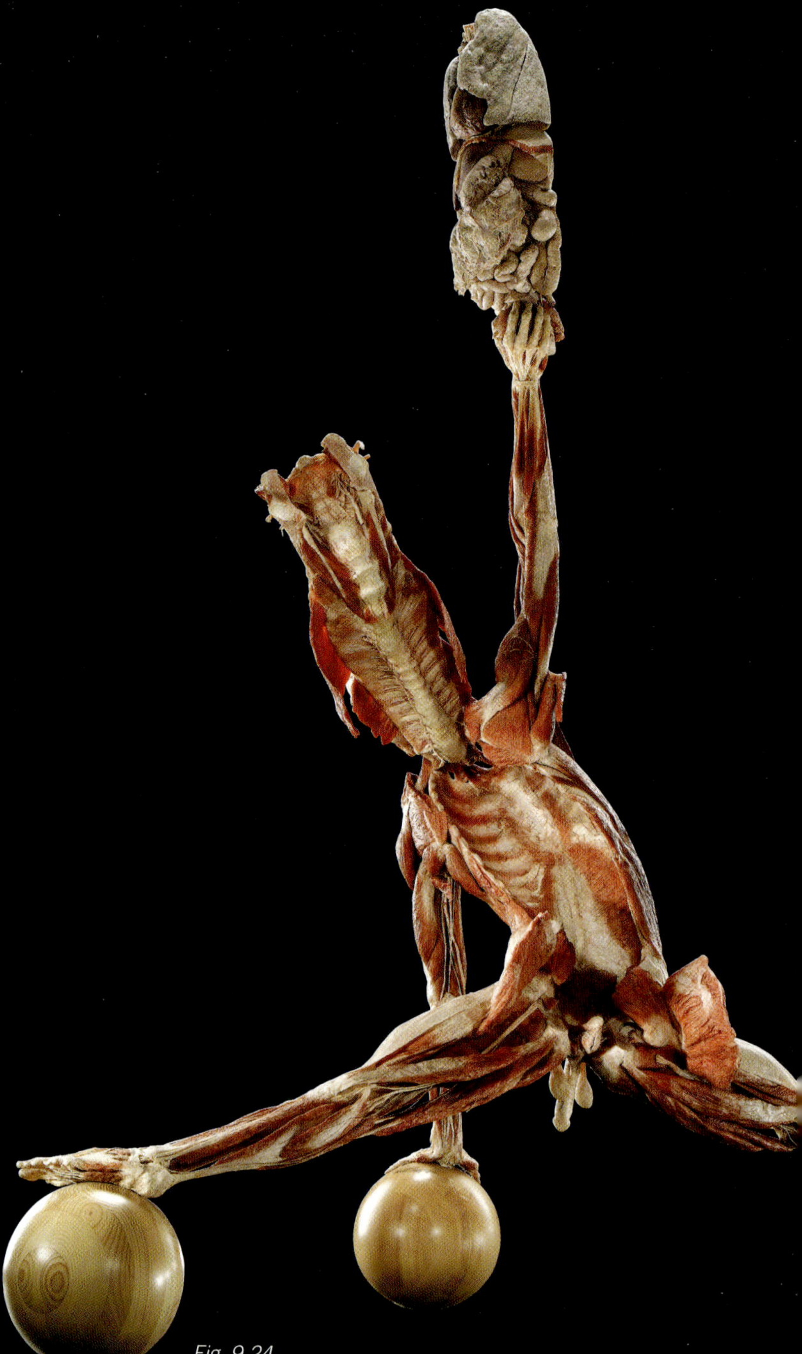

*Fig. 9.24*

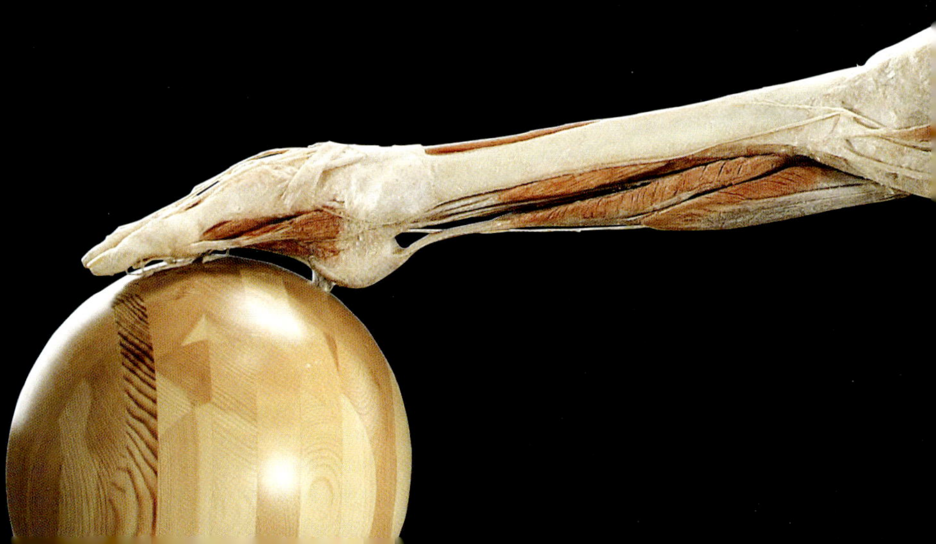

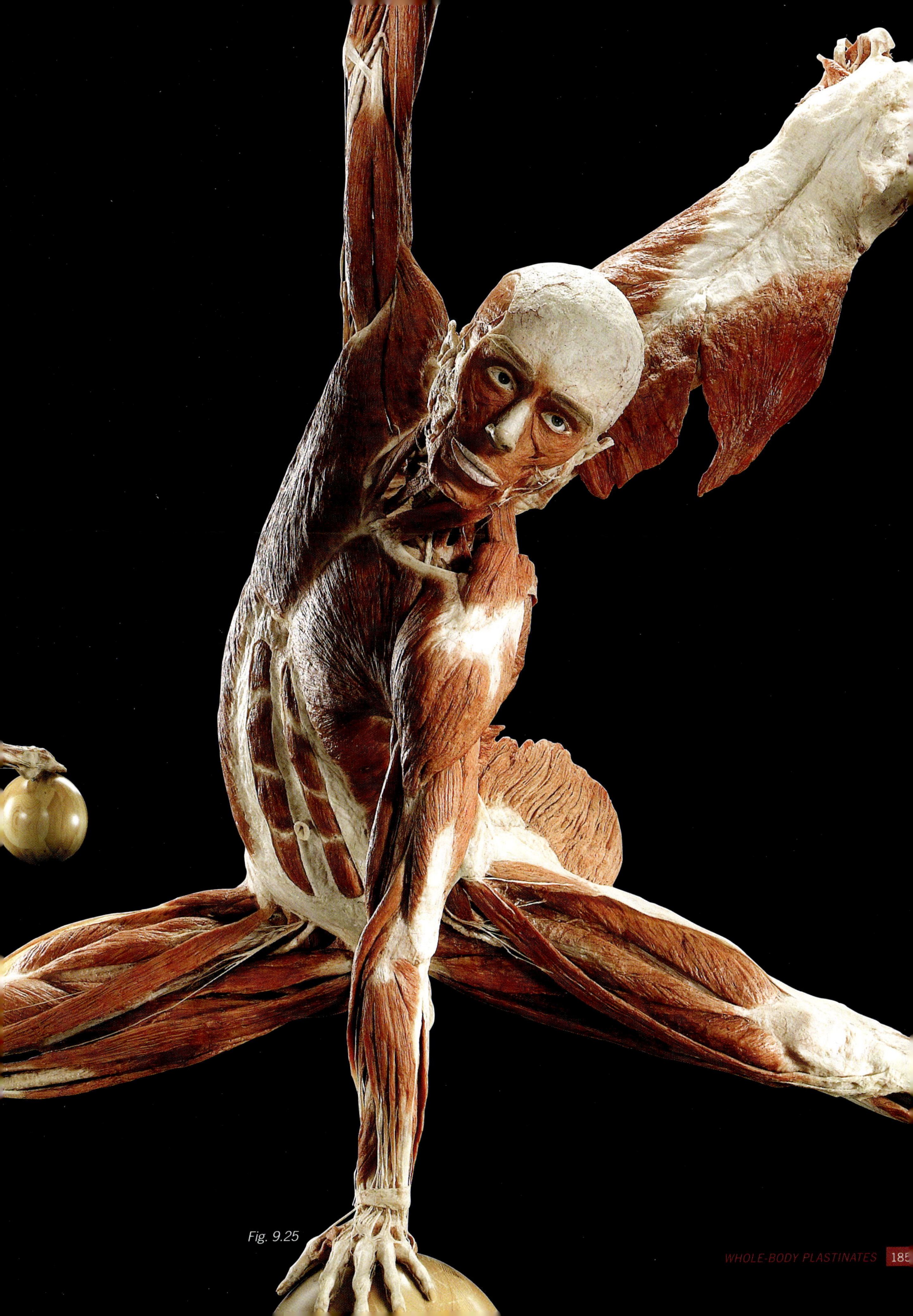

Fig. 9.25

## The Ponderer

This sitting specimen shows the spinal cord
and the detailed pathways of nerves branching off it.
The spinal cord and brain
comprise the central nervous system.
This system controls and integrates body functions.
Because it is so crucial, it is very well protected.
It is embedded in three tough sheets
of connective tissue, called meninges.
The spinal cord is also enclosed in the backbone.
From between the vertebrae,
31 pairs of spinal nerves
connect the spinal cord to the rest of the body.
The bundle of nerves at the base of the spine
is the cauda equina – the 'horse's tail'.
The two sciatic nerves run from the lower spine
behind the hip joint down the leg.
They are the largest and longest nerves in the body.

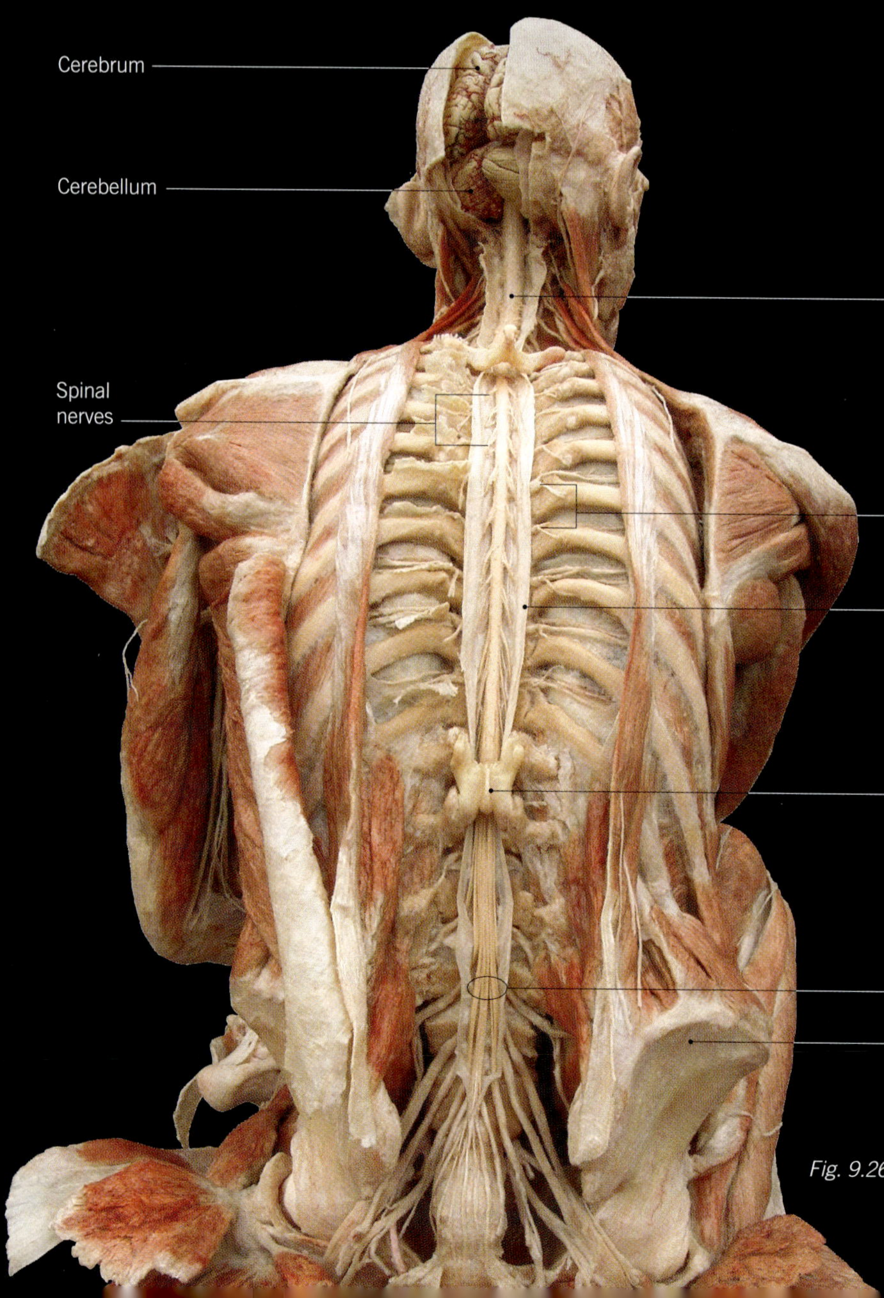


*Fig. 9.26*

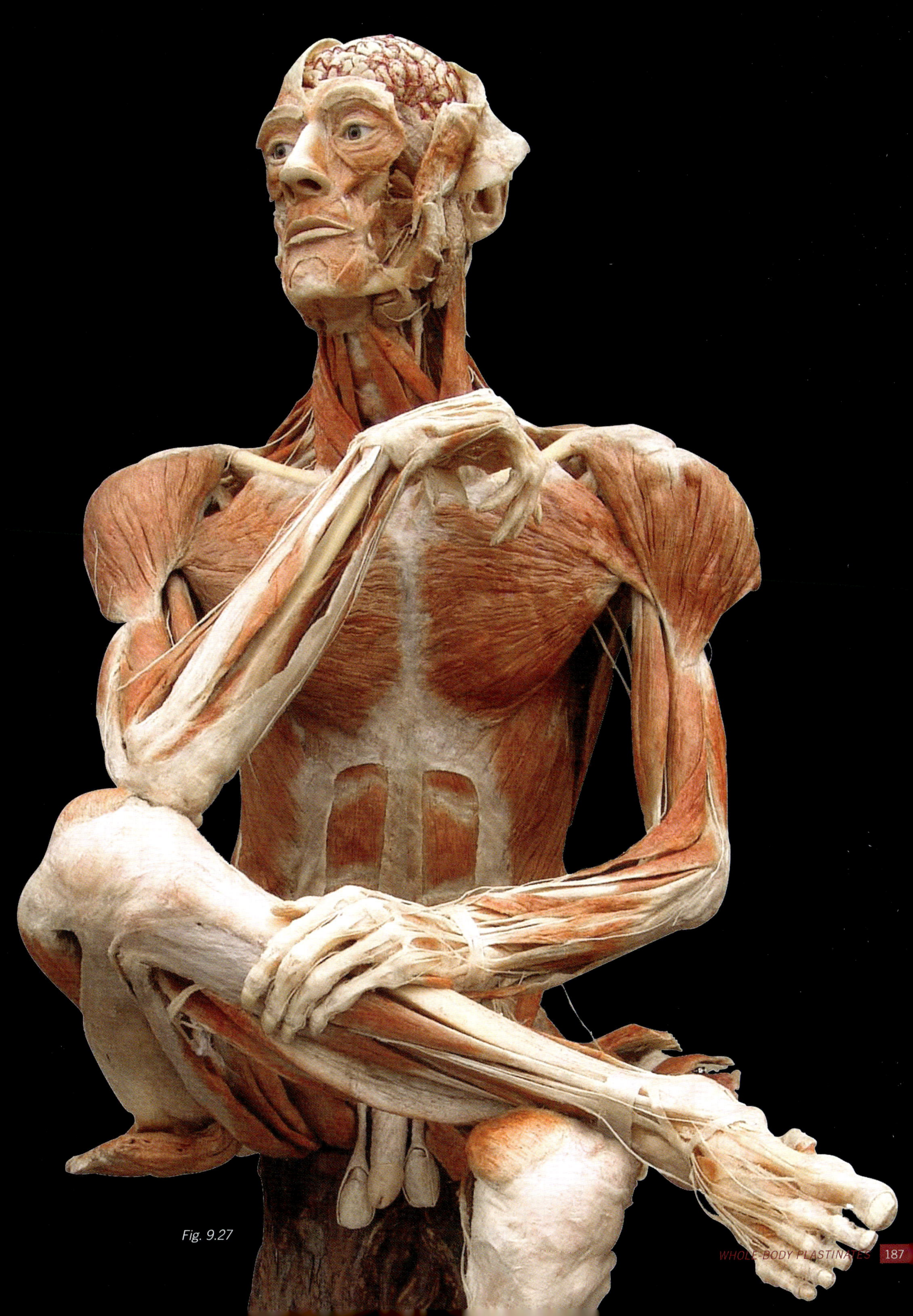

Fig. 9.27

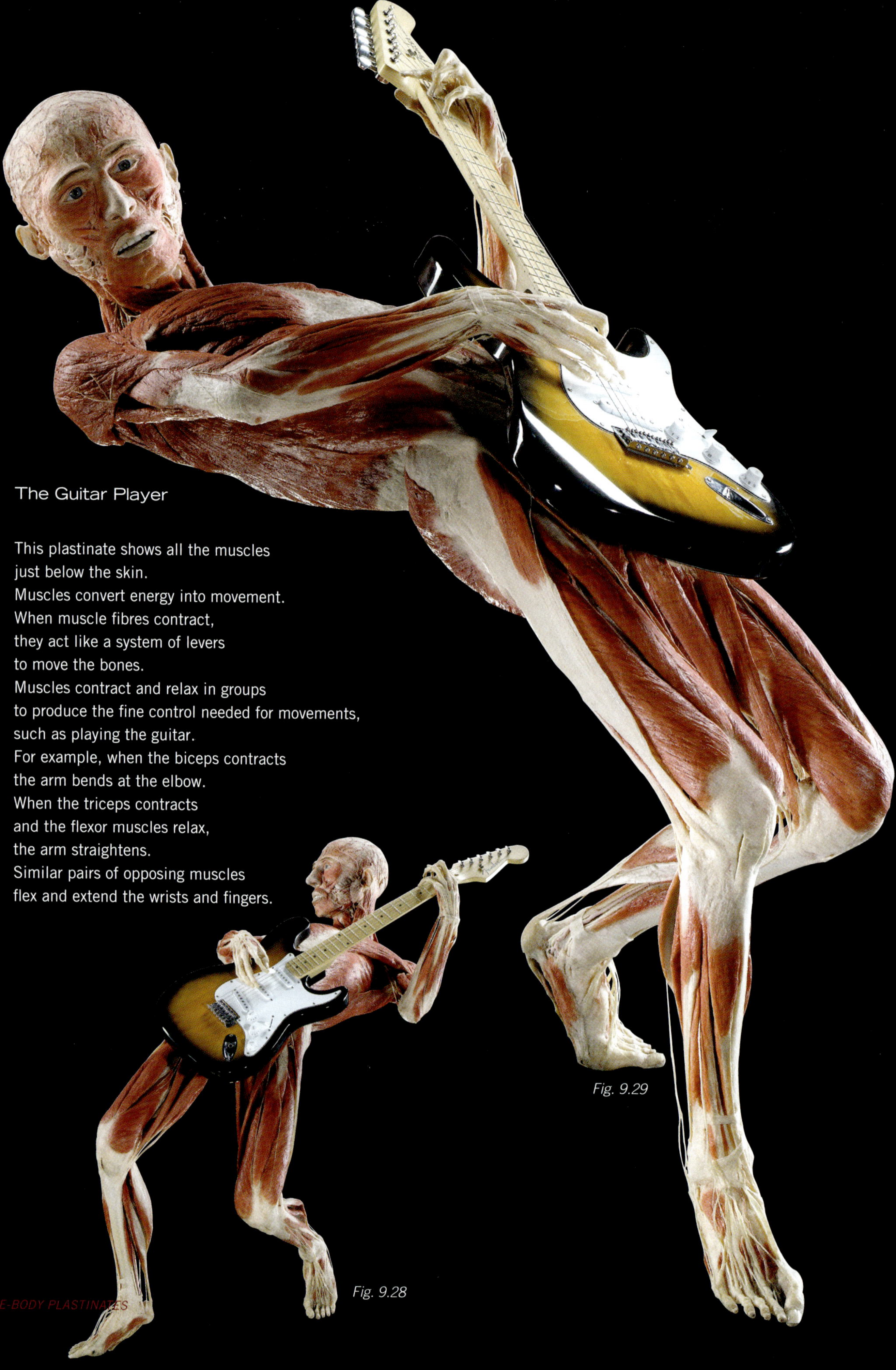

Fig. 9.29

## The Guitar Player

This plastinate shows all the muscles just below the skin. Muscles convert energy into movement. When muscle fibres contract, they act like a system of levers to move the bones. Muscles contract and relax in groups to produce the fine control needed for movements, such as playing the guitar. For example, when the biceps contracts the arm bends at the elbow. When the triceps contracts and the flexor muscles relax, the arm straightens. Similar pairs of opposing muscles flex and extend the wrists and fingers.

Fig. 9.28

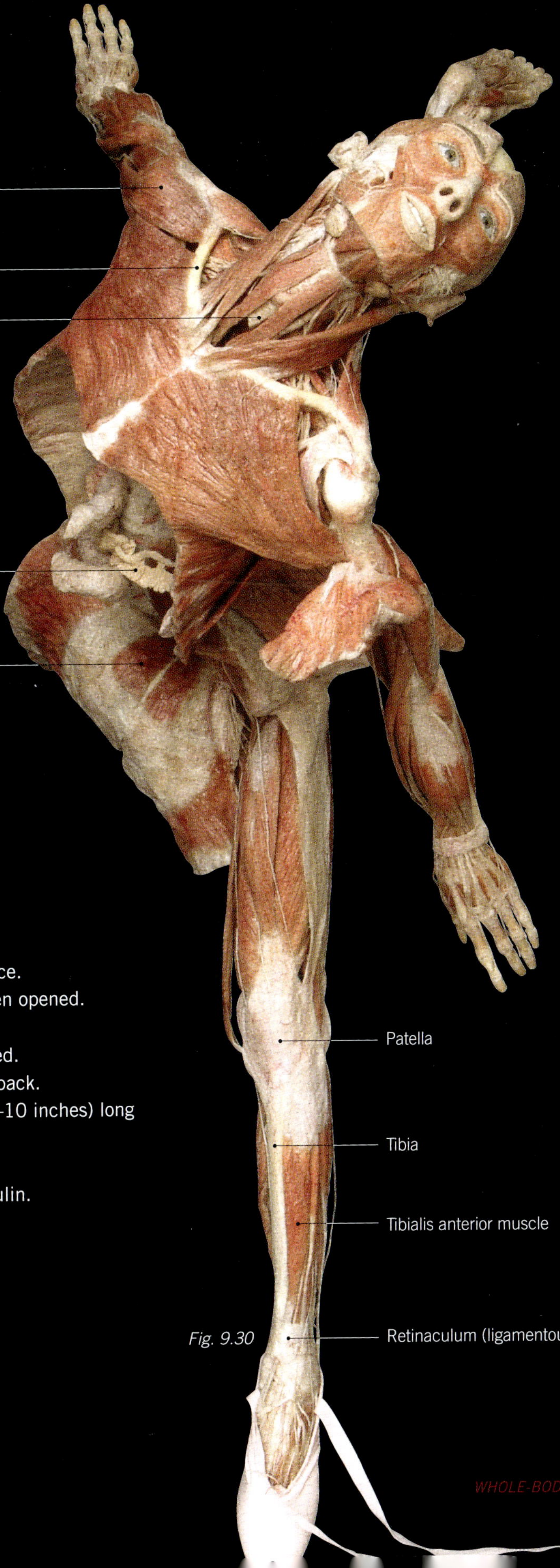


*Fig. 9.30*

## The Ballet Dancer

Dance and balance result from
perfect mental and physical harmony.
This plastinate shows perfect muscular balance.
The abdominal and thoracic cavities have been opened.
The abdomen's muscle wall is bent down,
and almost all inner organs have been removed.
The flat, elongated pancreas is visible at the back.
The pancreas is about 18–25 centimetres (6–10 inches) long
and is attached to the duodenum.
Pancreatic juices aid digestion.
The pancreas also produces the hormone insulin.
Insulin imbalance is one cause of diabetes.

## The Jumping Dancer

This particular preparation enables the simultaneous view of muscles from the front and inner organs from the back. The rear body wall together with the brain were flipped down to present the central nervous system, composed of brain and spinal cord, and the thoracic and abdominal inner organs. This arrangement enables us to view the inner side of the neck, thorax, abdomen, and pelvis upside down on the back of the specimen.

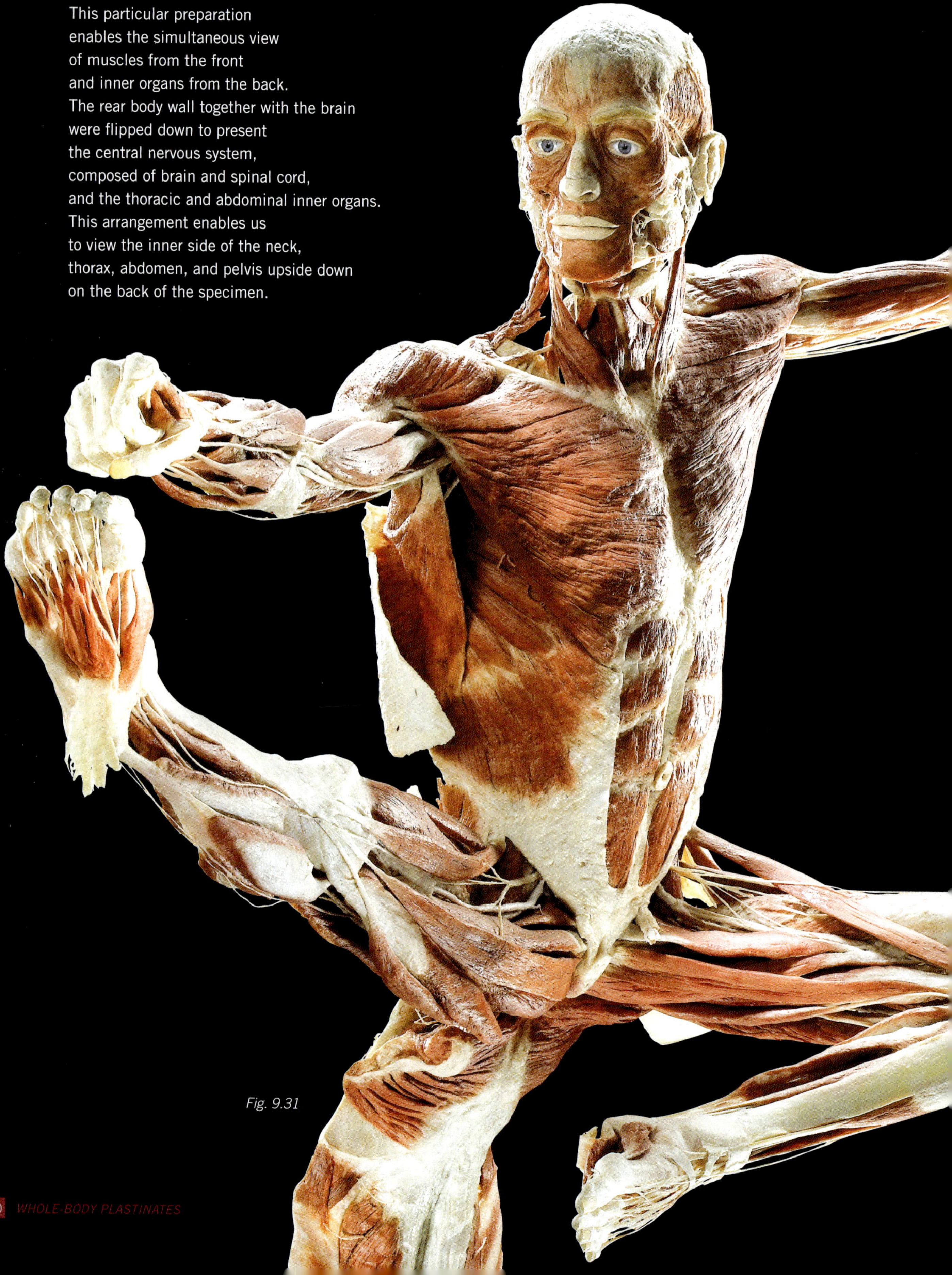

*Fig. 9.31*

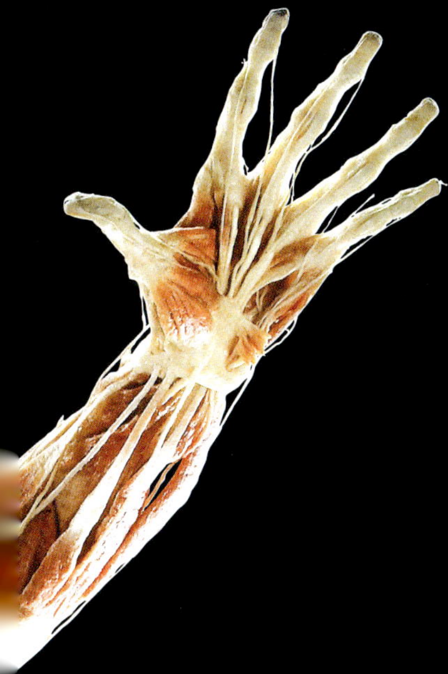

Also the thoracic and abdominal cavities
with lungs, kidney, and intestines
can clearly be seen.
Especially noticeable is the diaphragm,
a thin muscle plate
which, as the 'breathing muscle'
divides the thoracic cavity
with the heart and lungs
from the abdominal cavity
with the liver, intestines, and kidneys.
A small anatomical highlight of this specimen
is the exposure of the round heads
of the femoral bones from behind.

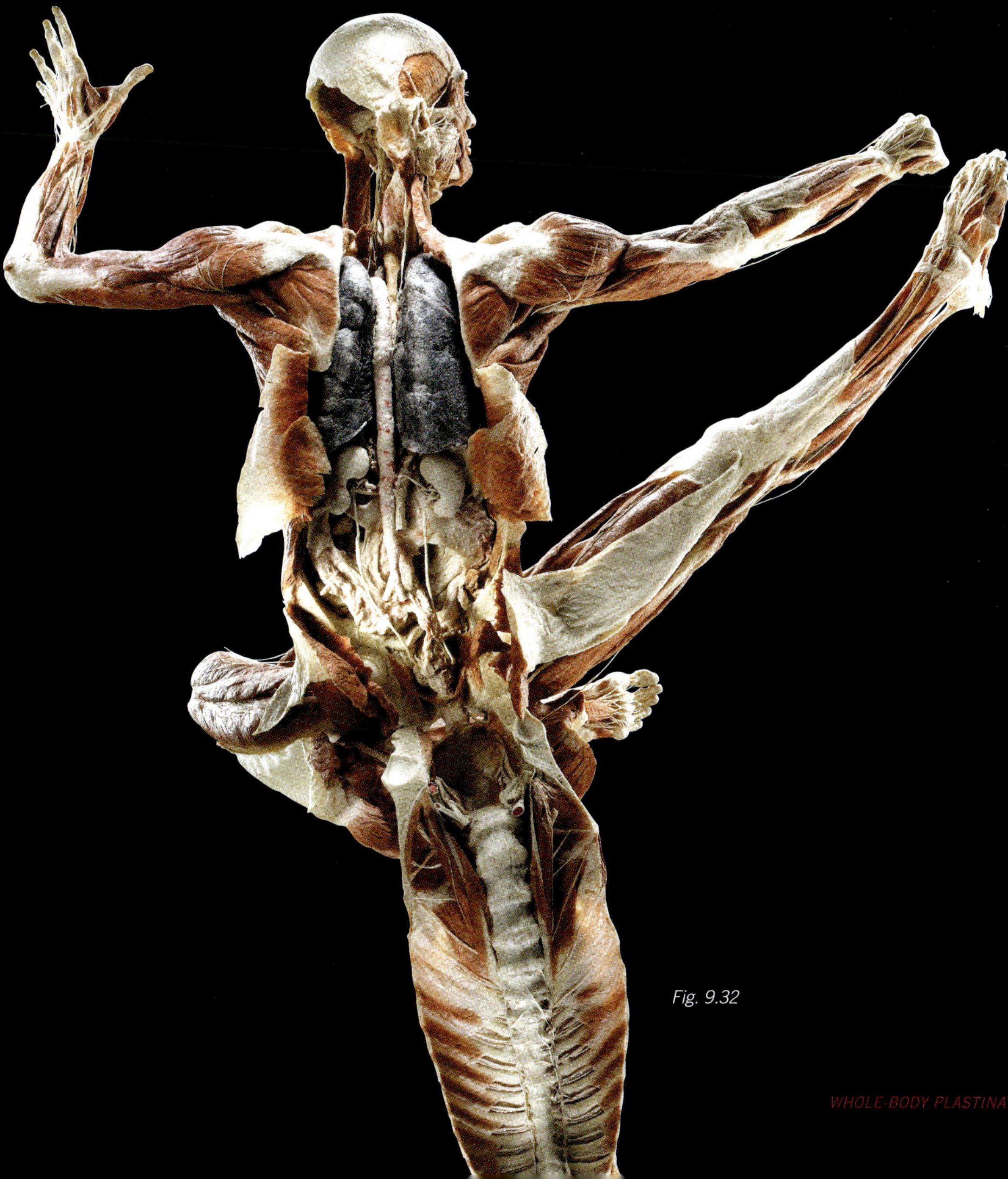

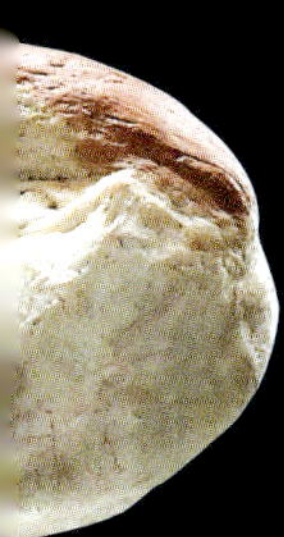

*Fig. 9.32*

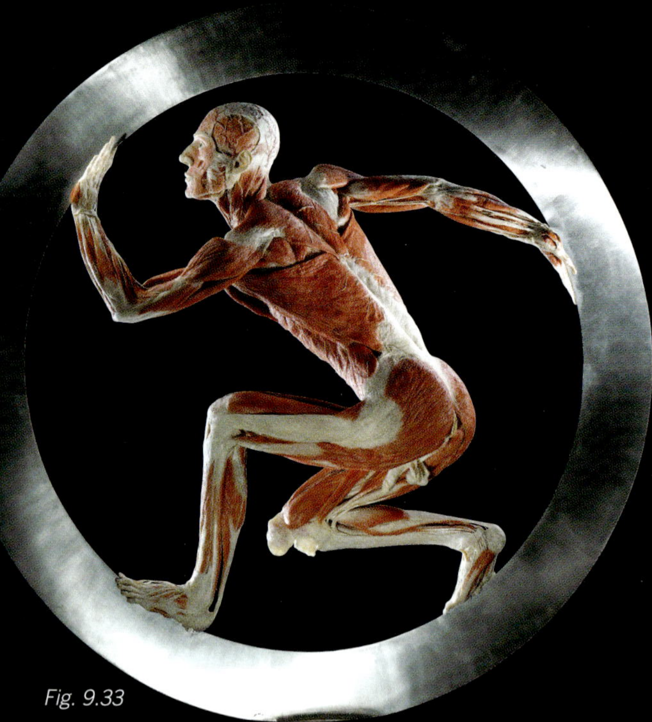

*Fig. 9.33*

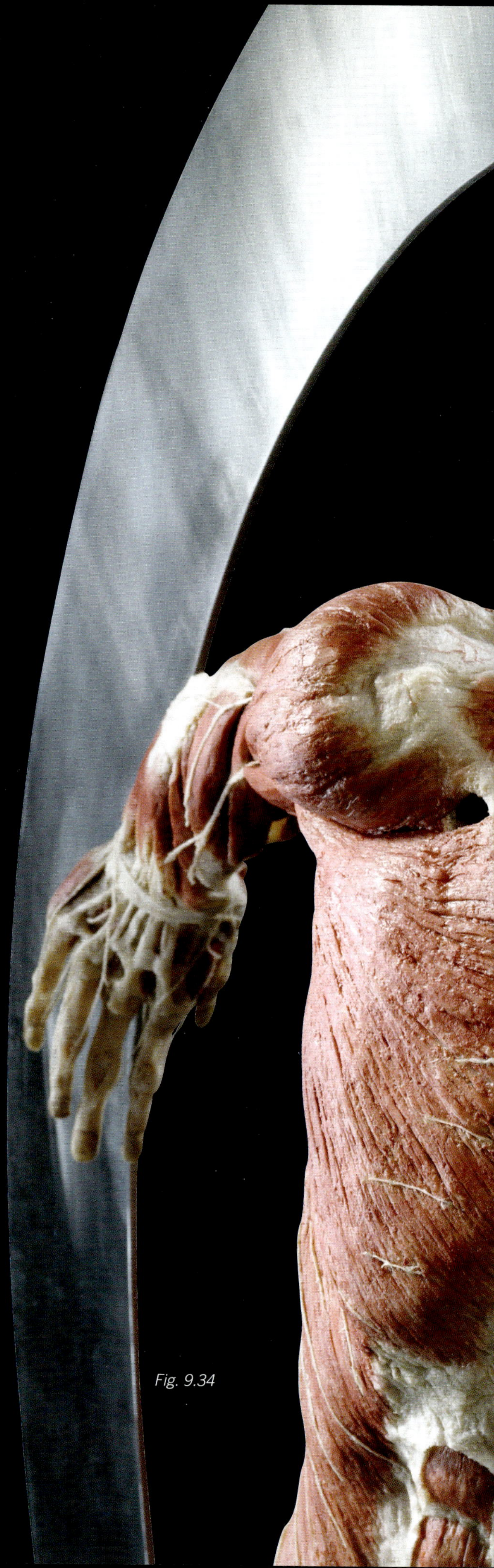

*Fig. 9.34*

## The Wave Roller

With his dynamic pose and ease of balance, the Wave Roller glides his steel wheel elegantly down the waterfall. His posture highlights his tensed muscles and the tendon-like aponeuroses. Aponeuroses are membranes with a whitish-silvery colour. They separate muscles from each other and are made of the same taut connective tissue as the round tendons of spindle-shaped muscles. The largest aponeuroses protectively cover the torso and the inner organs. The large dorsal lumbar aponeurosis – the lumbodorsal fascia – is the tendon-like continuation of the broad back muscles. It also serves as an elastic connective tissue for the muscles and tendons underneath. This soft connective tissue is called fascia. A network of fascia is found throughout the body and surrounds the muscles. The aponeurosis of a muscle can also be the fascia for other muscles lying deeper underneath.

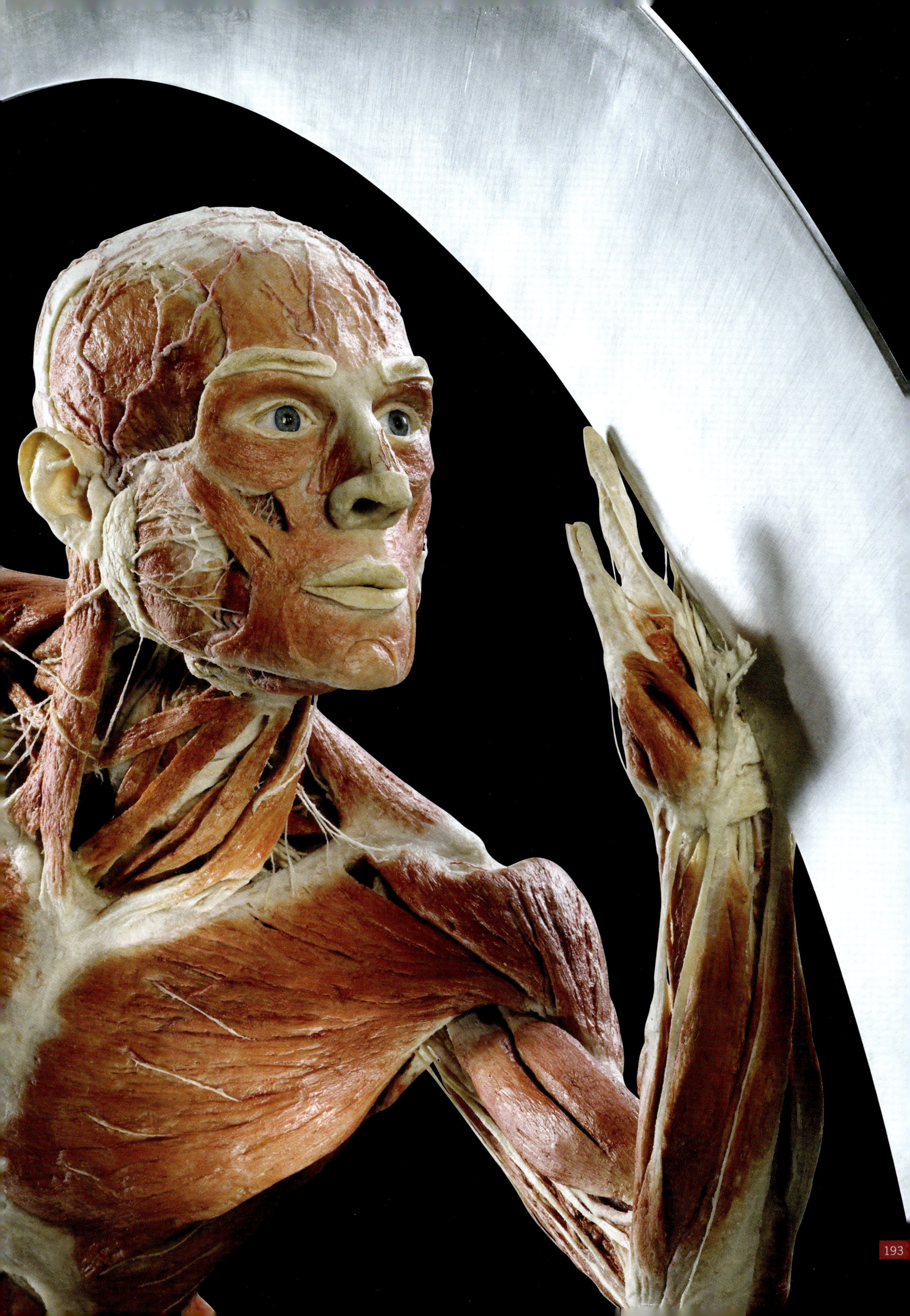

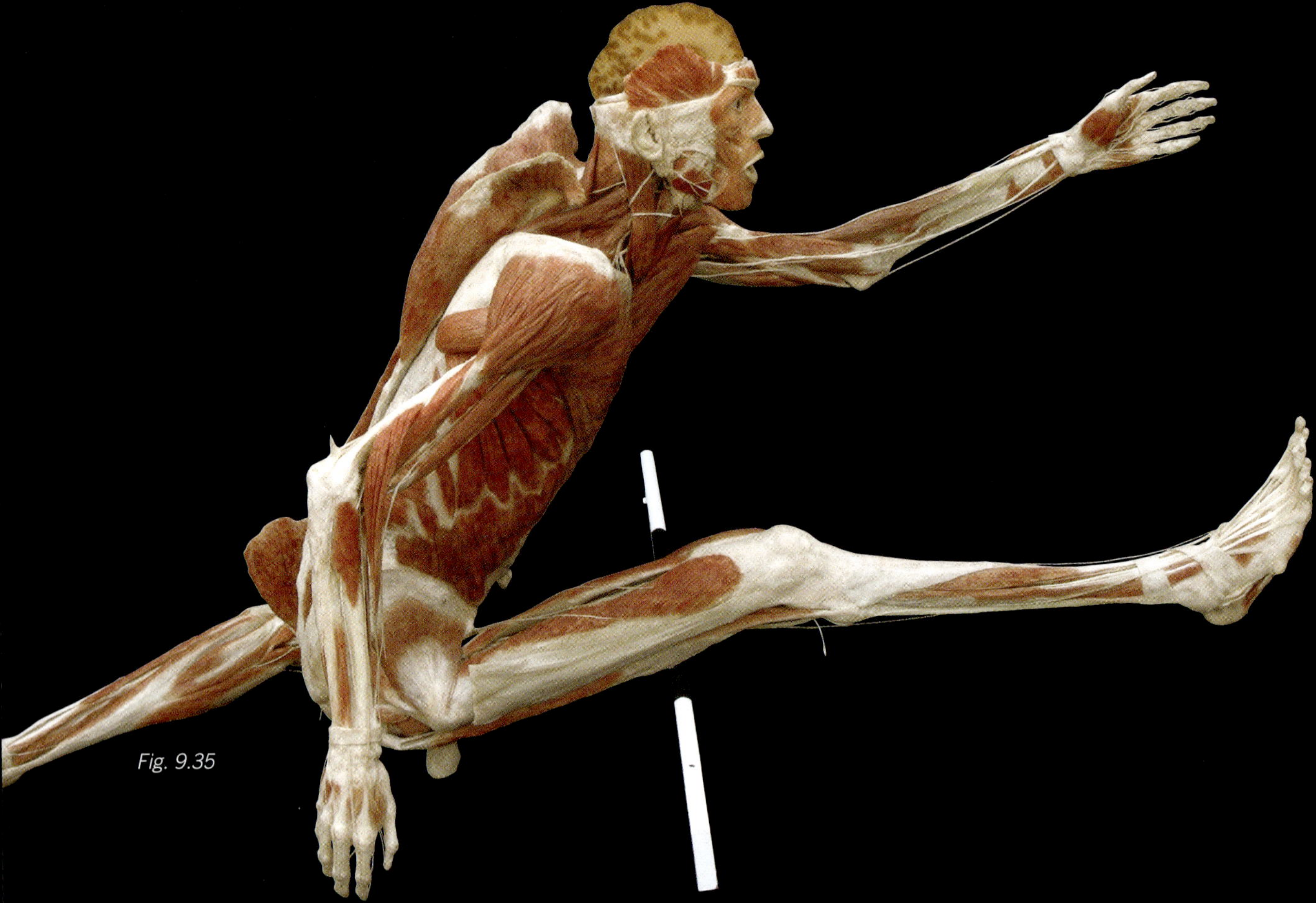

*Fig. 9.35*

## The Hurdler

This plastinate shows the interplay between surface and intermediate muscles.

A muscle can only shorten.
When we move, different muscles act on opposite sides of a joint, pulling it in the different directions in which it can move.
For example, the biceps flexes the elbow, while the triceps at the back of our arm does the opposite and extends the elbow.
When the biceps contracts, balancing activity in the triceps inhibits excessive movement.
This makes our movements fluid and controlled.

Any increase in energy expenditure requires rapid adjustments in blood flow that affect the entire cardiovascular system.
During extensive muscle activity, such as running and cycling at maximum intensity, muscle blood flow accounts for 80–85% of the total cardiac output.

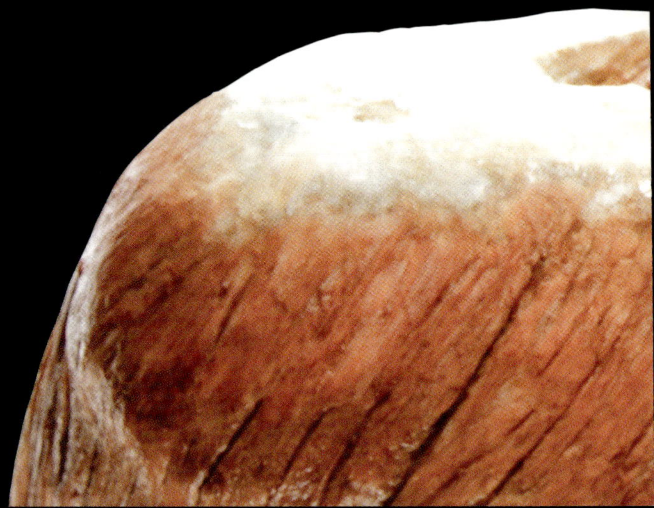

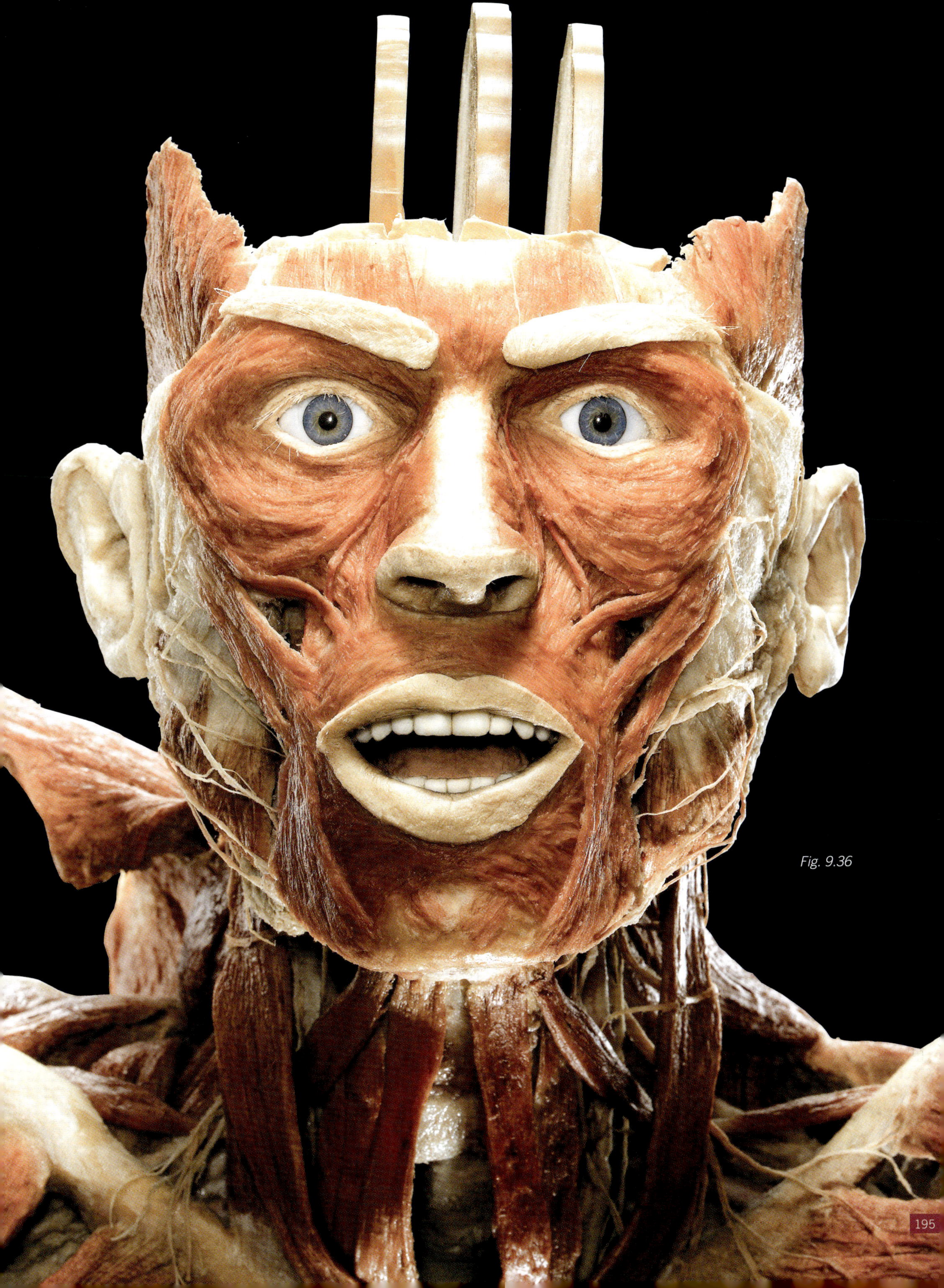

Fig. 9.36

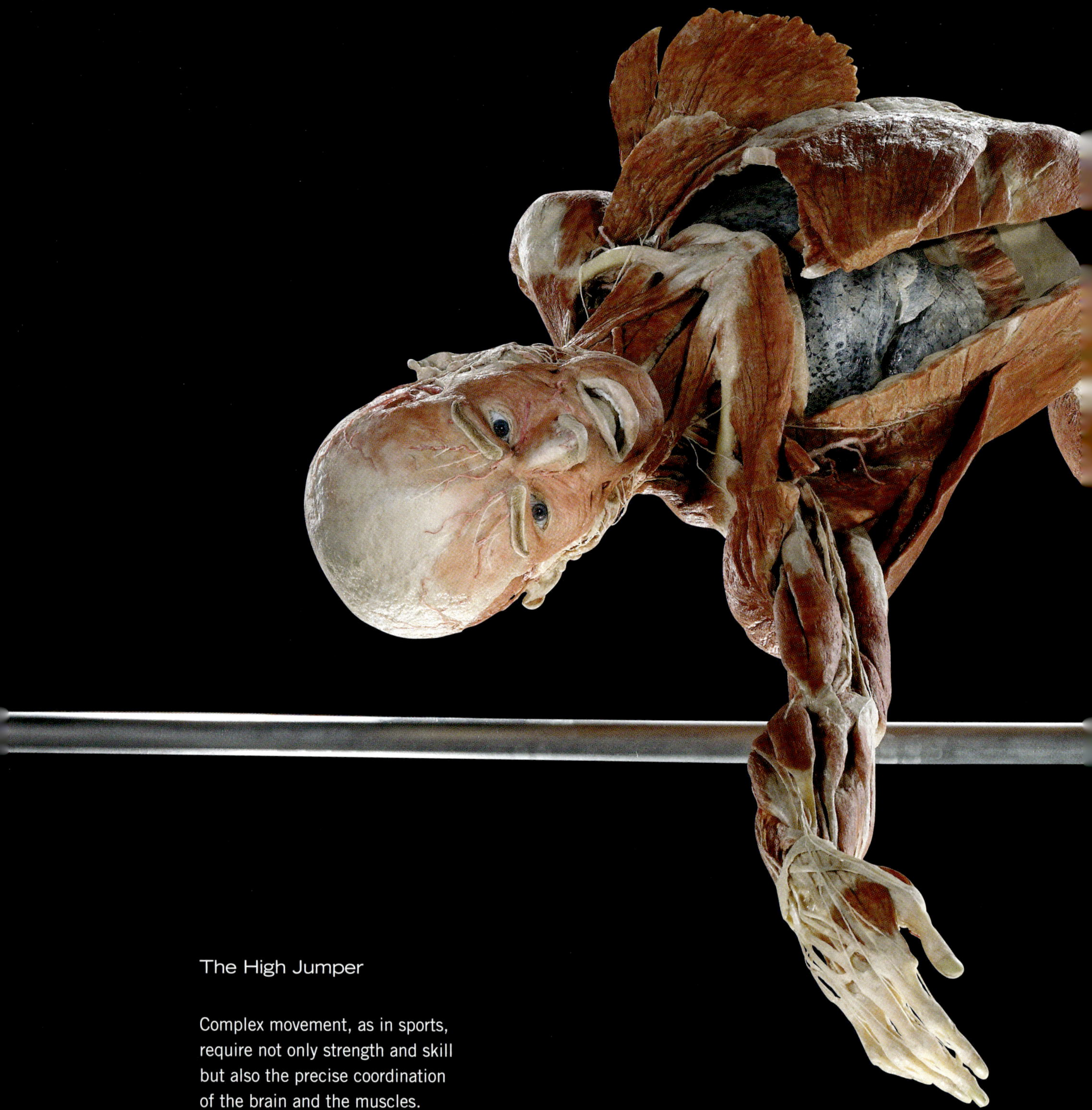

## The High Jumper

Complex movement, as in sports,
require not only strength and skill
but also the precise coordination
of the brain and the muscles.
This plastinate shows the muscles
of a high jumper in a functional pose.
His arms have been extended away from the body
to open the view on the anatomy of the arm pit.
The important vessels and nerves
supplying the arm
can thus be seen.
The inner organs in their natural positions
have been made visible by folding back
the walls of abdomen and chest.

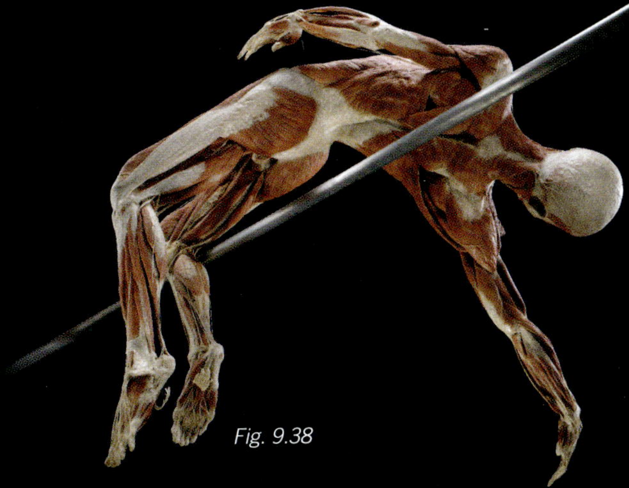

Fig. 9.38

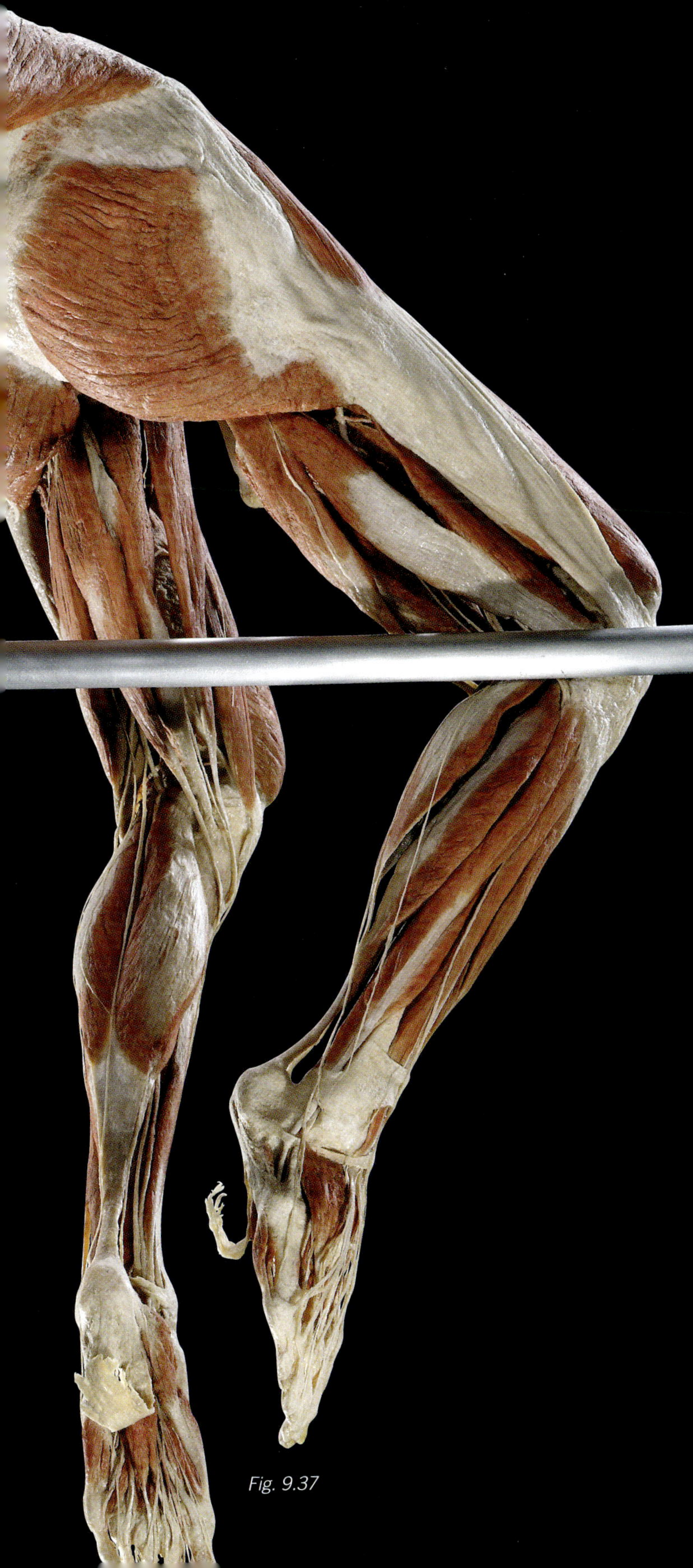

Fig. 9.37

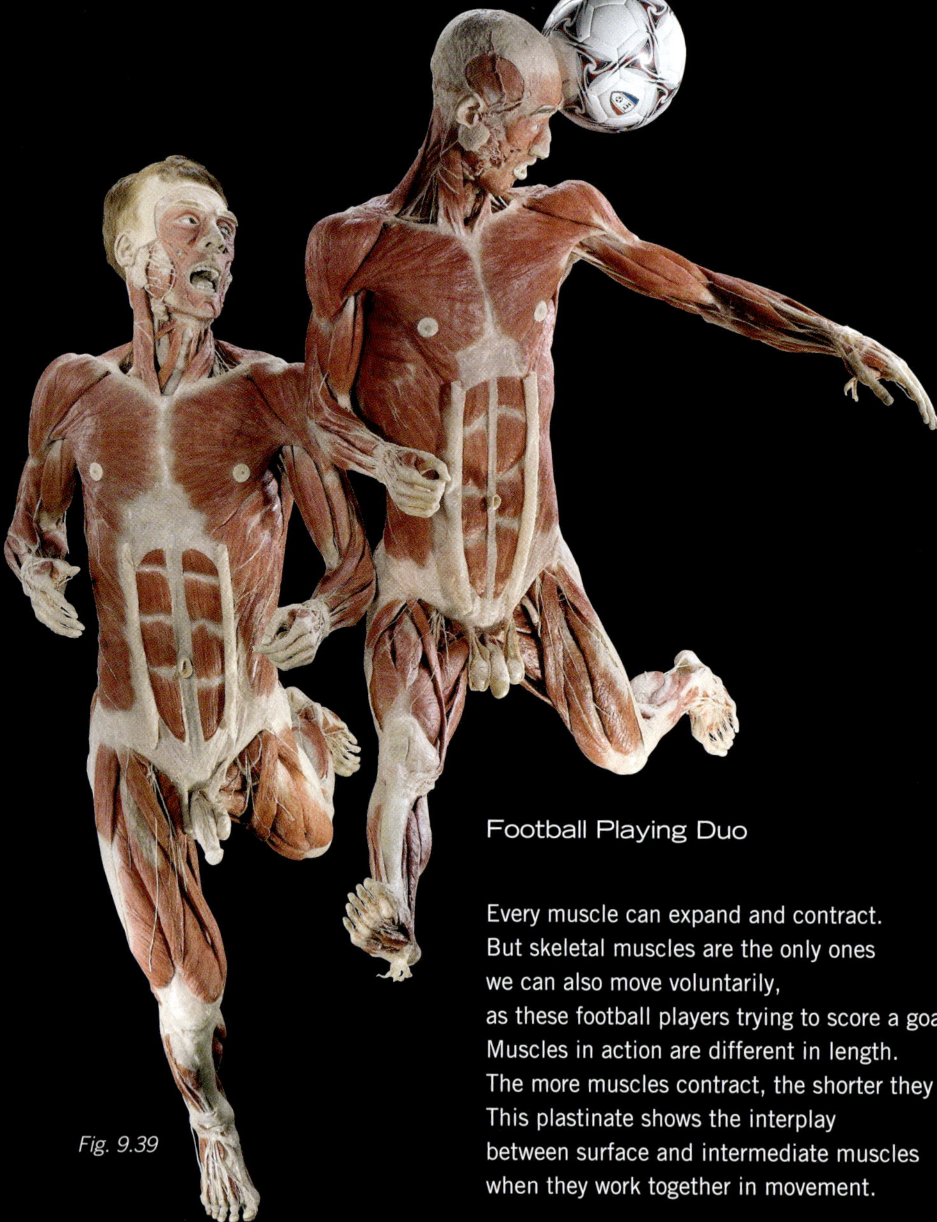

Fig. 9.39

## Football Playing Duo

Every muscle can expand and contract.
But skeletal muscles are the only ones
we can also move voluntarily,
as these football players trying to score a goal.
Muscles in action are different in length.
The more muscles contract, the shorter they are.
This plastinate shows the interplay
between surface and intermediate muscles
when they work together in movement.

The skeletal muscles all overlap intricately.
They play a big role in the way we look
and make up the largest proportion of our tissue:
roughly 23% of body weight in women
and 40% in men.

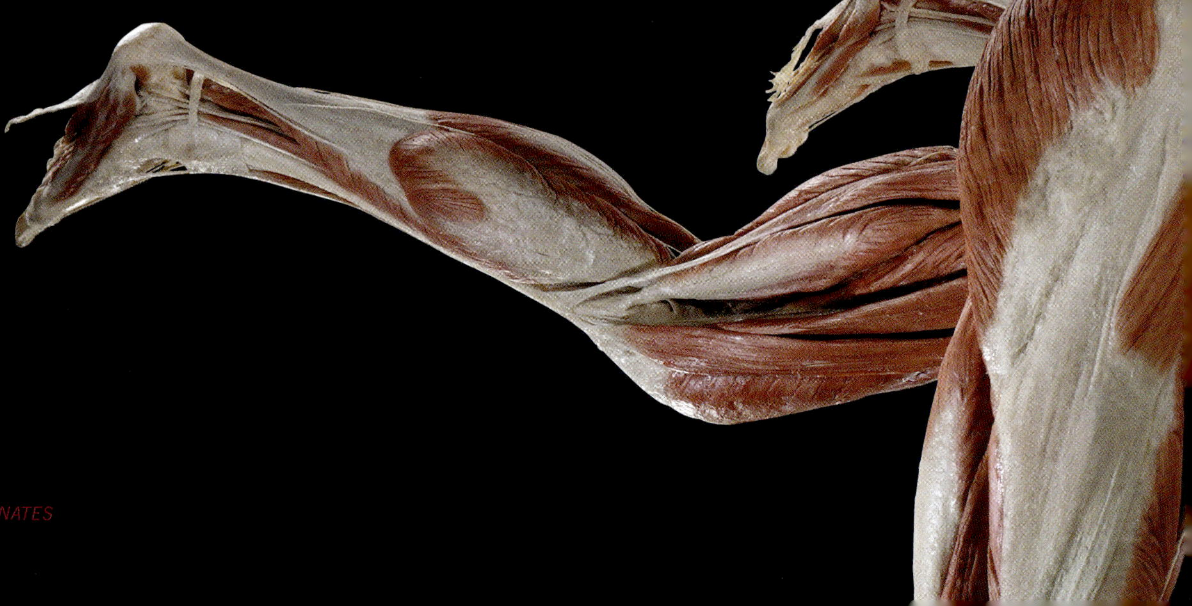

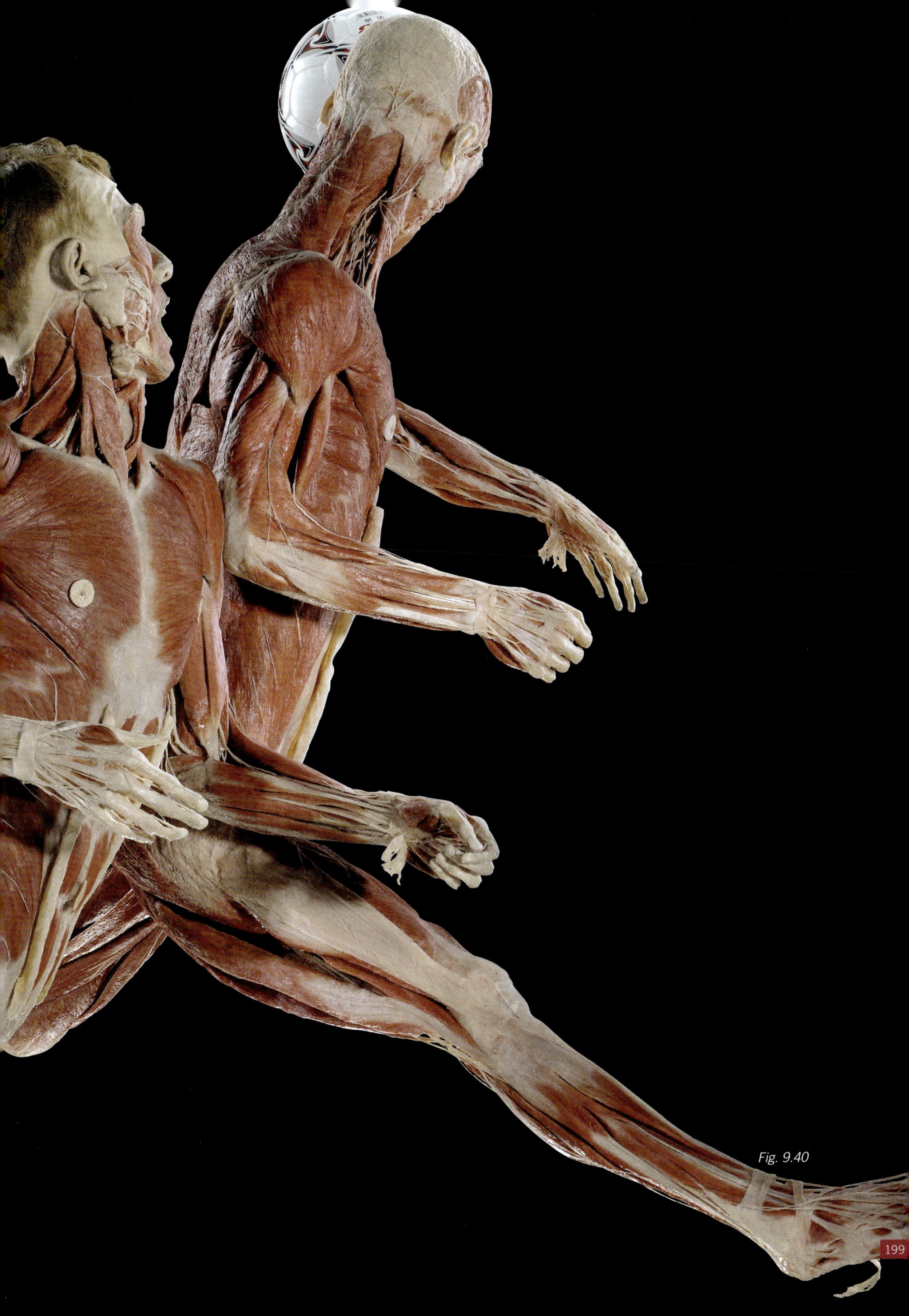

Fig. 9.40

## The Football Gladiators

Muscles are usually arranged in pairs with opposing functions. For example, the quadriceps muscle, the big bulky muscle on the front of the thigh, allows us to straighten the knee. The hamstring muscle on the back of the thigh allows us to bend the knee. The combination of all the skeletal muscles allows us a huge variety of movements, including walking, running, smiling, writing, or playing football.

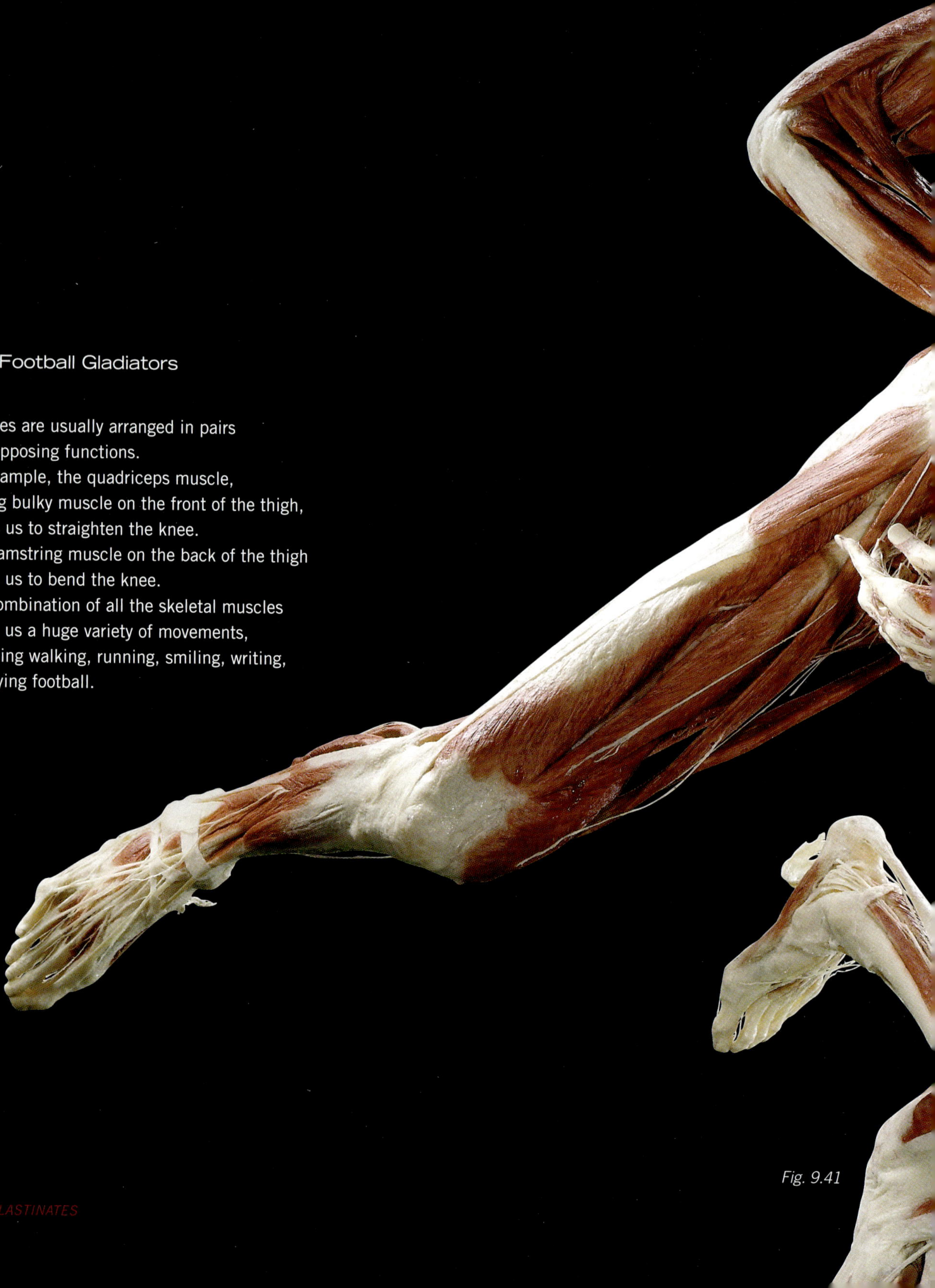

*Fig. 9.41*

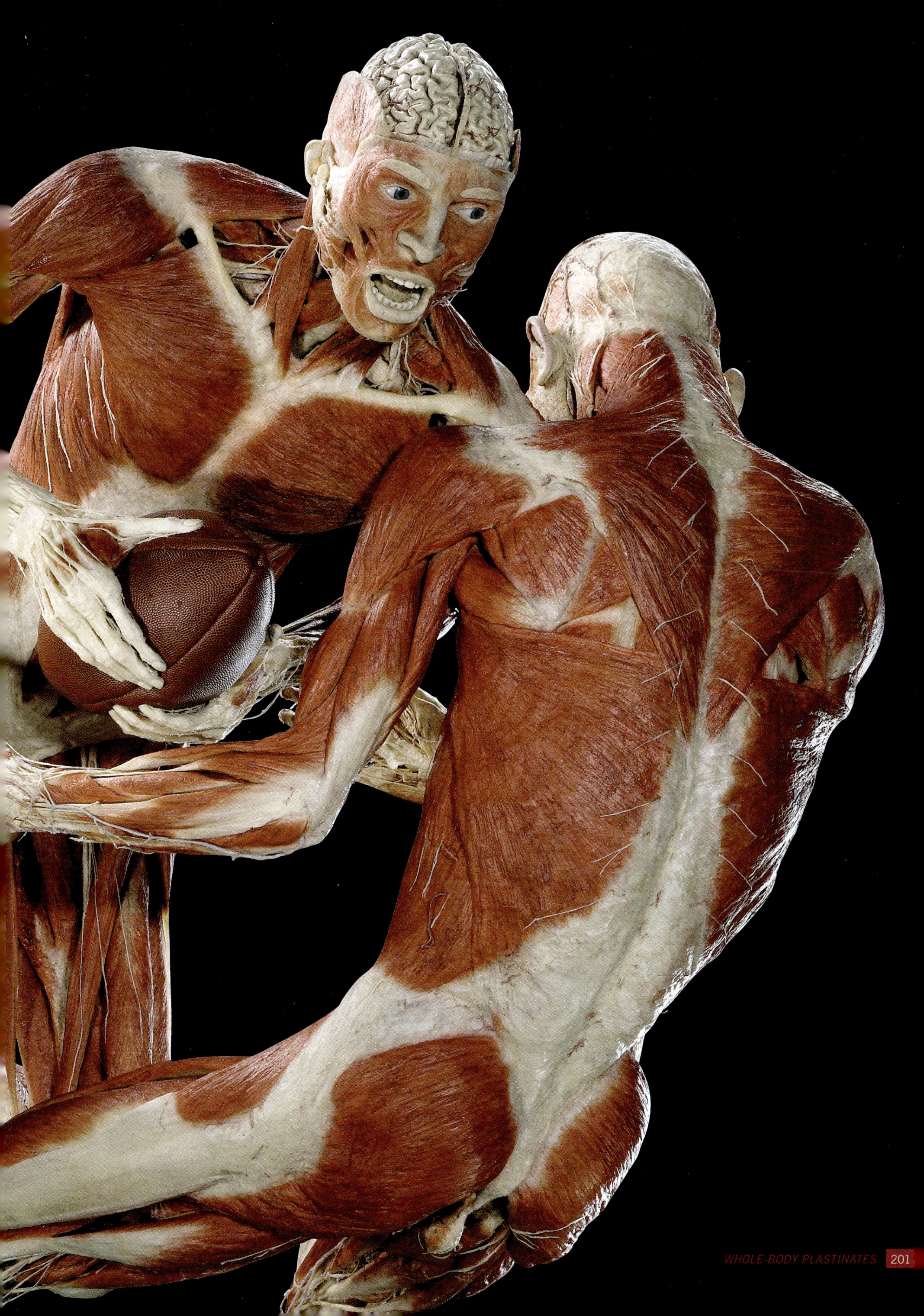

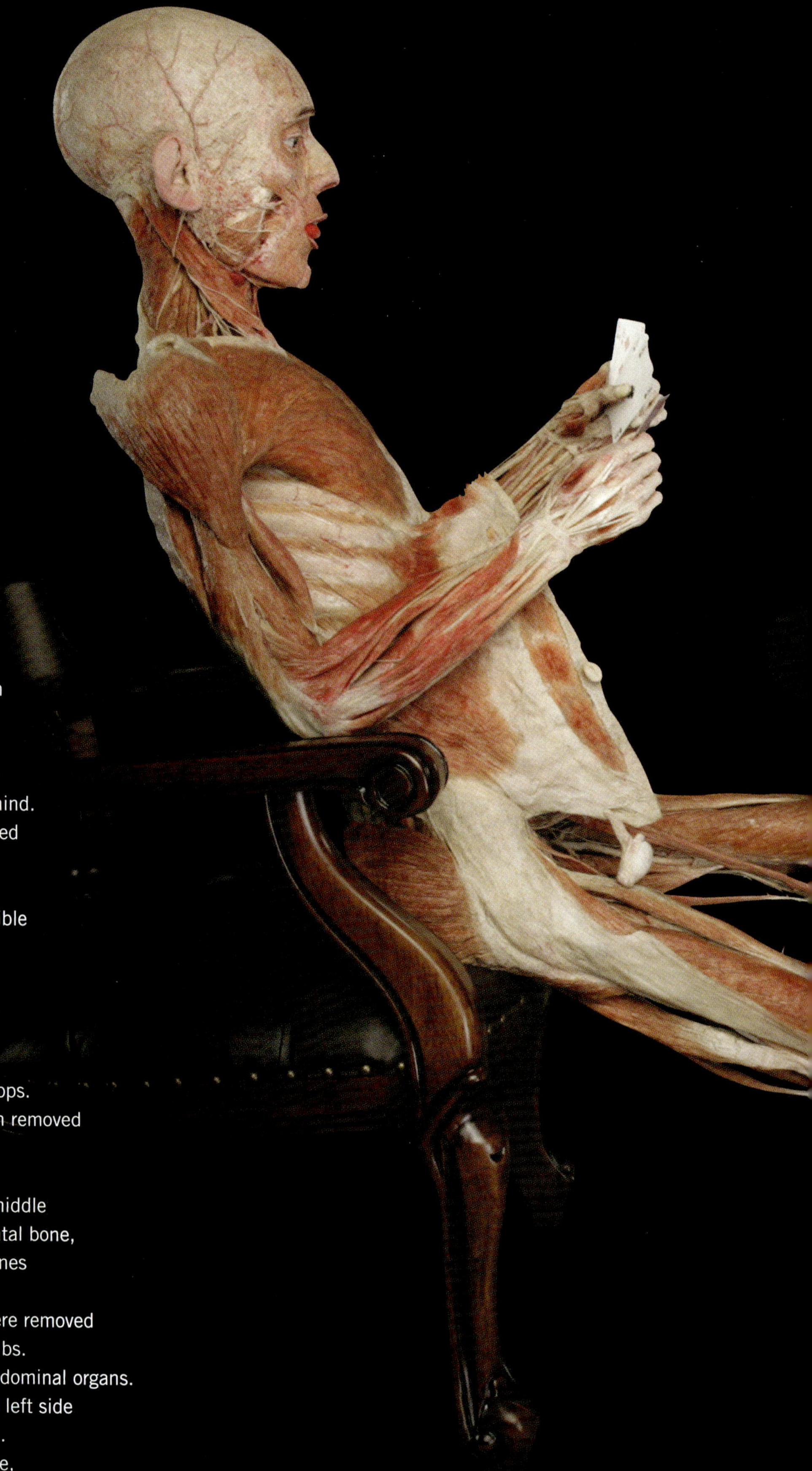

## Poker Playing Trio

Their presentations differ as much
as their poker playing strategies.
In the poker player on the right,
both parietal bones were lifted up
to make the brain visible from behind.
The brain was horizontally sectioned
and folded out.
Beneath it is the cerebellum,
below which the spinal cord is visible
inside the opened vertebral canal.
The large gluteal muscles
have been removed on both sides.
In the poker player on the left,
the abdomen was opened,
yielding a view of the intestinal loops.
The gluteal muscles have not been removed
but were simply folded back.
The unusual and striking head
of the poker player sitting in the middle
was created by separating the frontal bone,
the nasal bone, and both cheekbones
from the posterior skull bones.
The chest and abdominal walls were removed
down to the posterior part of the ribs.
The kidneys remain as the only abdominal organs.
This player's smoker's lung on the left side
covers up the left half of the heart.
The right half of the heart is visible,
because the tissue of the right lung
has been partially removed.

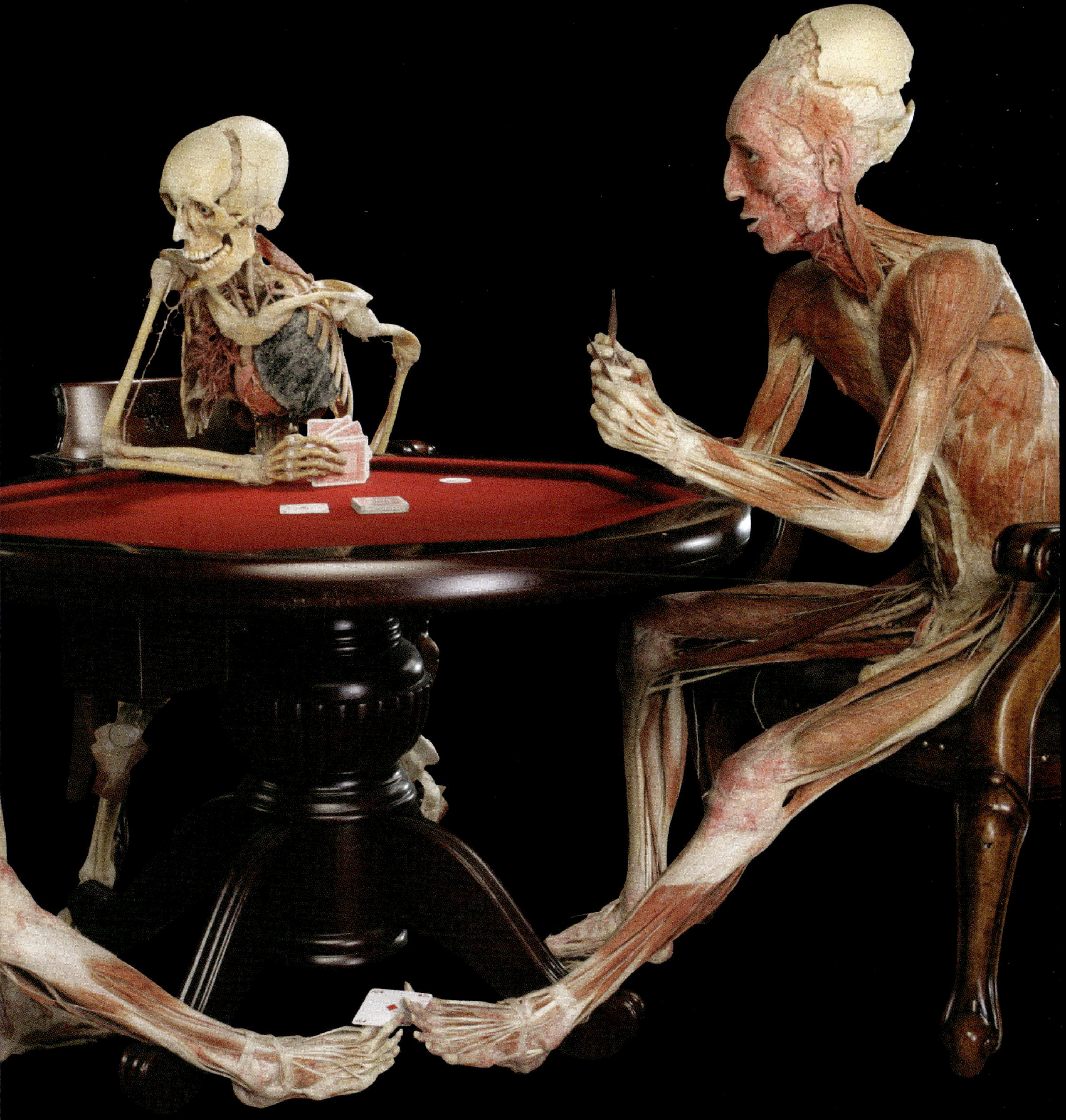

Fig. 9.42
This Trio played a round of poker in the James Bond movie, "Casino Royale".

Fig. 9.43

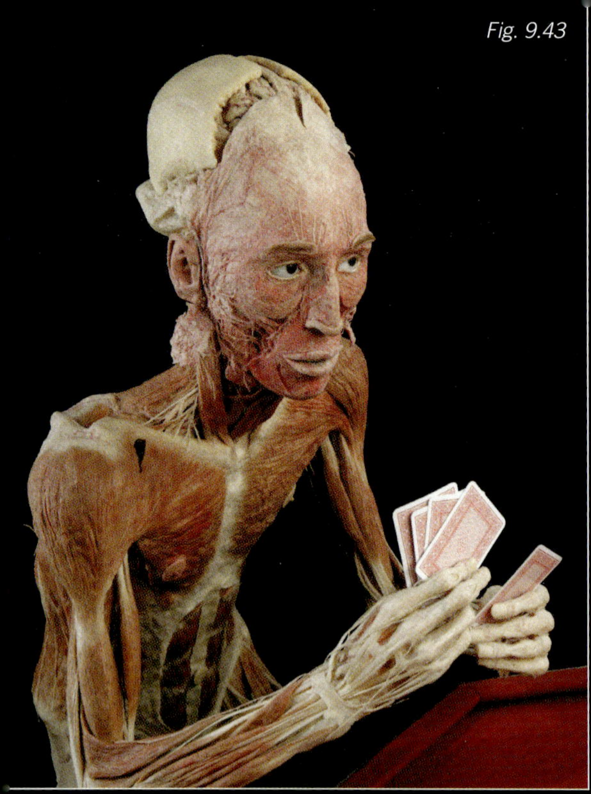

Fig. 9.44

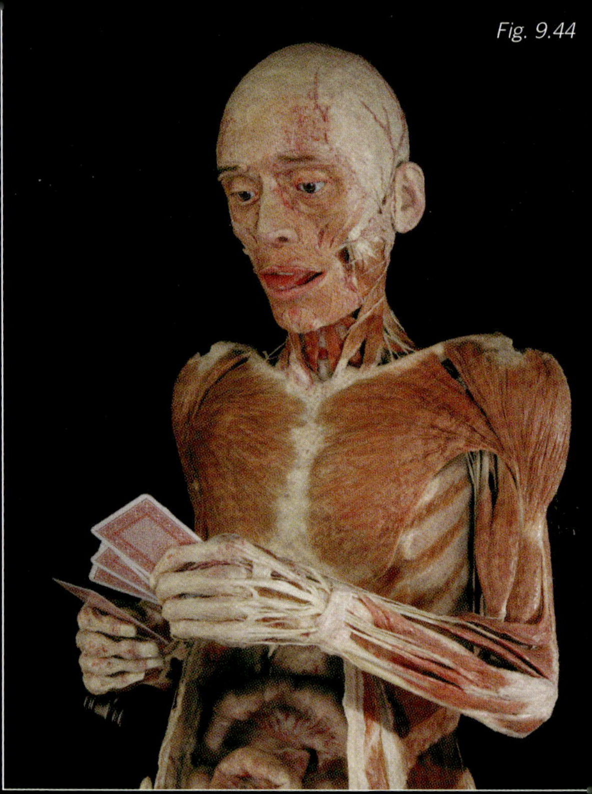

Fig. 9.45

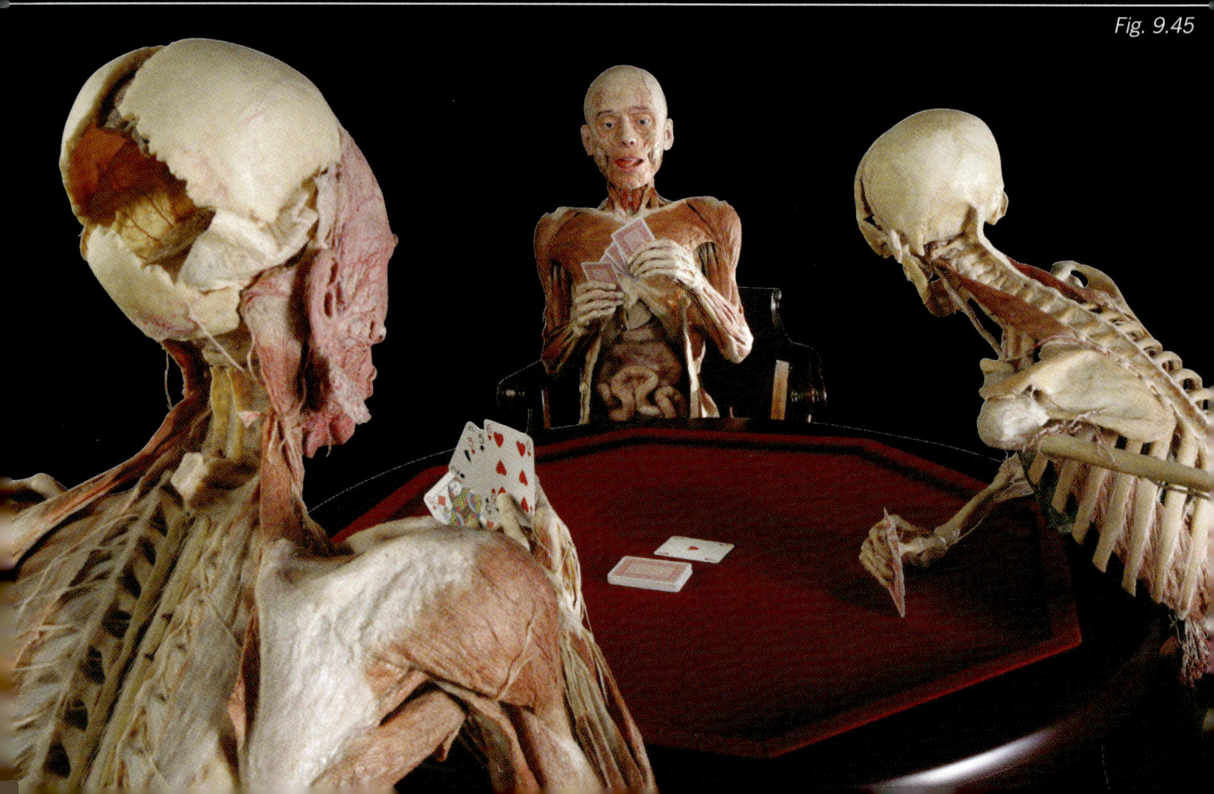

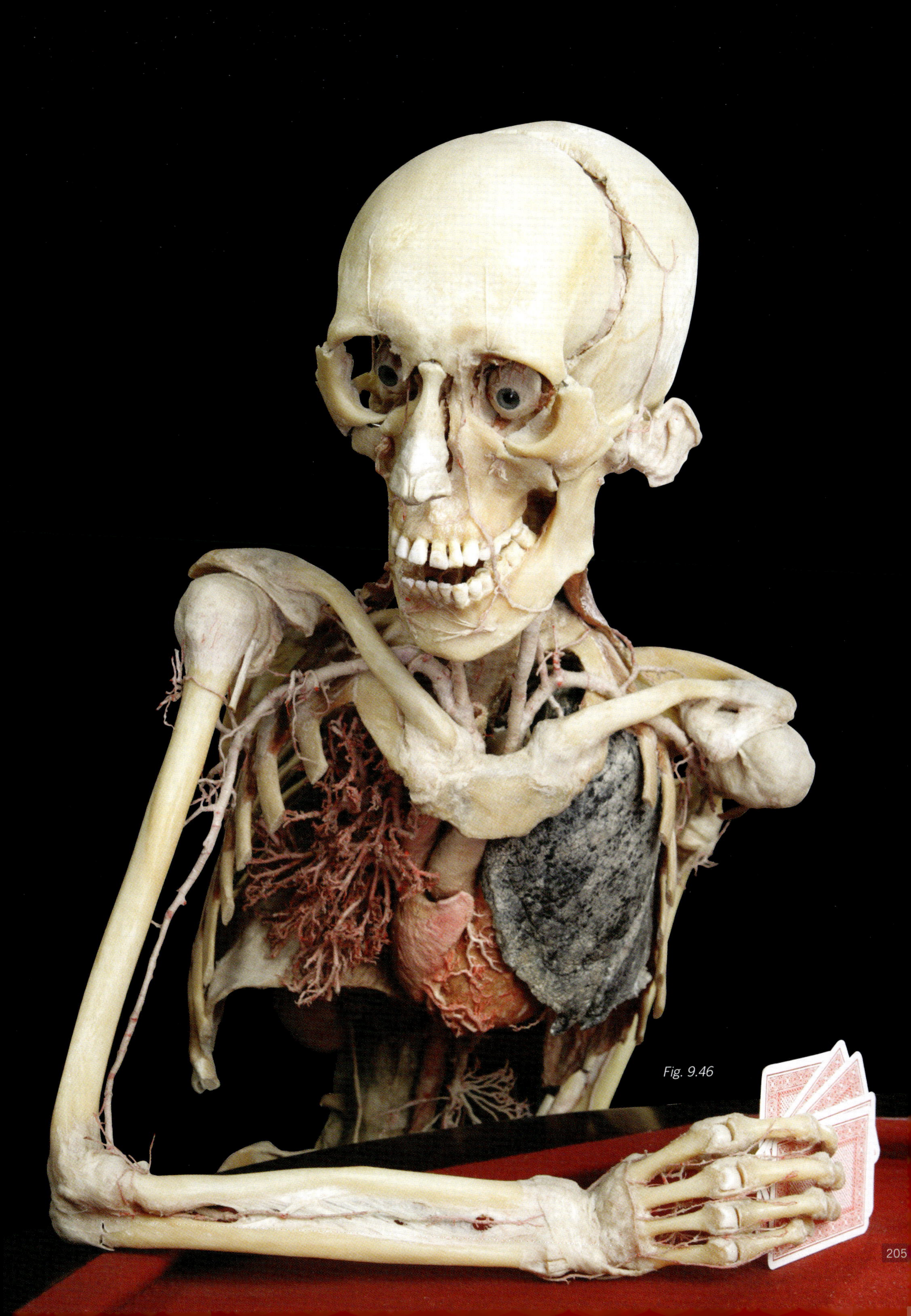

Fig. 9.46

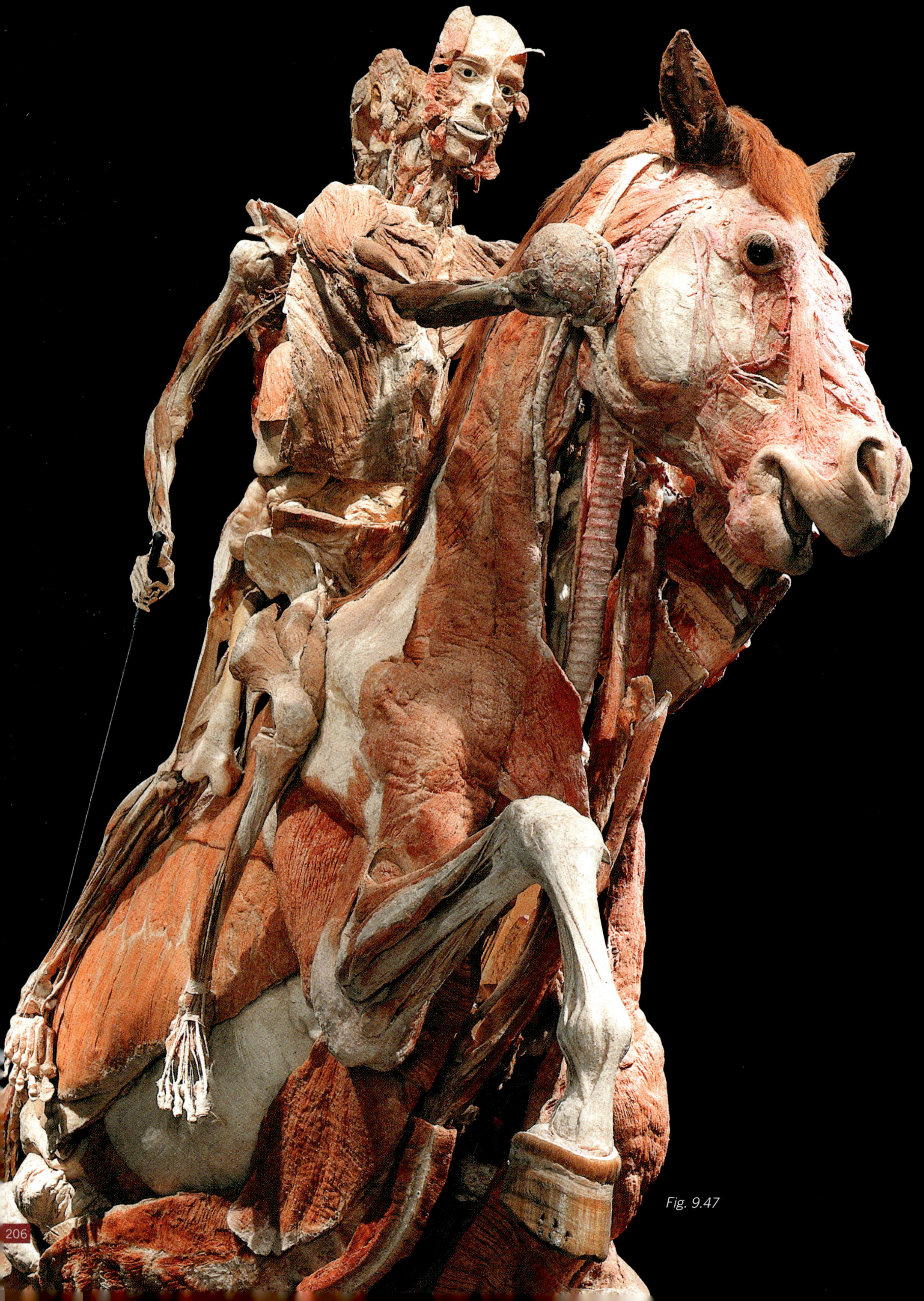

Fig. 9.47

## The Rearing Horse with Rider

Both the human and the horse
share a very similar anatomical arrangement
in the form, position, and microscopic structures
of their organs and muscles.
However, there are major differences in the proportions.
Compared to the horse, human musculature is rather puny,
while on the other hand, the larger human brain
results in significantly higher intelligence.

In humans, the humeri (long bones of the arm)
and thighbones are relatively long,
while the hands and feet are relatively short.
In horses, the bones of the fore and hind limbs
are by contrast relatively short and closer to the trunk.
However, the cannon bones, fetlocks,
pasterns, and hoofs are relatively long,
and the number of phalanges of the toes is reduced
so that the joints of the limbs have different positions.

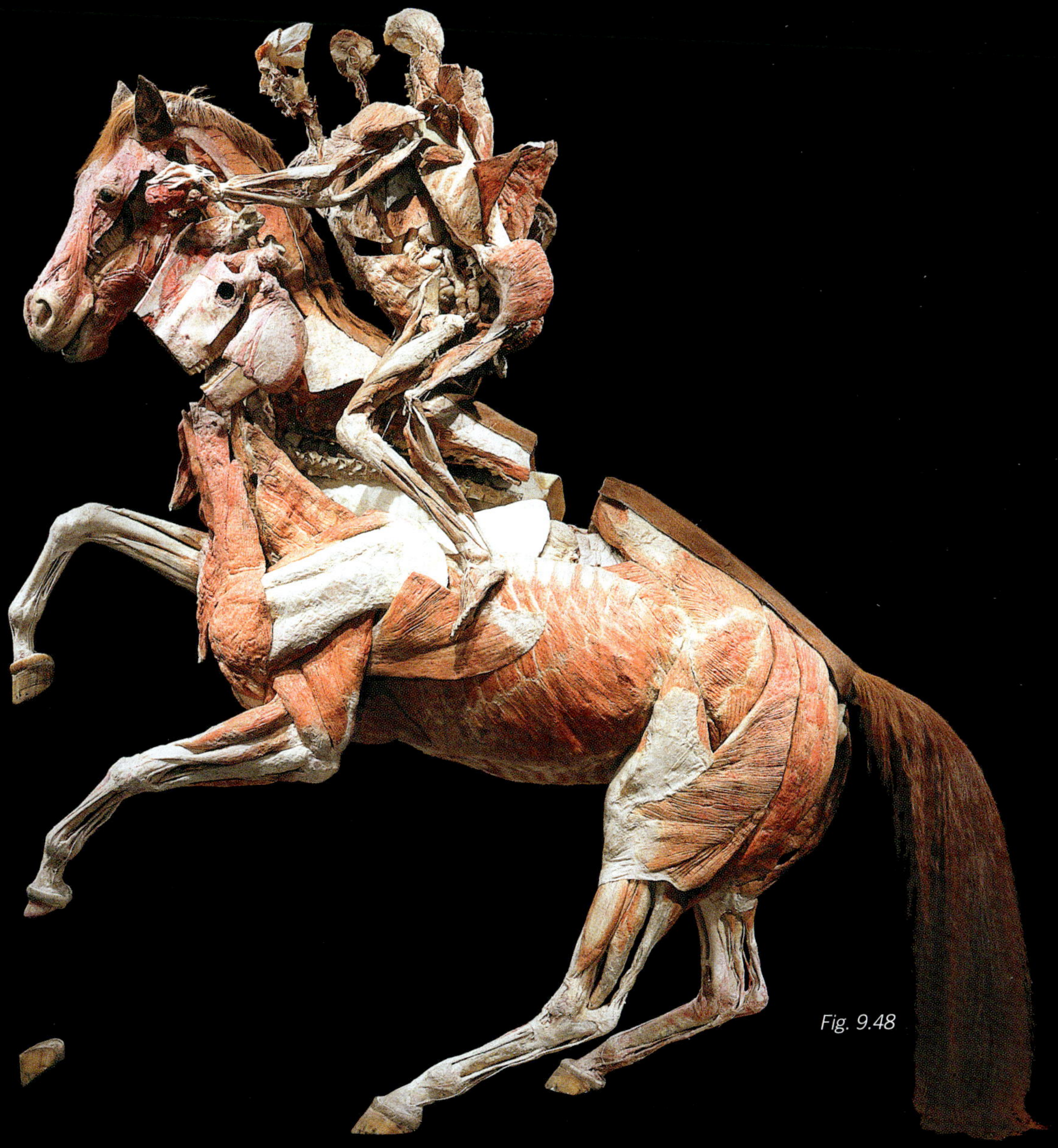

*Fig. 9.48*

rimates are mammals that most resemble humans
n their anatomy and behaviour.
This lowland gorilla weighs 200 kilograms (441 pounds),
s 1.85 metres (6.1 feet) tall,
measures 1.55 metres (5.1 feet) around the chest
and 2.4 metres (7.9 feet) from fingertip to fingertip
with its arms outstretched.
Female gorillas are shorter (1.3 metres/4.3 feet)
and only weigh half as much.
Gorillas generally walk on all fours.
Standing upright is straining for them
because of the slight curvature of their spine.
Compared to humans,
they have a deeper and broader chest,
wider jaws, and significantly longer bones
n the forearms, metacarpi, and fingers.
When standing, their arms extend down
beyond their knees.
Like other apes, gorillas do not have a tail.
The thumbs and big toes can be used
opposite the fingers and toes
for grasping or climbing.
The gorilla's internal organ structure displays
the long intestines typical of herbivores.
Gorillas spend 50% of their waking hours feeding,
aided by their powerful chewing muscles.

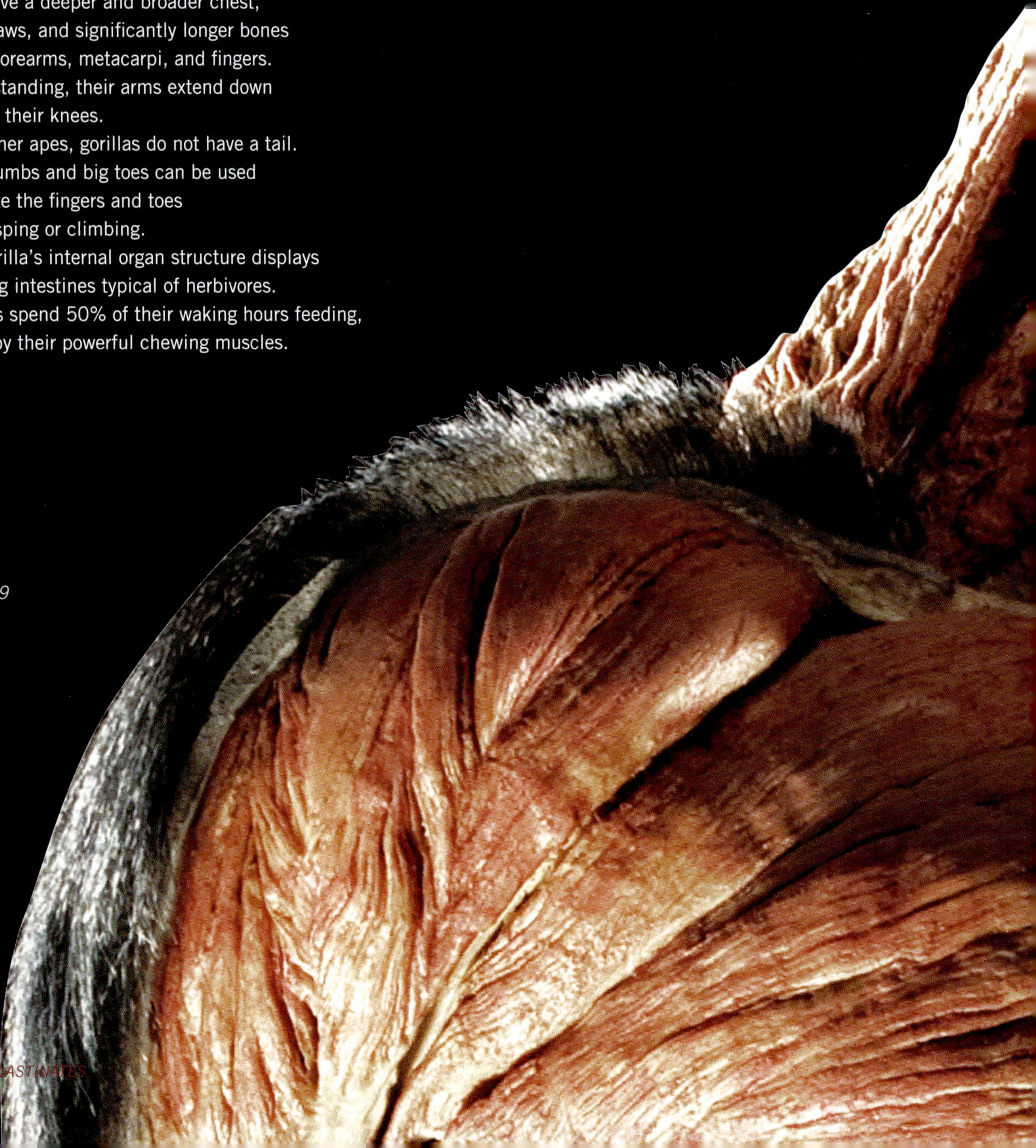

*Fig. 9.49*

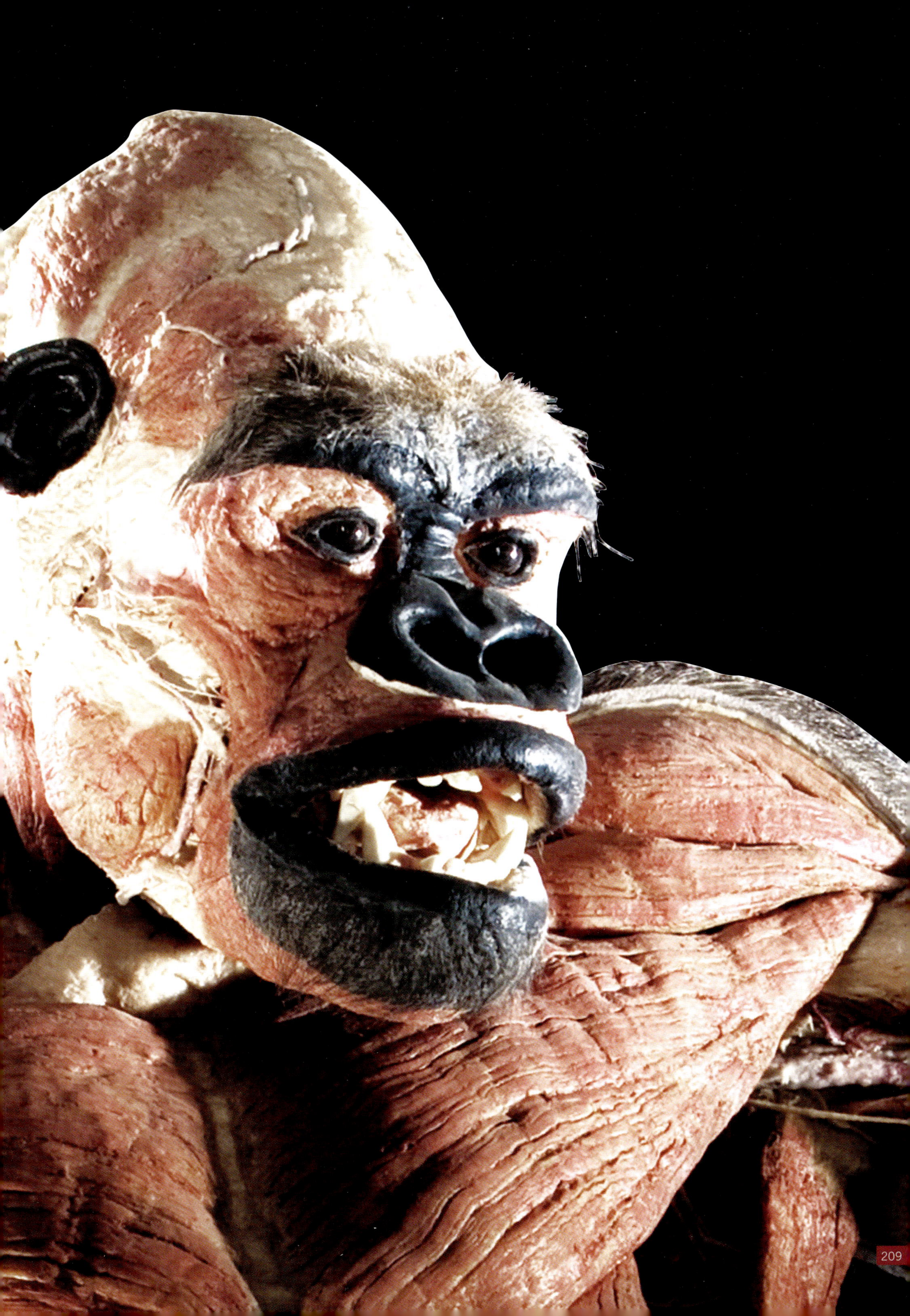

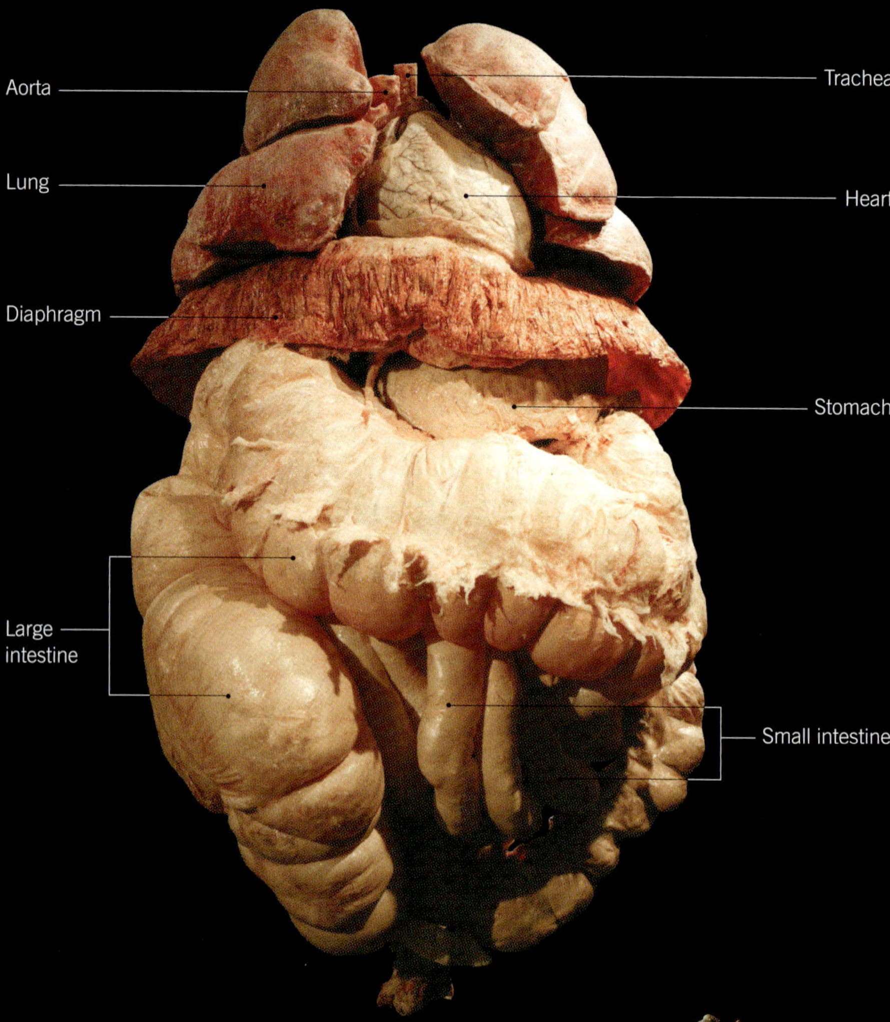


*Fig. 9.50* | *Internal organs of the Gorilla.*

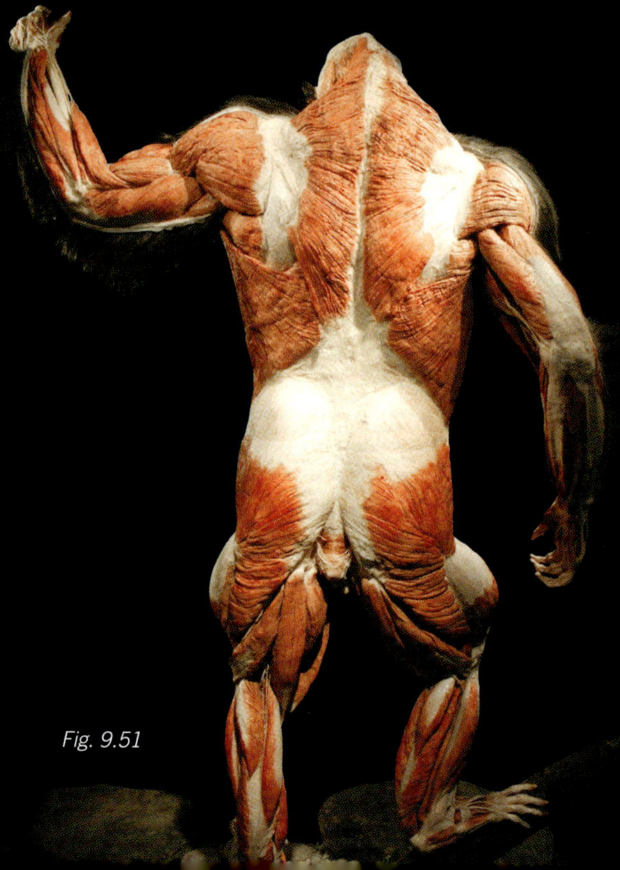

*Fig. 9.51*

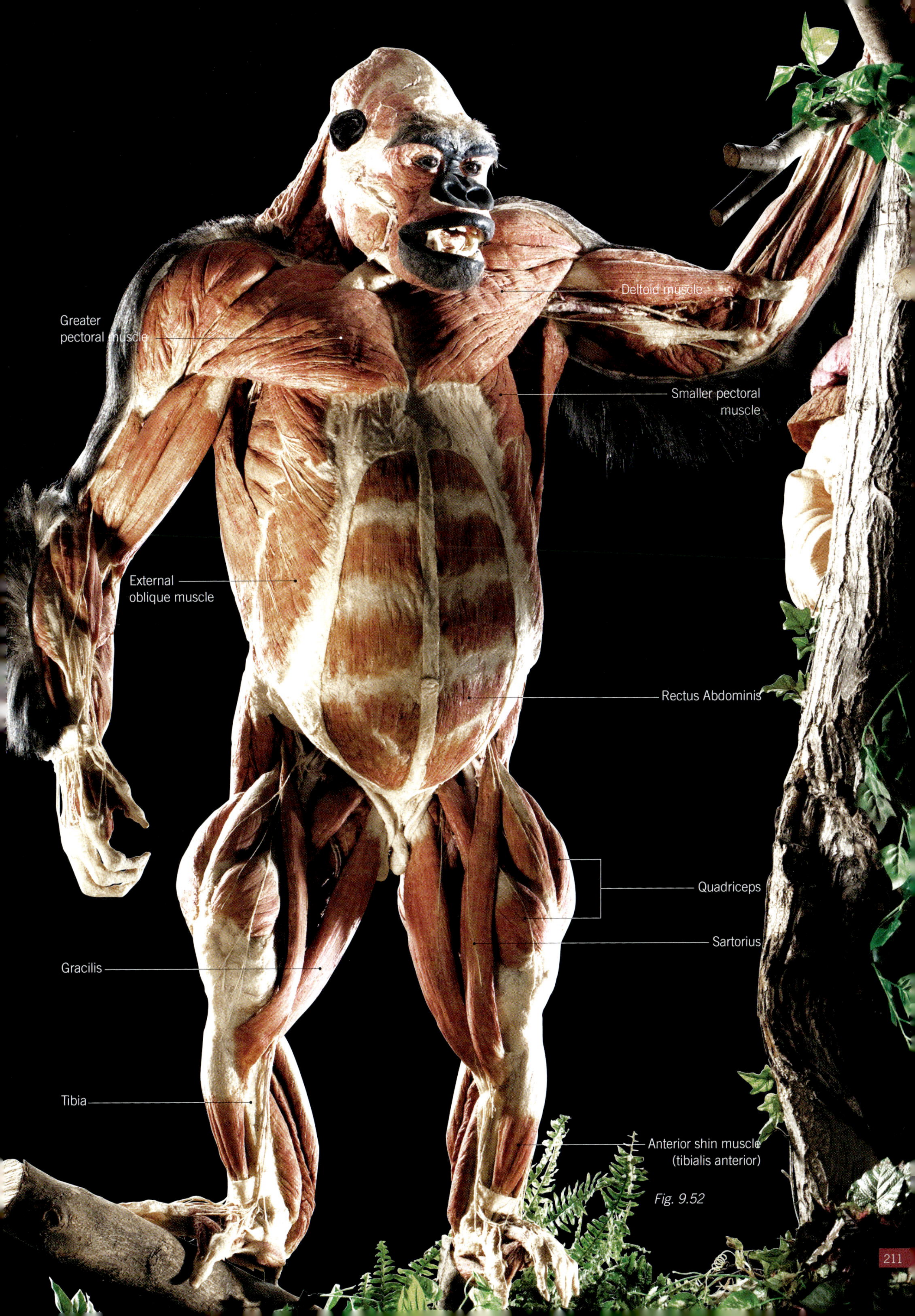
Deltoid muscle
Greater pectoral muscle
Smaller pectoral muscle
External oblique muscle
Rectus Abdominis
Quadriceps
Sartorius
Gracilis
Tibia
Anterior shin muscle (tibialis anterior)

*Fig. 9.52*

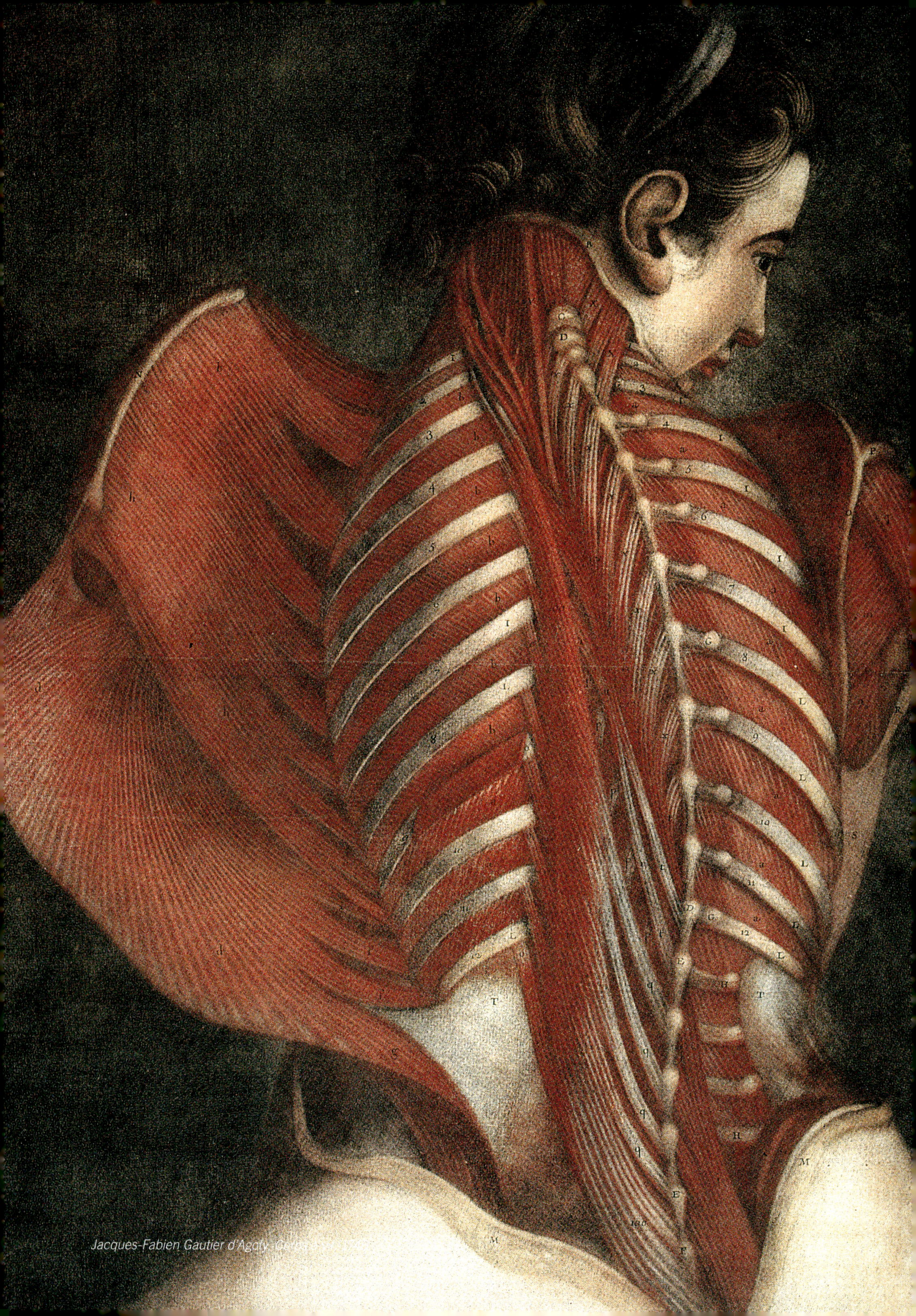

Jacques-Fabien Gautier d'Agoty,

## Prof. Dr. Franz Josef Wetz

# The Public Corpse

### The Dignity of Man

Man is something worth looking at; he presents a picture full of sublimity and dignity. At least, that is what the Renaissance philosophers thought. They one-sidedly emphasised the outstanding importance and sovereignty of this living creature that had the gift of language, and which had already once in its history – in the sculptures of classical Western antiquity – depicted itself, or at least its gods and heroes, as the ideal. With such a self-confident way of looking at themselves, numerous thinkers and artists between the 14th and 16th centuries clearly rejected the dismal mediaeval image, which, in contrast to the glorious Christian afterlife, frequently depicted the misery of existence here on Earth, its wretchedness and worthlessness.

However, what is truly special about the humanistic revaluation of man lies not merely in the emphasis of his worth, but above all in recognition of his beauty. It was as though it was only then that their unique upright posture enabled the inhabitants of Earth to gain an objective view of themselves. Not only at that time was the scope of what the world contained studied, comprehended and painted as an unending landscape as never before – for the Renaissance masters the body of mortal man itself, in ancient times often called the tomb of the soul, had become proof of God's existence. Now it was said that the human body had been designed so superbly in order for it to form a worthy vessel for the immortal soul. The heavenly perfection promised by the church was given an aesthetic earthly counterpart.

It was therefore not by chance that anatomy reached a peak for the first time during the Renaissance and was connected with the art of the time: as shown in countless portraits of the period – realistic even to the extent of dirt under the fingernails – man had become convinced that he could be seen as an individual; and he began systematically to discover the inner as well as the outer features of his form.

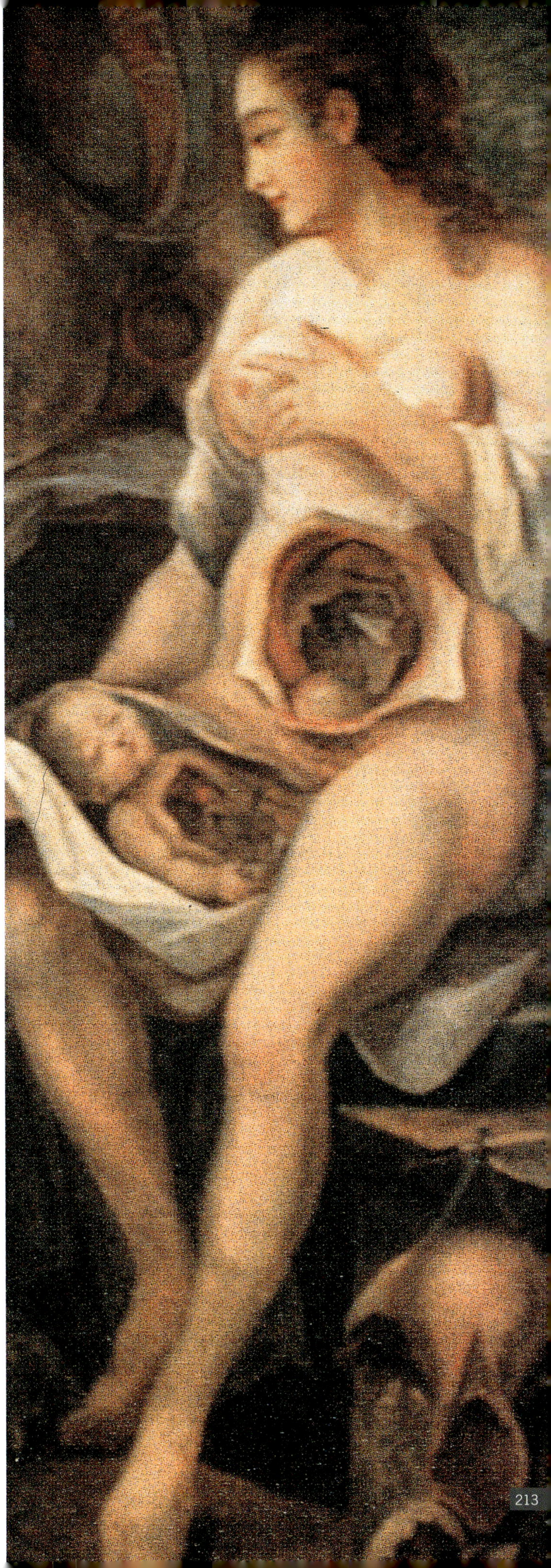

*Since the Renaissance, artists' representations of the human body have been based on anatomical studies, and from then onwards representations of anatomy, which was only founded as a medical discipline in that period, for a long time followed aesthetic rules and motifs taken from art. The "Dissected Woman with Opened Abdomen and Foetus" by French medical illustrator Jacques-Fabien Gautier (1711–1785), a pioneer in four-colour printing, was painted in 1746.*

However, to be looked at also means that we offer a target. For however highly developed we may be, we still remain vulnerable creatures, and frail ones at that. It is precisely our vulnerability in many respects and our great and varying sensitivities that cause us to perceive our own visibility as a danger; we therefore conceal ourselves in clothing and housing, and even hide ourselves when we by no means need to shun the light.

Thus on the one hand we consider ourselves worth looking at, do not want to be overlooked, and even seek publicity from time to time, but on the other hand we are also aware of our vulnerability. Ultimately possessing little security, most people are confronted with the need to shape their arduous and worrisome existence themselves throughout their lives. Those who are happy at most experience episodes of a carefree, unworried life.

This recognition of the greatness and misery of man raises the fundamental question of whether the individual also possesses a value that differentiates him from nature. Is he not ultimately only one transient being among others – a naked, narrow-nosed mammal with an overweight head on a spinal column that is rather unsuitable for his upright posture?

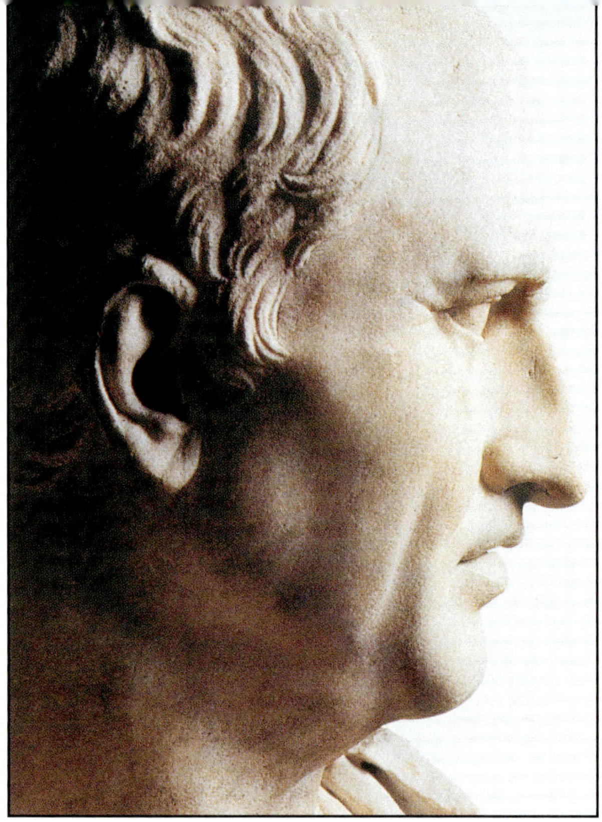

*Marcus Tullius Cicero, the most famous orator in ancient Rome, was the first to proclaim the idea of general human dignity – to be understood both as a distinctive characteristic of each individual as well as a way of individually shaping one's life.*

Precisely our neediness, imperfection and shortcomings, our insignificance in the boundless universe and our mortality repeatedly raise doubts today about the dignity of man in general, the latter of which, against this sobering background, appears to be a ridiculous presumption. Nevertheless, innate human dignity is a slogan of our time; sadly, however, it is burdened with an unbearable vagueness. Virtually nobody is able to provide clear information on the significance of, and justification for, this great idea. However, everybody uses the expression as if it were obvious. Thus one often reads and hears about the lack of dignity throughout the world, that this or that regime totally disregards human dignity, that something is beneath someone's dignity, even that the dead have a sacrosanct dignity. Unfortunately, what that all really means is generally impossible to find out.

The pathos that is always discernible in the expression all too easily masks its vagueness and openness. Instead of being inviolable, dignity appears to be elusive. One only needs to say the word 'dignity' out loud to be shocked by its hollow ring. Like many big words, this one too has largely worn thin today.

This is cause for concern if one considers the value that should be given to human dignity throughout the world. All of the United Nations' fundamental documents acknowledge this, and demand that it be recognised by all states and citizens. Accordingly, article 1 of the Universal Declaration of Human Rights from 1948 begins with the sentence: "All people are born free and equal in dignity and rights." But these declarations say nothing about what the expression implies, nor do the numerous state constitutions into which it has been incorporated.

An explanation is therefore urgently needed, especially as many people regard the expression "dignity" more as an empty phrase than a pure introductory word, as a commonplace word to be used in Sunday sermons, that – like edifying words intended as comfort – merely contributes to satisfying the need for general harmony. People like to refer to dignity because this word still sounds good and the fact that it is easy to remember gives the impression that it has a definition.

The fact that in truth it does not have one at all was proven by the examples to be found in the debates about the first major exhibition of plastinated whole-body specimens or plastinates in Germany. Like an all-purpose weapon, it was used against every reasonably justified argument, and was even ideologised. In debates like this, the reference to dignity – or rather to the lack of dignity – was often misused as a rhetorical phrase, either in order to silence unpleasant opponents or in order to help gain general recognition for one's personal interests and ideals associated with the traditional term. Who, by dissenting, would like to give rise to the suspicion that they supported infringements of human dignity? This explains why, in differences of ideological opinion, it can often be played as the joker, and why supporters of the widest range of opinions frequently like to refer to it.

Because dignity was one of the most widely used expressions in the controversy about BODY WORLDS, I shall discuss here in more detail its significance and justification in three general sections and in a fourth section the dignity of the dead.

**Sketches from Cultural History**

All highly advanced cultures maintain that they respect and protect human dignity. But the expression, if one looks more closely, is mainly of Western origin. In this traditional environment, it is almost always used in two ways.

Firstly, it is used to describe an innate quality. Accordingly, as a result of his humanity, the individual possesses a special dignity as an essential characteristic peculiar only to him, irrespective of his behaviour and the social conditions in which he lives: one comes into the world equipped with it in the same way as with arms and legs.

Secondly, dignity is a question of how to achieve it. Accordingly, it depends on us humans ourselves, on our life-style and manners, whether and to what extent we acquire and possess dignity. In this connection, it is sometimes considered more as an individual achievement, and sometimes more as a social skill.

In Western history, both views have almost always been connected with each other. It was said that man should satisfy his innate dignity – the natural characteristic – in his life through his thoughts and actions, i.e., prove himself worthy in accordance with what is required. But only the idea of dignity as a concrete task permeates the whole of Western culture, not its understanding as a natural basic condition and determination of being.

For the ancient Athenians and Romans, the idea that all human beings possessed dignity from birth onwards was foreign. At that time, it was considered to be solely the result of individual achievement and social recognition. Dignity was dependent on the ability and effort made to conquer passions and control feelings. A dignified personality observed the correct moderation and lived according to reason; he bore unhappiness, which did not unduly distress him, in just the same relaxed way as the happiness that he did not allow to result in excessive high spirits. In addition, he displayed dignity in his behaviour, his expressions and gestures, his body care and clothing, and in the calmness that he radiated. Such a person never spoke too loudly, and always walked circumspectly and gracefully. Social esteem, from which dignity could also grow, was bestowed by the general public either on aristocrats or persons with a particular social rank, who – as persons with dignity – generally occupied a high political office.

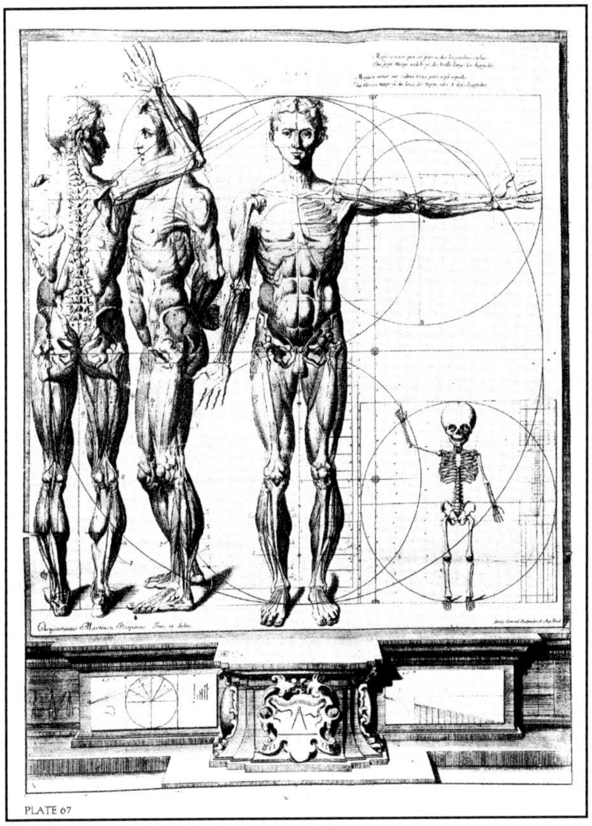


*With the fundamental change in Western philosophy at the beginning of the modern era, a humanistic view of man began to take hold, who now began to investigate both his interiors and exteriors at the same time. Beauty was understood not merely as a superficial quality, but was attributed to internal structures and harmonious proportions. The drawing "Skeleton and muscle figures to illustrate proportions" by the Spaniard Crisostomo Martinez (1638-1694), based on related studies by Renaissance artists such as Leonardo da Vinci and Albrecht Dürer, appeared in print in 1689 in Fontainebleau and in 1692 in Frankfurt and Leipzig.*

As far as is known, however, the Roman philosopher and politician Marcus Tullius Cicero (106-43 BC) was the first to express in his writings the idea of general human dignity, describing it both as an unmistakable characteristic as well as a requirement, which he attributed to all men; he based this kind of dignity, on which every individual should base his life, on human rationality. However, Cicero's wider understanding did not gain immediate acceptance; only Christianity brought his ideas to maturity.

If we combine the viewpoints of Christian teaching and of philosophy, the result is the following picture: According to these ideas, the dignity of man is based on the biblical God having created man in His image and allowing him to share His reason and might. As God's special creation, man has an absolute value, as a result of which he differs from all other creatures. In contrast to the natural world, he occupies the centre of the universe, which was created for him and for his sake. In addition, according to Christian opinion, the superior worth of man can also be seen in his upright posture, his personality, free will, his immortal soul and from the reason that enables him to recognise the world and God. In particular, however, it appears through God's becoming man – the Almighty becoming flesh – and through the redemption by Christ through His death and resurrection.

In all of these conceptions, human dignity is always seen as an essential characteristic possessed by each one of us, and which is not due solely to an elevated position, aristocratic origins or an impeccable life-style. It must be respected by every individual and all social institutions up to the state itself; all must protect and preserve it.

From the innate worth of man in this respect, however, an obligation is also derived, namely to live in an honest and God-fearing manner and to treat oneself and others kindly. People were convinced that although no-one can destroy the dignity innate in all men, the individual can nevertheless harm himself by allowing himself to revolt against God in sin and disobedience, and by being governed by his inclinations and unbridled egoism – instead of living a thoughtful, virtuous, considerate life.

Unlike the Middle Ages, from the 17th century onwards the dignity of man ceased to be attached to his being the image of God and to his position as the highest being in the world. Knowledge of the immensity of the universe had gradually become widespread, and even today this has the disturbing effect of making man aware of his minuteness and triviality. As a result of rational views, by the beginning of the modern age it had become impossible to deduce further the particular quality of man from his position in the world.

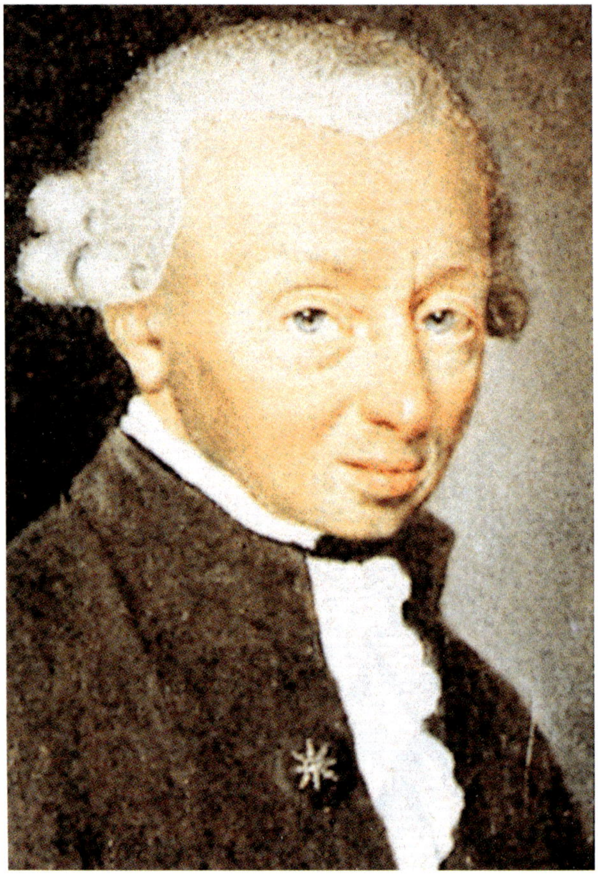

*Marcus Tullius Cicero, the most famous orator in ancient Rome, was the first to proclaim the idea of general human dignity – to be understood both as a distinctive characteristic of each individual as well as a way of individually shaping one's life.*

Consequently, the fact that the stars do not revolve around man became ever less essential for determining his importance. Man's overriding dignity was seen in the human ability to recognise nature and goodness. Thus, the French philosopher and mathematician Blaise Pascal (1623-1662) confirmed that although man was only one being among others, and as such was of only slight significance, he was a rational being – and as such he was far superior to all other creatures as far as dignity and rank were concerned.

The thinkers of the Enlightenment also speculated that only man possesses self-awareness, freedom, moral standards and reason. Their most important protagonist, Immanuel Kant (1724–1804), based the dignity of man exclusively on his particular intellectual gifts, on his capacity for self-contemplation and moral self-determination. On the one hand, Kant was convinced that man is a transitory part of nature; on the other hand he considered him as a person standing out from nature with a particular, indeed absolute, dignity. By this, Kant meant an absolute, incomparable value, higher than any price; having a price meant having only an external value, and thus capable of being bought, being exchangeable. Conversely, man as a rational being has an intrinsic value – dignity – and is therefore just as irreplaceable as he is unique. As an intellectual and morally rational being, he justly has the right to the respect of his peers, and conversely is obliged to heed others. In addition, the individual also has the same obligations toward himself, and these include never grovelling voluntarily to others. Whoever obsequiously bends the knee in search of favour is insulting himself. Whoever creeps to others should not be surprised if he gets kicked. Only a life in mutual acknowledgement and honest self-respect permits walking tall as the only physical and mental bearing appropriate for man.

According to Kant, the capacity for moral self-determination is expressed above all in the ability of the individual to free himself from his own desires, drives and instincts, and to decide on moral behaviour. One should always ask oneself what would happen if everyone acted like oneself, and then behave in such a manner that everyone in fact could act in the same way as oneself, without its resulting in chaos, injustice or pain.

For Kant, man was master, but not owner of himself. As a rational being with moral standards, the individual does indeed have power over himself, but he should not misuse this power to rid himself of it (that is why the sober thinker was also against intoxicants). Just as the respect-worthy value of the free man forbids his being treated simply as an object or tool, he as a person – that is, as a rational being bound to moral standards – must also never use himself merely as a means to an end or as an object; his dignity therefore forbids him from mistreating, selling or even killing himself. For Kant, human dignity as the embodiment of moral freedom is also a characteristic of man's being and form.

The following is clear: in the modern age, the idea of human dignity has detached itself from old religious bonds, but, as the one innate quality, it has continued to exist and has now found its ultimate foundation in rationality and morality.

**Uncertain Ideological Viewpoints**

In the meantime, major doubts about the traditional understanding of the term dignity have arisen: doubts about man occupying a special position in nature – whether as a result of his being in the image of God or as a result of his reason. Many reject this superiority over the animal and plant world and the resultant devaluation of all other beings as being doubtful, if not presumptuous or even unworthy. Doubts of a quite different nature weigh even more heavily.

It is still occasionally maintained that the political-legal idea of human dignity is inconceivable without religious assumptions. However, this is countered not only by the fact that in the secular, pluralistic society Christian beliefs have become incomprehensible for many people; the anchoring of human dignity in religion is in contradiction of the constitutionally guaranteed neutrality of liberal communities and of the ideological openness of the United Nations. Accordingly, neither the individual state nor the world community may stipulate an ideology for people – which would, however, be the case if the idea of human dignity were made generally subject to the Christian image of mankind. The liberal constitutional state and the world community should therefore take a neutral stance not only with regard to people's decision to adopt or reject a religion, but should also restrict itself to imparting only ideologically neutral values that are indispensable for the well-being of the individual and the peaceful co-existence of all. The idea of innate dignity based on the ideal of man as being in the image of God does not belong to this.

This is not to say that innate human dignity does not exist. State and law should merely act as though it did not exist, because no one should impose acknowledgement of one particular ideology on another. It should be pointed out, however, that the requirement of neutrality affects only the state and its citizens in their political-legal role; conversely, no one should be denied the right to advocate his religious-ideological opinions in his private and social sphere, or the right to live in accordance with these.

The same objections that oppose a Christian interpretation of human dignity can also be put forward against the rational-philosophical view. The human concept on which it is based is just as invalid universally. The idea of man as a rational being with an absolute value that is distinct from nature is almost as ideologically secure as a religious belief. Hence, the rational-philosophical interpretation of dignity contradicts the constitutionally guaranteed neutrality of our state and the ideological openness of the United Nations; it becomes incompatible with a liberal community and a pluralistic world public as soon as it becomes applicable and binding for all.

However, this does not prevent the individual from having good reasons for being convinced of the truth of a particular ideology. But he should not want to force it onto his neighbour, the State not onto its citizens, and the world community not onto its member states. Only ideologically neutral moral concepts can be asked of anyone and acknowledged by everyone. However, an ideologically completely neutral interpretation of the concept of innate human dignity is not possible; any such attempt must fail as a result of ideologi-

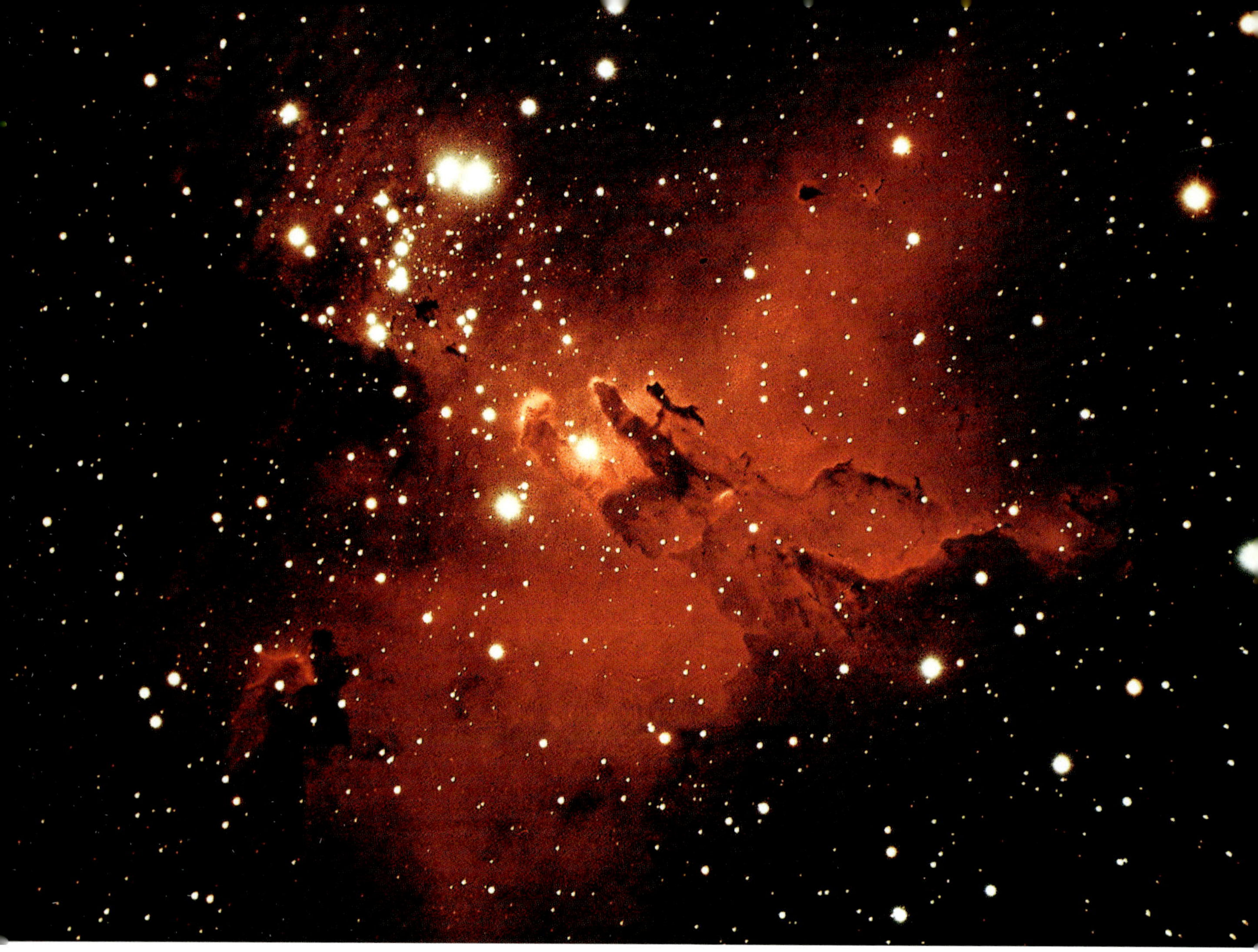

*The practice of stargazing, one of the oldest sciences known to man, developed from the 15th century into modern astronomy, and broke with traditional mystical ideas. In particular, the knowledge gained only 80 years ago, that even our familiar Milky Way system with its billions of suns, is only one of countless galaxies in the immeasurable universe, made the planet Earth, and thus mankind, into just a fleeting cosmic peripheral phenomenon. The photograph shows a highly active area of star formation in the Rosetta nebula, dark clouds of which will probably also compress and finally collapse to form new stars.*

cal controversies, because the ideas represented cannot be generalized. Consequently, in principle there can be no generally valid interpretation. It would either be definite with regard to ideology or vague with regard to content, for without ideological background assumptions, the assumption of dignity as an innate characteristic remains incomprehensible and empty. Admittedly one can go one step further. As stated, the need for ideological neutrality merely requires the political institutions to act as if innate human dignity did not exist; modern natural sciences suggest, however, that in fact it does not exist. Thus modern cosmology can at least teach modesty to the citizens of Earth: our planet is only one of nine in the solar system, our central star only one average star out of a good two hundred thousand million in the galaxy, and the latter only one of more than a hundred million such galaxies, which in turn form groups and super-groups with immense empty spaces between. Similarly, the knowledge that humanity is a chance result of undirected and often crisis-like biological evolution can place our proud self-awareness in proportion. For example, for about 150 million years of the earth's middle age, reptiles – the dinosaurs – were the predominant creatures living on land; the anatomically modern Homo sapiens has only existed for about 100,000 years. Moreover, according to modern genetics and the neurosciences, our behaviour and intellectual life are determined by hereditary factors and unknown cerebral processes to a greater degree than was previously assumed.

Apparently there are no signs in nature that man could point to himself as an indication of his dignity. On the contrary, he is a transitory part of nature, concerned with himself in a world that is not concerned with him. The earliest known traces of hominoids who walked upright were found in a forested area in Tanzania, the Laetoli. These footprints are more than 3.5 million years old. Like the already very human-like primates, who left these behind, we human beings – the last representatives of the species Homo – will at some point have disappeared from the surface of the earth.

There is no victory over the briefness of time. The many ruined walls, the weather-beaten columns and the torso sculptures from bygone phases of the very short – measured by geological ages – era of civilization very clearly bear witness to this. What is existentially important is not what the Roman Forum and the Acropolis once were, but what they are today: ruins and piles of rubble, which impressively remind us of the transient nature of everything human. In the nearer or more distant future nothing and no-one with the knowledge that there was once life on earth that claimed a particular value for itself will any longer exist. It requires no excessive pessimism, rather a sober realism, to recognise that man and all his works of intellectual culture have ultimately been condemned to disappear without a trace.

### Self-Assertion of Dignity

We shall neither want to accept nor be able to come to terms with complete rejection of the idea of innate dignity, even though it cannot be generalised, and will possibly prove to be merely a fantasy. The excess of suffering, oppression and injustice in the world makes such a rejection appear nothing less than irresponsible; rather, it calls for respect for this idea in everyday practice and for its preservation in philosophical theory. We therefore cannot escape the question of how, despite all reservations, it can be saved.

This question can never be disregarded when humanitarian principles are infringed. This means that our vulnerability and sensitivity in many respects, but also our longing for a successful life, self-determination in freedom and undisturbed self-development, reveal a need for help and protection in which an ideologically neutral right to dignified treatment is established. Consequently, the expression 'dignity' has a meaning for as long as we can still imagine anything in terms of human degradation and humiliation. The trembling body – ever a symbol of elementary vulnerability and need for protection – stands for such a need for respect, recognition and assistance. One can call this the self-assertion of human dignity as a result of becoming aware of it possibly and actually being disregarded.

This knowledge by no means contradicts the view that man is only one part of transitory nature, only one being among others. For in accordance with the same existentialist premise that each of us is condemned to shaping his needy and worried existence himself, oppression and injustice are perceived as distressingly cruel; nature by no means eliminates the difference between a successful and unsuccessful life.

However, one thing is no longer possible – adhering to the idea of innate human dignity. It is not only difficult to reconcile it with the natural scientific philosophy of our time – it already stands in contradiction to the fundamental principles of our liberal community and of those of the multicultural world community.

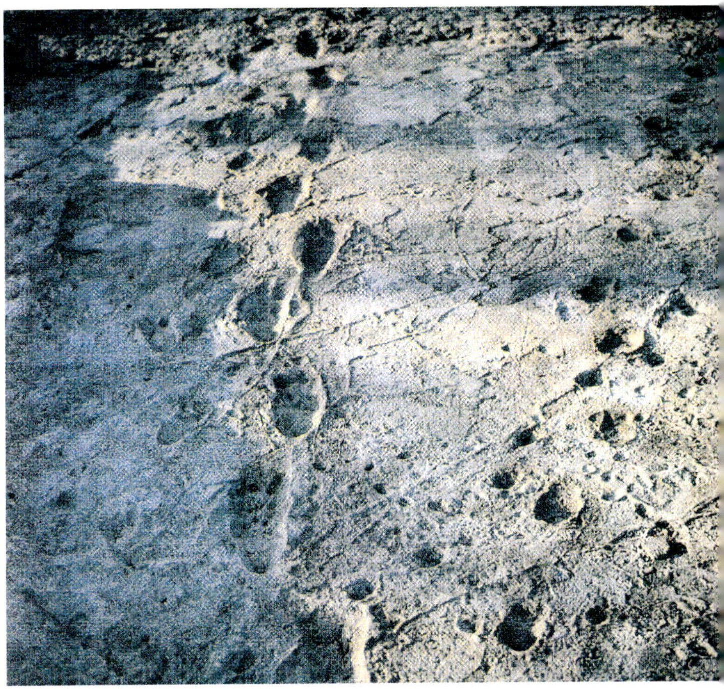

*Biologically modern man appears late in the evolution of organisms, and is the last hominoid. Anatomically, we are for the most part the heirs of earlier species of our genus; for example, fossilised footprints discovered in Tanzania confirm that as early as approximately 3.5 million years ago human-like beings were walking upright. Like its ancestors, humanity will not last forever despite all of its achievements in terms of civilization; the end of all life as we know it will come at the latest when the sun inflates into a red giant, and then our planetary system will be destroyed.*

Only dignity as an aim can be generalised. Understood in this way, it is less given to us than imposed on us, not a general sign of nobility, but a particular identification of that imperfect being – man. Yet it denotes an ethical ideal and the concrete task of preventing and eliminating intellectual oppression, material need and social injustice. The basis for this is the mutual respect of humans as vulnerable beings concerned for themselves and for others. Considered from the ideologically neutral point of view – that is from the radically secular viewpoint – dignity is not naturally a part of us, but results only from the individual's dealings with himself and his equals, and the dealings of the state with its citizens.

However, if dignity is only a matter of shaping the conditions under which we live, it becomes possible to think that humans have none. Whenever someone is brutally degraded or loses his self-respect, his dignity disappears – albeit not the ethical right to it.

In order to avoid misunderstandings: no-one should be stripped of his dignity; but on the basis of the existence of those who lead, or who are forced to lead, a wretched life without self-respect, one can no longer sensibly say that it has dignity if innate dignity is absent. But even if this existed, it would be of no help to those affected, for such a nobility of being could not give any consolation to them about their undignified conditions anyway. If, therefore, dignity in the religious or rational philosophical sense does not exist, it in no way means that it should no longer be respected as an objective to be striven for. The contrary is the case: human dignity should be respected precisely when it does not exist as the one so that it exists as the other.

In this ideologically neutral assessment, the rational philosophical principle, which the adherents of religious opinions also share, namely that no one may merely be misused as a means to an end or as an object, continues to be maintained. Such a demand is sensible and ethically justified even if we no longer regard man as a being in God's image or as an intellectual being removed from nature, but merely as a transitory part of nature concerned with himself.

Dignity as an ethical right is one thing, but its guarantee in law is another. In view of the general tendency of man to indifference, egoism and violence, in view of the fact that we cannot be gods creating perfection and general happiness, but are rather animals, the special protection of human dignity in the community – as in Germany as a result of article 1, paragraph 1 of the federal Constitution – appears to be absolutely justified. This arrangement is sensible even without ideological background assumptions.

**The Dignity of the Dead**

According to general opinion, the right to the protection of dignity also applies to those who have died. In this connection one talks of its continued influence and effect even beyond death. In the debate about BODY WORLDS, the dignity of the dead has become a key concept on which the questions, opinions, assertions and arguments concerning the permissibility and responsibility of a public exhibition of whole-body plastinates are focused.

**The Inevitability of Death**

Lifelessness is the norm in the cosmos, not a special circumstance; life, in contrast, is a borderline case. What is most natural for us humans – our own existence – is the great exception to which death is the rule.

If the whole of reality were full of life, death would have to remain a puzzle because in that case it would not fit into the world. However, the real puzzle is life, because ever since the big bang the universe has consisted mainly of a field of inanimate particles and forces. Measured against the universe's dimensions of time and space, the entire history of organisms known to us is a fleeting episode restricted to a tiny concentration of matter – the planet Earth.

This applies all the more so for the Homo sapiens phase: just as it was by chance that our species appeared in the biotic evolution characterised by erratic mutations and selection (also as a result of catastrophic mass death), the end of humanity is just as certain; and this will not have to wait for the annihilation of our planet when the sun explodes into a Red Giant in about five thousand million years, time.

Like the death of life in general, the death of the individual human being is neither mysterious nor profound. It is the end of a natural course. Admittedly, we can try to postpone this biological actuality with the aid of modern medicine and a healthy life-style, but we cannot avoid it. Our death is as natural as the ageing and decline of the human body, in the course of which nerves and muscle cells die, the skeleton becomes more brittle and the hair less rich in pigment, eyesight and heart and brain functions deteriorate and dark spots develop on sagging skin. For one thing, all these processes are due to the wear and tear to which tissues and cells are exposed in the everyday performance of their tasks; for another, ageing follows a genetic program that determines the life of the individual cells, organs and the entire body. Harbingers of the end of life are age-related illnesses, which often considerably reduce the quality of life. When, finally, the supply of oxygen to the body breaks down, the person who was alive a moment ago is now dead.

## Ambiguity of the Dead

But who are the dead after all? Without necessarily having to go into the medical question of definite signs of death, on closer consideration the term itself proves to be ambiguous. On the one hand, we understand the dead to mean the dead body, while on the other hand we mean the deceased.

The deceased is commemorated; the body is disposed of. Nowadays, and in Germany at least, it is either buried in a coffin or cremated and its ashes placed in an urn and interred or scattered at sea. Graves can be anonymous or furnished with names.

However, funeral practices, some of which are very old and carefully handed down, are as diverse as cultures. The ancient Egyptians, who for some of their Pharaohs built the pyramids that subsequently came to be considered wonders of the world, and provided them with costly gifts for the after-life, were generally buried in a linen cloth. The Parsees placed their dead, naked, on the towers of silence for the vultures. In many tribes, ritual cannibalism took place right up to modern times. The atheist Communist Party of the Soviet Union embalmed their first dictator Vladimir Ilyich Lenin and placed him on show. The Catholic Church allows bones and other physical relicts of its martyrs and saints to be revered as relics. Meanwhile, not only plagues, but above all wars and systematic murder like the fascistic genocide of the European Jews have also filled numerous mass graves. How a culture treats a body is one expression of the instinctive rejection of the idea that, with death, the definitive end of life has come. The other manifests itself in that, according to general opinion, the wishes of the deceased should remain valid even after death; thus wills that are valid in law must be adhered to by the surviving heirs. The specific instructions of a person concerning the fate of his body after death – such as how it is to be buried and how the grave is to be designed, or whether it is to be donated for anatomical purposes, plastination or transplantation surgery – are also always the provisions of the deceased; they cannot be those of the body. Although we associate the term 'the dead' with both the deceased and with the body, the two expressions do not mean the same thing. How otherwise could one sensibly talk about the "body of the deceased?"

Etymologically, the term 'body' refers to the (dead) physical shell. The expression, which is perceived to be more considerate, is often used instead of 'corpse'; and this latter word in its turn had already supplanted the Old and Middle High German words *hreo* and *re* with their blunt meaning of "cadaver." Yet one also talks about mortal remains, about the part of a human that can decay. The body, which after the death of the individual still retains its form for some time in silent motionlessness, showing features of its personality, is called a corpse until the flesh has disappeared from the bones and any connection with the former unmistakable whole no longer exists as a result of natural decay or other form of decomposition.

The corpse is no longer a person; its ego ceased to exist at the latest after brain death. The corpse as a physical thing or object reveals itself to the unprejudiced view as what it actually is – a possible object for decay or cremation, organ removal, anatomy or plastination. On death, the person comes to an end; he is no longer in this world. He has thus lost his subjective quality and has become an object.

Since time immemorial, man, needing not only direction about reality, but also reassurance about it, has invented symbols and stories in order to cope with death. These make it clear that our need for realism is limited. Glossing over the harshness of reality, even now one talks about peaceful sleep or the resting of the dead, and includes in this picture the body, which, lying on its back with eyes closed and hands folded, is laid out and placed in the coffin. Yet the terms rest, peace and sleep, when related to the body, say less about death itself than about life – its restlessness, restless effort and exhausting difficulty.

Yet the popular image of peace in death is also connected to religious ideas, especially those of the Christians, because they expect re-awakening and resurrection. This concept was often transferred to the body, which is the reason that the Catholic Church forbade cremation for many hundreds of years; the prohibition was only lifted in 1963.

However, if such religious expectations are not, or are no longer, convincing, many people suffer an existential trauma or fear such a trauma. Admittedly, even a religious person cannot seriously believe that a body rests and sleeps. Even though one usually does not wish to know what happens so precisely: A dead person does not rest, he decays; he does not sleep, he decomposes and disintegrates to dust or is burned to ashes. The disintegration of his body into organic and inorganic molecules is inevitable, until, in accordance with the old Latin proverb, *terra tegit terram*, earth again only covers earth.

Possibly the dead person remains an object of mourning the whole time. However, this, too, like respecting the last wishes, relates not to the body, but only to the deceased. The body is a lifeless object in appearance, but the deceased is a living subject in memory. Even the visible grave into which the body was lowered, and which those left behind visit, care for and decorate as a place of particularly intensive memories, almost always evokes for them the image of the person who once was, as they knew him, not the image of decaying flesh and disintegrating bones. Not least because this idea is difficult to bear, more and more people are deciding on cremation nowadays, and many are allowing their bodies to be used after death for the living – through transplant surgery, for anatomical purposes or for plastination.

Nameless gardens of rest and communal graves for ashes are a further sign of an absence of illusions in our society. History no longer grows on these grassy areas in many cemeteries. Like the graveyards without individual names that were common in earlier phases of European history, they are in advance of their time, for at some point all graves will reach this state of anonymity and inconspicuousness, and the bodies buried in them will have disappeared without a trace. Even the stone monuments and mausoleums disintegrate if they are not cleared away beforehand.

Memories are of even shorter duration. The mourning for the death of a person cannot hurt forever. The memory of his or her life pales, and finally the once inconsolable ones left behind die themselves; we cannot stop the past from slipping into nothingness. Finally, a veil of forgetfulness covers us all, and even this forgetting is ultimately forgotten.

**The Dignity of Plastinates**

It should always be made clear in what sense – religious, rational philosophical or ideologically neutral – the word dignity, which can be interpreted in different ways, is being used. If one must apply the word to the dead, in light of all that has been mentioned above, a strict differentiation must be made between the dignity of a body and that of the deceased.

This is not easy. One might think that the word refers only to the body, not to the deceased, since the highest value cannot logically be attributed to something that does not physically exist, that only lives on in memory, which, moreover, gradually pales. However, it is also feasible that dignity apply only to the deceased, but not to the body or even its ashes and the dust, into which it disintegrates, since, with death, the person is extinguished and has lost his subjective quality.

In the debate about plastination and the exhibition of plastinates, there was much talk about infringement of human dignity – that the dignity of the dead, that of their closest relatives, even that of the general public, if not the whole of humanity, had been disregarded. This criticism was expressed by representatives of the two major Christian churches in Germany, namely the Lutheran Church and the Roman Catholic Church who knew that they had the support of politicians from different camps, and also by doctors; and many journalists made themselves the mouthpieces of these accusations.

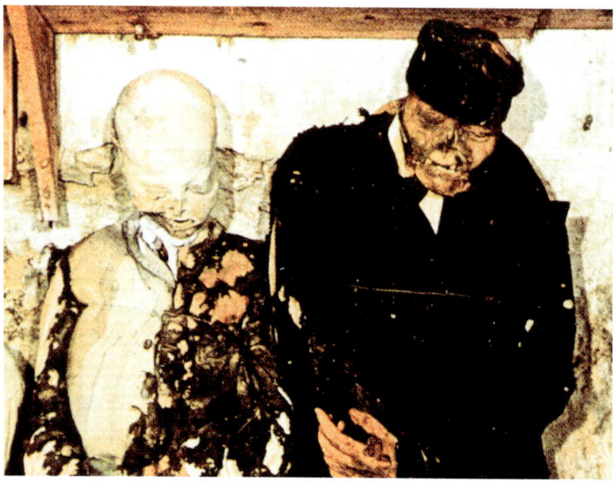

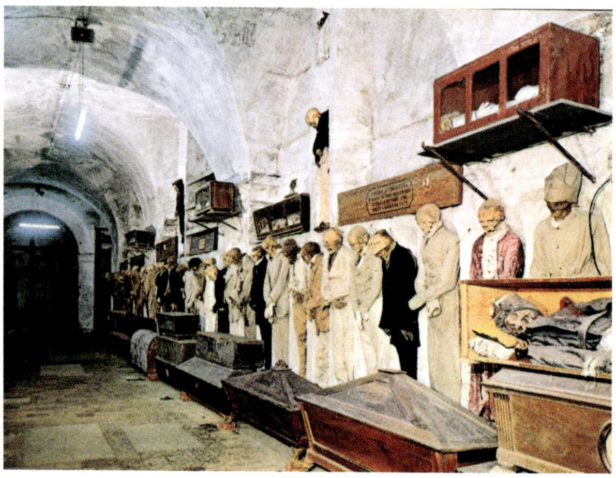

*Burying corpses or burning them and placing the ashes in an urn are merely cultural conventions – and by no means the only ones, and not the ones that are always adhered to in modern Europe. For example, the Capuchin tomb in Palermo is the largest cellar of mummies in the world. The picture on the left shows a young woman and her godfather, the one on the right the so-called corridor of scholars.*

It was striking, however, that mostly one only heard or read that human dignity had been infringed, rarely to the extent to which it was supposed to have been. Apparently the critics were confident that those who refer to dignity are correct from the outset, without a precise justification and closer definition of what is meant. Thus the very different questions that arise in this connection, and which I shall discuss below, remained largely disregarded:

- Does the individual infringe his own dignity if he makes his dead body available for plastination?
- For its part, does this type of anatomical dissection and preservation of the donated body infringe human dignity?
- In particular, does the aesthetic form of a plastinated body, and possibly its conversion into a work of art, jeopardise the dignity of the dead?
- Can public exhibitions of plastinates, which are acknowledged to be aesthetically attractive, offend human dignity?
- And to what extent would charging entrance fees for visiting such exhibitions and providing plastinates for scientific and educational purposes in return for money be compatible with the dignity of man?

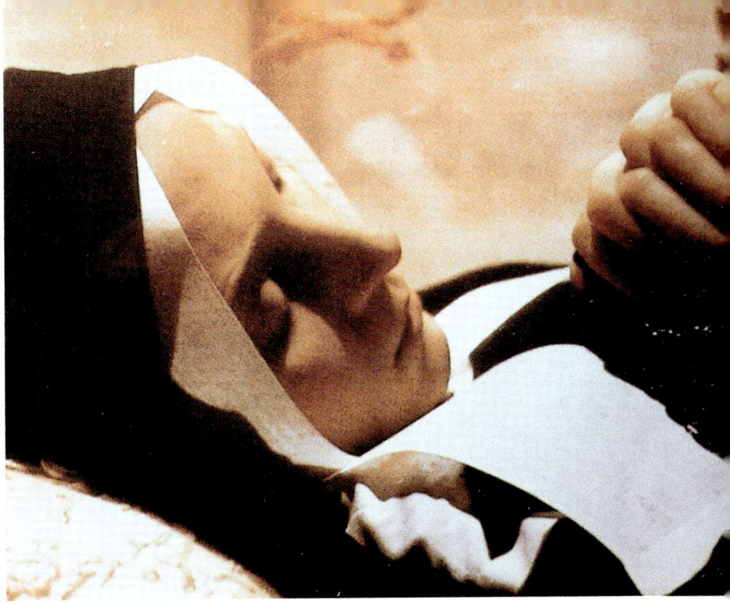

*The Christian religious ideas of resurrection are expressed in concrete terms in the traditional picture of the peace of death. Accordingly, the Catholic Church has dressed up relics and whole bodies of saints – here Marie-Bernarde Soubirous (1844–1879), known as Bernadette, in the chapel of the convent of St. Gildard in Nevers. The religious visions that she had at the age of 14 formed the basis for the pilgrimages to Lourdes; she was canonised by Pope Pius XI in 1933.*

**Limits of Self-Determination**

The supporters of the most varied of ideas of dignity are largely agreed that self-determination is one of its essential characteristics. Whether they represent a religious, rational philosophical or radically secular viewpoint – they are all convinced that one of the freedoms of man is being able to make binding arrangements about his estate for the time after death. Furthermore, it is then often simply maintained that the dignity of a person continues after death and even extends to the dead person.

However, on closer examination, this quite common argument proves to be extremely problematical. For it gives the impression that the dignity of a person can outlive the person himself. However, that is nonsensical, to some extent a misunderstanding of logic: Such use of language presupposes that the deceased, although he no longer exists, must nevertheless continue to be regarded as existent; for only something that exists can have properties such as human dignity. But an existent non-existent is a contradiction in itself.

Respect for the dignity of someone who has died can therefore only mean respect for the dignity that the person had when he was still alive. That therefore means respect not for something that is present, but merely for something that is past. To have this respect is obviously possible, just as the arrangements made by a deceased regarding what he leaves behind can remain binding for the survivors after his death.

The question is, however, where does this obligation come from? It is mainly a social agreement that can be justified both by the wish of the citizens to take decisions that are binding beyond death, and also by their right to self-determination and by the dignity that they can normally demand when they are still alive.

There are nevertheless generally acknowledged limits to the free development of the individual personality. Heading these is the freedom of the person in question. To illustrate the point: the right to swing his arm ends at just the point where somebody else's nose begins. For a similar reason, in some circumstances – despite the right of self-determination – personal disposition over one's body must be withdrawn.

According to religious opinion, man may not dispose of his body in any way that he wishes, because the body, as the image of God, is also God's property; even a corpse has dignity. According to rational philosophical thinking, man may be master of himself, but he is not the owner of himself; accordingly, the individual may not take an entirely free decision about his dead body, because as a former bearer of reason it is given a particular dignity. In contrast, according to radically secular understanding, the mortal remains of a person, considered by themselves, have no dignity whatsoever; only to the extent to which the body is respected and honoured is it given a certain dignity.

Does it follow from these three ideas that while the individual is alive he may not decide on the fate of his later dead body? If that were really the case, the dignity of the body would be in direct conflict with the dignity of the person who has died – his former right to self-determination.

Let us disregard the fact that in major natural disasters and epidemics and in wars, when the living count for virtually nothing and the corpses buried in mass graves count for nothing at all, and let us also disregard the numerous anonymous communal graves from former times that also lack special respect for the dignity of the corpses. Whether influenced by this or not – in the meantime man has come to the decision that the dignity of the deceased, i.e., his right to self-determination when he was alive, should be valued over the dignity of his dead body. It is said that the freedom of man includes being allowed to make arrangements about the fate of his mortal remains. Thus what has been said about its not being permissible to decide what is to happen to the corpse has already been partially countered.

Moreover, anyone who can decide between the different methods of disposal after death must decide on one possibility, and as a result of this situation he is inevitably master of his own corpse. Then, however, instead of burial or cremation of his body, he can stipulate that it be given to an anatomical institute for educational and research purposes, or to transplantation surgery for the removal of certain organs, organ parts and tissues in order to save the lives of others; and in view of these long-established possibilities, it would be absurd and inconsistent to forbid individuals from donating their own bodies for the relatively new procedure of plastination.

There is also another aspect. The authorities responsible may only approve a cremation if all suspicion of murder or manslaughter can be ruled out. In order to be sure of this, it is sometimes necessary to perform an autopsy; likewise the legal authorities can order an autopsy and the exhumation of a body that has already been buried – without the consent of the deceased and his relatives – in order to solve a crime. Not only the supporters of the radically secular understanding of dignity are in agreement with this, but usually also those who hold religious and rational philosophical views. However, by doing this, they also forfeit the idea of the unavailability of the human corpse. For apparently the fact that this is considered to be the property of God or a former bearer of reason, and the fact that relatives, friends and the general public would like to honour the person in the same way as they perceived him at the time of his death, apparently counts for less than the deceased's right to self-determination and the requirements of public safety.

This does not prevent religious or rational philosophical dignity from being conferred on the decaying body, the ashes of a cremated body, the anatomical dissection, the transplantation-surgery organs or a plastinate. It is merely that – as stated above – ideological opinions, which cannot be generalised, may not be imposed on anybody. The liberal State must therefore evaluate the concept "corpse" only from neutral and generally valid points of view, and not from points of view that are bound up with religious allegiance or intellectual history. However, the dignity of the corpse independent of all religious and rational philosophical convictions does not exist. Seen from an ideological point of view, the dignity of a corpse only arises when living persons are handling it; this also includes the respect for the last wishes of the deceased with regard to his mortal remains, as long as public order and health would not be affected by this decision.

Accordingly, with regard to the criticism of plastination and BODY WORLDS, it must be concluded that whoever, while he is alive and in full possession of his mental faculties, voluntarily and after comprehensive information makes his body available for this procedure, and gives his consent to exhibition of the denaturized and transformed dissection resulting from it, is not offending the dignity of his body. In contrast, whoever forbids such a donation of a body is infringing the dignity of the deceased – unless public order and health would be jeopardised.

### Objectification of a Dead Body as a Result of Plastination?

The object principle put forward in connection with the Supreme Court's definition and establishment of human dignity has recently also been applied to plastination. There was talk of degrading conversion of the dead into mere objects by making them into organ and whole-body specimens, of demeaning the dignity of their bodies by making them simply objects or things.

This accusation is untenable. It is untenable for the simple reason that while they were alive, the donors contractually agreed to plastination of their bodies after death and because plastination does not indicate contempt for the dead. Above all, the accusation is unjustified because a corpse, as the impermanent remains of a deceased person, is already an object or a thing. It becomes a thing before it comes under the hands of the plastinator. Consequently, the object principle can only relate to living persons, not to dead bodies, as these no longer have a subject quality.

Admittedly, considering the body as an exception to the 'either-or' classes of persons and objects has become established in law. However, this cannot seriously mean that the corpse is still somehow a person, rather that, being the mortal remains of a person who once was, possibly it should not be treated in the same way as other lifeless objects. It can be the object of respect and mourning; and for religious and ideological reasons, out of consideration for the wishes of the deceased and consideration of our own moral feelings, but also, with an eye to public order, we are obliged to treat it with respect. However, none of that would change anything with regard to the status of a corpse as an object. Otherwise in principle, it could not be used for the removal of organs and tissues for transplants or used for anatomical purposes, and it could not even be burned or left to decay in the ground.

According to Gunther von Hagens, the inventor of plastination, during its conversion into a whole-body specimen, a corpse goes through three stages: Firstly it becomes anonymous. Then it is turned into a durable specimen, physically and chemically denatured through and through, which can no longer be identified with the former person. Finally it becomes an object of scientific information. It is simply absurd to consider the rendering of a dead body anonymous (by its not being given the name of the deceased) to be degrading, and to see degradation in the subsequent elimination of its physiognomic individuality (as a result of the anatomical dissection). The person bearing the name did indeed have his own individual life and sickness history; but this is not taken away from the deceased as such, and thus nor is his dignity, whereas the corpse was an object even before plastination.

In this respect, the only thing that is new, and thus unfamiliar, about the otherwise truly revolutionary procedure is that its results, instead of showing the mere frailness and transitoriness of life as anatomical specimens preserved in the usual way do, show the human body in a state that is no longer alive but not yet decayed for a virtually unlimited period of time. In addition to the amazing functionality of our body, its inner beauty can also be revealed if the plastinator is sensitive to this and proceeds with sufficient skill.

**Improper Aestheticisation of Plastinates?**

As described at the beginning, anatomy blossomed for the first time in the Renaissance, and entered into an alliance with art. At that time, and for a long time afterwards, reproductions of medical discoveries and aesthetic depictions of the human body in paintings and sculptures were very closely connected.

Plastination, as Gunther von Hagens practices it, is in this tradition. A plastinate, if it is to fulfil the task of general enlightenment that is the aim, must be given an appropriate form, which could by no means be achieved with traditional methods of dissection and preservation. If the senses as well as the intellect are to be appealed to, aesthetically attractive solutions to the problem of form almost inevitably result.

However, von Hagens seems to have gone a step further when he oriented the shape of some of his whole-body plastinates on paintings and sculptures. Indeed, the opinion could arise that great works of art had served as models for him: the "Prototypes of Movement in Space" by the Italian futurist painter Umberto Boccioni (1882–1916) for The Runner; the "Anthropomorphic Cabinet" by Spanish surrealist Salvador Dali (1904–1989) for The Drawer Man; the figure of Bartholomew in the Sistine Chapel by the Renaissance genius Michaelangelo Buonarroti (1475–1564) for the Muscle Man with his skin draped over his arm; and "The Doll" by German-French graphic artist and sculptor Hans Bell–mer (1902–1975) for the Fencer. However, these similarities came about purely by chance, as Gunther von Hagens did not yet know of these works of art when he conceived these plastinates. Although this may indeed seem astounding, there is nonetheless no doubt about the aesthetic, virtually artistic presentation of his anatomical themes.

Various groups have protested vigorously against this ambitious structural transformation of anatomical specimens. In particular, they maintain that the plastinator is to some degree blasphemously making himself the Creator; in reality he is not concerned with passing on knowledge, but in self-expression. In the process, he is degrading the bodies of the dead in a demeaning manner into mere objects of art that allow the fact that they consist of parts of real bodies to be forgotten. The dead person serves him only as the means for an aesthetic purpose.

In addition, this criticism describes consequences that are to be expected after the supposed taboo has been broken. This leads to the question of how far one wants to go with the treatment of dead bodies. For if the fashioning of corpses so that they can be displayed in museums of art and galleries were once to be allowed, it would only be a small step to transforming dead men and women into armchairs, skeletons into hall-stands, skulls into soup bowls – most definitely infringements of dignity showing contempt for mankind.

The religiously biased accusation that the plastinator is playing the Creator with his whole body specimens carries as little weight as the suspicion that the workers in a crematorium are behaving like the assistants of the Old Testament's God of Wrath or mythical idols when they push the dead into large incinerators. If one were to argue in this way, one would have to ask whether every surgical procedure performed on humans – whether for health or aesthetic reasons – would not have to be condemned as pride and an offence against the omnipotence of God. Apart from the members of certain sects, the vast majority of people obviously consider this absurd.

Moreover, the criticism of the aesthetic quality of plastinates misses the point here insofar as it is claimed that they are clearly identifiable as objects of art. In principle, however, no object can stipulate how the human mind must perceive it; whether it is perceived as a work of art depends mainly on the eye and judgement of the beholder (although the difficult question of what art or beauty is can be ignored here).

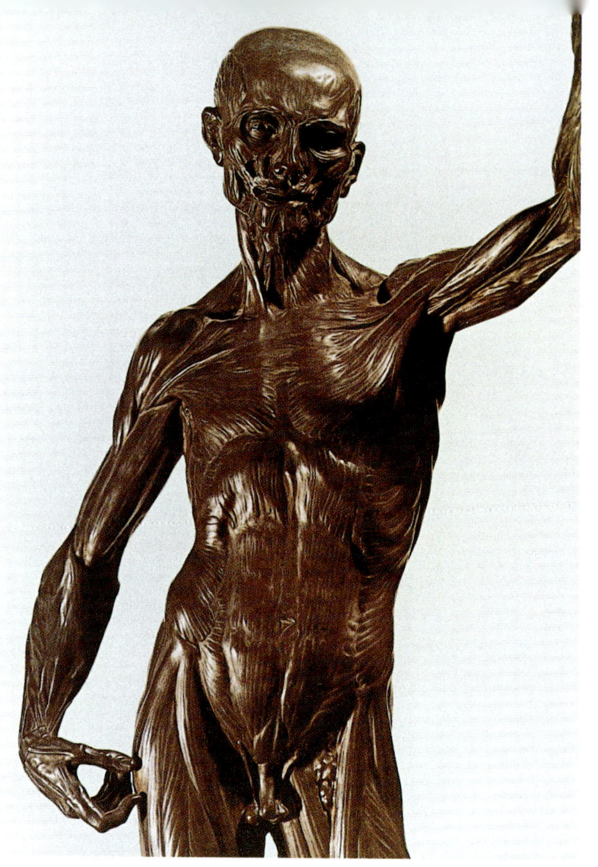

*At an early stage in the modern era, anatomy and art joined forces, and medical knowledge was depicted in aesthetic images of the human body. The sculpture "Scorticato" (The flayed one) by Lodovici Cigali (1559–1613) is in the Italian National Museum in the Bargello Palace in Florence, one of the most important collections of works of Tuscan sculptors of the 14th–16th centuries.*

According to what Gunther von Hagens himself says, he makes no claim to be a genuine artist. However, he by no means denies an intended affinity of his works with sculptures – in the same ways as was attempted for the first time with the anatomical portrayals of the Renaissance, and was realised with three-dimensional anatomical models that later became famous. It was for this reason that he even coined the term BODY WORLDS. He can, of course, give his reasons for this: Firstly he owes it to the body donors to give their cadavers an aesthetic form. Secondly, in addition to the functional aspect of the human body, his aim was to reveal the natural beauty of its inner structures. Finally, since traditional anatomy has become increasingly isolated from the public, his plastinates were intended to provide general enlightenment; therefore, among the non-medical lay public, he is trying to prevent the natural fear of death and the horror and revulsion that the usual anatomical specimens can provoke.

In the opinion of almost all the visitors to the BODY WORLDS exhibitions in Germany and abroad up to now, he has, in fact, succeeded in this. Apparently, with his plastinates, many people can be shown things that would otherwise cause existential trepidation and could stir up the emotions, something that, in a natural realistic form, i.e., a form left unaesthetic either through thoughtlessness or by intention, they would not be willing to look at, even if it were to interest them.

The critical observation that this aestheticisation is simply a means to an end that is superficial for, and alien to, a dead body is doubtlessly correct. However, to interpret aestheticisation as an infringement of dignity is nevertheless wrong. Firstly, this reproach does not hold water, because the intentions pursued – dispelling revulsion and creating beauty – are not in themselves offensive, and are fully in accord with the interests of the body donors, who expect their dead bodies to be preserved as perfectly as possible and to be made presentable for lay persons. They would certainly never have agreed to the degradation of their bodies. Secondly, this attack also misses its target because it implies, without explicitly stating it, that the inherently true purpose of a corpse is to be burned or to decay, and that to be plastinated in an aesthetic manner is missing its real purpose. If that were true, it would have to follow that every anatomical or legally ordered autopsy, and even the removal of organs for transplant purposes, would merely be a means to an end that is superficial for, and alien to the true purpose of the body and would thus infringe its dignity. To take that to its ultimate conclusion: the same argument could be used to object to any type of disposal of a body. The reason is that with hygienic disposal of bodies, one is pursuing the superficial purpose of preventing harm from the remains to the health of the living, which would result from being in close proximity to an untreated cadaver – not to mention the intolerability of the appearance and smell. None of these ways of treating a body can be regarded as an infringement of dignity, because a corpse is no longer a subject and thus there is no purpose inherent to it that could be disregarded.

Does this imply carte blanche to use the dead for any purpose whatsoever? If it is permitted to transform them into aesthetic objects, why not into useful objects – chairs, hallstands or bowls? After all, in the 17th and 18th centuries in France and Germany, corpses were used for supposedly very effective remedies; soldiers believed that carrying the finger of a fallen comrade would bring them luck, and candles made from human tallow were considered to be helpful when seeking treasure. Furthermore, in the Capuchin church in Rome, one can still admire pillars made from skulls, arch supports made from shinbones and chandeliers made from vertebrae, produced by an old monk.

To what extent does a plastinate differ from these? In principle, they do differ: Firstly, these products made from human remains were truly only in fact a means to an end (even though they did not fulfil any rationally comprehensible end). Above all, however, they depicted something that was not human. In order to be truly clear about this attribute, it is necessary to differentiate between relative unfamiliarity with a body and absolute alienation from it: Plastinated whole-body plastinates such as Gunther von Hagens offers to the public depict the human organism as such in order to educate the individual observer about the inside of his own body. In doing so, he uses anatomical specimens rendered durable through unusual techniques – but only relatively, because they still bear the image of man. Conversely, to transform bodies or parts of bodies into bowls or clothes racks would mean totally alienating the dead bodies, because they would then no longer appear to be anything human.

Nowadays, using bodies or parts of bodies for the wrong purpose would conflict not only with ideological opinions of dignity. Public opinion is almost unanimous in believing that the importance of a body as the remains of a person who has died and respect for his memory would be incompatible in such cases. Even if the deceased, when he was alive, had agreed in his will to his body's being used for useful purposes, or had even demanded this, in the opinion of most people compliance with this wish would not be possible for reasons of observing the established social order and because it would generally be too excessive to be acceptable. Conversely, the relative (mental) recycling of a body for purposes of serving life, maintaining order and providing education – such as removing organs and tissues for transplantation surgery, performing autopsies for forensic medical purposes or for pathological clarification of the causes of death and dissections for anatomical research and instruction – is basically compatible with any and all ideas of dignity. Plastination, as just expounded, is a relative recycling in the same sense; why then has criticism been sparked by the public exhibition of plastinates?

### Offensive Visibility of Plastinates?

Covering dead bodies is a cultural-historical phenomenon of particular importance. Many people find it difficult to bear, or even refuse to look at them. This is an expression of reluctance to face one's own death and the death of others, but also of the need to keep the physical picture of the deceased, whom one has known and loved, intact in one's memory – and possibly of the fear of being reminded of the future decay of one's own body.

This defensive attitude is particularly striking in highly civilised societies. A cloth is placed as soon as possible over the face of the person who has died. The catafalque is covered with flowers and wreaths. In the Federal Republic of Germany, even being waked in an open coffin requires a permit from the authorities.

However, it was not long ago that death was perceived to be natural to a far greater degree than it is today, and deal-

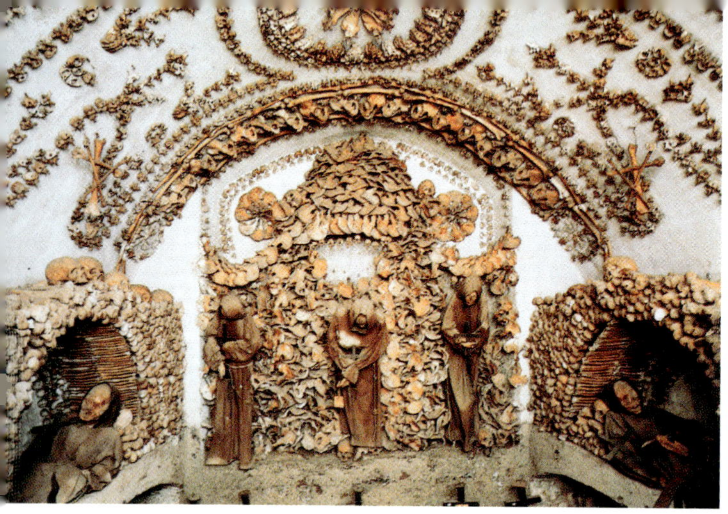

*In the not too distant past, dealings with the dead were far more uninhibited than they are today, as ossuaries in many places show. In these, skulls and bones from opened graves were stacked on top of each other. From time to time, however, the limits of piety were considerably exceeded, as in the Capuchin church in the Via Veneto in Rome, where a monk used human bones to make abstruse room decorations.*

ing with the dead was far more relaxed. Piles of bones and skulls can still be seen in ossuaries, and mummy cemeteries – as in Rome and Palermo – and can still be visited. Unlike Northern Europe, in many places in the Mediterranean countries, it is still the custom to leave the coffin half open until burial so that the immediate family as well as the relatives and friends who have travelled some distance, and all other members of the deceased's community can have a parting look.

In our artificial world, we are rather more inclined to suppress natural facts – the inevitable end of life and the physical disintegration of the body. Confrontation with anatomically dissected and preserved bodies is all the more confusing for many people. Many others, however, want to have them consigned to invisibility, so to speak; thus, in order to deter other interested parties from visiting the BODY WORLDS exhibition, attempts were made to prevent it from opening in Mannheim, with the objection that it lacked dignity; and when that failed, the public was accused of pure voyeurism, of seeking sensation and of having a tasteless thirst for horror. Just as the Jesuits at one time condemned Galileo Galilei because the knowledge that he had obtained by looking at the sky through one of the first telescopes threatened their traditional conception of the world, our contemporaries were now to be denied views of the human body that were not possible before the invention and development of plastination, or which, in a different and far less attractive manner were reserved exclusively for members of the medical profession.

There is no doubt that a particular attraction lies in the authenticity and originality of the plastinates. An exhibition of anatomical models that looked confusingly genuine would certainly not have had such enormous success or lasting impact as BODY WORLDS. Certainly many visitors came simply out of curiosity and with the expectation of ambivalent feelings – stunned oppressiveness as well as excited fascination. Yet a representative survey revealed that, instead of these feelings, almost all the visitors had an objective interest in, and concerned thoughtfulness for, the exhibits. The majority proved only to be interested in the structure of the human body, and at the same time recognised its greatness and misery, the physical quality and frailness of the interiors of their own bodies.

What had already been confirmed in the article entitled "Anatomy" published by Denis Diderot and Jean le Rond d'Alembert in the great French Encyclopédie that appeared from 1751–1780 all of a sudden became a happening: "Knowledge of oneself requires knowledge of one's body, and knowledge of the body presumes knowledge of such a wonderful chain of causes and effects that one can say that none leads more directly to the concept of an omniscient and omnipotent God; it is, so to speak, the foundation of natural theology." And further: "In addition to such an important motive, there is a benefit that cannot be disregarded, namely that of being informed of the means by which one feels well, by which one can prolong one's life, which explain the sites and symptoms of disease when one is ill... Knowledge of anatomy is important for everyone."

However, the question remains as to whether the use of plastinates in a way that provides an opportunity for emotional experiences and factual knowledge is generally compatible with the dignity of man. That would certainly not be the case if the public exhibition of anatomical objects were equivalent to a debasing heteronomy of the dead. No one is being debased; and nor is there any heteronomy, as a corpse does not possess any self-determination of purpose. Despite this, those representing a very wide range of ideas of what dignity is or should be are agreed that a body, as the remains of a person who has died, may never be used merely as a means to an end. However, this merely means that one should approach the specimens with a certain respect, and not that the right to view them must be reserved exclusively for the medical profession and should be refused to non-medical laypeople.

## Unseemly Exploitation of Plastinates?

Whoever respects the dignity of man respects his neighbour for his own sake and does not regard him merely as a replaceable object. Supporters of religious and radically secular viewpoints also share this rational philosophical principle of Immanuel Kant. Can it also be applied to plastinates?

Many people maintain that selling them (the only possible purchasers are research and teaching institutions and natural history museums) or charging admission to attend an exhibition of them is an infringement of dignity. But even if one concedes that the corpse as a mere thing should be given a certain degree of respect because it is the dead body of someone who has died, that does not apply to payment for a plastinate – considered with reference to Kant's idea regarding goods.

The practices of the Institute for Plastination do not permit any doubt whatsoever on this matter, because they already fulfil the strictest conditions: firstly, the Institute requires that the donation of the body carry no reward; and secondly, it is committed to the principle of never charging for a plastinate itself, only for the costs of producing it – i.e., the cost of dissection and preservation.

Thus the Heidelberg Institute is clearly a service-provider, just like the undertaker who transfers the body to the mortuary and sells the surviving relatives a coffin or urn, the newspaper that accepts death notices, the florist who supplies wreaths, the restaurant owner who prepares the funeral meal, the municipal authority that maintains the cemetery and the layman who speaks at the graveside – but it is also like the church, which is paid for providing spiritual support at the graveside through the church tax.

## Conclusion

All in all, it should have become clear that plastination and all of the activities connected with it do not infringe human dignity. These activities are not only compatible with the radically secular understanding of the concept, which as a result of its ideological neutrality can be generalised; but also those who hold an opinion connected with an ideology – religious or rational philosophical – which mainly belongs to the private sphere of the people, do not necessarily have to regard the plastination process or the exhibition of plastinates as an infringement of dignity.

The words 'human dignity' weigh heavily, even though they trip off the tongue so lightly. Precisely for that reason, they should also in future be used more judiciously and with greater circumspection in all respects with regard to plastination.

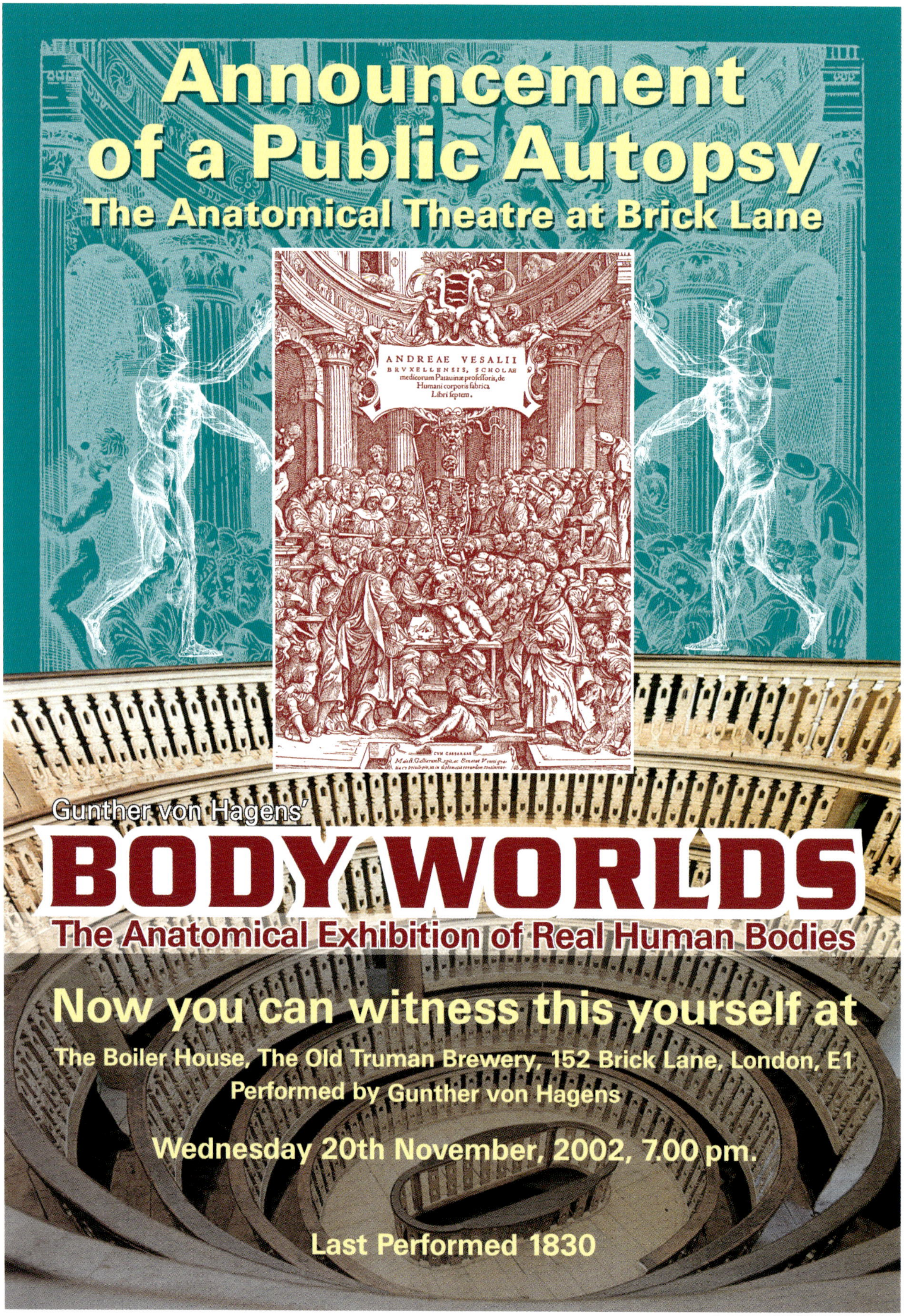


*Advertisement for the first public autopsy since 1830, performed by Gunther von Hagens*

Prof. Dr. Franz Josef Wetz

# Modern Anatomical Theatre – The First Public Autopsy in 200 Years

"At the end of every problem, you'll find a German," wrote Voltaire during the French Enlightenment in the 18th century. Even today, not much has changed, which has to do with the fact that Germany has always been an extremely nervous and very fundamental nation, which as such can be easily disconcerted in order to be able to discuss the issues thus awakened down to the last detail.

This was proven once again by the strong reactions and heated discussions about an "anatomical drama" played out in London. There on November 20, 2002, between 7:00 and 10:00 p.m., the first public autopsy in about 200 years took place. The 'scene of the crime' for this controversial event was the Boiler House of the Old Truman Brewery in Brick Lane. Together with two anatomists and two pathologists, plastinator Gunther von Hagens uncovered the secrets of the corpse of a 72-year-old German. This unusual spectacle was observed by about 500 spectators on the scene and thousands more on TV screens. As was to be expected, this public autopsy triggered heated debates among Great Britain's citizenry and even more in Germany, although it was performed with all due respect for the proprieties of the medical profession.

No matter how understandable such impulses appear to be at first glance, they still seem odd. What is actually so horrible about it when medically interested laypersons for once look over the shoulders of anatomists and pathologists at work in order to inform themselves first hand about the insides of their bodies? It is in fact human nature to have an interest in our own bodies, and it just so happens that the cultural answer to this question is indeed anatomy. In any case, it would be difficult to make medical laypersons understand why they should be barred from taking part in an autopsy while museums of medical history and the BODY WORLDS exhibition are readily open for them to visit.

It is correct to say that today the possibility of taking part in a public autopsy normally does not exist. However, how quickly do we ascribe universal applicability to truths bound up in time and space, which they ultimately never ever possessed as such? Some things that came about historically – and in the meantime have long since become history – were once considered to be perpetually valid. This includes the widespread though mistaken idea of bans on public autopsies. From the close of the 16th century until the end of the 18th and early 19th centuries, there was a long tradition of public anatomy that enjoyed considerable popularity among laypersons.

### Anatomical Theatres

In addition to scientific and medical researchers, many artists also showed great interest in anatomy. Hence, Leonardo da Vinci and Michelangelo (1475–1564) not only attended dissections of physician friends of theirs, but also performed anatomical studies themselves – in order to be able to depict persons even more faithfully in their art. Leonardo is supposed to have dissected more than 30 corpses in Florence in order to be better able to incorporate his figures on his canvases more perfectly through a better knowledge of the arrangement of bones, muscles, and tendons as well as of all the other organs. The body, which had been disparaged as the "grave of the soul" for centuries, was ennobled by the Renaissance as the "temple of the soul."

Since this upgrading of the body as an attractive form of expression for the human soul, the general public took greater interest in anatomy, which has been most decidedly demonstrated by the numerous anatomical theatres that were established throughout Europe. However, public dissections first took place outdoors or in temporary structures built out of wood especially for this purpose, which could easily be dismantled when not needed. Such so-called "temporaria theatra" could be assembled and disassembled as needed just as quickly as additions to existing buildings. Public dissections were even performed in vacant churches and in the chapels of former monasteries, such as San Francesco in Bologna, Italy, the Church of St. Elizabeth in Basle, Switzerland, or St. Jacob's Chapel in Tübingen, Germany. Nevertheless, permanent "theatra anatomica" soon followed in Montpellier, France, in 1530; in Padua, Italy, in 1594; in Bologna, Italy, in 1595; in Leiden, Netherlands, in 1597; in Uppsala, Sweden, in 1622; in Copenhagen, Denmark, in 1643; in Paris, France, in 1694; in Berlin, Germany, in 1720; and in Halle, Germany, in 1727, to mention just a few places. By the 18th century, nearly every medical school had its own anatomical theatre.

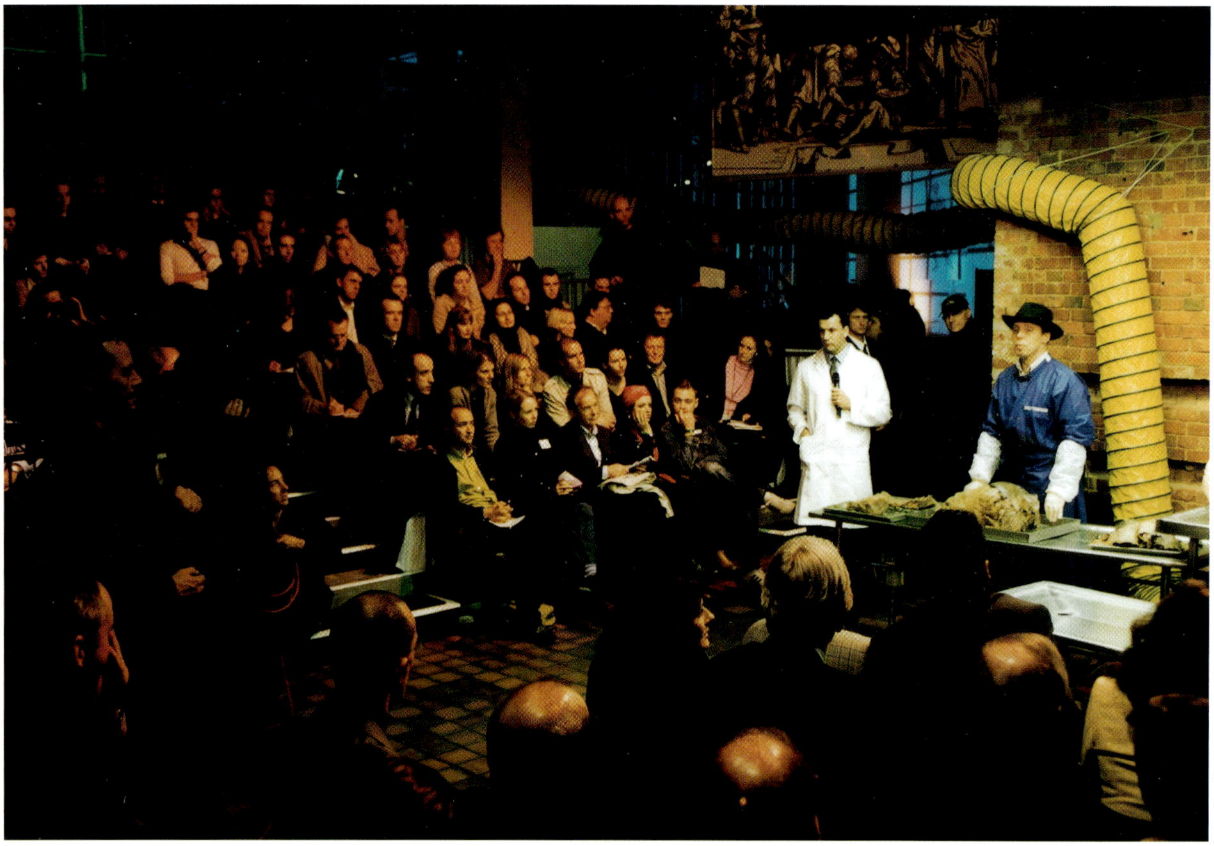

*Gunther von Hagens´ Public Autopsy, London 2002*

Nearly every dissection was performed in public and was thus accessible to a wider audience. They were not meant solely for a medical forum. This was proven by the title page of Andreas Vesalius' illustrated textbook De Humani Corporis Fabrica (1543). It shows Vesalius at the dissection table, closely surrounded by persons of the most widely varied social classes. The same can be seen in Rembrandt's famous painting, The Anatomy of Dr. Tulp (1632), in which Amsterdam mayor and anatomist Nicolaas Tulp is shown dissecting a corpse in an apparently private lesson in anatomy before a group of prominent citizens of that city.

In those days, such events gradually developed into social happenings – a new form of sociability and fashion, which soon came to be a part of gracious living. In addition to professors and students, there were also members of the upper class, the nobility as well as numerous clergymen and monks who took part in such events. Moreover, barbers, midwives, battlefield physicians, surgeons and apothecaries were in attendance, even though these were not yet academic professions, but only skilled trades. In addition, many artists, writers, and scholars, such as Johann Wolfgang von Goethe as well as the brothers Wilhelm and Alexander von Humboldt also numbered among the medically interested professional and lay publics. They were bound by a close friendship with the renowned anatomist Justus Christian Loder of Jena, under whose direction Goethe was able to deepen his knowledge of the inner structures of the human body.

Anyone who so desired and could afford it was allowed to attend public anatomical dissections. Even then, admission was charged to take part in such events. Admission to these demonstrations was only free of charge for faculty members, but not for students and medical laypersons.

In general, anatomy lessons resembled more exciting theatre performances than edifying instructional presentations. It was not only that they – like theatre performances – were announced by engraved invitations and were sometimes even accompanied by music, even the name "theatre" indicates a festive and entertaining framework for anatomical demonstrations that developed more and more into social highlights. They usually lasted several days, starting, for ex-

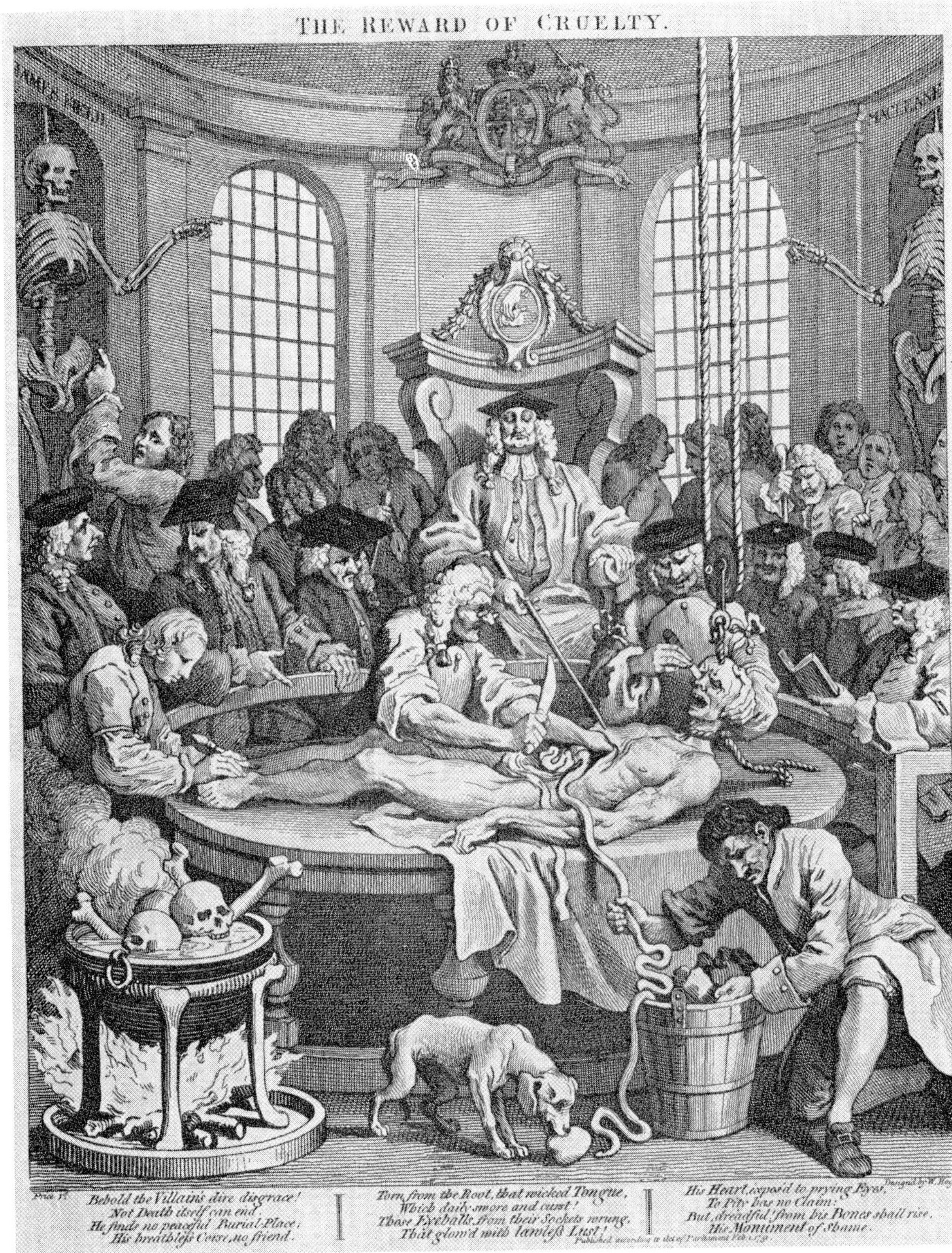


*William Hogarth, The Reward of Cruelty, plaste of The Four Stages of Cruelty, 1750–1751*

ample, with an examination of the abdominal organs on the first day, the contents of the chest cavity on the second day, continuing with the skull on the third day and ending on the fourth day with the limbs, including the muscles, nerves and blood vessels. The attraction of such performances was enormous, but not just because it was so unusual to open and dissect an otherwise closed corpse, but also because of certain non-medical aspects that went beyond the relatively narrow scope of anatomy.

In summary, it can be said that the view of the otherwise concealed interior of the body had the following benefits for visitors of anatomical theatres in those days:

- Instructional information (scientific)
- Satisfied curiosity (philosophical)
- Pleasantly spine-tingling experiences (aesthetic)
- Raptly reverent veneration of divine Creation (theological)
- Humble self-realisation on the part of the individual as a vulnerable, mortal, and insignificant part of Nature (existential).

After anatomy as a discipline was sequestered behind the walls of universities at the beginning of the 19th century, where it has been functioning solely as a scientific discourse ever since and still to the exclusion of medical laypersons. This was then accompanied by a development that left only the scientific interest of experts paramount to all the various perspectives on the deeper structures of the human body. Other forms of perception were either rejected as unscientific or were dismissed as immoral. However, even a non-scientific perspective possessed a certain justification, and what was once considered morally questionable could have been justified as ethically permissible even then.

**Renaissance of the Renaissance**

This is enlightenment: a kind of thinking with the sun at its zenith, which means the same as maximum light with minimum shadows. Thinking of this kind vigorously defies taboos and shadowy zones, where things seemingly mysterious remain out of the reach of the light of dissection. In this

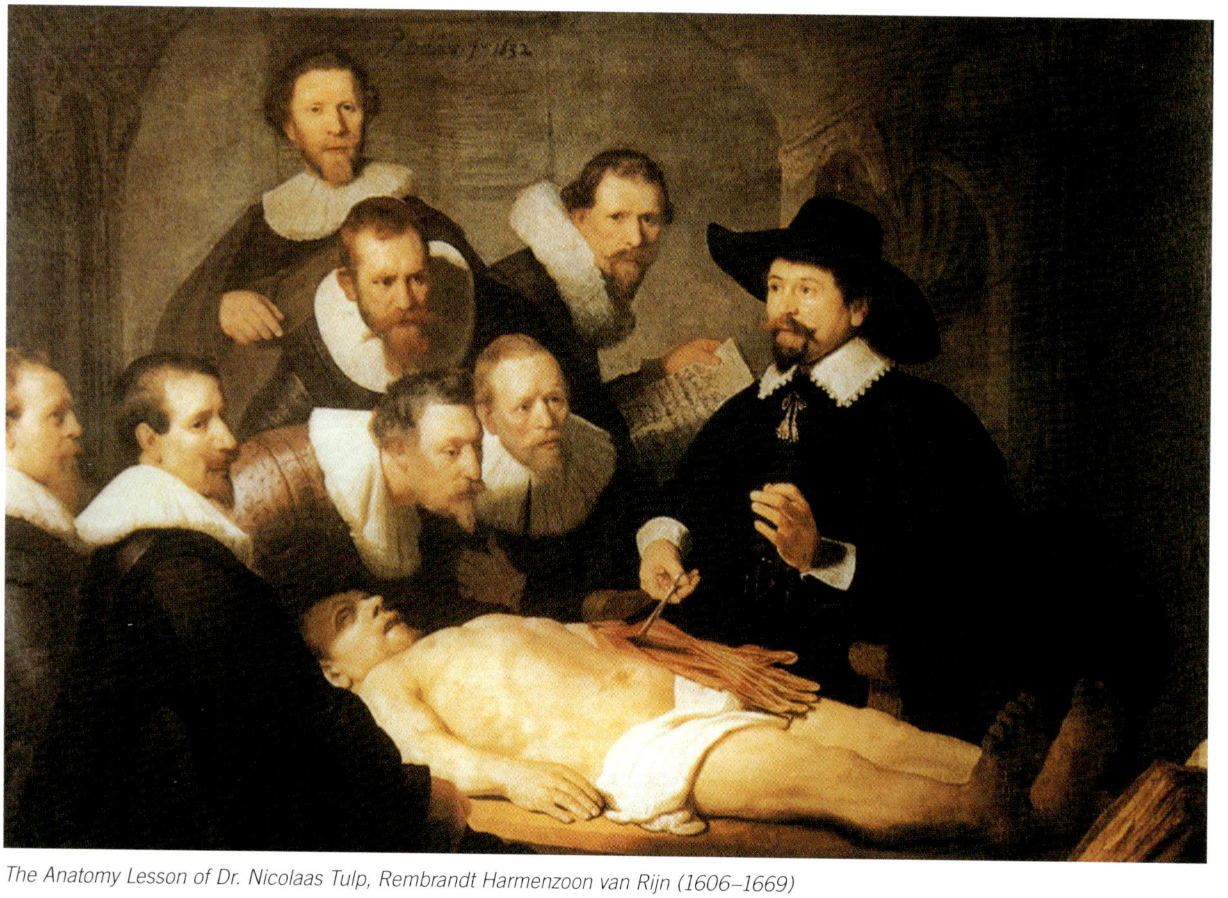

*The Anatomy Lesson of Dr. Nicolaas Tulp, Rembrandt Harmenzoon van Rijn (1606–1669)*

context, anatomical dissections of a corpse can be equated with illuminating the darkness of life with the light of death.

Through Gunther von Hagens, public dissections are being performed for the first time in just under two centuries. In resurrecting this old tradition, the Institute for Plastination aims to educate the public (and medically interested laypersons in particular) about anatomy, but at the same time he is returning to its proper place the thoroughly acceptable, human need to be curious about our anatomy and to feel a pleasant sensation of horror, a sense of awe, and a humble awareness of ourselves as vulnerable, mortal, insignificant creatures. To venture a glance into an unknown body is virtually the same as to discover our own body therein, as only that which can be uncovered and dissected can be comprehended. There is certainly nothing ethically reprehensible in this.

The criticism that such public spectacles have come to form a part of our thrill-oriented entertainment culture is pointless, as it could also be applied ultimately to almost every cultural event. High culture has been integrated into our general leisure-time activities for years, which have also had a certain justification despite our reservations. Apart from that, high expectations have always depended on the attitude of the beholder. The obnoxiousness of public dissections is primarily also a question of the standpoint, as an anatomical theatre is quite capable of becoming a site for contemplation as well as a place for the imagination. It can thus serve as a venue for thoughtful observation, which invites inquisitive, fascinated, and existentially involved viewers to become engrossed and offers them an unusual kind of encounter with themselves. Whoever becomes earnestly involved in this will emerge from this experience a changed person. For this purpose, the moralisers of our time should stop trying to make anyone interested in public dissections into politico-cultural invalids through their doting condescension.

It is in fact human nature to have an interest in our own bodies, and it just so happens that the cultural answer to this question is indeed anatomy. If, however, medical laypersons

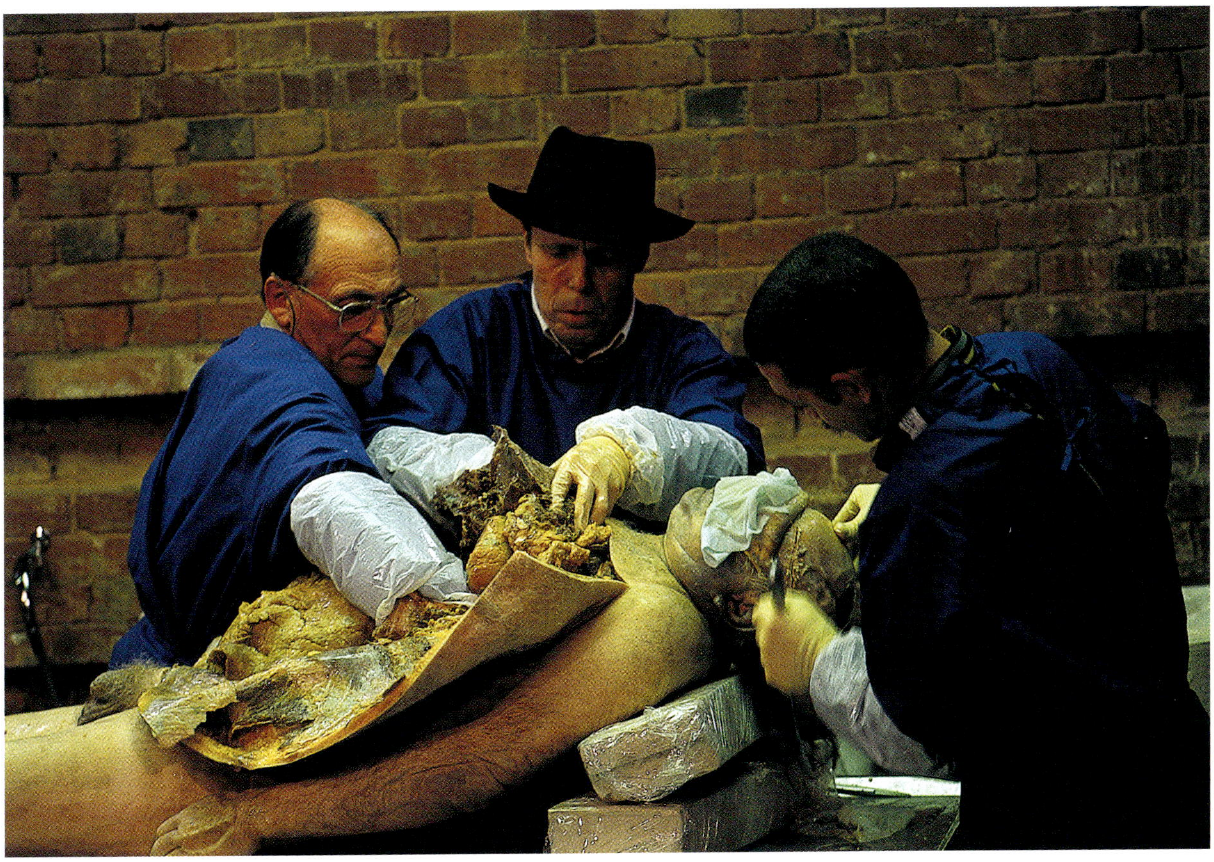

*Gunther von Hagens´ Public Autopsy, London 2002*

are permitted to look at anatomical specimens, then it is not understandable why they should not be allowed to view the dissection of corpses. However strong the fearful desire and pleasant dread may be, which autopsies evoke in their observers, most people will certainly witness such affairs with a straight face. The reason for this is not because the very sight of a dissected body would be shocking for them, but rather because it would be nearly impossible for any of us to treat looking at the fragile bases of our own existence in a light and frivolous way.

**Contemplating Oneself without a Mirror – An Eye-Witness Report**

Today there is a wide variety of possibilities for producing lifelike pictures of bodily interiors: anatomical atlases in colour, imaging and data technologies such as x-ray, ultrasound, CT, and NMR. In light of this background, the question arises whether direct viewing of dissected bodily organs while studying macroscopic human anatomy is becoming superfluous?

(Old anatomical plates, Florentine wax models and the figures made out of Plexiglas, aluminum and plastic in the Hygiene Museum in Dresden are as fascinating today as they ever were. To this, the 20$^{th}$ century has added numerous coloured anatomical atlases as well as new imaging technologies such as x-ray, ultrasound, CT and NMR, which can be used to generate lifelike images of the body's interiors. And let us not forget the computer-generated 3D representations of the human body, i.e., virtual anatomy, which are at the heart of the Visible Human Project launched in the US in 1988. Does this wide variety of anatomical imaging and data technologies make it unnecessary for students of macroscopic human anatomy to view the dissected organs of a corpse directly?) Are there not already enough books, illustrated reference works and CD-ROMs out there where laypersons can learn all that they need to know about the internal structure of their bodies? Now it is even possible for people to view highly realistic body models on their computer screens and dissect them for themselves. Medical laypersons can use a virtual scalpel to remove the outer layers of tissue to expose the underlying structures. So why would we still need anatomical theatres?

I personally witnessed the public dissection in London. I admit to having been highly sceptical when I went there. I was horrified by the media frenzy surrounding this 'event,' but my own morbid curiosity won out in the end. On the way to the actual venue, I felt a tingle of excitement and a pleasant sense of anticipation – a mixture of trepidation and heightened expectation – no matter how much I tried to visualise just being able to see the inside of a human corpse, i.e., not as something holy or demonic, but simply something natural. Since it was nothing more than this, all of my sensation-seeking voyeurism and comforting horror visions melted away as soon as the demonstration began. Like everyone else in attendance, I earnestly followed the work of the three anatomists and two pathologists. What struck me was how soberly they went about their work, their dispassionate explanations, and the quiet calm in the hall, which at the same time stood in such stark contrast to the heated, often emotional and grim debate conducted in the media and in the public about this demonstration both before and after it took place.

What I was witnessing was what had already been seen at the BODY WORLDS exhibition: a self-disciplined audience that did not first need to be brought to order or to its senses. I think this phenomenon is well worth noting since it is anything but a given in today's world; nevertheless it is not surprising if one realises that both the exhibition and the autopsy reveal a completely new, close-up look at human existence – and we as humans have always been curious about ourselves. In both instances, viewers are looking into someone else's body in order to discover their own, which is the reason that we can even speak of "discovery anatomy." Like a finished plastinate, a dissected corpse also gives us a visual bridge to our own vulnerable, mortal existence. As a result, it is almost inevitable that such a glimpse would function as a way of "viewing oneself without a mirror," which sufficiently explains the earnestness of those in attendance at both the exhibition and the autopsy. This earnestness does not arise because the people are seeing something gruesome that has left them speechless, as might easily be assumed, but rather because these events have simply allowed all of us to see clearly, in a bold or even shocking way, just how fragile the basis for our own lives ultimately is. BODY WORLDS is no more a baroque gallery of curiosities than a public dissection is a Renaissance fair; both provide room for contemplation and imagination, are places to reflect on oneself, and showplaces for contemplative observation that invites curious, fascinated viewers to lose themselves in existential questions.

Nevertheless, a question remains: How is it that knowing the plastinated specimens and dissected corpses to be real can bring viewers closer to themselves? There is, of course, no doubt that the authenticity of the exhibits at events such as these heighten the experience, making it more intense

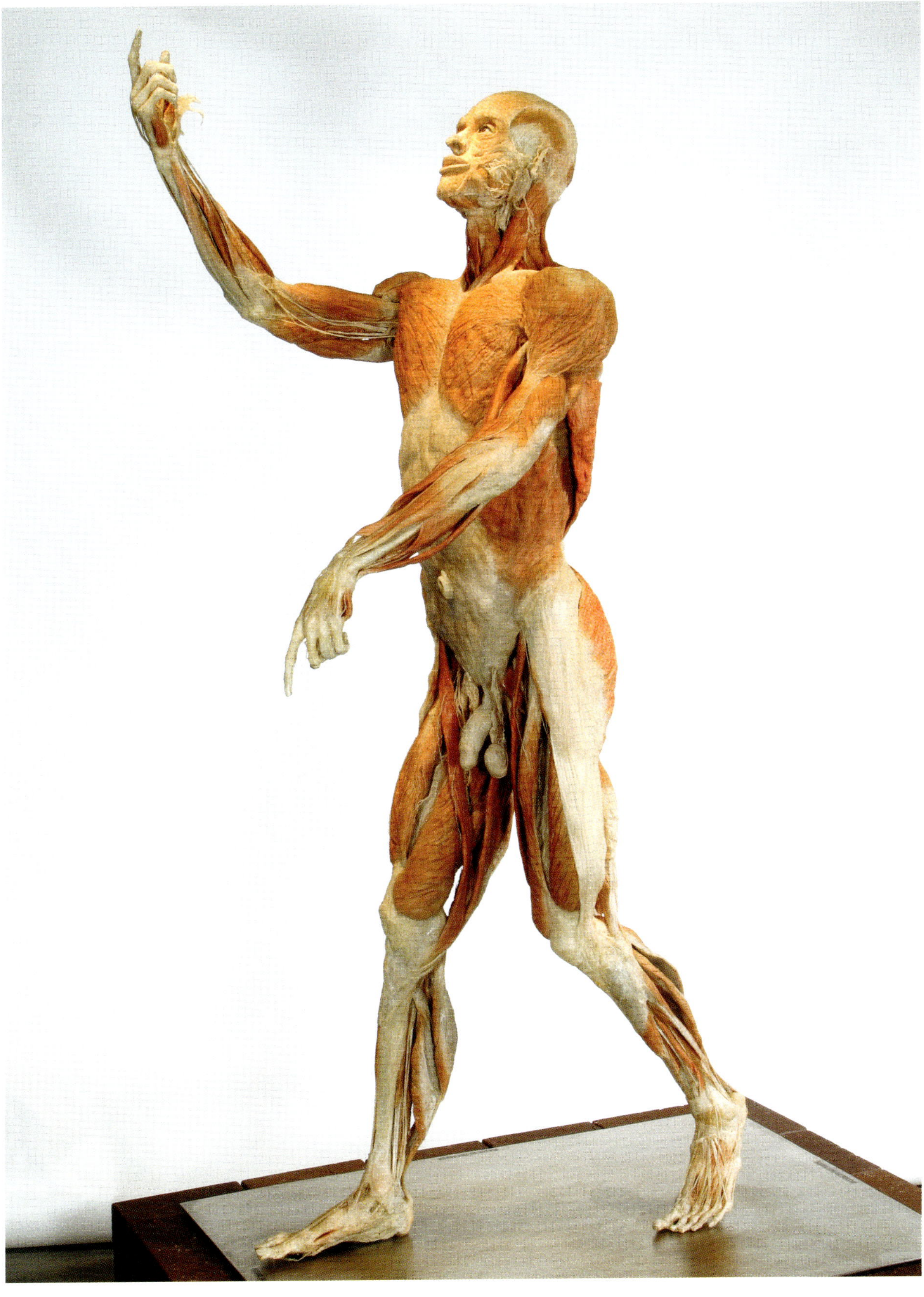

*The Autopsy Body*

and credible, but it is difficult to say precisely why that should be. What first comes to mind is to reflect on the difference between an original work of art and a copy. The first is usually considered more valuable than the latter, just as encountering a celebrity on the street will arouse greater attention from passers-by than will a life-size photograph of the same person in a store window. This belief in the superiority of seeing an original work of art or seeing a celebrity face-to-face is based on an outmoded superstition, however, and as such I will not pursue this line of thinking any further.

More revealing would be to contrast hiking in a natural setting with paging through a volume of nature photography, or going to the theatre or opera with reading a play or listening to an opera on CD. In these cases, one could also point out that, because we have books and CDs, we would no longer need nature, opera houses or theatres. This is not the conclusion that people would generally draw, however, convinced as we are of the superiority of the latter categories. A similar difference is that between attending BODY WORLDS or a public dissection and merely studying anatomical plates in a book or viewing virtual anatomical specimens on a computer screen. The contrast in this case is as stark as that between walking in nature and simply looking at it in a picture book. The depth of experience is different, and one must understand both to appreciate the difference fully.

I admit, of course, that the need for such an exhibition and for a public dissection has not yet been demonstrated. Where culture is concerned, however, such a necessity simply does not exist. The question we should be asking is not "Is that really necessary?" but rather "Is that really permissible?" When it comes to the permissibility of an event in a liberal state with an open society, the burden of proof does not lie with the organiser, but with whomever would attempt to deny permission in order to forbid it. This is the party that must provide a convincing argument against public dissections. Precisely such arguments, however, simply do not exist. As a result, it is difficult to convince interested parties that anatomical dissections, which medical students regularly attend throughout the course of their studies, must remain solely the privilege of medical experts. Excluding medical laypersons from anatomy can no longer be justified in a liberal democracy with an open society. The opportunity to attend publicly accessible dissections should therefore again become a right granted to all responsible citizens whenever facilities and staffing permit.

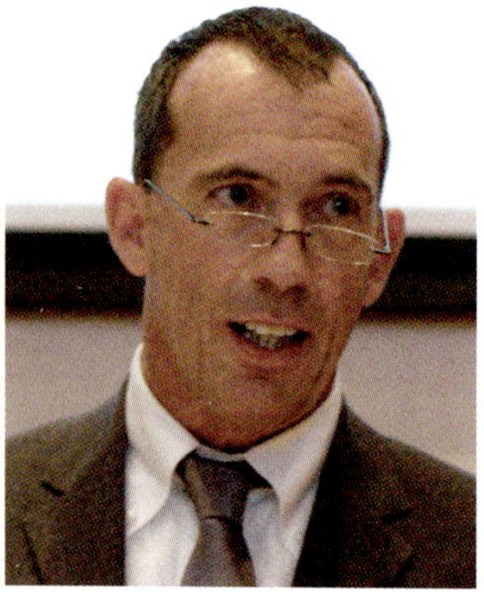

Franz-Josef Wetz has been a professor of philosophy at the University of Education in Schwäbisch Gmünd since 1994. He studied philosophy, German, and theology, and graduated from the University of Giessen. His main areas of work are hermeneutics, ethics and cultural and natural philosophy. To date, he has published more than 15 books such as *Die Kunst der Resignation* (The Art of Resignation); *Magie der Musik* (The Magic of Music); *Illusion Menschenwürde. Aufstieg und Fall eines Grundwerts* (Human Dignity – an Illusion. Rise and Fall of a Basic Right.); Baustelle Körper. *Bioethik der Selbstachtung* (Construction Site: Human Body. The Bioethics of Self-Respect.); and *Rebellion der Selbstachtung: Gegen Demütigung* (Rebellion of Self-Esteem: Against Humiliation). He often appears on radio and TV and wrote numerous scientific articles.

# PUBLISHING INFORMATION

**EXHIBITION** CATALOGUE
BODY WORLDS – The Original
Gunther von Hagens
Angelina Whalley

**EDITING**
Angelina Whalley

**SCIENTIFIC CONSULTANTS**
Eduard Borzyak
Vladimir Chereminskiy

**DESIGN**
DIE-**WERBE**AKTIVISTEN.DE
mArc Schumacher, Mannheim, Germany

17th printing



Arts & Sciences
Exhibitions and Publishing

**Arts & Sciences**
Exhibitions and Publishing GmbH, Heidelberg



ISBN 978-3-937256-36-8

www.bodyworlds.com